Behavior, Society, and Nuclear War

BEHAVIOR, SOCIETY, AND NUCLEAR WAR
A Series of Review Volumes

edited by Philip E. Tetlock, Jo L. Husbands,
Robert Jervis, Paul C. Stern, and Charles Tilly

Committee on Contributions of Behavioral and Social Science
to the Prevention of Nuclear War

Commission on Behavioral and Social Science and Education

National Research Council/National Academy of Sciences

BEHAVIOR, SOCIETY, AND NUCLEAR WAR

VOLUME ONE

Philip E. Tetlock
Jo L. Husbands
Robert Jervis
Paul C. Stern
Charles Tilly
Editors

Committee on Contributions of Behavioral and Social Science to the Prevention of Nuclear War

Commission on Behavioral and Social Sciences and Education

National Research Council

New York   Oxford
OXFORD UNIVERSITY PRESS
1989

Oxford University Press

Oxford New York Toronto
Delhi Bombay Calcutta Madras Karachi
Petaling Jaya Singapore Hong Kong Tokyo
Nairobi Dar es Salaam Cape Town
Melbourne Auckland

and associated companies in
Berlin Ibadan

Copyright © 1989 by Oxford University Press, Inc.

Published by Oxford University Press, Inc.,
200 Madison Avenue, New York, New York 10016

Oxford is a registered trademark of Oxford University Press

All rights reserved. No part of this publication may be reproduced,
stored in a retrieval system, or transmitted, in any form or by any means,
electronic, mechanical, photocopying, recording, or otherwise,
without prior permission of Oxford University Press.

Library of Congress Cataloging-in-Publication Data
Behavior, society, and nuclear war.
"Committee on Contributions of Behavioral and Social Science
to the Prevention of Nuclear War,
Commission on Behavioral and Social Sciences
and Education, National Research Council."
Bibliography: p. Includes index.
1. Nuclear warfare—Psychological aspects.
2. Nuclear warfare—Social aspects. I. Tetlock, Philip.
II. National Research Council (U.S.).
Committee on Contributions of Behavioral and Social Science
to the Prevention of Nuclear War.
III. National Research Council (U.S.).
Commission on Behavioral and Social Sciences
and Education.
U263.B45 1989 355'.027 88-33043
ISBN 0-19-505765-1 (v. 1)
ISBN 0-19-505766-X (v. 1 : pbk.)

9 8 7 6 5 4 3 2 1
Printed in the United States of America
on acid-free paper

Foreword

In recent years, scientists, including behavioral and social scientists, have expressed growing concern about the risk of nuclear war. New programs and research groups have sprung up at universities, and professional associations have paid increasing attention to the issue. In the National Academy of Sciences, many members felt a need to move beyond the academy's traditional focus on technical issues to explore the potential contributions of behavioral and social science research to the issue. The creation of the Committee on Contributions of Behavioral and Social Science to the Prevention of Nuclear War in the spring of 1985 thus reflected the recognition that scientists can work to reduce the risks of nuclear war by improving understanding of the cultural, institutional, political, and cognitive processes involved in making war or preventing it.

The National Research Council assembled a committee that brings knowledge and concepts from across the behavioral and social sciences to bear on international security issues. Committee members thus include individuals with experience in relevant international policy issues and individuals with broad knowledge in the behavioral and social sciences. The committee has five major objectives: (1) to foster innovative, multidisciplinary applications of social and behavioral science knowledge and methods to the problem of preventing nuclear war; (2) to synthesize and bring to the attention of policymakers and the public existing knowledge from the behavioral and social sciences that illuminates policy issues and the implicit assumptions guiding policy; (3) to serve as a bridge between social and behavioral scientists and potential users of their findings, including Congress, policymakers, and the interested public; (4) to encourage the interest and activity of scholars not previously involved in this issue; and (5) to foster cooperative research relevant to reducing the risk of nuclear war with Soviet counterparts of the U.S. behavioral and social science community.

As one of its first tasks, the committee set out to identify knowledge about behavior and society that may have value in developing policies to reduce the risk of nuclear war. It has called on behavioral and social science scholars to review work in specific areas to determine its relevance to understanding current defense and foreign policy issues. This volume is the first in a series that presents those reviews.

The series takes a measured approach out of conviction that scholars need to be especially cautious and self-critical when they seek to advise on practical decisions of grave consequence. Much that has been offered as knowledge in the past cannot be defended as more than educated opinion, and one aim of this series is to keep that distinction clear. The primary audience for the series, then, consists of scholars and students interested in international security issues and in the possible applications of knowledge in the behavioral and social sciences to those issues. The committee hopes that the critical distillations of knowledge presented here can offer a basis for developing more focused knowledge and better informed advice for preventing nuclear war.

The series is edited by committee members Philip E. Tetlock, Robert Jervis, and Charles Tilly and staff members Jo L. Husbands and Paul C. Stern. The editors have been responsible for developing ideas for chapters, selecting the authors, and managing the review process. Each chapter has been carefully reviewed by the editors, additional members of the committee, and scholars and practitioners who brought diverse perspectives to the topics. The views expressed in the chapters, however, are those of the authors.

We are indebted to the Carnegie Corporation of New York, the John D. and Catherine T. MacArthur Foundation, and the National Research Council Fund for their support of the committee. We wish also to acknowledge the important role of the Commission on Behavioral and Social Sciences and Education of the National Research Council, which was responsible for organizing this committee. Special thanks are due David A. Goslin, former executive director of the commission, for his unswerving support of the committee's efforts from its inception through the planning stages of this volume.

>William K. Estes and Herbert A. Simon, *Cochairs*
>Committee on Contributions of Behavioral and Social Science
>to the Prevention of Nuclear War

NOTICE: The project that is the subject of this report was approved by the Governing Board of the National Research Council, whose members are drawn from the councils of the National Academy of Sciences, the National Academy of Engineering, and the Institute of Medicine. The members of the committee responsible for the report were chosen for their special competences and with regard for appropriate balance.

This report has been reviewed by a group other than the authors according to procedures approved by a Report Review Committee consisting of members of the National Academy of Sciences, the National Academy of Engineering, and the Institute of Medicine.

The National Academy of Sciences is a private, nonprofit, self-perpetuating society of distinguished scholars engaged in scientific and engineering research, dedicated to the furtherance of science and technology and to their use for the general welfare. Upon the authority of the charter granted to it by the Congress in 1863, the Academy has a mandate that requires it to advise the federal government on scientific and technical matters. Dr. Frank Press is president of the National Academy of Sciences.

The National Academy of Engineering was established in 1964, under the charter of the National Academy of Sciences, as a parallel organization of outstanding engineers. It is autonomous in its administration and in the selection of its members, sharing with the National Academy of Sciences the responsibility for advising the federal government. The National Academy of Engineering also sponsors engineering programs aimed at meeting national needs, encourages education and research, and recognizes the superior achievements of engineers. Dr. Robert M. White is president of the National Academy of Engineering.

The Institute of Medicine was established in 1970 by the National Academy of Sciences to secure the services of eminent members of appropriate professions in the examination of policy matters pertaining to the health of the public. The Institute acts under the responsibility given to the National Academy of Sciences by its congressional charter to be an adviser to the federal government and, upon its own initiative, to identify issues of medical care, research, and education. Dr. Samuel O. Thier is president of the Institute of Medicine.

The National Research Council was organized by the National Academy of Sciences in 1916 to associate the broad community of science and technology with the Academy's purposes of furthering knowledge and advising the federal government. Functioning in accordance with general policies determined by the Academy, the Council has become the principal operating agency of both the National Academy of Sciences and the National Academy of Engineering in providing services to the government, the public, and the scientific and engineering communities. The Council is administered jointly by both Academies and the Institute of Medicine. Dr. Frank Press and Dr. Robert M. White are chairman and vice chairman, respectively, of the National Research Council.

Committee on Contributions of Behavioral and Social Science to the Prevention of Nuclear War

WILLIAM K. ESTES
Cochair, Department of Psychology, Harvard University

HERBERT A. SIMON
Cochair, Department of Psychology, Carnegie-Mellon University

KENNETH J. ARROW
Department of Economics, Stanford University

ROBERT M. AXELROD
Institute of Public Policy Studies, University of Michigan

SEWERYN BIALER
Research Institute on International Change, Columbia University

BARRY M. BLECHMAN
Defense Forecasts, Inc., Washington, D.C.

GEORGE W. BRESLAUER
Department of Political Science, University of California, Berkeley

TIMOTHY J. COLTON
Center for Russian and East European Studies, University of Toronto

PHILIP E. CONVERSE
Institute for Social Research, University of Michigan

CLIFFORD J. GEERTZ
The Institute for Advanced Study, Princeton University

ALEXANDER L. GEORGE
Department of Political Science, Stanford University

ROBERT JERVIS
Institute for War and Peace Studies, Columbia University

CATHERINE MCARDLE KELLEHER
School of Public Affairs, University of Maryland

HAROLD H. KELLEY
Department of Psychology, University of California, Los Angeles

ROY RADNER
Mathematical Sciences Research Center, AT&T Bell Laboratories

JACK P. RUINA
Center for International Studies, Massachusetts Institute of Technology

PHILIP E. TETLOCK
Department of Psychology, University of California, Berkeley

CHARLES TILLY
Center for Studies of Social Change, New School for Social Research

CHARLES H. TOWNES
Department of Physics, University of California, Berkeley

AMOS TVERSKY
Department of Psychology, Stanford University

PAUL C. STERN
Study Director

JO L. HUSBANDS
Senior Research Associate

DANIEL DRUCKMAN
Senior Staff Officer

Contents

Introduction, 3
    PHILIP E. TETLOCK, JO L. HUSBANDS, ROBERT JERVIS,
    PAUL C. STERN, AND CHARLES TILLY

1 Crisis Decision Making, 8
    OLE R. HOLSTI

2 Behavioral Aspects of Negotiations on Mutual Security, 85
    DANIEL DRUCKMAN AND P. TERRENCE HOPMANN

3 Democracy, Public Opinion, and Nuclear Weapons, 174
    BRUCE RUSSETT

4 The Causes of War: A Review of Theories and Evidence, 209
    JACK S. LEVY

5 Methodological Themes and Variations, 334
    PHILIP E. TETLOCK

Contributors and Editors, 387
Index, 391

Behavior, Society, and Nuclear War

Introduction

PHILIP E. TETLOCK, JO L. HUSBANDS, ROBERT JERVIS, PAUL C. STERN, AND CHARLES TILLY

The search for the causes of war is a long-standing intellectual project. Since Thucydides's account of the Peloponnesian War in the fifth century B.C., scholars have been trying to construct explanations for the diverse forms of conflict among nations. Never before in human history, however, has the search for causes—and preventive measures—been as critical as it is in the late twentieth century. Rapid qualitative advances in military technology have given extraordinary destructive power to the leaders of an expanding group of nations. The brutal consequences of war were once limited to the local populations involved; we now face the specter of a thermonuclear war that could threaten the very existence of civilization (Solomon and Marston, 1986).

We find as close to unanimity as ever encountered in the political world on one key point: nuclear war must be avoided. The consensus reflects the deep revulsion that civilized people feel on contemplating the massive devastation and long-term suffering that such a war could so easily produce. But that consensus is intellectually and politically shallow. Political commentators and decision makers in the United States who agree on the necessity of avoiding nuclear war disagree sharply over exactly how to achieve that objective. Different analysts advocate as diametrically opposed policies as arms procurement and arms reduction in the name of avoiding nuclear war. Some analysts believe that the only true security against nuclear adversaries comes from convincing them that one possesses the capability and resolve to "prevail" at any level of nuclear conflict. Some believe that the use of nuclear weapons as instruments of foreign policy is morally abhorrent and support partial or even total unilateral disarmament. Others argue that nuclear deterrence between the superpowers is not highly demanding—it can be accomplished as long as each side fears that it would be destroyed in the event of nuclear war.

Preference for more or less nuclear weaponry is not the only issue at stake in these debates. Advocates of the competing positions differ on a range of complicated factual and moral issues that is difficult to disentangle: What type of risks is the Soviet Union prepared to take to achieve its geopolitical objectives? What are these objectives? What types of risks should the United States be prepared to take to achieve its geopolitical objectives? What should these objectives be? What are the likely short- and long-term consequences of pursuing new policy initiatives—whether nuclear weapons systems, arms control agreements, or military, political, or economic interventions in zones of contested influence? Under what conditions might a conflict among Third World countries escalate to nuclear war? Debates on these questions tend to be acrimonious, with each side often simply reiterating its own position and disparaging the arguments of the other side. The acrimony is not surprising given the variety of important issues at stake and the confusion about the meaning of key terms on both sides. What, for example, does "prevailing" in a nuclear war really mean? What exactly is "minimal deterrence" or "vital interest"?

Our goal with respect to these issues is to explore the contributions that the behavioral and social sciences can make to the understanding both of how a nuclear war might come about and of how such a war could be prevented. These contributions can be divided into two broad categories, methodological and theoretical. On the methodological side, the behavioral and social sciences remind us of the dangers of making vague causal claims that are difficult to falsify and that rest on superficial and highly subjective readings of the historical record. The quality of analysis that underlies public debates over the political and strategic functions of nuclear weapons is often strikingly inferior to the quality of analysis that was required to invent and construct these weapons in the first place. One rarely hears policy advocates specifying the types of evidence that would induce them to change their minds, clearly articulating the causal assumptions that undergird their prescriptive recommendations, or dispassionately assessing the strengths and weaknesses of alternative research methods for testing these causal assumptions. In short, the policy debate seems to encourage the suppression of ambiguity and doubt. Although the contributors to this series were asked to explore the policy implications of the research literatures they reviewed, they were also asked not to slip into roles of policy advocacy. Indeed, we encouraged contributors to be methodologically self-conscious, to make careful note of both the strengths and weaknesses of the data and methods from which they derived their theoretical and policy conclusions.

On the theoretical side, the behavioral and social sciences remind us of the dangers of making sweeping, undifferentiated claims concerning the causes of war. Simple theoretical generalizations tend to have poor empirical track records. The causes of international conflict are extremely complex. Variables operating at a number of levels of analysis appear to play key causal roles. Moreover, the effects of these variables appear to be both interactive (the effects of variable A on war depend on the levels of variables B, C, D, . . .) and probabilistic (variables influence the likelihood of various types of war and peace but rarely make a particular outcome inevitable). A reasonable inductive inference from the relevant research literatures is that there are many possible pathways to nuclear war (Allison, Carnesale, and Nye, 1985), with the relative likelihoods of the different paths shifting as a largely unknown function of complex configurations of psychological variables (the belief systems and motives of the decision makers), bureaucratic variables (the standard procedures of national security organizations and the rivalries among organizations), domestic political variables (the pressures from various internal constituencies to be firm or conciliatory), and the nature of the international environment (the military–technological–economic balance of power).

The behavioral and social sciences have established lines of research and theory that promise to clarify the factors affecting both the likelihood of war in general and of nuclear war in particular. Although there is no well-accepted theory of the conditions promoting nuclear war, there is knowledge bearing on important parts of the problem: the behavior of decision makers under uncertainty, the effects of different kinds of organizations on their members, the circumstances under which threats deter dangerous behavior, the processes of negotiation when stakes are high, and so on.

Our strategy in developing this series has been to identify existing work that bears on issues of this kind and then to persuade a well-informed researcher to summarize the current state of the literature and reflect on its implications for preventing nuclear war. The contributions to this volume present and assess knowledge about decision making in crisis situations (Holsti, Chapter 1), domestic political pressures to go to war (Russett, Chapter 3; Levy, Chapter 4), the rhythms and patterns of international negotiations (Druckman and Hopmann, Chapter 2), and the conditions under which various types of international influence tactics (especially deterrence) do and do not work (Levy,

Chapter 4). Contributions to future volumes will address these issues and others, such as the functioning of complex national security bureaucracies; the processes of judgment and decision making in foreign policy contexts; the role of arms races in international conflict; and the relevance of current knowledge about aggressive behavior, cooperation, international interdependence, and nationalist ideology to reducing the risk of nuclear war.

Given the difficulties of conducting research on these issues—the limited number of observations, the large number of confounding variables, and the fallibility of the research methods at our disposal—it is impressive, as Tetlock argues (Chapter 5), that we have achieved as much as we have. Given the magnitude of the problem of nuclear war, it is discouraging, as Tetlock also argues, that so much remains to be accomplished.

The behavioral and social sciences do not offer decisive solutions to the international predicaments confronting us; they do, however, identify considerations that prudent policymakers should take into account in performing the difficult act of balancing "vital national interests" against the necessity of avoiding nuclear war. The behavioral and social sciences can help illuminate and specify for the policy community the dangers of cognitive conceit (of thinking we know more than we do); the limitations of the most widely accepted theory of international influence (deterrence theory); the multiplicity of potential pathways to nuclear war; the impact of crisis-induced stress on human thought; the difficult trade-offs in crisis management; the ease with which both intended and unintended signals can be misinterpreted; and the egregious errors that can arise from relying on selective and superficial readings of the historical record.

In brief, we draw on the behavioral and social sciences to make a case for new intellectual approaches to the subject of international security. The approaches need to be conceptually rigorous (key ideas should be well defined and their links to empirical reality explicitly noted), theoretically eclectic (drawing on a broad range of interacting levels of analysis, from the psychological to the international system), and methodologically self-conscious (carefully scrutinizing the distinctive strengths and weaknesses of different research methods that underlie claims to knowledge about the sources of war). Taking a new approach, to be sure, is not easy; it requires increased tolerance of ambiguity and complexity. There are no neatly packaged answers to the pressing policy dilemmas posed by the multifaceted and rapidly changing international environment. To contribute to policy deliberations, we need to understand and take account of the complex interactions of human and societal processes. Appreciating the difficulties, we attempt here to mobilize new resources for the task.

References

Allison, G.T., Carnesale, A., and Nye, J.S., Jr., eds. 1985. *Hawks, Doves, and Owls: An Agenda for Avoiding Nuclear War*. New York: Norton.

Solomon, F., and Marston, R.Q., eds. 1986. *The Medical Implications of Nuclear War*. Proceedings of a symposium sponsored by the Institute of Medicine. Washington, D.C.: National Academy Press.

1

Crisis Decision Making

OLE R. HOLSTI

Crisis Decision Making: Perspectives from Four Levels of Analysis, 13
THE NATION-STATE, 13   THE BUREAUCRATIC ORGANIZATION, 16
DECISION-MAKING GROUPS, 19   THE INDIVIDUAL DECISION MAKER, 22

Crisis, Stress, and Decision Making: Some Evidence from Experimental
and Field Research, 25
REDUCED SPAN OF ATTENTION, 30   COGNITIVE RIGIDITY, 30
TIME PERSPECTIVE, 31

Decision Making in Foreign Policy Crises, 37
THE 1914 CRISIS, 37   THE CUBAN MISSILE CRISIS OF 1962, 41
OTHER INTERNATIONAL CRISES, 43

Crisis Management, 48
PRESCRIPTIVE THEORIES, 53   ASSESSMENT, 57

Conclusion, 59
Notes, 65
References, 69

"When the going gets tough, the tough get going" is a favorite aphorism of countless football coaches and Marine drill instructors. It also appears to be deeply embedded in the mind-sets of many students and practitioners of foreign policy. Although usually worded more elegantly, the essence of this proposition may be found in both theoretical treatises on international relations and in the memoirs of statesmen. According to this view, when the stakes in a situation are low and the costs of miscalculation are limited, various constraints and nonrational elements may reduce the quality of decisions but in a major crisis, when even national survival may be at risk, leaders and governments will rise to the challenge by performing at their best.

Nowhere is this proposition expressed as clearly as in memoirs written by Richard Nixon some years before he assumed the presidency. He described crises as "mountaintop experiences" in which his performance reached its peak: "Only then [in crises] does he discover all the latent strengths he never knew he had and which otherwise would have remained dormant" (Nixon, 1962:xvi). He added that:

> It has been my experience that, more often than not, taking a break is actually an escape from the rough, grinding discipline that is absolutely necessary for superior performance. Many times I have found that my best ideas have come when I thought I could not work for another minute and when I literally had to drive myself to finish the task before a deadline. Sleepless nights, to the extent that the body can take them, can stimulate creative mental activity (Nixon, 1962:105).

Others have appraised the effects of crisis on decision making in a similar vein, suggesting, for example, that "a decision maker may, in a crisis, be able to invent or work out easily and quickly what seems in normal times to both the 'academic' scholar and the layman to be hypothetical, unreal, complex or otherwise difficult" (Kahn, 1965:38), and "routine experience may lead us imperceptibly to ignore a slowly changing or suddenly new reality, but we do sometimes rise to a challenge with heightened alertness and an increased sense of responsibility, especially on matters of great moment" (Wohlstetter and Wohlstetter, 1971:263). These observations share the assumption that, like the prospect of hanging in a fortnight, crisis "concentrates the mind" and increases the decision maker's motivation and ability to cope with threat, complexity, and uncertainty.

Many theories of international relations and specific elements of them—for example, theories of deterrence—also presuppose rational and predictable decision processes, even during intense and protracted international crises. They assume that threats and ultimata will enhance calculation, control, and caution while inhibiting recklessness and risktaking. In short, many observers tend to be sanguine about the ability of policymakers to be creative when the situation requires it—and never is that requirement greater than during an intense international crisis.

These observations appear to confirm the conventional wisdom that in crisis decision making necessity is indeed the mother of invention. Is there any reason to question the universal validity of that view? If the ultimate contemporary criterion of effective crisis decision making is the avoidance of nuclear war, the burden of proof would appear to be on those who doubt the conventional view. Despite frequent confrontations and crises during the past four decades, the major powers have not only avoided a nuclear war but in only two instances have their armed forces come into direct conflict with each other, resulting in casualties: China and the United States in Korea during the early 1950s, and various clashes between the Soviet Union and China on their common border.

Nevertheless, although scenarios of decision-making malfunctions resulting in a nuclear war are limited to novels and movies, not all of the relevant evidence is totally reassuring. The recollections of those who have experienced intense and protracted crises suggest they may be marked at times by great skill in policymaking and at others by decision processes and outcomes that fail to meet even the most permissive standards of rationality. Some recall the "sense of elation that comes with crises" (Argyris, 1967:42), whereas others admit to serious shortcomings in their own performance during such situations. Dwight Eisenhower, for example, recalled, "You see a poor, rather stupid fellow behind a desk and you wonder why he couldn't do better than that. Unfortunately, that picture comes up too often" (Eisenhower, 1965). Indeed, although the definitive history of the Watergate episode remains to be written, the evidence suggests that Nixon's performance during that culminating crisis of his presidency was at best erratic, certainly falling far short of his self-diagnosis. This gap between one's assessments of one's abilities to cope and one's actual performance in crises is probably not limited to Nixon. That in itself is somewhat sobering.

But anecdotes do not provide a sufficient basis for evaluating the impact of crisis on policymaking. Is there any systematic evidence about how individuals, groups, and organizations respond to the challenges and demands of crises? Do they tend to approach such situations with high motivation, extraordinary energy, more accurate perceptions of the situation and relevant actors, an enhanced ability for processing information, and increased capabilities and resources for creative problem solving? Or, is the capacity for coping with complex problems sometimes impaired, perhaps to the point suggested by Richard Neustadt's (1970:116) phrase, "the paranoid reaction characteristic of crisis behavior?"

To explore the relationship between crisis and decision-making performance, this chapter examines three very diverse bodies of literature and focuses on several different levels of analysis for insights and evidence. First, theories of international relations, foreign policy, and deterrence provide a rather varied set of answers to the central questions about crisis decision making. Second, psychologists and other social scientists have also undertaken experimental and field research about various aspects of decision-making performance under conditions that replicate at least some aspects of crises, notably high stress. There is a large and growing literature of field studies on how individuals, groups, and organizations cope with disasters, including floods, earthquakes, tornadoes, chemical accidents, civil disturbances, riots, and the like.[1] Owing to important differences between the laboratory and foreign offices, experimental evidence is more appropriately used as a source of insights and hypotheses rather than as direct answers to questions about the impact of crisis on foreign policy decision making. Third, in order to overcome these limitations on experimental evidence, it is fortunate that we can also draw on a growing body of systematic and comparative research on actual international crises of both the prenuclear and contemporary eras. The concluding section of this chapter examines several approaches to improving policymaking performance in crises—that is, crisis management.

Before proceeding it may be useful to identify several aspects of the issue that will *not* be discussed here and to discuss briefly two of the terms that will appear frequently throughout this chapter: *crisis* and *stress*.

The discussion that follows will not deal with the psychobiological aspects of crisis decision making (the impact of aging, sleep deprivation, diurnal cycles, etc.) or with pharmacological issues (the effect of heavy intake of caffeine, nicotine, or various prescription drugs during a crisis). Although it is well known that some key policymakers have suffered from serious illnesses during major crises—for example, Anthony Eden had a severe case of ulcers and John Foster Dulles was stricken with cancer during the simultaneous Suez and Hungarian crises of 1956—this aspect of the question will receive little attention.[2]

It is also important to emphasize that the focus here is on "normal" rather than psychopathological foreign policy leaders. This is not to deny the dangers of a Stalin or Hitler, or even a Khaddafi or Khomeini, who might have access to nuclear weapons, but a focus on such cases might suggest that the central questions of crisis decision making are confined to pathological personalities and, therefore, that the policy problem is essentially to ensure that such leaders are denied access to the levers of power, especially if those levers are linked to nuclear weapons. This seems to be a misplaced focus for two reasons. First, it may establish unrealistically narrow boundaries around the issue of crisis decision making in the nuclear age by suggesting that it is limited to the clearly abnormal leaders, thereby perhaps leading to a neglect of potentially important types of decision-making malfunctions that may occur among normal leaders, advisory groups, and organizations. Second, it is doubtful that the best use of behavioral science knowledge is the identification of future Stalins and Hitlers and the prescription that they be denied office. The willingness of many psychiatrists to undertake negative evaluations at a distance of Senator Barry Goldwater in 1964 and to pronounce him unfit for the presidency was not one of the shining episodes in the history of the behavioral sciences.

Crisis and stress are two of the central concepts that will be used repeatedly in the discussion that follows, but in neither case is there a consensus in the literature on how they should be defined. Students of crisis tend to adopt either a systemic or a decision-making definition. The latter perspective, focusing on the policymaker's definition of the situation, is clearly more relevant for present purposes. Although there is a lack of complete agreement on definitions of crisis, even among those who have adopted the decision-making perspective, some common elements may be found.[3] There is general agreement that crises are marked by a *severe threat* to important values and that *time* for coping with the threat is finite. That definition will be adopted here.

Two other potential attributes of crisis also merit mention. Some have included *surprise* as an element of crisis. Although there is reason to believe that the behavioral consequences of surprise may be significant, the evidence on this point is not strong enough to indicate that it should be a necessary condition for the existence of a crisis. Several other students of crisis have included the stipulation that a crisis must involve the policymaker's perception of a significant *probability of armed conflict*. This requirement may be valid for many foreign policy situations, but it also seems overly restrictive. Perhaps two examples will illustrate the point. When a major drug manufacturer learns that its products have been tampered with, resulting in a number of deaths, even though there is no perceived threat of war, one might want to conceive of it as a crisis for the organization and its top executives. Or, if a consortium of major Third World debtor nations were to declare a default on all of their external debts, officials in Washington, London, Bonn, Tokyo, the World Bank, the International Monetary Fund, and major private banks might believe that they are confronted with a major crisis (high threat to important values and a limited time for coping with the problem), even though there would be little danger of armed conflict.

There is widespread agreement among students of crisis, whatever definition of that term they may adopt, that it is likely to give rise to *stress* among those who must cope with it. However, there is not a corresponding consensus on operational measures of stress among those who have contributed to the research to be reviewed here. Some define it as the stimulus (severe threat), whereas others view it as the perceptual and behavioral response to threat.[4] The latter definition will be used here, but the review of the research literature is not limited to any single conceptualization of stress.

Crisis Decision Making: Perspectives from Four Levels of Analysis

To survey theories and evidence about crisis decision making, it is useful to distinguish among four levels of analysis—the nation, bureaucratic organizations, decision-making groups, and the individual—because each tends to focus on and highlight different aspects of the question and to yield a somewhat different modal diagnosis (Table 1.1). As a rule, theories that focus on larger units (nations, organizations) tend to be somewhat more optimistic about the impact of crisis on the quality of decision making than those that deal with smaller ones (groups, individuals).

The Nation-State

The traditional and still-dominant "realist" theories usually incorporate the assumption that nation-states are best characterized as "unitary rational actors." Consequently, they attach relatively low explanatory power to cognitive and behavioral aspects of decision making in crises. As the most useful perspective for understanding the relations between nations, realists assume that in an international system characterized by structural anarchy policymakers are guided by the "national interest." Unwise leaders may at times miscalculate their interests, the resources available to various national actors, or the motives of adversaries. Worse, they may succumb to utopian or ideological thinking or to the parochial priorities and values of domestic politics, perhaps even creating crises in order to avoid coping with domestic difficulties. As the dean of the realist school wrote, "the rational requirements of good foreign policy cannot from the outset count upon the support of a public opinion whose preferences are emotional rather than rational" (Morgenthau, 1967:547).

Realist theories rarely distinguish between policymaking in crises and noncrisis situations; when they do so they tend to predict better performance in the former circumstances because of a reduced likelihood that irrelevant or

TABLE 1.1 Crisis Decision Making: Perspectives from Four Levels of Analysis

	The Nation-State	The Bureaucratic Organization	The Decision Making Group	The Individual Decision Maker
Conceptualization of decision making	Realism: unitary rational actor	Decision making as the result of bargaining within bureaucratic organizations	Decision making as the product of group interaction	Decision making as the result of individual choice
Sources of theory, insight, and evidence	Political science History Philosophy	Organization theory Sociology of bureaucracies Bureaucratic politics	Social psychology Sociology of small groups	Cognitive psychology Dynamic psychology
Premises	Decisions guided by the national interest and the logic of an anarchical international system	Central organizational values are imperfectly internalized Organizational behavior is political behavior Structure and standard operating procedures affect substance and quality of decisions	Most decisions made by elite groups Group is different from the sum of its members Group dynamics affect substance and quality of decisions	Importance of subjective appraisal and cognitive processes

Constraints on rational decision making	Inadequate understanding of the national interest Miscalculations of resources or motives of rivals Utopian thinking Lack of prudence Intrusion of domestic politics	Imperfect information resulting from centralization, hierarchy, or specialization Organizational inertia Conflict between individual and organizational utilities Bureaucratic politics and bargaining dominate decision making	Groups less effective for some decision making tasks Pressures for conformity Quality of leadership "Groupthink"	Cognitive limits on rationality Information processing distorted by cognitive consistency dynamics Systematic and motivated biases in causal analysis Individual differences on abilities related to decision making (e.g., problem-solving ability, tolerance of ambiguity, defensiveness and anxiety, information seeking) Cognitive dissonance
Prognosis: decisions made in crises versus "normal" situations	Tends to be higher, as impact of domestic politics, etc., is likely to be reduced	Variable to higher, as higher-quality information and superordinate values are likely to dominate parochial ones	Variable to lower, depending heavily on the ability of leader to make use of group, avoid "groupthink," etc.	Tends to be lower, as high stress tends to erode abilities needed to cope with complex problems.

inappropriate values will intrude into leaders' calculations. Even when the outcome of a crisis is war, the explanation is usually one of calculated political choice. Michael Howard (1983:22) makes the point clearly: "Whatever may be the underlying causes of international conflict . . . wars begin with conscious and reasoned decisions based on the calculation, made by both parties, that they can achieve more by going to war than by remaining at peace." The same point is made even more strongly in another treatise on war. "In every case, the decision [to go to war] is based upon a careful weighing of the chances and of anticipating consequences. . . . In no case is the decision precipitated by emotional tensions, sentimentality, crowd behavior, or other irrational motivations" (Abel, 1941:855).[5]

Theories of deterrence are especially sanguine about the calculated aspects of decision making. Although there are several approaches to deterrence and none of them is free from controversy, most of them share two central propositions. First, foreign policy can best be characterized as a process of rational calculation. As Thomas Schelling (1963:4) has put it, the premise is "not just of intelligent behavior, but of behavior motivated by a conscious calculation of advantage, a calculation that in turn is based on an explicit and internally valid value system." Second, as the stakes in a situation increase—for example, when a nation faces a major threat to core values, or perhaps even to its existence—policy processes will even more closely approximate the norms of calculated decision making. Conversely, deterrence, whether in criminal law or nuclear strategy, is of doubtful efficacy against madmen, the suicidal, or those who welcome martyrdom. Some critics have suggested that challenges to deterrence (which may precipitate a crisis) are only partially explained by the "unitary rational actor" model of foreign policy behavior. They may, for example, arise from domestic political considerations or from calculations of weakness rather than from strength (Jervis et al., 1985). These and other reasons suggest that a complete explanation of crisis decision making cannot be achieved by focusing solely on the nation-state level of analysis.

The Bureaucratic Organization

Traditional theories of bureaucratic organizations focused on a division of labor dictated by expertise, rationality, obedience, and clear boundaries between politics and decision making on the one hand, and administration and implementation on the other. Following the pioneering work by Barnard (1938), Simon (1947), March and Simon (1958), and others, more recent theories depict organizations quite differently. The central premise is that decision making in bureaucratic organizations is heavily constrained, and not only by the legal and formal norms that are intended to enhance the rational and eliminate the capricious aspects of bureaucratic behavior. There is an *emphasis,* rather than a denial, of the political character of bureaucracies as well as on other constraints on organizational behavior. Complex organizations are regarded as being composed of individuals and units with conflicting perceptions, values, and interests that may arise in part from parochial self-interests ("what is best for my bureau is also best for my career") and also in part from different perceptions of problems arising naturally from a division of labor ("where you stand depends on where you sit"). Organizational memories and standard operating procedures (SOPs) constrain the search for and evaluation of policy options and, more generally, innovation. Consequently, organizational decision making is essentially political in character, dominated by bargaining for resources, roles, missions, and compromise, rather than by analysis.[6]

These and other aspects of bureaucracy are also likely to constrain information processing, with the consequence that, as one observer has put it, "Intelligence failures are built into complex organizations" (Wilensky, 1967:179). Information normally enters the organization at middle levels or lower, and the need to reduce it to a manageable quantity as it flows upward may result in qualitative distortions arising from both motivated and unmotivated biases. Incoming information may be filtered through and fitted into existing images, preconceptions, preferences, expectations, and plans. Officials may screen out some data adverse to their own interests and magnify others that are favorable; information may also be distorted by a tendency to make it reflect, more closely than reality warrants, what superiors are believed to want to hear (Downs, 1967:265–266, 282). Aside from these more or less deliberate distortions, the taller the organizational hierarchy, the greater the "uncertainty absorption" as information moves upward (March and Simon, 1958:165; Wilensky, 1967:57; Downs, 1967:269).

In light of these somewhat jaundiced views about the performance of bureaucracies, it is perhaps not surprising that some students of organizational behavior tend to view the impact of crises in a favorable light. Crises provide both the motivation and the means for reducing some of the pathological aspects of "normal" bureaucratic behavior. They are likely to move the locus of decision making to the top of the organization where higher-quality intelligence is available; information is more likely to enter the top levels of the hierarchy directly, reducing the distorting effects of hierarchy on information processing; and broader, less parochial values—for example, "the national interest"—may be invoked. Several analysts place special emphasis on the salutary effects of short decision time in reducing the opportunities for decision making by bargaining, logrolling, incrementalism, lowest-common-denominator values, muddling through, and the like (Wilensky, 1967:76–81, 175–179; Lowi, 1969:158–160)

> Thus, it may be, paradoxically, that the model of means-ends rationality will be more closely approximated in an emergency when the time for careful deliberation is limited. Though fewer alternatives will be considered, the values invoked during the decision process will tend to be fewer and more consistent, and the decision will less likely be the result of bargaining within a coalition (Verba, 1961a:115).

The optimistic interpretation of organizational responses to threat and stress is not universally accepted. Drawing from evidence at the individual, group, and organizational levels, Staw et al. (1981) developed a model in which threat gives rise to restrictions in information processing and constriction of control, both of which contribute to rigidity in response—a "tendency toward well-learned or dominant responses" rather than creativity or innovation. The critical intervening variable is the nature of the threat, because the "well-learned" response may be appropriate for familiar threats but less so for unknown dangers. Finally, even those who believe that the organizations are capable of rising to the challenge of a crisis caution that repeated crises are likely to have significant deleterious efforts, including the inhibition of creativity, the enhancement of ideological preconceptions in decision making, the increased reliance on "worst case" contingency plans, and the premature narrowing down of alternatives (Wilensky, 1972:8).

Perhaps owing to the dominant position of the "realist, unitary rational actor" perspective cited earlier, students of foreign policy have only in recent years incorporated bureaucratic/organizational theories and insights into their analyses. There is an ample literature of case studies of budgeting, weapons acquisition, and similar noncrisis situations confirming that foreign and defense policy bureaucracies rarely conform to the Weberian "ideal type" of rational organization.

However, even studies of international crises from an organizational perspective are not uniformly sanguine about decision-making performance in such circumstances. Allison's (1971) study of the Cuban missile crisis revealed a substantial number of malfunctions, especially in the implementation of some key decisions, including, but not limited to, the dispersal of U.S. aircraft in Florida, the location of the naval blockade, and the grounding of weather-sampling flights near the Soviet Union. As the president complained at the time, "There is always some son of a bitch who doesn't get the word."[7] Perhaps equally sobering is the conclusion of Neustadt's (1970) analysis of two crises involving the United States and the United Kingdom. Despite sharing many political and cultural values, leaders of even these long-time allies significantly misperceived each others' interests and policy processes during the Suez and Skybolt missile crises. And a study of three U.S. nuclear alerts revealed substantial gaps in understanding and communication between policymakers and the military leaders who were responsible for implementing the alerts (Sagan, 1985).

Decision-Making Groups

Because foreign policy decisions are usually made in a group context, some analysts have drawn on sociological and sociopsychological insights and evidence to assess the impact of group dynamics on decision making (De Rivera, 1968; Paige, 1968; George, 1974; Janis, 1972, 1982). Underlying this perspective are the premises that the group is not merely the sum of its members (therefore decisions emerging from the group are likely to be different than what a simple aggregation of individual preferences and abilities might suggest), and the dynamics of group interaction are likely to have a significant impact on the substance and quality of decisions.

Groups often perform better than individuals in coping with complex tasks, owing to diverse perspectives and talents, an effective division of labor, and high-quality substantive debates centering on diagnoses of the situation and prescriptions for coping with it (Vroom, 1969; Collins and Guetzkow, 1964). Groups may also provide decision makers with emotional and other types of support that may facilitate coping with complex problems. But there is less agreement on the relative merits of individuals and groups in generating alternatives approaches to a problem (Maier, 1970; Taylor et al., 1958; Dunnette et al., 1963; Vroom, 1969; Vroom et al., 1969; Feldman and Kanter, 1965). Extensive evidence indicates that interaction within groups reduces variance in behavior, crystallizes attitudes and beliefs, and generally exerts pressures for conformity to group norms (Festinger, 1965). The classical experiments by Asch (1953, 1965) revealed the extent to which group members will suppress their beliefs and judgments when faced with a majority adhering to the contrary view, even a counterfactual one.

Some social psychologists have also suggested that groups are more prone than individuals to making high-risk decisions (Ziller, 1957). Neither risk taking nor risk avoidance are, per se, indications of nonrational decision making. If, however, accepting high risk is the result of group dynamics rather than of conscious calculations and careful assessment of the situation, then it does deviate from rationality. Some experiments suggest that groups are more prone to choose high-risk options and that group discussions are likely to cause individuals to shift to riskier choices. The interpretation of these findings has become somewhat controversial, however (see, for example, Pruitt, 1971a, 1971b; Schneider, 1974; George, 1980), and even the basic concept of the "risky shift" has been challenged. Cartwright (1971) suggests that the risk-taking propensities of groups might better be explained by reference to social influence and conformity. Perhaps the most persuasive explanation is the "group polarization" hypothesis, which is based on attitude change theory. It suggests that groups make decisions that are "more extreme in the direction of the norm than the initial responses of members," whether in experimental groups (Moscovici, 1985:397; Myers and Lamm, 1976) or in juries (Rodin, 1985:818–819). Thus, initial inclinations of group members are important because the outcome is likely to be an exaggerated version of initial individual judgments. Perhaps this hypothesis explains the anecdotal evidence that groups or committees may also produce conservative, low-risk decisions (Whyte, 1957; de Rivera, 1968:140–141). Thus, existing data on risk taking are less than conclusive. Experimental studies must necessarily be confined to situations of low to moderate stakes. The relationship between group dynamics and risk taking when the stakes are immense, as they often are in foreign policy crises, is of special interest, but the evidence on this is virtually nonexistent.

There is some evidence that groups perform best with respect to task orientation, efficiency, adaptability, and consistency in circumstances of moderate stress, whereas high stress tends to have a negative effect on their performance. Both experimental and historical studies have consistently shown that in high-stress situations decision groups tend to become smaller. This was true, for example, of the groups that developed policy in many international crises, including Indo-China (Roberts, 1954), Korea (Paige, 1968), Cuba (Kennedy, 1969), Vietnam (Hoopes, 1969), and Cambodia (Maxey, 1970; Smith, 1970). The reasons may be related in part to the belief that smaller groups can cope more effectively with crises because they can act more quickly, with better insulation against domestic political pressures and constraints and with a reduced risk of premature "leaks" of sensitive information to the media and the public.

However, limiting the number of participants in a decision group can also be viewed as a strategy for coping with some sources of stress; for example, the need for coordination within the group declines as the group becomes smaller. As another step to reduce stress, leaders may also take steps to restrict the diversity of viewpoints by selective recruitment or by elimination of known dissenters. However, these steps may have other consequences as well. Other things being equal, a smaller group is likely to represent neither the same range of diversity in values, beliefs, and attitudes as a larger one nor the knowledge and analytical skills. On balance, the evidence suggests that a reduction in size may lead to reduced decision-making effectiveness.

Among the most widely cited social science axioms is that external threat, when experienced as common fate, increases group cohesion.[8] This may facilitate effective teamwork on common tasks, provide psychological and emotional supports, and reduce the stresses associated with conflict within the group. However, cohesion may also become a superordinate rather than instrumental value, thereby creating greater pressures for conformity to group goals and norms, reducing tolerance for critical analysis and dissenting viewpoints, and eroding judgment (Janis, 1972, 1982; Festinger et al., 1950; Vroom, 1969; Verba, 1961b; Blake and Mouton, 1962). To the extent that conflict within the group is itself perceived to be a source of stress rather than of better analysis (decision makers appear to differ in their ability to tolerate such conflict), there will be added pressures for conformity.

Because most of these data were developed by experimental methods, a series of case studies by Janis (1972, 1982; see also Tetlock, 1979; and the critique by Etheredge, 1985:112–114), including a number of foreign policy crises, is an especially relevant source of evidence about group decision-making performance. Groups are vulnerable to a variety of serious malfunctions. As a means of dealing with the stresses of having to cope with consequential problems and in order to bolster self-esteem, the frequency and intensity of face-to-face interaction may increase, resulting in greater identification with the group and less competition within it. According to Janis, "groupthink"—defined as a deterioration of mental efficiency, reality testing, and moral judgment—occurs when concern for group solidarity supersedes the effective performance of vital decision-making tasks. As a consequence, groups may be afflicted by unwarranted feelings of optimism and invulnerability, stereotyped images of adversaries, inattention to warnings, and powerful, if sometimes subtle, pressures against dissent.

Janis' case studies of "successful" decisions, including development of the Marshall Plan by the Policy Planning Staff and the response to the Soviet deployment of missiles in Cuba, indicate that "groupthink" or other decision-making pathologies are not inevitable. The nature of the threat may be a critical variable (Staw et al., 1981) but, even in high-stress situations, the potential range of group performance is moderately wide. Various structural attributes may affect group performance, and there is also strong evidence that the nature of leadership in managing the decision process accounts for a good deal of the variance. Effective and imaginative leadership appears to be a necessary condition for averting some of the vulnerabilities of group dynamics. However, leaders themselves are not immune to high stress, and leadership performance becomes more variable under such circumstances (Torrance, 1957, 1961).

The Individual Decision Maker

Many approaches to the individual as a decision maker emphasize the gap between the demands of the classical model of rational decision making and the substantial body of theory and evidence about various constraints that come into play even in relatively simple choice situations. (For a review of the alternative models and the vast literature, see Abelson and Levi, 1985.) The more recent perspectives go well beyond some of the earlier formulations that identified various types of psychopathologies among political leaders, including paranoia, authoritarianism, and the displacement of private motives on the public objects (Lasswell, 1931). Although interest in these concerns persists, much recent theory and research has been directed at cognitive and motivational constraints that, in varying degrees, affect the decision-making performance of "normal" rather than deviant subjects. Thus the relevant universe includes all leaders, not merely those who display evidence of clinical abnormalities, such as Hitler and Stalin.

The major challenges to the classical model have focused in various ways on limited human capabilities for performing the tasks required by objectively rational decision making. Skepticism about the classical decision model has given rise to several competing conceptions of the decision maker and his or her strategies for dealing with complexity, uncertainty, incomplete or contradictory information, and, paradoxically, information overload. They variously characterize the decision maker as a problem solver, naive or intuitive scientist, cognitive balancer or dissonance avoider, information seeker, cybernetic information processor, and reluctant decision maker.[9] Of these conceptions, three that seem especially relevant for present purposes can be described briefly.

• The decision maker is a "bounded rationalist." As Herbert Simon (1957:198) has put it, "The capacity of the human mind for formulating and solving complex problems is very small compared with the size of the problems whose solution is required for objectively rational behavior in the real world—or even a reasonable approximation of such objective rationality." Moreover, it is not practical for the real-world decision maker to take the time and effort to make optimal choices, for example, because of the costs associated with the search for information.

• The decision maker is an "error-prone intuitive scientist" who is likely to commit a broad range of inferential mistakes: "attempts to understand, predict and control events in the social sphere are seriously compromised by specific inferential shortcomings" (Nisbett and Ross, 1980, quoted in Abelson and Levi, 1985:233). Thus, rather than emphasizing the limits on costs of search, information processing, and the like, this conception views the decision maker as a person who, through a variety of flawed heuristics or decision rules, uses data poorly; for example, there are tendencies to underuse base rate data in making judgments, believe in the "law of small numbers," underuse diagnostic information, overweigh low probabilities and underweigh high probabilities, and commit other violations of the requirements of consistency and coherence. These deviations from classical decision theory are traced to the psychological principles that govern perceptions of decision problems and evaluations of options (Tversky and Kahneman, 1974, 1981; Kahneman et al., 1982).

• The decision maker is dominated by motivational forces that will not or cannot be controlled (Janis and Mann, 1977; Steiner, 1983; Lebow, 1981).

Common to virtually all of these approaches is an interest in belief systems, images of relevant actors (including self-images), perceptions, information processing strategies, heuristics, certain personality attributes (ability to tolerate ambiguity, cognitive complexity, etc.), and the impact that these may have on decision-making performance. A subject of special relevance for this chapter is research on the impact of high stress—for example, that induced by an intense crisis—on cognitive performance.

Despite this diversity of theoretical perspectives and concepts and the difficulty of choosing between cognitive and motivational models (Tetlock and Levi, 1982), there has been some convergence on three types of cognitive constraints that may introduce systematic biases into the decision process (Kinder and Weiss, 1978).

THE IMPACT OF EFFORTS TO ACHIEVE COGNITIVE CONSISTENCY ON PERCEPTIONS AND INFORMATION PROCESSING

Several kinds of systematic bias have been identified in both experimental research and historical studies of foreign policy and other kinds of decisions. Among them are propensities to assimilate and interpret incoming information in ways that conform to, rather than challenge, existing beliefs, preferences, hopes, and expectations; denial of, rather than acceptance of, the need to confront trade-offs; and postdecision rationalizations to bolster the selected options while denigrating those that were rejected ("spreading the alternatives").

SYSTEMATIC BIAS IN CAUSAL ANALYSIS

An extensive literature on styles of attribution has revealed several types of bias. Perhaps the most important for present purposes is the basic attribution error—a tendency to explain the adversary's behavior in terms of personal characteristics (for example, inherent aggressiveness or hostility) instead of the context or situation, while attributing one's own behavior to the latter (for example, legitimate security needs arising from a dangerous and uncertain international environment) instead of the former (Jones and Nisbett, 1972; Ross, 1977; and a fuller review in Ross and Fletcher, 1985). A somewhat related type of double standard in assessing oneself and the adversary has been noted by George Kennan (1978:87–88).

> Now is it our view that we should take account only of their capabilities, disregarding their intentions, but we should expect them to take account only of our supposed intentions, disregarding our capabilities? . . . If we are going to disregard everything but their capabilities, we cannot simultaneously expect them to disregard everything but our intentions.

ASSUMPTIONS ABOUT ORDER AND PREDICTABILITY IN THE ENVIRONMENT

Whereas one may have an acute appreciation of the disorderly environment in which one operates (for example, arising out of the domestic political process), there is a tendency to assume that others, especially adversaries, are free of such problems. Allison (1971), Jervis (1976), and others have demonstrated that there is a tendency to believe that the unitary rational actor model (Model I) is the appropriate representation of the opponent's decision processes. Stated differently, whatever happened was the direct result of deliberate action by the adversary. The Korean Airlines flight 007 tragedy offers a relevant example. The hypothesis that the Soviet action may have resulted from intelligence failures and bureaucratic foul-ups, and not from a deliberate decision to commit an act of mass murder against civilian passengers, was either not given serious consideration or was suppressed for strategic reasons (Hersh, 1986).

A related but somewhat different perspective, emphasizing *the impact of stress*, is especially relevant for the present discussion. This approach goes beyond the observation made earlier that the perception of a severe threat to important values is likely to result in stress for those who must cope with the problem. It also regards the requirement of having to make nontrivial decisions as in itself a major source of stress. Janis and Mann (1977:3) have developed a conflict-theory model that conceives of a human being as a "reluctant decision maker" and focuses on "when, how and why psychological stress generated by decisional conflict imposes limitations on the rationality of a person's decisions. . . ." According to Janis and Mann's model, an individual may employ five strategies for coping with a situation calling for a decision: unconflicted adherence to the existing policy, unconflicted change, defensive avoidance, hypervigilance, and vigilant decision making. The first four strategies are likely to yield low-quality decisions owing to incomplete search, appraisal, and contingency planning, whereas the fifth strategy, characterized by a thorough performance of vital tasks, is more likely to result in a high-quality choice. The mediating processes that will affect the employment of decision styles are information about risks, expectations of finding a better option, and time for adequate search and deliberation.

These constraints are likely to be operative in all cases of consequential decision making. The next two sections of this chapter consider how these and other aspects of the decision process are likely to be affected by stress.

Crisis, Stress, and Decision Making: Some Evidence from Experimental and Field Research

One of the most extensive systematic bodies of theory and evidence on crisis behavior focuses on the impact of stress on certain aspects of cognitive performance that are integral to decision making. In assessing the potential impact of crisis on cognitive performance, it is important to do so against realistic standards and not against an idealized model of rational decision making that can never be matched, even for relatively simple problems. The cognitive constraints on rationality include limits on the individual's capacity to receive, process, and assimilate information about the situation; an inability to generate the entire set of policy alternatives; fragmentary knowledge about the consequences of each option; and an inability to order preferences for all possible consequences on a single utility scale (March and Simon, 1958:138). Because these constraints exist in all but the most trivial decisions, it is not instructive to assess the impact of crises against a standard of synoptic rationality. A more modest and realistic set of criteria might include the ability to deal effectively with the following cognitive, information-processing, and management tasks.

- Define the main elements of the situation; for example, what are the nature and sources of the threat, and what is at stake?
- Identify and consider adequately the major values, interests, and objectives to be fulfilled.
- Search for and evaluate the major alternative courses of action.
- Estimate the probable costs and risks, as well as the probable consequences, of various alternatives (and, as a corollary, distinguish the possible from the probable).
- Search for new information relevant to assessment of the options.
- Maintain receptivity to new information, even that which calls into question the validity of preferred courses of action (and, as corollaries, discriminate

between relevant and irrelevant information, resist premature cognitive closure, and tolerate ambiguity).
- Consider the problems that may arise in implementing various options.
- Assess the situation from the perspective of other parties.
- Deal with the possibility that one of many conceivable but highly unlikely events will occur as a result of system failures or "normal accidents."
- Resist both the Scylla of defensive procrastination and the Charybdis of premature decisions.
- Monitor feedback from a developing situation.
- Make adjustments to meet real changes in the situation (and, as a corollary, distinguish real from apparent changes).[10]

A substantial body of theory and evidence suggests that intense and protracted crises may erode rather than enhance the ability to perform these tasks. As a shortcut to the vast literature, Figure 1.1 presents a series of hypotheses linking the defining attributes of crisis, first to stress and then to selected aspects of decision-making performance. These propositions are presented not as iron laws but as a checklist of points at which decision making may be vulnerable to the effects of stress.

The psychological literature suggests that crises are characterized by high stress for the individuals and organizations involved. That a severe threat to important values is stress inducing requires little elaboration. The element of surprise, if present in the situation, may also be a contributing factor; there is evidence that unanticipated and novel situations are generally viewed as more threatening (Korchin and Levine, 1957). Moreover, crisis decisions are rarely if ever analogous to the familiar multiple-choice question in which the full range of options is neatly outlined. The theoretical universe of choices usually exceeds by a substantial margin the number that can, will, or even should be considered. Unanticipated situations for which there are no established standard operating procedures or decision rules make it necessary to search out and perhaps create options. Alternatively, there is a danger that planned routines—what one historian has called "drills"—will be employed even if they are not especially appropriate for the problem at hand (Keegan, 1981).

Finally, crises may be marked by almost around-the-clock work schedules, owing to both the severity of the situation and the absence of extended decision time. During the Cuban missile confrontation, for instance, many U.S. officials slept in their offices for the duration of the crisis: "We had to go on a twenty-four hour basis here in the Department of State" (Rusk, 1963). Premier Khrushchev also seems to have had little sleep during that week: "I must confess that I slept one night in my studio fully dressed on the sofa. I did not want to be in the position of one western diplomat who, during the Suez crisis, rushed to the telephone without his trousers" (*New York Times,* June

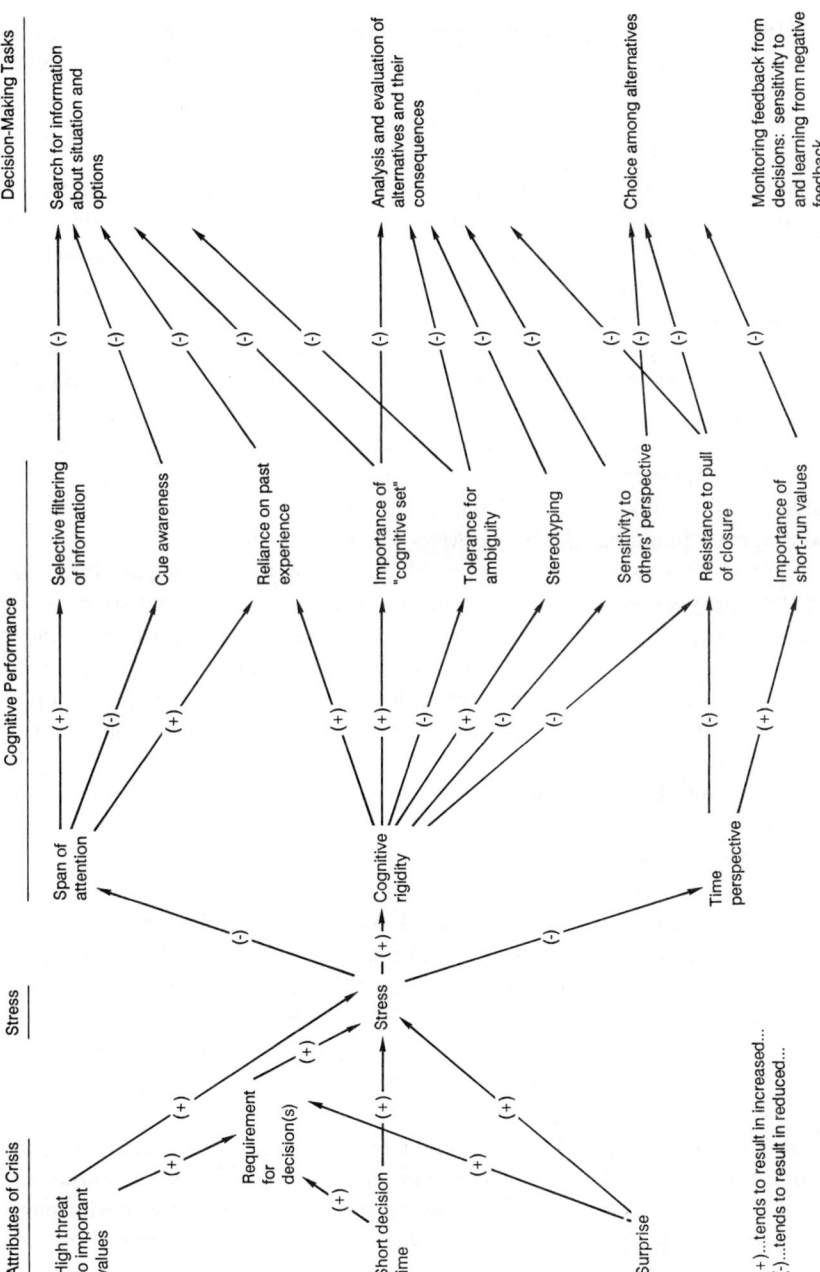

FIGURE 1.1. Individual decision making in crisis: some hypotheses. *Source:* Holsti (1979:106).

27, 1967). Even during the much less intense Middle East situation created by the Six Day War in 1967, the Soviet Politburo had at least one all-night meeting (according to the *San Francisco Chronicle,* June 9, 1967). Excessively long working hours without rest or recreation are likely to magnify the stresses inherent in the situation.

Thus, quite aside from the threat to be dealt with, the requirement of having to make decisions may itself be a significant source of stress, arising from efforts to cope with value complexity, cognitive constraints on rationality, and fatigue, as well as role factors, small group dynamics, and bureaucratic politics (George, 1975).

Some degree of stress is an integral and necessary precondition for individual or organizational problem solving, since in its absence there is no motivation to act. Even very low levels of stress may not be sufficient to alert one to the existence of a situation requiring attention, increasing vigilance, and stimulating preparations to cope with it. One may thus resort to "unconflicted adherence" or "unconflicted change" without adequate search, appraisal, and contingency planning (Janis and Mann, 1977:70).

Moderate levels of stress may heighten one's motivation and ability to find a satisfactory solution to the problem. A study of research scientists revealed, for example, that an environment of moderate stress, characterized by "uncertainty without anxiety," is the most conducive to creative work.[11] Indeed, for some elementary tasks a rather high degree of stress may increase performance, at least for limited periods of time. If the problem is qualitatively simple and performance is measured by quantitative criteria, stress can increase output. The threat of a severe flood may result in exceptional physical performance by emergency work crews who are filling and stacking sandbags, and a severe international crisis may give rise to improved output by foreign-office clerical staffs. The primary concern here, however, is not with the effects of stress on persons engaged in manual or routine repetitive tasks, but with its consequences on the performance of officials in leadership positions during international crises. These are nearly always marked by complexity and uncertainty, and they usually demand responses that are judged by qualitative as opposed to quantitative criteria. It is precisely these qualitative aspects of performance that are most likely to suffer from intense and protracted stress (Lowe, 1961; Kiesler, 1966).

The preponderance of experimental evidence indicates that intense and protracted stress, although it may improve simple psychomotor output, impairs cognitive performance. The relationship between cognitive performance and stress is often described as an "inverted U." Low to moderate stress may facilitate better performance but, according to most of the experimental evidence, protracted high stress degrades it. Birch (1945) determined that intermediate rather than high or low motivation was most conducive to the efficient solution of problems requiring both high and low insight. A related finding is that persons with moderate fear were better able to cope with the problems arising from major surgery than were those with high or low fear (Janis, 1958). Observational evidence from related field research (for example, studies of natural disasters, performance in combat, or other dangerous circumstances) and from analyses of foreign policy decision making—studies that are more directly relevant with respect to subjects, setting, and decision-making task, but are often considerably less rigorous and systematic—also tend to suggest that intense and protracted stress erodes rather than enhances the ability of individuals to cope with complex problems. Specifically, much of the disaster literature suggests that anxiety and stress give rise to withdrawal, reduction in effective information processing, and constriction of behavioral responses.[12] The following are some typical conclusions about the effects of high stress on aspects decision-making performance.

> Perceptual behavior is disrupted, becomes less well controlled than under normal conditions, and hence is less adaptive. The major dimensions of perceptual function are affected: selection of percepts from a complex field becomes less adequate and sense is less well differentiated from nonsense; there is maladaptive accentuation in the direction of aggression and escape; untested hypotheses are fixated recklessly (Postman and Bruner, 1948:322).

> [A] shift to a more rigid, primitive, less adequate and less realistic efforts at mastery . . . ineffective, rigid, and primary forms of coping, such as reality-distorting defenses (Lazarus et al., 1974).

> There is a narrowing of the cognitive organization at the moment; the individual loses broader perspective, he is no longer able to "see" essential aspects of the situation and his behavior becomes, consequently, less adaptive (Krech and Crutchfield, 1964:63).

> There is a tendency for more recent and usually more complex behavior to disappear and simpler and more basic forms of behavior to reappear (Milburn, 1972:265).

> When political leaders are faced with the necessity of making decisions the outcomes of which they cannot foresee, in crises which they do not wholly understand, they fall back on their own instinctive reactions, traditions and modes of behavior. Each of them has certain beliefs, rules or objectives which are taken for granted (Joll, 1968:6).

Because the evidence is far too voluminous and complex to summarize in detail, only a few of the main findings are outlined next, with a focus on three intervening variables identified in Figure 1.1: span of attention, cognitive rigidity, and time perspective.[13]

Reduced Span of Attention

Aside from the experience or anticipation of harm, the sources of stress in a decision-making situation may include task overload, information overload, and task or role conflicts. One way of coping is to narrow one's span of attention to a few aspects of the decision-making task: "the number of cues utilized in any situation tends to become smaller with an increase in emotion" (Easterbrook, 1959:197; see also Miller, 1960, 1962; Baddeley, 1972; Williams, 1957; Hermann, 1963). This is a functional strategy to the extent that it permits the executive to eliminate trivial distractions, filter out irrelevant information, and develop an agenda of priorities. However, these benefits may be offset by a number of costs.

Attention to fewer cues can be helpful if only trivial and irrelevant ones are overlooked but, as stress increases, filtering is likely to be less discriminating. As a consequence, important dimensions of the situation may escape scrutiny, conflict of values may be overlooked or suppressed, and the range of perceived alternatives is likely to narrow, but not necessarily to the best ones. In these circumstances search activity may be dominated by predispositions, operational codes (George, 1969), scripts (Abelson, 1976, 1981), schemata (Axelrod, 1976), or past episodes, either experienced first hand or vicariously as "lessons of history," the misapplication or overgeneralization of which is often a primary source of low-quality decisions (Broadbent, 1971; Paige, 1968; Milburn, 1972; Maier, 1963; Jervis, 1976; May, 1973; Neustadt and May, 1986; Vertzberger, 1986).

Cognitive Rigidity

Charles Lindblom (1968:22) suggests that, "A serious emergency or crisis often transforms a policy analyst's perception (and sometimes galvanizes his energies) with the result that he gets a new grasp on his problem." There is also some evidence that persons experiencing intense stress tend to suffer increased cognitive rigidity, an erosion of general cognitive abilities, including creativity and the ability to cope with complexity. The decision maker is likely to establish a dominant percept through which he or she interprets information and to maintain it even in the face of information that might seem to call for a reappraisal. Often this percept is a familiar one transferred from previous situations (for example, lessons of history), even though it may be inappropriate for the circumstance at hand. It is more likely to be characterized by stereotypes than by subtletly as the complexity of the psychological field is reduced.

It is neither possible nor wise to change one's beliefs and theories each time some discrepant information is received, but it is at least useful to be aware that evidence about an unfolding situation may be consistent with more than a single explanation. Tolerance for ambiguity is likely to suffer from high stress, with the result that conclusions may be drawn more quickly than is warranted by the evidence. Finally, caricatures of motivational structures may develop: the anxious become more anxious, the energetic become more energetic, the repressors become more repressive, and so on (Nalven, 1961; Manis, 1966; Kilpatrick, 1969; White and Lippitt, 1960; Smith et al., 1956; Jervis, 1968, 1976; Smock, 1955; Milburn, 1972).

Time Perspective

It has been observed that high-ranking public officials typically have a high discount rate, assigning high value to immediate achievements and discounting heavily the value of those that might be realized in a more distant future (Allison and Halperin, 1972). This tendency may be heightened by stress. For example, the ability to judge time is impaired in situations that increase anxiety (Cohen and Mezey, 1961). There thus appears to be a two-way relationship between time and stress. On the one hand, the common use during crisis of techniques such as ultimata and threats with built-in deadlines is likely to increase the stress under which the recipient must operate. On the other hand, increasing levels of stress tend to heighten the salience of time and distort judgments about it. It has been found in real life crisis situations as well as experimentally that as danger increases there is a significant overestimation of how fast time is passing (Williams and Rayner, 1956; Langer et al., 1961). This suggests that not only does short decision time distinguish crises from other types of situations, but also that the increasing stress will further heighten the salience of time. One consequence may be a reduced resistance to closure (Cohen, 1964; Usdansky and Chapman, 1960; Pepinsky and Pavlik, 1960; Mackworth and Mackworth, 1958; Birch, 1945; Bruner et al., 1956; Dubno, 1963; Horvath, 1959; Hoffeld and Kent, 1963). Finally, time pressure may result in more cautious behavior and greater sensitivity to negative information (Wright, 1974; Ben Zur and Breznitz, 1981); alternatively, it may give rise to hypervigilance (Janis and Mann, 1977).

The consequences of these three intervening variables for decision-making tasks may include some of the following.

The *search* for information about the situation and alternative courses of action, although likely to become more active, may also become more random and less productive. A loss of ability to make subtle discriminations often accompanies intense and protracted stress. As a result, search behavior may be adversely affected in several ways: other actors and their motives are likely to be stereotyped, and the situation itself may be defined in overly simple, one-dimensional terms, for example, that it is a zero-sum situation, or that everything is related to everything else.[14] The ability to invent nonobvious solutions to complex problems may be impaired.

The extent of the search for satisfactory solutions to a problem depends in part on the belief that the environment is benign and that such options in fact exist, but it is the nature of crisis that most policy alternatives, if not all, are likely to be perceived as involving undesirably high risks. The frying pan and the fire rather than Burian's ass (who starved to death when unable to choose between equally delectable bales of hay) is usually the more appropriate metaphor for choices in an international crisis. As noted earlier, when stress increases, problem solving tends to become more rigid: the ability to improvise declines; previously established decision rules are adhered to more tenaciously, whether appropriate to the circumstances or not; and the ability to "resist the pull of closure" is reduced (Korchin, 1964; Moffitt and Stagner, 1956; Pally, 1955; Korchin and Basowitz, 1954). Janis and Mann (1977:70) suggest that when there is little hope of finding a satisfactory alternative, policymakers may engage in defensive avoidance. The evidence thus suggests the paradox that as the intensity of a crisis increases, it makes creative policymaking both more important and less likely.

Identification of alternatives can also be related to the element of surprise that exists in crises. Snyder (1961) has suggested that more options will be considered when the need for a decision is anticipated instead of suddenly imposed. In circumstances such as those following the attack on Pearl Harbor we would not expect a lengthy review of potential responses by decision makers, but even during the unanticipated Korean crisis of 1950, in which the situation was somewhat more ambiguous (the precise role of the Soviet Union in the invasion was not wholly clear), only a single alternative course of action was considered: "The decision-making process in the Korean case was not characterized by the consideration of multiple alternatives at each stage. Rather a single proposed course of action emerged from the definition of the situation" (Snyder and Paige, 1958:245; Paige, 1968).

The extreme situation of constricted search occurs when only one option is perceived and the policymaking process is reduced to resigning oneself to the inevitable, for example, "We have no alternative but to go to war." In that case considerable dissonance may be generated. The dissonance between what the decision maker does (pursues policies that are known to carry a high risk of war) and what he or she knows (that war can lead to disaster) can be reduced by absolving oneself from responsibility for the decision. This solution has been described by Festinger (1957:43–44).

> It is possible, however, to reduce or even eliminate the dissonance by revoking the decision psychologically. This would consist of admitting to having made

the wrong choice or insisting that really no choice had been made for which the person had any responsibility. Thus, a person who has just accepted a new job might immediately feel he had done the wrong thing and, if he had it to do over again, might do something different. Or he might persuade himself that the choice had not been his; circumstances and his boss conspired to force the action on him.

This process may also be related to the widespread inability to perceive and appreciate the dilemmas and difficulties of others: the grass is always greener on the other side of the fence. This has been noted with respect to the motives, general capabilities, military strength, and freedom of action ascribed to the adversary (Boulding, 1959; Osgood, 1959; Bauer, 1961; Huntington, 1958).

One way of coping with dissonance in a crisis is to persuade oneself that the adversary is free from the very situational constraints that restrict one's own options. Only the other side can prevent the impending disaster, and a failure to do so is further confirmation of his or her bad faith. For example, during the frantic last-minute correspondence between the kaiser and the tsar in July 1914, Kaiser Wilhelm wrote: "The responsibility for the disaster which is now threatening the whole civilized world will not be laid at my door. In this moment it still lies in your power to avert it" (Montgelas and Schucking, 1924:480).[15]

Finally, complex problems are more likely to be defined by the decision maker's beliefs, expectations, and cognitive and emotional predispositions than by the "objective" attributes of the situation. In ambiguous situations or in circumstances of information overload one may also be more likely to screen information and to respond in terms of personal predispositions (March and Simon, 1958; Milburn, 1972; Singer, 1968; Streufert et al., 1967; Miller, 1956; Weick, 1968).

Analysis and evaluation may also be impaired. The ability to identify side effects and unintended consequences of various policy options, especially "preferred" options, is reduced (Milburn, 1972). There is a tendency to overestimate the benefits of certain alternatives and to underestimate the costs of others. As propensities to apply all-or-nothing criteria to the assessment of policy options increase, decision makers may find themselves more persuaded that a single policy would permit all values to be satisfied—that is, they may deny the existence of value conflicts.

In making *choices,* individuals vary widely in the decision rules that they fall back on when faced with uncertainty and in the types and degrees of error they are willing to tolerate. Cordell Hull relied on a set of maxims from Jefferson and Gladstone, Harry S. Truman tended to look for applicable lessons from history, and Calvin Coolidge attempted to avoid decisions ("sit down and keep still") in the expectation that many problems would disappear

(Hull, 1948:24–25, 37, 169, 173, 197; Fenno, 1959:35). Other decision rules might include: in case of uncertainty, select policies that have brought success in the past; alternatively, if in doubt, choose the option that will relieve the most proximate danger or will gain the easiest acceptance by the policymaking group, the legislature, the public, or others.

When experiencing stress, decision makers are likely to cope by relying on familiar or readily available decision rules, possibly employing increasingly crude and undifferentiated versions of them as stress increases (Zajonc, 1966). For example, they might find parallels between the present and previous situations and draw on historical analogies that are based on superficial rather than fundamental similarities (Kilpatrick, 1969; White and Lippitt, 1960; Milburn, 1972; May, 1973; Neustadt and May, 1986; Jervis, 1976). When faced with an intransigent Egypt in 1956, Anthony Eden drew an analogy between Nasser and Hitler. Harry Truman likewise saw a basic similarity between the Communist invasion of South Korea in 1950 and the expansion of other totalitarian systems during the 1930s. In these examples Eden and Truman drew on the history of the 1930s, the period in which each achieved political prominence, as a source of guidance, the latter more successfully than the former.

Rarely does a situation permit the decision maker to maximize all values with a single option; whatever exceptions exist are trivial and of limited interest. Although policymakers often do confront value trade-offs (Janis, 1972, 1982; Maoz, 1981; Snyder and Diesing, 1977), in circumstances of high stress there is an increased likelihood that the decision maker may fail to recognize adequately the existence of a conflict between utilities or to believe that a policy option that satisfies one important value will somehow also enable him or her to satisfy others: "We are not skilled in speaking to more than one value at a time. . . . When our values compete, we . . . return to singular emphasis on our favorite value" (Hammond and Mumpower, 1979, quoted in Abelson and Levi, 1985:288). In this event, motivational conflict and cognitive imbalances are overlooked or suppressed. On the other hand, if the decision maker does recognize the conflict over utilities and the probability that no available alternative will maximize or even satisfy all of them, then this will add another source of stress to the decision process. This observation illustrates again the point made earlier that stress may be created not only by the external situation (threat to important values) but also by the tasks and processes associated with formulating a response to it.

As stress increases, resistance to pressure for closure declines. In some cases any choice may be seen as preferable to prolonging a decision process that is itself a source of stress.[16] Concomitantly, priorities are likely to shift, with greater emphasis being placed on satisfaction of short-run values. In many circumstances this may be highly functional, but in others it may entail heavy long-run costs.

Sensitivity to and learning from negative feedback about a developing situation may also be affected. Simple learning may be facilitated by stress, but complex learning is generally disrupted. The more difficult the decision and the processes leading up to it, the greater the tendency to engage in cognitive dissonance reduction through information processing that is biased in favor of evidence supporting the choice—for example, by bolstering—and the lower the probability that the decision will be subject to dispassionate reexamination in the light of subsequent feedback.[17] If a decision was reached as a result of intensely divisive or otherwise stressful deliberations, there may be substantial reluctance to go through a similar experience to reconsider the decision, even in the face of information indicating that it might be wise to do so. Thus, sensitivity to subtle cues, especially those that suggest the inadequacy of the original decision, may tend to decline.

It is important to emphasize, however, that individuals seem to differ widely in the ability to tolerate stress, the threshold at which it begins to impair performance, and in strategies for coping with stress. For example, anxious persons tend to suffer a greater decline in cognitive performance, and those with experience in stressful situations may fare better (Kogan and Wallach, 1964; Baddeley, 1972). The personality and other correlates of performance under stress are at best imperfectly understood, however, and it is hazardous to predict from behavior under normal conditions, or even those of simulated stress. In this connection, Robert Kennedy's recollections of the Cuban missile crisis are worth noting.

> The strain and hours without sleep were beginning to take their toll. However, even many years later, those human weaknesses—impatience, fits of anger—are understandable. Each of us was being asked to make a recommendation which would affect the future of all mankind, a recommendation which, if wrong and if accepted, could mean the destruction of the human race. That kind of pressure does strange things to a human being, even to brilliant, self-confident, mature, experienced men. For some it brings out characteristics and strengths that perhaps they never knew they had, and for others the pressure is too overwhelming (Kennedy, 1969:22).

A high-ranking member of the Kennedy administration recently revealed that two of the president's advisers were unable to cope with stress during the missile crisis, "becoming quite passive and unable to fulfill their responsibilities" (George, 1986b:541).[18]

This brief overview is suggestive, not exhaustive. Moreover, the emphasis has been on processes rather than on decision outputs and, just as we cannot assume that "good" processes will ensure high-quality decisions, we cannot assume that erratic processes will always result in low-quality decisions and fiascoes. But neither is the relationship between process and outcome a random one. As George Ball (1962) put it shortly after resolution of the Cuban missile crisis, "the process was the author of the policy."[19] Janis' (1986) careful analysis of U.S. decision making in 19 crises indicates a rather strong correlation between symptoms of defective decision making and undesirable outcomes. Even if the hypotheses in Figure 1.1 describe only some modal tendencies rather than unvarying relationships, there is sufficient evidence to call into question the universal validity of the expectation that we always rise to the occasion in crises drawing, if necessary, on hidden reservoirs of strength and creativity. The evidence cited here suggests that the casualties of crises and the accompanying high stress may include the very abilities that are most vital for coping effectively with such situations: establishing logical links between present actions and future goals; searching effectively for relevant policy options; creating appropriate responses to unexpected events; communicating complex ideas; dealing effectively with abstractions; perceiving not only black and white, but also distinguishing them from the many subtle shades of gray that fall in between; distinguishing valid analogies from false ones, and sense from nonsense; and, perhaps most important of all, entering into others' frames of reference. With respect to these vital cognitive abilities, the law of supply and demand may sometimes operate in a perverse manner; as crisis increases the need for them, it may also diminish the supply.

The vast experimental literature on stress, only a small part of which was just summarized, is suggestive and can serve as an important source of insights and hypotheses. For several reasons, however, it must be used with caution by the foreign policy analyst. Research ethics limit the range of stress-inducing stimuli that may be employed in the laboratory. The situation must of necessity be relatively benign and of short duration. Failure in an assigned task, the method often employed to induce stress among experimental subjects, is presumably different than the real possibility of war that may face foreign policy leaders in a crisis. Many laboratory studies limit themselves to a single type of stress in order to isolate more precisely the effects of the independent variable whereas, as previously emphasized, policymakers must often confront multiple sources of stress. The tasks undertaken by subjects who have been exposed to stressful stimuli have tended to be either psychomotor problems such as repairing field telephones or cognitive problems for which there is a clearly defined answer. Relatively few laboratory studies have involved more complex cognitive processes or highly intellectualized tasks that often confront the real-world policymaker. Experimental subjects have usually been students, who differ from political leaders by virtue of age, experience and, perhaps, motivation. Finally, many experimental studies isolate the subject instead of placing him or her into a context of groups or organizations, either of which may provide the political leader with supports or constraints in performing the required decision-making tasks.

In short, the important advantages of the laboratory—internal validity, control of key variables, ease of replication, and the like—are not sufficient to offset skepticism about the external validity of the results. The ultimate test of relevance and validity is not how often one can replicate laboratory experiments on the consequences of stress for performance of complex cognitive tasks, but whether some of the same effects may be found in foreign offices and other venues of policymaking in crises.

Decision Making in Foreign Policy Crises

Fortunately, a growing body of comparative systematic research on actual international crises provides less precise but more directly relevant evidence. Before summarizing some of these studies, it may be worth examining briefly two of the most dramatic episodes of the twentieth century—the crisis leading up to World War I in 1914 and the 1962 Cuban missile crisis between the United States and the Soviet Union.

The 1914 Crisis

The events that gave rise to what is arguably the most consequential war in modern history—World War I—provide perhaps the most compelling evidence of misperceptions, inadequate information processing, and other decision-making malfunctions that significantly shaped the dynamics and outcome of a major international crisis.[20] The state of military technology, European alliance commitments, the balance of power and threats to its stability, contingency plans of foreign and war offices, bureaucratic and other factors that gave rise to a "cult of the offensive" among general staffs, historical enmities, economic competition, and imperial rivalries undoubtedly created a setting fraught with potential for conflict, and no explanation of how events unfolded in 1914 can fail to take them into account. Nevertheless, they do not appear sufficient to explain the many decision-making malfunctions that characterized the crisis. Nor do they fully account for the outbreak of war in 1914 instead of in 1909, 1911, or other years, when essentially the same background conditions existed and when dangerous events—seemingly more threatening in many respects than the royal assassination—precipitated confrontations between two or more of the major European powers.

Decision-making deficiencies that contributed to the escalation of a limited, local conflict into a general war in 1914 included:

- Misperception of other nations' vital interests, intentions, and likely responses to certain contingencies; examples include misperceptions of Russia's willingness to tolerate the humiliation and possible subjugation of Serbia, and Great Britain's likely response to a German implementation of the Schlieffen Plan by striking France through Belgium.
- Insensitivity to warnings, even from a nation's own diplomats abroad. The German kaiser and some of his colleagues in Berlin were sufficiently convinced by sketchy evidence (bolstered by fervent hopes) that Great Britain would remain neutral even if France were drawn into war that they consistently dismissed warnings to the contrary.
- Suppression, distortion, or rejection of information that called into question familiar or comforting premises. Kaiser Wilhelm eagerly grasped for information that supported his hopes and expectations for a quick and easy resolution of the crisis that would simultaneously result in a triumph over Serbia for his allies in Vienna and acceptance of that outcome in St. Petersburg, Paris, and London.
- Failures to recognize miscalculations as the crisis developed, or to deny one's own responsibility, while attributing them to the adversary's perfidy. The kaiser and his colleagues were especially adept at employing this form of bolstering; Lebow's (1981:119) assessment that German policy during the crisis can best be understood in terms of "the cognitive closure of the German political system" is very close to the mark, and comparable evidence could also be found in some of the other capitals of Europe.
- A tendency to attribute almost complete freedom of action to adversaries, while insisting that virtually insurmountable barriers constrained one's own policy choices.[21]

As the crisis deepened, an increasing sense of helplessness and resignation to the irrepressible course of events is evident. On the day of the Serbian reply to the Austro-Hungarian ultimatum, Paul Cambon stated that he saw "no way of halting the march of events" (France, 1936: Document no. 38). In contrast to Edward Grey, who maintained the hope that the European powers would find a way to prevent a general war, Arthur Nicolson asserted on July 29: "I am of the opinion that the resources of diplomacy are, for the present exhausted" (Great Britain, 1926: Document no. 252). At the same time, in St. Petersburg Sazonov wrote of the "inevitability of war" (Russia, 1931–1934: Document no. 221), while in Berlin, the kaiser, in one of his most vitriolic marginal notes, concluded that "we have proved ourselves helpless" (Montgelas and Schucking, 1924:401).

To students of strategy the assertions of the kaiser, the tsar, and others that they were helpless once they had set their military machines into motion may appear to be a real-life application of the tactics of commitment, "a device to leave the last clear chance to decide the outcome with the other party, in a manner that he fully appreciates; it is to relinquish further initiative, having rigged the incentives so that the other party must choose in one's favor" (Schelling, 1963:37); but there were also military reasons for these perceptions. Significantly contributing to the belief that options were severely restricted was the rigidity of the various mobilization plans (Taylor, 1969). Austria-Hungary and Russia had more than one plan for mobilization, but once any of them was set in motion it was impossible to change to another. The Russians could order either a general mobilization against both Germany and Austria-Hungary or a partial one directed only at the latter. But, as Russian generals were to argue vehemently during the crucial days at the end of July, a partial mobilization would preclude a general one for months to come, leaving Russia completely at the mercy of Germany. Although Austria-Hungary also had a number of different military plans, the condition of its army served as a constraint. One of the proposals to confine the Balkan dispute to a local area was the "Halt in Belgrade" plan. But this proposal broke down because the Austrian army was not even in a condition to occupy Belgrade. The other two continental powers—France and Germany—each had but a single plan for calling up their armed forces and, in the case of Germany, political leaders were ill informed about the rigidity of mobilization and war plans.

All the mobilization plans existed only on paper: except for the Russo-Japanese War, no major European power had mobilized since 1878. This fact rendered the plans all the more rigid and made military leaders responsible for carrying them out less likely to accept any last-minute modifications. It may also have added to the widely believed dictum that one did not mobilize for any purpose other than war.

Finally, military plans that stressed rapid offensive action contributed to a sense of urgency arising from a fear that adversaries could mount a decisive first strike. Whether they could in fact do so is perhaps open to question, especially in the light of the deployment of weapons that might favor the defense, for example, the machine gun. "Objectively," time was of far less importance than in the present nuclear age. In contrast to the current ability of the Soviet Union and United States to strike each other in a matter of minutes, estimates of the time required for Austria-Hungary to field a full army in 1914 ranged from three to four weeks. The necessity of harvesting summer crops was a factor in military calculations. Russia's ability to mount a rapid offensive against Germany could be discounted; indeed, the entire Schlieffen Plan was predicated on the assumption that Russia's lack of speed would permit German strength to be massed on the western front during the early weeks of the war. It is thus not certain that a distinct military advantage could be gained by striking first or, conversely, that a delay of a day or two in mobilizing would have resulted in catastrophic consequences.

Yet the "reality" as defined by European leaders was quite different. In the situation of high tensions the decision makers of 1914 perceived that time was of crucial importance—and they acted on that assumption. During the final stages of the crisis, foreign policy officials increasingly perceived that their enemies were capable of delivering a sudden punishing blow. In doing so they attributed to their adversaries a flexibility and speed of military operations that they knew was impossible for their own forces. As a consequence, the penalties for delaying immediate military action were perceived as increasingly high. Or, to use the language of deterrence theory, leaders perceived that their adversaries were able and willing to launch a decisive first strike, and thus they hastened their own military preparations.

In summary, the crisis leading up to World War I was characterized by a fatal interaction between dangerous political and strategic environment and seriously flawed decision processes, neither of which by itself seems sufficient to explain the catastrophe that ensued and both of which are a necessary part of the explanation. In a less dangerous strategic environment, the decision-making malfunctions probably would have been inconsequential. Indeed, in a different environment the European policymakers would no doubt have felt themselves under less stress. On the other hand, the strategic environment and the security dilemmas the crisis posed are not sufficient to explain the flawed decision processes and choices in Berlin, St. Petersburg, and the other capitals of Europe. There are numerous accounts of the deleterious impact of stress on officials who were making the fateful decisions that led to war. For example, Admiral von Tirpitz wrote of his colleagues: "I have never seen a more tragic, more ravaged face than that of our Emperor during those days. . . . Since the Russian mobilization the Chancellor gave one the impression of a drowning man" (Tirpitz, 1919:279, 280). Prince von Bulow asked the German chancellor why diplomacy had failed to avert war: "At last I said to him: 'Well, tell me, at least, how it all happened.' He raised his long thin arms to heaven and answered in a dull exhausted voice: 'Oh—if I only knew'" (von Bulow, 1932:166). Possibly these and similar observations, written after the disastrous war, are self-serving efforts at "impression management" (Tetlock and Manstead, 1985), with an eye on the historical record. However, these accounts are also consistent with other evidence (for example, contemporary observations of officials from nonbelligerent nations) as well as documents and marginal comments written during the crisis. Thus, unless one is prepared to accept the thesis that competing and incompatible national interests rendered war "inevitable" in 1914, the disastrous outcome (for both the ultimate victors and the vanquished) gives rise to some sobering thoughts about decision making in crises.

The Cuban Missile Crisis of 1962

Because relatively few crises result in war, we can assume that the decision processes that seem to have contributed to the outcome in 1914 are neither inescapable nor beyond the possibility of some human control. The Cuban missile crisis, the most intense Soviet-U.S. confrontation of the nuclear age, seems to have been characterized by higher-quality decision processes than those that marked the events of July–August 1914.[22]

The success of the United States in obtaining the removal of the offensive missiles from Cuba without provoking a war has led many analysts to conclude that President Kennedy and his advisory group (the executive committee of the National Security Council, or "Ex Comm") did so by avoiding many of the more egregious errors of their counterparts almost a half century earlier, or even of their own badly flawed deliberations leading up to the failed invasion of Cuba in 1961. Indeed, some observers have noted that Kennedy had recently read and had been influenced by Barbara Tuchman's *Guns of August*, a best-selling account of the misperceptions and miscalculations that characterized policymaking in European capitals during the summer of 1914. Kennedy and his advisers are often credited with taking a number of steps that contributed to the ultimate peaceful resolution of the crisis:

- They created a decision-making environment that encouraged spirited debate on policy options. In at least one instance the president absented himself from the deliberations in order to stimulate frankness.
- They exhibited a sensitivity to likely perceptions, calculations, and responses of Nikita Khrushchev and his colleagues. Kennedy was especially concerned not to reduce Soviet alternatives to two: total humiliation or war.
- They adopted a less violent strategy of coercive diplomacy in the first instance, albeit after debates that initially seemed to point toward a "bomb-and-invade" strategy.
- They employed some creative means to lengthen, rather than constrict, the time for the Kremlin to ponder its options and policy. For example, an order to pull the blockade line back toward Cuba was sent "in the clear" rather than in code to ensure that the Soviets would intercept the message and understand that they had additional time to consider whether to challenge the blockade.
- They exercised tight control over the deployment of the naval blockade and other military forces. Secretary of Defense McNamara risked a major confrontation with the chief of naval operations to ensure that a naval war did not begin because of details that might be overlooked (were there Russian-speaking personnel on the ships that might be required to stop one of the Soviet vessels?) or because of unauthorized use of force (shooting at the rudders of Soviet ships should they attempt to run the blockade).
- They created and used multiple channels of communication with the Soviet leaders before the permanent "hot line" was established.

Whereas the 1914 crisis is frequently described as the classic case of decision-making malfunctions, the missile crisis is almost equally often cited as the textbook example of ways to avert some of the impediments to effective policymaking in high-stress situations. However, just as some students of the World War I crisis are unprepared to accept an interpretation that accords a significant role to the effect of crisis-induced stress, some revisionist interpretations of the missile crisis have questioned whether President Kennedy and his advisory group deserve high marks for their performance in October 1962. Leaving aside several examples of crude psycho-McCarthyism that have depicted Kennedy as bringing the world to the brink of a nuclear holocaust as the result of deep-seated character or personality defects, the revisionist interpretations deserve a serious hearing, even if they are not fully sustained by summaries or verbatim records of the Ex Comm deliberations that have recently been declassified (White House, 1985; Bundy and Blight, 1987–1988). Among the more thoughtful critiques from a decision-making perspective, several are especially relevant for present purposes.

- Lebow (1981) and Snyder (1978) have questioned whether Kennedy permitted, much less encouraged, open debates in the Ex Comm, citing, for example, the derisive treatment accorded to U.N. Ambassador Adlai Stevenson, who proposed bargaining rather than coercive diplomacy or "compellance" to gain removal of the missiles from Cuba. Lebow depicts Kennedy's leadership as "promotional" rather than open. Snyder's conclusion is that, despite frequent descriptions of the Ex Comm's decision processes as models of openness and rationality, the president and his advisers perceived only the single option of a relentless policy based on coercion, denying any trade-off between the values of obtaining removal of the missiles and averting nuclear war. These are the characteristics of a cognitive decision maker, not an analytical one.
- Several analysts have concluded that Kennedy and his advisers were strongly motivated by domestic political concerns, which dictated the choice of a coercive rather than bargaining strategy to deal with the missiles. According to this thesis, the choice of a naval blockade, which could not remove the missiles already in Cuba, can best be explained by a perceived domestic political requirement for dramatic action (Hampson, 1984–1985; Nathan, 1975; but see also Patterson and Brophy, 1986, and Welch and Blight, 1987–1988:24–25, who find no evidence that domestic politics played any role in the decision making).
- Two scholars who generally give both Kennedy and Khrushchev high marks for coping with the crisis (and who find no evidence in the events of 1962 for the hypothesis that crisis-induced stress adversely affects decision making) conclude that officials in both Washington and Moscow made poor risk estimates (Wohlstetter and Wohlstetter, 1971; see also Leng, 1984).

Aside from underscoring the obvious point that crisis processes and outcomes may differ significantly, the evidence from 1914 and 1962 raises further questions about the relevance of explanation that focus on decision-making performance with an emphasis on information processing and other cognitive tasks. That is, were decision-making variables crucial in 1914 and 1962, or should one look elsewhere to explain the different outcomes? Specifically, can a sufficient explanation be found in changes in the international system between 1914 and 1962? For example, did the existence of nuclear weapons, resulting in different constraints and strategies for pursuing national interests, account for the different behavior in the two crises? Even if one accepts an interpretation that attaches substantial significance to the impact of crisis-induced stress in 1914 (some do not), was this a deviant case of limited theoretical and policy relevance, especially for the dramatically different international system of the late twentieth century? A somewhat similar argument could, of course, be developed with respect to the missile crisis.

Other International Crises

Fortunately, it is not necessary to rely solely on evidence adduced from these two frequently studied cases. Recent years have witnessed the development of a substantial literature of systematic and comparative crisis studies, providing a significant base of evidence.

- Glenn Snyder and Paul Diesing undertook a study of 16 crises, including five occurring prior to World War I, three during the interwar period, and eight since World War II. Their impressive research draws on three bodies of theory: systems, bargaining, and decision making. It is impossible to summarize briefly, but a few findings of special relevance are worth citing. They found ample evidence of stereotyped thinking, restricted search for alternatives, and impaired ability to estimate the consequences of action but, unlike some students of crisis, they question whether these decision-making malfunctions can be traced to time pressures. Rather, "the cause must lie in some other stress-producing aspect, such as having to make difficult trade-offs between important values and high risks in a situation of considerable uncertainty" (Snyder and Diesing, 1977:492). Of special relevance is the finding that information processing during crises was generally poor; as only 40 percent of the messages between governments were correctly interpreted, with the remainder incorrectly interpreted (52 percent) or distorted in transmission (8 percent). Although they found that the accuracy of interpretation increased during the culminating stages of crises, incorrect information processing ranks high among the authors' tentative conclusions about the causes of war (Snyder and Diesing, 1977:316, 503). A partial replication of these case studies, using a different data base, provided at least partial support for the Snyder and Diesing findings (Leng and Walker, 1982; see also Leng and Wheeler, 1979).
- The International Crisis Behavior Project directed by Michael Brecher, the most extensive undertaking of its type, is investigating a larger number of crises

from the perspective of a common decision-making framework (Brecher, 1979). Included are analyses of major and minor power crises that resulted in war and that were resolved peacefully. Studies completed to date have yielded somewhat mixed results about the impact of crisis and stress on the quality of decision making. For example, in their study of Israeli policy during the 1967 and 1973 crises, Brecher and Geist (1980) found strong support for the hypotheses that time will be perceived as more salient, leaders will become concerned with the immediate rather than the distant future, and they will perceive the range of alternatives open to themselves to be narrow. But they also concluded that "intense and increasing stress impaired cognitive performance in Israel's two crises but not drastically or fundamentally so" (Brecher and Geist, 1980:347).

Dowty's (1984) analysis of U.S. policy during the Middle East crises of 1958, 1970, and 1973 also found that crisis pressures had both positive and negative consequences for decision making. Despite some evidence pointing to an avoidance of value trade-offs, he characterized much of U.S. policymaking as displaying a mixture of cognitive rigidity and tactical rationality (Dowty, 1984:370–371).

On the other hand, Shlaim's (1983) analysis of U.S. decision making during the Berlin blockade of 1948–1949 found relatively few adverse consequences of the crisis. Despite manifestations of cognitive rigidity and fatigue, "the widely held assumption that high stress is necessarily dysfunctional finds little support in the Berlin case study" (Shlaim, 1983:410). Oneal (1982), who examined the Berlin blockade case (as well as the early Cold War crises revolving around Iran and Greece), but from a different perspective, came to essentially the same conclusion as Shlaim.

• Richard Ned Lebow's (1981) study of international crises casts considerable doubt on rational actor models of decision making. His research is based on 26 cases, spanning the period from 1898 (Fashoda, Cuba) to 1962 (missiles in Cuba), ranging in duration from a week (Dogger Bank) to 311 days (Berlin blockade), and resulting in a variety of outcomes, including war, both diplomatic victories and defeats for the initiator, and compromise settlements. Although his analysis is not limited to psychological aspects of decision making, Lebow effectively uses both cognitive and motivational models, drawing on the work of Jervis and Janis, respectively, to explain the erratic behavior of policy makers in crises. They often pursued strategies based on unrealistic judgments of how their adversaries would respond. The initiators' expectation that opponents would back down was justified in only 3 of 14 "brinksmanship" crises, 2 of which involved Nazi Germany (Rhineland, Munich); the remaining cases resulted in war (5), compromise settlement (2), or the initiator being forced to back down (4) (Lebow, 1981:271; for a critique and rejoinder, see Orme, 1987; Lebow, 1987a).

It may be worth noting that although Lebow's definition of crisis and case studies overlap substantially with those selected by Snyder and Diesing—nine of the crises appear in both studies—their interpretations of the evidence do not always coincide. For example, whereas Snyder and Diesing found that decision makers in crisis are often able to change their strategies in the face of new information about adversaries, Lebow concludes that "learning during a crisis is likely to be hindered by the same impediments that caused the initiator to misjudge his adversary's resolve in the first place" (Lebow, 1981:272). Another of several important disagreements concerns the impact of time pressure. Snyder and Diesing indicate that the longer a crisis lasts, the more likely it is to get out of control, but Lebow comes to the opposite conclusion.

- Richard Smoke's (1977) analysis of escalation processes culminating in war encompasses five case studies, including the Seven Years' War, the Crimean War, the Austro-Prussian and Franco-Prussian wars, and the Spanish Civil War. Although not strictly focused on crises, his results are nevertheless relevant. Escalation of conflict was accompanied by some of the same perceptual and cognitive consequences found in crisis studies, including a narrowing range of expectations and a sense of a closing future created by the adversary's actions. "The subjective future closes in faster than one anticipates it should because it is closing in from psychological, not just objective, reasons" (Smoke, 1977:295).

- Peter Suedfeld, Philip Tetlock, and their colleagues have undertaken an interesting series of crisis studies from a psychological perspective. Many of them have focused on "integrative complexity," a behavioral, information processing variable that they distinguish from "cognitive complexity," a personality trait. Integrative complexity is defined as the ability to make subtle distinctions along multiple dimensions, flexibility, and the integration of large amounts of diverse information to make coherent judgments; integrative simplicity is characterized by simple responses, gross distinctions, rigidity, and restricted information usage. A standard content analysis technique has been used to code the levels of differentiation and integration revealed in documentary materials generated by policymakers before, during, and after a wide range of international crises (World War I, Cuba [1962], Morocco [1911], Berlin [1948–1949 and 1961], Korea [1950], the Middle East wars of 1948, 1956, 1967 and 1973, etc.), as well as by other subjects facing very different kinds of stressful situations.

Their findings reveal substantial, although not uniform, support for hypotheses linking crisis-induced stress to integrative simplicity on the one hand, and nonviolent conflict resolution to integrative complexity on the other (Suedfeld and Tetlock, 1977; Suedfeld et al., 1977; Levi and Tetlock, 1980; Raphael, 1982; Tetlock, 1985).[23] However, these studies also found some deviations from this pattern that suggest the need for further theorizing and research. For example, Soviet officials (notably Andrei Gromyko) tended to exhibit *increased* integrative complexity in times of crisis, as did some of the prominent leaders of the nineteenth century, including Talleyrand, Castlereagh, Wellington, Metternich, and Bismarck (Wallace and Suedfeld, 1985).

The findings from all these studies are not surprising. Although laboratory results overwhelmingly indicate that intense and protracted stress erodes cognitive performance, the pattern of findings on decision-making performance in foreign policy crises is much more mixed and therefore requires going beyond the individual or decision-making level of analysis for a satisfactory explanation. Stated differently, psychological theories, insights, and findings may be necessary for an adequate understanding of political behavior, but they cannot be sufficient. Just as not all wars are the result of crises, not all crises spin out of control, and even among those that do, misperceptions, miscalculations, and other decision-making malfunctions are unlikely to provide a full explanation. Although the period since World War II has witnessed repeated crises and many instances of deterrence failure, it has been relatively free of direct violence between the major powers. Several explanations have been offered.

- *The existence of nuclear weapons has dramatically changed the ratio of risks and rewards of armed conflict.* According to this explanation, whatever decision-making shortcomings may occur in crises, the threat of nuclear war is such a dominating aspect of reality that any group of leaders, short of the clinically suicidal, will act in a calculating, restrained, and cautious manner. Even a defense analyst who had earlier argued that the nuclear "balance of terror" was "delicate" rather than robust wrote of the missile crisis that "the possibility of irreparable harm" resulting from nuclear war "makes clear why neither Nikita Khrushchev nor John Kennedy behaved like the irrational juvenile delinquents who are sometimes assumed to occupy the seats of power today, strapped by their seatbelts in a carefree game of chicken" (Wohlstetter and Wohlstetter, 1971:262–263). However, several recent studies of deterrence have posed important questions about whether it is a policy for all seasons or whether it has been implemented effectively (George and Smoke, 1974; Jervis, 1984; Steinbruner, 1976; Morgan, 1985; Green, 1968; Allison, et al., 1985; Huth and Russett, 1984, 1988; Ben-Zvi, 1987; Betts, 1987; Jervis et al., 1985; see also the critique of Jervis et al. in Blight, 1986–1987).

- *Crises may serve as surrogates for war, offering relatively safe means for effectuating needed changes in the international system* (Waltz, 1964; Aron, 1965; Bell, 1971, 1984). The reasoning, somewhat analogous to the thesis that if one could induce regular minor earthquakes in geologically unstable regions it would be possible to forestall catastrophic ones, is that crises can bring about incremental changes, thus averting cataclysmic ones that might result in war. The period immediately following the missile crisis, which witnessed several major steps to stabilize relations between Washington and Moscow, is often cited in support of the somewhat related thesis—that crises can have sobering effects on leaders who experienced them. Aside from the obvious danger that crises can get out of control, there is no certainty that policymakers who have experienced crises will draw identical lessons from their experiences. For some the missile crisis may have reinforced the belief that caution is appropriate in nuclear confrontations, others saw it as confirmation that firmness will cause the adversary to back down, and still others regarded it as a lost opportunity to achieve even more, such as the elimination of the Castro regime. It may also have contributed to the view in the Kremlin that strategic parity is necessary to avoid a similar outcome in the future, thus setting the stage for an arms race.

• *Because policymakers learn from their experiences, crises tend to become "routinized" and therefore less dangerous.* Charles McClelland (1961:199), one of the pioneers of crisis research, wrote:

> Outputs received from occurrences and situations in the international environment and from sequences of international interaction are processed by the advanced modernizing social organizations according to their perceived characteristics: if these outputs are recognized as familiar and expected experiences met repeatedly in the remembered past, they will be treated in a highly routine fashion.

The participants gain experience in ways of coping with the environment and adversaries and, although threats and challenges may continue to characterize relations between parties, uncertainty is reduced. Thus, "repeated exposure to acute crises may reduce the probabilities of an outbreak of general war" (McClelland, 1961:200).

This line of reasoning assumes that policymakers conduct effective postcrisis analyses to learn appropriate lessons from them and, perhaps even more important, to avoid learning the wrong ones. Moreover, it assumes that governments have cadres of professional "crisis managers" and effective "institutional memories" for collecting, preserving, and transmitting such knowledge and wisdom from administration to administration. There is some evidence that neither of these premises is wholly valid, at least for the U.S. government. Dowty found that effective crisis postmortems were not always held and that, ironically, "the bigger the success, the less the learning experience" (Dowty, 1984:376). Lebow (1981), Oneal (1982), and Etheredge (1985) also question the effectiveness of learning from crises. More generally, there is evidence that each administration comes to office with a crisis management tabula rasa and then undergoes a period of on-the-job training in learning how to cope with them (Smith, 1984).

No doubt there are important elements of truth in each of these three rather optimistic interpretations. Yet the suspicion lingers that even the experience of more than four decades without nuclear war—what one of the most perceptive defense analysts has dubbed "the Long Peace" (Gaddis, 1986)—does not establish conclusively that policymakers have become immune to decision-making malfunctions that could result in an unwanted and unforeseen war. Five times during 1954 alone, President Eisenhower resisted substantial pressure from his advisers in the National Security Council, Joint Chiefs of Staff, and State Department to use nuclear weapons against China (Ambrose, 1984:229–230). Interpreting this evidence is not unlike determining whether the glass is half empty or half full. Are we reassured by Eisenhower's rejection of the advice, or do we worry that another leader, with less experience in military affairs or possessing a different value or belief system, might have decided differently?[24]

The past record of coping with crises is certainly no guarantee of continued success in avoiding nuclear war, especially if one can identify significant changes (for example, in the strategic environment) that might alter the probabilities of failure in the future. Most of the past four decades were marked by U.S. strategic superiority, limited nuclear proliferation, and widespread if not universal consensus that the nuclear "balance of terror" was stable in that a first-strike attack offered no substantial advantage to the initiator. Moreover, some of the notable innovations in military technology, such as the orbiting surveillance satellite and deployment of the submarine as the basing mode for retaliatory weapons, tended to further reduce the incentives for a first strike. From the perspective of crisis decision making, some of these developments were especially important because they tended to reduce time pressures on policymakers. These and other features of the international system would appear to have contributed to crisis stability. Therefore, in turning to the prospects for crisis management it will be useful to consider whether recent developments in weapons and doctrines are likely to have a significant impact on the context in which crisis decisions will be made.

Crisis Management

There are many well-known reasons for skepticism about game theory, including "prisoners' dilemma" scenarios, as a *prescriptive* guide to deterrence, crisis decision making, and other aspects of foreign affairs (George and Smoke, 1974). But the prisoners' dilemma can serve as a *diagnostic* tool for identifying elements of the situation that may lead the participants to make choices that are "rational" but that may nevertheless result in mutual losses because each calculates that defection will yield a better payoff than cooperation, regardless of the other's choice.

Aside from the high stakes, three aspects of the situation are crucial. In line with the dictum that "there is no honor among thieves," *the prisoners do not wholly trust each other*. The sheriff immediately separates the suspects, *restricting their ability to communicate,* thus also providing a greater opportunity for increasing their mutual distrust. Finally, by offering better terms *only* for the first confession, the sheriff places the prisoners under severe time pressure. In short, the sheriff has structured the situation to maximize the probability that at least one of the prisoners, and probably both, will calculate that defection (confession), rather than cooperation (silence), is the rational choice. These three attributes of the situation are analogous to some key elements of decision making in crises, and they suggest some of the steps that might be taken to reduce crisis instability.

It is almost axiomatic that adversaries in an intense international crisis will not trust each other very much and, over the short-to-intermediate term it is hard to be sanguine that much can be done to alter that condition. There are likely to be historical reasons for the lack of trust—certainly this is true of U.S.-Soviet and Sino-Soviet relations—and images of the adversary as aggressive and untrustworthy may persist over substantial periods of time, even in the absence of direct and incontrovertible evidence of continued hostility. Indeed, images of the enemy may even have a self-sustaining character for several reasons; for example, they may be nurtured, sustained, or even exacerbated by belief systems, ideologies, domestic political needs, and the like. Strategies such as Osgood's (1962) graduated reduction in international tensions (GRIT) or Axelrod's (1984) "tit for tat" may offer some means of eroding intense distrust but, at best, these appear to be long-term steps that can serve the goal of crisis avoidance rather than measures that can easily and effectively be implemented during a crisis. Studies of bargaining indicate that "firm-but-fair" reciprocity strategies that combine sticks (demonstrations of military resolve) and carrots (an openness to diplomatic accommodation) are most likely to be effective for dealing with crises (Leng and Walker, 1982), but implementation also requires that policymakers be capable of performing complex information processing and related tasks to implement a relatively subtle and mixed influence strategy.

Problems of effective and instantaneous communication during the Cuban missile confrontation led to the establishment of a hot line between Moscow and Washington, and subsequent modifications have improved the ability of Soviet and U.S. leaders to communicate with each other directly during a crisis. As important as these steps are, however, effective crisis communication cannot be assured merely by deploying more efficient and foolproof equipment. Recall the Snyder and Diesing (1977) finding, cited earlier, that a substantial number of communications in crises were misunderstood or misinterpreted. Although not without some risks of deliberate misuse, suggestions for "backtranslating" messages and the creation of a joint Soviet-U.S. crisis control center are among the proposals to facilitate more effective communication during crises (Kahan et al., 1983; Ury and Smoke, 1984).

There is some consensus that intense time pressure is potentially the most dangerous element of many crises. A situation that gives rise to the calculation that there is a substantial advantage to be gained by striking first, as is clearly the case in the prisoners' dilemma, is inherently unstable. Recent years have witnessed the revival of a long-standing debate about the stability of nuclear deterrence and whether the Soviet-U.S. arms race has created a "window of vulnerability" that might make a preemptive first strike seem to be a reasonable alternative during an intense superpower crisis. The weapons and doctrinal requirements for enhancing (if not ensuring) deterrence stability at the strategic level are well known and need not be reviewed in detail here. In essence, they emphasize the need for secure, second-strike capabilities that simultaneously convey a message of threat (assured devastating punishment of an attacker) and reassurance (that one's forces do not increase anxiety by threatening a successful preemptive attack on the adversary's retaliatory forces), as well as effective command, communication, and control of strategic forces.

It would seem that, of the three elements highlighted by the prisoners' dilemma, efforts to lengthen rather than reduce decision time offer an especially fertile area for steps to enhance crisis stability. Unfortunately, developments and trends of the past decade offer few grounds for optimism. There appears to be have been an almost calculated disregard in Moscow and Washington for the dangers of placing policymakers under greater time pressure. A partial list of these developments include the following.

- The *increasing accuracy of missile guidance systems* tends to increase fears that one's retaliatory forces may be at risk, heightening incentives for "launch-on-warning" policies. To be sure, there is more than a little controversy about the extent to which a first strike could in fact bring any advantage to the attacker (for example, missiles have never been tested on polar routes, raising some questions about estimates of accuracy based on east-west trajectories), and the Scowcroft Commission has cast authoritative doubts on the notion of a "window of vulnerability" that would tempt an initiator (see also Lebow, 1984; Schelling, 1984; Steinbruner, 1984). But perceptions count, and fears leading to "use them or lose them" reasoning in a severe superpower confrontation, whether objectively justified or not, would surely erode crisis stability.

- The ability to launch *multiple warheads* from a single missile, and to do so with great accuracy, may also have deleterious effects on crisis decision making. Missiles such as the Soviet SS-18 and the U.S. MX, which have "hard target" capabilities, may lead policymakers to fear that the adversary may gain substantial advantage in striking first; in a worst-case analysis, the initiator may be perceived as capable of disarming as many as 10 missiles (and, therefore, 100 warheads) with each of its own missiles. There are potent arguments to be raised against this type of reasoning (including the fact that more than a single warhead must be assigned to each target in order to ensure its destruction), but once more the point is that multiple independently targetable reentry vehicle (MIRV) technology has at least potentially affected the decision calculus of crisis decision makers by increasing perceived time pressures.

- According to one school of strategic thought that has its roots in the writings of Bernard Brodie, deterrence is the sole function of nuclear weapons and deterrence is assumed to be robust. An alternative line of reasoning, *a doctrine that one must be prepared to fight, limit, and win a nuclear war,* has gained ascendency in recent years, as evidenced by National Security Decision Memorandum 242 and Presidential Directive 59 (Bracken, 1983:241; Gray and Payne, 1980; Gray, 1982; and the critiques in Ball, 1982–1983; and Jervis, 1984). Although the Presidential Directive 59 was made public during the final year of the Carter presidency, there is no indication that it was abandoned by the Reagan administration.[25] Of special relevance for present purposes is the proposition that targets should include highly vulnerable national command structures, communication and control networks, and the like—that is, one should pursue a "decapitation" strategy (Steinbruner, 1981–1982). The U.S. policy follows the Soviet lead in this respect by at least a decade. That such a strategy places decision makers under greater stress and time pressure is obvious and requires no elaboration.

- Both the United States and the Soviet Union have deployed weapons with very short flight times. Pershing II missiles deployed in Western Europe can reach targets in the Soviet Union within a few minutes, and Soviet missiles launched from submarines deployed off the east coast of the United States can reach their targets in comparably short times. As Bracken (1983:231) has pointed out, aside from underscoring the threat of a decapitation attack, deployment of these weapons has injected a significant element of ambiguity into Soviet–American confrontations by requiring commanders to recognize that their own command structures will not survive more than a few minutes in any nuclear war. In this respect, the intermediate-range nuclear forces (INF) treaty signed by President Reagan and General Secretary Gorbachev at the 1987 Washington summit conference represents a useful step.

- Development and deployment of *antisatellite (ASAT) weapons* will put at risk one of the more stabilizing elements of military technology that has been introduced during the past several decades. Although orbiting surveillance satellites have not provided the superpowers with complete assurance about the adversary's actions, they have served a useful function in reducing the dangers from what Schelling (1963) has called "the reciprocal fear of surprise attack." Any attack on satellites during an intense crisis can only increase the uncertainties, fears, and time pressures on those who are attempting to cope with the crisis. (For a less pessimistic assessment, see Carter, 1986.)

- Since President Reagan's March 23, 1983 proposal for a multilayered, space-based *strategic defense initiative (SDI) program,* it has become the dominant and most controversial defense issue of the 1980s. Along with a substantial research and development program, SDI has generated a vigorous debate and an extensive literature. Much of this focuses on questions of scope (Is SDI intended to protect all potential targets, or is it essentially a ballistic missile defense program?), role (Should it be confined to a research and development program, used as a "bargaining chip," or should it be fully deployed?), feasibility (Can effective hardware be developed? Can reliable software be written?), cost, and impact on strategic stability. Expert opinion is sharply divided on most of these issues. The last is of most interest for present purposes because it will have an impact on the strategic environment in which crisis decisions may have to be made.

Virtually all experts agree that SDI cannot achieve President Reagan's repeatedly stated goal of rendering nuclear weapons "impotent and obsolete," if only because even a fully effective system cannot cope with all means of delivering nuclear warheads (for example, cruise missiles). According to one study, the prospect of reaching the president's goal "is so remote that it should not serve as the basis of public expectation or national policy about ballistic missile defense (BMD). This judgment appears to be the consensus among informed members of the defense technical community" (Ashton B. Carter, quoted in Glaser, 1985:25).

Although proponents of SDI are typically pessimistic about the robustness of deterrence based on mutual assured destruction (Payne and Gray, 1984), they tend to base their case for the intermediate term on strengthening deterrence by protecting land-based missiles against a first strike. By doing so, SDI contributes to crisis stability by reducing a potential attacker's incentives to strike first. As the author of the *Hoffman Report* puts it, "Defenses of relatively moderate capability can make [ballistic missiles] obsolete to a military planner long before they are impotent in terms of their indiscriminate destructive potential" (Hoffman, 1985:23). In reply to the argument that SDI cannot cope with cruise missiles, the supporters answer that these air-breathing delivery systems are slow and thus, compared to intercontinental ballistic missiles (ICBMs), they provide decision makers with more reaction time. Thus, if SDI creates incentives for the Soviets to shift from ballistic to cruise missiles, it will have contributed further to a more stable strategic environment. Finally, supporters of the program point out that it permits the United States to exploit its unquestioned lead in several areas of advanced technology.

Opponents of SDI base their case on several points. A former Republican defense secretary emphasizes the strategic instabilities that will be inherent during the deployment period in which one side or the other has achieved a significant lead in defensive capabilities (Schlesinger, 1985). (Virtually no one takes seriously President Reagan's suggestion that the SDI system will be shared with the Soviets in order to allay fears that a combination of U.S. offensive and defensive weapons threatens their legitimate security interests.) Critics also assert that, on balance, defense is inherently destabilizing (Glaser, 1984, 1985). They further argue that SDI will harm the strategic environment because, legal interpretations of the Reagan administration to the contrary notwithstanding, it is incompatible with one of few remaining threads in the fabric of the arms control regime, the Antiballistic Missile (ABM) Treaty of 1972 (Bundy et al., 1984–1985; Drell et al., 1984; McNamara, 1986). Finally, the opponents of SDI assert that the cost of the program will not only place an intolerable burden on an already deficit-ridden U.S. economy, but it will also require abandonment of other programs that could contribute more effectively to national security (Schlesinger, 1985). As the president of a major military electronics firm, who believes that the minimum price tag on SDI is $5 trillion, said, "While we and the Soviets will be draining our resources in military competition in space, our economic competitors will be eating our lunch" (O'Keefe, 1986:192).

At this point the only safe generalizations about SDI are that the program will continue well into the 1990s, if not beyond; it will continue to generate a heated debate among defense analysts; and it is part of a much broader effort by the super powers to militarize space (Roberts, n.d.). Even critics favor a research and development effort, as permitted by the ABM Treaty, as a hedge against a Soviet breakthrough in this area, or as "the quintessential bargaining chip" (Schlesinger, 1985:12). The termination of the SDI program would not end efforts to achieve space-based defenses. The debate about SDI has often taken on an almost theological dimension; is SDI a "dangerous hoax and a cruel and potentially expensive exercise in self-deception" (Burrows, 1984:844), or does it hold out "the possibility of transforming, though not transcending, the Soviet-American deterrence relationship" (Payne and Gray, 1984:842)? It is less clear that in this debate, and in Soviet and U.S. policy decisions about strategic defense, crisis stability requirements will be a dominant consideration.

This list is necessarily incomplete but it does indicate that, on balance, recent technological and doctrinal developments are not likely to contribute to crisis stability, especially to the extent that they reduce perceived reaction times. Several analysts have suggested important parallels between the "cult of the offensive" in 1914 and current Soviet and U.S. military doctrines (Van Evera, 1984; Snyder, 1984). Whether or not such analogies and the "lessons of history" drawn from them are appropriate, it is hard to be especially sanguine about a situation in which weapons deployments and doctrines seem to reflect an almost complete inattention to attributes that would enhance crisis stability by lengthening rather than reducing decision time. As the military historian John Keegan has pointed out, among the important reasons we should fear speed is a haunting prospect: "Must we then foresee some future crisis which will either overcome a president or drive him to the resort of pre-packaged decisions—i.e. drills" (Keegan, 1981:148).

Prescriptive Theories

The questions and concerns described to this point have provided the impetus for a good deal of attention to the subject of crisis management. The basic task is far more easily described than accomplished: to influence the adversary through a skillful blend of coercion and accommodation in order to protect one's most vital national interests, without provoking war or stumbling into war by losing control of events.

Prescriptive theories of crisis management span a broad range. Differences among them are usually rooted in varying perspectives on the causes of war, images of the opponent and his probable responses to coercion and accommodation, and the primary threats against which one must guard. Three different viewpoints illustrate but do not describe exhaustively the extensive literature (Allison et al., 1985; see also Jervis, 1976; Cleveland, 1963; Roderick, 1983; Lebow, 1985; Caldwell, 1986; Gray, 1986, Ch.6; Ury, 1986).

One position identifies the unwarranted appeasement of expansionist powers as the primary danger of war. The shortsighted policies pursued by the British and French during the 1930s, culminating in the Munich agreements of 1938, are often invoked as examples. The adversary is usually depicted as a thoroughly rational actor, rarely if ever constrained by internal politics, whose policies reflect a careful calculation and appreciation of the opportunities and dangers in an emerging situation. The primary task of crisis management is therefore to communicate one's interests and demands as unambiguously as possible while avoiding concessions, since they will merely encourage the opponent to make further demands. Accommodation and appeasement not only reward aggression, thereby strengthening the adversary for the next round of demands, they may also give rise to dangerous miscalculations (for example, leading the adversary to believe that there are no limits to one's ability and willingness to comply with aggressive demands). Whereas appeasement postpones rather than averts war, a clear exposition of one's interests and an unconditional determination to protect them will force the opponent either to back down (thus ending the crisis on favorable terms for oneself) or to escalate (thus exposing the opponent's lack of interest in resolving it on terms short of one's capitulation). An inventory of arms that provides "escalation control"—military superiority at each rung on the ladder of escalation—will go a long way toward ensuring that the opponent will choose the former rather than the latter option. Strategies of crisis management may include "burning one's bridges," "chicken," and other steps that will convey an unambiguous signal of one's resolve and commitment while making it clear that only the adversary can take steps to prevent escalation.

A second approach to crisis management places emphasis not only on protecting one's primary interests but also on avoiding actions that might provoke a desperate and frustrated opponent into a mutually undesirable process of escalation, ending in war. According to this perspective, the opponent's capacity for absorbing humiliation is not boundless, if only because of domestic political concerns. American policy toward Japan prior to Pearl Harbor is sometimes cited to illustrate the danger posed by a cornered opponent. Accommodation on some points may serve a useful function in defusing a situation by providing the opponent a reasonable alternative to escalation, enabling him to "save face." The first rule of sound crisis management is therefore that one should not reduce the adversary's options to two—escalation toward war or humiliation.

A third perspective on crisis management focuses on the danger that decision makers will lose control of events, resulting in unintended, but no less costly, war. Just as the events leading up to World War II serve as sources of historical lessons for the first two approaches to crisis management, advocates of the third view often cite the denouement of the 1914 crisis as supporting evidence. This view incorporates somewhat less heroic assumptions about either side's ability to overcome constraints on rational decision making, especially under the pressures of a crisis. Consequently, crisis management proposals deal with both decision processes and the substance of policies.

Analysts whose diagnoses give substantial consideration to the possible loss of control by decision makers have also developed crisis management prescriptions for reducing the incentives for the opponent, whose rationality may not be without limits in high-stress situations, to escalate or even launch a preemptive attack out of fear ("he who hesitates is lost"), miscalculation, or similar motives. A very small sample of such suggestions is presented in Table 1.2. These prescriptions are usually offered on a contingent basis that will serve well regardless of circumstances and with a recognition that policymakers may have to face difficult trade-offs, for example, between the requirements of crisis management and coercive diplomacy (George et al., 1971; George, 1984).

The relevant literature is not narrowly confined to crisis studies, however. It also includes prescriptive theories that deal more broadly with the various cognitive, bureaucratic, and other constraints on rationality in the decision-making process. Contributions of this type include the following.

- George (1972) has offered suggestions for improving the quality of information and advice available to top-ranking leaders through a system of "multiple advocacy."
- Janis' (1972, 1982) analysis of high-quality decisions and fiascoes provides the basis for a number of steps to reduce the likelihood that decision groups will be afflicted by "groupthink," as well as other types of pitfalls (Janis and Mann, 1977).
- Allison (1971) and Steinbruner (1976) offer a number of suggestions for improving the quality of organizational decision making. For example, both discuss the limitations and possible dangers of the conventional premise that governments behave like unitary rational actors.
- Hermann and Hermann (1975) have addressed directly some disruptive

TABLE 1.2   A Sample of Crisis Management Prescriptions

Decision time
Each side shall slow down the tempo and momentum of crisis development, if necessary, in order to provide enough time for the two sides to assess the situation, make decisions, and exchange signals and proposals (G)
Do not adopt a launch-on-warning policy (A)
Make every effort to slow down the pace of crisis event (H)
Avoid military doctrines that emphasize rapid offensive action (H)
Do not issue ultimatums (F)

Decision making
Top-level political authorities must maintain knowledge and informed control over the selection and timing of military alerts, movements, and actions (G)
Do take decapitation seriously (A)
Do send top leaders out of Washington during crises (A)
Responsible policymakers should be in control not only of broad strategic decisions, but also of the details of implementation (H)
Do not accept military advice uncritically (H)
Assess the opponent's motives and actions from multiple perspectives (H)
Establish agreed-on crisis procedures between the United States and the Soviet Union (US)

Crisis communication
Do install bilateral hot lines between all nuclear powers (A)
Do not cut off communications as a sanction (A)
Keep communication channels open and communications specific (F)
Create a joint U.S.–U.S.S.R. nuclear crisis control center (US)
Establish a crisis consultation period (US)

Signaling and bargaining with the adversary
Each side shall ensure that military alerts and force movements undertaken to reduce vulnerability, increase readiness, and signal resolve are consistent with its limited diplomatic objective (G)
Each side shall avoid military moves and threats that give the mistaken impression that it is about to resort to large-scale warfare, thereby forcing the other side to consider preemption (G)
Do not plan for a nuclear demonstration shot in Europe (A)
Do meet regularly with Soviet leaders (A)
Do encourage nongovernmental contacts with the Soviets (A)
Have a sensitivity to the opponent's frame of reference (H)
Avoid taking steps that seal off "escape routes" (H)
Reduce the adversary's incentives to escalate with a combination of incentives and threats (H)
Do not threaten the core of the opponent's value system (F)
Do not pressure the other side beyond certain limits and/or by using force (F)

Force structures and the uses of force
Top-level political authorities must carefully coordinate movement of military forces and use of force options with diplomatic actions as part of an integrated strategy for pursuing crisis objectives at acceptable cost-risk levels (G)
Diplomatic and military options should be chosen that signal, or are consistent with, a desire to negotiate a way out of the crisis rather than to seek a military solution (G)

(continued)

TABLE 1.2 *(Continued)*

Each side shall select diplomatic proposals and military moves that leave the other side a way out the crisis that is compatible with its fundamental interests (G)
Do develop a survivable ICBM (A)
Do not seek a first-strike capability (A)
Do not engage U.S. and Soviet forces in direct combat (A)
Do not use nuclear weapons against third parties (A)
Do not treat nuclear weapons like other weapons (A)
Deploy invulnerable retaliatory forces (H)
Employ forces wisely, with flexibility and self-control (F)

Others
Do prepare decision makers to deal with nuclear crises (A)
Do work with the Soviets to prevent and manage crises (A)
Do not try to change rapidly the situation in Eastern Europe (A)
Do expect the unexpected (A)
Do not exaggerate military imbalances (A)
Be wary of initiating or increasing alliance commitments during a crisis (H)
Solicit third-party involvement (F)
Disregard provocative actions (F)
Fractionate the conflict to diffuse the situation (F)
Do not mix moral principles with conflicts of interest (F)
Hold semiannual nuclear risk-reduction talks with the Soviet Union (US)
Establish a presidential crisis control seminar to pass on accumulated learning about crisis management (US)
Enhance third-party roles in defusing regional conflicts (US)

Key: A: Allison et al., 1985; F: Frei, 1982; G: George, 1986a; H: Holsti, 1972; US: Ury and Smoke, 1984.

manifestations of stress on decision making with special emphasis on: fixation on only one reasonable option, simplification of the adversary and his or her limitations, physical fatigue, collapsed time perspective and neglect of future consequences, and excessive concurrence seeking. They suggest some indicators that may be used for monitoring decision processes as well as some possible prescriptions for coping with them (see also Hermann, 1979).

Assessment

Although there is some assessment convergence in crisis management prescriptions (for example, on the importance on slowing the pace of events to relieve time pressure on policymakers), it is nevertheless hard to take strong exception to the conclusion of a recent survey undertaken at the Rand Corporation: "a confident assessment that behavioral research findings can be plucked 'off the shelf' to solve crucial international problems remains incomplete" (Kahan et al., 1983:v). In fact, the effort to develop and use the behavioral sciences in this manner has elicited some sharp critiques. One is that these prescriptions are banal and "about as useful as general advice to hospital room personnel—keep calm, have equipment ready, and make no premature diagnoses" (Paul Schroeder, cited in Gilbert and Lauren, 1980:657). Another survey of the literature concludes that the results adduced from crisis research are deficient in several important respects: claims for crisis management prescriptions are insufficiently modest; much of the advice consists of epigrams that are, at best, little more sophisticated than common sense and thus hardly merit extensive research and are, at worst, dangerously simplistic; many crisis situations are intractable and thus impervious to crisis management advice; and prescriptions are too heavily oriented to process (Gilbert and Lauren, 1980). No doubt there is some validity to these points, but the criticism also seems to be based in part on a misunderstanding. Most crisis research has been motivated less by naive aspirations to create cookbook recipes for all crises than by hopes of at least laying open to serious scrutiny, through rigorous research, some of the received truths that often underlie official thinking about deterrence, coercive diplomacy, crisis management, and other aspects of international affairs.

A somewhat different charge is that the same analysts who are critical of the rational actor model of foreign policy propose antidotes to decision-making failures based on precisely that model. The belief that crisis can be managed more effectively is described as a defense mechanism that policy-makers and social scientists have erected to protect themselves from anxiety about the consequences of nuclear war (Lebow, 1981:298; see also Lebow, 1987b).

This is not the place to speculate about the deeper motives of crisis management theorists or to engage in a thorough analysis of the "epigrams" that they have offered. Perhaps their enterprise is indeed a delusion, but what is the alternative? There is surely no guarantee that systematic probes into cognitive and other decision-making malfunctions will yield greater wisdom and ultimately enable us better to defuse crises—and it is even less likely that the results will find their way into the councils of government. But is it a more dangerous delusion than reliance on the epigrams that so often guide foreign policies: the *para bellum* doctrine, the "domino theory," the "lessons of Munich," the "lessons of Vietnam" (of which there are many, often mutually exclusive versions), or the other, often unexamined axioms that have at times served as shortcuts to, if not substitutes for, sophisticated analyses of foreign policy situations (Halperin, 1974; May, 1962, 1973; Neustadt and May, 1986)?

However, one criticism cannot be easily dismissed. Even far better crisis management theories than are presently available—or foreseeable—would be an inadequate basis on which to pin too many hopes. It is instructive to recall the point made by those who claimed responsibility for the unsuccessful attempt to assassinate Prime Minister Thatcher and her cabinet in October 1984: "We failed this time, but *we* only have to be lucky *once.*" In nuclear crises, we only have to be unlucky once. Crisis management, in short, is no substitute for crisis avoidance. Even decision making in the Cuban missile crisis, often depicted as a source of important lessons about sensitive and effective crisis management, has attracted some thoughtful critics. Perhaps the most authoritative words of sobriety, addressed to those who may have become overly enthusiastic about adducing formulas for crisis management from the missile episode, came from President Kennedy himself. He remarked, some weeks after the crisis, "You can't have too many of those."

Conclusion

Can the behavioral sciences contribute to improving the quality of crisis decision making? Does the evidence summarized to this point have any policy implications? If these questions suggest that we can adduce some recipes that will enable us to transcend the often cruel paradoxes and dilemmas of the nuclear age, the answer must be negative. Beyond that, the answer depends on how one diagnoses the problem. The evidence surveyed in the preceding pages suggests that the potential loss of control of events by officials who must operate under conditions that generate substantial stress is one of the central problems of crisis decision making. If one accepts that diagnosis, then useful prescriptions can indeed be adduced, especially because the literature yields some important convergences of findings from several research domains and disciplinary perspectives. Thus, the proposals of George, Allison et al., and Ury and Smoke listed in Table 1.2 are examples of prescriptions that deserve serious consideration by policymakers, because they address key elements of central problems and they appear to have strong theoretical and empirical foundations. However, an assessment of policy implications is not complete unless it also addresses some of the political and other barriers that might impede implementation of crisis management prescriptions.

The tasks that constitute effective crisis management are demanding and difficult to carry out even if one could isolate the contending parties, most importantly, the United States and the Soviet Union. The nature of the difficulty is suggested by Henry Kissinger's colorful metaphor of the superpowers as "heavily armed blind men feeling their way around a room, each believing himself in mortal peril from the other whom he assumes to have perfect vision" (Kissinger, 1979, cited in Lambeth, 1982–1983:149). This may be overstated in some respects, but one can also argue that it does not fully describe the dilemmas and difficult trade-offs that may complicate life for top officials trying to cope with crises. One cannot separate crisis decision making and crisis management from other major elements of international politics and foreign policy. Specifically, policymakers may not be able to divorce themselves completely from pressures and constraints arising from two other sources—the alliance and domestic political arenas.

Most superpower crises have revolved around efforts to promote or protect the interests of allies and client states, including West Germany (the status of West Berlin), Cuba, Israel and its Arab neighbors, and many areas in the Third World. These have often confronted policymakers with potentially serious tensions between alliance management and crisis management. This is especially true for the United States because its allies are far more independent and vulnerable to domestic political pressures than are those of the Soviet Union. In a crisis the alliance leader may face a number of critical tasks, not all of which may be compatible with each other.

1. To convey to the adversary:
   a. A determination to maintain existing commitments, by force if necessary.
   b. Sufficient reassurance to reduce the adversary's motivations for significant military escalation and, perhaps, to permit bargaining on crisis issues.
2. To convey to allies:
   a. Assurance to some allies that their vital interests will not be sacrificed in seeking accommodation with the adversary.
   b. Assurances to other allies that they will not be drawn into a general war over issues of peripheral interest to them.
   c. A resolve not to be drawn into a strategy of escalation on behalf of an ally who is willing to run unduly high risks in the pursuit of purely parochial interests.

It is not easy for national leaders to coordinate their efforts in ways that will simultaneously achieve each of these goals. This point is illustrated by some examples of crises involving the United States (Table 1.3). The most obvious strategy for coping with the tensions between alliance and crisis management is to send one set of signals to allies and another to adversaries, but successful use of this ploy depends on airtight communication channels, something that cannot be assumed in an era that has not always prized secret diplomacy, is marked by public pressures for "instant history," and is notable for deliberate leaks to the media by supporters or opponents of specific policies. It need hardly be added that these dilemmas may be another source of stress for top officials.

The domestic political arena may also be a source of difficulties for crisis management. The reference here is *not* to the sometimes valid charge that the

TABLE 1.3 U.S. Crisis Management and Alliance Management

Crisis	Critical Task	Objectives
Quemoy-Matsu, 1954–1955	1a	To convey resolve to support Taiwan against any attack on offshore islands by China
	2a	To assure Taiwan that its security would not be compromised.
	2b	To assure NATO allies that they would not be drawn into war with China (and possibly the Soviet Union) over tiny offshore islands
Berlin "deadline" crisis, 1958–1959	1a	To demonstrate to Soviet leaders that there had been no reduction of resolve to maintain the freedom of West Berlin
	1b	To assure the Soviet Union sufficiently to reduce motives for rash policies and to permit negotiations over the status of Berlin
	2a	To assure Bonn that vital West German interests in Berlin would not be sacrificed
Quemoy-Matsu, 1958	1a	To convey to China and the Soviet Union a determination not to evacuate offshore islands under threat of force
	2c	To convey to Chiang Kai-shek a determination not to be drawn into war with Mainland China—in pursuit of Chiang's unrealistic goals
Cuban missile crisis, 1962	1a	To convey determination to the Soviet Union that offensive missiles in Cuba had to be removed
	1b	To reassure Soviet leaders sufficiently to reduce motivation for military escalation or for a preemptive attack
	2b	To assure skeptical allies (e.g., Canada) that they would not be drawn into a nuclear war over peripheral issues
Yom Kippur War, 1973	1a	To deter the Soviet Union from sending "volunteers" to the Middle East
	2a	To assure Israel that its vital interests and security requirement would not be compromised
	2b	To assure NATO allies that they would not be drawn into war
	2c	To restrain Israel when the opportunity for a military breakthrough threatened the ceasefire

Source: Holsti, O. R. 1976. Alliance and coalition diplomacy. In J. N. Rosenau, K. Thompson, and G. Boyd, eds. World Politics. *New York: Free Press.*

leaders may deliberately provoke crises in order to avoid having to cope with intractable domestic problems, or take advantage of the familiar "rally-round-the-flag" phenomenon that may characterize the responses of public opinion and opposition leaders, at least in the short run.[26] Rather, the point is that pressures and constraints from the domestic political arena represent a major barrier to the already difficult task of improving the strategic environment within which crisis decisions may have to be made. This is not the place for a full discussion of a very complex set of issues, but several examples will at least illustrate some dimensions of the problem.

As indicated earlier, recent developments in Soviet and U.S. weapons acquisition and strategic doctrine reveal a limited sensitivity to the requirements of crisis stability. Part of the reason is that there is at least a partial trade-off between key elements of crisis management and other techniques of statecraft such as deterrence or coercive diplomacy (George et al., 1971). Weapons acquisition processes are also driven by domestic political considerations, including calculations about the bureaucratic and electoral consequences of decisions on specific military systems. For example, whatever the merits of the B-1 bomber program, the fact that its contractors and subcontractors are located in all of the 48 contiguous states and hundreds of congressional districts makes it politically difficult to assess the program purely in terms of its contributions to national security, much less in terms of what some may regard as the more esoteric requirements of crisis stability. By 1989, the strategic defense initiative program may have developed a sufficiently large domestic constituency that it will persist, almost without regard to its merits. Thus, the requirements of crisis stability may not be completely lost in the shuffle but, at best they must compete with many other considerations, including those arising from the domestic political arena. Building an effective constituency for improving crisis management is not an easy task, but perhaps the support of Senators Nunn (D, Georgia) and Warner (R, Virginia) for useful steps in this direction suggests that it is not impossible.

Second, although there is very substantial public support for arms control and general efforts to stabilize relations with the Soviet Union (Holsti, 1987), specific efforts directed at those goals have run afoul not only of such Soviet actions as the invasions of Czechoslovakia and Afghanistan or the destruction of the Korean Airlines flight 007, but also of the electoral cycle in U.S. politics and the perceived needs of some leaders arising from it. President Ford's decision to delay sending the Strategic Arms Limitation Talks (SALT) II Treaty to the Senate until after the 1976 election, President Carter's initial decision to scrap the Vladivostok formula, and Senator Church's decision to make an issue of the "Cuban brigade" (Duffy, 1983) were related to electoral politics, and they gave opponents of the agreement such as the Committee on the Present Danger time to mobilize forces against it. The Soviets signed the death warrant for the SALT II Treaty by their brutal invasion of Afghanistan, but domestic politics in the United States had already inflicted serious, if not mortal, wounds on it.

Finally, the tasks of crisis management may be complicated not only by the rapid turnover of leaders in the United States, but also by the increasingly partisan and ideological tenor of U.S. politics. It is not a very useful exercise in nostalgia to yearn for the return to prominence in foreign and defense policy of the "establishment" leaders who provided a good deal of continuity during the pre–Vietnam era, but proposals for coping more effectively with crises can have a practical impact only if there is some cumulation of theory and practice that transcends the four- or eight-year cycle of a U.S. administration.

In addition to substantive proposals on crisis management, Allison, George, Janis, Jervis, May, Neustadt, and others have offered useful prescriptive theories on the uses of advisers and the management of information in order to reduce the risks that policymakers will make poor decisions based on unexamined or flawed premises, biased information, miscalculations, and the like. There are, to be sure, limits on how far this approach can take us. It is by now a truism that top-ranking leaders bring to their offices a variety of decision-making styles, each with its strengths and vulnerabilities (Johnson, 1974; Barber, 1977). They are unlikely to alter dramatically the habits, preferences, beliefs, and values that have worked sufficiently well to bring them to high office, even if these were developed in settings that bear little resemblance to those in which critical foreign and defense policy decisions are made.

Nevertheless, a good deal more can be done to provide better cumulation and transmission of relevant crisis management knowledge, insights, and skills from one administration to another. Simulations, war gaming (George et al., 1985), process debriefing, and related techniques could be used to provide some sensitivity training for top-ranking officials during the long transition period between elections and inaugurations. At least some of the efforts to provide continuity in the relevant knowledge and procedures should be directed at the middle-to-upper range officials whose tenure is not dependent on the current administration. It must be recognized, however, that a corps of "crisis specialists" will not automatically ensure effective continuity or even be easy to establish. The U.S. political culture has never been especially hospitable to an idea that may resemble the permanent staff of the British Foreign Office, and each of the past several presidents has come to office, after a successful "anti-Washington-establishment" electoral campaign, with the avowed goal of confronting the bureaucracy. Moreover, as three perceptive critics of U.S. foreign policy have shown, the use of partisan and ideological litmus tests for appointments has increased sharply in recent years, resulting in more rather than less continuity between administrations (Destler et al., 1984).

Efforts toward improving the prospects for effective crisis decision making must also be directed more broadly at the strategic environment and, more specifically, at reversing a rush toward arms races that seems likely to erode rather than enhance crisis stability. In light of observations about the many forces driving weapons programs there should be no illusions about the difficulties of reversing some of the more dangerous elements of the arms race. On the other hand, even some relatively modest steps—certainly far less radical than the proposals put forward by President Reagan at the 1986 Reykjavik summit meeting—could be helpful in reducing the time pressure and stress under which crisis decisions may have to be made. In this respect, some of the trends and developments identified earlier—specifically relating to warfighting doctrines, deployment of weapons with very short flight times, ASATs, and SDI—are areas that deserve the most serious examination in terms of crisis stability. The near certainty that the late 1980s will be marked by stringency for the defense budget, if only because current programs are underfunded by some $325 billion (Korb, 1987), suggests that weapon programs may undergo more careful scrutiny but this does not, of course, ensure that crisis-stability criteria will be invoked as top-priority values when trade-offs have to be faced.

A second and related type of threat to crisis decision making arises from vulnerabilities in command, communication control, and information (C^3I) structures. Traditionally, students of strategy have tended to focus on weapons and doctrines, but a number of recent studies have posed some disturbing questions about C^3I (Steinbruner, 1978; Steinbruner, 1981–1982; Bracken, 1983; Blair, 1985; Sagan, 1985). According to Steinbruner (1981–1982:18), for example:

> The United States does not have a strategic command system that could survive deliberate attack of a sort that the Soviet Union could readily undertake. . . . Even 50 nuclear weapons are probably sufficient to eliminate the ability to direct U.S. strategic forces to coherent purposes.

Summarized briefly, these studies of command structures suggest serious flaws and vulnerabilities that could result in lethal consequences, especially during a tense confrontation between the superpowers: "Under conditions of an intense crisis, the existing U.S. command system is subject to strains powerful enough to trigger an unintended war" (Steinbruner, 1981–1982:22). The combination of highly accurate weapons with short flight times, doctrines that emphasize "decapitation" attacks, and vulnerabilities in C^3I clearly poses a danger to crisis stability. The prospective costs of effective measures may be a major constraint. In a stable, but not growing, budgetary environment, proponents of other major defense programs will correctly perceive that significant efforts to deal with C^3I may pose a threat to other, preferred projects. Will there be an effective constituency for improving C^3I? Can one be developed that can compete effectively, for example, with proponents of SDI or comparable programs?

It seems appropriate to end on a cautiously optimistic note, with emphasis on the caution. On the one hand, much of the existing research points to a number of frailties to which human beings whether acting alone, in groups, or in organizations are vulnerable, and some of these vulnerabilities may be exacerbated in situations of intense and protracted stress. It is not overstating the case to say that this is a part of the human condition. On the other hand, imperfect and incomplete as our understanding of human behavior may be, systematic knowledge about decision making has surely increased substantially during the past several decades. It is unlikely that the behavioral sciences will ever be in a position to offer lawlike prescriptions that will enable those who must make decisions in crises to transcend the awful dilemmas they may have to face, but theoretically informed and empirically based diagnoses of the potential frailties and weaknesses in decision-making systems, capabilities that are within reach, constitute a not-insignificant contribution toward the prevention of nuclear war. Conversely, policy prescriptions that fail to take these diagnoses into account may be dangerously flawed. Even if one accepts this moderately hopeful conclusion, however, it would be naive to end without mentioning yet another gap—that between the behavioral science and policy communities. Only the most optimistic will believe that it will bridged easily or soon. Steinbruner's (1983:5) observation about the C^3I issue may have broader relevance: "The problem therefore is one of telling current policymakers things they are not at all prepared to hear about issues they think they already understand."[27]

Notes

Parts of this chapter have drawn on several previous publications: Holsti (1972, 1979), and Holsti and George (1975). For valuable research assistance, I am indebted to Cherie Morris, a Duke University undergraduate student. I also benefited greatly from helpful comments and suggestions on an earlier draft of this chapter by Alexander George, Roy Melbourne, Richard Preston, Darryl Roberts, Ted Ropp, and Philip Tetlock, as well as seven anonymous reviewers for the National Research Council.

1. See, for example, Barton (1969), Brouillette and Quarantelli (1971), Dynes (1976), Turner (1976), and Quarantelli (1978) for an introduction to this literature. The Disaster Research Center, at Ohio State University until 1985 and the University of Delaware since then, has undertaken nearly 500 field studies since 1963. For further details, see Disaster Research Center (1987).

2. The stresses of high political office are discussed from psychiatric, medical, and biological perspectives by Rogow (1963, 1969), L'Etang (1970), Wiegele (1973, 1977), and Wiegele et al., (1985).

3. For extended discussions and evaluations of the concept of crisis, see McClelland (1961, 1972), Hermann (1963, 1969a, 1969b), Miller and Iscoe (1963), Robinson (1972), Hermann and Brady (1972), Brecher (1974, 1977, 1979), Snyder and Diesing (1977), Brecher and Wilkenfeld (1982), Lebow (1981), Parker (1977), Tanter (1975), Head et al. (1978), Young (1968), and Haas (1986).

4. In field research the stimulus is often stressful for virtually all subjects; examples include soldiers in combat or persons caught in various types of natural disasters and catastrophes (see the literature cited in note 2). In such cases the problem of circularity between the stimulus and response is minimized. The problem can be significant in laboratory research, however, because ethical researchers cannot easily create equally unambiguous threatening situations.

5. See also Levi (1981) and Stein (1982). Stein develops the thesis that misperceptions rarely cause conflict or its escalation into war. Some recent studies of war have also approached the topic from the perspective of the "expected utility" of decisions to engage in armed conflict. See, for example, Bueno de Mesquita (1981, 1985).

6. For summaries of the bureaucratic politics perspective on foreign affairs, see Neustadt (1970), Allison (1971), Allison and Halperin (1972), Destler (1972), Halperin (1974), Caldwell (1977), Williamson (1979), and Rosati (1981), as well as the critiques in Krasner (1972), Art (1973), Ball (1974), and Perlmutter (1974). See also the general reviews on organizations under stress in McGrath (1976) and Staw et al. (1981).

7. However, the most widely cited illustration of a bureaucratic failure to implement a decision—the order to withdraw obsolete missiles from Turkey—is apparently incorrect (Hafner, 1977; Bernstein, 1980). Recently published transcripts of Ex Comm deliberations do not offer a great deal of evidence in support of the bureaucratic politics model of decision making. However, they indicate clearly that concern for what to do about the missiles in Turkey was a critical factor during the crucial meetings of October 27, and that President Kennedy probably would have traded the missiles in Turkey for those in Cuba if necessary to avoid violent escalation of the Soviet-U.S. confrontation (Welch and Blight, 1987–1988; Bundy and Blight, 1987–1988).

8. The classic studies are Sherif and Sherif (1953) and Sherif et al. (1961). Cohesion is unlikely to increase if the threat is unevenly felt or if it strikes at the very basis of common interests. For example, a group is likely to experience increased cohesion in the face of an external threat to reduce all salaries by 20 percent, but not if the external threat takes the form of an order to effect a similiar saving by firing 20 percent of the group members. Moreover, cohesion may be affected by the level of group success in coping with the threat (Staw et al., 1981).

9. This literature is huge. Among the works with more direct application to political decision making are: Festinger (1957), Janis and Mann (1977), George (1980), Steinbruner (1974), Jervis (1976), Axelrod (1976), Holsti (1972, 1976), Lebow (1981), Cottam (1977), Simon (1947), March and Simon (1958), White (1970, 1984, 1986), Ableson and Levi (1985), and Hermann (1986).

10. Somewhat different lists appear in Morgan (1977:102–103), Janis and Mann (1977), and George (1980:10).

11. Cited in Back (1961). But in at least one study it was found that even mild stress interfered with problem solving (Ray, 1965). Excellent if somewhat dated introductions to research on the impact of stress are two extensive reviews of the literature: Lazarus et al. (1952) and Horvath (1959).

12. Among the many studies supporting this conclusion are: Korchin et al. (1957), Murphy (1959), Schroeder et al. (1967), Anderson (1976), Grinker and Spiegel (1945), Torrance (1961), Baker and Chapman (1962), Baddeley (1972), and Staw et al. (1981). The psychobiological effects of crisis and stress are discussed in Wiegele (1973, 1977) and Wiegele et al. (1985).

13. More comprehensive summaries may be found in Lazarus et al. (1952), Easterbrook (1959), Horvath (1959), Janis and Leventhal (1968), Lazarus et al. (1974), Holsti (1972), Milburn (1972), Hermann and Brady (1972), Janis (1973), and Broadbent (1971).

14. The tendency to see events as linked to each other is illustrated by two episodes in October 1962. When news that China had invaded India reached those who were grappling with the problem of Soviet missiles in Cuba, some of them initially assumed that the two events were linked as part of a worldwide assault on the noncommunist world, even though by that time there was no shortage of evidence indicating a deep split between Moscow and Peking.

15. Citations to the 1914 diplomatic documents identify the document number, not the page number.

16. On the basis of the six crises that he experienced up to the 1960 election, Richard Nixon (1962:113) observed: "Decisive action relieves the tension which builds up in a crisis. When the situation requires that an individual restrain himself from acting decisively over a long period, this can be the most wearing of all crises."

17. This is one of the nonobvious predictions of cognitive dissonance theory that has been supported in repeated experiments (Festinger, 1957; Englander and Tyszka, 1980). The thesis that cognitive dissonance may occur prior to a decision is effectively developed in Janis and Mann (1977).

18. At the Hawk's Cay meeting in 1987, Theodore Sorensen recalled of the crucial meeting on the night of October 27: "The only word which can describe the meeting that night is 'rancourous'—we *did* show the effects of stress and fatigue, and the air strike *was* gaining strength and its proponents were becoming more vigorous" (Welch and Blight, 1987–1988:21). Arthur Schlesinger (1978:546–547) has written that Dean Rusk "had a virtually complete breakdown mentally and physically." However, two analysts who have read transcripts of the Ex Comm deliberations conclude: "We see no indication of stress- or fatigue-induced dysfunction in the transcript, and certainly no

indication that Dean Rusk, the member of the Ex Comm whose name is usually linked with rumors of breakdown, had in fact become passive or unable to fulfill his responsibilities" (Welch and Blight, 1987–1988:22).

19. This view was shared even by those who were in fundamental disagreement with the ultimate decisions. Dean Acheson, perhaps the most notable of the critics, wrote that not only was U.S. strategy during the Cuban crisis wrong—that it succeeded in gaining withdrawal of the missiles was attributed to "dumb luck"—but also that ascribed errors can be traced back to the "leaderless" meetings and almost endless, freewheeling discussions and debates of that 13-day period. Elsewhere Acheson wrote that the doctrine of keeping options open is synonymous with "avoiding decisions" (Acheson, 1969a, 1969b).

20. The outbreak of World War I continues to attract attention from students of foreign policy and strategy, including some of the ablest young scholars of the past decade. See, for example, Kahler (1979–1980), Lebow (1984), Kennedy (1984), Snyder (1984), Van Evera (1984), Levy (1986), Lynn-Jones (1986), and Sagan (1986). In virtually all cases, the analyses are driven by assessments of parallels between 1914 and the contemporary situation.

21. For quantitative evidence on this point, see Holsti (1972:143–168).

22. The literature on decision making during the missile crisis is extensive and is certain to grow as new materials become available for scholarly research. A partial list includes: Allison (1969, 1971), Snyder and Diesing (1977), George et al. (1971), Holsti (1972), George and Smoke (1974), Wohlstetter and Wohlstetter (1971), Snyder (1978), Nathan (1975), Wohlstetter (1965), Lebow (1983), Anderson (1983), Hampson (1984–1985), Trachtenberg (1985), Neustadt and May (1986), Garthoff, (1987), and Blight et al. (1987). There are also many memoirs and journalistic accounts of the crisis. In 1987, on the twenty-fifth anniversary of the crisis, meetings of surviving participants were held at Hawk's Cay, Florida, and at Harvard University. The latter were joined by Soviet leaders (Welch and Blight, 1987–1988).

23. The studies listed here focus on international relations. Among the many strengths of the Suedfeld and Tetlock approach is the fact that it has been tested among a broad range of subjects in a wide variety of settings other than international politics. See, for example, Suedfeld (1979, 1985), Suedfeld and Rank (1976), Suedfeld et al. (1986), Tetlock (1979) and Tetlock et al. (1984).

24. Although Ambrose gives Eisenhower high marks for his handling of the 1954–1955 Quemoy-Matsu crisis, two scholars with access to recently available materials are much more critical (Brands, 1988, Chang, 1988).

25. Of four categories of Soviet targets, the third listed by Secretary of Defense Brown was "leadership and control." However, he went on to state, "At the same time, of course, we recognize the role that a surviving supreme command could and would play in the termination of hostilities, and can envisage many scenarios in which destruction of them would be inadvisable and contrary to our own best interests. Perhaps the obvious is worth emphasizing: possession of a capability is not tantamount to exercising it" (Department of Defense, 1981:41–42).

26. For example, on the eve of the Civil War, Secretary of State Seward advised Abraham Lincoln to provoke a war against Spain or France to remedy the problem

that, "We are at the end of a month's administration, and yet without a policy, either domestic or foreign." Fortunately for the United States, the president had the wisdom to reject Seward's suggestion, which was appropirately offered on April Fool's Day, 1861 (Nicolay and Hay, 1890:446). For other examples, see the case studies in Jervis et al. (1985).

27. For a somewhat different perspective on this gap, see Gaddis (1987).

References

Abel, T. 1941. The element of decision in the pattern of war. *American Sociological Review* 6:853–859.

Abelson, R.P. 1976. Script processing in attitude formation and decision making. In J.S. Carroll and J.W. Payne, eds., *Cognition and Social Behavior*, pp. 33–45. Hillsdale, N.J.: Erlbaum.

———. 1981. Pyschological status of the script concept. *American Psychologist* 36:715–729.

Abelson, R.P. and A. Levi. 1985. Decision making and decision theory. In G. Lindzey and E. Aronson, eds., *Handbook of Social Psychology*, Vol. I, pp. 231–309. New York: Random House.

Acheson, D. 1969a. Dean Acheson's version of Robert Kennedy's version of the Cuban missile affair. *Esquire* (February) 71:76–77, 144.

———. 1969b. *Present at the Creation*. New York: Norton.

Allison, G.T. 1969. Conceptual models and the Cuban missile crisis. *American Political Science Review* 63:689–718.

———. 1971. *Essence of Decision: Explaining the Cuban Missile Crisis*. Boston: Little, Brown.

Allison, G.T., A. Carnesale and J. Nye, Jr., eds. 1985. *Hawks, Doves and Owls*. New York: Norton.

Allison, G.T., and M. Halperin. 1972. Bureaucratic politics: A paradigm and some policy implications. *World Politics* 24:40–79.

Ambrose, S. 1984. *Eisenhower: The President*. New York: Simon and Schuster.

Anderson, C.R. 1976. Coping behavior as intervening mechanisms in the inverted-U stress-performance relationship. *Journal of Applied Psychology* 60:30–34.

Anderson, P. 1983. Decision making by objection and the Cuban missile crisis. *Administrative Science Quarterly* 28:201–222.

Argyris, C. 1967. *Some Causes of Organizational Ineffectiveness within the Department of State*. Washington, D.C.: Center for International Systems Research, Department of State Publication 8180.

Aron, R. 1965. *The Great Debate*. Garden City, N.Y.: Doubleday.

Art, R.J. 1973. Bureaucratic politics and American foreign policy: A critique. *Policy Sciences* 4:467–490.

Asch, S.E. 1953. Effects of group pressure upon modification and distortion of judgment. In D. Cartwright and A. Zander, eds., *Group Dynamics, Research and Theory*, pp. 189–200. Evanston, Ill.: Row Peterson.

———. 1965. Opinions and social pressure. In A.P. Hare, E.F. Borgatta, and R.F. Bales, eds., *Small Groups: Studies in Social Interaction*, pp. 318–324. New York: Knopf.
Axelrod, R. 1976. *The Structure of Decision*. Princeton, N.J.: Princeton University Press.
———. 1984. *The Evolution of Cooperation*. New York: Basic Books.
Back, K. 1961. Decisions under uncertainty: Rational, irrational, and non-rational. *American Behavioral Scientists* 4:14–19.
Baddeley, A.D. 1972. Selective attention and performance in dangerous environments. *British Journal of Psychology* 63:537–546.
Baker, G.W. and D.W. Chapman, eds. 1962. *Man and Society in Disaster*. New York: Basic Books.
Ball, D.J. 1974. The blind men and the elephant: A critique of bureaucratic politics theory. *Australian Outlook* 23:71–92.
———. 1982–1983. U.S. strategic forces: How would they be used? *International Security* 7:31–60.
Ball, G. 1962. Lawyers and diplomats. Department of State Bulletin 47 (December 31):990.
Barber, J.D. 1977. *The Presidential Character: Predicting Performance in the White House*. Englewood Cliffs, N.J.: Prentice Hall.
Barnard, C.I. 1938. *The Functions of the Executive*. Cambridge, Mass.: Harvard University Press.
Barton, A.H. 1969. *Communities in Disaster: A Sociological Analysis of Collective Stress Situations*. Garden City, N.Y.: Doubleday.
Bauer, R.A. 1961. Problems of perception and the relations between the United States and Soviet Union. *Journal of Conflict Resolution* 5:223–229.
Bell, C. 1971. *The Conventions of Crisis*. London: Oxford University Press.
———. 1984. Decision-makers and crises. *International Journal* 39:324–336.
Ben Zur, H., and S.J. Breznitz. 1981. The effect of time pressure on risky choice behavior. *Acta Psychologica* 47:89–104.
Ben-Zvi, A. 1987. *The Illusion of Deterrence*. Boulder, Col.: Westview.
Bernstein, B.J. 1980. The Cuban Missile Crisis: Trading the Jupiters in Turkey. *Political Science Quarterly* 95:97–126.
Betts, R.K. 1987. *Nuclear Blackmail and Nuclear Deterrence*. Washington, D.C.: The Brookings Institution.
Birch, H.G. 1945. Motivational factors in insightful problem-solving. *Journal of Comparative Psychology* 37:295–317.
Blair, B. 1985. *Strategic Command and Control*. Washington, D.C.: The Brookings Institution.
Blake, R.F., and J.S. Mouton. 1962. Overvaluation of own group's product in intergroup competition. *Journal of Abnormal and Social Psychology* 64:237–238.
Blight, J.G. 1986–1987. The new psychology of war and peace. *International Security* 11:175–186.
Blight, J.G., J.S. Nye, Jr., and D.A. Welch. 1987. The Cuban Missile Crisis revisited. *Foreign Affairs* 66:170–188.

Boulding, K. 1959. National images and international systems. *Journal of Conflict Resolution* 3:120–131.

Bracken, P. 1983. *Command and Control of Nuclear Forces*. New Haven, Conn.: Yale University Press.

Brands, H.W., Jr. 1988. Testing massive retaliation: Credibility and crisis management in the Taiwan strait. *International Security* 12:124–151.

Brecher, M. 1974. Research findings and theory-building in foreign policy behavior. *Sage International Yearbook of Foreign Policy Studies* Vol. 2, pp. 49–122.

———. 1977. Toward a theory of international crisis behavior. *International Studies Quarterly* 21:63–74.

———. 1979. State behavior in international crisis. *Journal of Conflict Resolution* 23:466–480.

Brecher, M., and B. Geist. 1980. *Decisions in Crisis: Israel, 1967 and 1973*. Berkeley, Calif.: University of California Press.

Brecher, M., and J. Wilkenfeld. 1982. Crisis in world politics. *World Politics* 34:380–417.

Broadbent, D.E. 1971. *Decision and Stress*. London: Academic Press.

Brouillette, J.R., and E.L. Quarantelli. 1971. Types of patterned variation in bureaucratic adaptations to organizational stress. *Sociological Inquiry* 41:39–45.

Bruner, J., J.J. Goodnow, and G.A. Austin. 1956. *A Study of Thinking*. New York: Wiley.

Bueno de Mesquita, B. 1981. *The War Trap*. New Haven, Conn.: Yale University Press.

———. 1985. The war trap revisited: A revised expected utility model. *American Political Science Review* 79:159–177.

Bundy, M., transcriber and J.G. Blight, ed. 1987/1988. October 27, 1962: Transcripts of the meetings of the Ex Comm. *International Security* 12:30–92.

Bundy, M., G.F. Kennan, R.S. McNamara, and G. Smith. 1984–1985. The President's choice: Star Wars or arms control. *Foreign Affairs* 63:264–278.

Burrows, W.E. 1984. Ballistic missile defense: The illusion of security. *Foreign Affairs* 62:843–856.

Caldwell, D. 1977. Bureaucratic foreign policy-making. *American Behavioral Scientist* 21:87–110.

———. 1986. *American Styles of Crisis Management*. Malibu, Calif.: Pepperdine University.

Carter, A.B. 1986. Satellites and anti-satellites: The limits of the possible. *International Security* 10:46–98.

Cartwright, D. 1971. Risk taking by individuals and groups: An assessment of research employing choice dilemmas. *Journal of Personality and Social Psychology* 20:361–378.

Chang, G.H. 1988. To the nuclear brink: Eisenhower, Dulles, and the Quemoy-Matsu crisis. *International Security* 12:96–123.

Cleveland, H. 1963. Crisis diplomacy. *Foreign Affairs* 41:638–649.

Cohen, J. 1964. Psychological time. *Scientific American* (November) 211:116–124.

Cohen, S.I., and A.G. Mezey. 1961. The effects of anxiety on time judgment and time

experience in normal persons. *Journal of Neurology, Neurosurgery and Psychiatry* 24:266–268.
Collins, B.E., and H. Guetzkow. 1964. *A Social Psychology of Group Processes for Decision-Making*. New York: Wiley.
Cottam, R. 1977. *Foreign Policy Motivation*. Pittsburgh: University of Pittsburgh Press.
Department of Defense. 1981. *Annual Report, Fiscal Year 1982*. Washington, D.C.: U.S. Government Printing Office.
de Rivera, J. 1968. *The Psychological Dimension of Foreign Policy*. Columbus, Ohio: Merrill.
Destler, I.M. 1972. *Presidents, Bureaucrats and Foreign Policy*. Princeton, N.J.: Princeton University Press.
Destler, I.M., L. Gelb, and A. Lake. 1984. *Our Own Worst Enemy*. New York: Simon and Schuster.
Disaster Research Center. 1987. *Publication List*. Newark, Del.: University of Delaware.
Downs, A. 1967. *Inside Bureaucracy*. Boston: Little, Brown.
Dowty, A. 1984. *Middle East Crisis: U.S. Decision-making in 1958, 1970 and 1973*. Berkeley, Calif.: University of California Press.
Drell, S.D., P.J. Farley, and D. Holloway. 1984. Preserving the ABM treaty: A critique of the Reagan SDI. *International Security* 9:51–91
Dubno, P. 1963. Decision time characteristics of leaders and group problem solving behavior. *Journal of Social Psychology* 59:259–282.
Duffy, G. 1983. Crisis mangling and the Cuban brigade. *International Security* 8:67–87.
Dunnette, M.R., J. Campbell, and K. Jaastad. 1963. The effects of group participation on brainstorming effectiveness for two industrial samples. *Journal of Applied Psychology* 47:30–37.
Dynes, R.R. 1976. *Organized Behavior in Disaster*. Lexington, Mass.: Heath.
Easterbrook, J.A. 1959. The effects of emotion on cue utilization and the organization of behavior. *Pyschological Review* 66:183–201
Eisenhower, D.D. 1965. Address to *Washington Post* book and author lunch. *Palo Alto Times*, 1 October.
Englander, T., and T. Tyszka. 1980. Information seeking in open decision situations. *Acta Psychologica* 45:169–176.
Etheredge, L.S. 1985. *Can Governments Learn?* New York: Pergamon.
Feldman, J., and H.E. Kanter. 1965. Organizational decision-making. In J.G. March, ed., *Handbook of Organizations*, pp. 614–649. Chicago: Rand McNally.
Fenno, R. 1959. *The President's Cabinet*. Cambridge, Mass.: Harvard University Press.
Festinger, L. 1957. *A Theory of Cognitive Dissonance*. Evanston, Ill.: Row, Peterson.
———. 1965. A theory of social comparison processes. In A.P. Hare, E.F. Borgatta, and R.F. Bales, eds., *Small Groups: Studies in Social Interaction*, pp.146–169. New York: Knopf.

Festinger, L., S. Schachter, and K. Bach. 1950. *Social Pressures in Informal Groups.* New York: Harper.
France, Commission de publication des documents relatif aux origins de la guerre, 1914. 1936. *Documents Diplomatique Français (1871-1914),* 3rd series, Vols. 10 and 11. Paris.
Frei, D., ed. 1982. *Managing International Crises.* Beverly Hills, Calif.: Sage.
Gaddis, J.L. 1986. The long peace: Elements of stability in the postwar international system. *International Security* 10:99–142.
———. 1987. Expanding the data base: Historians, political scientists, and the enrichment of security studies. *International Security* 12:3–21.
Garthoff, R.L. 1987. *Reflections on the Cuban Missile Crisis.* Washington, D.C.: The Brookings Institution.
George, A.L. 1969. The "operational code": A neglected approach to the study of political leaders and decision-making. *International Studies Quarterly* 13:190–222.
———. 1972. The case for multiple advocacy in making foreign policy. *American Political Science Review* 66:751–785, 791–795.
———. 1974. Adapation to stress in political decision-making. In G.V. Coelho, D.A. Hamburg and J. Adams, eds., *Coping and Adapation,* pp. 176–245. New York: Basic Books.
———. 1975. Toward a more soundly based foreign policy: Making better use of information. *Report of the Commission on the Organization of the Government for the Conduct of Foreign Policy,* Vol. 2., Appendix D. Washington, D.C.: U.S. Government Printing Office.
———. 1980. *Presidential Decision-making in Foreign Policy: The Effective Use of Information and Advice.* Boulder, Col.: Westview.
———. 1984. Crisis management: The interaction of political and military consideration. *Survival* 26:223–234.
———. 1986a. Crisis management: Lessons from past U.S.-Soviet crises. Stanford University. Mimeo.
———. 1986b. The impact of crisis-induced stress on decision-making. In *The Medical Implications of Nuclear War,* pp. 529–552. Washington, D.C.: National Academy Press.
George, A.L., D.M. Bernstein, G.S. Parnell and J.P. Rogers. 1985. *Inadvertent War in Europe: Crisis Simulation.* Stanford, Calif.: Center for International Security and Arms Control.
George, A.L., D.K. Hall and W. Simons. 1971. *The Limits of Coercive Diplomacy.* Boston: Little, Brown.
George, A.L. and R. Smoke. 1974. *Deterrence in American Foreign Policy.* New York: Columbia University Press.
Gilbert, A.N., and P.G. Lauren. 1980. Crisis management: An assessment and critique. *Journal of Conflict Resolution* 24:641–664.
Glaser, C.L. 1984. Why even good defense may be bad. *International Security* 2:92–123.

———. 1985. Do we want the missile defense we can build? *International Security* 10:25–57.
Gray, C. 1982. What deters? The ability to wage nuclear war. In J.F. Reichart and S.R. Sturm, eds., *American Defense Policy*, 5th ed., pp. 171–187. Baltimore: Johns Hopkins University Press.
———. 1986. *Nuclear Strategy and National Style*. Lanham, Md.: Hamilton Books.
Gray, C.S., and K. Payne. 1980. Victory is possible. *Foreign Policy* 39:14–27.
Great Britain, Foreign Office. 1926. *British Documents on the Outbreak of War*, Vol. 9. London: His Majesty's Stationery Office.
Green, P. 1968. *Deadly Logic*. New York: Schocken.
Grinker, R.R., and J.P. Spiegel. 1945. *Men Under Stress*. New York: McGraw-Hill.
Haas, M. 1986. Research on international crisis: Obsolescence of an approach? *International Interactions* 13:23–58.
Hafner, D.L. 1977. Bureaucratic politics and "those frigging missiles": JFK, Cuba and U.S. missiles in Turkey. *Orbis* 21:307–334.
Halperin, M.H. 1974. *Bureaucratic Politics and Foreign Policy*. Washington, D.C.: The Brookings Institution.
Hammond, K.R., and J. Mumpower. 1979. Risks and safeguards in the formation of social policy. *Knowledge: Creation, Diffusion, Utilization* 1:245–258.
Hampson, F.O. 1984/1985. The divided decision-maker: American domestic politics and the Cuban crises. *International Security* 9:130–165.
Head, R.G., F.W. Short and R. McFarlane. 1978. *Crisis Resolution: Presidential Decision Making in the Mayaguez and Korean Confrontation*. Boulder, Col.: Westview.
Hermann, C.F., 1963. Some consequences of crises which limit the viability of organizations. *Administrative Science Quarterly* 8:61–82.
———. 1969a. *Crises in Foreign Policy: A Simulation Analysis*. Indianapolis: Bobbs-Merrill.
———. 1969b. International crisis as a situational variable. In J. N. Rosenau, ed., *International Politics and Foreign Policy*, 2d ed. New York: Free Press.
Hermann, C.F., and L.P. Brady. 1972. Alternative models of international crisis behavior. In C.F. Hermann, ed., *International Crises: Insights from Behavioral Research*, pp. 281–320. New York: Free Press.
Hermann, M.G. 1979. Indicators of stress in policymakers during foreign policy crises. *Political Psychology* 1:27–46.
———. 1986. *Political Psychology*. San Francisco: Jossey-Bass.
Hermann, M.G., and C.F. Hermann. 1975. Maintaining the quality of decision-making in foreign policy crises: A proposal. *Commission on the Organization of the Government for the Conduct of Foreign Policy*, Vol. 2, pp. 124–136. Washington, D.C.: U.S. Government Printing Office.
Hersh, S.M. 1986. The target is destroyed. *Atlantic* (September) 258:46–69.
Hoffeld, D.R., and S.C. Kent. 1963. Decision time and information use in choice situations. *Psychological Reports* 12:68–70.
Hoffman, F. 1985. The SDI in U.S. nuclear strategy. *International Security* 10:13–24.

Holsti, O.R., 1972. *Crisis, Escalation, War*. Montreal: McGill-Queens University Press.
———. 1976. Foreign policy decision-makers viewed cognitively. In R. Axelrod, ed., *The Structure of Decision*, pp. 18–54. Princeton, N.J.: Princeton University Press.
———. 1979. Theories of crisis decision making. In P.G. Lauren, ed., *Diplomacy*, pp. 99–136. New York: Free Press.
———. 1987. Public opinion and containment. In T.L. Deibel and J.L. Gaddis, eds., *Containing the Soviet Union*, pp. 20–58. New York: Pergamon-Brassey's.
Holsti, O.R. and A.L. George. 1975. The effects of stress on the performance of foreign policymakers. In C.P. Cotter, ed., *Political Science Annual VI*, pp. 255–319. Indianapolis, Ind.: Bobbs-Merrill.
Hoopes, T. 1969. *The Limits of Intervention*. New York: David McKay.
Horvath, F. E. 1959. Psychological stress: A review of definitions and experimental research. *General Systems: Yearbook of the Society for General Systems Research* 4:203–230.
Howard, M. 1983. *The Causes of War*. Cambridge, Mass.: Harvard University Press.
Hull, C. 1948. *Memoirs*. New York: Macmillan.
Huntington, S.F. 1958. Arms races. Prerequisites and results. In C. Friedrich and S. Harris, eds., *Public Policy, 1958*, pp. 41–86. Cambridge, Mass.: Harvard University Press.
Huth, P., and B. Russett. 1984. What makes deterrence work?: Cases from 1900 to 1980. *World Politics* 36:496–526.
———. 1988. Deterrence failure and crisis escalation. *International Studies Quarterly* 32:29–26.
Janis, I.L., 1958. *Psychological Stress*. New York: Wiley.
———. 1972. *Victims of Groupthink*. Boston: Houghton Mifflin.
———. 1973. *Stress and Frustration*. New York: Harcourt.
———. 1982. *Groupthink*. Boston: Houghton Mifflin.
———. 1986. Problems of international crisis management in nuclear age. *Journal of Social Issues* 42:201–220.
Janis, I.L., and H. Leventhal. 1968. Human Reaction to Stress. In E.F. Borgatta and W.W. Lambert, eds. *Handbook of Personality Theory and Research*, pp. 1041–1085. Chicago: Rand McNally.
Janis, I.L., and L. Mann. 1977. *Decision-Making*. New York: Free Press.
Jervis, R. 1968. Hypotheses on misperception. *World Politics* 20:454–479.
———. 1976. *Perception and Misperception in International Politics*. Princeton, N.J: Princeton University Press.
———. 1984. *The Illogic of American Nuclear Strategy*. Ithaca, N.Y.: Cornell University Press.
Jervis, R., R.N. Lebow, and J.G. Stein. 1985. *Psychology and Deterrence*. Baltimore: Johns Hopkins University Press.
Johnson, R.T. 1974. *Managing the White House*. New York: Harper & Row.
Joll, J. 1968. *1914: The Unspoken Assumption*. London: Weidenfield and Nicolson.
Jones, E.E. and R.E. Nisbett. 1972. The actor and observer: Divergent perceptions of

the causes of behavior. In E.E. Jones et al., eds., *Attribution: Perceiving the Causes of Behavior*. Morristown, N.J.: General Learning Press.

Kahan, J. P., R. E. Karilek, M. H. Graubard, and N. C. Brown. 1983. *Preventing Nuclear Conflict: What Can the Behavioral Sciences Contribute?* Santa Monica, Calif.: Rand Corporation.

Kahler, M. 1979–1980. Rumors of war: The 1914 analogy. *Foreign Affairs* 59:374–396.

Kahn, H. 1965. *On Escalation: Metaphors and Scenarios*. New York: Praeger.

Kahneman, D., P. Slovic, and A. Tversky. 1982. *Judgment Under Uncertainty: Heuristics and Biases*. Cambridge, England: Cambridge University Press.

Keegan, J. 1981. The human face of deterrence. *International Security* 6:136–151.

Kennan, G.F. 1978. *The Cloud of Danger*. Boston: Little, Brown.

Kennedy, P.M. 1984. The first world war and the international power system. *International Security* 9:7–40.

Kennedy, R.F. 1969. *Thirteen Days*. New York: Norton.

Kiesler, S.B. 1966. Stress, affiliation and performance. *Journal of Experimental Research in Personality* 1:227–235.

Kilpatrick, F.P. 1969. Problems of perception in extreme situations. In R.R. Evans, ed., *Readings in Collective Behavior*, pp. 168–173. Chicago: Rand McNally.

Kinder, D.R., and J.R. Weiss. 1978. In lieu of rationality: Psychological perspectives on foreign policy decision making. *Journal of Conflict Resolution* 22:707–735.

Kissinger, H.A. 1979. *The White House Years*. Boston: Little, Brown.

Kogan, N., and M. Wallach. 1964. *Risk-Taking: A Study in Cognition and Personality*. New York: Holt.

Korb, L.J. 1987. Spending without strategy: The FY 1988 annual defense department report. *International Security* 12:166–174.

Korchin, S.J. 1964. Anxiety and cognition. In C. Sheerer, ed., *Cognition: Theory, Research, Promise*, pp. 58–78. New York: Harper & Row.

Korchin, S.J., and H. Basowitz. 1954. Perceptual adequacy in life stress. *Journal of Psychology* 38:501.

Korchin, S.J., and S. Levine. 1957. Anxiety and verbal learning. *Journal of Abnormal and Social Psychology* 54:234–240.

Korchin, S.J. et al. 1957. Visual discrimination and the decision process in anxiety. *AMA Archive of Neurology and Psychiatry* 78:424–438.

Krasner, S.D. 1972. Are bureaucracies important? *Foreign Policy* 7:159–179.

Krech, D., and R.S. Crutchfield. 1964. Anxiety and cognition. In G. Murphy, ed., *Cognition: Theory, Research and Promise*, pp. 58–78. New York: Harper & Row.

Lambeth, B.S. 1982–1983. Uncertainties for the Soviet war planner. *International Security* 7:139–166.

Langer, J., S. Wapner and H. Werner. 1961. The effects of danger upon the experience of time. *American Journal of Psychology* 74:94–97.

Lasswell, H.D. 1931. *Psychopathology and Politics*. Chicago: University of Chicago Press.

Lazarus, R., J. Averill and E. Opton, Jr. 1974. The assessment of coping. In G.V.

Coelho, D.A. Hamburg, and J. Adams, eds., *Coping and Adapation*, pp. 249–399. New York: Basic Books.

Lazarus, R., J. Deese and S. Osler. 1952. The effects of psychological stress upon performance. *Psychological Bulletin* 49:293–317.

Lebow, R.N. 1981. *Between Peace and War*. Baltimore: Johns Hopkins University Press.

———. 1983. The Cuban Missile Crisis: Reading the lessons correctly. *Political Science Quarterly* 98:431–458.

———. 1984. Windows of opportunity: Do states jump through them? *International Security* 9:147–186.

———. 1985. Practical ways to avoid superpower crises. *Bulletin of the Atomic Scientists* 41:22–28.

———. 1987a. Deterrence failure revisited. *International Security* 12:197–213.

———. 1987. *Nuclear Crisis Management: A Dangerous Illusion*. Ithaca, N.Y.: Cornell.

Leng, R.J. 1984. Reagan and the Russians: Crisis bargaining beliefs and the historical record. *American Political Science Review* 78:338–355.

Leng, R.J., and S.G. Walker. 1982. Comparing two studies of crisis bargaining. *Journal of Conflict Resolution* 26:571–591.

Leng, R.J., and H.G. Wheeler. 1979. Influence strategies, success and war. *Journal of Conflict Resolution* 23:655–684.

L'Etang, H. 1970. *The Pathology of Leadership*. London: William Heinemann.

Levi, A., and P. Tetlock. 1980. A cognitive analysis of Japan's 1941 decision for war. *Journal of Conflict Resolution* 24:195–211.

Levi, W. 1981. *The Coming End of War*. Beverly Hills, Calif.: Sage.

Levy, J.S. 1986. Organizational routines and the causes of war. *International Studies Quarterly* 30:193–222.

Lindbolm, C.E. 1968. *The Policy-Making Process*. Englewood Cliffs, N.J.: Prentice-Hall.

Lowe, A. 1961. Individual differences in reaction to failure: Modes of coping with anxiety and interference proneness. *Journal of Abnormal and Social Psychology* 62:303–308.

Lowi, T. 1969. *The End of Liberalism: Ideology, Policy and the Crisis of Public Authority*. New York: Norton.

Lynn-Jones, S.M. 1986. Detente and deterrence: Anglo-German relations, 1911–1914. *International Security* 11:121–150.

Mackworth, N.H., and J.F. Mackworth. 1958. Visual search for successive decisions. *British Journal of Psychology* 40:210–221.

Maier, N.R.F. 1963. *Problem-Solving Discussions and Conferences*. New York: McGraw-Hill.

———. 1970. *Problem Solving and Creativity in Individuals and Groups*. Belmont, Calif.: Brooks/Cole.

Manis, M. 1966. *Cognitive Processes*. Belmont, Calif.: Wadsworth.

Maoz, Z. 1981. The decision to raid Entebbe: Decision analyses applied to crisis behavior. *Journal of Conflict Resolution* 25:677–708.

March, J.G., and H. Simon. 1958. *Organizations*. New York: Wiley.
Maxey, D.R. 1970. How Nixon decided to invade Cambodia. *Look*, 11 August.
May, E.R. 1962. The nature of foreign policy: The calculated versus the axiomatic. *Daedalus* 91:653–667.
———. 1973. *"Lessons" of the Past: The Use and Misuse of History in American Foreign Policy*. New York: Oxford University Press.
McClelland, C.A. 1961. The acute international crisis. *World Politics* 14:182–204.
———. 1972. The beginning, duration and abatement of international crises: Comparisons in two conflict arenas. In C.F. Hermann, ed., *International Crises*, pp. 83–105. New York: Free Press.
McGrath, J.E. 1976. Stress and behavior in organizations. In M. Dunnette, ed., *Handbook of Industrial and Organizational Psychology*, pp. 1351–1396. Chicago: Rand-McNally.
McNamara, R.S. 1986. *Blundering Into Disaster: Surviving The First Century of the Nuclear Age*. New York: Pantheon.
Milburn, T.W. 1972. The management of crisis. In C.F. Hermann, ed., *International Crises: Insights from Behavioral Research*. New York: Free Press.
Miller, G.A. 1956. The magical number seven plus or minus two: Some limits on our capacity for processing information. *Psychological Review* 63:81–97.
Miller, J.G. 1960. Information input overload and psychopathology. *American Journal of Psychiatry* 116:695–704.
———. 1962. Information input overload. In M. C. Yovits, G.T. Jocobi, and G. D. Goldstein, eds., *Self-Organizing Systems*, pp. 61–78. Washington, D.C.: Spartan Books.
Miller, K., and I. Iscoe. 1963. The concept of crisis: Current status and mental health implications. *Human Organization* 22:195–201.
Moffit, J.W., and R. Stagner. 1956. Perceptual rigidity and closure as a function of anxiety. *Journal of Abnormal and Social Psychology* 52:355.
Montgelas, M., and W. Schucking, eds. 1924. *Outbreak of the World War, German Documents Collected by Karl Kautsky*. New York: Oxford University Press.
Morgan, P.M. 1977. *Deterrence: A Conceptual Analysis*. Beverly Hills, Calif.: Sage.
———. 1985. Saving face for the sake of deterrence. In R. Jervis, R.N. Lebow, and J.G. Stein, eds., *Psychology and Deterrence*, pp. 125–157. Baltimore: Johns Hopkins University Press.
Morgenthau, H.J. 1967. *Politics Among Nations*, 4th ed. New York: Knopf.
Moscovici, S. 1985. Social influence and conformity. In G. Lindzey and E. Aronson, eds., *Handbook of Social Psychology*, Vol. II, pp. 347–412. New York: Random House.
Murphy, R.E. 1959. Effects of threat of shock, distraction, and task design on performance. *Journal of Experimental Psychology* 58:134–141.
Myers, D.G., and H. Lamm. 1976. The group polarization phenomenon. *Psychology Bulletin* 83:602–627.
Nalven, F.B. 1961. Defense preference and perceptual decision-making. Ph.D. dissertation, Boston University.
Nathan, J.A. 1975. The missile crisis: His finest hour now. *World Politics* 27:256–281.

Neustadt, R.E. 1970. *Alliance Politics*. New York: Columbia University Press.
Neustadt, R.E., and E.R. May. 1986. *Thinking in Time: The Uses of History for Decision Makers*. New York: Free Press.
Nicolay, J.G., and J. Hay. 1890. *Abraham Lincoln: A History*, Vol. III. New York: Century.
Nisbett, R.E., and L. Ross. 1980. *Human Inference: Strategies and Shortcomings of Social Judgment*. Englewood Cliffs, N.J.: Prentice-Hall.
Nixon, R.M. 1962. *Six Crises*. New York: Doubleday.
O'Keefe, B.J. 1986. The SDI and American R&D. *International Security* 11:190–192.
Oneal, J.R. n.d. The appropriateness of the rational actor model in the study of crisis decision making. Vanderbuilt University. Mimeo.
———. 1982. *Foreign Policy Making in Times of Crisis*. Columbus, Ohio: Ohio State University Press.
Orme, J. 1987. Deterrence failures: A second look. *International Security* 11:96–124.
Osgood, C.E. 1959. Suggestions for winning the real war with communism. *Journal of Conflict Resolution* 3:295–325.
———. 1962. *An Alternative to War or Surrender*. Urbana, Ill.: University of Illinois Press.
Paige, G.D. 1968. *The Korean Decision*. New York: Free Press.
Pally, S. 1955. Cognitive rigidity as a function of threat. *Journal of Personality* 23:346–355.
Parker, R.W. 1977. An examination of basic and applied international crisis research. *International Studies Quarterly* 21:225–246.
Patterson, T.G., and W.J. Brophy. 1986. October missile and November elections: The Cuban Missile Crisis and American politics, 1962. *Journal of American History* 73:87–119.
Payne, K.B., and C.S. Gray. 1984. Nuclear policy and the defensive transition. *Foreign Affairs* 62:820–842.
Pepinsky, P.N., and W.B. Pavlik. 1960. The effects of task complexity and time pressure upon team productivity. *Journal of Applied Psychology* 44:34–38.
Perlmutter, A. 1974. The presidential political center and foreign policy. *World Politics* 27:87–106.
Postman, L., and J. Bruner. 1948. Perception under stress. *Psychological Review* 55:314–323.
Pruitt, D.G. 1971a. Choice shifts in group discussions: An introductory review. *Journal of Personality and Social Psychology* 20:339–360.
———. 1971b. Conclusion: Toward and understanding of choice shifts in group discussion. *Journal of Personality and Social Psychology* 20:495–510.
Quarantelli, E.L., ed. 1978. *Disasters: Theory and Research*. Beverly Hills, Calif.: Sage.
Raphael, T.D. 1982. Integrative complexity theory and forecasting international crises: Berlin 1946–1962. *Journal of Conflict Resolution* 26:423–450.
Ray, W. 1965. Mild stress and problem solving. *American Journal of Psychology* 78:227–234.
Roberts, C.M. 1954. The day we didn't go to war. *Reporter*, September 14.
Roberts, D. n.d. Space and international relations. Duke University. Mimeo.

Robinson, J.A. 1972. Crisis: An appraisal of concepts and theories. In C.F. Hermann, ed., *International Crises,* pp. 20–35. New York: Free Press.

Roderick, H., ed. 1983. *Avoiding Inadvertent War: Crisis Management.* Austin, Tex.: LBJ School of Public Affairs.

Rodin, J. 1985. The application of social psychology. In G. Lindzey and A. Aronson, eds., *Handbook of Social Psychology,* Vol. II, pp. 805–881. New York: Random House.

Rogow, A. 1963. *James Forrestal: A Study of Personality, Politics, and Policy.* New York: Macmillan.

———. 1969. Private illness and public policy: The cases of James Forrestal and John Winant. *American Journal of Psychiatry* 125:1093–1098.

Rosati, J.A. 1981. Developing a systematic decision-making framework: Bureaucratic politics in perspective. *World Politics* 33:234–252.

Ross, L. 1977. The intuitive psychologist and his shortcomings: Distortion in the attribution process. In L. Berkowitz, ed., *Advances in Experimental Social Psychology,* Vol. 10, pp. 173–220. New York: Academic Press.

Ross, M., and G.J.O. Fletcher. 1985. Attribution and social perception. In G. Lindzey and E. Aronson, eds., *Handbook of Social Psychology,* Vol. II, pp. 73–122. New York: Random House.

Rusk, D. 1963. Interview of Secretary Rusk by David Schoenbrun of CBS News. In D. Larson, *"The Cuban Crisis" of 1962,* pp. 267–270. Boston: Houghton Mifflin.

Russia, Komissiia po izdaiiu dokumentov spokhi imperializma. 1931–1934. *Mozhdunarodnye otnosheniia v ipokhu imperializma: dokumenty iz arkhivov tsarkogo i vrmennogo pravitel'stv 1878–1915.* 3d series, Vols. 4 and 5. Moscow and Leningrad.

Sagan, S. 1985. Nuclear alerts and crisis management. *International Security* 9:99–139.

———. 1986. 1914 revisited: Allies, offense, and instability. *International Security* 11:121–150.

Schelling, T. 1963. *The Strategy of Conflict.* New York: Oxford University Press.

———. 1984. Confidence in crisis. *International Security* 8:55–66.

Schlesinger, A., Jr. 1978. *Robert Kennedy and His Times.* New York: Ballantine.

Schlesinger, J.R. 1985. Rhetoric and realities in the Star Wars debate. *International Security* 10:3–12.

Schneider, B. 1974. Danger and opportunity. Ph.D. dissertation, Columbia University.

Schroeder, H., M. Driver and S. Steufert. 1967. *Human Information Processing.* New York: Holt.

Sherif, M., and C.W. Sherif. 1953. *Groups in Harmony and Tension: An Introduction to Studies in Intergroup Relations.* New York: Harper & Row.

Sherif, M., Harvey, O.J., White, B.J., Hood, W.R., and Sherif, C.W. 1961. *Intergroup Cooperation and Competition: The Robbers Cave Experiment.* Norman, Okla.: University Book Exchange.

Shlaim, A. 1983. *The United States and the Berlin Blockade 1948-1949.* Berkeley, Calif.: University of California Press.

Simon, H.A. 1947. *Administrative Behavior*. New York: Macmillan.
Singer, J.E. 1968. Consistency as a processing mechanism. In R. P. Abelson et al., eds., *Theories of Cognitive Consistency*, pp. 337–342. Chicago: Rand McNally.
Smith, H. 1970. Cambodian decision: Why the president acted. *New York Times*, 30 June.
Smith, M.B., J. Bruner and R. White. 1956. *Opinions and Personality*. New York: Wiley.
Smith, R.J. 1984. Crisis management under strain. *Science* 225:907–909.
Smock, C.D. 1955. The influence of psychological stress on the "intolerance of ambiguity." *Journal of Abnormal and Social Psychology* 50:177–182.
Smoke, R. 1977. *War: Controlling Escalation*. Cambridge, Mass.: Harvard University Press.
Snyder, G.H., and P. Diesing. 1977. *Conflicts Among Nations: Bargaining, Decision Making and System Structure in International Crises*. Princeton, N.J.: Princeton University Press.
Snyder, J. 1978. Rationality at the brink: The role of cognitive processes in failures of deterrence. *World Politics* 30:345–365.
———. 1984. Civil-military relations and the cult of the offensive, 1914 and 1984. *International Security* 9:108–146.
Snyder, R.C. 1961. *Deterrence, Weapons, and Decision Making*. China Lake, Calif.: U.S. Naval Ordinance Test Station.
Snyder, R.C., and G. Paige. 1958. The United Nations decision to resist aggression in Korea: The application of an analytical scheme. *Administrative Science Quarterly* 3:341–378.
Staw, B.M., L.E. Sanderlands, and J.E. Dutton. 1981. Threat-rigidity effects in organizational behavior. *Administrative Science Quarterly* 26:501–524.
Stein, A.A. 1982. When misperception matters. *World Politics* 34:505–526.
Steinbruner, J. 1974. *The Cybernetic Theory of Decision*. Princeton, N.J.: Princeton University Press.
———. 1976. Beyond rational deterrence: The struggle for new conceptions. *World Politics* 28:223–245.
———. 1978. National security and the concept of strategic stability. *Journal of Conflict Resolution* 22:411–428.
———. 1981–1982. Nuclear decapitation. *Foreign Policy* 45:16–28.
———. 1983. Memorandum to the Carnegie Corporation.
———. 1984. Launch under attack. *Scientific American* 250:37–47.
Steiner, M. 1983. World of foreign policy. *International Organization* 37:373–414.
Streufert, S., M. Driver and K. Haun. 1967. Components of response rate in complex decision-making. *Journal of Social Psychology* 3:286–295.
Suedfeld, P. 1979. Stressful levels of environment stimulation. In I.G. Sarason and C.D. Spielberger, eds., *Stress and Anxiety*, pp. 109–127. Washington, D.C.: Hemisphere.
———. 1985. APA presidential addresses: The relation of integrative complexity to historical, professional and personal factors. *Journal of Personality and Social Psychology* 49:1643–1651.

Suedfeld, P., R. Corteen, and C. McCormick. 1986. The role of integrative complexity in military leadership: Robert E. Lee and his opponents. *Journal of Applied Social Psychology* 16:498–507.

Suedfeld, P., and A.D. Rank. 1976. Revolutionary leaders: Long-term success as a function of changes in conceptual complexity. *Journal of Personality and Social Psychology* 34:169–178.

Suedfeld, P., and P. Tetlock. 1977. Integrative complexity of communications in international crises. *Journal of Conflict Resolution* 21:169–186.

Suedfeld, P., P. Tetlock and C. Romirez. 1977. War, peace and integrative complexity. *Journal of Conflict Resolution* 21:427–442.

Tanter, R. 1975. Crisis management: A critical review of academic literature. *Jerusalem Journal of International Relations* 2:71–101.

Taylor, A.J.P. 1969. War by time-table. In *History of the Twentieth Century*, Vol. 1, pp. 442–448. London: Purnell for BBC Publishing Ltd.

Taylor, D.W., P.C. Berry, and C.H. Block. 1958. Does group participation when using brainstorming techniques facilitate or inhibit creative thinking? *Administrative Science Quarterly* 3:23–47.

Tetlock, P.E. 1979. Identifying victims of groupthink from public statements of decision-makers. *Journal of Personality and Social Psychology* 37:1314–1324.

———. 1985. Integrative complexity of American and Soviet foreign policy rhetoric: A time series analysis. *Journal of Personality and Social Psychology* 49:1565–1585.

Tetlock, P.E., K.A. Hannum, and P.M. Micheletti. 1984. Stability and change in the complexity of senatorial debate: Testing the cognitive versus rhetorical style hypotheses. *Journal of Personality and Social Psychology* 46:979–990.

Tetlock, P.E., and A.S. Levi. 1982. Attribution bias: On the inconclusiveness of the cognition-motivation debate. *Journal of Experimental Social Psychology* 18:68–88.

Tetlock, P.E., and A.S.R. Manstead. 1985. Impression management versus intrapsychic explanations in social psychology: A useful dichotomy? *Psychological Review* 92:59–77.

Tirpitz, A. 1919. *My Memoirs*. London: Hurst and Blackett.

Torrance, P.E. 1957. Group decision-making and disagreement. *Social Forces* 35:314–327.

———. 1961. A theory of leadership and interpersonal behavior under stress. In L. Petrullo and B.M. Bass, eds., *Leadership and Interpersonal Behavior*, pp. 100–117. New York: Holt.

Trachtenberg, M. 1985. The influence of nuclear weapons in the Cuban missile crisis. *International Security* 10:137–163.

Turner, B.A. 1976. The organizational and interorganizational development of disasters. *Administrative Science Quarterly* 21:378–397.

Tversky, A., and D. Kahneman. 1974. Judgment under uncertainty. *Science* 211:453–458.

———. 1981. The framing of decisions and the psychology of choice. *Science* 211:453–458.

Ury, W.L. 1986. A "warm line" to avert war. *New York Times*, 27 August.
Ury, W.L., and R. Smoke. 1984. *Beyond the Hotline: Controlling a Nuclear Crisis*. Cambridge, Mass.: Harvard Law School.
Usdansky, G., and L.J. Chapman. 1960. Schizophrenic-like response in normal subjects under time pressure. *Journal of Abnormal and Social Psychology* 60:143–146.
Van Evera, S. 1984. The cult of the offensive and the origins of the first world war. *International Security* 9:57–107.
Verba, S. 1961a. Assumptions of rationality and non-rationality in models of the international system. *World Politics* 14:93–117.
———. 1961b. *Small Groups and Political Behavior*. Princeton, N.J.: Princeton University Press.
Vertzberger, Y.Y.I. 1986. Foreign policy decision-makers as practical-intuitive historians; applied history and its shortcomings. *International Studies Quarterly* 30:223–247.
von Bulow, B. 1932. *Memoirs of Prince von Bulow*. Boston: Little, Brown.
Vroom, V.H. 1969. Industrial social psychology. In G. Lindzey and E. Aronson, eds., *The Handbook of Social Psychology* 2d ed., Vol 5, pp. 196–268. Reading, Mass.: Addison-Wesley.
Vroom, V.H., L.D. Grant, and T.S. Cotton. 1969. The consequences of social interaction in group problem solving. *Organization Behavior and Human Performance* 4:77–95.
Wallace, M.D., and P. Suedfeld. 1985. Leadership performance in crisis: The longevity-complexity link. Paper for the Canadian Political Science Association.
Waltz, K. 1964. The stability of a bipolar world. *Daedalus* 93:881–909.
Weick, K.E. 1968. Processes of ramification among cognitive links. In R.P. Abelson et al., eds., *Theories of Cognitive Consistency*, pp. 512–519. Chicago: Rand McNally.
Welch, D.A., and J.G. Blight. 1987–1988. An introduction to the Ex Comm transcripts. *International Security* 12:5–29.
White House. 1985. Tapes and minutes of the Cuban missile crisis. *International Security* 10:164–203.
White, R.K. 1970. *Nobody Wanted War: Misperception in Vietnam and Other Wars*. New York: Doubleday/Anchor.
———. 1984. *Fearful Warriors: A Psychological Profile of U.S.-Soviet Relations*. New York: Free Press.
———. 1986. *Psychology and the Prevention of Nuclear War*. New York: New York University Press.
White, R.K., and R. Lippitt. 1960. *Autocracy and Democracy: An Experimental Inquiry*. New York: Harper and Bros.
Whyte, W.H., Jr. 1957. *The Organization Man*. New York: Doubleday.
Wiegele, T.C. 1973. Decision making in an international crisis: Some biological factors. *International Studies Quarterly* 17:295–335.
———. 1977. Models of stress and disturbances in elite political behaviors: Psycho-

logical variables and political decision-making. In R.S. Robins, ed., *Psychopathology and Political Leadership*, pp. 79–111. New Orleans: Tulane Studies in Political Science.

Wiegele, T.C., G. Hilton, K.L. Oots and S.V. Kisiel. 1985. *Leaders Under Stress: A Psychophysiological Analysis of International Crises*. Durham, N.C.: Duke University Press.

Wilensky, H. 1967. *Organizational Intelligence: Knowledge and Policy in Government and Industry*. New York: Basic Books.

———. 1972. Intelligence, crises, and foreign policy: Reflections on the limits of rationality. University of California, Berkeley. Mimeo.

Williams, H.B. 1957. Some functions of communication in crisis behavior. *Human Organization* 16:15–19.

Williams, H.B., and J.F. Rayner. 1956. Emergency medical services in disaster. *Medical Annals of the District of Columbia* 25:655–662.

Williamson, S.R., Jr. 1979. Theories of organizational process and foreign policy outcomes. In P.G. Lauren, ed., *Diplomacy*, pp. 137–161. New York: Free Press.

Wohlstetter, A., and R. Wohlstetter. 1971. Controlling the risks in Cuba. In R.J. Art and K.N. Waltz, eds., *The Use of Force*, pp. 234–273. Boston: Little, Brown.

Wohlstetter, R. 1965. Cuba and Pearl Harbor. *Foreign Affairs* 43:691–707.

Wright P. 1974. The harassed decision maker: The pressures, distractions, and the use of evidence. *Journal of Applied Psychology* 59:555–561.

Young, O.R. 1968. *The Politics of Force: Bargaining During International Crises*. Princeton, N.J.: Princeton University Press.

Zajonc, R.B. 1966. *Social Psychology: An Experimental Approach*. Belmont, Calif.: Wadsworth.

Ziller, R.C. 1957. Four techniques of group decision-making under uncertainty. *Journal of Applied Psychology* 41:384–388.

2

Behavioral Aspects of Negotiations on Mutual Security

DANIEL DRUCKMAN
P. TERRENCE HOPMANN

The Security Dilemma, Security Regimes, and Negotiation Theory, 89

Negotiating in the International Context, 91
ARMS CONTROL NEGOTIATION AS A TYPE OF INTERNATIONAL NEGOTIATION, 93

One or Many Theories? 96
GAME THEORETIC MODELS, 97   THE SOCIAL PSYCHOLOGICAL PERSPECTIVE, 98   ORGANIZATIONAL BARGAINING MODELS, 98   INTERNATIONAL SYSTEM MODELS, 100

A Note on Research Methodology, 102

Negotiation Processes and Influences, 103
PRENEGOTIATION PHASE, 104   BARGAINING PROCESSES, 107   CONTEXTUAL INFLUENCES, 119

Two Cultures: Theory and Practice, 137

Conclusion: Retrospect and Prospect, 145

Appendix: Issues of Research Methodology, 151
GENERAL METHODOLOGICAL ISSUES, 152   CONTENT ANALYSIS IN NEGOTIATION RESEARCH, 154

Notes, 163
References, 163

On December 8, 1987, President Ronald Reagan and Soviet General Secretary Mikhail Gorbachev met in Washington, D.C., to sign a treaty eliminating all nuclear delivery vehicles in their arsenals with ranges between 500 and 5,500 kilometers. Known as the Intermediate-range Nuclear Forces (INF) Treaty, this agreement requires the United States to dismantle about 400 nuclear delivery vehicles, while the Soviet Union will have to dismantle approximately 1,500 such weapons within three years. This represents the first time since the nuclear arms race began in 1945 that an entire category of nuclear delivery vehicles has been eliminated from the arsenals of either superpower.

The agreement on the INF Treaty represented the outcome of almost eight years of negotiation. The process began in December 1979, when the North Atlantic Treaty Organization (NATO) adopted its so-called Dual Track decision. NATO declared its intention to deploy 572 new U.S. missiles in five Western European countries beginning in 1983 in response to the deployment by the Soviet Union of its SS-20 missiles, which had commenced several years earlier. However, the alliance also committed itself to begin immediate negotiations for the elimination of this category of weapons, thereby making the new NATO deployments unnecessary. Thus, NATO's actual deployment was made contingent on the failure of those negotiations to produce results prior to the 1983 deployment date.

The opening of the actual negotiations was delayed, however, due to both the U.S.S.R. intervention in Afghanistan just two weeks after the NATO decision in 1979 and the election of a new U.S. president in 1980. Negotiations finally opened in late 1981, but they were unable to reach any concrete results prior to the 1983 deadline. Therefore, negotiations were suspended during 1984, while the United States began deploying missiles in the Federal Republic of Germany, Italy, and Great Britain. In early 1985 the Soviets agreed to reopen discussions within the context of a tripartite negotiation dealing simultaneously with intercontinental or strategic nuclear weapons, space-based weapons, and intermediate-range nuclear forces. These negotiations remained largely stalemated until the summit conference at Reykjavik, Iceland, on October 11–12, 1986, between General Secretary Gorbachev and President Reagan, at which time major breakthroughs were accomplished. Throughout the following year a series of Soviet concessions, especially an agreement to break a prior linkage between space-based defenses and INF weapons, as well as progress on the complex issues of verification, enabled the two leaders to sign the INF Treaty in Washington on December 8, 1987.

At the same time, Reagan and Gorbachev reaffirmed their agreement in principle, reached at the Reykjavik summit meeting, to reduce their strategic weapons with ranges of greater than 5,500 kilometers by about 50 percent over five years. By that time each superpower had accumulated approximately 10,000 nuclear warheads poised on intercontinental-range delivery vehicles, in addition to many thousands more on intermediate-range and short-range delivery vehicles. The agreement in principle at Reykjavik to move toward a 50 percent reduction of these strategic arsenals over a five-year period represented the first time during the postwar period when there was serious hope for an accord calling for major reductions of strategic weapons as opposed to a limitation on further increases in the number and quality of weapons.

Of course, the relationship between the number of nuclear weapons in the hands of the superpowers and the dangers of nuclear war is far from a simple one, and it would be facile to suggest that a simple reduction in the number of nuclear weapons, even by 50 percent, would be directly correlated with a reduction in the probability of a nuclear war. Indeed, there are many—including President Reagan—who have long asserted that a reduction in nuclear weapons would be virtually impossible until a prior improvement had been achieved in Soviet-American relations. These individuals argue on the basis of Singer's (1962:173–176) "tensions-first approach," in which political differences between adversaries must be reduced prior to negotiating on disarmament. The armaments are seen by proponents of this view as largely symptoms of the underlying political conflict, which cannot be removed as long as the basic problems remain unresolved. To analysts of this school, the kind of reductions discussed at Reykjavik and Washington would seem to be "putting the cart before the horse."

An alternative view holds that armaments may be in part a consequence of preexisting political conflict, but that they also reinforce that conflict. As Claude (1963:298) has observed: "The truth is that this is a circular problem, in which causes and effects, policies and instruments of policy, revolve in a cycle of interaction and are blurred into indistinguishability." The arms race may not be a first cause of political conflict, but it is extremely difficult to resolve conflicts with parties who have the capacity to destroy one's own country many times over. Therefore, controlling the arms race may be a necessary condition for improving the climate of East-West relations, which may in turn be an important factor in reducing the probability of nuclear war.

Among those who believe that arms control agreements can contribute to preventing nuclear war there remain those who believe that quantitative reductions are not the best means to do so. In this view, there are many aspects of the arms race that are more directly connected to the likelihood of nuclear war than the number of weapons, including the survivability of weapons (or, conversely, the first-strike capabilities of weapons). As Sigal (1981:80) has observed, "proposals for deep cuts seldom deal with the forces that most endanger stability—improvements in accuracy; some forms of mobility; antisubmarine warfare capabilities; ABMs; and the possibility of more exotic systems, such as lasers." An arms control regime that truly is to have a significant impact on reducing the risks of nuclear war must deal with such issues as well as with quantitative reductions in weapons.

Although the Reagan-Gorbachev agreements were unique in their dramatic and comprehensive character, they also reflected the fruits of a long process of negotiation on arms control that goes back at least to the mid-1950s and that received its major impetus from the negotiation of the Partial Nuclear Test Ban Treaty in 1963. Although the new proposals broke from past negotiating traditions in many important ways, they also reflected a frustration with the many impasses that have blocked agreements in previous arms control negotiations. Furthermore, if they are to yield important long-term results beyond the 1987 INF Treaty, a long and extremely complex process of negotiation will have to continue.

There are clearly a large number of *substantive* obstacles to arms control that have received extensive attention in hundreds of books and articles. Yet the frustrating history of efforts to achieve arms control since the 1950s and the obstacles to reaching agreement in the present are due only in part to these many and complex substantive problems. They are also in important ways a consequence of the *process* through which the nuclear superpowers have sought agreement on arms control, that is, on the process of international negotiation.

In spite of this fact, the vast majority of studies on prospects and obstacles for agreement in arms control have placed relatively little attention on the negotiation process, especially on those aspects of the process that may make a difference between creating a stalemate and overcoming impasses. Most studies of the negotiation process have been conducted by social psychologists and other social scientists, often in laboratory research far removed from the burning issues of the arms race and the threat of nuclear war. Although much of this literature has begun to become cumulative and to suggest some commonalities about the negotiation process in a wide variety of contexts, there has been surprisingly little effort to extract systematically the major conclusions of this research and to try to apply those insights to achieve a better understanding of the process of negotiation in the case of nuclear arms control. The purpose of this chapter is to do just that—to identify relevant findings in the vast theoretical and experimental literature on negotiation and to employ these findings as hypotheses that may enable us to develop a deeper understanding of the negotiation process on nuclear arms control and on the resolution of related political conflicts that may threaten to escalate into nuclear war. We then examine the growing, but still insufficient, number of studies that attempt to test these hypotheses systematically in international negotiations on nuclear weapons issues.

Before dealing with the specific research findings and their application to theories of international negotiations, however, some clarification of the conceptual domain of a theory of international negotiation is in order. It is to that task that we will address ourselves in the next several sections of this chapter. Our task is to relate work on negotiations in general to the more specific problem of international negotiations and to apply the major findings in this work to an analysis of negotiations on arms control and disarmament and to the resolution of political conflicts where the risk of nuclear confrontation is high. Our effort is thus parallel to Walton and McKersie's (1965) work on labor-management negotiations. As they note, their work is distinguished from previous syntheses of the research in the broader field of conflict resolution by its focus "on the negotiation process in general and labor negotiation in particular" (Walton and McKersie, 1965:9). In a similar sense, we are interested in theories of negotiation in general, but also in their specific application to international negotiations, especially to negotiations on nuclear arms control and disarmament.

The Security Dilemma, Security Regimes, and Negotiation Theory

A theory of international negotiations that will shed light on these problems need not be a full-blown theory of international relations, nor should it be reduced to a narrow and abstract model of bargaining. Rather, it should reflect borrowings from these literatures to document the complex interplay between context and process. The theory should be developed analytically by building on research that adheres to standards of precision while taking into account the processes and influences that operate at several levels of analysis. And it should attempt to address concerns articulated by a research community whose goal is understanding and by a policy community oriented primarily toward action. While a theory of international negotiation need not constitute by itself a theory of international relations, it can best be developed within the context of such a theory. It is essential to link the set of studies focused on the negotiation process with the issues of nuclear war prevention. It is likewise necessary to embed our analysis within a more general framework for understanding international relations.

Of particular relevance to both of these domains is the recent work directed toward the effort to overcome the "security dilemma" in superpower relations and to establish a "security regime." The Soviet-U.S. arms race seems to be an excellent example of the operation of the security dilemma, originally identified by Herz (1950:157–180) and more recently defined by Jervis (1983:184) as referring to a situation in which "policies that are designed to increase a state's security automatically and inadvertently decrease the security of others." This approach to the arms race assumes that each state embroiled in such a race prefers not to arm. However, seeing its potential "enemy" arming, it may feel that it must arm itself in response. This may be a consequence of both "realistic" perceptions of the capabilities and intentions of its potential enemy and of the reluctance of states to engage in risk-taking behavior when their national survival is at stake. But it may also be in large part a consequence of the psychological tendency to exaggerate the degree of threat from "outsiders" or "enemies" and to attribute all responsibility for the conflict to the other party, without any recognition of the part that each state plays in this vicious cycle (see the Nisbett and Ross [1980] discussion of the "fundamental attribution error"). Yet whatever the cause of this "defensive" reaction, when the "enemy" responds according to the same logic, the result may be an arms race.

Such competition is likely to leave both sides less secure, due both to the larger quantity and improved quality of armaments and the hostilities engendered by the arms race itself. Each would find it advantageous to disarm if it could know with some certainty that its opponent was doing likewise, thus leaving both better off. However, in an international system of anarchy, such a mutually beneficial agreement may be difficult to achieve and to enforce.

On a broad scale, then, the effort to overcome this arms race may require a set of agreements to create what has recently been called by Jervis (1983) a "security regime." This concept was given prominence in the field of international politics by the pathbreaking work of Keohane and Nye (1977) (see also Young, 1983). A regime was considered as a governing relationship created in international relations intended to affect and to build on the condition of "complex interdependence." Interdependence in turn refers to situations involving reciprocal effects among nation-states. These effects need not be perfectly symmetrical, but they must be at least bidirectional. Complex interdependence applies in situations where there are multiple actors who are interconnected across national boundaries and where multiple issues may be aggregated to affect interdependence. In their analysis, Keohane and Nye dealt primarily with international relations in areas such as political economy, which they presumed were replacing security issues as a central focus, at least in the period of the mid-1970s. While recent events have illustrated that issues such as nuclear war remain central to the agenda of international politics, most of the studies on the formation of regimes and the growth of complex interdependence have concentrated on these political and economic areas.

However, as Jervis has suggested, regime analysis may be equally appropriate for security issues, especially in a world where more formal and institutionalized efforts to reduce the security dilemma seem largely to have failed to live up to expectations. A security regime is then defined as "those principles, rules, and norms that permit nations to be restrained in their behavior in the belief that others will reciprocate" (Jervis, 1983:173). Yet those norms, principles, and rules do not arise out of thin air; on the contrary, they are usually either the explicit or the implicit result of a process of negotiation between parties seeking to create such a regime (Caldwell, 1978). Fundamental to the negotiation of a security regime is some common understandings between the United States and the Soviet Union about the concept of mutual security. A security regime requires that concepts about unilateral security be replaced by a common realization that, in the nuclear age, neither superpower is secure unless both are secure. Thus, mutual security must be based on a recognition, as Smoke (1987:3) has observed, that the threat of nuclear catastrophe means that the security interests of the two nuclear superpowers are literally "wired together." Once this fundamental recognition of mutual interdependence is achieved, the essential problem becomes how to negotiate specific arrangements in arms control and in the settlement of related political disputes that will make it possible to create such a mutual security regime and thereby reduce the risks of nuclear war.

In this light, our goal in this chapter is to evaluate the existing literature on negotiation processes with a view to understanding the dynamics through which a security regime may be negotiated. Most of the studies to be considered pursue more limited objectives, so that one of our tasks is to review these studies systematically in order to derive insights that might be applied in imaginative ways to seek a way out of the contemporary "security dilemma" and the superpower arms race that has resulted from it. Another task is to develop themes for organizing the research on negotiation processes and influences as these are analyzed in the literature and as they relate to concerns of the policymaking and diplomatic communities.

Negotiating in the International Context

Until the late 1950s virtually all studies of international negotiations consisted of historical case studies, from which the author may have tried to derive useful "lessons" (see, for example, Nicolson's [1946] classic study of the negotiations in the Congress of Vienna). By contrast, the first systematic studies of international negotiations relied very heavily on formal theories of bargaining, largely developed by economists (Nash, 1950; Schelling, 1956), although a pioneering work by Iklé and Leites (1962) argued that political issues could be represented on utility scales. These models were applied to international negotiations in the now classic work of Thomas Schelling, *The Strategy of Conflict* (1960). Such bargaining models generally assume that negotiations are purely bilateral, involving two unified actors who have clearly defined utilities and complete information about one another's utilities. Given this information, the analyst may then "solve" the bargaining problem analytically and thereby arrive at either a unique outcome or a range of outcomes within which the parties *should* reach agreement. Different analysts have produced different procedures to solve this problem, including maximizing the product "of the differences between the values of the game and the utilities of the situation where the players do not cooperate" (Nash, 1953:72), Kalai and Smorodinsky's (1975) solution based on "equal resistance" points, and Felsenthal and Diskin's (1982) "minimum utility point" solution. (For a review of this literature, see Schellenberg and Druckman [1986]). All of these solutions assume an approach to negotiation that is essentially static. As Bartos (1974:23) has observed, "the Nash solution presupposes that the players can analyze the game in their mind, anticipating each other's moves, so that the game really need not be played at all: if they are rational, they realize what agreement must be made and make it at once."

Yet the conditions assumed by such formal models of bargaining seldom pertain in the "real world" of international negotiations. Often more than two parties are involved, and seldom are those parties internally unified. The utilities of the actors are often complex and changing, so that each party is uncertain even about its own utilities, and the preferences of the other party are usually unknown due to deliberate concealment or even deceit (see Cross, 1983). Therefore, very few international negotiation problems are "solvable" in this analytical sense, and some game theorists such as Shubik (1985) have expressed skepticism about their applicability to real-world contexts. Formal bargaining models have certainly suggested useful concepts for negotiation theory, such as the "security level" (Luce and Raiffa, 1957:65–68), "targets" and "resistance points" (Walton and McKersie, 1965:41–44), and the "best alternative to a negotiated agreement" (BATNA) (Fisher and Ury, 1981), all of which suggest that rational negotiators will reach agreement within some specified range or "bargaining space" (Hopmann, 1978:153–156). Yet attempts to produce deductively valid "solutions" to the bargaining problem have largely failed to produce satisfying results when applied to international negotiations. The outcomes of negotiations on international issues are generally determined through the *process itself,* rather than through an analytical derivation of some clearly defined set of initial conditions.

It is largely for this reason that there has been a definite trend in the study of international negotiations away from formal models of bargaining, except as heuristic devices that may be useful in clarifying certain parameters and conditions of the negotiation problem. While most contemporary analysts acknowledge that bargaining is part of international negotiations, most would also insist on embedding their analysis of negotiation within a broader framework that encompasses a variety of processes, activities, and influences (see Druckman, 1983). The basic objective of a theory of international negotiations is, thus, to analyze how nation-states seek agreement operating within a complex international context. In analyzing research on international negotiation, we will therefore concern ourselves largely with negotiations as defined by Iklé (1964:3–4): "a process in which explicit proposals are put forward ostensibly for the purpose of reaching agreement on an exchange or on the realization of a common interest where conflicting interests are present."

Defined in this way, a framework for the analysis of international negotiation must involve far more than a process of mutual concession making between two parties with essentially conflicting preferences. Rather, as Fisher and Ury (1981) have emphasized, it must also involve the process of identifying mutual benefits, often through problem solving rather than through confrontation and concession making. As Zartman and Berman (1982) have suggested, it entails a three-stage process: (1) the diagnostic phase, where negotiable issues are identified and separated from nonnegotiable issues; (2) the formula phase, where formulas are created through a complex process of developing packages of agreements across many subissues, which thereby serve as a framework of principles that give structure and coherence to an agreement; and (3) a detail phase, where the parties converge on specific arrangements that give substance to the formula. The negotiator's primary challenge is to manage complexity in an environment where setting the stage in the early or exploratory phase of the negotiation is essential and where the process of negotiation merges into the general practice of diplomatic politics (Winham, 1977; Saunders, 1984). All of these processes are very much a part of any negotiation on complex security issues such as arms control and disarmament.

Arms Control Negotiations as a Type of International Negotiation

Negotiations on arms control and disarmament represent only one special type of international negotiation that is particularly relevant to the endeavor to prevent nuclear war. In this instance the topic involves high politics while, at the same time, there is great technical and substantive complexity of detail that must also be negotiated. These negotiations are often very sensitive, because they involve the highest stakes for which nations play, yet they are also the subject of intense public discussion and pressure. Many of the negotiations are long term, institutionalized and, in some cases, are conducted more for "side effects," such as demonstrating a general interest in peace (Iklé, 1964:42), rather than for actual results in reducing the dangers of nuclear warfare.

There is a large and growing literature on the substance of many recent arms control negotiations, including the Partial Nuclear Test Ban Treaty (Jacobson and Stein, 1966; Seaborg, 1981), the Nuclear Nonproliferation Treaty (Fischer, 1971), Strategic Arms Limitation Talks (SALT) I (Newhouse, 1973; Wolfe, 1979; Smith, 1980); SALT II (Talbott, 1979); Strategic Arms Reduction Talks (START) and INF (Talbott, 1984; Coffey, 1985), and Mutual and Balanced Force Reductions (MBFR) (Ruehl, 1982; Dean, 1987), as well as more general treatments of the long-term history of arms control negotiations (Myrdal, 1976; Blacker and Duffy, 1984). Unfortunately, much of this literature has remained largely oblivious of the analytical literature on the negotiation process.

Yet issues of process are very much relevant to the task of achieving agreements on arms control. This may be illustrated by recent difficulties that the United States and the Soviet Union have encountered in reaching an agreement on the reduction of strategic nuclear weapons. Both have strong interests in reversing the arms race. Among the many shared interests, two are paramount. First, there is the fundamental recognition that a nuclear war would absolutely destroy both countries and, in all likelihood, all of human civilization; therefore, insofar as nuclear arms control can reduce the possibility of this mutually destructive event occurring, it represents an overwhelming joint interest. Second, both countries need to free economic resources from military spending to meet other domestic goals, especially to reduce the national budget deficits in the case of the United States and to facilitate a restructuring of the domestic economic system in the case of the Soviet Union. Yet, in spite of these common interests, the two nations were unable to achieve major agreements on nuclear weapons at least between the SALT II Treaty of 1979 and the INF Treaty of 1987, which actually represented only a first step toward significant reductions of nuclear arms.

Much of the difficulty in reaching agreement seems to have derived from different definitions that the two parties have of "mutual security." There are several components of these different definitions. One component is the different perceptions that each side has of the other's "missions" or objectives, because each perceives that the other wants to extend its political, economic, and social system throughout the entire globe. Another element is simply the lack of any agreement about the relative strength of the nuclear arsenals of the United States and the Soviet Union. There is no broad consensus about which side is "ahead," although each side tends to be cautious and to perceive that the other has the lead. In addition, when viewed from this perspective, each side tends to see key aspects of the arms control proposals of the other side as enhancing its lead in the components of the other's force that it fears most. The Soviets are particularly concerned about a wide variety of U.S. technological advantages in both warhead accuracy and in strategic defenses; U.S. proposals are thus perceived as being intended to protect these advantages and perhaps to secure a first-strike advantage for U.S. nuclear forces against an increasingly vulnerable Soviet land-based missile force. Similarly, Americans tend to be preoccupied with Soviet heavy-weight land-based intercontinential ballistic missiles (ICBMs), which are perceived to give the Soviets a first-strike capability based primarily on the large number of multiple warheads that these missiles might potentially be capable of delivering against strategic targets in the United States.

These different perceived threats have generally led to very different proposals for the reduction of strategic weapons. Early in the 1980s in the START negotiations the Soviets tended to align their positions fairly close to the "nuclear freeze" movement within the United States, not only for propaganda reasons, but largely because this seemed to offer the best hope to constrain a technological arms race that they perceived they might end up losing. As Hough (1985) has noted, the Soviets are particularly cognizant of the fact that arms control agreements have never been applied to U.S. technologies that have much chance for success. By contrast, the United States emphasized throughout the START negotiations, especially in its "build-down" proposals, the reduction of strategic delivery vehicles that highlighted the Soviet heavyweight missiles. While the United States perceived that this would eliminate the most threatening element of the Soviet strategic arsenal, the Soviet Union saw it as cutting at the very core of its strategic nuclear deterrent, permitting the United States to speed ahead with new technological innovations without being constrained by such a proposed START agreement.

Much of the negotiating effort in Geneva, and indeed many of the analyses of these negotiations in the academic literature, have focused on technical solutions to these sources of impasse, including restructuring of forces and banning defensive systems or destabilizing offensive systems such as anti-satellite (ASAT) weapons (see, for example, Warnke and Linebaugh, 1985). Others have argued that such technical solutions were unlikely to come to fruition without a prior improvement in the overall political relationship between the United States and the Soviet Union (see, for example, Sloan, 1985). Yet both of these perspectives fail to focus on the role that the negotiation process itself could play to induce these two superpowers to redefine the problem of their strategic relationship in ways that would promote agreements intended to produce *mutual security* rather than promoting their own perceived needs for unilateral security. In addition to these technical and political improvements, attention must also be paid to the format, structure, and timing of negotiations in an effort to create or to sustain momentum toward agreement.

Social science has a place in these debates. Its unique contributions are its emphasis on problem solving through research and its attempt to go beyond individual case studies to seek general explanations. This ability to generalize, however, depends on the extent to which social scientists can accomplish the following tasks: (1) to identify in theoretical and conceptual terms the major relationships that link negotiating processes with substantive outcomes; (2) to test these relationships with common methodologies that are capable of producing results that are valid across different cases; and (3) to fine tune the generalizations through sensitivity to the impact of different contexts, thereby seeking the highest level of generalization possible given the limitations presented by a complex and often variable set of phenomena. A systematic approach thus makes its primary contribution through the cumulation of knowledge about international negotiations that, in turn, is enhanced through the use of common conceptual categories, theoretical frameworks, and research methodologies.

In the following section we will indicate some important areas in which social science research, employing these standards, may shed light on the improvement of the negotiation process. Our long-term goal is to enhance the prospects of actually reaching agreements in arms control and disarmament that will in fact improve U.S. and Soviet mutual security interests, in spite of continuing conflicts about many other political and economic issues.

One or Many Theories?

Although the goal of a social scientific perspective on negotiations is cumulation, the development of the literature in this field to date suggests that the results fall well short of this goal. Diversity, rather than cumulative progression or overarching concepts, characterizes much of the theoretical work in this field (see the appraisal by Haas [1980]). Yet some of these diverse elements have begun to come together in what Guetzkow (1957) has referred to as "islands of theory." The general outlines of this condition of diversity, and partial convergence, can be put into perspective by tracing the various traditions and noting key reviews that attempt to synthesize them. In this section we will consider four such traditions, proceeding from the most abstract to the most contextually rich: (1) game theoretic models, (2) social psychological models, (3) organizational bargaining models, and (4) international system models.

Game Theoretic Models

One tradition is derived from game theory and the analysis of utilities, reflected in the bargaining models discussed earlier. Although this approach has been limited by its simplified assumptions already discussed, it has found some applications in the literature on international negotiations. The most ambitious effort to bring the international negotiation literature together under this rubric is found in Raiffa's (1982) important work, *The Art and Science of Negotiation,* although the analysis in that work goes far beyond the bounds of a narrow game theoretic presentation. One recent example of an interesting application of game theory may be found in Brams' (1985) analysis of the verification of arms control agreements, presented in terms of strategies for the signaler and the detector. He showed that it pays to induce the signaler to be mostly truthful or for the detector to believe generally the signals that he or she receives. Similarly, Zagare (1981, 1983) has used game theory to analyze bargaining in the 1967 and 1973 Middle East crises, arguing that Soviet and U.S. leaders both effectively tried to create the structure of a "prisoner's dilemma" situation to facilitate resolution of these crises. Finally, Brams and Hessel (1984) have argued that the ability to threaten the other is an important factor in affecting the outcome of bargaining situations, and they illustrate this with an example of bargaining between the Polish Communist Party leadership and the Solidarity Union in Poland in 1980–1981.

Another example is Hopmann and Druckman's (1981) analysis of Kissinger's strategy in his "shuttle diplomacy" in the Middle East. They applied a bargaining framework to identify the range of possible bargaining space between Israel and its two negotiating partners, Egypt and Syria. They then show how Kissinger manipulated the strategic environment to expand the bargaining space available to the competing parties, making it easier for the parties to converge on agreements that avoided the perception of unequal outcomes.

The game theoretic perspective purports to offer a deductive model of negotiations, starting with fundamental axioms from which hypotheses may be derived. The application of this framework to international negotiations, however, may be characterized more as a contribution to a vocabulary for discourse than as a tool for more deductive analyses. A case in favor of the latter position is made by Raiffa's (1982) recent analyses of complex preference structures for negotiators on the Panama Canal Treaty and Philippine base-rights talks (these applications are discussed more fully later in the section entitled "Two Cultures: Theory and Practice").

The Social Psychological Perspective

A second approach that has provided a core of concepts around which some cumulation has occurred is the social psychological perspective on negotiations. Like game theory, the work done in this tradition has been most often applied to two-party negotiations. Unlike the models based on utility approaches, however, this perspective focuses on the processes of negotiation rather than on analytically derived outcomes. Instead of assuming, for example, a certain type of interaction between opponents, social psychologists have considered forms of interaction to be an empirical issue whose resolution is sought primarily through experiments (see Pruitt and Kimmel [1977] for a review and evaluation of the tradition of experimental gaming).

The social psychological perspective on negotiations was first integrated by Sawyer and Guetzkow (1965), and the extensive literature in this area has been reviewed by Druckman (1973, 1977a), Rubin and Brown (1975), and Pruitt (1981). This vigorous research tradition has produced findings on a variety of influences that impede attempts to reach agreement. Among the factors of interest are the following: differences in culture and in values; size of the difference in interests and in preferences for solutions to the problem; amount of stress induced, for example, by deadline pressures; strength of obligations to various constituencies; need to save face; perception of the other's concession behavior; the impact of tactics used by a bargainer and his or her opponent; and the effects of third-party interventions.

This perspective has to date had a limited impact on the field of international negotiations, especially in the arms control area. Fisher (1981:107–110) has shown the utility of "single-negotiating-texts" in promoting face saving in the 1978 Camp David negotiations between Israel's Prime Minister Begin and Egypt's President Sadat; similarly, Kelman (1982) has suggested ways for conflicting parties to develop empathy through techniques such as role reversal in his work with Israelis and Palestinians. The attempts to apply hypotheses from experimental, laboratory-based research to arms control negotiations, as well as the future potential for making use of this rich source of relevant insights, will be discussed in the sections to follow.

Organizational Bargaining Models

An intraorganizational process model of international negotiations largely takes its inspiration from Walton and McKersie's (1965) pioneering work on behavioral aspects of labor negotiations. This model emphasizes that international negotiations take place not between unified nation-states, but between large bureaucracies reflecting diverse and competing interests. Before nation-states may advance positions in international negotiations, they must first resolve their internal disputes about objectives and priorities in negotiations. Therefore, bargaining occurs not only among states but within states as well, and the negotiations between a diplomat and his or her home government may often be as intense as negotiations with other countries. This latter point was developed by Walton and McKersie in their concept of the "boundary role conflict," which refers to the negotiator's dilemma of being caught between the conflicting expectations of the home constituency and the other party or parties to the negotiations.

The importance of this problem to international arms control negotiations has been noted by numerous recent studies, which place a good deal of emphasis on the impact of both Soviet and U.S. bureaucracies on the negotiation process (Jensen, 1988; Talbott, 1979, 1984; Smith, 1980). While these studies stress the importance of bureaucratic effects, they are missing a fully developed model for their analysis; in this area, as in many others on arms control negotiations, systematic investigation lags behind descriptive work.

Some attempts have been made to apply theoretical concepts from the bureaucratic organization model to the study of international negotiations. For example, Druckman (1978a) has focused on the negotiator as a representative who must construct an overall negotiating package that is potentially acceptable to the other party, yet who must also take into account the influences of the various bureaucratic agencies that want to affect the contents of that package. He then assigns weights to the different components of a negotiating package and analyzes the extent to which the negotiator is loyal to various constituencies in representing the different parts of the package. Similarly, Hopmann (1977) has applied Walton and McKersie's formulation of the intra-organizational bargaining model to an analysis of the negotiations on MBFR, the conventional arms reduction negotiations between NATO and the Warsaw Pact that began in 1973. He demonstrates how the positions of the NATO alliance emerge from bureaucratic bargaining within various NATO committees, as well as how many of the positions taken by different alliance members within these committees reflect the result of bargaining among bureaucratic agencies back home. These multiple layers of bargaining, and the high levels of complexity that they helped to create, were partially responsible for the long-term stalemate in which these negotiations became entrapped. These analyses will be discussed in more detail in the section entitled "Contextual Influences."

International System Models

A fourth tradition stems from the literature on international politics, emphasizing the context provided for negotiations by the structure of the international system. At the broadest level, negotiations within this tradition may be thought of as a necessary part of the process of regime formation, as emphasized in the introduction to this chapter. Yet the tradition of work on international negotiations, including the impact of system level factors, has been most heavily influenced by the works of Iklé (1964), Lall (1966), Zartman (1975, 1976), and Zartman and Berman (1982).

For many decades international politics was dominated by the realist school, which emphasized the central role of power in all international politics, including the politics of negotiation. In the classic work in this tradition, Morgenthau (1967:521) argues that the primary means of diplomacy are three: "persuasion, compromise, and threat of force." The great negotiator was someone who could put "the right emphasis at any particular moment on each of these three means"; the diplomat "must at the same time use persuasion, hold out the advantages of a compromise, and impress the other side with the military strength of his country." Thus power was defined in this tradition quite broadly to include skills of persuasion and artful compromise, but always in the context of military force. This tradition has been carried on in more contemporary scholarship by so-called neorealists such as Waltz (1979), who argues that the critical factor explaining the conduct of international politics is the structure resulting from the distribution of capabilities within the international system. All interactions among states, including bargaining and negotiation, are conditioned by the structure of the system, that is, by the distribution of capabilities within that system. Thus, bargaining for Waltz is largely determined by the number of actors engaged in the process—two or more—and by their relative capabilities. Negotiations on disarmament are especially affected by the distribution of military resources between the negotiating parties and vis-a-vis third parties.

This realist tradition in international politics has had a significant impact on the way many political scientists approach the study of negotiation. Because of their emphasis on power, which consists in absolute terms of state capabilities and in relational terms of influence, they tend to emphasize the role of tactics within the negotiation process. Therefore, much of the early work on international negotiations, especially that of Schelling (1960) and Iklé (1964), concentrates on the role of commitments, threats, and promises. These are contingent statements made in the context of negotiations about future positions and/or about the future allocation of rewards and/or punishments, here linking in part with the social psychological tradition (Tedeschi,

1970). A state's negotiating position is thus determined largely by its ability to employ these tactics in ways that will be believable or credible to the other party. Credibility, in turn, is dependent on both the perceived will power of the other state to carry out the tactics and on its perceived capability to implement rewards and punishments. Thus, the distribution of power in international politics translates into differential ability to employ these negotiating tactics successfully, so that, *ceteris paribus,* states with greater capabilities have an advantage in negotiations.

Yet more recent analyses have adopted the stance of Walton and McKersie (1965), suggesting that tactics that may be useful for conflictual or "distributive" bargaining may turn out to be dysfunctional for more cooperative or "integrative" bargaining. This conclusion has been adopted particularly by scholars who emphasize the role of negotiations in the construction of international regimes (Jervis, 1983), as defined earlier. The objective of negotiations, even in the international arena, is not primarily to win in conflict of interest situations, but to solve common problems (Fisher and Ury, 1981).

This approach has often been applied in the analysis of international conferences, stressing the relationship between timing—rhythms and patterns—within the negotiations and those occurring in the larger systemic context. Such concepts as stages and turning points have been used to describe the linked unfolding of behavior in both formal negotiations and in the external environment. Druckman's (1986) analysis of patterns of soft and hard negotiating rhetoric showed that events such as impasses and turning points emerge from patterns of interstate interaction over time. Similarly, Zartman (1986) has argued for the necessity of careful attention to the timing of negotiations, especially for identifying the precise moment of "ripening" within negotiations when the necessary preconditions for agreement all seem to fall into place. At the systems level, coding of international events has provided indicators of tension between negotiating states, such as the United States and the Soviet Union, and this has been used as a forecasting device in crisis management. By charting trends in cooperation and conflict, we may obtain an ongoing record of the content of interstate relations. These coding systems have also been used to study the linkages between events taking place outside negotiations and interactions occurring within conferences. Results have indicated that context and process may be related in a reciprocal fashion (see also Strauss [1978] and Young [1983] for a discussion of this relationship). More generally, this approach has proven useful for hypothesis testing and has provided tools for monitoring and signaling in extended arms control talks. They may prove to be particularly useful in identifying turning points or ripe opportunities for overcoming impasses in negotiations. Cases illustrating these principles will be discussed in some detail in the sections entitled "Negotiation Processes and Influences" and "Two Cultures: Theory and Practice."

Each of the four perspectives on negotiation can be viewed as an island of theory in itself, although we have suggested that there are many differences of approach even within each of these perspectives. On the other hand, many similar concepts cut across all of the approaches, suggesting that there is some potential for integration. Perhaps these can form the basis for a general framework that focuses on both the process and context of international negotiations, as they influence negotiation outcomes (see Druckman, 1983; Hopmann, forthcoming). Clearly there is no single theory of negotiation; rather, there are many theories, rooted in different traditions, that may be woven together to provide a broad perspective on this complex activity.

A Note on Research Methodology

Before proceeding to evaluate the literature within these various traditions, a brief digression on issues of methodology is in order. Insofar as cumulation is a goal of the behavioral science approach to the study of negotiation, then some common research methodologies may enable us to enhance the degree of comparability and cumulativeness across different theoretical traditions and substantive domains.

Until recently the study of negotiation was characterized by an even greater disparity of methodologies than of theories. The techniques of analysis ranged from tightly controlled laboratory experiments involving issues such as the making of sequenced choices in a prisoner's dilemma game to rich and detailed histories of various negotiations. These methodologies thus tended to emphasize precision and reliability on the one hand or contextual validity on the other, and there was very little linkage among studies using the different approaches. Therefore, findings developed within narrowly defined disciplines were seldom, if ever, applied to the analysis of real international negotiations, while the study of international negotiations often proceeded as a set of case studies emphasizing the uniqueness of each instance. Little or no effort was made to generalize or to develop valuable lessons that could be applied from one situation to another.

We contend in this chapter that the details of context (uniqueness) and general aspects of negotiation process (theory) can be woven together in analysis. We make no assumption here, however, about the relative importance of context and process. Whether findings are mostly specific to the particular situation examined or are more general characterizations of processes that occur in many negotiating situations is an empirical issue whose resolution depends on the results of numerous studies. Ultimately, it should be possible to develop contingent generalizations that "specify the circumstances in which a given relationship is likely to be observed, and where it is unlikely to appear" (Manis, 1975:451). But our success in actually doing this depends in part on the development of methodologies that can be applied equally well in studies under controlled laboratory conditions, under more loosely structured simulation exercises, and in actual international negotiations.

Fortunately recent developments in techniques of content analysis have enabled us to begin to draw generalizations across these different kinds of studies, analyzing the content of negotiations systematically in a wide variety of settings. Of particular interest here is a content analysis tool called "bargaining process analysis," especially developed for the study of negotiation (Walcott and Hopmann, 1978). This technique has been applied to generate hypotheses from experiments and simulations of the negotiation process, which may then be tested systematically in detailed case studies of actual international negotiations. (Content analysis procedures, especially bargaining process analysis, are discussed in detail in the appendix to this chapter.) Further development of such cross-level methodologies should greatly enhance our ability to apply the hypotheses derived from experimental research on negotiations to the complexities of real-world negotiations on vital issues such as arms control.

Negotiation Processes and Influences

We turn next to a review of the multiple studies of the negotiation process and its impact on the outcomes reached in negotiations. We discuss process in terms of three sets of factors: (1) the influence of the prenegotiation phase; (2) the effects of the bargaining process itself; and (3) the influence of contextual factors. The analytical case studies to be reviewed in this section were intended primarily to contribute to the development of theory about processes and influences on international negotiations. Combining context with process, the studies reflect both the rigor of the laboratory, on the one hand, and the somewhat broader perspectives of international politics, on the other.

In particular we search the experimental literature for hypotheses that can be tested at the international level, and we seek wherever possible to present the results of initial attempts to test such hypotheses in actual international negotiations. Thus, some studies are closer to the experimental tradition, and we must forfeit a degree of rigor in order to extend them into the somewhat more complex realm of international politics. Such findings can at best be considered to be "suggestive," indicating possible areas for further exploration at the international level. Other studies attempt to operationalize the more elusive concepts treated in the literature of international politics and to test those concepts with increasingly rigorous and replicable research methods. Overall the studies have been innovative within the confines of manageable extrapolation from laboratory work or established behavioral science traditions.

Prenegotiation Phase

Activities that occur prior to a negotiation present a special problem. While they are not part of the bargaining process per se, they play a large role in the shaping of that process. An interesting question is whether to stretch negotiation theory to take account of these activities or to treat them as part of the context, to wit, the diplomatic politics surrounding the negotiation. Saunders (1984) calls for a broader framework that would consider these activities as part of the negotiation process itself. Husbands (1979) calls for a separate model of prenegotiation experience, distinguishing it from negotiation. These contending positions suggest fundamental differences about the status of prenegotiation phases.

The fine line between context and process is illustrated by Saunders' (1984) proposal that foreign policy issues be incorporated into the negotiating process. His four-stage process consists of defining the problem, committing to negotiate, arranging the negotiation, and negotiating. This scheme emphasizes the activities involved in setting the stage for a negotiation. The stage is set when all parties agree on a common definition of the problem, that is, to reach understandings about interests and objectives as well as what might be expected. These understandings are most difficult to achieve among states where value differences are the primary obstacle to negotiation. This is clearly the case in Middle East diplomacy, the region from which Saunders draws his examples. It is less problematic when value differences are either not at issue (for example, between allies) or are subservient to common interests likely to be served by an agreement (for example, superpower arms reductions). The understandings reached are often formalized in documents such as a "declaration of principles." They symbolize a commitment to negotiate and enable the parties to work on preparations, including choosing a site and setting an agenda. Such a foundation for the December 1987 summit conference between President Reagan and General Secretary Gorbachev to complete an INF agreement was reached in Washington between Secretary of State Shultz and Foreign Minister Shevardnadze in September 1987.

Unresolved issues concerning the nature of the relationship between the parties frequently hamper efforts to initiate serious negotiating. The parties may be stuck in a prenegotiation phase, as Saunders illustrates with the example of Middle East diplomacy. Similar problems may occur in the area of arms control, as Husbands (1979) makes evident in her analysis of the Conventional Arms Transfer (CAT) talks. These talks never got beyond the prenegotiation stage, a result that was due in part to doubts about the sincerity of the other side (Soviet Union or United States) and in part due to a controversial domestic issue.[1]

The issue of restraints on arms transfers is complex. Both political and economic pressures drive policy in this area. And these pressures are further complicated by a large number of potential players representing a broad spectrum of nations (superpowers, European allies, third-world nations) and interest groups (within supplier and recipient nations). Questions suggested by this analysis, and unresolved in the CAT talks, concern the negotiability of the issues and the identity of the parties. Considered a part of the prenegotiation phase referred to by Saunders as "defining the problem," these questions must be resolved before serious negotiating can begin.

The discussions in CAT were preliminary. They did not mature to a stage where a bargaining framework evolved. What, then, is needed to move discussions to this stage? Some clues are provided by the literature on experimental bargaining processes. One prerequisite is assurances from all parties that they will negotiate in "good faith." These assurances may take the form of "contracts" to protect each party against being exploited by or suffering disloyalty from one or more of the other parties (Thibaut, 1968). Another clue is informal discussions focused on the issues. Such discussions are a basis for gauging the prospects for a successful negotiation (Druckman, 1968). Both these elements were missing in CAT, as Husbands makes clear in her hypothesis-testing analysis.

Experimental evidence suggests that prenegotiation activities affect both the prospects for entering negotiations and the ease with which parties negotiate. Thibaut (1968) illustrates the delicate balance of power among the parties needed to preserve a common interest in negotiation. Parties are more likely to enter into a negotiation when negotiation can help them avoid a mutually unsatisfactory breakdown in their relationship: for example, when one party is in a better position to be exploitative, as in the case of a powerful nation demanding a high price for armaments from a weaker ally, and when another party is in a better position for being disloyal, as in the case of a weaker nation threatening to leave an alliance. Results indicated that most protective contracts were entered into when these threats were highest.

Druckman (1968) and Bass (1966) illustrate the impact of prenegotiation communication on subsequent negotiations. Bargaining was facilitated to the extent that parties avoided intensive strategy preparation and focused on the issues per se during prenegotiation caucuses. Moreover, it made little difference whether the caucuses were unilateral (teammates only) or bilateral (members of opposing teams): informal, issue-oriented discussion was more effective than both tactical preparation and no prenegotiation communication.

These results have implications for Dean's (1986) analysis of the preparation of U.S. negotiators for arms control talks with the Warsaw Pact states. Dean (1986:102) stresses the importance of bringing the U.S. negotiator "into the U.S. concept at the outset." However, we would add that this suggestion may be limited only to informal and issue-oriented discussions. While a negotiator's participation in the development of national positions may give him or her a better understanding of the country's position, as Dean suggests, it may also enhance his or her commitment to those positions with a corresponding unwillingness to compromise, as the laboratory research suggests. Development of a negotiating concept would also benefit from exploratory discussions with the *other side* prior to formal negotiations. Dean recognizes the importance of such nonbinding exchanges for the formulation of opening positions, taking into account differences and similarities in perceptions of the purpose of the negotiation. While highlighting the importance of the prenegotiation phase, these activities may also be necessary conditions for bargaining.

It may, however, be necessary to broaden these concepts to take account of complexity and nuance overlooked in models and experiments, but reflected in real-world cases. A wide range of prenegotiation activities may improve the "atmospherics" of the bargaining process itself. For example, attention must be paid to the physical setting of the negotiation—including both its symbolic significance and its physical facilities—and to the provision of adequate logistical support; actual changes in interactions among the parties—such as through the taking of unilateral conflict reducing initiatives—may lay a better foundation for constructive negotiations; informal channels of communication may be opened for issuing trial balloons and for widening the range of options under consideration. Effective use of prenegotiation preparations may significantly differentiate successful from unsuccessful negotiations. They form part of the larger diplomatic context for negotiation.

Whether to consider them as context or process remains an issue: as context, they influence decisions to negotiate and the atmosphere of negotiation; as process, they frame a negotiation at the beginning just as an implementation phase frames it at the end. Theorists who conceive of negotiation primarily as a subfield of international politics are likely to emphasize the prenegotiation phase as an essential aspect of the context, whereas theorists who seek to develop negotiation theory per se are likely to view this as just an initial stage in the process itself (see the distinction between the confrontation and conference perspectives in Druckman, 1977b). Whichever perspective one takes, however, the prenegotiation phase is primarily of interest because of the impact that it has on the bargaining process itself; it is to that process that we turn in the next section.

Bargaining Processes

A central theme of research on the bargaining process has dealt with factors that facilitate and impede agreement in negotiations. Particular attention has been given to processes such as negotiator responsiveness and debate, including the effectiveness of persuasion and role reversal. Responsiveness concerns largely the process of moves and countermoves through which concessions are exchanged and positions converge or, conversely, through which previous offers are retracted and positions diverge. Recent work on this process documents the ways in which bargaining behavior moves on a trajectory toward or away from agreement. Debate, by contrast, has been defined by Rapoport (1960:273) as the process through which one party tries "to modify the image of the other." Thus, rather than trying to induce the other to change position due to the tactical manipulation of rewards and punishments, debate seeks to induce cognitive change in order to bring about a shift in positions. It most often takes the form of either direct persuasion or the development of empathic understanding through role reversal. Whereas tactical manipulation seems to be characteristic of a primarily distributive bargaining process, debate tends to be characteristic of a more integrative bargaining process. While these processes have generally been studied separately, they usually operate together in any particular negotiation. As we will see, we still need additional studies that take into account and analyze the interplay between these two dimensions of the bargaining process.

RESPONSIVENESS

Negotiator responsiveness has been the subject of a large experimental literature (for example, Wilson, 1971; Bartos, 1974). It is treated as an incremental process where concessions by both sides lead to convergence or agreement. A question has been raised concerning whether this is the best model for international negotiation. As noted, an alternative, proposed by Zartman and Berman (1982), claims that the process proceeds in three stages—from diagnosis to formulas to details. This alternative emphasizes that the negotiation process is driven by a search for an organizing framework; concession-making dynamics occur, if at all, only toward the end, when details of the agreement are being hammered out. The few empirical studies that have attempted to arbitrate between these alternatives have generally supported a concession to convergence process (Hopmann and Smith, 1978; Jensen, 1984). In reviewing these studies, however, it will be noted that the tests are not definitive. Support for one model or the other may be due largely to methodology: Hopmann/Smith and Jensen employ content analysis of negotiation transcripts that may emphasize the incremental steps taken in formal negotiations, while Zartman and Berman base their conclusions largely on interviews with negotiators who may remember especially well the formulas that provided the basis for breakthroughs in their own experience as negotiators. Furthermore, the two approaches may not be completely opposed, as Hopmann and Smith, and Jensen may be emphasizing the convergent nature of negotiations on details after negotiable issues have been identified and general formulas have been established. In any event, both of these perspectives as well as the more general literature on negotiations acknowledge the importance of some form of responsiveness in reaching agreement.

The issue of forms of responsiveness can be summarized in terms of alternative models. One views this in terms of a stochastic learning process and computes the probability that cooperative behavior will be reciprocated by a positive response (Apfelbaum, 1974). Another incorporates the expectation/evaluation/adjustment aspects of the process in order to identify junctures where strategy changes will occur (Coddington, 1968; Snyder and Diesing, 1977; Druckman, 1978*a*). Both types of models are designed to capture the interaction process by which cooperation or competition evolves. A difference between them, however, is their emphasis on either the mutual-conditioning aspects (Apfelbaum) or the information-processing (Coddington) parts of the process.

Coddington's model departs from the mechanical assumptions of most other models of responsiveness. Bargaining is not construed simply as actions and reactions; it is characterized by staged sequences of information processing by the participants. Key elements in this process are the monitoring of trends (in concessions or rhetoric) and delayed responsiveness to earlier moves. These elements are present particularly in long and complex interactions such as those that occur in international negotiations. Specifically, Druckman's (1986) study of a U.S.-Spain base-rights negotiation describes a pattern of responsiveness similar to Coddington's model and referred to as "threshold adjustment." Snyder and Diesing (1977) extend Coddington's notion of sequence, capturing more subtle elements as they are manifest in a variety of cases of crisis bargaining. Both studies suggest implications for identifying when a response is likely to occur (after monitoring the trend) and the type of response (for example, an adjustment toward synchrony).

Further evidence has been obtained about responsiveness in interpersonal interactions that may be relevant to the negotiation context. For example,

Hammer (1983) has demonstrated how "matching" may be used as an influence strategy, Druckman and Bonoma (1976) have illustrated the use of reciprocal concession making in bilateral monopoly and duopoly bargaining, and Apfelbaum (1974) has developed stochastic models of cooperative moves in matrix games. There is also ample evidence to suggest that nation-states in general do not respond to one another's moves (Zinnes, 1980), with two notable exceptions: (1) regions involved in intense conflict such as the Middle East (Wilkenfeld et al., 1972), and (2) negotiations on issues such as arms control (Hopmann, 1972; Hopmann and King, 1976; Hopmann and Smith, 1978).

The issue of responsiveness has been studied systematically in several arms control negotiations, and successful negotiations have generally been found to be characterized by high levels of responsiveness among the opposing parties. For example, Jensen (1968) found that the negotiations leading to the Partial Nuclear Test Ban Treaty were characterized by a responsive pattern resembling an approach-avoidance process. As the United States and the Soviet Union made more concessions and as their positions began to converge, they tended to draw back and even to retract previous concessions. This may be explained by several factors. First, the last concessions often involve the most difficult issues about which the negotiators are least prepared to compromise. Second, early concessions have a certain air of unreality, since the distance from an agreement makes the likelihood that one will actually have to live with those concessions appear remote. By contrast, the final concessions may actually make it possible to consummate an agreement, and they, therefore, constitute concessions that both sides will almost certainly have to live with. This may make parties more reluctant to offer these last minute concessions or even to retract prior concessions.

In the Nuclear Test Ban negotiations this tendency was most noted with respect to the principle of on-site inspections. The United States and the Soviet Union started from widely divergent positions, with the United States demanding large numbers of inspections each year and the Soviet Union arguing that no specific compulsory inspections were necessary. By the end of 1962, the differences had narrowed to eight to ten annual inspections in the U.S. proposal and three in the Soviet version, although there were rumors of a private understanding between the U.S. ambassador and the Soviets at about two to four per year. In anger over the alleged breach of faith when President Kennedy rejected this compromise publicly, the Soviets retracted their acceptance of on-site verification early in 1963, so that agreement on a Comprehensive Test Ban became impossible. The consequence was an agreement in July 1963 on a Partial Nuclear Test Ban Treaty that permitted testing to continue underground, the only venue where inspections had been a serious issue.

A similar study by Hopmann and King (1976:137) found that "the test ban negotiations were clearly characterized by substantial behavioral reciprocity among the three major negotiating nations [United States, Great Britain, and Soviet Union], both inside and outside the negotiations." Particularly noticeable was a decline in negative interactions in 1963, beginning several months after the successful resolution of the Cuban missile crisis. This decline continued through June 1963, when the overall pattern became relatively neutral in contrast to the highly conflictual interactions of earlier periods. Thus a cycle of reciprocally positive interactions appears to have been an important feature, perhaps contributing to the successful outcome of this, the first major arms control agreement of the postwar period (see Druckman's [1983] reanalysis of the Jensen [1976] and Hopmann and King [1976] data).

Responsiveness can also be considered from a tactical standpoint, as a strategy used to influence the other or to encourage cooperation. A renewed interest in responsive strategies has resulted from Axelrod's work on *The Evolution of Cooperation* (1984). He makes the case for a particular tactic referred to as tit-for-tat, namely, cooperating when the other cooperates and failing to cooperate when the other fails to cooperate. His argument is based on certain qualities of the strategy: (1) it is never the first to defect, (2) it is easily provoked and hence cannot be taken advantage of, (3) it is forgiving, quickly providing a reward when the other returns to cooperation, and (4) it is easily recognized and understood by the other party (see also Beer, 1986). Results of his computerized contests showed that tit-for-tat was the most effective strategy: it encouraged cooperative behavior by most of the opposing strategies, ending up with the most points overall across the contests. Laboratory studies with human subjects are somewhat more mixed. Rapoport and Chammah (1965) reported 46 to 72 percent cooperation over 300 trials of a prisoner's dilemma game. Oskamp's (1971) computed average cooperation across seven studies was 62 percent. Wilson (1971), however, shows that a tit-for-tat strategy produces higher levels of cooperation than several variants, including both a more conciliatory and a more retaliatory variant.

A number of experimental studies provide insights into the conditions under which tit-for-tat is likely to be effective. The target of influence is likely to respond cooperatively if he or she sees himself or herself gaining more from mutual cooperation than from mutual noncooperation and is concerned primarily with his or her own gains, that is, individualistically motivated (Kuhlman and Marshello, 1975). The strategist may elicit cooperation to the extent that he or she carefully monitors the other's behavior and does not over- or undermatch the other's level of noncooperation, that is, makes the "punishment fit the crime" (Lindskold et al., 1976). It is also likely to be more effective when the parties move sequentially than when they move simultaneously (Oskamp, 1971). Variants on the tit-for-tat theme may enhance its effectiveness. Bixenstine and Gaebelein (1971) found that a strategist who was slow to retaliate but also slow to forgive was more effective than tit-for-tat. Komorita and Mechling (1967) showed that the effects of tit-for-tat are enhanced by an earlier period of unconditional cooperative behavior, and the more cooperation the better. For discussion of other moderating variables, see Deutsch (1973) and Pruitt and Rubin (1986).

The tit-for-tat strategy has shortcomings that require auxiliary procedures. One of these is that actions desired of the other may not be obvious. Possible remedies include calling the target's attention to the desired response, making clear the link between the desired response and the reciprocated cooperation (for example, the reinforcer), and building the credibility of this link through prior experience. Another problem is that tit-for-tat may be viewed as being unnecessarily escalatory: the other party is immediately punished if he or she lapses even once into noncooperation. One solution is Axelrod's (1984) "tit-for-two-tats"—retaliate only after the other's second or third lapse. Another is to combine the delayed retaliation with a verbal warning to the effect that one will not keep on giving the other "one last chance to reform."

Even more serious, however, is the problem of mutual escalation of conflicts. Tit-for-tat is hopeless for this situation, since it refuses to cooperate until the other party cooperates; in the jargon of negotiators, this implies that at all times "the ball is in the other side's court." Put another way, it lacks a way to break the cycle of noncooperation; it needs a starting mechanism. As Fisher (1987:326) has remarked concerning the U.S.-Soviet relationship, if "we behave no better than we think they are behaving, the relationship is likely to get steadily worse." This problem is especially severe in situations of low trust. Some possible remedies include signals, backchannel communications, and the use of intermediaries. The mechanism receiving the most attention, however, is unilateral initiatives.

Unilateral initiatives are a form of mismatching, since they are cooperative responses to the other's noncooperative behavior. The goal is to encourage a positive (cooperative) response from the other party, usually reciprocity. The best-known theory about unilateral initiatives was developed by Osgood (1962, 1979). The most systematic research on the subject has been done by Lindskold and his collaborators (1976, 1986). Both these investigators recommend a number of ways by which the strategy can be executed effectively. The strategy assumes a history of mistrust and mutual misperceptions between antagonists that must be overcome. One party thus must take the initiative to announce unilateral steps that it will take to reduce tensions, while inviting reciprocation. The initiator must make clear that these steps will continue for a limited time in an effort to induce reciprocation, but that they will not continue indefinitely in the absence of reciprocation. Thus, for example, Osgood proposed that the United States should begin to initiate significant unilateral measures of disarmament that would clearly be sufficiently important so that the Soviets could not simply dismiss them as a trick. Then the United States should invite Soviet reciprocity. At the same time, the United States should make it clear that these initiatives would stop short of the abandonment of its fundamental nuclear deterrent, so that it would be clear to the Soviet Union that it could not exploit these unilateral measures to achieve quick and easy military victories.

These measures could be reinforced by clarifying explicitly the intention behind the strategy, not requiring reciprocity too soon, rewarding reciprocity when it occurs, and making it difficult for the other party to explain away the initiatives. Conditions under which initiatives are likely to be effective are when the other (target) feels dependent on the initiator, when he or she feels that the initiator cannot be exploited, and when he or she regards the benefits of cooperation to outweigh those of competition. These conditions were present for the dramatic foreign policy initiatives taken by two national leaders, Sadat's 1977 trip to Jerusalem and Kennedy's announcement in June 1963 of a unilateral suspension of U.S. nuclear tests and his call for a relaxation of East-West tensions. Each move followed a period of heightened tensions where the conflict was seen by both sides as being costly. They suggest that unilateral initiatives may be more effective when the parties are experiencing a "hurting stalemate" (Touval and Zartman, 1985).

All of these approaches suggest the desirability of employing unilateral initiatives for a limited time only in order to try to create a cycle of positive reciprocity. Going one step further, however, Fisher (1987:326) has argued that the best strategy for the United States to build a constructive relationship with the Soviet Union is to be "unconditionally constructive. That is, we should do those things, and only those things, that are good for the relationship and good for us whether or not they are reciprocated."

Based on the experimental evidence, nevertheless, it would seem that the strongest case can be made for a combination of reciprocity (tit-for-tat) and unilateral conciliatory initiatives. This would consist of responding in kind equally to conciliatory and to coercive moves made by an adversary, while retaining the option of unilateral moves if the interaction became locked into a cycle of mutual competition. The posturing here is intended to convey the message of being firm but fair. Indeed, evidence from different settings support this observation as Patchen (1987:182) notes in his review. Experiments, computer simulations, and field studies of actual interactions among nations show a "remarkable convergence of findings." In most cases, the use of conciliatory initiatives to break out of competitive spirals would be effective. The rare exception noted by Patchen is the case of an adversary that is more powerful than one's own side and that has exploitative aims. Few cases can be cited where the costs of attempting to dominate the other are not excessive, and this includes current Soviet-U.S. relations.

Osgood's proposal, referred to as GRIT, was designed to reduce tensions in order to conduct successful negotiations. It is intended to "create an atmosphere in which political, rather than military, resolution of conflict becomes feasible" (1979:31). His rules of communication are quite specific, serving as guidelines to policymakers and analysts alike. Lindskold, Betz, and Walters (1986:113) have provided laboratory tests of GRIT, concluding that there is a "readiness on the part of subjects to follow an adversary's lead in changing the climate of a relationship from competitive to cooperative." They thus conclude somewhat optimistically that it is possible to disrupt conflictual cycles "with honesty, conciliation, and responsiveness—all unambiguously communicated."

The issue of unilateral initiatives has also been discussed in terms of alternatives to formal negotiations. Both Sharp and Adelman, from quite different perspectives, call attention to the dysfunctions of arms-control negotiations. Sharp argues that arms-control talks encourage increased defense spending under the guise of bargaining chips. The surplus arms or forces are chips to be cashed in later, and "to the extent they are not cashed in become part of the permanent force structure" (Sharp, 1976:1). The apparent emphasis of negotiations on "the narrow security aspects of international relations at the expense of more cooperative and functional interaction" leads Sharp (1976:3) to conclude that the United States should "plan our forces unilaterally and flexibly as required, rather than in lockstep with our political adversaries."

Adelman (1984:261) shares these concerns, noting that "the arms-control process itself has contributed to keeping obsolete and even dangerous nuclear weapons in the arsenal in order to bolster bargaining leverage for ongoing or prospective negotiations". Even more interesting, perhaps, are his observations on process and negotiating format. Adelman identifies several impediments to agreement that have also been shown to produce extended impasses in social-psychological experiments, for example, bargaining reputations, constituency pressures, a need for binding agreements, visibility and publicity about the process, and stress (see Druckman [1977a] for a review of experiments along these lines). Indeed, these aggravating factors may be exaggerated in formal international negotiations. Their influence may well be reduced in the informal discussion procedures advocated by Adelman and others. The key question, however, is whether these sorts of initiatives will produce the desired response.

Another type of unilateral initiative consists of posturing. Certain types of communication styles may be effective in inducing an opponent to cooperate. One of these styles is referred to by Deutsch (1985:286) as being firm but friendly: "Firmness in contrast to belligerence is not provocative, and thus, while aborting development of vicious spirals, it does not abort development of cooperation." His research indicates that it is just this kind of firm nonbelligerent, self-confident, friendly attitude that is most effective in inducing cooperation. This is similar to Pruitt and Lewis' (1977:183–184) concept of "flexible rigidity," in which they conclude that cooperation is improved over the long run if negotiators remain "relatively rigid with respect to ends (i.e., goals or aspirations)—holding fast to them over a period of time," while being "flexible with respect to means, trying out various options in search of one that satisfies both sides." Deutsch's experimental findings also seem to be consistent with Fisher and Ury's (1981:13) invocation to negotiators to be "soft on the people, hard on the problem."

When these concepts are applied to current U.S.-Soviet relations, however, there remains some doubt about whether the psychological preconditions for such communication exist. A willingness to communicate in this open manner with others as people requires a certain degree of self-confidence that, Deutsch contends, may be lacking at the present time in the United States. But even if this obstacle is overcome, it is necessary that the messages sent be interpreted as intended, namely as indicating a desire to cooperate. Opportunities for misinterpretation abound given the system of mutual threats that has prevailed in East-West relations for many decades. Yet, it is that system itself that may be changed by repeated and varied attempts to achieve mutually beneficial interactions. By taking a proactive stance in one's efforts to transform an adversary into a collaborator, it may be possible to move from a destructive to a constructive system of relationships.

The issue of unilateral initiatives remains largely unresolved, pending research using actual historical materials. A start along these lines has been made recently by Rose (1985). He used four cases to illustrate some conditions for the successful execution of unilateral initiatives: U.S. initiatives taken in 1962 (moratorium on putting weapons into orbit), 1963 (postponement of underground tests, moratorium on atmospheric tests), and 1967 (conditional restraint on ABM production). Conditions for reciprocity include a clear signaling of demands, no internal bureaucratic conflicts concerning the response, and no threats to political status, security, economic, or military capabilities. Of the various conditions, he suggests that risks to security are the most important reason for nonreciprocation. This conclusion must be regarded as tentative. Shortcomings in the choice of cases suggest that these findings should be regarded as hypotheses rather than as conclusions: for example, there was little variation among the cases in presence or absence of these conditions; in no case were U.S. interests harmed by Soviet nonreciprocation; and in all there were significant conflicts of bureaucratic interest present. They do, however, provide a framework for further investigation of a new set of cases, including those where international tension is high, economic gains are an issue, and security consequences compete with bureaucratic interests.

DEBATE AND ROLE REVERSAL

A large portion of the activities of international negotiators consists of debate, that is, a discussion of issues and concepts toward "a mutual appreciation and adjustment of the perception and preferences of the parties" (Deutsch, 1968:131). The complex substantive context of most international negotiations encourages a debating format, including both formal and informal interchanges. Even a casual reading of publicly available negotiation transcripts makes evident the extent to which national representatives engage in this activity (see, for example, the records of the U.N. Conference on Disarmament available for each plenary meeting held at the Palais des Nations in Geneva). However, the activity per se does not suggest a particular intention. Debate may be competitive, cooperative, or a mix of these motives. As a competitive activity, debate is used to improve one side's position at the expense of the other and is referred to as persuasive debate. As a cooperative activity, it is used as a device for promoting problem solving toward mutually acceptable agreements and is discussed in the context of conflict resolution. This dual theme makes much of the research on international negotiations only partially relevant: while the process is likely to be characterized by competitive elements, most of the relevant research has emphasized the cooperative aspects of debate. This is understood most clearly when an attempt is made to investigate the use by international negotiators of cooperative techniques and the effects of those techniques on the negotiation process or outcome.

One particular cooperative technique, role reversal, has received the most attention. As formulated by Rapoport (1960, 1964), the procedure consists of three parts: stating the opponent's case as clearly as possible to the opponent's satisfaction (role reversal), exploring the areas of agreement in the opponent's position (identifying the region of validity), and inducing assumptions of similarity in background and values (empathy). Various renditions of the technique have been evaluated in laboratory studies. Most of these renditions have in common the first two aspects of Rapoport's procedure, which we will refer to as "bilateral focus," and they compare its effects on outcomes with a form of debate referred to as "self-presentation" (emphasis on defending one's own position). Taken together, the results from numerous experiments suggest that bilateral focus is not more effective than self-presentation in producing agreements. It may, however, produce attitude change (assumptions of similarity) or cognitive change (understanding the other's position) (Hammond et al., 1966). The development of understanding, however, may actually reveal irreconcilable positions that, once discovered, render agreement less likely.

Certain conditions have been identified that may enhance the effects of bilateral focus: examples include the adequacy with which the procedures are performed (Johnson, 1967), the degree of compatibility of the opposing positions (Johnson, 1967; Muney and Deutsch, 1968), the direct proposal of compromises (Johnson, 1971), the perceived warmth of the interaction (Johnson, 1971), and the initial orientation of the negotiators (Johnson and Dustin, 1970) (further discussion of these results can be found in Druckman [1973] and Walcott [1977]). It can be argued that the effectiveness of bilateral focus remains an open issue. One shortcoming of the laboratory studies is that they have concentrated primarily on outcomes, such as the number of agreements, not process, such as the tone and content of the discussion. Debate is an activity that occurs during the negotiation with consequences for its outcome. Bilateral focus and its variants are debating techniques. As such, their effects may be felt more strongly on the process than on outcomes.

Implications for process effects are found in Neale and Bazerman's (1983) work on perspective taking, which is defined as the tendency to adopt the opponent's viewpoint in structuring bargaining strategy. They found that both a negotiator's perspective-taking tendencies and his or her perception of the opponent's perspective taking influenced the negotiating process in several ways. High perspective takers in a simulated bargaining exercise were less likely to escalate demands needlessly, tended to reframe their proposals in positive terms, and had a strong sense of control over the situation. When negotiators perceived their opponents as being good perspective takers, they tended to reciprocate their concessions often (see also Bazerman, 1986). By improving one's perspective taking, bilateral focus techniques should result in process effects similar to those obtained in the Neale and Bazerman research. Whether these effects occur also in international negotiations, however, is less clear.

An evaluation of this issue entails the development of systems to code relevant aspects of the negotiating interactions. Coding categories have been developed by Zechmeister and Druckman (1973) and by Walcott and Hopmann (1978): the former categories consist of revealed similarities and differences in values and in descriptive statements; the latter system, called bargaining process analysis (BPA), is divided into the categories of substantive, strategic, task, affective, and procedural behavior. (A further description of this coding scheme is found in the appendix to this chapter.)

Another shortcoming of the laboratory work is the attempt by investigators to impose the procedures on negotiators, whether or not they are ready for such an exploration. Few positive effects are likely to be found if participants do not feel comfortable with the procedures. Timing may be critical, and it is the negotiators' sense of timing, not the experimenters', that counts. Attempts to code the debate process as it occurs in situ take advantage of the spontaneous, though infrequent, occurrence of role reversal. They rely on the participants' readiness to engage in such a process rather than their willingness to accede to the experimenters' instructions.

This feature is also reflected in King's (1976) analysis of transcripts from the negotiation on the nuclear test ban issue in the Eighteen Nation Disarmament Conference, 1962–1963. King's effort was primarily descriptive. He sought to determine the extent to which the negotiations leading to the Partial Nuclear Test Ban Treaty were characterized by the use of bilateral focus procedures. He used Zechmeister and Druckman (1973) and BPA categories to define and count the frequencies of occurrence of each of the three steps in Rapoport's procedure, role reversal (restatements of the other's position), region of validity (perceived similarity codes), and assumptions of similarity (positive affect codes). Results obtained for each step were as follows.

1. Each party stated its own position more often than it stated the position of any opponent. The largest discrepancy was found for U.S. negotiators, who stated their own position more than twice as often as they stated the positions of the Soviet Union.

2. Each of the three major parties (United States, Soviet Union, and Great Britain) perceived dissimilarities in positions considerably more often than similarities. Perceived similarity scores for the entire negotiation were less than 25 percent of the total (similarity plus dissimilarity) for each of the parties. However, the parties perceived more similarity in their positions later in the negotiations, following substantial modifications in their initial positions.

3. None of the parties expressed much positive affect toward its opponents. The United States was high, with only 7 percent of the total statements coded as positive affect directed towards the East; the Soviet Union was low, with a mere 1 percent of the total coded as positive toward the West. By contrast, each country expressed positive affect about its own side 100 percent of the time; self-criticism was thus totally absent from the debate.

These results suggest that the debate within these talks was primarily competitive, not cooperative. The parties rarely engaged in bilateral focus and showed little inclination to reverse roles or to explore regions of validity as these activities are defined by Rapoport. The codes used by King provided few clues to the eventual agreement that was obtained. Therefore, it is not surprising that the bilateral focus procedures did not produce the results expected by Rapoport, since the process was not pursued in a cooperative fashion and since at most only the first stage of the three-stage process was followed. It is necessary to look elsewhere for reasons why these talks produced an agreement. One factor is the important intervening role of the Cuban missile crisis and of its resolution (Hilsman, 1967; Hopmann and King, 1980); another is the private meetings between the United States and the Soviet Union that occurred almost daily along with informal interactions at the United Nations (see King, 1976); still another is the important pressure of domestic politics, especially agitation against environmental pollution from atmospheric nuclear testing (Seaborg, 1981). Access to external and internal discussions surrounding the formal negotiation would provide a more complete understanding of the forces that eventually led to agreement.

King's analysis implies a limited role for cooperative debating procedures in past arms-control negotiations. This implication is supported also by findings showing a high percentage of "hard" (compared to "soft") statements in related venues (see Hopmann and Walcott [1977] for a review of the studies). In fact, even less cooperation may be seen in other international forums as suggested by a preliminary comparison between an inter- and an intra-alliance negotiation: considerably less hard behavior was observed between the superpowers in the former than among the allies (Spain and the United States) in the latter negotiation. However, these findings are limited to the cases examined to date. They do suggest that the limited success of arms control negotiations in the past owes more to external considerations than to the constructive processes of debate that have been employed in the course of the negotiations. We may only hypothesize that a more cooperative use of debating techniques might lead to better results in future negotiations. The suggestive evidence reviewed in this section is a basis for the systematic work that must be done on a range of cases and formats where arms-control issues are "debated" before any firm conclusions may be drawn about the utility of debate in advancing the negotiation process.

The idea of role reversal is frequently viewed by policymakers with skepticism. They tend to be particularly cautious about according any legitimacy to the beliefs and positions of their opponent, which is implied by stating the opposing position to the satisfaction of the opponent, not for the purpose of refutation but rather for the purpose of developing empathy. Note here that we get little guidance from the laboratory—the situation is contrived, the stakes are low, and the experimenter has a good deal of control. Experience with full-fledged role reversal in real international negotiations is virtually nonexistent. Therefore, while the ultimate value of this technique remains in doubt, it is nonetheless an approach that may well deserve a more thorough trial in actual negotiations.

There is, however, another tack that may appeal more to policymakers.

Role reversal may be useful in unilateral planning exercises as part of simulations designed to increase understanding of the other side's intentions. We do know that the technique is effective in this way even if it does not lead to faster or better agreements (see the review by Walcott et al. [1977]). One illustration is instructive. Members of the U.S. delegation to the MBFR negotiations enacted role-playing scenarios between rounds of the formal sessions. Particularly noteworthy was the discovery that the exercises could alert the delegates to proposals likely to be made by other parties in the next session. Such "short-term forecasting" depends for its effectiveness on the quality of the expertise displayed by those playing the roles of members of the other side's delegation. It also depends on the extent to which surrogates (role players) are able to make comparable judgments to those that would be made by the delegates whose roles they enact. In any event, this use of role reversal is a promising avenue in need of further exploration.

Contextual Influences

Context refers to the structures, interactions, and events in the broader system within which negotiation occurs. It is regarded in the literature on negotiation as an external influence (Druckman, 1983), but it also consists of the relatively enduring aspects of nation-states and relationships, including the various differences among them, that impinge on the negotiating process. These factors are difficult to control and are often obstacles to agreement. Three types of influences are discussed in this section: external influences, structural factors, and cultural factors. The research reviewed covers both the systemic (specific events and general atmosphere) and the relational (structure and culture of parties) influences on negotiation. Our primary concern in this review is the way that these factors affect negotiating behavior.

EXTERNAL INFLUENCES

Events in the international system or in domestic politics are external only from the standpoint of the negotiation analyst. They are the phenomena of primary interest to both the scholar of international relations and to the policy analyst. These differences of perspective raise the larger issue of the role of negotiation in the international system. For the policy analyst and international relations specialist, negotiation is just another setting for playing the game of international politics. It is a microcosm of international relations where parallel interactions or cross linkages among many types of diplomatic activities occur, each influencing the other. For the negotiation analyst, negotiation is regarded as a special type of interaction among a small group of national representatives. It is a relatively self-contained system subject to the influence of outside events. Our treatment of external influences in this section is based on this latter perspective.

Perspectives only serve to bound the problem, without probing deeply into its ingredients. Unresolved conceptual problems turn on issues of definition: What is meant by external? What aspects of the process are influenced? Sometimes the meaning is clear, as when we examine the effects of public opinion (external) or team composition (internal) on negotiating tactics. Other times the distinction is blurred, as when we try to determine whether the parliament or the embassy is an outside influence on the process or a key player in the process.

Some clarification may be obtained by considering external influences in terms of their dimensions. Three distinctions are relevant: proximal and distal events, domestic or international influences, and specific events versus the international atmosphere. Each type of event may have a different influence on the process, as Druckman (1988) illustrates in the setting of base-rights talks. Some effects are direct, as when Franco's death (proximal, domestic) produced a rush to agreement in the 1975–1976 talks about U.S. basing rights in Spain. This contrasts with Soviet involvement in Afghanistan (distal, international), which turned the U.S. government against immediate ratification of SALT II. Other influences are indirect, exerting an impact on negotiations through effects on the relationship among parties. For example, the development of a Sino-American rapprochement during the early 1970s (distal, international) seemed to enhance Soviet interest in a SALT I agreement, although the full extension of diplomatic recognition between the People's Republic of China (PRC) and the United States in 1979 became a disruptive influence on Soviet behavior in the final stages of the SALT II negotiations. The effects of such indirect events on negotiations may be particularly strong if they are used as part of a deliberate strategy, as when Secretary of State Henry Kissinger or National Security Advisor Zbigniew Brzezinski frequently played "the China card" to put pressure on the Soviets to concede in other settings.

A conscious strategy for bringing external events into the negotiation process is referred to as linkage. These are attempts to link a negotiated agreement to the settlement of issues outside the negotiation. Linking political settlement with arms reductions has a long history in disarmament talks, as Jensen (1979) observes. He found that the United States used this strategy considerably more often than did the Soviet Union in SALT. Whether it interferes with or promotes the prospect for agreement depends on two variables: the domain of the linked issue and interest in a negotiated agreement. Linkage between issues in the same (different) domain and an equal (unequal) interest in attaining an agreement will facilitate (hinder) progress (Tollison and Willett, 1979). This is a sensitive business. It leads invariably to an extended agenda where issues of relationship come into prominence. The type of issue linkage used or the extent to which matters of relationship are probed depends on the motives of the party making the linkage (Jensen, 1979). By joining Soviet involvement in Afghanistan with ratification of SALT II, the United States effectively prevented ratification of the treaty. By holding a base agreement hostage to NATO membership, Spain clarified its overall defense relationship with the United States.

External factors influence other aspects of the process such as preconditions for negotiation and Iklé's (1964) classic threefold choice (agree, continue negotiating to improve the terms, or abandon negotiations). These influences are generally observed through detailed, substantive case studies, a literature which is better suited for illustrating effects than for determining with any precision the relationship between events and negotiating behaviors. These case studies typically do not address the analytical questions concerning the size and direction of impact of external factors.

In order to model these relationships more precisely, a careful coding of both external events and internal processes is necessary, as well as statistical analysis of the relationships between events and negotiating behaviors. Recent behavioral science research, however, has begun to undertake such systematic analyses along two dimensions: (1) the impact of specific events or activities outside the negotiation on the bargaining process, and (2) the effects of a tense or relaxed international environment on the internal dynamics of negotiation. We turn now to a review of these studies.

External events

Relationships between external events and internal negotiating behaviors have been the subject of several studies. Hopmann and King (1976) and Hopmann and Smith (1978) analyzed responsiveness to internal and external factors in the 1962–1963 rounds of the Partial Nuclear Test Ban negotiations, while Druckman and Slater (1979) focused on the impact of external actions on negotiating behavior in the 1975–1977 rounds of the MBFR negotiations, and Hopmann (1979) has analyzed MBFR from its inception through Round 16 at the end of 1978.

The test ban studies examined interactions among the United States, Great Britain, and the Soviet Union outside and inside the negotiations. Outside interactions were coded from chronologies of events in the *New York Times* (for the United States), *Keesing's Contemporary Archives* (for Great Britain), and the *New Times* (for the Soviet Union). These events were coded along dimensions of cooperation and competition, as defined by Corson (1970), and aggregated on a monthly basis in terms of the balance of cooperative versus competitive interactions. Internal interactions were coded in terms of the categories of the bargaining process analysis system described in the appendix to this chapter. These codes were combined into categories of soft and hard bargaining and aggregated on a monthly basis as the difference between hard and soft negotiating behavior. The primary difference between the studies is mode of analysis: Hopmann and King used correlational methods to test their modified stimulus-response models, while Hopmann and Smith examined alternative regression equations, derived from Richardson's work on arms races (see, among others, Rapoport [1960] for a discussion of the Richardson process model), for goodness of fit.

Hopmann and King's (1976) correlations showed a continuous sequence of mutual interactions among the nations inside and outside the negotiations. Symmetrical behaviors were reflected in high levels of reciprocation of cooperative (soft) or conflictual (hard) responses. Consistent behaviors were reflected in high correspondences between interactions outside (either conflictual or cooperative) and inside (either hard or soft bargaining) the negotiation. The negotiators reacted in similar ways to both the internal and external actions taken by their opponents. More interesting, however, is the relative impact of the internal and external stimuli on their perceptions and responses. Using partial correlations, the authors evaluated this question for each nation separately. The United States responded primarily to external events in the previous month, while the British and Soviet negotiators responded primarily to the other's negotiating behavior in the same or previous rounds.

Regression analysis is better suited for providing estimates of the relative importance of external versus internal variables. The Hopmann and Smith (1978) results largely confirmed the findings obtained by Hopmann and King: U.S. negotiating behavior, in terms of hard or soft postures, was influenced by the actions taken by the Soviets toward the United States outside the negotiation. However, Soviet negotiating behavior was not affected by U.S. actions toward the Soviet Union outside the negotiations; the Soviets were influenced more by their own past negotiating behavior. Similar results were obtained for influences on changes in the negotiating process, assessed by beta weights. Since these results might have been influenced by the statistical problem of multicollinearity, resulting from correlated independent variables, the authors applied techniques for reducing the impact of this problem, which is common to all research applying statistical analyses to data such as that derived from coded negotiation transcripts. The results produced more conservative (lower) estimates of the importance of both internal and external factors on the behavior of negotiators in the test ban talks.

But, going beyond the issue of evaluating the size of impacts, Hopmann and Smith provide insights into the role of perceptions in mediating between the other party's behavior and one's own response. They found, for example, that when the U.S. negotiators perceived the Soviet actions as being "softer," they became "tougher" in their negotiating behavior. This apparent exploitation of the other's conciliatory behavior was explored further in the analyses performed by Druckman and Slater (1979).

Two forms of response to external events were identified by Druckman and Slater's analysis of negotiating behavior in MBFR: reflective and reactive. The former refers to effects of a nation's previous behavior outside negotiation on its negotiating behavior, as when increased Soviet conflictual behavior toward the United States in overall relationships is followed by increasingly negative Soviet reactions in the next round; the latter refers to effects of another nation's behavior outside the negotiation on a nation's negotiating behavior, as when increased Soviet-to-U.S. cooperation is correlated with increased U.S. commitments in MBFR, suggesting an attempt by the United States to take advantage of a positive relationship with its negotiating opponent. Both types of findings were obtained in this study.

Hopmann's (1979) study of MBFR, however, revealed only weak relationships between the international events and the progress of these negotiations. There was a modest tendency for NATO's behavior in the Vienna talks to be consistent with the external behaviors of all Warsaw Pact states toward the West. However, the behavior of the Warsaw Pact in Vienna was correlated with NATO external behaviors only for the first 28 months of the negotiations. From 1976 to 1978, in spite of a deterioration in East-West relations, the Warsaw Pact generally made positive changes in their negotiating positions in MBFR. This tendency for the Vienna negotiations to diverge from the general state of East-West diplomacy in the second half of the 1970s may have been indicative of the state of confusion within these negotiations, which approached agreement but failed to overcome the final obstacles, in 1979. From that time forward, MBFR has been characterized by a high degree of stalemate.

International environment

A large experimental literature on stress-related effects is the source for hypotheses about the relationship between stress and negotiating behavior. Stress in this context refers to the way individuals interpret a situation, especially to situations where they perceive that they have little control over events. Typical effects of stress reported in the experimental research include oversimplified perceptions, reduced tolerance for ambiguity, cognitive rigidity, less efficient problem solving, and increased hostility or aggressive behavior (see the chapter by Holsti in this volume; see also the reviews by Hopmann and Walcott [1977] and Druckman [1973]). The psychological literature is quite clear about the conditions that tend to produce stress, namely, a lack of information about the future leading to feelings of uncertainty (Lazarus and Folkman, 1984; Levine and Ursin, 1980). They were present during SALT I as Smith (1980:Chap. 7) notes in his discussion of the backchannel. The U.S. delegates were not told what was happening in the high-level informal discussions between Kissinger and Dobrynin. Smith's strong recommendation to avoid a second channel reflected the difficulties encountered by the delegates in resolving issues at their level. It may also have reflected the anxiety experienced by him and the other delegates due to a lack of information.

In addition to sources of tension that may originate within the negotiation, tensions may be projected onto the negotiations from the international environment. It has frequently been hypothesized in the literature that this reduction of tensions is a necessary condition for negotiated agreements. Singer's (1962) "tensions first" and Osgood's (1962) GRIT approaches assert that arms-control talks are likely to be most successful when tensions have been reduced. Druckman's (1973) propositions emphasize the dysfunctions of high levels of tension (that is, they lead to overreaction's to provocations) and the functions of low levels of tension (that is, they lead to underreactions to another state's provocations). These hypotheses contrast to an approach often taken by U.S. policymakers that emphasizes the advantages of external tensions: tensions may be increased in order to reinforce threats and commitments, and armaments may be procured and deployed to serve as bargaining chips to induce the opponent to make concessions.

Behavioral research suggests, however, that this relationship may actually be more complicated. Reciprocal effects may be found that produce either vicious or benign cycles. High or low levels of international tension may affect whether negotiations lead toward or away from agreements; these negotiating outcomes may, in turn, affect the level of tension in the international system. Such cyclical processes are demonstrated in results obtained by Hopmann and Walcott (1977).

The Hopmann and Walcott research is particularly notable for parallel analyses conducted in the laboratory and in situ. Results obtained from 24 runs of a simulation of the Partial Nuclear Test Ban talks (1962–1963) were buttressed by analyses of the actual discussions among the delegates from the three nuclear states participating in these negotiations (United States, Great Britain, Soviet Union). Three environments were created in the laboratory: a malign condition (a news bulletin announcing the onset of a crisis), a benign condition (a bulletin announcing a tension-reducing agreement on nondisarmament matters), and a neutral condition (in which no intervention occurred). Differences among the conditions showed the expected effects on several indices of negotiating behaviors and perceptions: the malign condition (compared to both the benign and neutral conditions) produced more hostility in mutual perceptions, more hard relative to soft tactics, more commitments, more negative relative to positive affect, a higher ratio of disagreements to agreements on substantive issues, and fewer overall agreements; no differences were obtained between the benign and neutral conditions. The direction of these effects suggests that high-stress environments hinder performance but that low-stress environments do not necessarily enhance performance (compared to a neutral-control condition). Tension reduction was not a necessary precondition for agreements in the simulation runs. The application of these simulation results to the actual negotiations was addressed in the parallel analyses.

Hopmann and Walcott's analyses of the test-ban discussions followed the procedures just outlined in our review of research on external events. Tensions were defined in terms of Corson's (1970) cooperative-competitive dimension and coded across the entire range of external interactions among the participating nations. Several results reinforced the laboratory findings. Coded levels of tension in external interactions correlated significantly in the hypothesized direction with indices of negotiating behavior and perceptions. Unlike the laboratory results, however, lower levels of tension (compared to the benign condition) were related to more positive perceptions and softer bargaining tactics (for the Western nations); this relationship became stronger as they approached the agreement. Thus, as expected, the Cuban missile crisis of October 1962 exerted a dampening effect on the test ban negotiations in the short run. However, when President Kennedy announced a coordinated set of measures to reduce tensions in his address at American University on June 10, 1963, a positive cycle of reduced tensions and greater cooperation within the test ban negotiations followed immediately thereafter.

Moreover, these analyses demonstrated reciprocal effects. Harder bargaining tactics taken by the negotiators in an earlier month led to increased external tension in their interactions during the next period. Such spiraling effects suggest similar patterns for interactions inside and outside the negotiations. Further work might explore the threshold problem, that is, the amount of tension needed to produce negative effects on negotiation. This may depend, at least in part, on the relative importance of the negotiations to the countries involved. Another topic of interest involves the possible positive functions of stress for performance in negotiations. Below some critical threshold stress may actually motivate negotiators to work harder to solve problems and to overcome obstacles to agreement. Many analysts have suggested that the long-term impact of the Cuban missile crisis on the test ban negotiations was to produce just this sort of stress (see Hopmann and King, 1980).

Spiraling effects of internal and external tension have implications for breakdowns of negotiations. From the practitioner's standpoint, it would be useful to monitor tension levels for warnings of the conditions that lead to crises. To do this effectively, however, may require a statistical approach that differs from the regression-correlation analyses used in the studies reviewed here. In this regard statistical techniques that depend less on patterns from the past and more on the conditions that signal an abrupt departure from normal activities would be appropriate. One such technique is stochastic modeling. Duncan and Job (1980) demonstrate the value of this approach for ascertaining characteristics of an interaction process that shift a system from one state (minor tension) to another (major tension). Their calculated transition probabilities enabled analysts to fine tune their estimates of tension in Israeli-Syrian interactions and of stability in the southern Rhodesia-Zimbabwe situation. Taking this process a step further, it would be useful to join the monitoring of external conditions to internal negotiating stages; this would enable analysts to warn of conditions that might lead to stalemate or to identify conditions that might provide opportunities to break through prior impasses.

STRUCTURAL FACTORS

Turning in a different direction, the international relations literature calls attention to structural determinants of international behavior including negotiation (for example, Haskel, 1974). These kinds of structural factors may operate at both the domestic and the international level.

Domestic structure

Domestic structures refer generally to national attributes such as capabilities, the organization of policymaking bureaucracies within states, and the patterns of relationship among critical domestic political and societal forces that influence national decision makers (see Druckman and Mahoney, 1977). The impact of structural factors on negotiations received early attention in the literature on labor-management bargaining. Walton and McKersie's (1965) intraorganizational bargaining model emphasized the importance of the within-group bargaining that occurs together with the between-group negotiation. Highlighted in particular are two sets of demands on the chief negotiator—one from his or her own organization and one from across the table, a process referred to as a "boundary role conflict." Applied by Druckman (1978a) to international negotiations, this concept implies two different models: the negotiator as bargainer and the negotiator as representative. The former reflects the process of monitoring *the other* for evidence of movement and attempting to persuade the other to accept one's own preferences; the latter describes the process of monitoring *one's own side* for evidence of preferences and frequently trying to persuade one's home government to respond to movement from the other side.

As originally defined, the boundary role conflict involves the conflicting aspects of a negotiator's role obligations: the expectations of his or her own side that emerge from an internal consensus on the positions he or she is to take and the expectations of the opponent that must be taken into account if an agreement is to be reached. However, the models developed and the evidence reported in Druckman (1978*a*, 1978*b*) suggest that these parts of the boundary role conflict are not simply competing demands but are fundamentally different processes. Responsiveness to the other takes the form of a sequence of comparisons and adjustments leading either to impasses or to agreement, which is in the tradition of dynamic equilibrium models. Responsiveness to one's own side consists of ascertaining the relative emphasis to be placed on presenting and defending one's own negotiating positions, which is in the tradition of linear statistical models. The former model emphasizes perceptions and concessions, while the latter highlights group commitments and priorities.

The two models are complementary and intertwined. Whereas the negotiator-as-bargainer model identifies the juncture where a change in position is likely to occur, the negotiator-as-representative model suggests the probable nature of the change. According to the former model, modifications in position occur when the other's strategy is discerned and after a comparison is made with one's own position. Which concessions are made and the extent of the concessions depend on the relative importance of the various parts of the package and on the degree of commitment to one's "agency." These variables are estimated by the latter model.

The negotiator's problem may be even more complex. The diverse interests of various roles and structures influencing the negotiation serve to expand the range of goals sought by a state which, in turn, reduces the available bargaining space with other states. Diversity in preferences is due to bureaucratically defined vested interests, compartmentalized access to information within an organization, ambiguity of novel situations, and assumptions about the opponent, including associated emotional reactions.

Internal structural factors have been explored in several studies. An interplay among levels of bargaining is demonstrated in a simulation of labor-management negotiation by Evan and MacDougall (1967). These investigators showed that differences within bargaining teams may facilitate the process of reaching agreements. More agreements were attained in a bilateral dissensus condition than in unilateral dissensus (disagreements within one team only) or bilateral consensus (no disagreements within either team) conditions: the moderates in the bilateral dissensus condition acted as mediators in bringing their more extremist teammates together. A similar process is described by Jonsson (1979) with regard to Soviet and U.S. decision making during the test ban negotiations. Support for a treaty depended on whether the moderate or extremist factions within each country were more influential. It was the efforts of the moderates in both countries to achieve similar objectives at the same time that seemed to account for the initial (1958–1960) agreement in principle on verification of a test ban and for the final (1963) treaty, as well as more flexible and conciliatory Soviet behavior in Geneva. In both examples, crosscutting lines of division played a facilitating role in the bargaining process.

International structures—alliances and coalitions

Structural factors also operate at the international level, especially in multilateral negotiations where alliances and coalitions can influence the process of negotiations. In this situation the internal decision-making process within an alliance or coalition may resemble similar structures within individual states in bilateral negotiations; for example, Hopmann (1977) has illustrated how the NATO bureaucracy in Brussels took on many of the traditional attributes of national bureaucracies in preparing its negotiators for the MBFR negotiations. One of the consequences is procedural complexity. Simply stated, there are a great many gates for a proposal to pass through on its way to the formal negotiating table. In order to develop a common negotiating position to present to the Warsaw Pact, not only must proposals be screened by multiple and often competing organizations at the domestic level, but they must then be screened again by complex international bureaucracies—such as the NATO structure in Brussels. Different national preferences must be reconciled with each other and with the preferences of the allies' military and political organizations, the Supreme Headquarters of the Allied Powers in Europe (SHAPE) and the North Atlantic Council (NAC).

But there may also be benefits from this complex decision-making process. Dean (1986) points to certain aspects of the process as facilitators of intraalliance coordination and cohesion as well as interalliance understandings: examples include the sustained discussions among small and large countries, opportunities for speculative discussions with the other side, and recognition of the need to coordinate force planning on an alliancewide basis. These structural factors and effects suggest that the negotiation can serve purposes other than to reach agreements. This idea is discussed later in relation to case studies.

The role of structural factors in larger multilateral conferences may be illustrated by such arms-control cases as the Seabeds Denuclearization Treaty, the Conference on Security and Cooperation in Europe (CSCE), the U.N. Special Session on Disarmament (UNSSOD), and the Mutual and Balanced Force Reduction talks (MBFR).

In his analysis of the process leading to the Seabeds treaty, Hopmann (1974) discovered an important cleavage that was considered, at that time, to be a "new pattern of interaction" among states. The division between nuclear and non-nuclear states cut across the traditional East-West blocs. The nuclear powers in both blocs often found that their common interests (due to shared national attributes) were reasons for cooperation. This new alignment within the negotiation had a strong impact on both the process and the outcome. More time was devoted to bargaining between the nuclear and the non-nuclear powers than among either the nuclear or non-nuclear states, and the treaty reflected several provisions favored by the non-nuclear states.

Extending the analysis further, Hopmann (1978) examined impacts of structural asymmetries on the interactions within CSCE. Influence over the outcome, defined as the portion of the text authored by each member state, was related to threat potential (defined as how little a country stands to lose by no agreement which, in turn, is a function of their alternatives to accepting a negotiated agreement within CSCE) and to resources (defined as military and economic assets). While the findings generally supported the hypotheses, there were notable exceptions. On the one hand, as in the earlier Seabeds analysis, there is evidence for a "bilateral condominium" between the superpowers: they acted together to preserve their joint interest in domination over their blocs and the nonaligned states. On the other hand, some countries with low threat potential (Yugoslavia, Rumania, France) became influential by acting together on the basis of their common interest to change the prevailing structures. These "renegades" were held in check to some extent by their more powerful bloc leaders: exercising the right to use a veto over the agenda, the superpowers demonstrated that "nondecision making" can also be a source of influence.

Continuing in the analytical tradition of the Seabeds and CSCE studies, King (1979) examined the jockeying for advantage among the players in UNSSOD. Textual changes from the draft final document, referred to by the conferees as "bracketing," were used as a measure of influence. This measure reflected attempts by participating nations to protect their interests. And, once again, we have evidence for a bilateral condominium between the superpowers: acting together, they used this mechanism to prevent the nonaligned states from making gains and, by doing so, restricted the range of bargaining. Indeed, the conference could be viewed as an exercise in damage limitation rather than bargaining with a goal of mutual accommodation of interests in mind. More broadly, this analysis implies that international negotiation can be modeled more appropriately as an attempt by nation-states to use their power to exert influence instead of to reach mutually satisfactory agreements.

Taken together, these three case studies suggest that negotiation may serve goals other than to reach agreement. (Iklé, 1964, describes this process as negotiating for "side effects.") The conference may be a "cover" for making gains sought more directly in other settings. Competitive interests are reflected in rhetoric and in decisions: the quantitative studies of negotiation transcripts frequently reveal a high percentage of statements coded in the categories of commitments and threats (Hopmann, 1974; King, 1976) and the common usage of vetos and text bracketing (Hopmann, 1978; King, 1979). These are mild forms of coercion intended to elicit compliance, and they are likely to be effective in the kinds of asymmetrical bargaining situations found in the cases reviewed earlier. They generally sit at the juncture where bargaining and influence processes overlap.

Particularly germane are Tedeschi and Bonoma's (1977) conditions for effective coercion in bargaining: moves supported by norms of the situation, moves seen as being defensively motivated, and moves seen as being unselfish or as nonpunitive actions. A negotiator's attributions of the other bargainer's intentions are critical; the line between justified and unjustified coercion is thin. When viewed by the coerced as being unjustified or extreme, the coercive moves can lead to a deteriorated relationship and, as Tedeschi and Bonoma caution, should be used only as a last resort.

As noted previously, the interplay between intra- and inter-bloc bargaining is the subject of Hopmann's (1977) analysis of the MBFR negotiations. Four models are superimposed on this complex negotiation, which opened in 1973: bargaining, strategic, attitudinal, and intraorganizational. Of the four, the intraorganizational model is the "best fit," revealing structural complexity and the effects of this complexity on position consensus. In particular, there were frequently different perspectives taken on the issues by the NATO headquarters staff in Brussels and the Vienna-based negotiators. For instance, the Vienna-based negotiators seemed to develop a better understanding of Warsaw Pact positions, and they were more prone to develop some empathy for those positions than were staff members in Brussels, who had little or no contact with the Warsaw Pact delegates.

Not only were there frequently different perspectives between the viewpoints of the negotiators and of officials at alliance headquarters, but there were also important differences within and among members of the NATO alliance. This tended to reduce the range of space available for negotiation; possible agreements were restricted to the area between the minimum acceptable positions of those organizational (domestic and alliance) members with the toughest positions. Within the NATO structure in Brussels, the Federal Republic of Germany (FRG) frequently took strong positions with regard to the MBFR negotiations through the 1970s, which in turn largely reflected the preferences of the foreign minister, Hans Dieter Genscher of the Free Democratic Party, rather than of his coalition partner, Chancellor Helmut Schmidt of the Social Democratic Party. For example, the FRG insisted that force ceilings should be on a collective, alliancewide basis rather than on an individual country basis, or that negotiations should be limited to manpower and not deal with associated armaments. Although these positions were not widely shared by the FRG's partners in NATO, they effectively limited the NATO position throughout the long history of these negotiations. Since these positions were generally opposed by the socialist states, the FRG position within NATO effectively narrowed the range of bargaining space in the interalliance negotiations, contributing to stalemate. By analyzing the various interests of major parties to the negotiations, Hopmann (1977) was able to show how fundamental interests could be made to overlap in order to create a plausible framework for agreement, in spite of the narrow range of bargaining space created by both domestic and alliance structures.

A similar analysis describes the evolution of Warsaw Pact cohesion through the course of the negotiations. In their Mathtech report, Druckman and Hopmann (1978) identified factors within the process that related to changes in cohesion. This study was based on a content analysis of the transcripts of all informal sessions held in Rounds 4 to 11 (1974–1977). Topics discussed (manpower reductions, counting rules, and so on), behavior styles (soft and hard rhetoric), and types of statements (demands, offers, justifications) were coded. In addition to an analysis of cohesion, the methodology permitted a detailed examination of the use of threats and promises, areas of compromise based on accusations made by the countries in each of the topic areas, models of responsiveness (see preceding discussion), and the identification of national and bloc objectives. This study was intended to be useful to policymakers in analyzing how their various negotiating behaviors might affect the response of their Warsaw Pact counterparts, especially the degree of unity expressed between the Soviet Union and its Eastern European allies. Advantages, and some possible disadvantages, of this methodology are discussed in the Appendix and in the section entitled "Two Cultures: Theory and Practice."

CULTURAL FACTORS

Cultural differences in negotiating styles have been a subject of speculation for some time. Writing on the eve of World War II, Harold Nicolson (1939) characterized the differences in diplomatic theory and practice that existed among Great Britain, Germany, France, and Italy. Thirty years later, Young

(1968) noted that the style of diplomats from the PRC, in contrast to the Western style, consists of a tough offensive posture, a rejection of the rhythm of bargaining and reciprocal concession making, moves calculated to induce tension, and an unwillingness to consider smaller issues in a stepwise progression toward a resolution of larger issues. Other contemporary writers have made similar observations (Samelson, 1976) and have offered advice to U.S. negotiators on how to deal with negotiators from the PRC (Solomon, 1985). Some differences in styles among countries have been documented by experimental results, notably those showing differences in competitiveness, strategy, preferred outcomes, and procedures. (See the literature reviewed in Druckman et al. [1976].)

The issue of cultural effects on the negotiation process has been discussed in some detail elsewhere (Druckman, 1977b, 1983). Here we are primarily concerned with the impact of culture on Soviet and U.S. behavior in arms control negotiations. Scholarly interest in this topic has been buttressed by the observations of diplomats and other "insiders." These insights, derived from the experience of diplomats, can be treated as hypotheses to be explored in a more systematic fashion or as preliminary guidelines for developing approaches to negotiation.

Many insights about Soviet negotiating behavior appear in articles and books written between 1977 and 1979, when U.S. optimism about arms control negotiations was high due largely to the earlier successes of SALT I and to the forthcoming conclusion of SALT II (for example, Garthoff, 1977; Smith, 1977; Muromcew, 1978; Whelen, 1979). Less has appeared on this topic during the early 1980s, a period marked by a Soviet walkout in reaction to the U.S. deployment of intermediate-range nuclear missiles in Europe and by a general cooling of relations following the arrival of the Reagan administration in Washington and preceding General Secretary Gorbachev's rise to power. More attention has been given by scholars and practitioners to the broad relationship between the superpowers and its implications for arms control (for example, Adelman, 1984; Krepon, 1984).

More generally, we detect a shift in theorizing from actor-specific theories of national negotiating styles to an emphasis on transnational bureaucratic politics, including external determinants of negotiating behavior. Rather than referring to a unique and invariable Soviet negotiating behavior, it seems more meaningful to speak of many Soviet styles adapted to changing circumstances (Jonsson, 1979). An emphasis on the impact of generational changes in the Soviet leadership has appeared in recent years, focusing on a shift in the Soviet world view from the dominance of ideological considerations to a dominance of more pragmatic approaches based on "objective" national interests. In particular Tetlock (1988) has noted the significant increase in the "integrative complexity" of Soviet foreign policy rhetoric in the period since Gorbachev's ascent to power.

Actually, cultural effects are probably understood best in relation to change. Whelen's (1979) distinction between the enduring and changing aspects of Soviet diplomacy is useful. It separates approaches to negotiation rooted in cultural traditions from those that are tactical and temporary and, in so doing, highlights the analytical problem of determining the relative importance of culture versus circumstance, ideology versus interests, or internal versus external factors. Observed differences in negotiating behavior between national representatives may be due to culture, or they may be a product of a particular political period. It is necessary to disentangle cultural from political regime interpretations of negotiating style. For example, some aspects of Soviet style may reflect the residual influence of Stalin's regime and, therefore, were likely to decline after Khrushchev's first attempt at de-Stalinization in 1956 or after Gorbachev's renewed attack on Stalinism in 1987. Other aspects of Soviet style may transcend governing regimes or perhaps may even reflect aspects of Russian culture that transcend the socialist political system.

A concern about the issue of the relative importance of different kinds of cultural influences moves us closer to a more analytical treatment of cultural effects than currently exists in the literature. An interesting question is, "How important is culture?" The answer can only be provided (at least tentatively) by experiments where culture and situation are varied systematically. But, the results of such experiments may answer the wrong question. How we think about culture is as much a matter of perspective as it is of methodology. A close reading of Whelen's study suggests a more complex perspective for evaluating cultural effects. His cultural imperatives are broad constraints within which a wide range of diplomatic behaviors can occur. Culture and situation are interacting factors, the one influencing the other in a reciprocal fashion. Stated simply, negotiating behavior is sensitive to circumstances and historical time periods that are themselves shaped by traditions, ideologies, and institutions. Many possibilities exist in any culture; which is chosen depends on the situation. Clues to the motives for particular negotiating moves are to be found in the interplay between the enduring (cultural) and changing (situational) aspects of diplomacy.

Reciprocal effects between culture and situation suggest that cultural traditions and habits may influence the way a situation is defined: the extent of influence depends on the strength of the link, as when perceptions (or interests) derive explicitly from cultural traditions (or ideologies) as opposed to when perceptions are momentary or are rooted in the immediate situation that confronts negotiators (Druckman and Zechmeister, 1973). But this is not a static model. Changes in traditions and situations occur through time and along with repeated interactions among the parties; the dynamics of relationships must also be elucidated. Druckman, Rozelle, and Zechmeister (1977:129) report some progress in specifying this process but also suggest that "more work on the descriptive phases of theory development" is needed. With respect to culture, this work entails a clearer definition of the difference between enduring and changing aspects of diplomacy and the negotiating behaviors that accompany them.

This perspective gains relevance in the more substantive treatments of Soviet styles by Whelen (1979) and Garthoff (1977), as well as in the developing literature on organizational cultures (Schein, 1985). A common theme is changing approaches to negotiation within the broad confines of an institutional structure that changes more slowly. For Whelen, it is the "imperatives of security, ideology, and the political system [that] endow Soviet diplomacy and negotiating behavior with a certain institutional permanency. But within these institutions significant changes are taking place" (Whelen, 1979:526). The imperatives are manifested in views of the world (respect for power, appreciation of realism), approaches to negotiation (value of total diplomacy, toughness), and relationships between negotiators and their bureaucracies (control from center and binding bureaucracy). For Garthoff (1977), the enduring structures produce unity in negotiating objectives and positions; they are also responsible for sluggishness. Changes appear evident in areas such as the willingness to compromise, a readiness to consider agreements on a wider range of subjects, and a less defensive posturing in negotiations. These observations have implications for U.S. tactics. Garthoff recommends a strategy of controlled flexibility: take advantage of moments when the Soviets seek agreements; be resolute when they demand unrealistic concessions or place the burden of concession making on their opponent. And, for Schein (1985), culture is revealed in basic assumptions from which observed behaviors, referred to as artifacts, are derived. Assumptions about the nature of reality or about human relationships provide a broad framework from which a variety of behaviors can emerge. While reflecting the assumptions, the artifacts are also responses to circumstances.

All of this suggests that changing patterns of negotiating behavior occur within relatively unchanging structures. Culture is context, not process. It shapes behavior but is not synonymous with it. A lesson suggested by this observation is to avoid imputing "cultural traits" that, like stereotypes, can blind one to flexible or changing behavior by others. While the concept of cultural traits remains elusive, there is a limited role for it in the analysis of negotiating behavior. We will attempt, in the remainder of this section, to elucidate that role.

The traitlike language used to depict Soviet negotiating behavior may serve useful analytical purposes, even if it is frequently inaccurate. It provides categories for monitoring changes in Soviet behavior. Whelen (1979) and Garthoff (1977) direct attention to "tendencies" such as toughness, realism, willingness to compromise, and defensive posturing. Other observers highlight timing (patience and perseverance), style and format (use of vague and obscure terms, formality, control by chief of delegation, obsessive note taking), and tactics (start with high demands, alternating soft and hard rhetoric, salami tactics, beating the price down). Muromcew's (1978) anecdotes provide good illustrations of these behaviors (see also Wedge and Muromcew, 1965). Many of these characteristics are indicated by language that can be coded, such as the indicators of soft and hard bargaining discussed in the section on content analysis in the appendix to this chapter. Trends in these indicators can be quite revealing, as when a nation's negotiators display increasingly soft rhetoric prior to making a proposal, followed by increasingly tough rhetoric when the proposal is rejected or tabled for later consideration (Druckman and Hopmann, 1978). Language can be revealing in other ways, such as when soft statements (accommodations, praise, promises) are used to suggest areas of compromise or when tough statements (retractions, criticisms, threats) define the boundaries of the bargaining space or suggest negotiating objectives.

It is important to recognize, however, that this is a one-sided analysis. Negotiation is an interactive process, requiring that we focus on both parties. Patterns that emerge are the result of a counterpoising of styles, moves, and proposals. In this respect, it is curious to note the relative absence of discussions of U.S. style or cultural influences in the literature on negotiating behavior. The subject is often treated as if the Soviets reflected an aberrant style of negotiation, perhaps even reflective of a "pathological" culture, in contrast to a "normal" U.S. style.

Nonetheless, a few studies have compared Soviet and U.S. negotiating styles systematically, often noting the differences in their general approach to negotiation. American negotiators seem to prefer a process that converges gradually and in stepwise fashion toward an agreement. Their Soviet counterparts seem to take an approach consisting of high initial demands and patience, often followed by rapid concession making as agreement approaches (Jensen, 1963). The U.S. penchant for steady progress and compromise is contrasted to a Soviet strategy of "first position, then delay." Given this difference, U.S. negotiators often become the side pressing toward agreement or introducing new elements into the negotiation. For example, in the test ban negotiations, the Soviet Union held out on a partial agreement, proposed jointly by the United States and Great Britain in August 1962, for a period of almost a year. Only in the final week of secret negotiations in Moscow in July

1963 did the Soviets accept this major compromise proposal. Similarly, the Soviets resisted frequent Western concessions on the Intermediate-range Nuclear Forces negotiations from 1981 to 1986. Suddenly, beginning with the Reykjavik summit in November 1986, they began a series of rapid and major concessions: they dropped insistence on the inclusion of British and French intermediate-range missiles in the agreement, they no longer insisted on linking an INF agreement to limitations of the U.S. Strategic Defense Initiative (SDI), they agreed to abandon INF missiles worldwide rather than just in the European parts of the Soviet Union west of the Urals, they agreed to eliminate short-range as well as intermediate-range missiles and, finally, they agreed to extensive on-site verification of the destruction of all of these weapons. Thus during the 12 months following the Reykjavik summit, the Soviets made numerous major concessions with virtually no reciprocation in kind by the United States. It was this series of Soviet last-minute concessions that made it possible to sign an INF Treaty in Washington in December 1987.

Kelleher (1976) has argued that this tendency of the Soviets to hold off making concessions until the final stages of negotiations creates a dilemma for U.S. negotiators. Frequently the United States is negotiating with itself in the early stages of the bargaining, and the provisions of past agreements frequently are supported by a public that believes in the logic of precedent. What is, however, acceptable to the U.S. public may not be acceptable to the Soviets. Thus, for long periods of time changes in U.S. negotiating behavior may be influenced more by domestic and bureaucratic considerations than by the dynamics of interaction with the Soviets. It is little wonder, then, that most popular treatments of arms control focus primarily on U.S. bureaucratic politics. (See Newhouse [1973] and Smith [1980] on SALT I; Talbott [1979] on SALT II, and Talbott [1984] on INF and START.)

But even two-sided analyses of national styles are limited. They assume that certain styles transcend the particular circumstances of a negotiation. Considerable evidence, reviewed earlier in the section entitled "Responsiveness," suggests an internal dynamic in which negotiators are very sensitive to each other's moves. Such responsiveness may be leading, over time, to the development of negotiator subcultures, especially in the long-term, institutionalized forums on arms control in the United Nations (for example, the U.N. Special Committee on Disarmament) and alliance-to-alliance (for example, MBFR) contexts. Negotiator subcultures may serve to moderate the effects on process of national styles. As Alger's (1963) study of diplomats interacting within a U.N. committee and Modelski's (1970) analysis of foreign ministers suggest, this common socialization may produce a cadre of diplomats who are more similar to one another than to their compatriots. To date, we know little about this phenomenon in arms control negotiations. It is a topic that needs to be examined carefully, perhaps in the manner of Schein's (1985) deep probes of an organization's values and operating assumptions.

Continuing along these lines, in the next section we will discuss the different assumptions made by practitioners and theorists of negotiation. These "cultural" differences have implications for the way that analytical work is used in the diplomatic community.

Two Cultures: Theory and Practice

This section examines the gulf that exists between the theory of international negotiation and the practice of diplomacy. We have reviewed thus far a large number of studies designed to derive and test theories of the negotiation process, beginning with simple models and laboratory experiments and expanding into much richer empirical analyses of the process of bargaining in real-world international negotiations. Yet both researchers and practitioners are hesitant to accept these tentative findings as advice for policymakers. There are several explanations for this reluctance to apply the results of this research directly to policy.

Perhaps the most fundamental reason is due to the different purposes and goals of basic research in the social sciences and policy research of direct relevance to governments and international institutions. The primary purpose of basic research is to produce general findings that *explain* to the greatest extent possible what accounts for variations in international negotiating behavior, in particular what kinds of conditions contribute to stalemate or facilitate agreement. The goal of such research is thus to produce generalizations that will apply across the largest number of possible cases and that can help to describe, explain, and predict the critical relationships. A crucial attribute of theory development is cumulation, namely the extent to which one set of findings builds on others to create a more complex and veridical model of the process in general.

By contrast, the policy community is more interested in specific advice for action in concrete circumstances. A set of general principles is not regarded as having much value unless it provides a guide for action in a particular instance. Thus, the policy analyst generally prefers knowledge that relates to specific cases in time and space where context is essential. They are also more interested in prescription than in explanation. Furthermore, to be useful, research must not only identify which variables account for the greatest variance, but it must also be sensitive to the extent to which variables can be *manipulated* by concrete human actions. Forces that may affect negotiations but that are largely beyond the control of the policymaker are generally of little or no relevance. Finally, the policymaker wants advice about how to act in novel circumstances, which may be unique and where there is a high degree of uncertainty about the consequences of alternative actions.

In a literal sense, no research can possibly satisfy the *ideal* needs of the policymaker. Insofar as each situation is in some sense unique (that is, the variables that are present may have been observed previously but seldom interrelated in quite the same way), no research can provide a certain guide for what actions to take in order to produce a desired outcome or to avert an undesired consequence. By definition, all past generalizations tend to hold context largely constant, and thus new contextual factors in the present situation always confront the policymaker with unique conditions. Even past case studies may be only relevant to those particular cases in their own unique contexts. It is for this reason that many policymakers assert that negotiations are primarily "art," and that there can be no science of international negotiation. The best guide for action is thus assumed to be the experienced diplomat whose "feel" for the situation allows him or her to respond creatively to the conditions at hand.

We do not accept this conclusion, however, about the inevitable gulf between theory and practice. Even the intuitive diplomat is undoubtedly carrying around in his or her head some "theory" of international negotiations that he or she uses to interpret any new situation. The task of the negotiation theorist is thus to help the diplomat recognize these implicit assumptions about how the negotiation process operates in order to aid in making these theoretical underpinnings of action more explicit and more subject to empirical verification. Quite frequently the intuitive theories of diplomats correspond to the theoretical generalizations of social scientists, as Zartman and Berman (1982) have demonstrated in their analysis of interviews with dozens of experienced and highly successful diplomats. At times, however, the assumptions diverge, and it is at this point that the two communities need to pay more attention to one another. Perhaps the diplomats know of some critical factors that the social scientists have omitted from their models or, alternatively, the social scientists may be able to point out to the diplomats that their assumptions are based on a limited set of cases that may represent the exception rather than the rule. Comparative research across a wider variety of contexts and conditions can produce more valid and useful generalizations than those that may be gleaned from the experiences of any single individual, no matter how experienced. But corrective feedback for theorist and practitioner alike can come only from extensive interaction across the two widely divided communities.

As Winham (1979) has suggested, there are at least five dimensions of difference between the research and policy communities that serve as obstacles to more effective communications between them: focus on external (intergovernmental) versus internal (interagency, alliance) negotiations; focus on strategic interactions versus problems of management; focus on styles or background factors versus substance and issues; emphasis on the negotiation process per se versus the context of policy formulation; and concentration on general principles versus case-specific details. Being concerned with execution and policy, the practitioners have concentrated on interagency and alliance bargaining, managing structural and substantive complexity, evaluating options and preparing position papers. By contrast, the most sophisticated academic models have focused on the interstate negotiation process. Little wonder then that difficulties arise when scholar-researchers enter into consultative relationships with practitioner-bureaucrats. Relevance, as defined by practitioners, has consistently been a sticking point in the relationship.

Still another difficulty for collaboration between the two cultures seems to be related to the distinction between research as a public and a private good. The "product" produced by the research community can be regarded as a "public" good. Three aspects of the product support this observation: results are more general than specific, explanatory rather than prescriptive, and discipline rather than practice-oriented (virtually all of the results of behavioral science research reported here have appeared in scholarly journals). Practitioners seek out consultants whose services are tailored to specific problems and whose advice is more prescriptive (Which option to choose?) than explanatory (What were the consequences of concessions in past negotiations for achieving a balanced agreement?). Appropriate consultants are likely to be identified either from policy-oriented articles or from a track record of relevant experiences. Rarely is advice sought from contributors to the scholarly journals. The two communities overlap only slightly: a public-oriented enterprise versus a client-oriented practice.

Yet despite these problems the two communities have a great deal to gain from one another. At a minimum the conceptual frameworks produced by the scholarly community may be useful organizing devices when superimposed on the case studies typically utilized by the policy community in the manner described by Druckman and Iaquinta (1974) and Druckman (1985). We illustrate here several examples of attempted communications between these communities, beginning with an example based on our own experience as consultants to the U.S. delegation in the early phases of the negotiations on MBFR (Druckman and Hopmann, 1978). In this instance, the consultants attempted to tailor various tools of content analysis to serve as an aid in solving bargaining problems identified by the negotiators. The delegates were interested in keeping track of statements and proposals through the course of a long negotiation (monitoring), anticipating key events such as the tabling of a proposal (signaling), anticipating reactions to their own statements or moves (predicting and posturing for effect), and constructing plausible packages based on areas where compromises were likely. Content analysis techniques were adopted to provide the delegation with a wide variety of information in response to these needs, including an information retrieval and data management system (a monitoring aid), measures of behavioral patterns or trends before and after proposals were introduced (signaling tool), and empirical models of responsiveness among the participating countries (an aid for posturing and influence), and a system of indicators for detecting areas of compromise from "soft" and "hard" rhetoric on different topics (aids for constructing packages). This system was designed to enhance relevant psychological properties such as memory, expectations, and problem solving. To the extent that these processes were improved, the consultative relationship was sustained.

This project contributed to both theory and practice. Benefits for the negotiation theorist and methodologist include the following.

1. A refined and extended bargaining process analysis system was developed (see the appendix to this chapter). It could capture details of verbal style and substance in a complex, multilateral negotiation extending over a period of several years.

2. This exercise, based on an application to an arms control case, also added to the ability to make comparisons across types of negotiations, since the results were compared with a previous study of base-rights negotiations. Differences between the two types of negotiations included technical and political complexity as well as the nature of negotiating patterns as regular (MBFR) or irregular (base rights) progressions through stages, turning points, and crises. Systematic case comparisons are a step in the direction of a more sophisticated discipline of negotiation analysis.

3. A number of interesting findings were obtained. These included discovery of a consistent trend for negotiators to change from hard to soft rhetoric before tabling a proposal, followed by increasingly hard statements after the proposal was introduced (the trend was depicted as a U-shaped function, going from pre- to postproposal sessions); patterns of responsiveness among the participants in each bloc were discovered to serve as predictors of tough or soft behavior in the next round; and a refined index of group cohesion was developed based on difference scores in relative hardness of negotiating rhetoric for pairs of nations within the Warsaw Pact and NATO alliances.

4. We developed a new conceptualization of negotiation processes as these occur in international conferences. This approach, discussed elsewhere (Druckman, 1983, 1986), highlights the many dimensions of difference between the processes observed in these cases and those depicted by bargaining theory.

Some of the contributions made to the practice of negotiation and, in particular, to delegates and supporting staffs included the following.

1. The computerized codes provided on-line support to the U.S. MBFR delegation. Especially valuable was the monitoring function that provided answers to questions such as: "When and how did the Soviets address the Western concern with the phasing of reductions in Rounds 4, 5, and 6 of the informal sessions?" "How often did the Soviets address the topic of the phasing of reductions?" "How often did the Soviet representative disagree with each element of the Western position?" "Has the Eastern bloc changed its style of argumentation on certain topics?" The answers to questions such as these enabled the consultants to support modifications of the NATO position, such as offering to trade some reductions in Western tactical nuclear weapons in exchange for greater reductions in Soviet manpower and tanks.

2. The project answered specific questions asked by analysts supporting the delegation. Examples are: "What accounted for the Czech representative's 'tough' postures in early rounds of MBFR?" "Who among the Warsaw Pact and NATO states were the strongest proponents of their bloc's positions?" "On which aspects of the Pact position was each state most strongly committed?" "What were the determinants of changes in bloc cohesion?" These questions could be answered in part with the results of time-series and path analyses of verbal exchanges during the negotiations. The coding scheme proved to be particularly rich in suggesting trends in both substantive topics of discussion and of negotiating style.

3. The approach taken by the project stimulated a debate among supporting analysts on the delegation's staff. The issue concerned the value of oral statements at informal sessions as indicators of parties' objectives or preferences. One camp argued against statistical trend analyses, claiming that only statements made in highly confidential conversations outside the sessions had "real" value. Another camp supported the idea of careful analysis of changes in verbal style over long periods of time. Although not resolved in favor of one or the other camp, the issue (and the project) served to call attention to the possibilities of systematic analysis of negotiating behavior.

More generally, the insights gained from this project were a basis for theoretical work on the monitoring function in negotiation (Druckman, 1978*a*, 1978*b*) and for a recognition by diplomats of the need to manage the complexity of the process: by keeping abreast of its progression, by getting a better grasp of changing situations, and by discerning those aspects that can be controlled (see Winham, 1979).[2]

Another example of a good working relationship between consultants and policymakers is the Ulvila and Snider (1980) approach to analytical consultation, as they prepared negotiators for an international conference on oil tanker standards. Analysts and negotiators worked together to refine a model that incorporated the views of many of the negotiating countries. The modeling effort helped the negotiators to identify a compromise proposal similar to the one finally adopted by the conference. Focusing on preferences, the modeling exercise charted changes in evaluations through simple algorithms based on decision (multiattribute value) theory. Of particular interest are complementary applications of the two approaches, the one focusing on process (Druckman and Hopmann, 1978), the other on preferences (Ulvila and Snider, 1980). They can be used effectively in tandem, first to assess progress and then to update the configuration of preferences as these change during the unfolding negotiation.

The multiattribute utility approach was used also with the U.S. teams on the Panama Canal and Philippine base-rights negotiations (Barclay and Peterson, 1976; summarized by Raiffa, 1982:Chap. 12, and Ulvila, 1988). The approach here involves the construction of package agreements based on trade-offs. Essential issues are defined and each issue is assigned an importance weight by each delegation. That is, each delegation may have 100 points to distribute across, for example, the 10 essential issues under negotiation for the Panama Canal Treaty. These weights are thus supposed to reflect the substantive value of attaining one's preferred outcome on each issue for each delegation. If a mediator is able to obtain such information from all parties, then these points may be assigned by each delegation. In the case of the Panama and Philippines negotiations, the U.S. delegation assigned their own points, whereas analysts who were knowledgeable about the other country attempted to estimate weights for Panama and the Philippines. Then a package was constructed matching the different preferences of the two parties, so that, for example, the United States could get a larger portion of the settlement on issues such as U.S. defense rights, which it regarded as especially important, whereas Panama could get an agreement on a treaty of short duration (in which the Panama Canal is rapidly turned over to Panama), since that issue was of special importance to it. By making trade-offs in this fashion, one can demonstrate that the results can be far better for both sides than agreements made by simple compromise or "splitting the difference." Such a model also helps states identify issues on which they should be prepared to be firm versus those on which greater flexibility may be beneficial.

Such a model has been designed as a formula for strategic arms reductions (Salter, 1984; Hopmann, 1987), and it has been used as the basis for a simulation developed at the U.S. Naval War College (Lamkin and Fought, 1988). This approach seeks to create packages for arms reductions where the principle of "equal reductions" is desired, but where asymmetrical force structures make these difficult to operationalize. Under this proposal (sometimes dubbed by the old child's rule for cutting cake, "You cut, I choose") each side has 10,000 points to distribute across all of its strategic nuclear forces. These points are to be assigned by each state unilaterally in proportion to the relative importance that the United States and the Soviet Union attribute to all elements of their forces. Then, if the two states have agreed in principle to reduce their forces by 10 percent per year over five years, each side is allowed to select any 1,000 points worth of cuts from the arsenal of the other in each of the five years.

There is no incentive to cheat in the assignment of points, since any state that undervalues certain items that it wants to retain must necessarily overvalue others and risk that the former will be chosen by the adversary in greater numbers than had the weights been assigned honestly. Thus, for example, if the Soviets overvalue their heavyweight ICBMs in an effort to protect them, they run the risk that the United States will be able to select a much larger number of other weapons for elimination. The price that they would pay for retaining their limited number of heavyweight ICBMs would be a much larger quantitative reduction of other weapons. In order to avoid this, each side has an incentive to estimate the value of its weapons honestly. Such a formula would permit each side to reduce its strategic forces in such a way that each assures itself that no more than 50 percent of its forces *as it values them* will be cut, while also permitting each side to eliminate from its enemy's arsenals those particular systems that each fears the most.

In an area somewhat removed from international negotiations but of potential applicability, Hammond, Stewart, Adelman, and Wascoe (1975) have developed a "lens-model" paradigm for dealing with the cognitive sources of conflict (that is, different interpretations of the same data). The aids are in some respects a substitute for the kinds of discussions and debates that usually occur in negotiation. With the help of computer graphics, negotiators are encouraged to think analytically about the problem, especially about their own judgment policies and task characteristics. In a well-publicized application, this approach was employed for the resolution of a community controversy in Denver over an acceptable bullet for the police department, one that would have more stopping power than the current bullet with no increase in injury. Hammond and his colleagues concluded that task clarification achieved what discussion could not: more accurate information about the technical aspects of the problem. This approach is likely to prove effective for conflicts where emotions and ideologies are not significant elements. The technical aspects (weapons capabilities) of arms control negotiations are sometimes of this type. Other aspects involve national interests and pride, calling perhaps for a different form of mediation. One possibility is the single, integrated text approach suggested by Fisher (1981).

Like Hammond and his colleagues, Fisher emphasizes the problem-solving aspects of negotiation. A difference, however, is that while Hammond concentrates on scaled positions ("quantities"), Fisher focuses his attention on interests that need to be protected and reconciled but that are often covered by rhetoric and position taking. He does this through a procedure referred to as the "single negotiating text" strategy. Successive drafts of an initial text are produced by a mediator, who then submits the drafts to the disputing parties for their criticism. Fisher argues that the parties are less likely to dig in their heels around fixed positions when asked to criticize a text and, furthermore, that it is easier to accept the draft recommendations of a mediator than to concede to an opponent, especially when the two opponents are initially kept apart. The mediator then responds to criticisms made by all parties, revising the drafts until one is produced that all find to be acceptable. At that point the parties may be brought into face-to-face negotiations to reach formal agreement. Citing the Camp David process as an example, in which President Carter used such a drafting technique to mediate between President Sadat and Prime Minister Begin, Fisher argues for the advantages of the technique: for example, it serves as an organizing framework, it avoids hard bargaining, and it promotes joint ownership of the drafts and final product. The effectiveness of this procedure follows from its general focus on interests, which may be disguised by rhetoric. This procedure thus seeks to improve the atmosphere of negotiations so that hard bargaining based on fixed positions can be overcome by a search for mutually overlapping interests or "integrative" solutions that at least incorporate the most fundamental objectives of all parties to a conflict.

One evident conclusion is that behavioral science research will become more meaningful and relevant to practitioners insofar as it is able to treat negotiations as complex processes where context is important. As we noted previously, some significant progress has been made in that direction in the most recent research, especially when the results of laboratory studies have been applied and tested with real-world cases. For example, Bonham (1971) and Ramberg (1977) have done an excellent job of applying the broad conceptual framework of Sawyer and Guetzkow (1965) to the study of specific negotiations.

The application of theoretical frameworks such as those just described can provide negotiators with better tools for evaluating the many aspects of problems under negotiation; however, to accomplish this, the frameworks must be adapted to each problem, changing some categories while retaining others within the broad architecture of their structures. As noted, for example, Druckman and Hopmann have adapted, expanded, and increased the complexity of methodologies for coding and analyzing negotiations in response to the demands of negotiators such as those representing the United States at the MBFR negotiations. Frameworks and methods must thus be modified constantly in response to feedback from experienced diplomats. Similarly, diplomatic practice could be improved by giving greater attention to a thorough analysis of the negotiating process, in which often implicit and incomplete theory is raised to the level of consciousness, inconsistencies and contradictions are resolved, and a more systematic effort is made to apply theory to the practice of negotiating. Thus, through the refinement of frameworks and methods, theory and practice may be joined, even though the theory must enter through the "service door."

Conclusion: Retrospect and Prospect

The preceding survey of theory and research about the process of international negotiation has revealed a substantial amount of progress in the development of a cumulative approach to this field of study. Although there are many more important research questions that need to be asked and answered, we are now beginning to learn enough about the negotiation process to apply some of the concepts, hypotheses, and methodologies to the study of actual international negotiations. Our goal, as set out at the beginning, was to apply this behavioral science research to find ways to negotiate an improved mutual security regime between the nuclear superpowers that would make nuclear war less likely in the years ahead. When President John F. Kennedy (1963:257) presented the first nuclear arms control agreement, the Partial Nuclear Test Ban Treaty, to the U.S. public in 1963 he noted the ancient Chinese proverb: "A journey of a thousand miles must begin with a single step." Just as the Partial Nuclear Test Ban Treaty represented for Kennedy the first step on the road to nuclear arms control, so the research reviewed here represents at best the first few steps in a long journey to a better understanding of how to negotiate a regime of *mutual security* between the nuclear superpowers.

Of course, the negotiation of an East-West security regime requires fundamentally a better understanding of the many substantive differences that separate the two major camps of the postwar world, as well as the identification of superordinate interests that may transcend those issues of mutual conflict. But this chapter has been based on the assumption that the identification of these interests will not be sufficient unless we also have a better understanding of how to use the negotiation process both to uncover such mutual interests and then to consummate them in actual agreements. Without such an improved understanding of the process, efforts to reach a mutual security regime may go unfulfilled.

The preceding review has suggested that there has been considerable growth in the various "islands" of theory about the negotiation process, to borrow Guetzkow's (1957) metaphor. What is still missing is a central organizing theme for this entire literature that will enable the islands to expand and eventually form a "continent." While our conceptualizations in this field do not yet provide sufficient clarity to indicate what that continent is likely to look like, we may at this stage offer some suggestions about ways to proceed in the development of such a unified theory. In so doing, we must keep in mind two essential, albeit partially contradictory, criteria for a theory of international negotiation: (1) the theory should be parsimonious, in that we should try to explain as much as possible about the negotiation process with as few key variables as possible, and (2) the theory should be sufficiently rich that it can be applied to a wide variety of problems and contexts in a very complex international setting.

With these guidelines in mind, we can suggest at least one way to proceed. We will begin by identifying the major factors or independent variables that may explain the unfolding of the negotiation process, starting with the simplest assumptions, to see how much we can derive from them in explanation. We will then introduce increased complexity until we have a theory that is sufficiently rich and flexible to be applied to a wide variety of international issues. After identifying the major factors in the process model, we will turn our attention to what it is we want to explain, the dependent variable, namely, the outcome of the negotiation process. Finally, we will conclude with a few words about applying such a theoretical framework for policy analysis on international issues relevant to the prevention of nuclear war.

First, beginning with the simplest assumptions, we can construct a basic model of two rational, symmetrical, unitary individuals negotiating about a simple issue that can be treated on a single dimension. Such a model would probably rely heavily on the game theoretic traditions of bargaining, for which such simple assumptions are appropriate. In this model, the negotiators are assumed to be utility maximizers, who strive to achieve agreements that provide them with the greatest possible benefits compared with the utilities associated with nonagreement (or, equivalently, their best alternative to a negotiated agreement). For reasons that we pointed out much earlier, this model lacks many features required for a valid theory of international negotiations, but it does offer some fundamental axioms on which almost all other work is based. Insofar as these simple assumptions do suggest valid hypotheses, they are to be preferred to more complex theories because of their high degree of parsimony.

Second, we may relax the assumption that these individuals are fully rational. Rather, as Simon (1957:198) has suggested, they operate according to a kind of "bounded rationality," within the constraints of their own world views. At this point, the perceptions of the individuals of one another and of the issues under negotiation become critical, and the models of the social psychologist become increasingly relevant. The individuals may then take on "personalities," which respond in different ways to similar situations. Furthermore, their world views become subject to the constraints of the culture within which they developed. Thus, the goals that negotiators seek are defined by their perceived interests within a cultural context, and their responses to one another are affected by the psychological dynamics of the interaction itself. The criterion for an agreement now becomes one of perceived satisfaction, in which the nature of the interpersonal relationship with the other party is also important.

Third, we may relax the assumption of symmetry and introduce the effects of asymmetry in several characteristics, but especially in capabilities to exert influence and alternatives to negotiated settlements. In this case, differences in capabilities among the parties may affect their ability to issue threats and promises, since capabilities are necessary to provide the contingent rewards and punishments implied by these tactics. Differences in alternatives to a negotiated agreement also create asymmetries in outcomes due to the different potential to threaten the break-off of negotiations. Thus, the introduction of variability in these elements of bargaining power may directly affect the degree of "equity" in negotiation outcomes.

Fourth, we may drop the assumption that we are dealing with unitary actors, and we may then introduce into the process the role of organizations and bureaucracies, as well as the "boundary roles" that link negotiators as representatives with the agents that they represent. In this sense, the negotiating positions are defined by the outcome of a process of within-group bargaining, in which the preferences of different organizations and the perceptions by the incumbents of different roles are somehow combined and reconciled in order to reach national positions. Negotiators are thus viewed as operating in a highly constrained environment, in which the development of understanding and empathy at the interpersonal level is complicated by the perceived needs and interests of many agents who are not necessarily direct participants in the process itself.

Fifth, we may relax the assumption that we are dealing only with negotiations between two parties, so that third parties may participate as mediators or the negotiations may become genuinely multipolar. This adds an element of complexity to our model, since the range of bargaining is now defined by parameters set by a large number of parties, often with very different interests and perceptions. Lines of division, rather than falling just between two individuals, may now be crosscutting or overlapping in complex patterns. Conflicts among negotiators on some issues may be offset by common interests on other issues. The negotiations are less likely to be characterized by bargaining, and problem solving is more likely to be an effective technique for conflict resolution.

Sixth, and finally, we may drop the assumption that these negotiations are occurring in a vacuum and at least introduce some of the most important elements of the context. These elements would include, among other things, the history and the current state of the relationship among the parties to the negotiation, especially with regard to internation tensions or détente; the structure of the international system within which the negotiations are embedded; the structure of the domestic political system in each of the countries participating in these negotiations; and the degree of cultural similarity or difference among the parties.

After evaluating the impact of all six of these elements in a model, we may still find that we cannot fully account for the kinds of outcomes reached through the negotiation process. In this instance, it will be necessary to resort to an explanation based on the substantive context of the negotiations, including the idiosyncratic nature of the issues under negotiation. Some progress has been made in this area in work on "organized complexity" within negotiations (Winham, 1977, 1987). This is part of an expanded conceptualization that takes into account some of the more elusive aspects of the process. Nonetheless, we are still far from understanding, much less modeling effectively, some of these elements of complexity, and there are probably serious limits to our ability to incorporate all of these elements into a single model without destroying completely any trace of parsimony. In other words, a comprehensive model of regularities in the negotiation process will almost inevitably fall short of providing a complete explanation. Once we reach the limits of explanation that can be found in the kinds of regularities normally considered by behavioral scientists, the element of art must be introduced. Beyond the limits of science, the intuitive understanding of the diplomat can well contribute to a more complete rendering of the negotiation process.

Having looked at the major elements of a comprehensive model of the negotiation process, we may turn next to an analysis of what it is that we want such a model to explain, namely, the outcome of negotiations. In particular, we are interested in developing models that will help to explain the difference between successful and unsuccessful negotiation outcomes, by analyzing in each of the components of the model the factors that facilitate or impede the process of reaching negotiated agreements. For example, we have found that tactical manipulations of the bargaining process may sometimes facilitate agreement by helping to clarify the range of mutually acceptable bargaining space but, more often than not, they may impede agreement by creating appearances of stalemates, hard bargaining styles, and hostile patterns of interpersonal interaction. Each component of the model must be examined in a similar way to try to identify the elements in each set of variables that may exert a positive or negative impact on the negotiated outcomes. In the end, a theory of negotiation will be valuable insofar as it helps us to identify ways to improve the conflict resolution process through negotiation. In order to be policy relevant, such research must not only identify which factors in the process make a difference in outcomes, but it must also call our attention to the aspects of the process that can be manipulated through human actions. In this manner, we may identify policy-relevant "handles" with which to make more effective use of the negotiation process in achieving successful outcomes in negotiations such as those on arms control and disarmament.

Once we have achieved somewhat greater consensus about the nature of the outcomes to be explained, and when we have identified the key aspects of the process amenable to being modeled systematically, we will be in a better position to conduct research that will be cumulative. However, some common conceptual frameworks are not alone sufficient to produce greater cumulation; we will also need greater commonality in research methods. This can be facilitated both by the use of common measuring instruments and the conduct of more truly comparative case studies, where a common focus on similar explanatory variables is used in a wide variety of cases. Especially relevant here may be the methodology of "focused comparisons" utilized by George and Smoke (1974) to evaluate and compare decision making in deterrence situations. They argue for the necessity of making systematic comparisons across cases in terms of the same set of analytical questions in order to enhance generality without reducing the richness of each individual situation.

The content analysis methodology discussed several times previously and in the appendix to this chapter can be used to compare two or more cases. This may be illustrated by the comparison of Hopmann's (1974) data on the Seabeds Denuclearization Treaty with data from Druckman's (1986) analysis of the base-rights negotiations between the United States and Spain using the BPA coding system. An interesting finding was that there was harder posturing between the allies in the base-rights case than between the adversaries in the arms control negotiations. Another comparative effort may be illustrated by the U.S. Foreign Service Institute's exercises on "lessons learned" from past negotiations. Here diverse cases were juxtaposed to produce propositions about negotiating behavior that can be tested in other settings (Bendahmane and McDonald, 1986). Both of these efforts contribute to the refinement of methodology and to the goal of theory building by distinguishing clusters of similar and dissimilar cases.

In short, we believe that progress in the behavioral science treatment of negotiation is likely to emerge from two directions. One consists of more comparative work using similar methodologies in order to achieve greater cumulation to link the various islands of theory that currently characterize the field. Another is the need to develop even broader conceptualizations that span across and link current frameworks and that include more explicitly elements from theories of international relations and of policy formulation both within and between governments. While the agenda of research that needs to be done is long, the progress that has been made to date by a relatively small group of scholars, working too often with limited resources, is nonetheless quite impressive. With more resources commensurate with the seriousness of the issue under investigation, and with more communication and explicitly comparative work, we are confident that further progress can be made by the dedicated community of scholars cited in this chapter.

Finally, we turn to a consideration of the application of these theoretical developments to the practical problems of bringing the Soviet-U.S. arms race under control and of creating the foundations for a mutual security regime. The relevance of this literature, we believe, is both direct and frequently overlooked. First, we must recognize explicitly that arms control agreements and more basic security regimes do not emerge out of thin air—they must be negotiated, sometimes tacitly but more often formally. Second, we must recognize that the success of those negotiations depends not only on the configuration of national interests and the changing structure of international relations; it also depends intimately on the process of negotiation itself.

What, for example, made the INF Treaty possible in 1988 when all efforts to reach agreement failed in 1983? Many of the differences are to be found in the international context, including the changed military balance after NATO had begun to deploy its own intermediate-range missiles, and in domestic changes within the Soviet government after Mikhail Gorbachev became general secretary of the Communist Party as well as within the U.S. government. But we would also venture to suggest that some of the differences lay within the negotiation process itself. Talbott (1984) has documented some of the many conflicts within the Reagan administration and in NATO that made flexibility almost impossible in U.S. negotiating positions; furthermore, the United States seemed to believe at that time that the Soviets could be pressured through hard bargaining tactics to reach an agreement along the lines preferred by NATO. Such tactics generally backfired and created stalemates and hostility rather than the problem-solving atmosphere necessary for successful negotiations.

Conversely, a greater openness on the part of the Soviets during the Gorbachev era, combined with greater pragmatism in a more mature and moderate Reagan administration in its final years in office, all seemed to contribute to a more integrative and problem-solving approach to negotiations than had been evidenced in earlier years. Yet the substantive terms of the agreement could in principle have been reached in 1983, and it is possible that a more effective negotiating process could have produced an equally fair and beneficial agreement five years earlier. In other words, at its worst a poorly managed negotiation process may create a stalemate on issues where the parties in principle have common interests that could provide the basis for an agreement; and even in the best cases, the negotiation process could have perhaps produced more rapid and effective results had it been managed more effectively.

As we noted at the outset, the INF Treaty marks only a small additional step along John F. Kennedy's "one thousand mile journey." Many more negotiations will have to take place and many more agreements will have to be reached on multiple and complex issues before we can truly say that the nuclear arms race has been brought under control; progress in arms control will have to be accompanied by the resolution of numerous other conflicts and by the attainment of higher levels of interdependence in political and military relations before we can claim that a mutual security regime has been established between the United States and the Soviet Union. The success or failure of this endeavor, on which the survival of human civilization depends, may in turn be affected by whether we are able to manage the process of negotiating on nuclear arms control and mutual security effectively. In this light, the recent progress in behavioral science research on negotiations reported in this chapter is impressive, but it still leaves us far short of the goal that we so greatly need to attain. But we have, indeed, taken the first steps on our "thousand mile journey," and we must now push forward to improve our theory and to find new ways of applying it effectively to the effort to prevent nuclear war.

Appendix: Issues of Research Methodology

Many of the issues involved in the development of behavioral science approaches to international negotiations entail questions of research methodology. Research methodologies involve the procedures through which one tests hypotheses and gains confidence in the validity of the results of one's research. A cumulative "science" of international negotiation certainly requires the development of methodologies that can be applied to a wide variety of different cases or circumstances in the hope of drawing valid generalizations, as well as for determining the limits of generalization across cases. Furthermore, the application of different methodologies to the analysis of identical cases and hypotheses may be a means for reinforcing the confidence that the research community has in its findings. For example, to the extent that statistical analyses of cases and qualitative, in-depth case studies produce reinforcing results, the community of scholars has greater confidence in the validity of those findings.

Therefore, in this appendix we consider some methodological implications of our approach to the application of behavioral science research to international negotiations on questions of relevance to survival in the nuclear age. We begin by exploring some general methodological issues and trade-offs and then turn to an examination of content analysis techniques that have been employed by scholars seeking to advance the systematic study of international negotiations.

General Methodological Issues

MICRO- AND MACROLEVELS OF ANALYSIS

The distinction between micro- and macrolevels of analysis is an issue at the interdisciplinary juncture where political sociology or culture, social psychology, and strategic analysis intersect. Construed in terms of linkages, the issue is treated as reciprocal effects of behaviors at one level (for example, negotiating rhetoric) on structures at another (for example, power asymmetries). The research reviewed in the section on "Structural Factors" concentrates on one part of the relationship, namely, the impact of structures on negotiating behaviors. The results suggest that negotiating processes generally reflect structural factors such as cleavages within and between countries, relative power, and bloc cohesion. These findings support the conclusion drawn from small-group research that structures set the tone for unfolding patterns of behavior (see Galtung, 1968). They provide a framework for international transactions referred to also as "regularizing effects on behaviors" (Druckman, 1980) or as "structurally conditioned effects" (Weede, 1975). They may even further rigidify these structures, as Sharp (1976) illustrates in her analysis of the effects of the MBFR process on superpower arms control regimes.

Sharp's analysis concentrates on the other part of the relationship, the impact of negotiating processes on structures. This direction has received less attention due largely to difficulties both in assessing effects on structures and in isolating the negotiating process as a primary influence on structures. The literature does suggest, however, several hypothesized relationships for focusing the analysis. Along one line, Sharp (1976) argues that arms control talks are frequently dysfunctional; instead of directing attention to the larger context of security regimes, they tend to place the emphasis on military priorities at the expense of other dimensions of security. Along another line, Galtung (1968) and Chayes (1972) emphasize possibilities for change: for Galtung, the informal interactions among representatives provide a route to more creative negotiation of arms reduction; for Chayes, it is the creation of domestic bureaucracies in many countries that serves to institutionalize the new relationships forged in negotiations. These ideas merit closer examination in conjunction with a broader (recursive) model of micro-macro linkages.

A major methodological issue that has preoccupied us throughout much of the literature review in this chapter is the issue of bridging one aspect of the micro-macro gap, that is, how and to what extent data from experimental laboratories can be used to further our understanding of arms negotiations. This issue is usually discussed in terms of problems of generality, noting in particular the dimensions of difference between the laboratory and the real world of international relations (see Druckman, 1983). Arguments often turn on judgments of the importance of observed differences in terms of their impact on negotiating behavior (for example, Druckman, 1971). Rather than contribute further to this debate, however, we prefer to make the case for the usefulness of laboratory findings regardless of generality.

More important, perhaps, is the heuristic value of experimentation. Ideas generated initially in the laboratory are often applied to the analysis of case materials. Examples have already been presented on topics such as responsiveness, debate and role reversal, stresses, and structural factors. Here, the laboratory work generally precedes the case studies. The reverse sequence also has merit: relationships obtained in field studies can be subjected to more rigorous evaluation in a laboratory setting; the laboratory evidence might elucidate mechanisms not identified easily in situ. For example, Hopmann and Walcott (1977) conducted a simulation of the same negotiation problem under conditions of conflictual and cooperative international interactions in order to test hypotheses about the effects of such events on the Partial Nuclear Test Ban negotiations at the Eighteen Nation Disarmament Conference in Geneva.

Further, the laboratory can be construed as an adjunct to real-world analyses. For analysts outside government, it provides a setting for exploring processes that are largely inaccessible. For negotiators and their support staffs, it allows for the playful exploration of strategies in a "safe" environment. (These and other advantages of experimental work are discussed in Mahoney and Druckman [1975].) For these reasons, among others, the issue is not one of generality or analogy. We do not seek isomorphisms. Conversely, we do promote taking advantage of the different strengths of alternative methods that contribute to understanding—for the theorists as well as the practitioners.

STATIC AND DYNAMIC APPROACHES

Another important and general methodological issue in the analysis of negotiation is how the analyst handles the passage of time. Both static and dynamic conceptions of negotiation are represented in the literature surveyed in this chapter. The key distinguishing element is time: static conceptions discount variation within a case while dynamic models trace an unfolding process as it changes through time. General frameworks and descriptive analyses are examples of static approaches. Frameworks are useful devices for organizing research at an early stage of investigation; they also provide a basis for comparing cases at a later stage. Time-series analysis and causal modeling are examples of techniques employed within a dynamic approach. For example, these techniques enable investigators to address problems of reciprocal effects of internal negotiating processes and external influences. The approaches can be regarded as complementary, the one being used to refine concepts, the other to test their implications (see, for example, Bonham [1971]).

Much of the conceptual work on negotiation has consisted of identifying the various parts of the process. These are general dimensions that can be used to describe a large variety of cases. The primary contributions of this approach are those found in most taxonomic work, namely, to define a field, to distinguish between similarities and dissimilarities, and to identify connections or hypothesized relationships among the categories. (See Fleishman and Quaintance [1984] for a discussion of taxonomies in social science.) These functions have been served best by one particular framework proposed originally by Sawyer and Guetzkow (1965) to organize empirical work done in the 1950s and 1960s.[3]

Sawyer and Guetzkow's basic structure, which relates preconditions to processes, conditions, and outcomes, has guided both basic research and applications, including Ramberg's (1977) study of tactics used in the Seabeds arms control talks, Bonham's (1971) analysis of factors influencing the 1955 East-West talks in the U.N. Disarmament Subcommittee, Druckman and Hopmann's (1978) models of the MBFR process, and Druckman's (1973, 1977a) attempts to organize the large social-psychological literature on bargaining. However, there are shortcomings. By itself, an organizing framework lacks sufficient penetration of details to capture subtle processes in particular cases; it is also primarily a descriptive, not explanatory, exercise. These disadvantages are compensated in part by an approach that focuses on negotiating dynamics.

Like many fields in social science, the study of negotiations has evolved toward a more dynamic conception of the phenomenon. Both Cross (1983) and Zartman (1986), for example, depict negotiation as a learning process where alternatives are gradually eliminated and solutions emerge through both successful and unsuccessful encounters. Central to this process are adjustments made in reaction to new information. These adjustments may become turning points that define junctures of a ripening process leading to either agreements or impasses; they may be alternating currents as between periods of intense or moderate conflict. Hopmann's (1972) "decaying lag" models of the reciprocal effects of internal and external factors are one attempt to capture these processes in arms control negotiations. He found that the degree to which negotiators were acting responsively toward one another could best be captured by a time-series approach that gives greatest weight to contemporaneous events, and that treats the impact of previous periods as being successively less important as one moves farther into the past. Related applications include the use of stochastic models in international relations and social psychology. (See Duncan and Job's [1980] use of Markov-chains analysis for analyzing transitions in cooperative interstate interactions, and Apfelbaum's [1974] work on probabilistic models of bargaining.) Also relevant are concepts that derive from a more qualitative tradition. Particularly notable is Schein's (1985) work on the development and change of organizational cultures, a process that appears to be similar to the unfolding interactions among representatives in long-term negotiating forums.

Content Analysis in Negotiation Research

Two themes have emerged in this chapter: one theme, organized complexity, has served as a guide for many of the frameworks that have been developed to study negotiations. Negotiating in the international context consists of many parts that need to be organized for coherence. Another theme emerges from theoretical developments: how context affects the process of bargaining and how that process in turn may facilitate or impede the attainment of agreement in negotiations. Process and context are intertwined, the one having an impact on the other in a reciprocal manner. Both affect the outcomes of international negotiations. These themes were evident in most of the detailed research and applications reviewed in this chapter. Much of this research is based on a particular methodology, content analysis, which more than any other technique has played an important role in the development of the systematic study of international negotiations.

Content analysis has been defined succinctly by Holsti (1969:14) as "any technique for making inferences by objectively and systematically identifying specified characteristics of messages." It is thus a technique that can be applied to any verbal communications, written or oral, and that enables the analyst to make systematic comparisons of the content of communications across a wide variety of contexts. The technique is suited to the kinds of documentation found in negotiation records and has been used in a variety of case studies. Most of the applications to date have consisted of providing data for time-series analyses of discussions within negotiations. One result of these applications has been the development of more sophisticated versions of earlier systems. One version in particular, referred to as bargaining process analysis (BPA), merits special attention due to its frequency of use and to its theoretical heritage. This system can be understood best by placing it in the context of general conceptual and technical issues.

Like any measurement technique, content analysis derives its meaning from a research design. The technique is one part of a design that "ensures that theory, data gathering, analysis, and interpretation are integrated" (Holsti, 1969:27). The distinction between description and inference summarizes the variety of designs for which content analysis is used: those that address the questions, What?, Who?, and To whom? versus those studies designed to address, Why?, How?, and With what effect? Inferential studies illustrate some of the more creative uses of the technique. For example, inferences about negotiating "intentions" can be drawn from assessments of several types of statements, especially those that indicate the relative importance that a negotiator assigns to particular issues or approaches. Relationships between communications made within the negotiation and underlying intentions may sometimes be corroborated by statements made by the negotiators in other settings, such as interviews. The negotiation messages are used to assess independent variables (statements by negotiator A at time 1) and dependent variables (statements made by negotiator B at time 2), while the outside statements by A and B are used to infer intentions (explanations for observed negotiating behavior). The same design could also be used to assess outside actions in order to bolster the validity of the interpretations. (See Holsti [1969] for a detailed discussion of illustrative research designs used for descriptive and inferential purposes.)

The largest problem for content analysis, as for all social science techniques, is the validity of the inferences. The issue can be understood in terms of trade-offs between accuracy (reliability) and meaning (validity). Attempts to maximize agreement between coders in order to enhance reliability, as in mechanical coding, may result in a distortion of the concept being assessed, thereby detracting from validity. The difference between the meaning of concessions in laboratory and field settings provides an example. A concession in a bargaining experiment is usually defined simply as the difference in offers made at time t and at $t + 1$. In this case coding of concessions is mechanical. A concession made in an international negotiation, on the other hand, is more difficult to identify. It must be inferred from suggestions, exploratory proposals, and packages that combine several offers. Coding is an interpretive exercise done with a system designed to capture these elements as they appear in negotiating rhetoric. The room for interpretation afforded by such a system is likely to reduce intercoder agreement while possibly enhancing validity. The extent to which it enhances validity depends, however, on the adequacy of the coding categories and on the sampling of appropriate materials.

The technical aspects of content analysis include coding categories, recording units, and a sampling design. Aided by general guidelines (see Holsti, 1969:95), the analyst must rely largely on his or her understanding of the theory or problem that inspired the investigation. As indicators of concepts, the categories should reflect the various dimensions of the phenomenon under investigation. As variables to be manipulated, the categories should guide coders to produce reliable judgments. Good systems of coding categories should meet both these criteria. Attempting to meet them, however, reveals a source of tension in the use of the methodology.

Responding to the criterion of validity, analysts have frequently opted for original systems designed to capture the essence of the phenomenon. A focus on the criterion of reliability has led analysts to promote standard categories that can be used repeatedly. Typically, the former requirement is favored more than the latter. A premium on originality, a reluctance to adopt others' categories, and the atheoretical basis of general schemas are reasons cited for the infrequent usage of standard categories. More basic, however, is the realization that categories may not be independent of the data at hand. Since few different applications deal precisely with the same content attributes, diverse category systems are the result. Some of this diversity is found in the area of negotiation research.

Other decisions include "What will be coded?" and "How will it be counted?" Answers to these questions are based also on an understanding of negotiating rhetoric and process as well as considerations of research costs. Diplomatic communication may best be analyzed in terms of themes, taking context and intensity of expression into account. The location of a theme within a text, and the adjectives used to describe it, may be quite important. A system for measuring these aspects of diplomatic communications may be found in the Stanford General Inquirer program for political analysis (see Holsti, 1969:Chap. 7), which attempts to identify the underlying dimensions of communications along the three dimensions of Osgood, Suci, and Tannenbaum's (1957) "semantic differential": (1) evaluative (positive to negative); (2) potency (strong to weak); (3) activity (active to passive). Hopmann and King (1976) used a computerized version of this schema to evaluate the attitudes expressed among the three nuclear powers in the Partial Nuclear Test Ban negotiations.

Two problems may arise with regard to the application of computerized content analysis systems such as the Stanford General Inquirer. First is the problem of sampling. The length of most arms control negotiations prohibits coding of the entire proceedings. Of particular concern, then, is the question whether the uncoded data differ qualitatively from that which has been coded. Thus, sampling procedures must be adopted for the selection of material to be coded. This question addresses the problem of bias that, if systematic, is a serious consequence of limited information. In fact, loss of information occurs both with respect to the thematic unit and the sample of material chosen. These decisions have implications for the validity of inferences drawn from the analysis. Case interpretations are, by necessity, tentative, although sophisticated scaling and sampling design technologies provide tools for estimating the likely consequences of information loss.

A second problem is that of the generality of the system. Programs such as the Stanford General Inquirer provide categories that can be applied in a wide variety of political contexts, international and domestic. The results of such analyses are often presented at a high level of generality. On the other hand, the considerations just outlined suggest that a particular kind of content analysis system may be especially appropriate for the analysis of international negotiations. It should be a flexible system that captures key dimensions of the phenomenon, to wit, negotiation, while permitting adaptations on a case-by-case basis. Adaptations might include improving the sensitivity of the categories to varying types of material, units of analysis, aggregations, and research questions. Such sensitivity is found most often in a continually evolving system tested by diverse applications in the substantive domain of interest. Such a system is provided by BPA.

BARGAINING PROCESS ANALYSIS

As already noted, current conceptualizations of international negotiations support the use of content (or process) analysis. Negotiations are depicted as a process of interactions among a small group of negotiators where debate is the central activity (see Druckman, 1983, 1986). Settlements sometimes emerge from the ongoing verbal exchanges—a process referred to as accumulating a settlement from the bottom up, or "building a package" (Winham, 1977). In other cases, the process influences the form and substance of formulas that frame the settlement. In both cases content analysis can document the stream of interactions that move toward (or away from) agreement. Capturing this ebb and flow, however, entails the development of coding categories that are sufficiently rich to represent some of the subtleties of the bargaining process.

Most extant systems for coding bargaining-type interactions can be traced to Bales' (1950) popular interaction process analysis (IPA). An early application of IPA to labor-management disputes demonstrated its relevance to bargaining (Landsberger, 1955). Recognizing the distinction between problem solving, as reflected in IPA, and bargaining, McGrath and Julian (1963) devised a new system that incorporated the interpersonal influences and affect dimensions characteristic of negotiation, that is, mixed-motive conflict. Other variants on these themes have included Zechmeister and Druckman's (1973) codes for the debating aspects of negotiation, Pruitt and Lewis' (1977) codes for integrative bargaining, and the Stephensen, Kniveton, and Morley (1977), system which recognizes the distinctions among kinds of statements (offer, accept, reject, seek), activities (structuring, outcome), and referents (self, person, party) as well as the connections among them. Particularly relevant to international negotiations are the distinctions made between content and style and between substance and strategy. These dimensions are represented in the adaptations developed for coding verbatim transcripts of arms control talks.

The categories vary from recording what is actually said (the topic discussed) to what may be inferred from a statement (underlying intention or strategy). Druckman and Hopmann (1978) coded the topics discussed in three years of the MBFR talks according to eight categories: manpower reductions, arms reductions, counting rules/data, participation, argumentation, associated measures, procedures, and other. Jensen (1984) charted concessions from changes in proposals made in SALT I and II (1969–1979); magnitude of change was inferred from movements toward (concession) or away (retraction) from the other's proposals. Bonham (1971) coded the earlier U.N. Disarmament Subcommittee talks (1955) for insecurity, propaganda, and hostility. Both content and style are represented by these categories: insecurity about the stability of disarmament is determined more or less directly from the actual statement (for example, fears of scientific breakthroughs, or fears of evasion of the agreement), while hostility is the affect inferred from statements such as, "Your note is a direct affront to the Soviet people." Walcott and Hopmann's (1978) BPA combines elements from most of the earlier approaches, although style is emphasized more than substance. When combined with the Druckman and Hopmann topic codes mentioned earlier (which could be varied as appropriate according to the substantive issue under negotiation), BPA provides an elaborate menu of options for coding diverse materials. It is the basis for our discussion of inferential problems in the remainder of this section of the appendix.

Bargaining process analysis has evolved from an earlier version, applied by Hopmann and his colleagues to simulation data, to a later version used to code complex multilateral conferences. The early versions consisted of 13 categories within 5 classes: substantive behavior (initiatives, accommodations, and retractions), strategic behavior (commitments, threats, and promises), task-oriented behavior (agreements, disagreements, questions, and answers), affective behavior (positive and negative), and procedural statements. The revised version of 33 categories expands the system into areas of persuasive behavior, procedural behavior, and a number of additions made within each of the original classes. Among the system's advantages are its theoretical heritage and analytical flexibility. The several theoretical traditions include work on strategic bargaining (Schelling, 1960), small-group interactions (Bales, 1950), the process of debate (Rapoport, 1960), theories of influence (Singer, 1963; Tedeschi, 1970), and integrative bargaining (Walton and McKersie, 1965). These traditions endow the categories with general meaning, permitting them to be used broadly in many negotiating arenas as well as for comparative studies. The large number of categories increases options for coding and analysis. Categories may be aggregated or disaggregated, as when substantive and strategic categories are combined to create indices of soft or hard bargaining behavior. The coverage also enables an analyst to capture a variety of meanings conveyed in the discussions. One distinction of interest is between the temporary, tactical aspects of bargaining and the sincere, actual components. Another is between substantive and affective behavior.

The same features may also be regarded as disadvantages. The large number of categories places a burden on the coder. He or she is required to make many fine distinctions among partially overlapping categories: for example, between threats and demands, between threats and/or commitments on the one hand and negative affect on the other, and among substantive disagreements/agreements, perceptions of dissimilarity/ similarity, and procedural disagreements/agreements. The larger number of categories may lead to a reduced intercoder agreement in assignment of categories. Thus, the shorter BPA version I generally produced higher intercoder reliabilities than did the longer BPA version II. The system's roots in theory renders it somewhat abstract, removed from the content of discussions. As a result, category assignment depends on inferences that must often be made on the basis of several statements: for example, the strategic categories (threats, promises, commitments, demands) may be understood best in the context of arguments that develop over a sequence of exchanges; the coder must be familiar with the entire history of a negotiation to code such behaviors accurately. Similarly, the affect categories may depend on access to spoken statements for tone, loudness, pitch, and so on; such judgments are difficult to make on the basis of written transcripts. Some of these problems may be remedied in part by adding categories to the system, for example, topic codes such as those developed by Druckman and Hopmann or nonverbal codes for video materials. However, the addition of more categories is likely to reduce reliability further, making the system even more cumbersome for tasks such as on-the-spot coding of live negotiations.

Bargaining process analysis illustrates a central dilemma for the content analyst, referred to earlier as a trade-off between reliability and validity. This is the difference between a few well-defined categories for enhancing intercoder agreement and many complex categories for capturing intentions and subtle meaning. While it may be that the analyst cannot have it both ways, he or she can make certain adjustments that would reduce the dilemma. These include developing a mix of content and style codes, extensive pretesting of categories against a variety of materials, and carefully prepared training regimens for coders. But even these precautions would not satisfy opponents of this approach to the analysis of negotiation. Their arguments often address problems associated with the statistical analysis of diplomatic behavior in general.

A number of arguments have been made against the use of content analysis. Four of them emphasize the limited purview of the process afforded by the method: for example, (1) the codes miss nuances and innuendoes that are the essence of negotiation; (2) the content analyst focuses exclusively on rhetoric, missing other aspects of the process including its structural and substantive complexity; (3) the coding process must necessarily be restricted to formal negotiations so that private meetings away from the negotiation site that may be crucial to the outcome may not be coded at all; and (4) the approach isolates a negotiation from its broader diplomatic or international political context.

While acknowledging these limitations, we would claim that they do not preclude the use of content analysis. They suggest a broader conceptualization of negotiation that includes the detailed study of interactions at several levels. Content analysis plays a role in a more encompassing study that examines both context and process. As noted earlier, categories can be developed for capturing the more subtle aspects of communication. The "broader context" can be regarded as influences on various aspects of the negotiating process, including trends in rhetoric. Such linkages are at the heart of a context-relevant approach to negotiation research. Obviously, when content analysis studies can be validated by other techniques, such as interviews with participants who may have been involved in private communications and other aspects of the process not reflected in the written record, the results of such studies may be accepted with greater confidence. Content analysis, like all methodologies, when used to the exclusion of other sources of information may produce distorted results. But when used as one method among many to obtain different and systematic insights into the process that cannot be readily obtained through other existing methods, it may help identify important aspects of the negotiation process.

Other critics dismiss content analysis either because it produces trivial results or because it distorts the phenomenon under investigation. Some claim that conclusions drawn from the analysis are often not surprising. Indeed, we may agree—but only after an appraisal of findings taken one at a time and independent of events that transpired since the research was undertaken. Sometimes observers tend to evince a "hindsight" bias, claiming to have known certain things all along, even though the evidence provides greater confidence in the findings than those that could be derived from intuitive observations alone. On the other hand, some "obvious" findings may be desirable as "proof" for the face validity of the approach. Nonobvious findings have been treated by the critics as evidence of errors introduced by the method. Another claim is that detailed coding results in lost meaning due to "atomizing" the content. In their search for broad themes, these critics overlook the fact that the methodology does not preclude the emergence of contextual meanings. The issue concerns the way that the technique is used. The unit of analysis could be a word or sentence, on the one hand, or a large chunk of text, on the other. What is of greatest interest to the researcher is the developing sequence of action within the negotiation process over some period of time that can be identified through this kind of textual analysis.

It may often be the case that conclusions that analysts had intuitively assumed to be *obvious* turn out not to be so, or even to be inaccurate when subjected to systematic scrutiny. Thus, content analysis may force us to challenge some of our truisms and assumptions about negotiations. Whether the intuitive claims of the traditional expert are valid, or whether the findings produced by techniques such as content analysis are more accurate, cannot be determined definitively. However, discrepancies between the two should at least encourage theorists and practitioners of negotiations to question many of the assumptions that they have traditionally taken for granted. This alone may be valuable, even if further research fails to substantiate the conclusions suggested through studies using content analysis. In short, research involves a process of gaining confidence in certain general findings. Discrepant findings should cause the theorist to raise new questions and to design new tests of the hypotheses, whereas confirmation of previous hunches should be viewed as part of the process of building confidence.

Many practitioners and diplomats argue that negotiation is an art, not a replicable phenomenon that can be depicted in terms of general categories. We do not reject this argument entirely. We contend that details of context (uniqueness) and general aspects of negotiation (theory) can be woven together in analysis. Indeed, such weaving is the defining feature of a context-relevant approach, serving both theory and practice. Similar themes are evident in Raiffa's (1982) treatment entitled *The Art and Science of Negotiation*. They are also a basis for our treatment in the section on "Two Cultures: Theory and Practice," where analysis is shown to contribute to, and improve, the art of negotiating.

Models derived from methodologies such as content analysis, and analyzed with statistical procedures, will probably never be able to explain most of the variance in negotiating processes or outcomes. Thus, some room will always be left for the creative negotiator to respond to the unique features of every negotiating situation. Yet it would be tragic if negotiators had to treat each and every negotiation as if it were an entirely new endeavor, with no lessons from the past to draw on. Systematic theories of negotiation, tested through research methodologies such as those just outlined, should enable us to improve substantially the knowledge base on which negotiators may function. With this understanding of the general aspects of negotiations, the individual negotiator may then apply his or her inventiveness and creativity to fashion the kinds of agreements that may be necessary if human civilization is to avoid the threat of nuclear catastrophe.

Notes

1. Laurance (1979) takes issue with this view. Using Zartman's (1978) formula-detail conceptualization, he claims that the CAT talks are an example of an arms control negotiation. Two defining features were satisfied: the parties' expectations were perceived to be within range of each other, and they agreed on a framework of legal and military criteria, regional applications, and a consultative mechanism. While these are considered by Zartman as critical turning points that precede bargaining, it is not certain whether they should be construed as prenegotiation or negotiation activities. Clearly they are part of the necessary preparation for detailed bargaining, although Laurance's analysis is limited only to the superpower deliberations.

2. One major feature of this project was to call attention to the advantages of computerized retrieval systems for negotiators. It came at the beginning of an era of technological breakthroughs in the area of computer aids, especially in the storage and retrieval of the sorts of information generated by note takers on national delegations. However, the analytical accomplishments of this project had less impact. This difference of impact between routine processing, on the one hand, and analysis, on the other, may be another example of the two cultures' problem.

3. A similar framework was proposed by Randolph (1966). Her categories are organized under four headings: prenegotiation, negotiation, agreement, and implementation phases. While capturing most of the elements discussed in the negotiation literature to that date, this framework has not received the attention given to the Sawyer and Guetzkow construction.

References

Adelman, K.L. 1984. Arms control with and without treaties. *Foreign Affairs* 62:240–263.

Alger, C.F. 1963. United Nations participation as a learning experience. *Public Opinion Quarterly* 27:411–426.

Apfelbaum, E. 1974. On conflicts and bargaining. In L. Berkowitz, ed., *Advances in Experimental Social Psychology*, Vol. 7. New York: Academic Press.

Axelrod, R. 1984. *The Evolution of Cooperation*. New York: Basic Books.

Bales, R.F. 1950. *Interaction Process Analysis: A Method for the Study of Small Groups*. Cambridge, Mass.: Addison-Wesley.

Barclay, S., and C.R. Peterson. 1976. Multi-attribute utility models for negotiations. McLean, Va.: Decisions and Designs, Inc., Technical Report 76–1.

Bartos, O.J. 1974. *Process and Outcome of Negotiations*. New York: Columbia University Press.

Bass, B.M. 1966. Effects on subsequent performance of negotiators of studying issues or planning strategies alone or in groups. *Psychological Monographs*, Whole no. 614.

Bazerman, M.H. 1986. Why negotiations go wrong. *Psychology Today*, June, 54–58.

Beer, F.A. 1986. Games and metaphors. *Journal of Conflict Resolution* 30:171–191.

Bendahmane, D.B., and J.W. McDonald, eds. 1986. *Perspectives on Negotiation: Four Case Studies and Interpretations*. Washington, D.C.: Foreign Service Institute, U.S. Department of State.

Bixenstine, V.E., and J.W. Gaebelein. 1971. Strategies of "real" opponents in eliciting cooperative choice in a prisoner's dilemma game. *Journal of Conflict Resolution* 15:157–166.

Blacker, C.D., and G. Duffy. 1984. *International Arms Control: Issues and Agreements*. Stanford, Calif.: Stanford University Press.

Bonham, G.M. 1971. Simulating international disarmament negotiations. *Journal of Conflict Resolution* 15:299–315.

Brams, S.J. 1985. *Superpower Games*. Princeton, N.J.: Princeton University Press.

Brams, S.J., and M.P. Hessel. 1984. Threat power in sequential games. *International Studies Quarterly* 28:23–44.

Caldwell, D. 1978. International systems, arms control negotiations, and regimes. Paper presented at the International Studies Association, Washington, D.C.

Chayes, A. 1972. An inquiry into the workings of arms-control agreements. *Harvard Law Review* 85:905–969.

Claude, I.L., Jr. 1963. *Swords Into Plowshares: The Problems and Progress of International Organization*. New York: Random House.

Coddington, A. 1968. *Theories of the Bargaining Process*. Chicago: Aldine.

Coffey, J.I. 1985. *Deterrence and Arms Control: American and West German Perspectives on INF*. Monograph Series in World Affairs, Volume 21, Book 4. Denver, Col.: University of Denver Press.

Corson, W.H. 1970. *Measuring Conflict and Cooperation Intensity in East-West Relations: A Manual and Codebook*. Ann Arbor, Mich.: University of Michigan, Institute for Social Research.

Cross, J. 1983. *A Theory of Adaptive Economic Behavior*. Cambridge, England: Cambridge University Press.

Dean, J. 1986. MBFR: From apathy to accord. *International Security* 7:116–139.

———. 1987. *Watershed in Europe*. Boston: Lexington.
Deutsch, K. 1968. *The Analysis of International Relations*. Englewood Cliffs, N.J.: Prentice-Hall.
Deutsch, M. 1973. *The Resolution of Conflict: Constructive and Destructive Processes*. New Haven, Conn.: Yale University Press.
———. 1985. *Distributive Justice: A Social-Psychological Perspective*. New Haven, Conn.: Yale University Press.
Druckman, D. 1968. Prenegotiation experience and dyadic conflict resolution in a bargaining situation. *Journal of Experimental Social Psychology* 4:367–383.
———. 1971. The influence of the situation in inter-party conflict. *Journal of Conflict Resolution* 15:523–554.
———. 1973. *Human Factors in International Negotiations: Social-Psychological Aspects of International Conflict*. Sage Professional Paper in International Studies 02–020. Beverly Hills, Calif.: Sage.
———. 1977a. *Negotiations: Social-Psychological Perspectives*. Beverly Hills, Calif.: Sage.
———. 1977b. The person, role, and situation in international negotiations. In M.G. Hermann, ed., *A Psychological Examination of Political Leaders*. New York: Free Press.
———. 1978a. Boundary role conflict: Negotiation as dual responsiveness. In I.W. Zartman, ed., *The Negotiation Process*. Beverly Hills, Calif.: Sage.
———. 1978b. The monitoring function in negotiation: Two models of responsiveness. In H. Sauermann, ed., *Contributions to Experimental Economics: Bargaining Behavior*. Tubingen, West Germany: J.C.B. Mohr (Paul Siebeck).
———. 1980. Social-psychological factors in regional politics. In W.J. Feld and G. Boyd, eds., *Comparative Regional Systems*. New York: Pergamon.
———. 1983. Social psychology and international negotiations: Processes and influences. In R.F. Kidd and M.J. Saks, eds., *Advances in Applied Social Psychology*, Vol. 2. Hillsdale, N.J.: Erlbaum.
———. 1985. Analysis and strategic planning. In S.J. Andriole, ed., *Corporate Crisis Management*. Princeton, N.J.: Petrocelli Books.
———. 1986. Stages, turning points, and crises: Negotiating military base rights, Spain and the United States. *Journal of Conflict Resolution* 30:327–360.
———. 1988. Base-rights negotiations: Lessons learned. In J.W. McDonald and D.B. Bendahmane, eds., *U.S. Base-Rights Negotiations: Three Case Studies and Lessons Learned*. Washington, D.C.: Foreign Service Institute, U.S. Department of State..
Druckman, D., A.A. Benton, F. Ali, and J.S. Bagur. 1976. Cultural differences in bargaining behavior: India, Argentina, and the United States. *Journal of Conflict Resolution* 20:413–452.
Druckman, D., and T. Bonoma. 1976. Determinants of bargaining behavior in a bilateral monopoly situation II: Opponent's concession rate and similarity. *Behavioral Science* 21:252–262.
Druckman, D., and P.T. Hopmann. 1978. Negotiation assessment model II: Mutual

and balanced force reductions. Bethesda, Md.: Mathtech, Inc., Analytic Support Center, Report M-12.

Druckman, D., and L. Iaquinta. 1974. Toward bridging the international negotiation/mediation gap. *International Studies Notes* 1(4):6–14.

Druckman, D., and R. Mahoney. 1977. Processes and consequences of international negotiations. *Journal of Social Issues* 33:60–87.

Druckman, D., R. Rozelle, and K. Zechmeister. 1977. Conflict of interest and value dissensus: Two perspectives. In D. Druckman, ed., *Negotiations: Social-Psychological Perspectives*. Beverly Hills, Calif.: Sage.

Druckman, D., and R. Slater. 1979. External events and arms-control negotiating behavior. Bethesda, Md.: Mathtech, Inc., Analytic Support Center, Report P-14.

Druckman, D., and K. Zechmeister. 1973. Conflict of interest and values dissensus: Propositions in the sociology of conflict. *Human Relations* 26:449–466.

Duncan, G.T., and B.L. Job. 1980. Probability forcasting in international affairs. Final Report to the Defense Advanced Research Projects Agency.

Evan, W.M., and J.A. MacDougall. 1967. Interorganizational conflict: A labor-management bargaining experiment. *Journal of Conflict Resolution* 11:398–413.

Felsenthal, D.S., and A. Diskin. 1982. The bargaining problem revisited: Minimum utility point, restricted monotonicity axiom, and the mean as an estimate of expected utility. *Journal of Conflict Resolution* 26:664–691.

Fischer, G. 1971. *The Non-Proliferation of Nuclear Weapons*. Trans. by David Willey. New York: St. Martin's Press.

Fisher, R. 1981. Playing the wrong game? In J.Z. Rubin, ed., *Dynamics of Third Party Intervention: Kissinger in the Middle East*. New York: Praeger.

———. 1987. What is a "good" U.S.-Soviet relationship—and how do we build one? *Negotiation Journal* 3:319–328.

Fisher, R., and W. Ury. 1981. *Getting to Yes: Negotiating Agreement Without Giving In*. Boston: Houghton Mifflin.

Fleishman, E.A., and M.K. Quaintance. 1984. *Taxonomies of Human Performance: The Description of Human Tasks*. Orlando, Fla.: Academic Press.

Galtung, J. 1968. Small group theory and the theory of international relations: A study in isomorphism. In M.A. Kaplan, ed., *New Approaches to International Relations*. New York: St. Martin's Press.

Garthoff, R.L. 1977. Negotiating with the Russians: Some lessons from SALT. *International Security* 1:3–24.

George, A.L., and R. Smoke. 1974. *Deterrence in American Foreign Policy: Theory and Practice*. New York: Columbia University Press.

Guetzkow, H. 1957. Isolation and collaboration: A political theory of inter-nation relations. *Journal of Conflict Resolution* 1:48–68.

Haas, E. 1980. Why collaborate? Issue-linkages and international regimes. *World Politics* 32:357–405.

Hammer, A.L. 1983. Matching perceptual predicates: Effects on perceived empathy in a counseling analogue. *Journal of Counseling Psychology* 30:172–179.

Hammond, K.R., T.R. Stewart, L. Adelman, and N. Wascoe. 1975. Report to the

Denver City Council and Mayor regarding the choice of handgun ammunition for the Denver Police Department. Boulder, Col.: University of Colorado, Program of Research on Judgment and Social Interaction, Report No. 179.

Hammond, K.R., F.J. Todd, M. Wilkins, and T.O. Mitchell. 1966. Cognitive conflict between persons: Application of the "lens-model" paradigm. *Journal of Experimental Social Psychology* 2:343–360.

Haskel, B.G. 1974. Disparities, strategies, and opportunity costs: The example of Scandinavian economic market negotiations. *International Studies Quarterly* 18:3–30.

Herz, J. 1950. Idealist internationalism and the security dilemma. *World Politics* 2:157–180.

Hilsman, R. 1967. *To Move A Nation*. New York: Dell.

Holsti, O.R. 1969. *Content Analysis for the Social Sciences and Humanities*. Reading, Mass.: Addison-Wesley.

Hopmann, P.T. 1972. Internal and external influences on bargaining in arms control negotiations: The partial test ban. In B.M. Russett, ed., *Peace, War, and Numbers*. Beverly Hills, Calif.: Sage.

———. 1974. Bargaining in arms control negotiations: The seabeds denuclearization treaty. *International Organization* 28:313–343.

———. 1977. Bargaining within and between alliances on MBFR: perceptions and interactions. Paper presented at the International Studies Association, St. Louis, Mo.

———. 1978. Asymmetrical bargaining in the conference on security and cooperation in Europe. *International Organization* 32:141–177.

———. 1979. Detente and security in Europe: The Vienna force reduction negotiations. Paper presented at the 11th World Congress of the International Political Science Association, Moscow, USSR.

———. 1987. 'I cut—you choose': An approach to strategic arms reductions. Brown University, Center for Foreign Policy Development. Mimeo.

———. Forthcoming. *Resolving International Conflicts: The Negotiation Process*. Columbia, S.C.: University of South Carolina Press.

Hopmann, P.T., and D. Druckman. 1981. Henry Kissinger as strategist and tactician in the Middle East negotiations. In J.Z. Rubin, ed., *Dynamics of Third Party Intervention*. New York: Praeger.

Hopmann, P.T., and T.D. King. 1976. Interactions and perceptions in the test ban negotiations. *International Studies Quarterly* 20:105–142.

———. 1980. From cold war to detente: The role of the Cuban missile crisis and the partial nuclear test ban treaty. In A.L. George, O.R. Holsti, and R.M. Siverson, eds., *Change in the International System*. Boulder, Col.: Westview.

Hopmann, P.T., and T.C. Smith. 1978. An application of a Richardson process model: Soviet-American interactions in the test ban negotiations, 1962–1963. In I.W. Zartman, ed., *The Negotiation Process*. Beverly Hills, Calif.: Sage.

Hopmann, P.T., and C. Walcott. 1977. The impact of external stresses and tensions on negotiations. In D. Druckman, ed., *Negotiations: Social-Psychological Perspectives*. Beverly Hills, Calif.: Sage.

Hough, J.F. 1985. Soviet interpretation and response. In *Arms Control and the Strate-*

gic Defense Initiative: Three Perspectives, pp. 5–13. Occasional Paper 36. Muscatine, Iowa: Stanley Foundation.

Husbands, J.L. 1979. The conventional arms transfer talks: Negotiation as proseletization. Paper presented at the American Political Science Association, Washington, D.C.

Iklé, F.C. 1964. *How Nations Negotiate*. New York: Harper & Row.

Iklé, F.C., and N. Leites. 1962. Political negotiation as a process of modifying utilities. *Journal of Conflict Resolution* 6:19–28.

Jacobson, H., and E. Stein. 1966. *Diplomats, Scientists, and Politicians: The United States and the Nuclear Test Ban Negotiations*. Ann Arbor, Mich.: University of Michigan Press.

Jensen, L. 1963. Soviet-American bargaining behavior in the post-war disarmament negotiations. *Journal of Conflict Resolution* 9:522–541.

———. 1968. Approach-avoidance bargaining in the test-ban negotiations. *International Studies Quarterly* 12:152–160.

———. 1976. Soviet-American behavior in disarmament negotiations. In I.W. Zartman, ed., *The 50% Solution*. New York: Anchor Books.

———. 1979. Bargaining strategies and strategic arms limitations. Paper presented at the American Political Science Association, Washington, D.C.

———. 1984. Negotiating strategic arms control, 1969–1979. *Journal of Conflict Resolution* 28:535–559.

———. 1988. *Bargaining for National Security: The Postwar Disarmament Negotiations*. Columbia, S.C.: University of South Carolina Press.

Jervis, R. 1983. Security regimes. In S.D. Krasner, ed., *International Regimes*. Ithaca, N.Y.: Cornell University Press.

Johnson, D.W. 1967. The use of role reversal in intergroup competition. *Journal of Personality and Social Psychology* 7:135–142.

———. 1971. Role reversal: A summary and review of the research. *International Journal of Group Tensions* 1:318–334.

Johnson, D.W., and R. Dustin. 1970. The initiation of cooperation through role reversal. *Journal of Social Psychology* 82:193–203.

Jonsson, C. 1979. *Soviet Bargaining Behavior: The Nuclear Test Ban Case*. New York: Columbia University Press.

Kalai, E., and M. Smorodinsky. 1975. Other solutions to Nash's bargaining problem. *Econometrica* 43:513–518.

Kelleher, C. 1976. Predilections in negotiations. Unpublished manuscript, University of Maryland, College Park.

Kelman, H.C. 1982. Creating the conditions for Israeli-Palestinian negotiations. *Journal of Conflict Resolution* 26:39–75.

Kennedy, J.F. 1963. Radio-television address by President Kennedy, July 26, 1963. In *Documents on Disarmament 1963*. Washington, D.C.: U.S. Arms Control and Disarmament Agency.

Keohane, R.O., and J.S. Nye. 1977. *Power and Interdependence: World Politics in Transition*. Boston: Little, Brown.

King, T.D. 1976. Role reversal debates in international negotiations: The partial test

ban case. Paper presented at the International Studies Association, Toronto.
——. 1979. Bargaining in the United Nations Special Session on Disarmament. Paper presented at the American Political Science Association, Washington, D.C.
Komorita, S.S., and J. Mechling. 1967. Betrayal and reconciliation in a two-person game. *Journal of Personality and Social Psychology* 6:349–353.
Krepon, M. 1984. *Strategic Stalemate: Nuclear Weapons and Arms Control in American Politics.* New York: St. Martin's Press.
Kuhlman, D.M., and A. Marshello. 1975. Individual differences in game motivation as moderators of preprogrammed strategy effects in prisoner's dilemma. *Journal of Personality and Social Psychology* 32:922–931.
Lall, A. 1966. *Modern International Negotiation: Principles and Practice.* New York: Columbia University Press.
Lamkin, F.M., and S.O Fought. 1988. Teaching about arms control. *Naval War College Review* 41:94–104
Landsberger, H.A. 1955. Interaction process analysis of the mediation of labor-management disputes. *Journal of Abnormal and Social Psychology* 51:552–559.
Laurance, E.J. 1979. Negotiating conventional arms transfer restraint. Unpublished manuscript, Naval Postgraduate School, Monterey, Calif.
Lazarus, R.S., and S. Folkman. 1984. *Stress, Appraisal, and Coping.* New York: Springer-Verlag.
Levine, S., and H. Ursin. 1980. *Coping and Health.* New York: Plenum.
Lindskold, S., R. Bennett, and M. Wayner. 1976. Retaliation level as a foundation for subsequent conciliation. *Behavioral Science* 21:13–18.
Lindskold, S., B. Betz, and D.S. Walters. 1986. Transforming competitive or cooperative climates. *Journal of Conflict Resolution* 30:99–114.
Luce, R.D., and H. Raiffa. 1957. *Games and Decisions.* New York: Wiley.
Mahoney, R., and D. Druckman. 1975. Simulation, experimentation, and context: Dimensions of design and inference. *Simulation and Games* 6:235–270.
Manis, M. 1975. Comment on Gergen's "Social-Psychology as History." *Personality and Social-Psychology Bulletin* 1:450–455.
McGrath, J.E., and J.W. Julian. 1963. Interaction process and task outcome in experimentally-created negotiation groups. *Journal of Psychological Studies* 14:117–138.
Modelski, G. 1970. The world's foreign ministers: A political elite. *Journal of Conflict Resolution* 14:135–175.
Morgenthau, H.J. 1967. *Politics Among Nations,* 4th ed. New York: Knopf.
Muney, B.F., and M. Deutsch. 1968. The effects of role-reversal during the discussion of opposing viewpoints. *Journal of Conflict Resolution* 12:345–356.
Muromcew, C. 1978. Soviet negotiating behavior. *Open Forum* (Department of State) Spring: 5–14.
Myrdal, A. 1976. *The Game of Disarmament: How the United States and Russia Run the Arms Race.* New York: Pantheon.
Nash, J. 1950. The bargaining problem. *Econometrica* 18:155–162.

———. 1953. Two-person cooperative games. *Econometrica* 21:128–140.
Neale, M.A., and M.H. Bazerman. 1983. The role of perspective-taking in negotiating under different forms of arbitration. *Industrial and Labor Relations Review* 36:378–388.
Newhouse, J. 1973. *Cold Dawn: The Story of SALT*. New York: Holt.
Nicolson, H. 1939. *Diplomacy*. London: Thornton Butterworth.
———. 1946. *The Congress of Vienna: A Study in Allied Unity, 1812-1822*. New York: Viking.
Nisbett, R., and L. Ross. 1980. *Human Inference: Strategies and Shortcomings of Social Judgment*. Engelwood Cliffs, N.J.: Prentice-Hall.
Osgood, C.E. 1962. *An Alternative to War or Surrender*. Urbana, Ill.: University of Illinois Press.
———. 1979. GRIT for MBFR: A proposal for unfreezing force-level postures in Europe. *Peace Research Review* 8(2):77–92.
Osgood, C.E., G.J. Suci, and P.H. Tannenbaum. 1957. *The Measurement of Meaning*. Urbana, Ill.: University of Illinois Press.
Oskamp, S. 1971. Effects of programmed strategies on cooperation in the prisoner's dilemma and other mixed-motive games. *Journal of Conflict Resolution* 15:225–259.
Patchen, M. 1987. Strategies for eliciting cooperation from an adversary: Laboratory and international findings. *Journal of Conflict Resolution* 31:164–185.
Pruitt, D.G. 1981. *Negotiation Behavior*. New York: Academic Press.
Pruitt, D.G., and M.J. Kimmel. 1977. Twenty years of experimental gaming: Critique, synthesis, and suggestions for the future. *Annual Review of Psychology* 28:363–392.
Pruitt, D.G., and S.A. Lewis. 1977. The psychology of integrative bargaining. In D. Druckman, ed., *Negotiations: Social-Psychological Perspectives*. Beverly Hills, Calif.: Sage.
Pruitt, D.G., and J.Z. Rubin. 1986. *Social Conflict: Escalation, Stalemate, and Settlement*. New York: Random House.
Raiffa, H. 1982. *The Art and Science of Negotiation*. Cambridge, Mass.: Harvard University Press.
Ramberg, B. 1977. Tactical advantages of opening positioning strategies: Lessons from the seabed arms control talks 1967–1970. *Journal of Conflict Resolution* 21:685–700.
Randolph, L. 1966. A suggested model of international negotiation. *Journal of Conflict Resolution* 10:344–353.
Rapoport, A. 1960. *Fights, Games, and Debates*. Ann Arbor, Mich.: University of Michigan Press.
———. 1964. *Strategy and Conscience*. New York: Harper & Row.
Rapoport, A., and A.M. Chammah. 1965. *Prisoner's Dilemma: A Study in Conflict and Cooperation*. Ann Arbor, Mich.: University of Michigan Press.
Rose, W.M. 1985. Unilateral initiatives: A theoretical and historical analysis. Paper presented at the International Studies Association, Washington, D.C.

Rubin, J.Z., and B.R. Brown. 1975. *The Social Psychology of Bargaining and Negotiation*. New York: Academic Press.
Ruehl, L. 1982. *MBFR: Lessons and Problems*. Adelphi Paper No. 176. London: International Institute for Strategic Studies.
Salter, S.H. 1984. Some ideas to help stop World War III. Unpublished manuscript, University of Edinburgh.
Samelson, L. 1976. *Soviet and Chinese Negotiating Behavior: The Western View*. Sage Professional Paper in International Studies 02–048. Beverly Hills, Calif.: Sage.
Saunders, H.H. 1984. The pre-negotiation phase. In D.B. Bendahmane and J.W. McDonald, eds., *International Negotiation: Art and Science*. Washington, D.C.: Foreign Service Institute, U.S. Department of State.
Sawyer, J., and H. Guetzkow. 1965. Bargaining and negotiation in international relations. In H.C. Kelman, ed., *International Behavior: A Social-Psychological Analysis*. New York: Holt.
Schein, E.H. 1985. *Organizational Culture and Leadership*. San Francisco, Calif.: Jossey-Bass.
Schellenberg, J.A., and D. Druckman. 1986. The bargaining problem revisited. *Society* 23:65–71.
Schelling, T.C. 1956. An essay on bargaining. *American Economic Review* 46:281–306.
———. 1960. *The Strategy of Conflict*. Cambridge, Mass.: Harvard University Press.
Seaborg, G.T. 1981. *Kennedy, Khrushchev, and the Test Ban*. Berkeley, Calif.: University of California Press.
Sharp, J.M.O. 1976. MBFR as arms control. *Arms Control Today* 6:1.
Shubik, M. 1985. The uses, value and limitations of game theoretic methods in defense analysis. Discussion Paper No. 766. Cowles Foundation for Research in Economics at Yale University.
Sigal, L.V. 1981. Kennan's cuts. *Foreign Policy* 44:70–81.
Simon, H.A. 1957. *Models of Man: Social and Rational*. New York: Wiley.
Singer, J.D. 1962. *Deterrence, Arms Control, and Disarmament*. Columbus, Ohio: Ohio State University Press.
———. 1963. International influence: A formal model. *American Political Science Review* 57:420–430.
Sloan, S.R. 1985. A new dilemma for NATO. In *Arms Control and the Strategic Defense Initiative: Three Perspectives*, pp. 14–22. Occasional Paper 36, Muscatine, Iowa: Stanley Foundation.
Smith, G. 1977. Negotiating with the Soviets. *New York Times Magazine*, 27 February.
———. 1980. *Doubletalk: The Story of SALT I*. New York: Doubleday.
Smoke, R. 1987. Mutual security: A framework for analysis. Unpublished manuscript, Center for Foreign Policy Development, Brown University.
Snyder, G.H., and P. Diesing. 1977. *Conflict Among Nations: Bargaining, Decision-Making, and System Structure in International Crisis*. Princeton, N.J.: Princeton University Press.

Solomon, R.H. 1985. *Chinese political negotiating behavior*. Report No. R-3295. Santa Monica, Calif.: Rand Corporation.

Stephenson, G.M., B.H. Kniveton, and I.E. Morley. 1977. Interaction analysis of an industrial wage negotiation. *Journal of Occupational Psychology* 50:231–241.

Strauss, A. 1978. *Negotiations: Varieties, Contexts, Processes, and Social Order*. San Francisco, Calif.: Jossey-Bass.

Talbott, S. 1979. *Endgame: The Inside Story of SALT II*. New York: Harper & Row.

———. 1984. *Deadly Gambits: The Reagan Administration and the Stalemate in Nuclear Arms Control*. New York: Knopf.

Tedeschi, J.T. 1970. Threats and promises. In P. Swingle, ed., *The Structure of Conflict*. New York: Academic Press.

Tedeschi, J.T., and T.V. Bonoma. 1977. Measures of last resort: Coercion and aggression in bargaining. In D. Druckman, ed., *Negotiations: Social-Psychological Perspectives*. Beverly Hills, Calif.: Sage.

Tetlock, P.E. 1988. Monitoring the integrative complexity of American and Soviet policy rhetoric: What can be learned? *Journal of Social Issues* 44:101–131.

Thibaut, J. 1968. The development of contractual norms in bargaining: Replication and variation. *Journal of Conflict Resolution* 12:102–112.

Tollison, R.D., and T.D. Willett. 1979. An economic theory of mutually advantageous issue linkages in international negotiations. *International Organization* 33:425–449.

Touval, S., and I.W. Zartman, eds. 1985. *The Man in the Middle: International Mediation in Theory and Practice*. Boulder, Col.: Westview.

Ulvila, J.W. 1988. Turning points: An analysis. In J.W. McDonald, Jr. and D.B. Bendahmane, eds., *U.S. Base-Rights Negotiations: Three Case Studies and Lessons Learned*. Washington, D.C.: Foreign Service Institute, U.S. Department of State.

Ulvila, J.W., and W.D. Snider. 1980. Negotiation of international oil tanker standards: An application of multiattribute value theory. *Operations Research* 28:81–96.

Walcott, C., and P.T. Hopmann. 1978. Interaction analysis and bargaining behavior. In R.T. Golembiewski, ed., *The Small Group in Political Science: The Last Two Decades of Development*. Athens, Ga.: University of Georgia Press.

Walcott, C., P.T. Hopmann, and T.D. King. 1977. The role of debate in negotiation. In D. Druckman, ed., *Negotiations: Social-Psychological Perspectives*. Beverly Hills, Calif.: Sage.

Walton, R.E., and R.B. McKersie. 1965. *A Behavioral Theory of Labor Negotiations: An Analysis of a Social Interaction System*. New York: McGraw-Hill.

Waltz, K.N. 1979. *Theory of International Politics*. Reading, Mass.: Addison-Wesley.

Warnke, P.C., and D. Linebaugh. 1985. Breaking the deadlock. In *Arms Control and the Strategic Defense Initiative: Three Perspectives*, pp. 24–31. Occasional Paper 36. Muscatine, Iowa: Stanley Foundation.

Wedge, B., and C. Muromcew. 1965. Psychological factors in Soviet disarmament negotiation. *Journal of Conflict Resolution* 9:18–36.

Weede, E. 1975. World order in the fifties and sixties: Dependence, deterrence, and limited peace. *Papers, Peace Science Society (International)* 24:49–80.

Whelen, J.G. 1979. *Soviet Diplomacy and Negotiating Behavior: Emerging New Context for U.S. Diplomacy.* Report prepared for the Committee on Foreign Affairs, House of Representatives. Washington, D.C.: U.S. Government Printing Office.

Wilkenfeld, J., V.L. Lussier, and D. Tahtinen. 1972. Conflict interactions in the Middle East, 1949–1967. *Journal of Conflict Resolution* 2:135–154.

Wilson, W. 1971. Reciprocation and other techniques for inducing cooperation in the prisoner's dilemma game. *Journal of Conflict Resolution* 15:167–195.

Winham, G.R. 1977. Complexity in international negotiation. In D. Druckman, ed., *Negotiations: Social-Psychological Perspectives.* Beverly Hills, Calif.: Sage.

———. 1979. Practitioners' views of international negotiation. *World Politics* 32:111–135.

———. 1987. Multilateral economic negotiations. *Negotiation Journal.* 3:175–189.

Wolfe, T.W. 1979. *The SALT Experience.* Cambridge, Mass.: Ballinger.

Young, K.T. 1968. *Negotiating with the Chinese Communists: The United States Experience.* New York: McGraw-Hill.

Young, O.R. 1983. Regime dynamics: The rise and fall of international regimes. In S.D. Krasner, ed., *International Regimes.* Ithaca, N.Y.: Cornell University Press.

Zagare, F.C. 1981. Nonmyopic equilibria and the Middle East crisis of 1967. *Conflict Management and Peace Science* 5:139–162.

———. 1983. A game theoretic evaluation of the cease-fire alert decision of 1973. *Journal of Peace Research* 20:73–86.

Zartman, I.W. 1975. Negotiations: Theory and reality. *Journal of International Affairs* 9:69–77.

———. 1976. *The 50% Solution.* New York: Doubleday.

———. 1978. *The Negotiation Process: Theories and Applications.* Beverly Hills, Calif.: Sage.

———. 1986. Ripening conflict, ripe moment, formula, and mediation. In D.B. Bendahmane and J.W. McDonald, Jr., eds., *Perspectives on Negotiation: Four Case Studies and Interpretations.* Washington, D.C.: Foreign Service Institute, U.S. Department of State.

Zartman, I.W., and M.R. Berman. 1982. *The Practical Negotiator.* New Haven, Conn.: Yale University Press.

Zechmeister, K., and D. Druckman. 1973. Determinants of resolving a conflict of interest: A simulation of political decision making. *Journal of Conflict Resolution* 17:63–88.

Zinnes, D.A. 1980. Three puzzles in search of a researcher: Presidential address. *International Studies Quarterly* 24:315–342.

3

Democracy, Public Opinion, and Nuclear Weapons

BRUCE RUSSETT

Popular Support for the Use of Force, 176

Mass Opinion: Stable or Volatile? 179
OPINION CHANGE AND POLICY CHANGE, 181   HOW ATTITUDES
CHANGE, 181   INTEREST AND INFORMATION, 184

Rational Leaders, 185
FOREIGN POLICY AS SYMBOLIC POLITICS, 186   ELECTORAL POLITICS AND
INTERNATIONAL CONFLICT, 187   DEMOCRACY AND INTERNATIONAL
CONFLICT, 188

Nuclear Weapons and Nuclear War, 192
NO FIRST USE OF NUCLEAR WEAPONS, 192   DISARMAMENT AND TRUST, 194
YEARNING FOR PROTECTION, 195   EFFECTS OF FEAR OF WAR, 197

Strengthening Command and Control, 198
ORGANIZATIONAL AND POLITICAL OBSTACLES, 199

Notes, 200
References, 202

Political theorists have long been divided between those who trusted the masses and those who feared or despised them. The divergence may occur within the same head: an ambivalence between an anxiety that mass opinions will be fickle, based on ignorance and emotion, and a reluctant acknowledgment that the alternatives—one form or another of oligarchy—are even more dangerous. Discussions of national security policy exemplify the force of this divergence. Can something as vital to the life and independence of the nation safely be left to popular decision—and if something so central to individuals' lives cannot be subject to popular control, does "democracy" any longer have much meaning? Questions about the procurement, control, and possible use of nuclear weapons pose the problem most starkly of all.

At one level the debate seems to be over process and lofty principles, but that is deceptive. In the United States and most Western democracies the prevailing myth is closer to that of Locke, the Founding Fathers, and Bastille Day than it is to Plato's guardians or Marx's vanguard of the proletariat. One does not argue with the principle of democratic control—only with whether the outcomes will be desirable in particular cases. Thus, American liberal internationalists of the early post-World War II period were staunch promoters and defenders of democracy, but they distrusted the historic isolationist impulses of the American populace and feared that American democracy would not sustain the rigors of a long-term struggle against Communist expansionism (see, for example, Almond, 1950).

In contemporary debates, the division often seems to be one between "hawks" and "doves." Doves frequently are found in, or leading, mass organizations to protest involvement in foreign conflicts (Vietnam, Central America) or to promote arms control and disarmament (the freeze). They try to stimulate broad public debate and applaud or promote graphic presentations of the horrors of nuclear war in the belief that repulsion from the horrors will lead also to repulsion from possession of the weapons that could cause the horrors. Over the years there has been a strong protestation on the left that a procedural commitment to popular rule, justifiable on grounds of democratic theory, would also produce substantively preferable policy outcomes (Dahl, 1985).[1] Hawks (also sometimes self-styled "owls") castigate "fear mongering," try to reassure the populace that the government is following a responsible and informed course, worry about leaks of sensitive information to the public, and largely try to encapsulate any changes in policy within the bureaucracy rather than in the public arena (for example, the Iran-Nicaragua policies exposed in 1986). Many of these characterizations are nevertheless dependent on the nature of the elite consensus at the time, and advocacy of popular involvement may less reflect conviction about democratic process than about the wisdom of particular policies and whether one is in or out of power.

We have a great deal of information touching on the convergences and differences between mass opinion and that of particular elites and how a democratic political system may promote one over the other. These points will be clear from the following detailed examination:

- The general public typically supports firm policies and the use of force in the short run, but that support decays rapidly in any protracted conflict.
- Governments often change policies in response to shifts in public opinion, as well as attempt to change opinion.
- Public attitudes on foreign policy are not volatile but are either stable or variable in response to major world events. Opinion change can be triggered by world events or by the leadership of popular presidents under certain circumstances.
- Leaders' decision making tends to reflect a rational attempt to maximize their popularity by use of symbolic politics, both to maintain their political influence and to improve their chances of reelection.
- There are mixed and somewhat disturbing research findings concerning the tendency of democratic governments to engage in international conflict, especially near elections and when economic conditions are poor. In general, support for toughness is balanced by desires for conciliation and avoiding major war.
- The public supports many aspects of nuclear disarmament, opposes first use of nuclear weapons, and favors arms limitation agreements despite fears that the Soviet government will cheat. Fears of nuclear war are substantial and leave people susceptible to faith in utopian proposals such as the Strategic Defense Initiative (SDI) as a perfect defense of population. Nevertheless, the public is potentially responsive to leadership promoting serious measures of arms limitation and war prevention.
- It will become clear from examining problems of nuclear command and control that the failure to effect measures of arms limitation cannot persuasively be blamed on the public.

Popular Support for the Use of Force

Americans, and probably the citizens of other democratically governed countries, fear war and seek peace. But neither the elite nor the general populace are united on the means by which peace is to be achieved. For some, the primary means should be conciliation and negotiation; for others, the appropriate means are strength, toughness, and deterrence. Nor, of course, are these two classes mutually exclusive. One can "bargain from strength"—

be firm and unyielding right up to the last moment and then offer a major concession, as is a recognized negotiating strategy. Elements of both are in fact widely advocated by the same individuals. In a response to a survey question frequently asked by the Roper Organization, typically one fourth of the population chooses, "It's clear Russia can't be trusted and we will have to rely on increased military strength to counter them;" one fourth answers, rather, "We should do nothing that is likely to provoke an American-Russian conflict but instead should try to negotiate and reason out our differences;" and about half essentially combine the two: "We should take a strong position with the Russians now so they won't go any further but at the same time we should try to re-establish good relations with them" (Schneider, 1987:49; Schneider, 1984). Wittkopf (1987) reports that the public favors toughness more than does the elite, but has little evidence on relative willingness to negotiate.[2]

With this mixed base of support, it would be reasonable to expect that either tough or conciliatory actions, taken in moderation and appropriately timed by their government, would meet with approval from a majority. Such a situation seemed to apply early in the Vietnam War, when a majority of Americans approved options both for escalating the war (sending more troops, bombing North Vietnam) and for conciliation (allowing a coalition government including the Communists). Americans may have been muddled or inconsistent in so doing. Alternatively, they may have been expressing a desire to end the war, not necessarily by a clear-cut victory, and in effect giving the government a broad mandate to choose among various means to achieve that goal (Verba et al., 1967). Similarly, research on changes in the president's popularity rating in surveys long seemed to indicate that crises, presidential uses of force, and conciliatory acts such as engaging in summit negotiations all could be expected to produce at least a temporary gain in popularity through a "rally 'round the flag" effect (Mueller, 1973, and a refinement but basically replication by Kernell, 1978).[3]

This conclusion has recently been challenged by evidence that presidential popularity ratings typically were boosted by 4 to 5 percent in the short term by conflictual behavior toward the Soviet Union, but decreased by about 2 percent by cooperation with the Soviets (Ostrom and Simon, 1985). The reasons for the difference in results are not clear; they may include new data for a longer time span, different definitions of acts, and a better specification of the statistical equation. Another study reports that a president perceived by the public as dovish (Carter) gains approval when he acts hawkish, and a president perceived as hawkish (Reagan) is more approved for initiatives the public sees as dovish (Nincic, 1988a). More research is needed, yet this fits with the view that the Reagan administration seized on the Intermediate-range Nuclear

Forces (INF) agreement in 1987 as a means of recovering some popularity. It also fits with the popular response to the failure of the summit negotiations in Iceland in October 1986. The immediate public reaction was one of dismay. Then the administration "shovel brigade" cleverly pictured the events not as a breakdown of strategic arms negotiations but as a temporary, although not necessarily permanent, near-miss for dramatic disarmament in which the president hung tough and refused to give up his SDI for the sake of achieving an immediate agreement; his popularity rating rose moderately.[4]

Although mass support can be rallied for a variety of dramatic actions, it nearly always begins from a lower level than does the support of elites (Russett and Hanson, 1975:79; Reilly, 1983:31). Moreover, support for the use of military force is lower in the abstract than it becomes in concrete situations. Before President Johnson sent U.S. combat troops to Vietnam following the Gulf of Tonkin incident, only 42 percent of the populace supported involvement in Vietnam; shortly afterward 72 percent did so. Similarly, before it happened only 7 percent endorsed the idea of invading Cambodia; after Nixon did it 50 percent approved (Weissberg, 1976:235; cited in Nincic, 1988*b*).[5] The usual increase in a president's popularity is probably a result of political and media elites' reluctance to criticize him, at least immediately, because on national security matters there is always a substantial risk that the president has access to secret information that he can selectively release so as to make a critic look foolish or even disloyal. Lacking the cues of elite disapproval, majority popular approval is hardly surprising (Brody, 1984). This interpretation is strengthened by the pattern of behavior following exposure of the Iran and Nicaraguan Contra arms deals in November 1986. Unlike the usual situation, elite criticism was immediate and widespread; President Reagan's popularity rating dropped 20 points in two weeks.

That disastrous effect on Reagan's popularity can be traced to several factors, not easily sorted out. Importantly, criticism came from across the political spectrum: secret dealings with Iran were as unpopular on the right as clandestine aid to the Nicaraguan Contras was on the left. Both elements tapped large reservoirs of public hostility. Iran's popularity rating among 23 countries was down at the bottom, well below even Syria and the Soviet Union; two-thirds of the populace opposed giving military assistance to the Contras (Schneider, 1987:56–57, 60). Elite criticism of either element was therefore safe. Also, the acts themselves were mixed. One was a conciliatory move toward a hated adversary; the other was a step up the escalation ladder of military force. It is impossible to prove which of these elements was more damaging, but most likely it was the former. Finally, military action to repel an armed attack across international borders is more popular than is intervention against domestic Communists within a country. Significantly, the earlier action against Grenada (1983) met with public approval more "mainly to protect the Americans living there" than to overthrow a Marxist government (Mueller, 1977; Schneider, 1987:59). In 1986 the Nicaraguan government was posing no immediate threat to its neighbors or to the United States, so American popular sentiment to overthrow it was low.

Under the best of circumstances, however, the immediate rise in popularity ratings also decays rapidly as memory fades or success of the policy appears ambiguous and critics become bolder; rarely does the half-life of a president's popularity boost exceed two months (Kernell, 1978). Drawn-out wars are invariably unpopular, in proportion to their length and cost (in casualties as well as in money). Presidents Truman and Johnson suffered badly from their extended wars. A recent article examining the electoral fortunes of congressional and presidential candidates over nearly a century found that in every case candidates of the party initiating a war did more poorly both during and immediately after the war than would have been predicted by the now-standard models that quite accurately predict election results from the state of the economy. The longer and more costly the war, the greater the loss of votes (Cotton, 1986).

Mass Opinion: Stable or Volatile?

Much more needs to be said about the interplay of opinion leadership and followership between elites and mass. First, the early fears that mass opinion would be volatile, with whims changing in response to every contradictory international event, have proved groundless. Although large-scale swings in public opinion on foreign and security policy did characterize the early post-World War II years, opinion on the major issues stabilized by the early 1950s. Neither the early volatility nor the stabilization should be surprising, since it took most of the post-1945 decade to resolve vigorous intraelite debates over issues such as the nature of the Soviet Union, isolationism versus internationalism, containment-rollback, and the relative efficacy of military versus economic and diplomatic implements. Thereafter, opinions changed little until major policy events had their impact.

As one example, attitudes toward spending on national defense seem to have been quite stable for most of the 1950s and 1960s, with about 25 percent of the population wanting to spend more on defense and about 20 percent wishing to spend less. (The rest were satisfied with the current amounts or had no opinion.) Attitudes then became more changing, although not exactly volatile. The cumulative impact of events of the Vietnam War produced an aversion to things military, so that at the beginning of the 1970s 50 percent of the population wanted to spend less on defense. By the beginning of the 1980s, however, that had dropped to 10 percent and then rose recently to a level approximating that during the Vietnam era (see Figure 3.1 and Graham 1986*b*). Defense spending came to be viewed in a more favorable light during a period when continued Soviet strategic weapons acquisition, a decline of détente, the Iranian humiliation, and finally the Soviet invasion of Afghanistan coincided with a drop in U.S. military budgets as a fraction of national income. But then, as the Reagan defense budget soared, opinion shifted once more toward a conclusion that the defense buildup had gone far enough and it was time to emphasize other priorities. While change certainly occurred, the changes were neither sudden nor frequent and seem to have responded well to changes in the world. Overall, Figure 3.1 suggests that in the past two decades preferences for change in military expenditures seem to have corresponded fairly closely to changes in actual military spending as a percentage of gross national product (GNP).

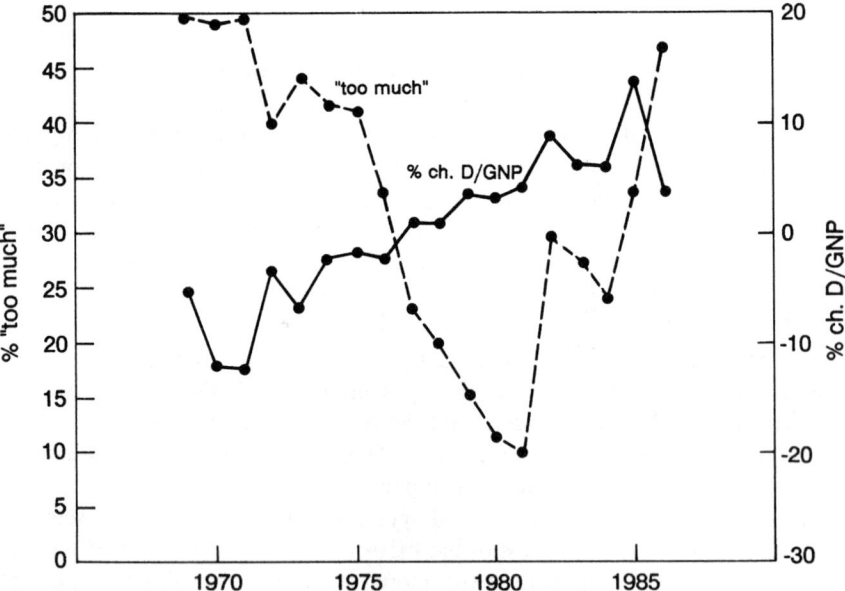

FIGURE 3.1. Defense spending as a percentage of GNP and opinions that the United States is spending "too much" on defense, 1969–1986. *Source*: National surveys as cited in Russett and DeLuca (1981), Russett and Starr (1985), and subsequent surveys.

Opinion Change and Policy Change

In fact, the data suggest that decisions about military spending levels respond to public opinion. I tried a simultaneous relationship and lags in both directions, and the strongest relationship is between opinion in one year and changes in actual military spending in the subsequent year. That is, the larger the proportion of the population that wants to reduce military spending, the greater the actual percentage reduction in the next year.[6] Other comprehensive studies of the interaction between attitudes toward defense spending and congressional decisions to increase or cut the president's military spending proposals have also found a strong relation between public opinion and subsequent congressional policy (Jacobson, 1985; Ostrom and Marra, 1986). Together, this evidence tends to support the hypothesis that on this issue the government does in some sense respond to the voice of the people. And in a systematic review of long-term public opinion and government policy change on many issues in the United States, Page and Shapiro (1983) found that government policy was more likely to change in the direction preferred by the public than public opinion was to change toward government policy.

How Attitudes Change

There were many exceptions to Page and Shapiro's generalization, and their work is not definitive. Figure 3.2 shows two matters on which the causal direction more plausibly runs from national policy and international events to opinion change. The graph plots, on a "temperature" scale of +500 to −500, changes in popular attitudes toward the Soviet Union and China as recorded by the American Institute of Public Opinion (AIPO) and National Opinion Research Center (NORC) national surveys. People are asked to rate a country on a scale of +5 "for something you like very much" to −5 "for something you dislike very much"; each of the scale positions is multiplied by the percentage of the population choosing that position, and these are then summed to produce the temperature rating for each survey. As Figure 3.2 shows, attitudes toward the Soviet Union improved slowly into the détente era (early 1970s) and then declined under the impact of détente's decay and the anti-Soviet rhetoric of the Reagan administration, recovering slightly in 1986 as the rhetoric warmed and there were no new major Soviet provocations. Attitudes toward China improved in response to changes in official policy in the 1970s, fell back a bit, and then resumed improvement at a slower and steadier pace.[7] Here is a case where attitude changes generally follow major policy shifts, but once set do not vary greatly in reaction to short-term ups and downs of policy. Not surprisingly, popular images of friends and adversaries

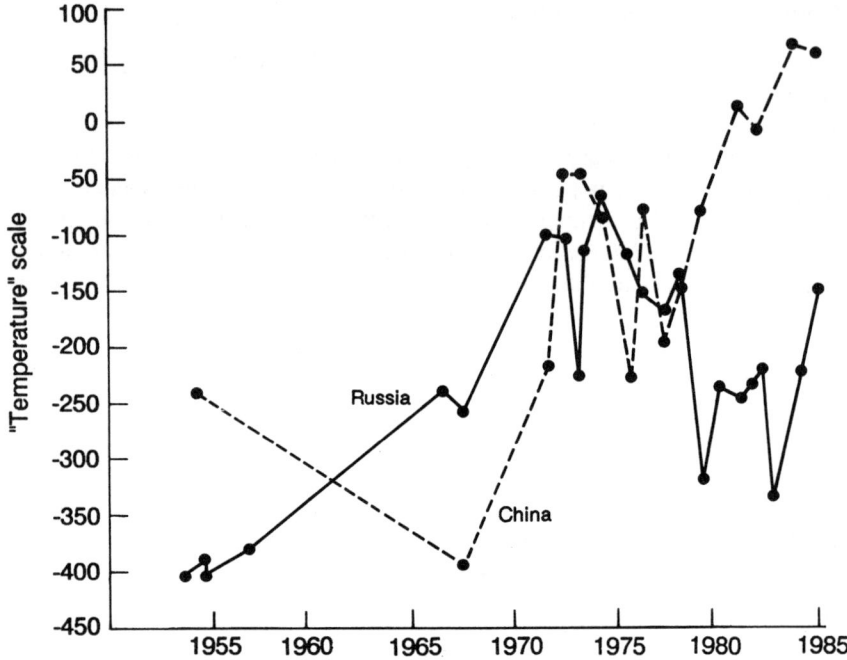

FIGURE 3.2. "Temperature" scale of attitudes toward the Soviet Union and China, 1953–1986. *Source*: AIPO and NORC U.S. national surveys.

depend on the general direction of foreign policy, including shifts in international alignment from enemy to ally.

Another clue to the pattern of opinion change emerges from examining the distribution of attitudes at any particular time. Instead of computing a summary temperature score for each survey, we can check to see whether the distribution of attitudes across the population is unimodal or bimodal. During the 1950s and 1960s the distributions were always unimodal, skewed toward the negative end of the scale with the largest number of respondents answering −5. But in the 1970s a second peak formed at the +1 point on the scale, and as many as 44 percent of the population rated the Soviet Union somewhere on the positive side, as did 36 percent of the population for China. In the early 1980s attitudes toward the Soviet Union chilled while those toward China continued to warm.[8] But whereas the distribution of attitudes toward the Soviet Union retained a minor secondary peak at +1 (with 10 to 12 percent of the population), that for China returned to unimodal form—but with the mode now at +1 and over 60 percent of the population on the positive side. During the 1980s, nowhere on the China scale is there a second peak.

Attitudes toward the Soviet Union and China have always been more positive among those with relatively high education and socioeconomic status, but the status differences were most marked in the early détente period of shift. In 1973, for instance, 51 percent of the college-educated population reported some degree of positive assessment of the Soviet Union, but just 30 percent of those with only a high school or grade school education did so (Gallup Report, June 1983). This constitutes dramatic evidence of the way attitudes can shift—not by the whole population at once, but by a change in part of what has long been known in the literature on public opinion and foreign policy as the "attentive public": those with relatively high status and media exposure. In the case of attitudes toward China, the movement eventually carried most of the population along; in the case of the Soviet Union it was aborted, leaving both mass and elite opinion sharply divided between the two modes.[9]

Some time ago Deutsch and Merritt (1965) established, for the United States and several European countries, that sustained change in such basic attitudes resulted only from repeated, dramatic events, and Caspary (1970) effectively challenged Almond's (1950) "mood theory" of volatility. More recently, Shapiro and Page (1988) examined 425 foreign policy items that had been repeated in national surveys at various times over a nearly 50–year period. They found that 51 percent of those items showed no statistically significant change at all, that about 50 percent of those that did change showed shifts of less than 10 percentage points, that foreign and defense policy items showed only very marginally greater change than did domestic policy items, and that there was very little fluctuation (defined as reversal of the direction of change) in foreign policy opinions. Foreign policy items did, however, show greater rates of change than did domestic policy items. These occurred primarily in war-related items, which Shapiro and Page regarded as basically appropriate opinion changes in response to rapid changes in the international environment as interpreted by the U.S. media and political leadership. They thus concluded (Shapiro and Page, 1988) that U.S. citizens "have formed and changed their policy preferences in a rational fashion—in a manner worthy of serious consideration in deliberation about the direction and content of U.S. foreign policy."

In other studies Shapiro and Page found that public opinion responds to television network commentators and to testimony by ostensibly nonpartisan experts and to popular presidents (those scoring over 50 percent at the time on the presidential performance scale) but not to unpopular presidents (Page et al., 1987). Also, "*Intensive efforts* over *several months* by *highly popular* presidents appear to bring about changes in opinion poll results of only some 5 or 10 percentage points, hardly a tidal wave" (Page and Shapiro, 1984:659, my emphasis).

These findings basically refer to the stability of opinion at the aggregate level; that is, the proportion of the population holding a given opinion is relatively stable. They do not tell us about the stability of individuals' opinion: if half the people changed their minds in opposite directions the aggregates would remain stable. For analyzing the consequences for the political system this may not matter much: politicians probably care less about shifts among individuals than about the proportion of votes that will be cast for them. Nevertheless, there remain important questions about who changes, how much, and why—questions that can be adequately answered only with a research design that repeatedly tracks the opinion of particular individuals.

This evidence suggests substantial public ability to form discriminating and stable opinions. People do not change their opinions frivolously, nor are they easily led. Many writers have contended that popular opinion is subject to manipulation by media and opinion elites. When the basic content of opinion is reasonably stable over time, this hypothesis is essentially untestable. Is mass opinion a function of elite opinion, or do the elites simply say what they know will be popular with the masses? If neither changes much, one cannot tell. Generally, individuals' foreign policy opinions seem less highly correlated with their socioeconomic status (which usually does not change much) than with their ideological perspectives on a broader range of public issues (which may be somewhat more malleable by political leaders whom they trust) (Russett and Hanson, 1975, on the United States; Arian et al., 1987, on Israel). Some analysts even have proposed that it is easier to manipulate opinion in a democracy—despite the greater range of opinion that can be expressed openly—than in authoritarian societies, because in the latter the level of skepticism is already great and people are psychologically prepared to handle suspected government manipulation (Jensen, 1982, as cited in Arian et al., 1987).

Doubtless there are circumstances when, for example, some elites first form a new opinion, then persuade opinion leaders in the media, who in turn persuade the mass public, so that finally the very people in government who initiated the change can "respond" to public opinion. The interaction between opinion change and policy change remains poorly understood and is much too complex for very satisfactory treatment here.[10]

Interest and Information

Some observers would contend that most people do not change their minds much about foreign and security policy simply because they do not care much about it. Admittedly, popular interest in such matters is only sporadically as high as the level of interest in domestic policy. Interest in foreign affairs and security was high during the early years of the Cold War, dropped in 1963, and was high again throughout the Vietnam War. Then it dropped sharply, and only twice in the next decade (in January 1974 for the oil shock, and January 1980 for Iran and Afghanistan) did the AIPO's regular question about "the most important problem" facing the country produce a plurality for a foreign policy problem (Smith, 1985). In 1983, however, international tension and fear of war emerged as most important and essentially have remained there, with 20 to 30 percent of the population giving such answers (Gallup Report, September 1986).

Information levels on security policy frequently do seem low across the broad public. For example, in 1964, 42 percent of the population did not know that the United States was a member of the North Atlantic Treaty Organization (NATO), and in 1985 only 36 percent were aware of the antiballistic missile (ABM) treaty. Those wary of greater popular participation in the formulation of security policy often like to cite these and similar data; for example, that in early 1979 only 34 percent of the U.S. population could correctly identify the two countries involved in the Strategic Arms Limitation Talks (SALT) negotiations. Yet even these indications of widespread ignorance can be deceptive, confusing active recall of information with somewhat more latent recognition. For instance, when respondents were given a list of possible purposes of SALT, 58 percent then correctly answered that the talks concerned long-range weapons (Graham, 1988*a*; Plous, 1988). Actual knowledge levels are higher than they appear from quiz-show questioning. And the number of people who could define the concept "NATO" (34 percent) is bracketed closely by the number who could define "welfare state" and "electoral college" (Neuman, 1986:17).

Rational Leaders

Just as we can speak sensibly of an inherent rationality in the way members of the general public change or retain their opinions on foreign policy issues, we can usefully consider the rationality of a leader who wishes to achieve or retain power in a democratic political system (Mayhew, 1974). To do so we begin with some observations on the rationality of voters and leaders regarding the state of the economy and then extend that reasoning to foreign and security policy issues.

Foreign Policy as Symbolic Politics

It is now well known that the governments of industrial democracies are vulnerable to electoral censure following periods of economic downturn. Inflation and unemployment both are unpopular and can even occur together, as happened during the 1970s. The best single predictor of the electoral fortunes of the governing party seems to be the direction and rate of change in real disposable personal income during the 9 or 12 months preceding the election. (For examples, not limited to the United States, see Kramer, 1971; Nordhaus, 1975; Tufte, 1978; Hibbs, 1982; Hibbs and Vasilatos, 1981; Ben-Haven and Temkin, 1986; however, see Monroe, 1984.) Voters react not only to changes in their own economic conditions, but to those they perceive in the economy at large. Some analysts even conclude that "citizens seem to pay principal attention to the nation's economic predicament, and comparatively little to their own" (Kinder, 1981:17). In this they react strongly to images and information in the mass media (especially television) and, as the focus is removed from immediate personal experience, many issues become subject to "symbolic politics" (Kinder and Kiewiet, 1979; Sears et al., 1980; but see the methodological critique by Kramer, 1983). Knowing the sensitivity of the electorate to the state of the economy, governments in turn stimulate public spending in advance of elections so as to enhance their prospects (Tufte, 1978). Some have claimed that military spending is an especially manipulable instrument (Nincic and Cusack, 1979). This last claim has been contested (Krell, 1981) and is hard to establish with annual spending data, but monthly data on Department of Defense contracting clearly indicate substantial increases immediately before national elections (Mayer, 1988:Chap.5). In Israel, where much military hardware is imported and total economic capacity is usually fully utilized, military spending typically declines just before elections so as to permit greater allocations to popular civilian functions (Mintz, 1988). In any case, economic conditions cannot always be controlled sufficiently to ensure electoral success (Alt and Chrystal, 1983; also Brown and Stein, 1982; Thompson and Zuk, 1983), and political leaders may seek out other means of enhancing their popularity.

In the "plebiscitary presidency" (Lowi, 1985) the chief executive is constantly under pressure to solve problems. Many problems cannot be solved even with the resources of the chief executive of the world's most powerful state, but the president must at least give the appearance of solving them. These pressures apply at all times during an executive's tenure in office. His popularity is perhaps his most important resource for accomplishing any of his goals; if he allows it to atrophy his legislative program will suffer. In the words of a congressional staffer, "When you go up to the Hill and the latest polls show Carter isn't doing well, then there isn't much reason for a member to go along with him" (quoted in Jacobson, 1983:179–80). But the pressures are greatest at election time. His election can never be certain enough, his victory margin never large enough. "As election nears, a president will be tempted to husband even what he regards as surplus support. Accordingly, an unpopular president nearing election should come as close to resembling a single-minded popularity maximizer as one will find" (Kernell, 1986:188).

Except in a protracted war, foreign policy is literally and figuratively distant from most citizens; its interpretation is thus particularly subject to selective information release and careful media presentation—a prime candidate for symbolic politics. It is also the area in which a president has the most authority to act, with the least congressional constraint. One possibility is to invoke the "rally 'round the flag effect." Short, low-cost military actions to repel an attack are almost invariably popular, at least at their inception; costly operations soon lose their appeal. Actions to avert loss from Soviet invasion of friends or allies are more acceptable than actions to achieve gains, as by rolling back a previous Soviet acquisition. Actions against small adversaries (for example, Grenada or Libya) are more popular than ones against the Soviet Union.[11] In their implicit cost-benefit equations, Americans seem not to put a high value on improvements in the U. S. international position as compared with substantial monetary costs, the loss of U.S. lives, or the risk of expansion to a wider and more costly war. These calculations are entirely consistent with models of rational economic and psychological behavior (see Kahneman and Tversky, 1979).

Faced with these popular preferences, economic sanctions provide a valuable instrument for government action. Sanctions—say against Cuba, the Soviet Union, or South Africa—offer an opportunity to express disapproval and impose (sometimes very limited) costs on an adversary while incurring virtually no risk of escalation to direct U. S. military involvement. Thus, despite evidence that economic sanctions rarely succeed in achieving their ostensible international goals, governments continue to employ them. They are eminently successful in satisfying a popular demand to "do something" (Lindsay, 1986).

Electoral Politics and International Conflict

Military force or threats against a foreign adversary may also be used, although perhaps with somewhat greater risk. The Soviet Union and those who are perceived as its allies constitute the United States' primary adversaries. Work by psychologists has established that U.S. presidents' foreign policy rhetoric toward the Soviet Union becomes more simplistic (its cognitive complexity declines) in the latter half of election years (Suedfeld and Tetlock, 1977; Tetlock, 1975), and that a decline in cognitive complexity by leaders is also associated with a greater likelihood of undertaking military interventions and a decreasing likelihood of arriving at international agreements (Tetlock and McGuire, 1985).

The direct connection between elections and military acts or threats is less well established. Stoll (1984) found that presidents are more likely to use force if they are seeking reelection during a developing or ongoing war. When this is the case, a president knows that voters will be more concerned than usual about foreign affairs and will therefore be especially likely to hold the war against him if things go badly. But if the year has been a relatively peaceful one, the risks that an initially limited use of military force may escalate to an unpopular war may discourage such acts. Another study shows that the international use of force since World War II, as authorized by a U.S. president, was especially common when the economic "misery index" (inflation and unemployment rates) was high and suggests (but in a statistically weak relationship) that force was more likely to be used in the months preceding an election[12] (Ostrom and Job, 1986).

A more recent report by the same authors (Job and Ostrom, 1986) refines and modifies some of these conclusions. The most important change is a better specification of the equation predicting use of force, namely, inclusion of terms for international conditions in recognition of the fact that a national leader has only a limited amount of choice about whether and when to use force. If an adversary conducts an aggressive act against what would typically be considered an important national interest, the state of the domestic political economy may be only marginally relevant to decisions about how to respond. With these revisions, the authors no longer found use of force to be more common in the quarter preceding elections; in fact, they report uses of force to be less common then. (They did not, however, report a test for all the nine months preceding elections, as would be suggested by work on how the state of the economy affects elections.) This more complete analysis fits Stoll's (1984) results when one recalls that most post-World War II elections in the United States have occurred in peacetime, as does their finding that presidents were more likely to use force when polls reported that the "most important problem" was one of domestic rather than foreign policy. Finally, they found that a president was more likely to use military force when his popularity rating was in the "critical" 40- to 60-percent range instead of very high or very low—in other words, when he needed the popularity boost most.

Democracy and International Conflict

One characteristic of all the studies of use of force reported in the preceding section is that they apply almost exclusively to the United States and to the nuclear era. In a sense that provides the best conditions for testing the relevant hypotheses: the United States in that period was the world's most powerful state—least constrained by external conditions and providing its leaders greater choice as to whether and when they would use military force. Yet the data base is relatively small, and an extension of the analysis to other times and countries, using data other than from opinion surveys, would be desirable for extending both the generality of the findings and our confidence in them. I have made several such extensions (Russett, 1987, 1989), as follows.

One large-scale cross-national statistical examination found that over a century-long period democratic states (but not authoritarian ones) were more likely to engage in international disputes involving the threat or use of military force in years after their GNP had declined. Limitation of this result to democratic states is consistent with the thesis that leaders of democracies are held more immediately and directly accountable than are autocratic leaders. Closer analysis disclosed that this result was substantially confined to the United States and Great Britain—the powers with the greatest international autonomy. Further analysis of U.S. behavior over nearly a century found that participation in international disputes was more common in years following periods of economic decline than in prosperous times, more common in years of congressional (off-year) elections than in nonelection years, and more common in years of presidential elections than in years of congressional elections. Disputes were most common in years when presidential elections and economic distress coincided. These results fit nicely with a model of a rational president seeking to maximize the chances that he (or his party) would retain the presidency and secondarily to maximize the number of his supporters in Congress.

Finally, another cross-national analysis, limited to the post-1953 era but adding several measures of domestic political conflict, found that economic downturn did not significantly increase the likelihood of involvement in international disputes. But domestic political protest was strongly associated with such involvement. Thus economic downturns per se may be less important in producing a tendency toward international conflict than is domestic political conflict, from whatever cause. "Rational" political leaders may thus seek to divert attention from many kinds of domestic troubles by engaging in foreign conflict.

At this point we must broaden the discussion to encompass wider perspectives on the degree to which democratic states are prone to engage in international conflict. First, these results apply only to engaging in international disputes, not to the large-scale exercise of international violence known as war (conventionally defined, in the scientific international relations literature, as producing more than 1,000 battle deaths). Whereas the initiation of rather low-level international conflict may be influenced by conditions of domestic politics, the dynamics of escalation are driven much more by the international environment and the behavior of one's adversary (Leng, 1984; Huth and Russett, 1988). And as noted, war—especially of any protracted nature—is not likely to enhance the electoral prospects of a government; regardless of economic conditions, democracies are not more likely than other states to escalate existing international conflicts (Russett, 1989). Nor do the findings reported here necessarily mean that democracies are more likely to engage in other forms of international conflict than are nondemocracies. In fact, the near-consensus of systematic studies is that political system type is not related in general to the probability that a country will be involved either in war or in other kinds of international conflict (Singer and Small, 1976; Chan, 1984; Weede, 1984; Domke, 1988). The findings reported apply only to the timing of conflicts, a matter that is partly under the control of a government. The United States has been more conflict prone than most governments, but not more so than other great powers; great powers have wider interests and greater capabilities for distant military engagement than do small powers, so they also are more conflict prone. This characteristic is distinct from anything peculiar to the United States or to democracies in general.

Second, the suggestion that states engage in international conflict partly as a means of managing or diverting domestic political conflict runs counter to most of the systematic research results heretofore reported (Stohl, 1980). We are concerned here with a fairly carefully delineated locus and type of domestic conflict. The locus is democratically governed states only, and the type is of only limited domestic conflict (little lethal violence; not revolution, civil war, coup d'état, nor even in most cases behavior that threatens the maintenance of the basic constitutional system). The large-scale or intense forms are not typical of the United States or Great Britain; where they occur, the state apparatus may engage in a degree of repressive behavior no longer compatible with terming it a democracy. Severe internal conflict is likely to engage the state's organs of institutionalized violence (primarily the military) to a degree that is inconsistent with also risking or seeking violent conflict with a foreign adversary. One recent study did find that countries experiencing political turmoil were less likely to engage in cooperative international behavior (which might be unpopular at home) and more likely to engage in foreign conflict (though not necessarily war) over issues of international security and status. Another found that escalation of military disputes was especially likely when domestic turmoil coincided with international opportunities (Hagan, 1986; James, 1987). If the investigation is conducted with careful theoretical specification, relationships can be found.[13]

We are therefore left with some disturbing implications about the difficulties of conducting national security policy in a democracy. We have evidence of a relationship between economic distress and involvement in international conflict and between election times and involvement in conflict. Electoral politics and economic distress (or perhaps domestic political disputes stemming from other causes) may be an especially dangerous combination for international relations. Together they constitute grounds for concern that the interests of governing elites, rather than broader "national" interests, may often drive security policy and foreign policy. The political elites have a clear interest in keeping themselves in power. They must conduct a foreign policy with a sharp eye to its domestic political consequences and may confound their personal interests with the national interest—believing, for example, that the national interest would be ill served by allowing the domestic opposition to take power.

These results also suggest serious concerns about the appropriate timing for leaders to attempt cooperative or peace-making moves toward other states. Arms control treaties, for instance, may not be well received in times of economic adversity. By this principle, the timing of consideration of the SALT II agreement by the U.S. Senate was doubly unpropitious. President Carter finally withdrew the treaty from Senate consideration following the Soviet military move into Afghanistan. Coincidentally, however, the U.S. economy was in recession, which may not have been the most promising time for ratification of an agreement requiring trust and conciliation with the nation's leading adversary. Future leaders contemplating such agreements may wish to take into account the state of the domestic economy as they ponder the degree of popular support and try to adjust their timing accordingly. Yet the opportunities afforded by the electoral cycle may be brief. "It takes the first twelve or eighteen months for an administration to climb down from campaign rhetoric into even modest pragmatism. The last twelve to eighteen months are consumed by the ever-expanding Presidential election system" (Destler et al., 1984:269). If the president is elected for a second term, by the third year of that term he is a lame duck, with little ability to garner legislative support in a Congress that is absorbed in maneuvering by those who wish to succeed him (Quandt, 1986).

Moreover, it takes two to make an agreement. Soviet leaders have their own set of domestic constraints and cycles of leadership succession. Some observers believe that periods of economic downturn for the Soviet Union may, unlike in democracies, be the times when "peace" or coexistence is most attractive; for example, that slow domestic growth led Leonid Brezhnev to seek Western technological assistance and reduction of the Soviet military burden, and that success in those efforts promised to promote his domestic political authority (Volten, 1982). None of these generalizations are solidly established, but they identify important areas for further systematic research.

Nuclear Weapons and Nuclear War

A little international conflict, or least an assertive verbal policy toward foreign adversaries, may bring approval in domestic politics. But, if so, that in no way implies public enthusiasm for war, particularly nuclear war. On the contrary, Americans' aversion to nuclear war is evident and there is strong resistance to policies that seem more likely—even in the name of limiting its extent—to bring such a war about.

No First Use of Nuclear Weapons

Everyone can argue about whether a particular policy prescription would in fact produce a desirable outcome and about what is desirable. What kinds of policies would be produced by greater popular control will vary with issue and historical context. In some respects the result would seem to please the political left. A majority of Americans regularly opposed U.S. military involvement in Central America or aid to the Nicaraguan Contras favored a nuclear freeze or other arms control even though they were deeply suspicious of the Soviet Union's treaty compliance and have long favored—by approximately a three-to-one margin—a policy of no first use of nuclear weapons. Indeed, 81 percent erroneously think that the United States already has a no-first-use policy (Russett and Starr, 1985:Chap. 10; Yankelovich and Doble, 1984:45; Kramer et al., 1983). The precise distribution of responses varies over time, and is importantly dependent on how the questions are worded, but these broad generalizations are quite solid.

Similar attitudes prevail in Western Europe—for example, opposition to deployment of nuclear-armed cruise missiles and advocacy of nuclear no first use. In 1981, for instance, fewer than 20 percent of the population in any of the largest Western European countries (Great Britain, France, West Germany, Italy) thought that NATO should use nuclear weapons to defend itself even "if a Soviet attack by conventional forces threatened to overwhelm NATO forces." The sentiment has been much the same for three decades (almost never net approval, in any country, for NATO first use), but has become even stronger in recent years. The longer NATO has relied on a first-use posture—and the less credible that posture has become, with the loss of Western strategic nuclear superiority—the more negative European attitudes have become (Russett and DeLuca, 1983; Adler, 1986:585).

Nuclear weapons are relatively cheap, however, and whether people actually would be prepared to spend more to strengthen conventional (nonnuclear) defenses is an open question. Inquiries in Great Britain have produced about an even split between those who say they would be willing to spend more for conventional weapons in order to rely less on nuclear ones and those who say they would not—a split not terribly sensitive to question wording (Russett and DeLuca, 1983:193). In the United States, two-thirds have said they would be willing to pay higher taxes for defense if both the United States and the Soviet Union would reduce nuclear weapons and replace them with nonnuclear forces (Yankelovich and Doble, 1984:45). These results should be considered tentative, both in the United States and in Western Europe, because people are much more willing to say that they will spend more for something in the abstract than if they are faced with an explicit list of trade-offs (Mueller, 1977:324–325). Their true willingness is hard to measure with survey instruments. Political leaders basically have assumed that this particular trade-off would be unacceptable. But because so few leaders have tried to persuade Western citizens to pay more to reduce reliance on nuclear weapons, the true degree of popular willingness remains unknown.

Israel is arguably the state most economically pressed by defense burdens and most exposed in the sense of risking the physical existence of its people if attacked by a determined and capable enemy. Yet even there, popular sentiment for using nuclear weapons is hardly enthusiastic. One survey produced clear disapproval: "Are there circumstances in which it would be justified (36 percent) for Israel to use nuclear weapons (if it has or will have these weapons), or do you believe that under no circumstances should nuclear weapons be used (64 percent)?" When probed, popular resistance appears less vigorous, but only for major provocations: "In a state of absolute helplessness" (76 percent) or "to save many lives" (51 percent), and not "to save a small number of lives" (16 percent) or "as a warfare tactic, instead of mobilizing the regular army" (11 percent) (Arian et al., 1987).

The reluctance of Americans to use nuclear weapons did not emerge at the beginning of the nuclear era. In 1945 the vast majority approved use of the atomic bomb against Japan; indeed, a vengeful 23 percent said, "We should have quickly used many more of them before Japan had a chance to surrender." In 1951, 66 percent thought that if the United States gets into an all-out war with Russia "we should use atom bombs first" and not "only if used on us" (19 percent), and two years earlier had rejected by almost three to one the proposition, attributed to "a U.S. Senator," that "the United States should pledge that we will never use the atom bomb in warfare until some other nation has used it on us" (Erskine, 1963). Also, in 1949 half the population thought that the United States would be justified in using atomic bombs against the Soviet Union "if one of our allies in Western Europe was attacked by the Russian army" (Kramer et al., 1983).[14]

Enthusiasm for nuclear first use faded, however, as U.S. invulnerability to Soviet retaliation faded. Between October 1949 and November 1955 (during which time the Soviet Union deployed large numbers of operational nuclear weapons and exploded a hydrogen bomb) there was a 6 percentage point shift both toward opposition to using nuclear weapons in Western Europe and favoring a no-first-use international agreement. By the late 1960s a majority of Americans rejected the idea of using nuclear weapons to defend Western European allies, and opposition to use in Europe reached two-to-one majority status in 1982 (Kramer et al., 1983). In 1951, 42 percent of the population thought that they "would feel reasonably safe if an atomic war should come" (50 percent not safe), and although in 1952 and 1954 surveys most people expected nuclear weapons to be used in any attack, 75 percent of those with opinions thought that no more than a few enemy planes would get through. But by 1956 a majority of those with opinions thought that the area where they lived would be wiped out and that they and their families would not be likely to live through an atomic war (Erskine, 1963; Withey, 1954). By 1963 the "don't knows" had shrunk from 32 percent to 6 percent, and a majority (52 percent) of the entire population thought that their chances of surviving would be poor (Kramer et al., 1983). That percentage has continued to rise somewhat.[15]

Effectively, the public has led the way toward de facto rejection of the policy of first use of nuclear weapons as an instrument of extended deterrence (deterrence of attack against allies, not of attack on the United States itself) (Graham, 1988b). By the 1980s large portions of the national security elite—not just prominent members of the former national security establishment such as the "gang of four" (Bundy et al., 1982), but admirals and generals—had reached the same conclusion. In 1984, a survey of such flag officers found 61 percent saying they could not justify a nuclear first strike against the Soviet Union (Kohut and Horrock, 1984). Note, however, that despite ambiguities, in strategic parlance no first strike constitutes a less restrictive deterrence policy than does no first use, which might include small-scale demonstrative uses not constituting an "attack." Nor does the general population necessarily support a pledge (especially unilaterally) or formal agreement of no first use, perhaps making an implicit distinction that still allows the opportunity to bluff. Nor is there much support for withholding nuclear weapons if the other side uses them first.

Disarmament and Trust

Nuclear disarmament remains a popular goal in the United States. The nuclear freeze movement was supported across a wide variety of groups with divergent attitudes on other issues (Milburn et al., 1986). Partly to counter the freeze, President Reagan presented SDI as a way to make nuclear deterrence obsolete, and both he and Gorbachev have struck resonant chords with their calls to abolish all nuclear weapons.

Distrust of Soviet international behavior is deep and remains a fundamental political barrier to concluding international arms control agreements. Nonetheless, as Table 3.1 shows, the dislike of nuclear weaponry is also deep, and many people, even among those who expect the Soviets to cheat, say they would favor an agreement to build no more. By January 1985 a 76 percent majority agreed (18 percent disagreed) that "the United States should negotiate a nuclear arms limitation agreement even if there is risk that the Soviets would cheat" (Schneider, 1987). Whereas 81 percent of those familiar with the SALT II Treaty believed that the Soviet Union had not lived up to its terms, 53 percent believed that the United States had not done so either. Pluralities or majorities disapproved of the Reagan administration's decision to abandon the treaty, thought that decision would increase the chances of war and hurt the chances to reach future arms agreements, and thought that it would increase the arms race (Gallup Report, June 1986). A reservoir of support for bold, dramatic moves can be tapped by governmental effort, as suggested by the events of late 1987 and 1988. An earlier study of public expectations of war found that despite widespread hostility toward the Soviet Union and suspicion of Soviet conciliatory moves, a sustained period (several months) of Soviet international conciliatory behavior was followed by lowered expectations of war (Mueller, 1979:314).

Yearning for Protection

If the preceding suggested that partisans of the left would be pleased with greater popular control of foreign policy, there also is important evidence to

TABLE 3.1 American Attitudes Toward Nuclear Disarmament

Attitude Toward	Percentages		
	Favor	Oppose	No Opinion
U.S.–Soviet agreement to destroy all existing nuclear weapons	47	44	9
U.S.–Soviet agreement to build no more nuclear weapons	72	20	8
Of those (60 percent of sample) who think Soviet Union "not very likely" to abide by agreement	65	28	7
If a U.N.-sponsored referendum, would vote for nuclear disarmament	59	29	12

Source: *Gallup Report, May 1981:3–9.*

the contrary. We saw the changeable, although hardly frivolous, state of attitudes toward spending for national defense and the support for toughness and limited military action. Furthermore, if dovish arms control advocates approve of a freeze or no first use, they certainly do not typically favor SDI (also known as Star Wars). Yet the principle of strategic defense has long been highly popular among Americans and not much related to ideology. Majorities or pluralities regularly favored ABM during the controversy over it under the Nixon administration, and also favor recent proposals for SDI. A plurality (and more recently a majority) has regularly said it thinks that the United States should be doing more to protect people from nuclear attack. The support is not solid; reference to it as Ronald Reagan's proposal increased the approval rate, and the balance can be tipped against SDI by reference to high costs or possible Soviet countermeasures. Majorities fear it would speed up the arms race and that the Soviets would go all out to frustrate it (Graham, 1986a; Graham and Kramer, 1986; den Oudsten, 1986; Gallup Report, December 1985). Popular support might therefore deteriorate under a different administration or different world conditions.[16] SDI's proponents have nevertheless tapped a deep vein of popular sentiment.

Popular support for SDI stems from real fears about the risks of nuclear war and the low probability of surviving it. Support varies directly with the degree to which SDI is seen as enhancing those survival prospects, from 86 percent support for a "system that was perfect and could successfully defend against all incoming nuclear weapons" to only 21 percent for "a system designed only to protect U.S. missiles, key military bases, and Washington, D.C., but not other areas" (Graham and Kramer, 1986:132). According to a Gallup (AIPO) survey in June 1981, 47 percent of the U.S. populace thought that a nuclear war was likely within the next 10 years, and 60 percent said that they did not expect that they personally would survive such a war. While those thinking a nuclear war to be probable are somewhat in the minority, they nonetheless constitute a larger proportion of the population than in almost any other country for which we have public opinion data. The populace of the U.S. superpower consistently ranks among the top two or three out of about 30 countries surveyed, sometimes matched by South Africans. (Western European countries typically showed only 20 percent thinking war likely, despite being much closer to Soviet military might.) The peak of fears of world war occurred during the Korean War, then declined and stayed relatively low until the early 1980s when, in common with virtually all countries, it peaked again. Fears remain high in the United States, at almost 60 percent in October 1986, for example. Fears are much higher in the mass public than among elites, negatively correlated with education and socioeconomic status (de Boer, 1981:131; Gallup Report, December 1986:6; Mueller, 1979).

Effects of Fear of War

Fear of war is likely to have corrosive effects on a broad range of attitudes and expectations. Psychiatrists have written about "psychic numbing" in the face of the nuclear danger (Lifton, Chap. 8 in Lifton and Falk, 1982) and have concentrated especially on the effects of nuclear war fears on U.S. and Soviet children and adolescents (American Psychiatric Association, 1982; Chivian et al., 1985; Mack and Snow, 1986). One author has declared, "It seems that these young people are growing up without . . . the sense of continuity upon which the development of stable personality structure and the formation of serviceable ideals depend. We may find we are raising generations of young people without a basis for making long-term commitments" (Mack, 1981). Psychiatric studies, however, often suffer from methodological difficulties with interviewing and with finding appropriate controls that would strengthen validity and generalizability. The same is true of many expositions on the effects of nuclear weaponry on contemporary culture (reviewed in Mandelbaum, 1981:Chap. 8). Possible psychological mechanisms for dealing with such fears could also include adaptive coping and vigilance, as well as evasion, buck passing, and "bolstering" (a form of "looking on the bright side") (Janis and Mann, 1977). Rigorous survey data are largely lacking and would be useful.[17]

Fears of war may even diminish people's willingness to save for the future. According to a rational expectations theory of saving, people save largely in anticipation of their retirement or to leave bequests. Beliefs (not necessarily conscious ones) that they are unlikely to live to retirement age or to have surviving progeny because of nuclear war could be expected to diminish readiness to save. Some macroeconomic analyses relating changes in the national savings rate to changes in expectation of war suggest that such a causal relationship may indeed operate, but the data on war expectations (from content analysis of elite publications) are of uncertain validity and the results therefore are intriguing rather than at all conclusive (Slemrod, 1986). Efforts to find a similar pattern with survey data on war expectations, either across time or across countries with different popular expectations, have failed to demonstrate a relationship. There is, however, some evidence that individual survey respondents who have high expectations of war are likely to save less than do those with lower expectations of war, even controlling for income, employment, socioeconomic status, and some other dimensions of optimism and pessimism (Russett and Lackey, 1987). The data nevertheless remain fragmentary, derived from survey instruments not designed specifically to test the hypothesis that there is a causal relationship. Further work is necessary.

To the degree that people's fears of nuclear war are deep and pervasive, they become subject to manipulation by cynical or politically utopian promises, whether those promises be to abolish nuclear weapons from the earth or to create a leakproof "peace shield" (SDI). But the basic yearning for protection could also be mobilized to support serious arms reduction and arms control agreements. Nuclear weapons provide the basis for a vivid form of symbolic politics, perhaps equivalent in foreign policy considerations to the Korean and Vietnam wars during their durations, and in similar ways (although not necessarily as severe) as unemployment does among domestic policy issues. Survey research directed specifically at the role of nuclear imagery (differences between expectation of nuclear war versus any kind of war; willingness to spend on nuclear weapons versus conventional ones or general defense spending) can help in understanding these phenomena.

Strengthening Command and Control

Many experts have recently written powerful critiques of the state of the command, control, communication, and intelligence (C^3I) facilities for nuclear weapons (Blair, 1985; Bracken, 1984). Their arguments are largely persuasive to many defense specialists across the political spectrum. They contend that whereas the vulnerability of strategic weapons themselves has been exaggerated, C^3I has been vulnerable at least since the early 1970s, with the result that U.S. strategic nuclear retaliatory capability has been unreliable in two senses. First—the continuing nightmare of doves—is the risk that in a crisis, faced with ambiguous information about an apparent Soviet attack and the knowledge that the C^3I capability to conduct any substantial, controlled response may not survive after that capability has been hit, the National Command Authority (NCA) will authorize a large-scale "retaliatory" nuclear strike under circumstances when the apparent attack is not in fact occurring or when the attack is so ragged or minimal as not to deserve such a response. The second sense relates to the stereotypical nightmare of the hawk—that the NCA will quickly lose the ability to retaliate and will lack the will to do so during the short period while it is still able; seeing this, the Soviet Union will be emboldened to attack in a confrontation.

It follows that there should be a convergence, across the political spectrum, on the need to strengthen C^3I. Yet whereas C^3I deficiencies have been well recognized in the community of defense intellectuals for many years, no adequate steps have been taken to correct them. Public discussions of deterrence and arms control have overwhelmingly focused on the traditional dimensions of weapons numbers and capabilities—a profound misallocation of attention. Minimal effort has been made to create a public constituency for debate on C^3I, and actions within the government to shift resources to improving C^3I have been insubstantial. At best, improvements have only kept pace with increases in the number and complexity of Soviet and U.S. weapons systems, producing no net improvement (Blair, 1985). To what degree may this failure be rooted in the nature of U.S. politics?

Organizational and Political Obstacles

Surely the reasons for this neglect are complex, and many of them are tangential to the subject of this chapter. They include problems of organizational behavior and bureaucratic politics. Each of the armed services has its major weapons, and those weapons substantially define a service's mission and are central to retaining both morale and budgetary resources. C^3I is the responsibility of no particular service. Hence, no service will fight political battles for it and will even resist increases in budgetary allocation for C^3I if the increases will endanger allocations for weapons. C^3I is largely in the domain of professional military officers; an effort to assert greater control by the president and other members of the NCA would raise divisive issues of civil-military relations. To confront C^3I problems seriously would also require the president and his staff to confront fears of their own personal vulnerability. If C^3I is vulnerable, they will be the first to die in a nuclear war. Thinking about this prospect requires overcoming powerful psychological defense mechanisms against thinking about one's own death.

In addition, fixing C^3I will be an expensive enterprise, requiring a public willingness to spend large sums. It has little political constituency. Professional politicians will be hesitant to take up its advocacy. It is not part of the way in which strategic issues have been framed in the public debate, hence there is no ready-made popular demand for it, as there is for arms reduction. Raising the C^3I matter in public discussion raises individuals' fears there, too. Improving C^3I is associated, both for the public and for the strategic community, with strategies for fighting limited nuclear war. Indeed, many of the measures needed to diminish the problems of C^3I could also have the effect of making limited nuclear war seem more feasible. Limited nuclear war is not politically popular; most people think it is an oxymoron, advocated by morons. (According to Yankelovich and Doble [1984:37], 83 percent of the population believe that there could be no such thing as limited nuclear war; any use of nuclear weapons would inevitably escalate to all-out war.) During the first two years of the Reagan administration talk about limited nuclear war proved politically counterproductive and had to be cut back. Similarly, the Kennedy administration's advocacy of fallout shelters was widely resisted and eventually abandoned because it made more imminent the specter of nuclear war without convincing people that it would significantly improve their prospects for survival.

An acceptable public case for C^{3}I improvement will require a more complex and nuanced presentation than has usually been feasible in discussions of strategic issues. Perhaps it is more amenable to a political "fix" than to technological ones. For example, Blair (1985:289–295) has suggested that strategic stability would be strengthened, in combination with technical improvements, by adopting a policy of "no immediate second strike." That is, the NCA would adopt, and be technically enabled to implement, a policy of retaliation only after at least 24 hours had elapsed following the first impact of an adversary's weapons on this country. With both weapons and C^{3}I suited to a secure second-strike posture, retaliation might become more certain at the same time as crisis stability was strengthened. Some aspects of this policy would undoubtedly be popular—as manifested, for example, in the existing support for no first use. Other aspects—such as the intent to defer vengeance—would not be so certain of popular acquiescence. Public preferences for toughness, conciliation, and war avoidance all need to be considered.

Further research on public attitudes and beliefs should be valuable in illuminating these and other complexities of the interplay between professional strategic analysis and the needs of democratic discussion and control. Simple propositions about public ignorance, volatility, or lack of interest simply will not do. The C^{3}I issue illustrates a problem of national and international security that demands sophisticated public attention. The elites have not satisfactorily dealt with it; it is a fundamental subject for democratic governance.

Notes

I am grateful to Thomas W. Graham for some of the data and insights in this chapter and also to Lloyd Etheredge, Scott Plous, Robert Shapiro, and Edward Tufte for extensive comments. George Randels provided valuable research assistance. Writing was partially supported by a grant from the U.S. Institute of Peace. Of course, only I bear responsibility.

1. Another dimension of the democracy/elitism debate not treated here directly concerns the need for secrecy to preserve national security, requiring restraint on the widespread diffusion of information even within the elites. Claims for restricting information often have a legitimate basis in security, particularly regarding the technology of nuclear weaponry. However, they also often are invoked merely to cloak the pursuit of policies not approved by, or even in violation of, democratic procedures. Nuclear weapons may contribute to the need for secrecy and to its abuse, but so do the whole range of policies associated with great power status. Serious restrictions on

public access to information about security affairs existed in both Great Britain and France during their imperial years, long before they became nuclear powers.

2. The extensive use of survey research materials in this chapter requires a methodological note. It has long been recognized that the answers obtained to survey questions depend importantly on cultural context, how the questions are worded, and—less well appreciated—the order in which they are asked. Indeed, there often is no truly "neutral" question wording. (A valuable if somewhat dated review is Hyman, 1972.) Consequently, the most valid and reliable use of survey data is for comparing different populations, within and between countries and over time. Where I have referred primarily to responses in one particular group I have tried to use several different questions to tap the range of attitudes for a concept.

3. Studies of the popularity of British Prime Minister Thatcher similarly attribute a boost to her vigorous response to Argentine seizure of the Falklands/Malvinas islands, although there is debate over the size of that increment relative to that of improving economic conditions (Norpoth, 1987; Sanders et al., 1987).

4. This image was consistent with popular preferences expressed in 1984, when people were asked, "If a nuclear freeze were negotiated, should development of such defensive space weapons continue (54 percent) or should development be abandoned (35 percent)?" (Graham and Kramer, 1986:133). A former member of the National Security Council has reported on the extensive use of survey data to shape both administration policy and the official justification of that policy; he indicates, for example, that data on U.S. attitudes toward terrorism influenced decisions of how to strike Libya in 1986 (Hinckley, 1988; Anderson, 1988).

5. This may be part of a general pattern of cognitive dissonance reduction, like postpurchase satisfaction.

6. $N = 18$ with annual data from 1969 to 1986 and the mean survey value used if there were two or more polls in the same year. Adjusted $R^2 = .55$; $p = .001$; autocorrelation is low as measured by the usual statistical tests. Similar results emerge using "too little" rather than "too much."

7. The apparent volatility of attitudes toward China is exaggerated by changes in the label used to identify the country. In the 1954 survey it was referred to simply as "China"; in 1967 (for a U.S. audience) by the unfavorable label of "Communist China"; and in 1972 and 1978 with the similarly unfavorable name of "Red China." Except for those, and three surveys in 1979, 1980, and 1983 using "Mainland China" with, if necessary, a supplementary "Communist China," other surveys simply used the neutral "China." Inspection of the data suggests that the score may be about 50 points higher for the neutral "China" than for "Mainland China (Communist China)."

8. Here and on other related matters (attitudes toward Soviet leader Gorbachev, trust of the Soviet Union to keep an arms control agreement, etc.) there was evidence of some shift toward more favorable attitudes in early 1988. At this time, however, the evidence was too fragmentary to discuss and too uncertain in its longer-term stability.

9. The fragmentation of elite opinion during the 1970s, on a variety of foreign policy issues, is well documented by Holsti and Rosenau (1984); fragmentation of both elite and mass opinion, with somewhat different analytical categories, is shown by Wittkopf and Maggiotto (1983).

10. Problems of issue, context, timing, political institutions, and the like contribute to the complexity. They are taken up, with further references, in Russett and Graham (1989).

11. This is also true of elites: "We saw a competitiveness engaged by challenges in underdeveloped countries but suppressed when the subjects faced a direct confrontation with the Soviet Union" (Etheredge, 1978:Chap. 4).

12. Lowi (1985:173) stresses the determined rather than volitional aspects of presidential behavior: "Carter did not take the risk of the Iranian hostage rescue mission merely to give himself leverage to move American public opinion. The leverage worked the other way: Public opinion had forced upon the president an act of the sheerest adventurism." A further constraint seems to be provided by Nincic's (1985) report that the U.S. public's hostility toward the Soviet Union varies inversely with the health of the U.S. economy. However, when one includes additional surveys now available, and controls for international events that might affect hostility levels, the effect of economic conditions disappears.

13. An excellent concurring review is Levy (1988). Small exposed countries such as Sweden dare not antagonize powerful neighbors merely because of the exigencies of electoral politics; their leaders may, however, safely criticize more distant powers (for example, the United States about its Vietnam or Nicaragua policy) (Goldmann et al., 1986:Chap. 1).

14. Graham (1988*b*) provides much additional documentation for such attitudes and for the shift discussed next. In the 1940s and 1950s there was a high level of concurrence with a no-first-use policy in the abstract and with the idea of an agreement with other countries that no one would use nuclear weapons, but that concurrence vanished in the specific reference to Soviet attack on Western Europe (Kramer et al., 1983).

15. Popular support for limited uses of military force—yet opposition to use of nuclear weapons—is reminiscent of Morgan's (1985) assessment that the U.S. government will use military force in limited ways against smaller states (presumably to demonstrate toughness and determination) precisely because its willingness to use force against a superpower adversary is so incredible.

16. Bobrow's (1969) fine analysis of attitudes toward ballistic missile defense found that support for it was essentially unrelated to perceptions of its cost or likely performance; it was, in the terminology of this chapter, an issue of symbolic politics.

17. Schuman et al. (1987) note that, save for the 1983–1986 period, Americans have not tended to cite the threat of nuclear war as one of the country's "most important problems" and that this is not sensitive to question format. As they note, this can neither confirm nor refute the proposition that, by protective psychic denial, fears of war are kept largely below the surface of everyday consciousness. Hence other measures, especially nonobtrusive ones, are needed.

References

Adler, K. 1986. West European and American public opinion on peace, defence, and arms control in a cross-national perspective. *International Social Science Journal* 38(4):589–600.

Almond, G. 1950. *The American People and Foreign Policy*. New Haven, Conn.: Yale University Press.

Alt, J.E., and K.A. Chrystal. 1983. *Political Economy*. Berkeley, Calif.: University of California Press.

American Psychiatric Association. 1982. *Psychological Aspects of Nuclear Developments: Aspects of Nuclear Developments: Task Force Report*. Washington, D.C.: American Psychiatric Association.

Anderson, J. 1988. White House took polls to make sure public would back bombing of Libya. *New Haven Register*, 28 February, 3.

Arian, A., T. Herman, and I. Talmud. 1987. *National Security Policy and Public Opinion in Israel: The Guardian of Israel*. Boulder, Col.: Westview.

Ben-Haven, U., and B. Temkin. 1986. The overloaded juggler: The electoral economic cycle in Israel. In A. Arian and M. Shamir, eds., *The Elections in Israel—1984*. New Brunswick, N.J.: Transaction.

Blair, B.G. 1985. *Strategic Command and Control: Redefining the Nuclear Threat*. Washington, D.C.: The Brookings Institution.

Bobrow, D. 1969. The organization of American national security opinions. *Public Opinion Quarterly* 33(1):221–239.

de Boer, C. 1981. The polls: Our commitment to World War III. *Public Opinion Quarterly* 45(1):126–134.

Bracken, P. 1984. *The Command and Control of Nuclear Forces*. New Haven, Conn.: Yale University Press.

Brody, R. 1984. International crises: A rallying point for the president? *Public Opinion* 6(6):41–43,60.

Brown, T.A., and A.A. Stein. 1982. Review of Tufte (1978). *Comparative Politics* 14(4):479–497.

Bundy, McG., G. Kennan, R. McNamara, and G. Smith. 1982. Nuclear weapons and the alliance. *Foreign Affairs* 60(4): 753–768.

Caspary, W. 1970. The "mood theory": A study of public opinion and foreign policy. *American Political Science Review* 64(2):536–547.

Chan, S. 1984. Mirror, mirror on the wall . . . are the freer countries more pacific? *Journal of Conflict Resolution* 28(4):617–648.

Chivian, E., J.E. Mack, J. Waletzky, C. Lazaroff, R. Doctor, and J. Goldenring. 1985. Soviet children and the threat of nuclear war. *American Journal of Orthopsychiatry* 55(October):484–502.

Cotton, T.Y.C. 1986. War and American democracy: Voting trends in the last five American wars. *Journal of Conflict Resolution* 30(4):616–635

Dahl, R. 1985. *Controlling Nuclear Weapons: Democracy versus Guardianship*. Syracuse, N.Y.: Syracuse University Press.

Destler, I.M., L. Gelb, and A. Lake. 1984. *Our Own Worst Enemy: The Unmaking of American Foreign Policy*. New York: Simon and Schuster.

Deutsch, K.W., and R.L. Merritt. 1965. Effects of events on national and international images. In H. Kelman, ed., *International Behavior: A Social-Psychological Analysis*. New York: Holt.

Domke, W. 1988. *War and the Changing Global System*. New Haven, Conn.: Yale University Press.

Erskine, H.G. 1963. The polls: Atomic weapons and nuclear energy. *Public Opinion Quarterly* 27(2):155–190.
Etheredge, L. 1978. *A World of Men: The Private Sources of American Foreign Policy*. Cambridge, Mass.: MIT Press.
Goldmann, K., S. Berglund, and G. Sjostedt. 1986. *Democracy and Foreign Policy: The Case of Sweden*. Aldershot, England: Gower.
Graham, T.W. 1986a. *Public Attitudes Toward Active Defense: ABM and Star Wars, 1945–1985*. Cambridge, Mass.: Center for International Affairs, Massachusetts Institute of Technology.
———. 1986b. Reducing Military Spending; Public Opinion and Strategic Planning for Progressives. Paper prepared for the Communications Consortium, Washington, D.C., November.
———. 1988a. The Pattern and Importance of Public Knowledge in the Nuclear Age. *Journal of Conflict Resolution* 32(2):319–334.
———. 1988b. Future fission? Extended deterrence and American public opinion. Occasional paper. Center for Science and International Affairs, Harvard University.
Graham, T.W., and B.M. Kramer. 1986. The polls: ABM and Star Wars: Attitudes toward nuclear defense, 1945–1985. *Public Opinion Quarterly* 50(1):125–134.
Hagan, J.D. 1986. Domestic political conflict, issue areas, and some dimensions of foreign policy behavior other than conflict. *International Interactions* 12(4):291–313.
Hibbs, D. 1982. On the demand for economic outcomes: Macroeconomic performance and mass support in the United States, Great Britain, and Germany. *Journal of Politics* 44(3):426–462.
Hibbs, D., and N. Vasilatos. 1981. Macroeconomic performance and mass political support in the United States and Great Britain. In D. Hibbs and H. Fassbender, eds., *Contemporary Political Economy*. New York: North Holland.
Hinckley, R.H. 1988. Polls and peacemakers: The case of the National Security Council. Paper presented at the American Association of Public Opinion Researchers, Toronto.
Holsti, O., and J. Rosenau. 1979. Vietnam, consensus, and the belief systems of American leaders. *World Politics* 32(1):1–56.
———. 1984. American leadership in world affairs: Vietnam and the breakdown of consensus. London: Allen & Unwin.
Huth, P., and B. Russett. 1988. Deterrence failure and escalation to war. *International Studies Quarterly* 32(1): 29–45.
Hyman, H. 1972. *Secondary Analysis of Sample Surveys*. New York: Wiley.
Jacobson, G.C. 1983. *The Politics of Congressional Elections*. Boston: Little, Brown.
Jacobson, H.K. 1985. *The Determination of the United States Military Force Posture: Political Processes and Policy Changes*. Washington, D.C.: The Woodrow Wilson Center, International Security Program.
James, P. 1987. Externalization of conflict: Testing a crisis-based model. *Canadian Journal of Political Science* 3(30):573–598.
Janis, I., and R. Mann. 1977. *Decision Making*. New York: Free Press.

Jensen, L. 1982. *Explaining Foreign Policy*. Englewood Cliffs, N.J.: Prenctice-Hall.
Job, B.L., and C.W. Ostrom, Jr. 1986. Opportunity and Choice: The U.S. and the Political Use of Force, 1948–1976. Paper presented at the American Political Science Association, Washington, D.C.
Kahneman, D., and A. Tversky. 1979. Prospect theory: An analysis of decision under risk. *Econometrica* 47(2):263–292.
Kernell, S. 1978. Explaining presidential popularity. *American Political Science Review* 72(2):506–522.
———. 1986. *Going Public: New Strategies of Presidential Leadership*. Washington, D.C.: Congressional Quarterly.
Kinder, D.R. 1981. Presidents, prosperity, and public opinion. *Public Opinion Quarterly* 45(1):1–21.
Kinder, D.R., and R.D. Kiewiet. 1979. Economic discontent and political behavior: The role of personal grievances and collective economic judgments in congressional voting. *American Journal of Political Science* 23(3):495–527.
Kohut, A., and N. Horrock. 1984. Generally speaking: Surveying the military's top brass. *Public Opinion* 7(5):42–45.
Kramer, B.S., M. Kalick, and M. Milburn. 1983. Attitudes toward nuclear weapons and nuclear war: 1945–1982. *Journal of Social Issues* 39(1):7–24.
Kramer, G. 1971. Short-term fluctuations in U.S. voting behavior. *American Political Science Review* 65(1):131–143.
———. 1983. The ecological fallacy revisited: Aggregate-versus individual-level findings on economics and elections and sociotropic voting. *American Political Science Review* 77(1):92–111.
Krell, G. 1981. Capabilities and armaments: Business cycles and defense spending in the United States, 1945–79. *Journal of Peace Research* 18(3):221–240.
Leng, R. 1984. Reagan and the Russians: Crisis bargaining beliefs and the historical record. *American Political Science Review* 78(2):655–684.
Levy, J.S. 1988. The diversionary theory of war: A critique. In M. Midlarsky, ed., *Handbook of War Studies*. London: Allen and Unwin.
Lifton, R., and R. Falk. 1982. *Indefensible Weapons: The Political and Psychological Case Against Nuclearism*. New York: Basic Books.
Lindsay, J.M. 1986. Trade sanctions as policy instruments: A re-examination. *International Studies Quarterly* 30(2):153–174.
Lowi, T. 1985. *The Personal President*. Ithaca, N.Y.: Cornell University Press.
Mack, J.E. 1981. Psychosocial aspects of the nuclear arms race. *Bulletin of the Atomic Scientists* 37(4):18–23.
Mack, J.E., and R. Snow. 1986. Psychological effects on children and adolescents. In R.K. White, ed., *Psychology and the Prevention of Nuclear War*. New York: New York University Press.
Mandelbaum, M. 1981. *The Nuclear Revolution: International Politics before and after Hiroshima*. Cambridge, Mass.: Cambridge University Press.
Mayer, K.E. 1988. *The Politics and Economics of Defense Contracting*. Ph.D. dissertation, Yale University.

Mayhew, D.A. 1974. *Congress: The Electoral Connection*. New Haven, Conn.: Yale University Press.

Milburn, M., P. Watanabe, and B. Kramer. 1986. The nature and sources of attitudes toward a nuclear freeze. *Political Psychology* 7(4):661–674.

Mintz, A. 1988. Electoral cycles and defense spending: American concepts and Israeli realities. *Comparative Political Studies* 21(1):368–386.

Monroe, K. 1984. *Presidential Popularity and the Economy*. New York: Praeger.

Morgan, P. 1985. Saving face for the sake of deterrence. In R. Jervis, R.N. Lebow, and J. Stein, eds., *Psychology and Deterrence*. Ithaca, N.Y.: Cornell University Press.

Mueller, J.E. 1973. *War, Presidents, and Public Opinion*. New York: Wiley.

———. 1977. Changes in American public attitudes toward international involvement. In E.P. Stern, ed., *The Limits of Military Intervention*. Beverly Hills, Calif.: Sage.

———. 1979. Public expectations of war during the cold war. *American Journal of Political Science* 23(2):301–329.

Neuman, W.R. 1986. *The Paradox of Mass Politics: Knowledge and Opinion in the American Electorate*. Cambridge, Mass.: Harvard University Press.

Nincic, M. 1985. The American public and the Soviet Union: The domestic context of discontent. *Journal of Peace Research* 16(2):345–357.

———. 1988a. The United States, the Soviet Union, and the politics of opposites. *World Politics* 40(4):452–475.

———. 1988b *U.S. Foreign Policy*. Washington, D.C.: Congressional Quarterly.

Nincic, M., and T. Cusack. 1979. The political economy of U.S. military spending. *Journal of Peace Research*, 22(4):101–115.

Nordhaus, W. 1975. The political business cycle. *Review of Economic Studies* 42(1):169–189.

Norpoth, H. 1987. Guns and butter and government popularity in Britain. *American Political Science Review* 81(3):449–460.

Ostrom, C.W., and B.L. Job. 1986. The president and the political use of force. *American Political Science Review* 80(2):541–566.

Ostrom, C.W., and R. Marra. 1986. U.S. defense spending and the Soviet estimate. *American Political Science Review* 80(3):819–842.

Ostrom, C.W., and D. Simon. 1985. Promise and performance: A dynamic model of presidential popularity. *American Political Science Review* 79(2):334–358.

den Oudsten, E. 1986. Public opinion on peace and war. In Stockholm International Peace Research Institute, ed., *World Armaments and Disarmament: SIPRI Yearbook 1986*. Oxford, England: Oxford University Press.

Page, B.I., and R.Y. Shapiro. 1983. Effects of public opinion on policy. *American Political Science Review* 77(1):175–190.

———. 1984. Presidents as opinion leaders: Some new evidence. *Policy Studies Journal* 12(4):649–661.

Page, B.I., R.Y. Shapiro, and G.R. Dempsey. 1987. What moves public opinion? *American Political Science Review* 81(1):23–44.

Plous, S. 1988. Disarmament, arms control, and peace in the nuclear age: Political objectives and relevant research. *Journal of Social Issues* 44(2):133–154.

Quandt, W.B. 1986. *Camp David: Peacemaking and Politics*. Washington, D.C.: The Brookings Institution.

Reilly, J.E., ed. 1983. *American Public Opinion and U.S. Foreign Policy*. Chicago: Chicago Council on Foreign Relations.

———. 1987. *American Public Opinion and U.S. Foreign Policy*. Chicago: Chicago Council on Foreign Relations.

Russett, B. 1987. Economic change as a cause of international conflict. In F. Blackaby and C. Schmidt, eds., *Peace, Defence, and Economic Analysis*. London: Macmillan.

———. 1989. Economic decline, electoral pressure, and the initiation of interstate conflict. In C. Gochman and A.N. Sabrosky, eds., *Prisoners of War? Nation-states in the Modern Era*. Lexington, Mass.: Heath.

Russett, B., and D.R. DeLuca. 1983. Theater nuclear forces: Public opinion in Western Europe. *Political Science Quarterly* 98(2):179–196.

———. 1981. "Don't tread on me:" Public opinion and foreign policy in the eighties. *Political Science Quarterly* 96(3):381–400.

Russett, B., and T.W. Graham. 1989. Public opinion and national security policy: Relationships and impacts. In M. Midlarsky, ed., *Handbook of War Studies*. London: Allen and Unwin.

Russett, B., and E.C. Hanson. 1975. *Interest and Ideology: The Foreign Policy Beliefs of American Businessmen*. San Francisco, Calif.: Freeman.

Russett, B., and M. Lackey. 1987. In the shadow of the cloud: If there's no tomorrow, why save today? *Political Science Quarterly* 102(2):259–272.

Russett, B., and H. Starr. 1985. *World Politics: The Menu for Choice*, 2nd ed. New York: Freeman.

Sanders, D., H. Ward, and D. Marsh, with T. Fletcher. 1987. Government popularity and the Falklands war: A reassessment. *British Journal of Political Science* 17(3):287–314.

Schneider, W. 1984. Public opinion. In J. Nye, ed., *The Making of America's Soviet Policy*. New Haven, Conn.: Yale University Press.

———. 1987. "Rambo" and reality: having it both ways. In K. Oye, R. Lieber, and D. Rothchild, eds., *Eagle Resurgent? The Reagan Era in American Foreign Policy*. Boston: Little, Brown.

Schuman, H., J. Ludwig, and J. Krosnick. 1987. The perceived threat of nuclear war, salience, and open questions. *Public Opinion Quarterly* 50(4):519–536.

Sears, D.O., R. Lau, T. Tyler, and H. Allen. 1980. Self-interest vs. symbolic politics in policy attitudes and presidential voting. *American Political Science Review* 74(3):670–685.

Shapiro, R.Y., and B.I. Page. 1988. Foreign policy and the rational public. *Journal of Conflict Resolution* 32(2):211–247.

Singer, J.D., and M. Small. 1976. The war-proneness of democratic regimes. *Jerusalem Journal of International Relations* 1(1):50–69.

Slemrod, J. 1986. Savings and the fear of nuclear war. *Journal of Conflict Resolution* 30(3):403:419.

Smith, T. 1985. The polls: America's most important problem part I: National and international. *Public Opinion Quarterly* 49(2):264–274.

Stohl, M. 1980. The nexus of civil and international conflict. In T.R. Gurr, ed., *Handbook of Political Conflict*. New York: Free Press.

Stoll, R.J. 1984. The guns of November: Presidential re-elections and the use of force. *Journal of Conflict Resolution* 28(2):231–246.

Suedfeld, P., and P. Tetlock. 1977. Integrative complexity and communication in international crises. *Journal of Conflict Resolution* 21(1): 169–184.

Tetlock, P. 1985. Integrative complexity of American and Soviet foreign policy rhetoric. *Journal of Personality and Social Psychology* 49(6):1565–1585.

Tetlock, P., and C. McGuire. 1985. Integrative complexity as a predictor of Soviet foreign policy behavior. *International Journal of Group Tensions* 14(2):113–128.

Thompson, W.R., and G. Zuk. 1983. American elections and the international economic cycle. *Journal of Conflict Resolution* 27(3):464–484.

Tufte, E.R. 1978. *Political Control of the Economy*. Princeton, N.J: Princeton University Press.

Verba, S., R. Brody, E. Parker, N. Nie, N. Polsby, P. Ekman, and G. Black. 1967. Public opinion and the war in Vietnam. *American Political Science Review* 61(2):313–333.

Volten, P.M.E. 1982. *Brezhnev's Peace Plan: A Study of Soviet Domestic Political Process and Power*. Boulder, Col.: Westview.

Weede, E. 1984. Democracy and war involvement. *Journal of Conflict Resolution* 28(4):649–664.

Weissberg, R. 1976. *Public Opinion and Popular Government*. Englewood Cliffs, N.J.: Prentice-Hall.

Withey, S.B. 1954. *Fourth Survey of Public Knowledge and Attitudes Concerning Civil Defense*. Ann Arbor, Mich.: Institute for Social Research, University of Michigan.

Wittkopf, E. 1987. Elites and masses: Another look at attitudes toward America's role. *International Studies Quarterly* 31(2):133–159.

Wittkopf, E., and M. Maggiotto. 1983. Elites and masses: A comparative analysis of attitudes toward America's world role. *Journal of Politics* 45(2):307–333.

Yankelovich, D., and J. Doble. 1984. The public mood. *Foreign Affairs* 63(1): 33–46.

4

The Causes of War: A Review of Theories and Evidence

JACK S. LEVY

Historical and Theoretical Context 213
THE HISTORICAL RECORD, 213   THEORIES OF INTERNATIONAL CONFLICT:
A PRELIMINARY OVERVIEW, 215   ORGANIZING FRAMEWORK, 219

Systemic-Level Theories 223
THE REALIST PARADIGM, 224   BALANCE OF POWER THEORY, 228   BUENO DE
MESQUITA'S EXPECTED UTILITY THEORY, 243   THEORIES OF POWER TRANSITION
AND HEGEMONIC WAR, 251   LATERAL PRESSURE THEORY, 258   LIBERAL ECONOMIC
THEORIES OF WAR, 260

Societal-Level Theories 262
MARXIST-LENINIST THEORIES OF WAR, 263   DEMOCRACY AND WAR, 267   DOMESTIC
POLITICS AND THE SCAPEGOAT HYPOTHESIS, 271

Decision-Making Theories 274
ORGANIZATIONAL POLITICS AND PROCESSES, 275   MISPERCEPTION AND WAR, 279

Implications for the Nuclear Era 289
Conclusions 295
Notes 298
References 315

There can be little doubt regarding the importance of the question of the causes of war. War has been a frequent and persistent pattern of behavior among and within states for millennia and has been enormously destructive of human life and property.[1] In addition to its human and material costs, war has had a profound impact on the behavior of states in the world arena, on the internal development of states, and on the welfare and behavior of individuals and groups within societies. War has been one of the primary vehicles for change in the international system, and the outcomes of major wars have been a primary determinant of the structure of political influence in world politics and of the structure of economic relations among states (Gilpin, 1981). The development of nation-states and capitalist economic structures nearly five centuries ago cannot be understood apart from patterns of warfare among states (Tilly, 1975; Howard, 1976), and the development of new states in the contemporary era continues to be influenced by warfare and preparations for war.[2]

The question of the causes of war is particularly urgent in the nuclear age, for the destructiveness of nuclear weapons and the range of intercontinental delivery systems mean that a major war between the nuclear powers could very well bring an end to modern civilization as we know it. If we are to have any hope of reducing the occurrence of war in the international system, it is imperative that we gain a better understanding of its causes. Such knowledge is also necessary if we are to achieve a better understanding of the more general patterns of the relationships among states, how those patterns have evolved in the past, and how they are likely to change in the future.

In spite of the enormous intellectual energy that has been directed to the question of the causes of war—by philosophers, historians, political scientists, theologians, anthropologists, sociologists, psychologists, economists, mathematicians, biologists, and others—a clear answer to that question has yet to be found. There is little agreement among scholars regarding the identity of the causes of war, the methodology by which those causes might be discovered, or the conceptual framework by which multiple causes might be integrated into a coherent theoretical explanation. Instead, there is a plethora of theories identifying a wide range of causal variables and combining them in a variety of ways. The only consensus is that the question is complex and that there is no single cause of war, although even this view is sometimes challenged.

This is not to say that we have learned little from the enormous amount of research on the conditions, processes, and events leading to the outbreak and escalation of war. Within certain research communities considerable progress has been made in identifying patterns of behavior that repeatedly occur under certain well-specified conditions and in providing plausible theoretical explanations for these observed patterns. Economists have taught us a great deal about what constitutes rational behavior under conditions of risk and uncertainty. Psychologists have demonstrated that individuals do not often behave as a rational economic model would predict and have taught us much about the behavior of individuals under stress, the dynamics of small group behavior, and the nature of heuristics and biases that affect the processes of judgment and decision making. We have also learned about mass psychology and the phenomenon of modern nationalism and about the internal dynamics of modern organizations. We have gained a good understanding of historical patterns of warfare in the modern world and of long cycles of war and peace. Certain empirical regularities have emerged, even if there are disagreements as to how to explain them.

Moreover, it is clear that some of this research has had considerable impact on policymakers. Theories of deterrence and crisis stability have had an important influence on the evolution of U.S. strategic doctrine and defense planning, and theories of coercion and limited war undoubtedly influenced U.S. policymakers during the 1960s (Kissinger, 1957; Brodie, 1959; Wohlstetter, 1959; Taylor, 1960; Schelling, 1960; Osgood, 1957). Recent research on the dangers of inadvertent war, the requirements of crisis management, and the performance of complex command and control systems (Roderick, 1983; Frei, 1983; George, 1983, 1984; Lebow, 1987; Bracken, 1983; Blair, 1985) has led to numerous proposals for organizational restructuring and behavioral changes to minimize the risks of nuclear war (Allison et al., 1985; Blechman, 1985). To take a more specific example, it has been argued that President Kennedy's skillful management of the Cuban missile crisis was influenced by his reading of Tuchman's (1962) account of the outbreak of World War I, which emphasized the dangers of miscalculation and policy rigidities in a crisis (Allison, 1971:218).[3]

Although it is true that within certain research communities there is consensus regarding the validity of certain hypotheses, it is also true that in other research communities sharing a different set of analytic assumptions these propositions might be rejected or considered to be theoretically inconsequential. Moreover, even when there is agreement on the validity of specific propositions, the point is that no one has been able to fit these different pieces together to complete the puzzle. No one has successfully integrated what we know into a single theoretical framework that provides a general explanation of the causes of war, at least in a way that has generated anything close to scholarly consensus on its validity. In particular, scholars have failed to integrate what we know about individual psychology with what we know about organizational behavior, political economy, and state-society relationships into a theory of how *states* make foreign policies on issues of war and peace. They have also failed to integrate theories of individual state behavior into a more comprehensive theory of strategic interaction and bargaining in a constantly evolving international system. Nor is there any consensus on whether the best of our existing theories have any relevance for the nuclear age. Some social scientists even doubt that it is possible to construct such a general theory and have joined historians in insisting that wars, like other social phenomena, are historically unique.

Given the importance of the question of the causes of war and its implications for contemporary policy, one might expect find a number of attempts to survey the general state of the literature in order to summarize what we know, assess the limitations of our knowledge, and suggest the most urgent and promising avenues for future research. Surprisingly, there are remarkably few surveys of this kind and none which is really comprehensive.[4] This chapter will fill this enormous gap in the literature by conducting a critical review of theories of the causes of war and, in the process, provide a general background for many of the essays in *Behavior, Society, and Nuclear War*.

The underlying theme of these volumes concerns the prevention of nuclear war, and that draws our attention to the likely causes of war between the superpowers. This leads to a primary focus on the causes of interstate war rather than on civil war, imperial or colonial war, or terrorism, although these other phenomenon will be considered to the extent that they are contributory causes of interstate war. My assumption is that the most appropriate historical referents for a superpower war in the future are interstate wars of the past, particularly great power wars. This interstate and great power orientation does not narrow our focus too much, of course, because this is the primary focus of the literature on the causes of war. The literature is still quite diverse, and this review will necessarily have to be selective. Some types of wars are more important than others and consequently deserve more attention. Some theories are more important than others, and these, too, require particular attention.

Before conducting a detailed examination of theories of the causes of war, therefore, it would be useful to step back and attempt to place this review within a larger historical and theoretical context. I will begin with a brief summary of historical patterns and trends in war in order to get a better sense of the phenomenon the literature is trying to explain and to assess the implications of historical trends for current theoretical and policy concerns, including the future evolution of war. I will then take a broad and somewhat reflective overview of the theoretical literature in order to help provide a broader context for our more detailed summaries of specific theories, justify the selective focus, and demonstrate the relevance of these theories for the nuclear age.

Historical and Theoretical Context

The Historical Record

One can find evidence of warfare as far back as prehistoric times (Ferrill, 1985), and written evidence is sufficient to trace a fairly comprehensive and continuous record of warfare since about 600 B.C. (Dupuy and Dupuy, 1977). It would be most useful, however, to restrict our attention to patterns of warfare in the modern state system, the origins of which most historians trace to about 1500 A.D..[5] The trends in warfare are complex and vary for different types of war, but some general patterns do emerge. We have a fairly good picture of the patterns of war involving the great powers in the Europe-based system prior to this century and in the larger global system after that, but we have a less accurate picture of other types of war.[6]

There have been approximately 120 wars involving a great power against another state since 1500, or about one every four years.[7] Of these, about half have been wars between great powers, or great power wars. Ten of these great power wars have been fairly long "general wars" involving all or nearly all of the great powers in the system, many smaller states as well, and enormous casualties; in fact, these 10 wars account for nearly 90 percent of the casualties from interstate wars involving the great powers over the last five centuries (Levy, 1983a:Chap. 4; 1985a).

There appear to be some very distinctive historical trends in war, trends that do not characterize the twentieth century alone but that apply to the entire five-century span of the modern Eurocentric state system. One is that great power wars have been declining in frequency but increasing in seriousness. Whereas a new great power war has occurred on average once every fifteen years in the twentieth century, they occurred once every four years in the sixteenth century. Those great power wars that have occurred, however, have become more serious in numerous respects: they have involved a larger number of great powers, more nation-months of war, and much higher casualties. They have not, on average, become longer in duration. The fact that the current "century of total war" (Aron, 1955) has witnessed enormously destructive wars but relatively few of them (by historical standards) is consistent with another pattern that has characterized the last five centuries of the modern great power system: there has been a slight tendency for wars in a given period to be either frequent but limited or infrequent but serious (Levy and Morgan, 1984; Morgan and Levy, 1989). One significant exception to these trends is the disproportionately low frequency and low seriousness of great power warfare in the nineteenth century (Levy, 1982).

The increasing destructiveness of warfare has been explained not only by changes in military technology, but also by the increasing rationalization of force as an instrument of state policy and the centralization of military power in the hands of the state; the commercialization of war and the increasingly symbiotic relationship between war and commerce; the popularization of war in the form of the nation in arms and conscripted manpower; the professionalization of military power, as evidenced by the development of a peacetime military establishment under the direction of a professional military elite and general staff system; and the scientific revolution, in which the entire scientific, engineering, and technological capacities of the state are mobilized for the conduct of war (Millis, 1956; Osgood, 1967; Howard, 1976; Levy, 1982).

Other types of war have followed different patterns over time. Wars involving the great powers against nonpowers have become less frequent and shorter but only somewhat more severe in terms of casualties (the most severe wars have become more severe, but the severity of most wars is on average only slightly greater). The frequency of colonial or imperial wars increased gradually, exploded in the nineteenth century, and then declined with the liquidation of the European colonial empires in the twentieth century.[8] Our picture of wars between smaller states is much less clear, particularly for the pre-nineteenth century period, but it is clear that the frequency of those wars has increased.[9] These increases should be put in context, however. Whereas the number of great powers in the system has been roughly constant over time (five or six), the number of states as a whole in the system, and hence the total number of opportunities for war, has increased dramatically. Proportional to the size of the system, the number of small state wars has not increased. Similarly, the number of civil wars has increased over time, but not disproportionately to the increasing size of the system (Singer and Small, 1972; Small and Singer, 1982).[10]

These trends have several important implications for a general review of the literature on the causes of war, particularly if one concern is the relevance of these theories for the nuclear age. One is that the pattern of warfare in the nuclear age appears to be different from the patterns of earlier eras. There are fewer great power wars but an increased number of wars between medium and smaller states, some of which are essentially proxy wars between the superpowers. There are also more civil wars, which may be largely indigenous in their origins but which often involve the interests of the superpowers. Consequently, there is an increased risk that one of these small interstate or civil wars might escalate through expansion into a superpower war.

These considerations have led some observers to argue that the most likely route to a superpower confrontation is through the escalation of a local conflict, that consequently traditional theories of great power war have diminished relevance for the nuclear age, and that the primary task for contemporary scholarship on war is to focus on proxy wars, wars of intervention, and processes of escalation that might involve the great powers. These observers would argue that a review of the conflict literature should focus more heavily on smaller wars, intervention, and escalation processes and less on the "traditional" literature on great power conflict. This is an important argument, but I think that it is wrong. In order to explain why and to justify the approach taken in this chapter, it is first necessary to take a brief and somewhat reflective look at the theoretical literature on international conflict.

Theories of International Conflict: A Preliminary Overview

The literature on the causes of war demonstrates a clear bias toward great power behavior. The majority of diplomatic historians have followed Leopold von Ranke ([1833]1973) in conceiving European history as the history of great power relations. A.J.P. Taylor (1954:xix), for example, argues that "the relations of the great powers have determined the history of Europe." Waltz (1979:72–73) reflects the argument of many political scientists in arguing that any theory of international politics must necessarily be based on the great powers, for they define the context for others as well as for themselves. Nearly all versions of balance of power theory are (whether explicitly or implicitly) theories of great power behavior, and current theories of hegemonic decline, power transition, and hegemonic war clearly focus on the causes and consequences of the behavior of the leading powers in the system (Organski, 1968; Modelski, 1978; Gilpin, 1981; Kennedy, 1987).[11]

The literature on the causes of war is biased toward the great powers in another sense: many of our theories of war and of international behavior in general are disproportionately influenced by a small handful of cases of great power war. The World War I case in particular has attracted an enormous amount of attention by historians and political scientists but also by military strategists, social psychologists, and others. Some theories of the balance of power, alliance behavior, economic imperialism, militarism, preventive war, misperceptions, organizational rigidity in the military, inadvertent war, and other behavior have been generated inductively from the 1914 case.[12] This raises the danger that some of our theoretical generalizations may be too closely tied to a single case and gives additional emphasis to the need for systematic empirical tests of theories of war across many cases.

It is important to note that the great power bias in the theoretical literature on war pertains primarily to systemic-level theories of war, those that trace war to the structure of the international system and the relationships among states. Much of the theoretical literature does indeed focus on systemic-level variables, and the impact of anarchic structures, power distributions, and alliance configurations is different for small states acting in the shadows of the great powers than it is for the great powers themselves. There has recently been increased attention to domestic political and decision-making variables and processes contributing to the outbreak of war (Holsti, 1972; Brecher, 1980; Lebow, 1981; Jervis, 1988a; Levy, 1989a), and many theories based on these variables are as applicable to smaller states as they are to the great powers. Admittedly, historical changes in the nature of economic systems, political structures, and other domestic variables have been more profound than changes in the structure of the international system itself (and probably also more profound than changes in individual threat perception and decision-making processes). This means that hypotheses linking domestic structures and war may be more difficult to generalize from earlier eras to the present as compared to systemic-level hypotheses, for great powers as well as for smaller states.

It is also true that relatively little serious attention has been devoted to the general theoretical questions of escalation, intervention, and proxy wars. Much has been written on likely scenarios for escalation to nuclear war (Kahn, 1965), and there have also been a number of simulations and other studies of the dangers of escalation of local conflicts (in the Middle East and elsewhere) to a superpower confrontation. The literature on limited war (Osgood, 1957, 1979; Halperin, 1963; Kissinger, 1957) and war termination (Fox, 1970; Iklé, 1971; Mitchell and Nicholson, 1983; Beer and Mayer, 1986) also deals implicitly with the question of escalation. Although the theoretical literature on the causes of war includes a great deal on the vertical escalation of a dyadic conflict; there is little on the horizontal escalation of local conflicts (Smoke, 1977; Bloomfield and Leiss, 1969; Blainey, 1973:Chap. 13–15; Barringer, 1972). There is no distinct *theory* of escalation, one that specifies under what conditions and through what processes local conflicts or low-level superpower conflicts escalate to superpower crises and war.[13] Similarly, there is no theory of intervention, which is one possible path to the escalation of war.[14]

What theoretical literature we do have on intervention and escalation processes essentially involves applications of more general hypotheses regarding the causes of war, including hypotheses linking war to balance of power considerations, alliances, domestic politics, bureaucratic processes, and misperceptions. Thus, a general grounding in theories of the causes of war is an essential point of departure for the development of a theory of intervention or escalation.

An understanding of escalation and intervention processes should be tied to the historical as well as traditional theoretical literature on war. The absence of any case of escalation to great power war in the nuclear age means that it is not possible to have an empirical test of a theory of escalation that is confined to the post-1945 period.[15] Our confidence in the validity of such a theory would be greatly enhanced if it were tested against the historical record of great power behavior while at the same time acknowledging the unique features of the nuclear era. The expansion of the data base to the prenuclear era would not only incorporate cases of escalation, it would also facilitate a more fully controlled empirical test by increasing the extent of variation in several important independent variables (for example, polarity, or the degree of diffusion of power in the system). In addition, in the absence of a comparative historical study there is little empirical basis for any argument that escalation processes in the nuclear age are distinct from those in the past, or that the processes of intervention in or escalation from a local war are important in the contemporary era but not in the past. In fact, there are a sufficient number of past great power wars growing out of smaller conflicts to suggest that their careful examination may help us understand escalation processes in the contemporary era.[16]

This discussion leads to a more general characteristic of the literature on the causes of war: the gap between (1) the theoretical and empirical literature on the causes of war, and (2) research by contemporary strategic analysts on deterrence, crisis stability, arms control, and superpower relations in general. Most of those who attempt to construct general theories of the causes of war focus on the pre-1945 period and make no explicit attempt to integrate the nuclear factor into their theories. Some go so far as to say that the causes of war are eternal, that nothing fundamental has changed in the nuclear age (particularly international anarchy and human nature), and that consequently their theories are as applicable today as in previous eras. Many quantitative empirical studies of international conflict, for example, include the nuclear era within the temporal domain of their analysis, but they rarely include a variable reflecting the presence or absence of nuclear weapons.[17]

Many of those who focus on strategic deterrence or on other contemporary strategic issues make the opposite argument, assert that the nuclear revolution has been so fundamental that everything has changed, that whatever happened before 1945 is no longer relevant, and that therefore they have little to learn from theorists or historians focusing on earlier eras. These theorists make little use of the theoretical or empirical literature on the causes of war in their work on contemporary policy. As a result, current strategic doctrines and the deterrence theories from which they are derived generally have little grounding in the theoretical literature on the causes of war or in the historical reality of great power behavior in the past.

While some insist that nothing has changed and others insist that everything has changed, others try to have it both ways. Many scholars demonstrate with ample historical evidence that war has been an integral part of international relations for millennia; argue that this pattern is a necessary consequence of any anarchic international system; acknowledge that the system is still anarchic; but then make an inferential leap and conclude that the nuclear era is sufficiently different and that past historical tendencies will be mitigated in the nuclear age. This argument is usually made with little rigorous theoretical analysis or empirical justification and with little attempt to integrate these two divergent tendencies into a single coherent theoretical explanation or model. There is an inability to come to terms conceptually with an important systemic transformation in the international system, but one that leaves the most basic structural characteristic of that system intact.

Although the impact (or lack of such) of the nuclear revolution on the causes of war is asserted far more often than it is rigorously argued and systematically analyzed, there have been some attempts to deal more thoroughly with the question. There have been a number of essays on the general question of the impact of the nuclear revolution on international politics (Brodie, 1946; Schelling, 1966; Mandelbaum, 1981; Gaddis, 1987; Jervis, 1984, 1988b, 1989; Mueller, 1988). Much has also been written on the question of the "utility of force" in the nuclear age (Knorr, 1966, 1977; Waltz, 1967; Gompart, 1977; Organski, 1968; Organski and Kugler, 1980:Chap. 4). Another body of literature attempts to assess the impact of nuclear weapons in specific deterrence situations in the nuclear age, either through case studies (Betts, 1987), quantitative methods (Stoll, 1982; Weede, 1983; Kugler, 1984; Morgan and Ray, 1988), or both (Blechman and Kaplan, 1978; Organski and Kugler, 1980). Many of these studies fail, however, to include any explicit comparisons with the prenuclear period. A related body of literature focuses explicitly on the question of how to explain the "long peace," the four decades of peace among the leading states in the system that is so rare by historical standards (Gaddis, 1987; Kegley, 1989).

Most of this literature is certainly relevant to the question of the causes of war in the nuclear age but fails to provide a complete answer to it. It explains why the likelihood of a major war is much less in the nuclear era than in previous historical eras (and also deals with the question of the likelihood of lesser wars) without answering the question of the specific conditions, processes, and events that might lead to such an admittedly low probability event. There has recently emerged a body of literature that makes a more explicit attempt to identify some of the specific conditions contributing to war. It attempts to ground middle-range theories of deterrence or hypotheses on the causes of war in historical experience, test those theories using a methodology of controlled comparison, and analyze their implications for contemporary policy issues. Among the more specific issues discussed by these scholars are the conditions under which deterrence is likely to succeed or fail (George and Smoke, 1974; Stern et al., 1989), the sources and consequences of offensive military doctrines (Posen, 1984; Van Evera, 1984a; Snyder, 1984b), the role of misperception in deterrence (Jervis, 1976, 1983, 1988a; Lebow, 1981), the ways in which domestic politics can undermine deterrence (Lebow, 1981; Stein, 1985a, 1985b), crisis management (Lebow, 1987; Levy, 1988d), and the sources of imperial overextension (Snyder, 1988).

These theoretical analyses and empirical studies are convincing enough to suggest that *some* of the causes of war are the same in the nuclear era as in previous eras. At this point there is insufficient empirical evidence to determine conclusively whether or not other factors that have been important in the past have ceased to be important in the nuclear age, or whether they carry much less (or much greater) weight now than in the past, or whether new causal variables have emerged in the nuclear era. The proposition that the causes of war have changed must be demonstrated and not just asserted, however, and this requires that we incorporate traditional theories of war into the analysis. In order to understand the extent to which the causes of war have changed over time we must first comprehend the nature of those causes in previous eras. From this foundation we will be better able to understand how the nuclear revolution has affected the impact of traditionally important causal variables and the relationships among them. Toward the end of this chapter we return briefly to the question of the impact of the nuclear revolution on the causes of war.

Organizing Framework

In reviewing the existing theoretical literature on the causes of war, we will be focusing primarily on interstate war, recognizing that is an important subset of a larger class of international violence that includes imperial war, civil war, terrorism, and the use of force short of war. These other phenomena will be examined to the extent that they contribute to the outbreak of interstate war under certain conditions. We will give somewhat greater emphasis to great power wars than to wars between secondary states, both because of the bias in the theoretical literature and because of our concern with the question of the prevention of nuclear war. The implications of particular theories for the nuclear age will be considered where relevant, although the relative silence of the literature on this question has already been noted.

I will focus on a relatively small number of major theories instead of presenting an extensive propositional inventory, since isolated hypotheses not integrated into a more general theoretical framework contribute little to the cumulation of scientific knowledge about war. For similar reasons I will also focus more on theories and their analytical problems than on the extensive empirical research on war. Systematic empirical findings and other forms of historical evidence designed to test specific hypotheses will be included to the extent to which they bear directly on the major theories. Specific findings relating to a particular case or to limited spatial and temporal domains, or those more reflective of narrow operational indicators than of broader theoretical concepts, will not be included, because they rarely produce generalizable knowledge about international conflict. This is based on a rejection of neopositivist epistemology that asserts that the primary path to knowledge is the cumulation of discrete empirical findings, and the adoption of a perspective that conceives of the growth of knowledge in terms of the development of better theories. This is consistent with a Lakatosian conception of science in which the validity of a theory is measured not only by its correspondence with empirical reality but also by its explanatory power relative to that of alternative theories (Lakatos, 1970).

This epistemological orientation has implications for the way in which empirical evidence will be utilized here. We can attempt to evaluate the extent to which the empirical evidence supports a particular theory, but we must recognize that other theories may be equally consistent with the same evidence. Thus, consistency with the evidence is not sufficient for the acceptance of a theory. Theories must be evaluated with respect to each other as well as compared to the evidence. Moreover, we must recognize that each theory is based on certain analytic assumptions, and the empirical evidence appropriate for testing each of the theories cannot be specified independently of these analytical assumptions. Thus, it is no simple task to evaluate the weight of the evidence in support of a theory. The relevance of various empirical studies for a particular theory depends on numerous aspects of its research design, including the appropriateness of its empirical domain, the validity and reliability of the empirical indicators used, the quality of the data, and so on.

There is insufficient space in this chapter to assess the evidentiary basis of various theories in this way. It is more important to emphasize the conceptual limitations of each of the theories, focusing on the evidence only where it seems to be overwhelming in support or contradiction. At this time, the primary limitations on our understanding of the causes of war are theoretical, not empirical. The central problem is not the lack of information or lack of data to test our theories, but the absence of theories that are sufficiently well specified and logically complete to provide a compelling explanation and one that facilitates a meaningful empirical test.

This leads to the question of the policy relevance of theories of war. Conflicting theories give rise to conflicting implications for contemporary policy debates. For most theories that posit that factor X causes war and that consequently statesmen should do Y, there is usually another theory positing that X contributes to peace and that consequently that statesmen should not do Y. In fact, many contemporary policy debates derive from these underlying theoretical debates regarding the causes of war. A careful examination of the theories will often make this clear, even if we do not have the time to trace explicitly all of the linkages between theory and policy. Another reason for giving greater emphasis to the theoretical dimensions of the literature is that many of the policy questions will be analyzed in much greater detail in other chapters in this series. Most of these chapters deal with more narrowly defined theoretical questions for which there is greater agreement as to the weight of the evidence and its implications for policy. This theoretical overview will serve as a useful reminder, however, that there is extensive debate regarding the validity of the broader theories within which each of these more specific hypotheses is embedded.

This chapter is concerned with the question of the conditions, events, and processes affecting the likelihood of the outbreak of war. It is less concerned with the more general philosophical question of why war occurs or with the questions of the "primary" or "permissive" causes that make it possible for war to occur but that are nearly always present. These are not very helpful with regard to the question of why war occurs at some times under certain conditions rather than at other times under other conditions, or between some states rather than other states. Consequently, they carry little explanatory or predictive power. Thus, this chapter will not examine the extensive literature on human nature and war (Waltz, 1954; Nelson, 1974). To the extent that human nature is a constant, it cannot account for the variation in war and peace. To the extent that human nature is conceived as variable, with aggressive drives varying in intensity and finding different types of outlets at different times and under different conditions, then the variation in war and peace is explained not by human nature itself but instead by these other conditions with which it interacts.[18]

The question remaining is exactly how our survey of the literature on the causes of war will be organized. One traditional mode of classification, which goes back to Thucydides, is based on the distinction between underlying (or remote or long-term) causes and immediate (or proximate or trigger or short-term) causes. This approach is common among historians and has the advantage of facilitating a dynamic analysis of the interaction of variables contributing to war.[19] Long-term processes of growth, uneven development, and changing power distributions establish the contexts within which interests intersect and crises occur, and then proximate causes are important in determining which of these crises escalate to war. One significant limitation of this classification scheme, however, is that some of the same variables can serve as both underlying and proximate causes of war. The prisoner's dilemma, for example, has been advanced as an explanation for the general tendencies of an anarchic environment to foster conflictual behavior, the long-term pressures for imperial expansion, the intermediate-term pressures for arms racing, and the immediate decisions to mobilize or initiate a preemptive strike in a crisis. Similarly, domestic political variables may be the primary determinants of long-term expansionist pressures within a state and also provide the political pressures that prevent statesmen from making necessary compromises with the adversary in a crisis. Each set of these sufficiently similar variables should be analyzed together rather than separated according to their temporal proximity to the outbreak of war.

For this reason I have adopted a *levels-of-analysis framework* to classify the independent explanatory variables and in this way to organize our examination of theories of war. I begin with *systemic-level* theories, in which the central causal variables are the structural characteristics of the international system that constitutes the external environment common to all states. These theories basically minimize the importance of the internal political and economic structure of states, domestic politics, the nature of the decision-making process, and the belief systems and psychological processes of individual political leaders in the processes leading to war. I then turn to theories that trace the roots of war to the *nature of state and society*. Here the focus is on the overall political structure of the state (for example, democratic or authoritarian), the structure of the economic system, political culture and ideology, nationalism and public opinion, and domestic politics more generally. Finally, I turn to theories that locate the sources of war in the nature of the political *decision-making process,* particularly during crises. These theories focus on bureaucratic politics and organizational processes, small group dynamics, psychological processes, individual beliefs and images, attitudes toward risk, misperception, and other factors. Because many of these factors are examined in other chapters in this series, I will focus here on theories of organizational politics and processes and on theories of misperception.

This framework constitutes a modification of other levels-of-analysis conceptions found in the literature of Waltz (1954), Singer (1961), and Rosenau (1966). One serious limitation of this organizing framework is that some important causal factors cut across levels of analysis (for example, trade patterns reflect both the structure of domestic economies and relationships among states in the international system). These variables affect the processes leading to war at different stages, and these dynamic processes involving multilevel variables are not easily accommodated into a basically static levels-of-analysis framework. My aim here, however, is not to construct a theory of the causes of war, for which a levels-of-analysis framework might not be optimum, but to organize a critical review of existing theories, for which this framework is quite useful. A curious feature of much of the literature on the causes of war and, in fact, one of its serious limitations, is that most of these theories either consist of essentially a single factor or integrate a cluster of variables from the same level of analysis. Consequently, most of these theories are relatively easy to classify into a levels-of-analysis framework. Cases of multilevel theories will be classified according to their primary explanatory variables, with particular attention given to cross-level relationships. Remote or proximate considerations will not be ignored, for they are relevant in the evaluation of the various theories. What we expect from a theory is in part a function of what it is attempting to explain, so that the standards for evaluating crisis decision-making theories must be somewhat different than the standards for evaluating theories focusing on the underlying causes of war. Neither type of theory is really complete without the other.

Systemic-Level Theories

Many systemic-level theories of war fall within the "realist" paradigm of international politics, and it would be useful to lay out the assumptions of this paradigm before examining any of the more specific theories of war that share realist assumptions. We will then turn to balance of power theory and many of the bivariate hypotheses that are often subsumed under it, including those focusing on the distribution of military capabilities in the system, alliance patterns, opportunities for expansion on the periphery of the system, and the dyadic balance of power. Power models will be contrasted with Bueno de Mesquita's expected utility theory of war, and static models will be compared with power transition theory, related theories of hegemonic war and change, and lateral pressure theory. Liberal economic theories of war will be examined as an alternative to the realist theories noted here. Although these structural theories focus primarily on the underlying conditions contributing to war, there are other structural variables that generate immediate pressures for war. Prisoner's dilemma models analyze the structural incentives for conflictive behavior in certain situations and have recently been receiving considerable attention, as have formal models of sequential games based on incomplete information, but these are treated elsewhere in this series and therefore will not be examined here. Similarly, the literature on deterrence, coercive diplomacy, and bargaining will not be covered in this chapter.

The Realist Paradigm

Of all the theoretical frameworks for the study of international politics, including the causes of war, the most widely accepted, at least in the West, is the realist paradigm.[20] Realist ideas can be traced back to Thucydides' *Peloponnesian War,* several centuries of balance of power theories, Morgenthau's (1967) elucidation of classical realism, Waltz's systematization of structural realism or neorealism, recent quantitative empirical (Singer, 1979a, 1979b, 1980) and formal (Wagner, 1986; Niou and Ordeshook, 1986) models of balance of power systems, and other contemporary analyses employing a range of different methodologies. There have also been a number of attempts to reconstruct or formalize realist theory (Keohane and Nye, 1977; Keohane, 1983; Vasquez, 1983). Although realism is often referred to as a theory, it is better conceived as a conceptual framework or paradigm (Kuhn, 1962). Realism itself is too general and cannot generate many specific predictions until some of its key concepts are given more precise definitions and hence greater empirical content. Realism has in fact spawned a number of more specific theories that often give different predictions but that share a hard core of common assumptions. These assumptions concern the nature of the actors in world politics and of the international system within which they interact.

One central assumption of the realist paradigm is that world politics is statecentric, that territorial states are the key actors in the system.[21] The key to understanding what occurs in world politics, and how the world system is likely to evolve in the future, is to understand the behavior of territorially defined states. A central determinant of state behavior, according to political realism, is the anarchic structure of the state system. Anarchy refers to the absence of any legitimate authority in the international system to make and enforce laws, adjudicate disputes, and regulate behavior among states. In the absence of an enforcement mechanism, sovereign states must provide for their own interests in a self-help system in which force is the ultimate arbiter of disputes. Thus, the system is often described as a Hobbesian state of nature, which is equivalent to a state of war because the absence of enforcement mechanism precludes effective cooperation among states to achieve their mutual interests (Hobbes, [1651] 1962).

Realist theories assume that states can be treated as if they are unitary actors with a single set of reasonably well-defined interests. Through this assumption realist theory minimizes the impact of any internal disagreements regarding the national interest or the optimum means of achieving those interests.[22] Realist theory also assumes that states can be treated as if they are rational as well as unitary: their interests are transitive, and they calculate the consequences of each policy alternative in terms of its costs and benefits for those interests (given uncertainty and informational constraints), and select the policy that maximizes their interests.[23] As we will see in our subsequent sections on societal-level and decision-making theories, serious objections have been raised against the unitary and rational actor assumptions.

Realist theory goes beyond the unitary and rational actor assumptions to assume that because of the potential for violence in an anarchic, high-threat system, the hierarchy of state interests is dominated by security. Although security interests and other interests reinforce each other over the long term, in the short term they occasionally come into conflict and, when that happens, security interests are given priority. The primary means to security is power. Realists have traditionally conceptualized power in terms of military power and the economic foundations of military power and potential, although some contemporary realists define power more broadly.[24] Regardless of how power is defined, it is assumed that power is fungible and applicable to a wide range of issue areas, that it is a universal currency that can be used to advance a wide variety of interests. It is also assumed that power (but not necessarily security) is relational and essentially zero sum in international politics: one's power is measured relative to the power of others. Because power is necessary to achieve other interests, and because power is relational, power becomes for all practical purposes an end in itself. As Morgenthau (1967) writes, international politics is a struggle for power, although one should add that since power is a means to security, the maximization of power is subject to the constraint that security not be impaired.

The rationality assumption is important because it provides a link among the structure of the system, the national interests of states, and their foreign policy behavior. It is assumed that a rational analyst can infer from a state's position in the system the security interests of the state, the systemic constraints and opportunities affecting those interests, the optimum policy alternatives for the achievement of those interests, and therefore a state's behavior. That is, realist theories generate a set of testable propositions linking the structure of the international system to the behavior of states. They assume that the identity of particular leaders, their individual belief systems and psychological processes, and the internal bureaucratic, domestic political and economic context within which they operate are of secondary importance in determining state behavior. These internal variables are important only insofar as they affect the economic and military power of the state. Because of the potential for violence in the international system, the imperatives of survival dominate other interests, and rational individuals respond to such danger in roughly similar ways.[25]

The central proposition of realist theory is that the distribution of power in the system determines the behavior of individual states within the system.

This proposition is often qualified to give negative rather than positive predictions: the distribution of power imposes constraints within which all states must operate if they want to maintain their security and other interests, but it does not generate positive predictions about behavior within this broad range of constraints (Waltz, 1979). That is, the proposition suggests necessary rather than sufficient conditions for behavior. Even the qualified proposition is not particularly discriminating, however, for it lacks much empirical content unless both the nature of power and the nature of the system are defined. At this point various realist theories begin to diverge, and these divergent theories will be examined in the following sections of this chapter.

Another very general set of propositions advanced by realist theories is that cooperation is relatively rare in a system in which sovereign states must provide for their own security in an anarchic world. The argument goes something like this. Because states may resort to force to preserve their security or advance their other interests if disputes cannot be resolved by nonviolent means, and because there is nothing to prevent a state from utilizing force, all states must be prepared to use force to protect themselves. The primary means by which security is enhanced is the accumulation of military power and the economic strength that underlie it, although alliances may also be useful, particularly as short-term solutions to the security needs of states.[26] But power is relative, rather than absolute, and, thus, with respect to power-related issues international politics approaches a zero-sum game (Wolfers, 1962:Chap. 10; Gilpin, 1975:Chap. 1), and consequently states are engaged in a continuous pursuit of power and security. This process is exacerbated by the inability to distinguish between the offensive and defensive intentions of others and between offensive and defensive weapon systems. The intentions of other states are inherently ambiguous and can change from one political leader to the next, and most weapons can serve both offensive and defensive functions (Jervis, 1978; Levy, 1984a). Even though there are risks in overreacting as well as in underreacting, statesmen generally prefer to err on the side of safety and assume the worst regarding the intentions and actions of other states, and this tendency toward worst-case analysis fuels the action-reaction spiral in international politics.

Because actions a state takes to increase its security often decrease the security of other states, which then feel compelled to take countermeasures to increase their own security, which in turn are threatening to others, and so forth, actions taken to increase security often generate an action-reaction spiral. This spiral may not only be costly, but it often fails to increase the security of any state and may actually decrease the security of all by increasing tensions and hence the probability of war and also by increasing the destructiveness of any war that might occur. This is the classic "security dilemma" (Herz, 1957; Jervis, 1978). It is important because it explains how states that prefer peace and that have no aggressive intentions can be induced by the structure of the system to take actions that none really wishes to take and that leave all states worse off than before. Under certain conditions, the security dilemma can lead to war in the absence of any "genuine" conflicts of strategic, economic, or ideological interests between states. Thus, states may prefer peace but rationally choose war.[27]

This is not the only causal sequence through which war might occur, of course, and not all security dilemmas lead to war. There may be "real" conflicts over territory, resources, and other issues that lead two states to perceive that their interests can best be served through the use of force, leading to war as the preferred outcome by both states.[28] Whether most wars arise from such conflicts of concrete interests is an interesting theoretical question, although the problem of analytically distinguishing between these concrete interests and other interests relating to power and prestige raises some very difficult questions. An interesting feature of the theoretical literature on international conflict, however, is that relatively little attention has been given to the actual *issues* involved in the processes leading to war.[29] It is recognized that some interests and some issues are more vital than others and more likely to lead to war than are conflicts over other issues. Analysts have not been very successful, however, in identifying an objective hierarchy of interests applicable to all states or even to all great powers, other than very general concerns for territorial and constitutional integrity, the maintenance of a minimal level of economic subsistence, the exclusion of hostile regimes from adjacent areas, and perhaps the prevention of any one state from achieving a position of dominance in the system. Instead, it is generally assumed that in an anarchic system conflicts of interests will naturally arise and that regardless of the long-term interests of states their immediate interests are the maintenance and if possible the improvement in their power position. Thus, international politics becomes, at least for the leading states in the system, a struggle for power (Morgenthau, 1967).

It should be emphasized that not all realist theories give equal emphasis to the anarchic structure of the system.[30] Whereas balance of power theories stress the importance of anarchy and the absence of order in the international system, recent versions of "hegemonic" theory acknowledge the existence of anarchy but emphasize the hierarchies of power and informal "regimes" within a formal sovereign state system. They assert that the leading state in the system uses its power to create and maintain a set of political and economic structures and certain norms of behavior (Keohane, 1980, 1984; Gilpin, 1981; Krasner, 1983; Modelski, 1978, 1987*b*) that serve its own interests. This will become more clear in our subsequent discussion of theories of power transition and hegemonic war.

In a general sense anarchy may explain why international political systems are more conflictual than domestic political systems that have centralized mechanisms of regulation and enforcement. Anarchy itself, defined as the absence of a higher formal authority, is a structural constant, however, and cannot really explain the enormous variations in war and peace in the modern Westphalian system or in any other sovereign state system. If at some times the system seems more anarchic than at others it is because of greater concentrations of power, a greater degree of cooperation among the great powers, greater compliance with informal rules and norms, and other factors. To the extent that state behavior is different in such a system, it is these other variables, not anarchy, that explains this variation in behavior. Anarchy itself says nothing about the conditions and processes under which the continuous struggle for power and security is likely to trigger a direct conflict of vital interests or an intense conflict spiral, and the conditions and processes under which these are likely to escalate to war. Within the general realist paradigm there are several distinct theories that advance more specific propositions regarding the conditions and processes contributing to war in an anarchic sovereign state system, and to these we now turn.

Balance of Power Theory

The balance of power is one of the oldest concepts in the literature on international relations, but also one of the most ambiguous and least tractable (Haas, 1953; Claude, 1962). The central concepts associated with the balance of power, including balance, power, equilibrium, and stability, are rarely defined in any rigorous manner. The balance of power concept itself has been used in a variety of different ways. It has been used descriptively to refer to the distribution of power in the international system; prescriptively to suggest how states should conduct their foreign policies; and analytically to refer to a universal law of history (Morgenthau, 1967), a particular kind of international system (Kaplan, 1957; Claude, 1962), or a theory of state behavior (Waltz, 1979; Wagner, 1986). Ambiguity is increased further by the tendency by some to equate balance of power theory with realist theory or with any theory utilizing power as a central organizing concept.

There is no single balance of power theory but, instead, a multiplicity of theories, each of which begins with the hard core assumptions of realism, adds more empirical content to the paradigm through more specific definitions of power and other key concepts, and introduces additional assumptions. As a result, various balance of power theories generate conflicting propositions about the actions and interactions of states. Each of these balance of power "theories" is not so much a theory as a loose collection of mainly bivariate hypotheses, which are based on a poorly defined set of assumptions and are without any well-developed connections between them.[31] Many of these propositions are inconsistent not only with propositions from other frameworks but also with each other.[32]

The confusion is all the greater because balance of power theorists cannot even agree on what it is they are trying to explain or, stated differently, what it is that a balance of power system is supposed to accomplish. Some argue that the purpose or function of the system is to maintain the peace (Wolfers, 1962:Chap. 8; Claude, 1962:55; Organski, 1968:280) but a majority of scholars reject this view. They argue that war is a means of achieving more important objectives. These other objectives are said to be the avoidance of hegemony (Morgenthau, 1967; Blainey, 1973:112), the maintenance of the independence of states—or at least of the great powers (Gulick, 1955; Organski, 1968:280; Wagner, 1986; Waltz, 1979), or the general maintenance of the status quo. Needless to say, this disagreement as to the identity of the dependent variable, and the possibility that there may be two or more dependent variables that are not collinear, inhibits the rigorous specification of the theory.

In spite of the variations in balance of power theories, these theories do share certain common features. The most significant are the emphasis on the prevention of hegemony through blocking coalitions as the fundamental rule of behavior and on the absence of hegemony as the most common state of affairs in world politics. As we will see, these features distinguish balance of power theory from hegemonic transition theories of various forms and from other power-oriented theories. Thus, balance of power theory is not the same as realist theory but is one version of realist theory. It is not restricted to a particular historical era and can be applied to bipolar systems involving two leading states as well as to multipolar systems characterized by five or so great powers of roughly equal strength. Balance of power theory is applicable in principle to (that is, its assumptions are satisfied in) the nuclear age as well as to previous eras (which is not to say that the theory gives equally accurate predictions in the nuclear and prenuclear eras).

This formulation is consistent in most respects with that of Waltz's (1979:Chap. 6) conception of balance of power theory as *the* theory of state behavior in any anarchic system (including the present one) consisting of two or more sovereign states (see also Wolfers, 1962:127). It is also consistent with Claude's (1962:Chaps. 2–3) conception of the balance of power as the system that exists by default in any international system unless it is consciously replaced by a world government or by a centralized and authoritative collective security arrangement. My formulation differs from these other conceptions by more clearly distinguishing balance of power theories from hegemonic theories, which downplay the behavioral consequences of anarchy and the importance of balancing mechanisms and emphasize the existence of hegemony as a common state of affairs within a formally anarchic system.

This formulation differs also from those that add a number of stronger assumptions to balance of power theory: the existence of four or five great powers, an equilibrium of military power in the system, a balancer, a colonial frontier, a consensus regarding the legitimacy of the system, and other considerations (Morgenthau, 1967:Chap. 14; Gulick, 1955:Chap. 1; Hoffmann, 1968; Wright, 1965:Chap. 20). These assumptions would deprive balance of power theories of much of their explanatory power by restricting their applicability to a very narrow set of theoretical conditions and, therefore, to a small number of specific historical eras. Within such systems several key propositions of the theory would become nearly tautological and validated by assumption (that is, when there is equilibrium in the system and a consensus regarding the legitimacy of the system, and when states have limited aims, there will be equilibrium and few major wars to overthrow the system and establish one's own hegemony). These "assumptions" are better conceptualized as variables that form the basis of testable hypotheses regarding the optimal conditions for the effective functioning of the system to avoid hegemony and the outbreak of major wars.

Balance of power theorists suggest a number of mechanisms by which states attempt to maintain an equilibrium and prevent any one state from achieving a position of dominance. One important distinction is between external balancing and internal balancing (Waltz, 1979:168). External balancing refers primarily to the formation of alliances as a blocking coalition against a prospective aggressor, but it also includes territorial compensations or partitions for the purposes of redistributing the sources of power and, if necessary, threats of force, intervention, and even war (Gulick, 1955:Chap. 3). Internal balancing refers to an internal buildup of military capabilities and the economic and industrial foundations of military strength. Although there have been few attempts to specify the precise conditions under which each of these means is used and in what combination, it is clear that alliances play a central role in most versions of balance of power theory.[33]

The central proposition of balance of power theory is that if one state threatens to achieve a position from which it would be able to dominate over the rest, a military coalition of most of the other great powers will form against it and a general war will follow. Thus the general perception that one state threatens to achieve a position of hegemony or dominance over the system is a sufficient but not necessary cause of general war involving nearly all the great powers in the system.[34] A number of general wars over the past five centuries of the modern system appear to fit this central balance of power proposition, including the wars against Philip II of Spain in the late sixteenth century, against Louis XIV in the late seventeenth century, against Revolutionary and Napoleonic France a century later, and against Germany twice in this century.[35] We will return to this proposition when we consider theories of hegemonic war.

It is important to recognize that the preceding proposition is concerned primarily with the war behavior of the great powers and that most versions of balance of power theory are essentially theories of great power behavior. When balance of power theorists refer to stability or to the avoidance of war in the system, they mean the avoidance of war among the great powers. They rarely make specific predictions about the outbreak of war between secondary states.[36] Smaller wars between great powers and secondary states or colonies are not considered as destabilizing, and many balance of power theorists view limited war as a particularly useful means of maintaining the stability of the system. To the extent that balance of power theory generates propositions about war, it is for the most part about fairly major wars between the great powers (Deutsch and Singer, 1964:315–316; Waltz, 1967:270; Levy, 1985b:44), which are assumed to have a different set of causes than wars in general. In addition, hypotheses regarding balancing behavior refer to the great powers more than to other states. Great powers balance against potential hegemons, whereas weaker states in the proximity of stronger states do what is necessary to survive, which often involves bandwagoning with the strong instead of balancing against them.[37]

There is less agreement among balance of power theorists regarding other conditions conducive to war, or at least great power war, although a number of discrete propositions are associated with the theory. These propositions, loosely connected at best, stress the impact of several independent variables on the frequency and seriousness of great power war. These include the distribution of power in the system, polarity, the number of great powers, the structure of the alliance system, and the opportunities for great power expansion in the peripheries of the system.

THE DISTRIBUTION OF POWER IN THE SYSTEM

The distribution of power in the international system, particularly among the leading actors in the system, is a central variable in realist theories of international politics, although there are conflicting views as to the consequences of a particular distribution of power. Most balance of power theorists argue that a relatively equal distribution of power among the great powers is conducive to peace as well as to the avoidance of hegemony and the preservation of the independence of the major units in the system. Approximate parity facilitates peace (defined as the avoidance of major wars) because it denies any single state the ability to enforce its will on others, provides several possible blocking coalitions that might form against any aggressor, and thus reinforces deterrence. Concentrations of power in the hands of a very small number of states are conducive to war because they reduce the number of blocking coalitions and hence undermine deterrence (Claude, 1962; Morgenthau, 1967; Gulick, 1955; Wright, 1965). Balance of power theorists concede that a given state is more likely to be deterred by a preponderance of power, and that preponderance by a nonaggressive status quo state would not necessarily be dangerous and would enhance deterrence. But because of the distrust of power in the abstract, the belief that power corrupts and that states' expansionist ambitions may be an increasing function of their power, and the fact that preponderance could not be made available as a deterrent without also being available as an instrument of aggression, balance of power theorists prefer the safety of parity.

These arguments are rejected by the "power preponderance" school, which reminds us of the Pax Romana under the overwhelming preponderance of ancient Rome and of the Pax Britannica in the nineteenth century. These scholars emphasize the deterrent functions of preponderance and argue that an equality of power is conducive to war rather than peace. Organski (1968:292), for example, argues that "periods of balance, real or imagined, are periods of warfare, while the periods of known preponderance are periods of peace." Parity increases the danger of war by tempting both sides to believe that they have a good chance of winning, whereas under conditions of preponderance war is unnecessary for the stronger and too risky for the weaker. Parity is particularly dangerous, according to Organski, in a situation in which power differentials are changing, but that question is better saved for our discussion of power transition theory.[38]

The theoretical debate over the relative war proneness of parity and preponderance is flawed in several respects. One problem is the confusion over the relevant level of analysis. Arguments relating to deterrence in a dyadic situation involving two states have been used to support hypotheses regarding the effects of the distribution of power in the international *system*, but there is no logical connection between the two. Preponderance and equality must be defined as systemic-level variables if they are to be meaningful in systemic-level balance of power hypotheses.[39] A related problem is that deterrence and the likelihood of war in an n-actor system is a function of the distribution of power among coalitions (and potential coalitions) of states as well as among individual states, but the effects of alliances are rarely considered in this debate.[40]

Another theoretical problem that has not been adequately explored is the precise form of the relationship between the distribution of power and the stability or war proneness of the system. Both balance of power and power preponderance formulations assume a linear (or at least monotonic) relationship between the two variables but, in the absence of a complete explanatory theory, this is not convincing. One could imagine a curvilinear relationship in which equality or approximate equality is destabilizing because it tempts aggression (particularly by risk-acceptant actors); a moderate level of power concentration is stabilizing because it deters aggression without threatening hegemony; and an extremely high level of power concentration is destabilizing because it generates fears of hegemony and a defensive military coalition of all other great powers.

The distribution of power in the system is also a central variable in the old debate over the relative stability or war proneness of bipolar and multipolar systems. Although there is little agreement on the precise meaning of polarity (Nogee, 1975) and there have been few successful attempts to operationalize it (Bueno de Mesquita, 1975; Rapkin et al., 1979), it is usually defined as some measure of the distribution of power among the major actors in the system.[41] Most balance of power theorists argue that multipolarity is more stable (that is, less prone to major wars) than bipolarity.[42] There is a larger number of possible coalitions that might form against a potential aggressor, and the greater uncertainty that this generates for the aggressor reinforces deterrence. Multipolar systems can incorporate the role of a "balancer," a normally unaligned state that helps to deter war by constantly threatening to shift its decisive political and military support to the weaker coalition (Morgenthau, 1967:332–338; Kaplan, 1957:34; Claude, 1962:48; Bueno de Mesquita, 1975:190). Deutsch and Singer (1964) argue that the increased number of interaction opportunities in multipolar systems generates pluralist crosscutting pressures that reduce the likelihood of mutually reinforcing antagonisms.

Waltz (1979:Chap. 8), on the other hand, argues that bipolar systems are more stable. They are characterized by fewer potential sources of conflict; the absence of peripheries that invite expansionist policies; the concentration of attention of the two leading states on each other; the insignificant impact of the behavior of third states; and the stabilizing effects of crises between the two leading states. In addition, in a system with two major poles there is a tendency for the behavior of other great powers to revolve around this bipolar axis, which increases the predictability of international behavior, reduces uncertainty, and hence reduces the likelihood of a war by miscalculation. Many of these arguments are disputed by Rosecrance (1966), who suggests that bipolar systems may increase the incentives for conflict because of the greater tendency to perceive international politics as a zero-sum game in which even minor shifts in influence in the periphery are important. Rosecrance (1966) concludes that wars in multipolar systems will be more frequent but less serious than those under bipolar systems, whereas Waltz (1979:172) suggests the opposite.

Note that both sides of the polarity/stability debate agree that bipolarity reduces uncertainty and that multipolarity increases it, but they disagree on the consequences of uncertainty. Advocates of bipolarity argue that the reduction of uncertainty reduces the likelihood of a war by miscalculation, whereas advocates of multipolarity argue that the reduction of uncertainty increases the likelihood of war by simplifying the calculations of the aggressor. Thus, uncertainty and the responses of statesmen to risk and uncertainty are critical intervening variables between the distribution of power and the likelihood of war.

One of the few to recognize this is Bueno de Mesquita (1980a, 1981b, 1985), who argues that in the absence of a consideration of the risk propensities of decision makers there is no logical or general relationship between the systemic distribution of power and the likelihood of war. He argues that some states and some statesmen are more willing to take gambles than others, and that the likelihood of war is a function of both the distribution of power and the risk propensities of decision makers.[43] This is a powerful, logically derived argument, the effects of which are demonstrated through a computer simulation (Bueno de Mesquita, 1981b). The addition of the risk orientation variable introduces enormous complications into any analysis of international politics, however, because the measurement of risk technically requires the extraordinarily difficult task of specifying the utility functions of the actors; but an analysis of the relationships between capability distributions and war is logically incomplete without it.[44]

Because of the absence of a coherent theory specifying the conditions under which parity is stabilizing and those under which preponderance is stabilizing, and because of the failure to incorporate the risk orientations of statesmen, it is not surprising that empirical research has not produced any consistent findings on this question. Singer, Bremer, and Stuckey (1972) find that concentrations of military capabilities among the great powers are associated with war in the nineteenth century and with peace in the twentieth century, while parity is associated with peace in the nineteenth century and war in the twentieth century. There are several possible explanations for this anomaly. One is that other variables, operating independently or through their interaction effects with the distribution of power variable, may be more important determinants of the likelihood of war, so that the failure to control for polarity, alliances, and other variables accounts for the instability of the hypothesized relationship over time. Bueno de Mesquita and Lalman (1988a) demonstrate, however, that the addition of these structural variables to the model is insufficient to account for variations in the outbreak of war, and that it is necessary to incorporate the risk propensities of decision makers and their evaluations of the utility of alternative outcomes (see also Bueno de Mesquita, 1981b). Alternatively, Vasquez (1986) suggests that the distribution of power affects the type of war that occurs rather than the likelihood of war.[45] The observed intercentury differences might also be the artifact of the particular methodological procedures used.

Although there has been a modest amount of work on polarity and war, the results are inconclusive, in part because of the ambiguity of the central concept of polarity (Wayman, 1984; Sabrosky, 1985; Most and Starr, 1987). This question does have some important implications for the nuclear era, and it is often argued that the "long peace" since 1945 is due to bipolarity as well as to the existence of nuclear weapons (Waltz, 1979; Gaddis, 1987). Theory provides conflicting answers to this question, and the failure to consider other cases of bipolarity precludes a controlled comparison that might enable the disentangling of the confounding effects of bipolarity and nuclear weapons in the contemporary era. Although alternative instances of bipolarity are rare, they do exist. The Greece of Athens and Sparta was essentially a bipolar system (Fleiss, 1966), as was Europe in the early sixteenth century with the Hapsburg-Valois rivalry dominating European diplomacy. The first was characterized by a hegemonic war for control over Greece and the second by a series of moderately intense great power wars for control over Italy and then Europe.[46] In the absence of further research on the relative stability of bipolar and multipolar systems, scholars and policymakers should be very cautious in assuming that bipolarity itself is a stabilizing force in world politics.

ALLIANCES

The lack of consistency among and within balance of power theories is illustrated by the role of alliances in those theories: some balance of power theorists claim that alliances contribute to peace while others insist that they increase the likelihood of war. Those in the first camp argue that alliances deter war by increasing the credibility of threats of military intervention in support of victims of aggression, so that alliances are an indispensable means of maintaining equilibrium in the system (Gulick, 1955:61–61; Holsti et al., 1973:31–32).[47] Others argue that alliances tend to generate counteralliances, which increase tensions, fuel the conflict spiral, and increase the likelihood of war, as demonstrated so clearly by World War I. As that case demonstrates, alliances can contribute to the scope of a war as well as its outbreak by increasing the likelihood that additional states will intervene. As in the debate over polarity and stability, there is agreement that alliances reduce the level of uncertainty in the system but disagreement as to whether this reduces the likelihood of a war by misperception or increases the likelihood of war by simplifying the calculations of the aggressor. This reflects a more general failure to identify the conditions under which alliances are stabilizing and the specific conditions under which they are destabilizing.

Many balance of power theorists make a distinction between ad hoc alliances and permanent alliances. Ad hoc alliances are formed in response to a dangerous shift in the distribution of power in the system or to a specific threat of aggression and are generally considered to be stabilizing (Wright, 1965:773). Permanent alliances are said to be destabilizing because they limit the "flexibility" of the alliance system by reducing the number of potential coalitions that could form against an aggressor and the number of states that might play the stabilizing role of a balancer (Morgenthau, 1967; Claude, 1962:47–48; Gulick, 1955:65–67). A related argument is that alliance commitments contribute to war by reducing the pluralist crosscutting pressures that minimize the likelihood of mutually reinforcing antagonisms (Deutsch and Singer, 1964). Thus, it is often argued that polarized alliance systems (characterized by two mutually distinct sets of alliances without crosscutting ties, as existed immediately prior to World War I) are destabilizing whereas nonpolarized alliances systems (as existed in Bismarckian Europe) are stabilizing.

There have been some quantitative empirical studies of the relationship between alliances and war. At the national level of analysis, Singer and Small (1966*b*) find that states involved in more alliances tend to be involved in more wars, although part of this relationship can be explained by a state's general level of diplomatic activity. At the systemic level, Singer and Small (1968) find that the number of alliances in the system is associated with peace in the nineteenth century but with war in the twentieth century, a discrepancy that has yet to be explained.[48] Levy (1981) finds that the formation of alliances over the last five centuries (but not in the nineteenth century) has generally been soon followed by war, but that most wars have not been preceded by alliances. He suggests that the tendency for wars to follow alliances may be explained by the tendency of states to form alliances for protection whenever they perceive that the probability of war is high, so that the causal linkage is from the anticipation of war to alliance formation and not from alliance formation to war. He suggests also that the conventional conception of the relationship between alliances and war is excessively static and theoretically misspecified. Attention should shift toward "the conceptualization of alliances as an intervening variable in a dynamic model of conflict escalation incorporating the reciprocal interactions among antecedent conditions, political tensions, alliances, and war" (Levy, 1981:612).

OTHER BALANCE OF POWER HYPOTHESES

Military capabilities and alliances are the central components of balance of power theory, but other variables have also been mentioned. One is the "openness of the colonial frontier," which reflects the availability of outlets for great power expansion on the periphery of the system. The hypothesis is that the larger the number of outlets for expansion, the lower the level of great power war, since imperial expansion provides a "safety valve" for the system. It diverts great power competition from the core to the periphery of the system, where their vital interests are not so directly involved and where concessions can more easily be made (Morgenthau, 1967:341–342; Hoffmann, 1968). As the availability of outlets for expansion on the periphery is reduced, the situation begins to approximate a zero-sum game, where further expansion of one great power can now come only at the expense of another (Chatterjee, 1975:150–151). The increased costs and risks of expansion reduces expansionist activity, but the activity that does occur is more likely to involve the great powers in direct conflict. Thus, the frequent but limited wars of an open colonial frontier give way to the less frequent but more serious great power wars of a system of closed peripheries.

Both arguments have been made with respect to the outbreak of World War I. Some historians argue that imperial expansion did indeed provide a safety valve and stabilized the system for several decades (Thompson, 1962:Chap. 20), whereas others, including Marxists, argue that the partitioning of the system closed off opportunities for low-risk expansion and contributed to great power conflict and war in 1914 (Lenin, [1917] 1939). If patterns of great power conflict and cooperation in the periphery are not congruent with those in the core, it is conceivable that the resulting crosscutting pressures might actually reduce the intensity of great power conflict and the probability of war, as Thompson (1962) argues with respect to the 1914 case. The availability of expansionist outlets may interact with the polarity of the system to generate more complex causal linkages leading to war (Morgan and Levy, 1986).

Balance of power theories also give some emphasis to the impact of the nature of military power on the stability of the system. Military power, it is argued, should be measurable, stable, and a viable instrument of policy. Military power must be measurable so that statesmen can calculate their relative strengths and behave accordingly to maintain an equilibrium (Gulick, 1955:24–29; Claude, 1962:91). One factor enhancing the stability of the balance of power systems of the eighteenth and nineteenth centuries, it is argued, was the ease of measuring power on the basis of territory, population, army size, and financial strength, whereas today the measurement of power is much more complex. However, the hypothesized causal impacts have yet to be demonstrated empirically.

Balance of power arguments regarding the importance of technological stability are more plausible (Kaplan, 1957:31–32; Burns, 1957; Wright, 1965:761; Claude, 1962:91; Hoffmann, 1968:507). The hypothesis is that rapid innovation in military technology is destabilizing and increases the likelihood of war, for several reasons. It creates uncertainties regarding the actual balance of military capabilities, and these uncertainties themselves are destabilizing. This line of argument is rarely developed, however, and we have seen that the consequences of uncertainty depend on the risk orientations of decision makers. A more plausible argument, although one that is rarely made, is that innovation in weapons systems or in transportation or communication technologies generates an temporary increase in the military capabilities of one state, which creates a window of opportunity before technological diffusion brings those same innovations to others. This window of opportunity itself is destabilizing because it creates temporary disparities in strength and incentives for preventive action (Van Evera, 1984a; Levy, 1987). Finally, rapid technological change may contribute to war indirectly by intensifying the arms race. It may create a new generation of weapons systems that thrust the arms race onto a new level that is less amenable to arms control agreements, as Kissinger (1982) argues with respect to the development of multiple independently targetable re-entry vehicles (MIRVs). This literature generally assumes that arms races contribute to the increased likelihood of war, but the evidence on this question is mixed (Wallace, 1979, 1981; Smith, 1980; Altfeld, 1983; Houweling and Siccama, 1988:Chap. 8).

Of course, some kinds of technological change may be more destabilizing than others. Huntington (1958) argues that quantitative arms races are more likely than qualitative ones to end up in war; however, this intriguing hypothesis has yet to be systematically tested. Others argue that military innovation favoring the offense are particularly destabilizing (Wright, 1965:761), especially when they create incentives to strike first. There is now a lively literature on the offensive/defensive balance of military technology, but this debate, like the debate on the connection between arms races and war, is no longer associated with balance of power theory (Jervis, 1978; Levy, 1984a; Van Evera, 1984a; Snyder, 1984a, 1984b; Sagan, 1986).

Balance of power theorists also assert that military force should be a viable instrument of state policy, because if alliances and armaments fail intervention and war may be necessary means for maintaining an equilibrium in the system. Thus, Claude (1962:91) argues, "war should be imaginable, controllable, usable." This is a common but exceedingly vague argument, for no attempt is made to specify the conditions under which force is not controllable and usable. Presumably the argument is motivated by the sense that the nuclear revolution has reduced the utility of some types of military power in the contemporary system, but few attempts have been made to refine this general argument into a set of theoretically meaningful propositions. The theoretical literature on the utility of military power in the nuclear age (Knorr,

1966, 1977; Gompart, 1977; Art, 1980; Organski and Kugler, 1980; Jervis, 1984, 1988b) has not been incorporated into the balance of power literature.

Another assertion often made by balance of power theorists, but one that is rarely developed into meaningful and testable propositions, is that the stability of a balance of power system is enhanced if statesmen are free to pursue realpolitik in the absence of domestic constraints. The hypothesis is that any internal bureaucratic or domestic constraints on the freedom of statesmen to conduct policy on the basis of power calculations alone reduces the effectiveness of the balancing mechanism and decreases the stability of the system (Claude, 1962; Wright, 1965:Chap. 20; Morgenthau, 1967). These things are difficult to measure, however, and the empirical literature on the balance of power generally focuses on structural hypotheses dealing with distributions of military power and alliances. There is a lively debate on the relative war proneness of democratic and nondemocratic systems, and this debate will be examined later.

Balance of power theorists point to a number of developments in the contemporary system that, according to the theory, should reduce the effectiveness of balancing mechanisms in maintaining the stability of the system. These include the reduction of the number of major actors and the transition from multipolarity to bipolarity, the increasing concentration of power in the hands of the two superpowers, the decreasing flexibility of the alliance system due to the rise of rigid ideologies, the disappearance of the balancer, the decreasing opportunities for great power expansion on the periphery, increasing technological instability, and the declining utility of military force as an instrument of policy for the great powers (Claude, 1962:88–93; Morgenthau, 1967:Chap. 21; Hoffmann, 1968). Thus, Claude (1962:92–93) concludes that while a balance of power system still exists, "all the most fundamental tendencies affecting the political realm in recent generations run counter to the requirements of a workable system of balance of power." The implication of these balance of power hypotheses, taken as a whole, is that the contemporary system should be less stable than those of the past (that is, there should be a higher incidence of major wars).

Although the four decades since World War II do not provide conclusive evidence, it appears that this period has been, if anything, more stable than previous historical systems. This clearly raises some serious questions about the applicability of balance of power theory in the contemporary era. The failure of balance of power theory to deal with the increased importance of economic variables has been frequently emphasized, but its failure to come to terms with the changing nature of military power may be even more important for its failed predictions regarding behavior on war and peace issues. In particular, there is a failure to incorporate a variable reflecting the infeasibility of population defense in the nuclear age (Schelling, 1966:Chap. 1; Art, 1980). The infeasibility of population defense has created a mutual system of hostages in which the very survival of states requires the cooperation of other states. This balance of terror has reinforced deterrence and reduced (but not eliminated) the likelihood of a major war between the leading great powers.

The question of the applicability of balance of power theories to the nuclear era is important, but perhaps the more basic question concerns the logical coherence of the theory and its validity in *any* historical era. The theory is in reality a collection of poorly integrated hypotheses with relatively weak links between them. Many of the hypotheses are mutually inconsistent. The empirical evidence suggests that some key conditions identified by the theory contribute to peace in one period and to war in another, and there has been little success in identifying the theoretical conditions under which each of these hypotheses might be true. The primary exception, and it is an important one, is that there appears to be rather strong evidence in support of the proposition that threats by any single state of achieving a position of hegemony in the system are a sufficient condition for a general war involving nearly all the great powers.

THE DYADIC BALANCE OF POWER

Although balance of power theories are basically systemic in orientation, in that they attempt to explain the interaction of great powers and other states in the system, there is one important dyadic-level hypotheses that is often associated with balance of power theories. It is argued that states will not initiate a war unless they expect to win, so that in a dyadic relationship a state's military superiority is a necessary (but not sufficient) condition for it to initiate a war. Stated differently, military superiority (perhaps modified by a loss-of-strength gradient) is sufficient for deterrence. This hypothesis forms the basis of many informal theories of deterrence and has generated some interesting empirical research.

This hypothesis is reflected in the old adage *si vis pacem para bellum* (if you want peace, prepare for war—presumably by building up one's military capabilities). The hypothesis states necessary but not sufficient conditions, so it does not imply that the strong will always attack the weak, but only that the weak will never attack the strong in a situation isolated from the possible intervention of allies. One can find, however, stronger versions of this hypothesis. Many realists distinguish between revisionist states and status quo states (how this distinction is operationalized is not always clear) and argue that for revisionist states the greater their military superiority over a particular rival the greater the likelihood that it will resort to military action to increase their power still further. This hypothesis is reflected in the Athenians' argument to the Melians in the Melian Dialogue that "the standard of justice depends on the equality of power to compel and that in fact the strong do what they have the power to do and the weak accept what they have to accept" (Thucydides, [431–411 B.C.]1954:V/89). It is also implicit in many theories of deterrence. These often assume that the adversary is inherently aggressive and that therefore military superiority (or at least parity) is not only a sufficient condition for deterrence (if A has superiority B will not attack) but also a necessary condition for deterrence (if A does not have superiority or at least parity, B probably will attack).

There are enough situations in which the strong fail to take advantage of opportunities to expand at the expense of the weak, as well as compelling theoretical arguments to disconfirm the second hypothesis. Even the weaker version of the hypothesis is open to question, however, because it is not clear that military superiority is sufficient for deterrence. The basis for the argument that militarily inferior states will not initiate wars is the assumption that military capabilities are a nearly perfect indicator of the probability of victory in war and that states will not go to war if they expect to lose. There are other factors affecting the probability of victory in war, of course (and military capabilities are not perfectly measurable in any case), but even if these are included there are still logical problems with the hypothesis.[49] It is more reasonable to hypothesize that states act more on the basis of expected utility than on the basis of probability alone. That is, actors consider the likely costs and benefits of war as well as the probability of victory. Actions, including the initiation of war, involving a low probability of success can be rationally undertaken if their outcomes, though unlikely, involve substantial benefits and if the costs of defeat are somehow limited. In addition, the costs and benefits of alternative actions must be compared to the costs and benefits of the status quo. Consequently, weaker states may initiate war if they have even a small chance of reaping substantial gains, or if the existing status quo is so unattractive that they feel that they have nothing to lose. These arguments are implicit in the concept of "asymmetry of motivation" emphasized by George, Hall, and Simmons (1971) and George and Smoke (1974), and in Jervis' (1979:314–317) emphasis on the importance of "intrinsic interests." The importance of both the expected probability of victory as reflected in military capabilities and the expected costs and benefits from war are integrated into a single integrated expected utility theory of war by Bueno de Mesquita (1981a, 1985).

Although these arguments would seem to be rather obvious, there are many proponents of a pure power model that posit that a state's military inferiority will preclude its initiation of war. In fact, the pervasiveness of the capability model has led to numerous empirical studies in an attempt to test several variations of the basic hypothesis. Many of these are quantitative empirical studies covering fairly extensive temporal domains. I have reviewed many of these studies elsewhere (Levy, 1989b), and here I will simply summarize the results.

Although some studies do support the dyadic preponderance hypothesis (Weede, 1976; Garnham, 1976a, 1967b; Organski and Kugler, 1980), much of the evidence runs against it. This evidence suggests that the dyadic balance of power between two states is a poor predictor of the probability of war between them and that the balance of resolve may be more important than the balance of military capabilities (Zinnes et al., 1961; Maoz, 1983; Wayman et al., 1983; Ferris, 1973; Karsten et al., 1984). Siverson and Tennefoss (1984) find that an equality of national strength, supplemented by major power alliances for weaker states, tends to reduce the likelihood of conflict escalation. This leads the authors to a cautious rejection of the power preponderance hypothesis.[50]

Analyses of the relative strength of war initiators and defenders generate similar conclusions. In an analysis of the nine wars between major powers since 1815, Singer and Small (1974:284–289) find that the initiator of the war was the weaker party in four of the nine cases. On the basis of this and other evidence they reject the "weakness leads to war" proposition. Bueno de Mesquita (1981a:Chap. 5) extends the analysis to all interstate wars. He finds that war initiators tend to be equal or stronger then their victims most of the time (in 59 of 76 cases). But this still leaves nearly a fourth of all initiators being the weaker party, which is more than sufficient to reject the hypothesis that military superiority is necessary for deterrence. Moreover, the relationship between expected utility and war initiation is even stronger and also more stable over time, reinforcing the argument that the dyadic balance of power is an insufficient predictor of the likelihood of war initiation in the absence of a consideration of the balance of interests or resolve.

There is also a body of literature on extended deterrence of aggression against an ally. The evidence suggests that although deterrence may be reinforced by the balance of military forces immediately available and proximate to the targeted ally, the overall balance of military power and potential between threatener and defender has no systematic impact on the likelihood of military action and the defender's possession of nuclear weapons has only a marginal impact (Huth and Russett, 1984; Russett, 1963, 1967; Huth, 1988). These quantitative empirical findings are reinforced by those from case studies by Lebow (1981, 1984) and Stein (1985a, 1985b), which emphasize the domestic incentives that often lead to the initiation of conflict in spite of the existence of a credible deterrent threat by the adversary. All of this adds support to the argument by George and Smoke (1974) that the emphasis of conventional deterrence theory on the defender's capabilities and on his or her ability to signal a credible commitment is mistaken, and that more attention needs to be directed to the conditions affecting the initiator's decision to undertake military action. The conclusion of the majority of these studies that a state's military superiority is not a sufficient condition to deter aggression by the adversary is of major significance for contemporary policy, and there is little reason to believe that it has been significantly affected by the development of nuclear weapons and delivery systems.[51]

Another theory that traces the causes of war to the dyadic power relationship between two states, but one which emphasizes the perceptions of this relationship rather than the objective balance of power, is suggested by Blainey (1973). He argues that war is a dispute about the measurement of power between two states and that wars usually begin when two nations disagree on their relative strength, defined in terms of military power. If states could agree on the "objective" balance of power they could predict the outcome of the war, settle their differences on the basis of compromises proportional to their shared expectations regarding the outcome of war, and therefore avoid the costs of fighting.[52]

Blainey's analysis is limited by a number of theoretical problems. One is his implicit assumption that military power is fungible across different issue areas (for example, that disputes over trade or ideology can be resolved by the threat or use of military power), and thus his failure to consider the potential use of other policy instruments as alternatives to war. This is a particularly serious limitation for the contemporary era, where the applicability of military power across issues has been severely restricted, especially for the advanced industrial states. Blainey also minimizes the importance of the issues at stake and implies that disagreements over the dyadic balance of power are equally serious for everything from minor cultural disputes to major territorial disputes. Another problem is the failure to include the expected costs of the war into decision makers' calculations. Although the difference in perceptions of relative power tap the relative costs that should be expected by each side, it fails to tap the absolute costs that are expected from a war. By failing to incorporate issues and costs, Blainey's theory fails to incorporate simple cost-benefit calculations regarding whether the expected gains from war outweigh its expected costs.

Bueno de Mesquita's Expected Utility Theory of War

Bueno de Mesquita's (1981*a*, 1985) expected utility theory of international conflict is an ambitious attempt to construct a parsimonious and formalized theory of decisions for war, to make operational the key theoretical concepts, and to use statistical techniques to test the theory against the historical evidence.[53] The theory purports to explain the necessary conditions for the rational initiation of international war or other forms of serious international disputes, but makes no attempt to specify sufficient conditions. Unlike most realist theories of war, which give primary attention to the great powers, Bueno de Mesquita's theory applies to all state actors. Key propositions derived from the theory have been tested against the historical evidence for the period from 1816 to 1980, and these empirical tests of the theory appear to confirm most of the key hypotheses at relatively high levels of statistical significance. The theory is recognized by some scholars as one of the most important theories of the causes of war, whereas others criticize it for its methodological limitations or its lack of theoretical or empirical content. Some aspects of the theory are highly technical, and partly for that reason a thorough presentation and critique of the theory would not be appropriate here. A briefer summary of the theory's key assumptions and some of the more important propositions derived from these assumptions, along with some of its limitations, would be more useful. The initial version of the theory has undergone some important modifications, and these also will be mentioned.[54]

Bueno de Mesquita (1981a, 1985) begins with a relatively small number of key assumptions: (1) decision making on issues of war and peace can be viewed as if there is a single dominant leader with the veto power to block decisions for war but not necessarily the power to impose war against the preferences of other internal actors[55]; (2) decision makers can be treated as if they are rational, expected-utility maximizers[56]; (3) differences in leaders' orientations toward risk taking influence their decisions; (4) uncertainty about the likely behavior of other states in the event of conflict influences decisions for war or peace; (5) the probability of success in a war or dispute is an increasing function of a state's (or coalition's) military capabilities relative to those of its adversary; (6) national power decays over distance; and (7) utilities are a function of the congruence of policy goals between states, as reflected by their formal military alliances. Note that the first five assumptions underlie the deductive theory itself, while the last two deal with its operationalization.

Rational, expected-utility maximizing with respect to war and peace decisions would involve the following calculations. Leaders calculate their expected utility from a bilateral war on the basis of an evaluation of the costs and benefits of victory and defeat, each weighted by its probability of occurrence.[57] They then calculate the additions or subtractions from their expected utility that would result from the intervention of third parties in support of their adversaries or themselves. The probabilities of victory and defeat are a linear function of the distribution of military capabilities, modified by a loss-of-strength gradient over distance. The costs and benefits of alternative outcomes are more difficult to determine. It is assumed that the purpose of war is to change the foreign policies of other states in order to bring them more in line with one's own policies and presumably one's own interests, and that the extent of congruence of the foreign policies of two states is reflected in the similarities of the alliance patterns of the two states. The more states ally with the same states, the greater the congruence of their policies and their interests. Thus, alliance patterns are a surrogate measure of the similarities of interests of states. Expected-utility calculations are then made on the basis of these factors.

It is important to note that Bueno de Mesquita (1981a:29–32) does not assume that political leaders actually make all of these calculations. He focuses not on their actual decision-making processes but instead on their subsequent behavior. He argues that the validity of the theory is to be judged by the empirical validity of the behavioral predictions of the theory regarding foreign policy decisions rather than by the empirical accuracy of the assumptions of the theory. Thus, the rather controversial assumption that political leaders act *as if* they are rational expected-utility maximizers.[58]

These assumptions generate numerous propositions about international conflict. The central proposition is that positive expected utility is a necessary condition for the initiation of war: states will not go to war if they have negative expected utility. Positive expected utility is not a sufficient condition for war, however, so that states may decide not to go to war even if they expect positive utility from doing so. There may be other policy options, for example, that are expected to bring even greater utility (although these are not formally incorporated into the theory). As we have seen, this expected-utility hypothesis is more theoretically plausible than the dyadic power preponderance hypothesis and, in fact, empirical tests show that it is more consistent with the historical record (Bueno de Mesquita, 1981a).

Because utility functions are invariant under a linear transformation (one can multiply all utilities by a constant value or add a constant), Bueno de Mesquita (1981a) is free to set the utility of the status quo at zero, which he does.[59] The necessary condition for war is thus that the expected outcome of the war is preferred to the status quo. This condition would seem to be reasonable, for states that expect that war will leave them worse off than the status quo should be disinclined to initiate war. The problem, however, is that this formulation assumes that doing nothing leaves one at the status quo. If one expected that the consequences of doing nothing would not be the absence of war but instead an attack by the adversary, and that the expected utility of an adversary's initiation of war would be worse than the expected utility of one's own preemption, it might very well be rational to initiate war in spite of war's negative utility. This aspect of strategic interaction cannot easily be captured in a decision-theoretic model such as expected utility theory. It should also be added that the utilities in Bueno de Mesquita's model capture only *state* interests. It is possible for a political leader to have bureaucratic, domestic political, or personal interests that generate a net positive expected utility for war, which would allow for the rational initiation of war in spite of the negative utility in terms of state interests.

The basic positive expected-utility hypothesis and other hypotheses deriving from the theory are tested empirically using the war, capability, and militarized interstate dispute data for 1816 to 1980 from the Correlates of War project. Empirical support for the basic proposition is extraordinarily high by normal social science standards. Of the 76 wars initiated since 1815, 65 (86 percent) had positive or zero expected utility as defined by Bueno de Mesquita (1981a:129–131), and only 11 (15 percent) had negative expected utility, a statistically significant ($p < .001$) difference. The fact that some cases of war initiation with negative expected utility have occurred suggests that positive expected utility is not technically a necessary condition for war initiation but, instead, that the likelihood of war initiation is a strongly increasing function of expected utility (Bueno de Mesquita [1981a:126–127] explains the anomalous cases in terms of measurement error.) Moreover, the fact that the probability of war initiation for states with positive expected utility is still very low (83 war initiations per 100,000 opportunities, if opportunity is defined on an annual basis in terms of the number of dyads in the international system) reinforces the notion that the theory does not specify sufficient conditions for conflict. These and comparable findings for related empirical tests seem to be robust and are valid for several different regions of the world and for both the nineteenth and twentieth centuries.[60] Comparisons with pure power models of war initiation (military superiority is a necessary condition for war initiation) demonstrates that the expected utility model is more consistent with the historical record (Bueno de Mesquita, 1981a:140–145). The statistical associations involved are considerably stronger and of a higher degree of significance than is normally found in quantitative empirical studies of international conflict.[61]

The initial version of the theory included numerous other propositions. (1) Nonaligned states cannot rationally attack more powerful nonaligned states.[62] (2) Great powers are more likely than lesser powers to fight in wars that are not of great significance for them. (3) Expectations of third state behavior may have a critical impact on decisions for war. (4) If i's positive expected utility from a war with j is less than j's expected loss from a war with i, both i and j prefer to negotiate rather than fight and war should not occur.[63] Although the preceding propositions are not particularly novel (but their axiomatic foundation is), the theory does generate some counterintuitive propositions. (5) Under some circumstances a nonaligned state can rationally attack a more powerful adversary even if the adversary is expected to attract allies, and it may also be rational for a state to attack the stronger of two aligned states. (6) Moreover, not only is it sometimes rational for allies to fight each other, but conflict should be more common between allies than between enemies.[64]

These other propositions also receive fairly strong empirical support for the period from 1816 to 1980. Regarding the counterintuitive proposition regarding wars between allies, for example, it is found that allies fight each other three times more frequently (five times in the European region) than would be expected by chance on the basis of the number of allied states in the system. The fact that these propositions are all derived from the same set of assumptions and integrated into a single framework makes the empirical results and their theoretical interpretation all the more powerful. The power of the theory is demonstrated further by its ability to resolve some contradictions between balance of power theory and power preponderance theory regarding the consequences of certain distributions of power and the role of alliances. It subsumes contradictory propositions from these other theories into a single framework that specifies the conditions under which the predictions of each are true (Bueno de Mesquita, 1988).

In spite of its theoretical elegance and strong predictive power Bueno de Mesquita's (1981a) expected utility model has some serious theoretical problems, and many of these have been pointed out by the critics (Zagare, 1982; Wagner, 1984; Majeski and Sylvan, 1984; Maoz, 1982a; Khong, 1984). These problems include the assumption that there are only two possible outcomes, war and peace; the failure to incorporate elements of strategic interaction and possible incentives for preemption; the failure to incorporate the costs of war into the model[65]; the interpersonal comparisons of utility; the strong tendency to treat conflict as a zero-sum game; the ad hoc treatment of risk orientation and the assumption that all major powers are risk neutral; the application of risk and uncertainty to third-party intervention but not to bilateral conflicts; the ambiguity of the identity of the initiator of a conflict, which is a central component of the theory; the tendency for a disproportionately large number of the expected utilities for war to cluster around zero and the resulting sensitivity of the results to small errors in the measurement of utilities; the use of formal alliance commitments as a measure of utilities; and some rather puzzling utility values in certain cases, which raise questions about the conceptualization and measurement of utility.[66]

Several of these problems are rectified, new theoretical questions are explored, and new propositions derived in later modifications of the theory by

Bueno de Mesquita and his students (Bueno de Mesquita, 1985; Morrow, 1985, 1987; Bueno de Mesquita and Lalman, 1986). Risk orientations have been endogenously derived and fully integrated into the theory. The tendencies toward interpersonal comparisons of utility have been eliminated and the tendency to treat conflict as zero sum has been greatly reduced. The initiation and escalation of conflict under conditions of differing perceptions as well as shared perceptions is analyzed, and the theory provides a potentially useful framework for the analysis of the consequences of misperception. The expected utility of the status quo has been made endogenous, and the expected costs of conflict have been integrated into the theory. The dichotomous treatment of outcomes has been expanded, providing a useful framework for differentiating among war, intervention, and peace (Bueno de Mesquita and Lalman, 1986), and a more generalized continuous-outcome expected-utility model has been proposed (Morrow, 1985). The transformation into polar coordinates (Bueno de Mesquita and Lalman, 1986) has facilitated the fuller incorporation of the costs of conflict into the model and the analysis of the dynamics of arms races. The most recent development is the application of a model of sequential games and incomplete information to the analysis of arms races (Bueno de Mesquita and Lalman, 1988b).

Thus modifications of Bueno de Mesquita's expected-utility theory of war have resolved some of the earlier inconsistencies and anomalies in the theory and have generated new propositions explaining a wider range of empirical phenomena. This is not to say, however, that all of the major problems have been resolved. The assumptions that there exist a single dominant decision maker who maximizes his or her expected utility, and that domestic and bureaucratic political considerations as well as individual belief systems and psychological processes have no impact on decisions for war, is open to question. There is substantial evidence from the case study literature and from some quantitative empirical studies, some of which we will cover later in this chapter, that individual, societal, and governmental variables have played critical roles in the processes leading to many wars.[67] There is also substantial evidence in social psychology that individual decision-making processes deviate significantly from the rational models postulated by microeconomic theory. These bodies of evidence raise important questions regarding the descriptive accuracy of the rational state-actor assumption and therefore of Bueno de Mesquita's expected-utility theory of war.

In the *as if* assumption, however, Bueno de Mesquita explicitly rejects the relevance of the descriptive accuracy criterion. He emphasizes instead the explanatory and predictive power of the theory, as reflected by the theory's logically deductive structure and by the empirical accuracy of its key propositions. If we accept this for the moment (and we are by no means obligated to do so), we are led back to the question of the theoretical content of these propositions and the strength of their empirical support.[68]

The fundamental conceptual problem lies in the measurement of utilities. The assumptions that one state's utility for war against another is a function of the similarity of their formal military alliances and that risk orientation can be derived from a state's best and worst possible alliance portfolios provide an ingenious way of measuring utilities with observable systemic-level indicators and have therefore been useful in permitting an empirical test of the theory. Conceptually, however, formal military alliances are an unsatisfactory measure of utilities or of risk orientation, and alternative measures need to be constructed in the future. Alliances are formed in response to threats to one's military security interests and do not necessarily reflect the congruence of two states' overall foreign policies and the similarity of their interests.[69] A formal military alliance is one component of a state's interests, but only one, and is neither a necessary or sufficient indicator of the congruence of interests and policies between states.[70]

I suspect that Bueno de Mesquita would respond that the validity of alliances as a measure of utilities is an important question, but one that has little relevance for the truth or falseness of his theory. He insists that "the truthfulness of a deduced relationship among variables in a world that complies with the theory's assumptions is a logical, and not an empirical question." Empirical analysis is relevant for the "usefulness" of a theory rather than its truth (Bueno de Mesquita, 1981a:9–10).

I have some difficulty with the epistemology underlying this argument. A theory is defined not only by its logical structure but also by its empirical content. It includes not only "internal principles" but also "bridge principles" linking the internal logical structure to the empirical world that it purports to explain (Hempel, 1966:Chap. 6; Nagel, 1961). Expected-utility theory itself is not a theory of war but a mathematical model with a logical structure but no empirical content. Bueno de Mesquita has constructed a theory of war by linking the abstract mathematical symbols of the expected-utility model with empirical phenomenon such as states and their dominant decision makers, military capabilities, military alliances, and so forth. In the absence of these linkages the model has no theoretical content and provides no explanatory power. Thus, the conceptualization of utilities in terms of alliance patterns is an essential element of the theory, and the validity of the theory should be judged in part by the validity of alliance patterns as indicators of utility.

This raises another point. Alliances are important not only in themselves but because they are manifestations of deeper communalities of interests between states and serve as surrogate measures of those interests. An important part of understanding the causes of war is to understand the nature of those deeper interests, and the specification of those interests would add greater empirical content to the theory. More generally, the concept of utility cannot be considered by itself to be an substantively meaningful independent causal variable, and the usefulness of that concept is ultimately dependent on the specification of the systemic, societal, economic, governmental, and individual variables that influence the utility calculations of decision makers.

Because the measurement of utilities is central to Bueno de Mesquita's expected utility theory, it would be useful to confirm the validity of the alliance indicator by demonstrating that it is consistent with other indicators of the congruence of the policies and interests of states. Otherwise, there is a danger that the operational hypotheses actually being tested may not be the same as the hypotheses formally derived from the theory, and that the empirical findings may say something about the connection between alliances and war but not necessarily about utilities. The possible use of a case study methodology to confirm decision makers' evaluations of the utility of war in a number of well-selected and critical cases should not be overlooked. Case studies cannot substitute for large-N correlational methodologies for testing most hypotheses because of their restricted ability to generalize over many cases, but their higher level of construct validity (congruence between theoretical concept and empirical indicator) suggests their potential use in confirming the validity of aggregate indicators.

The empirical findings in *The War Trap* are also affected in important ways by the classification of initiators and victims and of winners and losers. Bueno de Mesquita (1981a:99) conceives of the initiator as the state that had "the last reasonable chance to avert" the military conflict, that is operationalized in terms of the first state to engage in sustained combat on the opponent's territory. Although this appears to be a reasonable approach, the concept of a initiator is extremely complex, and so many of the statistical tests hinge on the proper identification of the initiator that further confirmation of the validity of this indicator is necessary. The classification of victory or defeat for members of coalitions is also difficult, as indicated by the classification of Poland as a victor in World War II and Serbia as a victor in World War I. Confidence in the strength of the empirical results would be greatly enhanced by a review of the data and refinement of classification and coding procedures.

These limitations only partly detract from the overall contribution of Bueno de Mesquita's expected utility theory to the study of international conflict. The core of the theory reflects the conventional idea that state behavior with respect to issues of war and peace are based on careful calculations of the costs and benefits of various policy options, which is a central assumption in realist international theory. The idea that statesmen think in terms of expected utility is not necessarily new, but it manages to integrate power-based notions that imply that statesmen think only in terms of probabilities with other

BUSINESS REPLY MAIL
FIRST CLASS   PERMIT NO. 4437   NEW YORK, N.Y.

POSTAGE WILL BE PAID BY ADDRESSEE

OXFORD UNIVERSITY PRESS
EDUCATIONAL SALES DEPARTMENT
200 MADISON AVENUE
NEW YORK, N.Y. 10157-0913

NO POSTAGE
NECESSARY
IF MAILED
IN THE
UNITED STATES

My comments on ....
                    Author or Editor   Title

.... Date   Name of course ....
May we quote you? ☐Yes ☐No   Level? ☐Fresh. ☐Soph. ☐Jun. ☐Sen. ☐Grad.
Will you adopt? ☐Definitely ☐Possible ☐No   For use as: Req'd Main Text ☐ Recom. Reading ☐
Decision date ....   Approx. Course enrollment? ....
Text used ....

Name (please print) ....
Dept. .... Position ....
Institution .... Tel. ....
City .... State .... Zip Code ....

concepts that give primary (but not exclusive) emphasis to value considerations (asymmetry of motivation, balance of interests). The contribution of the theory is its formalization of these simple notion into a parsimonious, logically integrated, and empirically testable theory of international behavior. Other theories may provide a richer explanation of the conditions and processes leading to war, but none combines as strong a combination of rigorous theorizing with rigorous and systematic empirical research. The further development of this expected utility theory—including its integration into a game theoretic framework to incorporate the strategic interaction between states (Morrow, 1986), the use of a sequential model to capture the dynamic processes involving both reputational effects and exogenous changes in relative power capabilities, the construction of alternative measures of utilities that incorporate both economic ties between states and the domestic political interests of political elites, the refinement of other operational indicators, and the incorporation of sufficient as well as necessary conditions for war—is one of the most important paths for future research on international conflict.

Theories of Power Transition and Hegemonic War

ORGANSKI'S POWER TRANSITION THEORY

One of Organski's (1968) criticisms of balance of power theory nearly three decades ago was that its conception of military power in terms of territory, population, armaments, and allies was basically static and ignored the role of internal economic development as a source of the changing military power of states. Organski argues that this conception may have been valid prior to the mid-eighteenth century, but for the last two centuries the primary source of national power has been industrialization, which leads to differential rates of economic growth between states and therefore to changing distributions of power in the international system. These changing power differentials are the primary source of war, or at least of major war, in international politics. They arise primarily from uneven rates of economic development and secondarily from institutional arrangements and social processes that affect the efficiency with which the state can extract human and material resources from society and aggregate it for use in serving state interests (Organski and Kugler, 1980:Chap. 1–2). This forms the basis of Organski's (1968) power transition theory, which has been further refined and tested by Organski and Kugler (1980).

Organski (1968:vii) summarizes the theory as follows

> The overall patterns of world politics in the modern era are caused by sharp differences in social, economic, and political modernization among and within nations. Differential modernization in turn causes shifts in the distribution of

world power among states. It is these changes that underlie the wars and other conflicts of our era. The immensely complex patterns that create these shifts in power, the shifts themselves, and their consequences are not easily deflected by diplomacy or military power.

Organski's basic argument is that the likelihood of a major war is greatest when the military power of a dissatisfied challenger begins to approach those of the leading state in the system, for the challenger will usually initiate a war to gain benefits, privileges, and influence commensurate with its newly acquired military power.[71] Thus the key condition for war is not the equality of capabilities per se nor the changes in those capabilities but, instead, the interaction effect between these two variables.[72] Organski also concedes that it is possible for world leadership to be transferred peacefully without violent conflict, but argues that this rarely happens: "the major wars of recent history have all been wars involving the dominant nation and its allies against a challenger who has recently risen in power thanks to industrialization" (Organski, 1968:376). Organski and Kugler (1980:Chap. 1) claim that their theory is confirmed by an empirical test based on the Franco-Prussian War, Russo-Japanese War, and two world wars.

The idea that changing power differentials are a primary cause of international war, particularly major wars involving the leading states in the system, is not really new. It can be traced to Thucydides'([431–411 B.C.] 1954:1/23) argument that "what made the Peloponnesian War inevitable was the growth of Athenian power and the fear which this caused in Sparta," and scattered references to the importance of uneven rates of growth can be found in a long history of realist thinking on international politics. The dominant orientation within the realist tradition, however, is balance of power theory, which focuses on the existing structure of the international system as the primary independent variable. Moreover, the condition of near equality is stabilizing in balance of power theory but destabilizing in power transition theory. To the extent that changing power differentials are explicitly recognized in balance of power theory, it is the increasing power of the already dominant state, leading to an opposing military coalition to block it from achieving a position of hegemony. In addition, the argument that alliances generally play a minimal role in the outbreak of major power war is also a distinct change in emphasis from balance of power theory (Organski and Kugler, 1980:24–28; Bueno de Mesquita, 1980a:377–380). Organski's systematic attempt to construct a theory of major war around the concept of power transitions driven by uneven rates of industrialization has led to a renewed emphasis on and systemization of this old idea.

Organski's (1968) focus on industrialization as the primary source of changing military capabilities and power transitions is somewhat limiting, because there were significant power transitions prior to the industrial era; several of these have been analyzed by Gilpin (1981) and others. The Organski and Kugler (1980) test of power transition theory, including the relevance of the Franco-Prussian and Russo-Japanese cases, has also been criticized (Bueno de Mesquita, 1980a:376–380; Thompson, 1983b; Levy, 1985a:353–354). One aspect of the Organski and Kugler formulation that is particularly open to question is their argument that the weaker but rising challenger initiates the war against the dominant power. It is not clear why the challenger should fight rather than wait until the trends in underlying economic and military power—which Organski and Kugler (1980:Chap. 4) claim are irreversible—propel it into the stronger position. An alternative hypothesis suggests a more plausible mechanism by which an impending power transition may lead to war: the leading state may launch a "preventive war" in an attempt to block or retard the rise of the challenger while that opportunity is still available.

The theoretical importance of preventive war has been widely recognized by political scientists (Vagts, 1956; Lebow, 1981; Gilpin, 1981:Chap. 5; Van Evera, 1984b:Chap. 2; Levy, 1987). Its historical importance has also been recognized. For Thucydides ([431–411 B.C.] 1954:1/69), Sparta's primary motivation was reflected in the Corinthians' argument for war against Athens: "instead of going out to meet them, you prefer to stand still and wait till you are attacked, thus hazarding everything by fighting with opponents who have grown far stronger than they were originally." Howard (1983:Chap. 1) suggests that Thucydides' explanation for the origins of the Peloponnesian War is true for most wars: "The causes of war remain rooted, as much as they were in the pre-industrial age, in perceptions by statesmen of the growth of hostile power and the fears for the restriction, if not the extinction, of their own." Taylor (1954:166) suggests that "every war between Great Powers [in the 1848–1918 period] . . . started out as a preventive war." The importance of the preventive motivation in the 1914 case in particular has attracted a great deal of attention from historians (Fay, [1928] 1966; Albertini, 1957; Fischer, 1961, 1975; Ritter, 1970).

One can find numerous instances, however, in which declining power has not led to preventive war, including Britain's decline relative to the United States in the late nineteenth century, Germany's decline relative to Russia for a decade before 1914, and the United States' decline relative to the Soviet Union after World War II (Lebow, 1984). This raises the obvious question of the conditions under which power shifts lead to war and the conditions under which they do not. Organski (1968:376) suggests (without elaboration) that:

> War is most apt to occur: if the challenger is of such a size that at its peak it will roughly equal the dominant nation in power; if the rise of the challenger is rapid;

if the dominant nation is inflexible in its policies; if there is no tradition of friendship between the dominant nation and the challenger; and if the challenger sets out to replace the existing international order with a competitive order of its own.

Van Evera (1984a:72–76) and Snyder (1985:160–61) argue that the likelihood of war under conditions of declining power is a function of the magnitude of the power shift, the offensive/defensive balance, and the expected probability the adversary will initiate a war in the future. Levy (1987) expands on this model and suggests that the probability of war is also affected by the preventer's expected probability of victory with tolerable costs in a preventive war now, decision makers' risk-taking propensities, the influence of the military in the political process, and domestic political factors undermining both the military potential of the state and the political position of decision makers. He notes that there are in principle other policy options available to a leading state in decline, including alliances against or negotiation with the rising challenger as well as industrial revitalization as a means of reversing the underlying sources of decline, and asserts that these considerations would have to be incorporated into any comprehensive theory of preventive war.

The implications of Levy's (1987) hypotheses are that the nuclear superpowers are less likely than great powers of the past to succumb to the temptations for preventive war. First, although power differentials continue to change, military superiority is more difficult to translate into political influence than in the past (at least for the leading states in the system), and therefore the political consequences of military decline, while not negligible, will be less than in the past. Second, pressures for preventive war in the past have been influenced by perceptions that a future war with the rising challenger was very likely if not inevitable, but perceptions of inevitability are much less likely in the nuclear age. Another important factor in the past was the perception by the declining leader that it had the ability to fight and win a preventive war now with acceptable costs, but such expectations should be far less likely in the nuclear age. Although all of these factors reduce the pressures for preventive war, the magnitude of their impact is more difficult to determine.

LONG-CYCLE THEORY

The power transition hypothesis has been incorporated into several recent theories of systemic change and hegemonic war in world politics.[73] One is "long-cycle theory," which has been developed by Modelski (1978, 1987a,b) and Thompson (1983c, 1988). They identify a global political system originating in 1494 and characterized by regular cycles of world leadership, system management, and global war over the last five centuries. Leadership in the system is based on control over military capabilities of global reach (sea power prior to the mid-twentieth century and air power since then). A world power emerges from a global war with monopoly control over sea power and world trade, which allows it to structure the global political and economic systems in its own interests and to maintain order in the system. The costs of world leadership and the emergence of new rivals invariably leads to a deconcentration of power and a decline in the leader's dominant position, and ultimately to a new struggle for world leadership and a renewed period of global war, a cycle that has repeated itself once every 100 hundred years.[74]

Long-cycle theory does not attempt to explain all wars in the system, but only a restricted class of global wars, defined as those wars that determine the constitution or authority arrangement of the global political system (Modelski, 1978; Thompson, 1983c).[75] They are the result of a structural crisis in the system and are basically succession struggles for leadership in the system. Thus, their fundamental cause is changing distributions of power arising out of states' uneven rates of economic development.[76] More specifically, they result from the rise of challengers who threaten to gain a dominant position on the European continent, which could provide the basis for a challenge to the global position of the world power. These wars do not begin as direct contests between the leader and challenger but instead as localized conflicts that escalate (Thompson, 1983c:349), although the conditions under which localized conflicts escalate into global wars have not yet been determined. The implication is that changing power concentrations in the global system arising out of some form of uneven economic development is a necessary but not a sufficient condition for global war. Note that the primary antagonism in the war is not between the declining leader and the global power that replaces it, but between the declining leader and the territorially based regional challenger.

Whatever the triggers leading from localized conflicts to global wars, the regional challenger always fails, for several reasons.[77] They do not augment their land-based military power with military power of global reach. They fail (at least before this century) to match the successful maritime powers in obtaining inexpensive credit to meet their enormous military expenses (Rasler and Thompson, 1983). Finally, they embark on expansion prematurely, before the power transition has been completed, and underestimate the seriousness of their threat to the global position of the world power and, hence, fail to anticipate the expansion of the war (Thompson, 1983b).[78]

Recent empirical research has provided some evidence in support of long-cycle theory. Thompson has generated data on the naval capabilities of the global powers over the last five centuries (Modelski and Thompson, 1988) and has used these data to test some key long-cycle propositions. Thompson (1983a, 1986b) examines the relationship from the perspective of the global system, in which power is defined in terms of naval capabilities, and finds that concentrations of power are consistently associated with periods of peace, as long-cycle theory would predict.[79] He also demonstrates that the consequences of global wars are significantly different than those of other interstate wars. In a study of the net impact of warfare on the economic growth of five leading states since 1500, Rasler and Thompson (1985b) show that global wars are more likely than other interstate wars to have a significant impact on the economic growth patterns of participating states, winners as well as losers. These wars increase state spending, state taxes, and state debts and contribute to the organizational expansion of the state without significantly expanding the material base for meeting the escalating overhead costs (Rasler and Thompson, 1985a), although the net economic costs even of global wars tend to be temporary. Thompson and Rasler (1988) also demonstrate that only global wars, and not other major interstate wars, result in a significant reconcentration of naval capabilities that provide a necessary foundation for systemic leadership in the world system.[80]

GILPIN'S THEORY OF HEGEMONIC TRANSITIONS

Gilpin's (1981) theory of hegemonic war and change is similar in many respects to long-cycle theory. The theory is based on an extension of hegemonic stability theory, which must be briefly examined. Hegemonic stability theory argues that stability in an international political economy requires the existence of a single dominant state, or "hegemon." The hegemon plays the leadership or system management role on the basis of its power and its will to bear the costs of maintaining order in the system in accordance with an informal system of norms and rules. In the absence of a leader to manage the system, the extent of economic conflict in the system will decrease. Similarly, the decline of a hegemon should lead to decreasing stability in the system (Kindleberger, 1973; Gilpin, 1975; Krasner, 1976; Keohane and Nye, 1977; Keohane, 1980, 1984).

A stable liberal, international political economy requires that the hegemon be both the most powerful state politically and the most efficient economically (Gilpin, 1981:129–131). Its comparative advantage leads it to prefer a liberal system, and its political strength facilitates the structuring of the international economic system along liberal lines to serve its own interests. On the other hand, political hegemony without economic efficiency tends to result in an imperial international system. It is precisely because of the historical rarity of the conjunction of political hegemony with economic efficiency that there have been so few liberal international systems. Thus, hegemonic stability theorists limit themselves primarily to two historical cases, the periods of Pax Britannica and Pax American in the last two centuries, and have not been concerned with behavior in nonliberal hegemonic systems or nonhegemonic systems.

Most versions of hegemonic stability theory attempt to explain the degree of stability in the world political economy rather than the frequency and seriousness of war in the system; for this reason hegemonic stability theory is not a theory of war and peace. This conclusion is reinforced by the fact that most hegemonic stability theorists are quite explicit in defining hegemony in terms of economic dominance and basically ignore the role of military power or the distribution of military power in the system.[81] There may be an implicit assumption that a stable liberal economy contributes to international peace and, in some cases, this argument is more explicit, as in Kindleberger's (1973) discussion of the role of the world depression of 1929–1939 in the processes leading to World War II and in other works as well. The theoretical linkages are rarely developed, however, and the hypothesized linkages between economic liberalism and peace are left to classical liberal theorists, who will be discussed later. Gilpin (1981) is one, however, who attempts to integrate aspects of hegemonic stability theory into a broader theory of hegemonic transitions and to extend the domain of the theory to previous historical eras and to cases of dominant but nonliberal states.

Gilpin recognizes that power consists of both military and economic dimensions and that these are not necessarily congruent, and gives greater emphasis to land-based power than do Modelski and Thompson.[82] National power is a function not only of economic development but also of structures of political and social organization and governance and of technological innovation in the military, transportation, and communication sectors. Gilpin suggests that historically one state has often (but not always) been dominant. The hegemonic state, such as Great Britain in the nineteenth century or the United States in the twentieth century, has the strength and motivation to structure the international political, economic, and cultural systems to serve its own interests. The resulting system provides a secure environment for trade and investment for all states, from which they can benefit without paying the costs.

Ultimately, however, the hegemonic power enters a period of decline while rivals catch up. The maintenance of a position of dominance brings increasing military and administrative overhead costs without a proportional increase in its resource base. In addition, resources tend to be diverted away from productive investment to the military sector for the purposes of protection, and the maintenance of a lead in military technology becomes increasingly expensive as that technology diffuses to other states in the system that do not have to pay the full costs of development or overhead. Wealth also diffuses, in part because the same economic processes that initially favor the hegemon ultimately work to the benefit of others (for example, the multinational corporation). Productivity declines further as prosperity creates both conspicuous consumption and domestic cartels with an interest in the maintenance of the status quo (Olson, 1982; Rogowski, 1983). Gilpin argues that attempts by the hegemonic power to reduce their commitments or expand their resource base usually fail, and that a preventive war against the rising challenger may be one of its most attractive policy options. More generally, the underlying cause of hegemonic wars is the increasing disequilibrium between the existing system of governance in an international system and the distribution of political, economic, and cultural benefits that follow from it, on the one hand, and the actual distribution of power in the system on the other.

These and other theories of hegemonic war (Wallerstein, 1984; Vayrynen, 1983; see also Toynbee, 1954) generally share the view that the underlying cause of major war is a power transition driven by some form of uneven economic development and perhaps other internal variables. There has yet to be a conclusive test of power transition theory or any of these hypotheses relating to the conditions under which power shifts lead to war.[83] This is a major gap in the literature because these hypotheses are important for contemporary policy as well as for theory. Uneven economic growth, changing power differentials, and the rise and fall of major actors have been persistent features of the international system throughout history. There is no reason to believe those processes have ceased to exist in the nuclear age. Because the consequences of systemic war would undoubtedly be far greater than ever before, the question of the conditions under which power transitions can be accomplished peacefully rather than through war, and what the rising state and others can do to reduce the pressures on the declining leader for preventive military action, are absolutely critical. Stated differently, a key question is whether there exists an alternative to hegemonic war as a mechanism for restoring an equilibrium between the existing patterns of governance and influence in the system and the changing distribution of power.

Lateral Pressure Theory

Another theory in which national growth is an important variable, but that does not necessarily involve power transitions and does not formally restrict itself to the class of hegemonic wars, is Choucri and North's (1975) lateral pressure theory of international conflict. Whereas much of the earlier work on North's 1914 project focused on misperceptions and other dimensions of the dynamics of crisis behavior (North, Holsti, and Choucri, 1976), the Choucri and North study examines the dynamics of national growth and the competitive processes of interstate interaction that result. The basic argument is that increasing population and advancing technology generate increasing domestic demands for resources, demands that cannot generally be satisfied by a state's domestic resource endowments or by existing levels of foreign trade. Resource demands generate "lateral pressure" for access to raw materials and markets and often for political control over external populations and areas. This lateral pressure often takes the form of colonial expansion, and when several states adopt expansionist policies their interests are increasingly likely to come into conflict. This generates an "intensity of intersections," which leads to internal pressures to defend one's expanding interests, which in turn leads to alliance formation and increased military expenditures. Alliances and military expenditures lead to reciprocal actions by adversaries, and the resulting action-reaction process often escalates to violent behavior and possibly full-scale war.

Choucri and North (1975) construct a simultaneous equation model to test the theory and apply it to the period from 1870 to 1914. They measure changing technology by a surrogate indicator, national income per capita; lateral pressure by colonial area under a state's control; and violence on a 30-point scale using events data. They conclude that national growth is indeed a primary determinant of the processes of national expansion, conflicts of interests, arms races, alliances, and violent conflicts, although there is some variation in the importance of specific linkages for the six great powers prior to World War I. In order to compare the dynamics of "war-prone systems" with those of "peace systems," Choucri and North (1972) apply their model to Scandinavia and the Netherlands over the last century. They find that none of the linkages from the pre-World War I great power model are strong in the Scandinavian cases and, in particular, that overseas commercial activities have not contributed to the growth of military establishments or led to war. The absence of a link between economic expansion and the growth of military establishments is found also in the case of Japan after World War II, although such links did exist for Japan in the previous seven decades (Choucri and North, 1986). The existence of hypothesized linkages in war systems and their absence in peace systems provide additional support for the theory. There is also evidence, however, that key linkages in the model also apply to the Sino-Soviet-U.S. triangle in the post-World War II period, which has been peaceful so far (Ashley, 1980).

The significance of the theory derives from its recognition of the importance of the processes of national growth, the specification of the ways in which it interacts with other variables, the integration of all of these variables into a dynamic model, the construction of operational indicators for the key theoretical concepts, and the testing of the model against the historical data. In this sense lateral pressure theory is an important advance over more static theories of international conflict, and the simultaneous equations used to model the theory constitute an improvement over the correlational methods commonly used to test systemic-level hypotheses. There are, however, a number of theoretical and methodological problems with the model. The validity of several of the operational indicators is open to question. National income per capita is a very weak indicator of technological development, particularly given the availability of the Correlates of War capability data on energy consumption and iron and steel production. Colonial area is a rather limited measure of lateral expansion and misses some other important forms of territorial expansion and intersections of interests (for example, the Austro-Russian conflict in the Balkans prior to 1914).

This raises a more general issue. The assumptions that resource demands are satisfied primarily through external sources and that these necessarily involve colonial expansion require more justification. There is a failure to consider the conditions under which free trade might be a viable alternative to colonization as a means of economic growth. The phenomenon of the "imperialism of free trade" (Gallagher and Robinson, 1953) is not captured in the model, and the relevance of the model to Japan and others after World War II and to the "trading state" (Rosecrance, 1986) in general is open to question. In addition, no attention is given to the overall structure of power in the international system and its effects on the feasibility of free trade. It may be that the absence of a linkage between economic expansion and the growth of military establishments can be explained in most cases by the existence of a leading state that provides for defense costs and enables others to concentrate on economic growth (for example, the U.S. nuclear umbrella facilitating Japanese economic expansive).

The link between colonial expansion and war needs to be further developed, especially in light of the safety valve hypothesis that suggests that colonial expansion may reduce the likelihood of major war by diverting great power competition away from the core of the system to the periphery of the system. The theory also fails to specify the direction of the colonial expansion and the identity of the adversary in military conflict. Some very serious colonial rivals prior to 1914 (Great Britain and France in Africa, Great Britain and Russia in Asia) became wartime allies rather than adversaries, contrary to the model (although the Franco-German rivalry in Northern Africa was also intense).

Liberal Economic Theories of War

Liberal economic theorists going back to Smith and Ricardo have argued that capitalist economies and an international market economy characterized by free trade are the best guarantors of peace.[84] As Montesquieu ([1750] 1949:I, Bk.20, Chap. 1) argued, "peace is the natural effect of trade." Manchester liberals believed that there exists a natural harmony of interests both between and within states and that free trade and other liberal reforms would facilitate this natural harmony of interests and the maintenance of peace (Silberner, 1946; Blainey, 1973:Chap. 2). Tariffs, quotas, and any other restrictions on the natural operation of the market mechanism reduces economic prosperity and increases the likelihood of war. In addition, an international market economy separates the pursuit of wealth from the pursuit of territory (Buzan, 1984). The traditional utility of force for the acquisition of territory is diminished if wealth is no longer based on territorial control. In relationships between liberal states difficult questions of production, distribution, price, and other dimensions of trade and finance can be resolved through impersonal market forces rather than through intergovernmental bargaining. Thus, international economic disputes are less likely to become politicized under liberal international economies. Because economic interests are more easily quantified than political interests and conflicts of economic interests are more conducive to negotiated solutions, the likelihood that conflicts of economic interests will increase the level of political tensions between states, and perhaps even lead to a violent resolution, is said to be lower in relationships among liberal capitalist states (Aron, 1968; Cohen, 1973). In addition, the interdependence generated by free trade increases the vulnerability of all states, the costs of any disruption, and hence the disincentives to use force.

The argument that liberal economies are more stable is made at the national as well as systemic level of analysis. Liberals endorse the argument of Comte, Spencer, and others that the underlying spirit of industrial societies runs counter to the spirit of military societies (Veblen, 1915; Schumpeter, [1919] 1951) because industrialism brings prosperity to the masses as well as to the business classes and diverts their interests from external expansion and conquest to making profits. People are "too busy growing rich to have time for war" (Blainey, 1973:10), and the demands of industrial capitalism require the diversion of resources from the military sector to the economic sectors. War is uneconomical because it results in depopulation, the destruction of industry, increased taxes and debt, the loss of profits, the reduction of international trade, and the general disruption of economic equilibrium, and generates a broad coalition of interests opposed to warlike policies.

There has been no convincing empirical test of these liberal hypotheses regarding the causes of war. The common references to the nineteenth century and post-1945 period (along with the interwar period as a case for comparison) to support the liberal case fail to come to terms with more compelling alternative explanations for the level of warfare in the system. It is true that the emergence of capitalist economic systems and an open international economy in the nineteenth century coincided with the most peaceful century in modern history, but it is not clear that the rise of an open international economic system was the cause and not the consequence of a stable security system

(Blainey, 1973:Chap. 2).[85] It has yet to be convincingly demonstrated that these economic considerations had a larger impact than the political and military structure of the international system created after the Napoleonic Wars. Both liberal and nonliberal economic systems have historically been too confounded with complex contextual factors to permit any simple inference that one is necessarily less war prone than the other.

This conclusion is reinforced by Buzan's (1984) theoretical arguments that although some features of liberal economic structures tend to reduce the level of international conflict, other features are destabilizing, just as mercantilist economic systems have some tendencies that reduce the tendency for states to resort to force as well as other characteristics that are more stabilizing. Thus, Buzan (1984:623) concludes that "liberal economic structure has neither a strong nor an unconditional constraining effect on the use of force," and that the impact of economic structure on international security is subordinate to military and political factors.

The systemic-level theories first surveyed locate the sources of war in the structure of the international system within which all states exist. It is assumed that the internal characteristics of states have only a marginal impact on their foreign policies, especially with respect to issues of war and peace. As we have seen, there has been some recent interest in the internal economic sources of national growth, but these affect war through their impact on the international distribution of military power. It does not require a detailed knowledge of international history to recognize, however, that different states in similar international situations, or even the same state in similar situations, do not always behave in similar ways and that factors internal to states often have a significant impact on their behavior with respect to issues of war and peace. Let us now turn to several societal-level theories of war focusing on the political and economic structure of states, political culture and ideology, and the impact of public opinion and nationalism. In the following sections we will turn to an examination of governmental-level decision-making theories relating to the issue of war and peace.

Societal-Level Theories

Attempts to trace war to conditions internal to states is an old tradition in the study of international relations. Plato argued that the likelihood of war is minimized if the population is relatively cohesive and if their economic system provides a moderate level of consumption: a loyal citizenry is necessary to deter external attacks, and a moderate level of prosperity both reduces one's own marginal economic benefits to be gained from war and at the same time reduces the potential economic gains to an adversary contemplating an attack (Haas, 1974:163). Shakespeare ([1598] 1845), in suggesting to leaders that they "busy giddy minds with foreign quarrels," recognized that internal discontent can motivate political elites to initiate external wars in order to promote internal unity and to consolidate their own internal political positions. Kant, Bentham, and other Enlightenment philosophers believed that the warfare that had plagued Europe for centuries could be traced to the imperatives of aristocratic societies and argued that representative governments are more peaceful because they invest ultimate political authority in the hands of those who must suffer the hardships of war (Kant, [1795] 1949; Waltz, 1954:Chap. 4). Marx and his followers have argued that modern war arises from the economic imperatives of capitalist societies and the inequitable distribution of wealth within them (Lenin, [1917] 1939). The importance of religious and ideological differences between states has long been recognized, and in the last century the destabilizing consequences of nationalism for the international system have been emphasized (Wright, 1965).

Yet, of all the factors involved in the processes leading to war, these societal-level variables have been given the least attention by modern political scientists. Their importance is minimized not only in realist theories emphasizing systemic constraints on states, but also in decision-making theories emphasizing the perceptions of leading decision makers and the interests and bureaucratic processes of governmental organizations. Although individual hypotheses linking war to societal-level variables have been tested, these tend to be analytically isolated propositions that have not been integrated into any general theoretical structure.[86] In addition, while earlier social theorists were quite interested in the question of war, that has not been true of post-1945 sociologists, although the threat of nuclear annihilation has aroused some recent interest (Bramson and Goethals, 1968:202). This relative lack of interest in societal causes of war by political scientists stands in marked contrast with recent trends among historians, whose work over the last couple decades has emphasized social and economic variables as among the most important causes of war (Levy, 1988a; Iggers, 1984).

This survey of societal-level hypotheses begins with Marxist-Leninist theories of war. It then turns to recent research on the question of the relative war proneness of democratic and nondemocratic regimes and, finally, to the role of domestic politics and the scapegoat hypothesis.

Marxist-Leninist Theories of War

The most comprehensive of all societal-level approaches to international conflict can be found in Marxist-Leninist theory. Our focus here is on those aspects of the theory relevant to the question of the causes of international war. In the Marxist-Leninist theory of imperialism, all international conflict can be traced to the internal dynamics of capitalist economic systems.[87] These systems are not self-sufficient and have an inherent tendency toward stagnation and collapse in the absence of an external stimulus. One problem is the disequilibrium between production and consumption resulting from the inadequate purchasing power of the proletariat and ultimately from the inequitable distribution of wealth in society. The surplus products resulting from this lack of demand in the economy generates pressures for imperialist expansion to secure external markets to absorb the surplus. This is the "underconsumptionist" theory of imperialism often associated with Hobson ([1902] 1954). A related problem, one given greater emphasis by Hilferding ([1910] 1981) and Lenin ([1917] 1939), is the existence of surplus capital resulting from the declining rate of return on capital. This also generates pressures for external expansion to secure better investment opportunities and higher rates of return on capital. Lenin ([1919] 1939) and others (Magdoff, 1969) have also emphasized the need for raw materials as another source of external expansion is the need for raw materials. The imperialist expansion of capitalist states for markets, investment opportunities, and raw materials leads to imperial and colonial wars to achieve those objectives.[88]

It is often assumed that imperial expansion and wars lead ultimately to interstate wars and great power wars.[89] One serious limitation of Marxist-Leninist theory from the perspective of the causes of war is that the theoretical linkages between imperialism and war have never been clearly specified or empirically confirmed. The *safety-valve* hypothesis, noted earlier, predicts precisely the opposite. There is little systematic empirical research on this question,[90] although there has been much debate about the World War I case. Marxists argue that World War I is a classic case of a war resulting from imperialist rivalries (Lenin, [1917] 1939). Others argue that imperial expansion served as a safety valve and that the crosscutting nature of the imperial and European interests of the great powers dampened the pressures for war.[91]

There may be a more direct path from capitalism to great power war in Marxist-Leninist theory. Capitalist economic systems tend not only to imperial expansion externally but also to generate high levels of military spending internally to serve as replacement markets to absorb excess capital and to reduce the level of unemployment. This argument was initially made by Luxemburg ([1913] 1951), who argued that the production of armaments was the only means by which surplus capital could be recirculated into the economy. The resulting "war economy" contributes to interstate war by triggering arms races and generally increasing levels of international tensions. This argument is not restricted to Marxist-Leninist theorists, of course. The internal dynamics driving lateral pressure theory (Choucri and North, 1975) are similar, although Choucri and North hypothesize that these linkages exist in any economic system and not only in capitalist states. The essential role of military spending and "militarism" in general in capitalist economies has been emphasized in recent theories of the "military-industrial complex" (Mills, 1956; Melman, 1970; Lens, 1970; Yarmolinsky, 1971; Sarkesian, 1972; Rosen, 1973). The primary difference concerns the extent to which the hypothesized behavior of capitalist states is believed to be inevitable; socialist and liberal theorists of economic imperialism recognize the feasibility of reform within capitalist states.

There are numerous critiques of the Marxist-Leninist theory of imperialism (Schumpeter, [1919] 1951; Robbins, 1939; Aron, 1968; Cohen, 1973; Waltz, 1979), and only a few brief comments are possible here. Although Marxist-Leninist theory appears to provide an elegant and powerful explanation of imperialism, it does raise some empirical questions that have not been rigorously and systematically investigated. If capitalist states by their very nature generate surpluses, and if these surpluses lead to external expansion to secure markets and investment opportunities, then we should expect a high correlation between capitalism and imperialist expansion.[92] Consider the period since 1870 or so, to which the theory should be most applicable. Noncapitalist as well as capitalist states have been imperialist, capitalist imperialism has not coincided with the monopoly stage of capitalism as predicted by Lenin, and a significant proportion of capitalist exports has been directed to other capitalist states.[93]

These theoretical and empirical problems in Marxist-Leninist theory raise some doubts regarding the validity of the theory. These doubts are compounded by the existence of alternative theories of imperialism that provide competing explanations for the phenomenon in question. Perhaps the leading alternative theory of imperialism is some version of structural realist theory emphasizing the anarchic structure of the international system and the absence of any mechanism to prevent the strong from dominating the weak. From this perspective imperialism is driven by the quest for power in the international system rather than the internal economic needs of the capitalist class. As the Athenians reminded the Melians, "the strong do what they have the power to do and the weak accept what they have to accept" (Thucydides, [431–411 B.C.] 1954:V/89).

A good example of such a theory is Waltz's (1979:Chap. 2) discussion of the imperialism of great power. He argues that the observed correlation between capitalism and imperialism in the last century does not reflect a direct causal connection between the two. According to Waltz, the leading capitalist states were imperialist not because they were capitalist but because they were the most powerful states in the system. In any historical era it is the great powers that build the large imperial empires, and the great powers are those states that have most efficiently exploited their available resources and have organized themselves most effectively for that purpose. In the modern era, Waltz argues, capitalism has been the most efficient form of economic organization. Imperialism results from the quest for power and security by the great powers. Capitalism is neither a necessary nor a sufficient condition for imperialism, although it can play a contributory role along with other variables on a causal chain leading to war.

The theory of great power imperialism provides a more general explanation for the historical tendency for the strong to expand at the expense of the weak and, for this reason, is more powerful than Marxist-Leninist theories of imperialism. It is a general theory applicable to any historical era and can explain the imperialism of the ancient Roman and Persian empires as well as the imperialism of the nineteenth century great powers, whereas Marxist-Leninist theory of monopoly capitalism is not applicable to the phenomenon of precapitalist imperialism or noncapitalist imperialism.[94]

One interesting variant of the theory of great power imperialism is Robbins' (1939) theory of "defensive economic imperialism." Robbins was typical of liberal economists who believed that states and individuals benefit most under a system of free trade and the uninhibited operations of an international market economy according to the law of comparative advantage. A few states—and, more particularly, a small number of groups within those states—perceive that they can make short-term gains by erecting trade barriers to lock out competition and by securing colonies for protected markets abroad. Once the process is initiated it becomes difficult to stop, as other states act to prevent their rivals from gaining control of key markets. Their motive in joining the scramble for colonies is not to reap gains from protected markets guaranteed by their own political control of colonies abroad, but to minimize their losses from being deprived of markets by rival states.[95]

Like Robbins, Schumpeter ([1919] 1951) argues that imperialism is contrary to the interests of capitalist states or to capitalist classes within those states. Whereas Robbins focuses on the systemic forces that lead states to adopt the imperialist policies they would prefer to avoid, Schumpeter focuses on the domestic incentives leading certain subnational groups to prefer imperialist and policies. Because capitalist societies are more concerned with profits and economic prosperity than with imperial expansion and war, and because both imperialism and war are bad for business, industrial workers as well as the capitalist class are generally opposed to imperialist policies. Nevertheless, capitalist states pursue imperialist policies because those policies serve the interests of a military elite. This "atavistic" warrior class first came to power in earlier feudal and aristocratic eras when war served as a useful instrument for the development and maintenance of the state. This elite has continued to maintain its power in part by using war and the threat of war to justify their policies and maintain their positions. Although one can question many of the details of Schumpeter's argument, it is important because it was one of the first to emphasize that under certain conditions the domestic political interests of the individuals or regime in power may be as important as the national interests of the state) in providing incentives for imperial expansion and war.

An alternative domestic political explanation for imperialism is Snyder's (1988) theory of imperial overextension driven by coalitional politics and strategic ideology. Snyder observes that states often expand beyond the point at which their imperial interests can be supported by available resources. He rejects both the Marxist-Leninist and Schumpeterian arguments that imperial overextension can be explained in terms of the interests of any single domestic elite, and he argues instead that each elite prefers some form of limited imperial expansion but recognizes the costs of too extensive expansion. The domestic coalition-building process among these different groups, especially when interest-based arguments are reinforced and exaggerated by strategic ideology, often generates a logrolled outcome leading to both external expansion and internal harmony. The consequences, however, are often a more aggressive and expansionist policy than is desired by any single domestic group, and the creation of more external enemies than can be managed by existing national resources and diplomatic arrangements. Historical examples supporting Snyder's theory would include the coalition of iron and rye in Germany before World War I and the phenomenon of social imperialism in Great Britain prior to the war (Kehr, 1970; Fischer, 1975). Snyder's (1988) theory provides a very plausible explanation for imperial overextension and perhaps imperial wars. Whether it provides an equally compelling explanation for great power war is a different question requiring further investigation.

The analytically distinct sources of imperialism represented in the theories just surveyed are not necessarily incompatible, however, and one cost of the effort to assert the superiority of one paradigm over the other is the failure to incorporate variables from different theories into a single integrated theory of imperialism and war. The theoretical task of constructing an integrated theory and the empirical task of testing these various theories against the historical record are important ones for future research.[96]

Democracy and War

Whereas the liberal theorists discussed earlier argue that both the system of free trade in an international market economy and the domestic characteristics of capitalist economic systems reduce the likelihood of war, another important body of liberal theory emphasizes the pacifying effects of democratic political institutions. Although many theorists make both sets of arguments, and although democratic political institutions often coexist with liberal capitalist economic institutions, the arguments are analytically distinct and will be treated separately here. The Kantian argument regarding the pacifying effects of republican political institutions is particularly interesting because it has generated considerable empirical research in recent years, and these theoretical and empirical debates continue to be relevant to the question of war in the nuclear age.

Kant's ([1795] 1954) argument is that republican regimes (characterized by a constitutional and representative government and a separation of powers) are more peaceful than nonrepublican regimes. People oppose war because they recognize that they would suffer from it, and if they are in a position of political power they can prevent war from occurring. Political leaders in democratic states are accountable to the electorate and incur domestic political costs for warlike policies. Those in authoritarian states, however, are immune from both the personal and the domestic political costs of war and therefore have less incentives to avoid warlike policies. In Kant's words (cited in Doyle, 1983a:229),

> If the consent of the citizens is required in order to decide that war should be declared (and in this constitution it cannot but be the case), nothing is more natural than that they would be very cautious in commencing such a poor game, decreeing for themselves all the calamities of war . . . having to fight, having to pay the costs of war from their own resources, having painfully to repair the devastation war leaves behind, and, to . . . load themselves with a heavy national debt that would embitter peace itself and that can never be liquidated on account of constant wars in the future. But, on the other hand, in a constitution which is not republican, and under which the subjects are not citizens, a declaration of war is the easiest thing in the world to decide upon, because war does not require of the ruler . . . the least sacrifice of the pleasure of his table, the chase, his country houses, his court functions, and the like. He may, therefore, resolve on war as on a pleasure party for the most trivial reasons, and with perfect indifference leave the justification which decency requires to the diplomatic corps who are ever ready to provide it.

Bentham makes a slightly different argument, relying on the pacifying effects not of domestic public opinion but, instead, of world public opinion (Waltz, 1954:Chap. 4). These arguments have been accepted by Thomas Paine, Woodrow Wilson, and countless other liberal theorists.

One serious logical problem with this argument and, in fact, with any national-level theory of foreign policy behavior, is that a reduced probability of a particular state initiating a war does not necessarily imply a reduced probability of that state being involved in a war. Under some conditions the unwillingness to prepare for war or to resort to threats of force to deter war will make war more likely by undermining deterrence and encouraging the adversary. At the systemic level, it has been argued that the institutional constraints against the effective use of threats of force, and even force itself, by democratic regimes may contribute to war by preventing those states from playing a stabilizing role in a balance of power system (Wright, 1965:842–848).

The question of the likelihood of war is analytically distinct from that of its seriousness, and many liberal theorists acknowledge that the low frequency of war involvement that they assume to be characteristic of democratic states is not matched by a comparable moderation in the seriousness of those wars that do occur. To the contrary, once begun, wars of liberal democratic states tend to be driven by ideological objectives, become transformed into crusades calling for total victory and the unconditional surrender of the adversary, and fought with unlimited means to achieve these unlimited ends. Thus, Churchill (speech in the House of Commons, May 13, 1901, cited in Gilbert, 1967:21–22) argued prior to World War I that "democracy is more vindictive than Cabinets. The wars of peoples will be more terrible than those of kings." Therefore, it is commonly argued that because of its national "style" growing out of its liberal democratic institutions and political culture, the United States is very reluctant to become involved in wars but, once forced into war, she treats it as a moral crusade to "make the world safe for democracy" and utterly destroy the evil enemy who alone had caused the war to occur (Spanier, 1985).

The question of the historical validity of these hypotheses has attracted considerable attention from researchers, many of whom have conducted some fairly rigorous quantitative empirical studies of the relative war proneness of democratic and nondemocratic regimes. Several of the early studies were cross sectional and focused on the characteristics and behavior of all states during certain periods since World War II.[97] Although the consistent conclusion was that democratic states are no more war prone than nondemocratic states (Rummel, 1968; Wilkenfeld, 1975; Russett and Monsen, 1975), the temporal domain is far too narrow to allow for generalizations about international behavior.[98] In addition, most of these early studies failed to distinguish between war involvement and war initiation.

Some of these problems have been corrected in recent studies, which have generally been based on more sophisticated research designs. Small and Singer (1976), Rummel (1983), and Chan (1984) each cover the entire period since the Congress of Vienna, and Babst (1972) and Doyle (1983a, 1983b) go back to the late eighteenth century. Even though these scholars use slightly different definitions of democracy, each is fairly rigorous within his own framework and the results are fairly consistent. The evidence shows that the proportional frequency of war involvement of democratic states has not been greater than that for nondemocratic states. Moreover, the severity of wars (generally measured by fatalities) involving democratic states has been no higher than the severity of wars in which democratic states are not involved. Democracies may be slightly less likely than nondemocratic states to initiate wars, but the evidence is not yet conclusive on this question (Small and Singer, 1976:64–66; Chan, 1984:638–639).

Although democracies have fought in wars as frequently as have nondemocratic states, they almost never fight each other. Moreover, in the world wars involving many states, democratic states always fight on the same side. Depending on precisely how one defines democracy, it is possible to find one or two exceptions,[99] but these would be marginal deviations from a robust conclusion demonstrated by rigorous and systematic empirical analyses. The consistency of results for different operational definitions of democracy only increases our confidence in the validity of the findings. This absence of war between democratic states comes as close as anything we have to an empirical law in international relations (Levy, 1988a:662).

This finding is particularly interesting because it runs counter to many of the leading theories of international conflict and war. Structural systemic theories, which claim that internal political structures and processes of states have far less impact on their behavior than the distribution of power (or changes in such) and the structure of alliances in the international system, clearly cannot account for the absence of war between democratic states. Because many states with democratic political structures also have capitalist economic structures, Marxist-Leninist theories would predict a higher than average incidence of war between democratic states. Although the correlation between democracy and capitalism is not perfect, the strength of the observed empirical findings is clearly contrary to the thrust of Marxist-Leninist theory. Following similar logic, we can conclude that liberal economic theories are consistent with the absence of wars between democracies but would incorrectly predict a lower overall war involvement for democratic as opposed to nondemocratic states. These considerations suggest that ideology, public opinion, and policy legitimacy have much greater impact on foreign policy behavior in general and decisions for war or peace in particular than is normally acknowledged. From several different theoretical perspectives, therefore, the absence of war between democracies constitutes an empirical anomaly that calls for further research.[100]

Domestic Politics and the Scapegoat Hypothesis

It is an article of faith of most liberal theorists that public opinion is inherently peaceful and that if a state initiates a war it is usually because political leaders choose war against the desires and interests of the public. Marxist-Leninist theorists agree that war does not serve the public's interest but argue that it is used by the capitalist class to serve its own economic interests. One can find, however, numerous historical examples of cases in which the public appears all too eager for war. One example would be the enthusiasm of people throughout Europe on the eve of World War I, which has been called "perhaps the most popular war in history" (Farrar, 1983). In some cases this popular enthusiasm for war may push political leaders into adopting more aggressive and risky policies than they would have preferred and thus be an important cause of the war. The pressure for war from public opinion and the press in 1898 has often been viewed as a primary cause of the Spanish-American War. Thus, May (1973:159) writes that because of domestic politics President McKinley "led his country unwillingly toward a war that he did not want for a cause in which he did not believe."

The immediate increase in public support for the president of the United States after the use of military force abroad, regardless of the wisdom or success of that action, is well known and is often explained by the tendencies of the public to rally around the flag, the president, and the party (Mueller, 1973; Brody, 1984). Presidents engaging in more conflictual behavior toward the Soviet Union, for example, usually find their popularity ratings in public opinion surveys to increase by 4 or 5 percent (Ostrom and Simon, 1985), although these effects may be temporary.[101]

The ultimate source of these rally-round-the-flag effects is the rise of modern nationalism and the tendency of the vast majority of people to center their supreme loyalties on the nation-state. They tend to conceive of the national interest as the highest interest and to acquire an intense commitment to the power and prosperity of the state. This commitment is strengthened by national myths emphasizing the moral, physical, and political strength of the state and by individuals' feelings of powerlessness and their consequent tendency to seek their identity and fulfillment through the state. Assertive and nationalist policies are perceived as increasing state power and are at the same time psychologically satisfying for the individual and, in this way, nationalism contributes to war (Fromm, 1941; Breuilly, 1985).

There are other more specific theoretical paths leading from nationalism to war. If the identity of the nation as a people sharing common ethnic and linguistic ties and common cultural and historical origins does not correspond perfectly with the territorial boundaries of the state as a political organization, nationalism may contribute to war by creating shared incentives for national unification, national independence, the integration into the state of national minorities living beyond state borders, the favorable resolution of territorial disputes and other historical antagonisms, and often the adoption of violent policies as a means to achieve those ends (Wright, 1965:Chap. 27). Nationalism can also contribute to war by creating or reinforcing militarism, either in the form of the increased influence of the military in the political process or the acceptance of military values as the dominant values in society (Berghahn, 1969; Vagts, 1959; Van Evera, 1984*b*). Germany before World War I would be a case in point.

Nationalism sometimes generates public sentiment that prefers more hawkish policies than those preferred by political authorities. Mass publics tend to be less sensitive than elites to the security dilemma and the possibility that attempts to increase one's security and power may actually result in a decrease in security and power. Under certain conditions this can impose serious constraints on decision makers who prefer more limited foreign policy objectives or the pursuit of those objectives through more limited means. Domestic political constraints of this kind may preclude significant compromises as viable policy options. For example, the possibility of a British leader compromising with Spain to prevent their commercial and naval rivalry of the early eighteenth century from escalating to war was basically precluded by the public's response after the Spaniards cut off the ear of a British seaman, leading to the War of Jenkins' Ear (1739–1748).

In spite of the widespread recognition of the importance of nationalism and jingoism, this phenomenon receives very little attention in the leading theoretical literature on international conflict and foreign policy decision making. There has been very little research on the conditions under which public opinion contributes to war or to peace or on the processes through which this occurs.[102] Nor is there much work on the reciprocal relationship between political elites and mass publics on foreign policy issues, on the conditions under which political authorities are pushed or constrained by the public, and on the conditions under which they are able to manipulate public attitudes and preferences to serve their own conception of the national interest or even their own personal interests.

The idea that political leaders may embark on risky foreign ventures in an attempt to achieve diplomatic or military gains that will help solve their domestic political problems is hardly a new idea. Four centuries ago Bodin ([1593] 1955:168–169) wrote that "the best way of preserving a state, and guaranteeing it against sedition, rebellion, and civil war is . . . to find an enemy against whom they can make common cause," and Sumner wrote that "the exigencies of war with outsiders are what make the peace inside" (Stein, 1976:143). This general proposition, often referred to as the scapegoat hypothesis or the diversionary theory of war, has also been endorsed by numerous modern international theorists. Wright (1965:727), for example, suggests that one of the more important causes of war is the perception that war is a "necessary or convenient means . . . to establish, maintain, or expand the power of a government, party, or class within a state," and Haas and Whiting (1956:62) argue that elites embark on foreign wars to create an outside target to divert the attention of the people from the inequities generated by rapid industrialization and social change.

The scapegoat hypothesis is theoretically grounded in the in-group/out-group hypothesis in sociology. As formulated by Simmel (1956), the hypothesis states that conflict with the out-group increases the cohesion and political centralization of the in-group. Coser (1956) modifies the basis hypothesis and argues that internal cohesion will be increased if and only if the external conflict is related to a threat that is perceived to menace the group as a whole (and not just part of it) and if and only if there exists some prior level of internal cohesion. Group leaders are aware of the cohesive effects of external conflict (but not always of the qualifying conditions), and sometimes act deliberately to create or maintain external conflict to serve their internal purposes.

The in-group/out-group hypothesis has also been subjected to systematic empirical research by international relations scholars. Most quantitative studies, utilizing research designs that correlate various indicators of the levels of internal and external conflict, have found that there exists no relationship between the two (Rummel, 1963; Tanter, 1966). More sophisticated studies, which attempt to control for other variables such as the type of regime, have found some positive but relatively weak relationships between internal and external conflict (Wilkenfeld, 1973). More thorough reviews of this quantitative literature can be found in Stohl (1980), Zinnes (1980), and Levy (1989*a*). One serious limitation of this body of research is that most of these studies are based on the period from 1955 to 1960, which is not only brief but also happens to coincide with an extraordinarily peaceful period of international politics, limiting the generalizability of the findings.[103]

The findings of these large-*N* correlational studies are not fully consistent with those of comparative historical studies or case studies of individual wars. In his comparative study of the European state system from 1740 to 1960, Rosecrance (1963) concludes that domestic instability and the domestic insecurity of elites was the primary determinant of international war and that this was true independently of the political structure or ideology of the regime. There have also been numerous studies of individual wars that have concluded that a primary cause of the war was the attempt by political leaders to solve their internal political problems through risky foreign policies in the hope of securing a diplomatic or military victory.[104]

This discussion calls attention to several significant puzzles in the literature on societal-level sources of international conflict. One is the gap between the general conclusion of large-N correlational studies that there seems to be little connection between domestic and foreign conflict and the findings of many individual case studies that the scapegoat motivation has an important impact in the processes leading up to many wars. Although the generalizability of the quantitative studies can be questioned because of their narrow temporal domain, and although there are alternative historical interpretations in each of the relevant historical cases, the discrepancy is still puzzling. On a more general level, there is a striking gap between the emphasis historians place on societal-level sources of the foreign policy and war behavior of states and the tendency of political scientists to minimize the importance of these variables. Both of these gaps raise serious conceptual and methodological issues regarding the linkages between theory, research design, and empirical findings, and point to an important agenda for further exploration.[105]

Decision-Making Theories

Decision-making theories focus on the individuals and governmental organizations that are empowered to make and implement policies on behalf of the state. Although historians have long talked about the beliefs, preferences, perceptions, and actions of heads of state and of their key advisors, as well as the "cabinet politics" in which decision makers engage, it is only in the last three decades that political scientists have begun to utilize systematic decision-making frameworks as a theoretical guide to the analysis of foreign policy behavior (Snyder, et al., 1954; Allison, 1971; Holsti, 1972; Janis, 1972; Steinbrunner, 1974; Halperin, 1974; Jervis, 1976; Snyder and Diesing, 1977; George, 1980; Brecher, 1980; Rosenau, 1966). Allison's *Essence of Decision* (1971) was particularly important because it was the first systematic application of theories of organizational behavior (March and Simon, 1958; Cyert and March, 1963) to the issue area of foreign policymaking.

Most of the applications of bureaucratic and organizational models have focused on defense spending, military procurement, or factors affecting the conduct of war, rather than on crisis decision making relating to the causes of war, although Allison's (1971) study of the Cuban missile crisis is an exception. There is a related body of literature on the "military-industrial complex" and on the ways in which the institutional interests of the military affect the processes of weapons development and military spending (Mills, 1956; Melman, 1970; Yarmolinsky, 1971; Sarkesian, 1972). There have also been case studies and quantitative work relating to the question of the relative impact of internal organizational variables on arms races (Allison, 1977; Ostrom, 1977).

Much of this literature on decision making and war is covered in Holsti's chapter in this volume and in subsequent volumes in this series. In this section we will examine some recent literature that focuses on more direct and immediate linkages between the organizational structure and processes of the military and the outbreak of war. In the following section we will examine the impact of misperceptions on the processes leading to war. Because the more general literature on crisis decision making is covered in Holsti's chapter in this volume, it will not be covered here. Other psychological and organizational models based on the operational codes of elites (George, 1969; Rogers, 1986), learning models (Etheridge, 1985; Leng, 1983), cognitive maps (Axelrod, 1976), artificial intelligence (Mefford, 1987), and other models (East et al., 1978; Falkowski, 1979; Tetlock and McGuire, 1985; Hermann et al., 1987) will not be examined because they do not focus primarily on issues of war and peace and because of space constraints. This survey of decision-making theories relating to war and peace is, is therefore, deliberately selective and incomplete.

It should also be noted that in this section we are not dealing with complete theories of the causes of war but, instead, with more restricted hypotheses that may very well be important components of a more inclusive theory. Psychological theories of individual behavior are incomplete as theories of war in the absence of a political theory that explains how individual goals and preferences are aggregated into the goals and preferences of the collective body, which makes and implements decisions for the state, and how the government interacts with the society within which it is embedded. A theory of foreign-policy decision making on issues of war and peace in turn must be subsumed within a larger theory of international politics and strategic interaction in order to explain how actions of one state result in the phenomenon of war involving two or more states.

Organizational Politics and Processes

Two related bodies of literature will be examined in this section. One concerns the hypothesized linkage among military organizations, offensive doctrines, and war. The other concerns the potential impact of rigid military mobilization and war plans on the processes leading to war. Both utilize certain concepts from organizational theory, and both incorporate some systemic-level variables.[106]

ORGANIZATIONAL INTERESTS, OFFENSIVE DOCTRINES, AND WAR

Just in the last several years there have been a number of theoretical and empirical studies linking the nature of military organizations, military doctrine, and war. The general argument is that military organizations prefer offensive doctrines and that offensive doctrines increase the likelihood of war. Several arguments have been advanced as to why military organizations should prefer offensive doctrines (Posen, 1984:47–51; Van Evera, 1984b; Snyder, 1984b:Chap. 1; Levy, 1986:215–218). First, the implementation of offensive doctrines and war plans requires larger numbers of troops and weapons systems, greater logistical support, and often more sophisticated military technology than do more static defensive strategies. For this reason offensive doctrines tend to require larger organizational budgets and manpower, which are high-priority goals in nearly all organizations and generally increase the influence of the organization. Second, offensive doctrines and plans also contribute to one's ability to seize the initiative, structure the battle, and thus fight the war on one's own terms, which serves a key organizational goal of uncertainty avoidance. It is also argued that the organizational autonomy of the military is greatest when its operational goal is the rapid and decisive disarming of the adversary by offensive means. Finally, the prospect of decisive victory through aggressive action tends to enhance military morale and prestige.[107] Once in place, and whether driven by the internal interests of organizations or external national security needs, offensive doctrines and war plans contribute to war by increasing the incentives to strike first; fueling arms races, tensions, and conflict spirals; encouraging aggressive policies; and increasing the destructiveness of war (Van Evera, 1984a:63–79; Posen, 1984:18–24).

These arguments have been applied to the 1914 case. Snyder (1984a:108) argues that the offensive doctrines and war plans of 1914 "were in themselves an important and perhaps decisive cause of the war," and Van Evera (1984a:58) argues that "the cult of the offensive was a principal cause of the First World War." In World War II, by contrast, the defensive character of the British and French doctrines contributed a great deal to the sitzkrieg or "phony war" after Hitler's attack on Poland (Posen, 1984). Each of these authors applies the theoretical generalizations and historical analogies to contemporary debates over offensive, defensive, and deterrent doctrines at the conventional as well as strategic levels.

The application of these theoretical generalizations and historical analogies is not without its problems. The distinctions among offensive, defensive, and deterrent doctrines is not always clear, and strategic nuclear deterrence confounds the traditional distinction between offense and defense. The important distinction between an incentive or policy of striking first and a strategy of deep penetration (Levy, 1984a) is rarely recognized.[108] The distinction is important because the former increases the probability of war but the latter does not. Deep territorial penetration was associated with the offense in 1914 but would be associated with deterrence today, so that some hypotheses about the consequences of offensive doctrines that are reasonable for the 1914 case may not be applicable for the superpowers in the nuclear age. It is not clear, for example, that the military prefers offensive doctrines and war plans in the contemporary era.[109]

RIGIDITY OF MILITARY DOCTRINES AND WAR PLANS

A related and overlapping literature traces crisis instability to the rigidity of military routines and war plans rather than their offensive character. This literature is not so much a well-developed body of theory as it is an application of certain concepts from organizational theory to the 1914 case and to command and control problems in the nuclear age. Although it is not clear that these processes are important in other cases,[110] the historical importance of the 1914 case and its relevance for the present makes this an important body of literature, and a brief survey would be useful.

Rigid military mobilization and war plans may be the product of technical military and logistical constraints, systemic imperatives and alliance politics, the vested interests of organizations, administrative arrangements, cognitive rigidity, and other factors (Snyder, 1984b; Levy, 1986). One important consequence is that once initiated, the process becomes difficult or impossible to delay, slow, or modify, and it may be impossible to switch from one mobilization plan to another. This means that once begun, the mobilization process acquires a momentum of its own, precludes the intervention of political leaders, and generates an inevitable slide toward war. There may be little opportunity for statesmen to interrupt the process and pursue diplomatic alternatives that might preserve the peace. Many historians and political scientists argue that the rigid military mobilization plans and railroad timetables of 1914 were an important cause of World War I because they created a situation in which "mobilization means war" and in which it was very difficult to slow or reverse the process (Taylor, 1969; Albertini, 1957; Fay, [1928] 1966; Van Evera, 1984a; Snyder, 1984b; Levy, 1986). Recent work suggests that certain organizational constraints and rigidities in U.S. command and control procedures may generate dynamics similar to those of 1914 (Bracken, 1983; Blair, 1985).

In addition, the inability to modify a plan or switch from one mobilization plan to another may seriously limit the feasibility of partial mobilization as a substitute plan, because once implemented it could not easily be replaced by full mobilization if circumstances warranted it. This leaves statesmen with no intermediate military option that would allow them to demonstrate their resolve without at the same time provoking a dangerous escalation by the adversary. Statesmen are deprived of the ability to fine tune their threats in a way that achieves an optimum balance between the twin objectives of coercive diplomacy and crisis management. This is an essential requirement for crisis management (George, 1984), and its absence in the Russian and German cases in 1914 was an important factor in the escalation of the conflict (Levy, 1986, 1988d). There are similar concerns that organizational rigidities may preclude U.S. and Soviet leaders from using military alert levels as a fine-tuned and easily manipulable instrument of signaling and influence in the nuclear age (George, 1984; Sagan, 1985; Allison et al., 1985).

There is a related set of hypotheses regarding the consequences of low levels of political-military integration (Posen, 1984), which refers to the congruence between the foreign policy goals of the state and the military means available to achieve those ends. Because of organizations' interests in autonomy and the tendency toward "factored problems" (Cyert and March, 1963), the technical specialization of the military and the general lack of civilian expertise, and the military's use of its control over information to enhance its autonomy, military organizations tend to focus on the military aspects of policy and to minimize its political component. There is a resulting danger that military doctrine will follow a "strictly instrumental military logic" and ignore important political considerations, particularly in the absence of strong civilian intervention (Posen, 1984:58). Many argue that in Germany in 1914, for example, the military plans were constructed without consultation with political decision makers and with total disregard for political considerations (Ritter, 1958; Taylor, 1969; Turner, 1979; Snyder, 1984b). The German Schlieffen Plan required movement through Belgium because it facilitated the invasion of France, which made British intervention, and thus a world war, inevitable.

The problem of low political-military integration is compounded if political leaders are ignorant of the details of military plans, because they may not realize the extent to which they lack the military options to support their foreign policy objectives. This ignorance was an important source of escalation in 1914. Whereas the military perceived mobilization as a means of preparing for a war that they perceived to be inevitable, political decision makers generally saw it as an instrument of deterrence or coercive diplomacy. They had little conception, until it was too late, that they lacked the means to support a coercive or deterrent strategy based on a fine tuning of military threats, or that their room to maneuver had been severely restricted. As a result, they did not realize that actions taken in all sincerity to avoid war while preserving vital interests only made war more likely (Levy, 1986:209–210).

Thus, Ritter (1958:90) concludes that "the outbreak of war in 1914 is the most tragic example of a government's helpless dependence on the planning of strategists that history has ever seen." Similarly, there are concerns that U.S and perhaps Soviet political leaders may not be fully aware of the extent to which existing rules of engagement leaves some authority in the hands of military leaders, restricting the politicians' ability to fine tune their threats in a nuclear crisis (George, 1984:227–228; Sagan, 1985:132–135).

George (1984) suggests several conditions conductive to effective crisis management. In addition to the limitations of one's political objectives, these include presidential control of military options, pauses in military operations, availability of discriminating military options, and coordination of military movements with political-diplomatic actions and with limited political objectives. The discussion of the World War I case demonstrates that rigid military mobilization plans contributed to the violation of every one of these requirements and suggests that this had profound consequences for the escalation of the July crisis to war. Although it is uncertain how frequently this particular causal path to war occurs in international politics, the severity of its consequences when it does occur and the potential resemblance of its antecedent conditions to certain conditions in the contemporary world makes it worth examining in more detail.

Misperception and War

The idea that wars are caused by misperceptions is very attractive in many ways.[111] For those who believe that the human and economic costs of war frequently far outweigh any benefits that it might bring to the states that initiate them, a theory based on misperception provides a satisfying explanation of how wars might occur in spite of their asserted irrationality. Misperception-based theories are also appealing to those who are frustrated by theories that trace war to inexorable systemic and societal forces that are for the most part beyond the ability of policymakers or citizens to control or influence. Perceptions and misperceptions are often viewed as variables that are more manipulable by policymakers and therefore more useful for a policy-relevant theory. In addition, scholars have been influenced by numerous historical cases in which misperceptions are so blatant and so consequential that many have concluded that the war would not have occurred in their absence. One can argue, for example, that Argentina would not have attempted to seize the Falklands/Malvinas from Great Britain had she anticipated that Great Britain would respond with military force (Hastings and Jenkins, 1983), or that the United States would have crossed the 38th parallel in Korea had she anticipated Chinese military intervention (George and

Smoke, 1974:Chap. 7). The "traditional" interpretation of World War I is that it was an "inadvertent" war driven by misperceptions, rigid railway timetables, and blunders as well as by underlying strategic necessities (Fay, [1928] 1966; Tuchman, 1962). Although this interpretation of World War I is no longer the dominant one, it has sensitized generations of historians and political scientists to the potential importance of misperceptions in the outbreak of war.

The role of misperceptions has probably been given greater emphasis by historians than by political scientists, in part because of the latter's concern for parsimonious theories and because of the enormous complexity added by the introduction of misperceptions to a theory of international politics. In addition, the analytical problems associated with the concept of misperception are extraordinarily difficult. Recently, however, political scientists have given much more attention to the question of misperception in foreign policy decision making, especially with respect to issues of war and peace (Jervis, 1976, 1983, 1988a; Lebow, 1981; Stein, 1982; Levy, 1983b; Snyder, 1984b; Van Evera, 1984b). Much of this literature has focused on the psychological processes generating misperceptions and has built on work in social psychology (Nisbett and Ross, 1980; Janis and Mann, 1977; Kahneman et al., 1982).[112] Less attention has been given to the linkages leading from misperception to war or to the difficult analytical problems involved in defining misperception. Since Holsti's chapter on crisis decision making in this volume and other chapters in this series on judgment and choice processes deal at length with the sources of misperception, the stress here will be on the linkages from misperception to war and on the meaning of the concept.

There are many different forms of misperception, and these contribute to war in different ways and under different conditions. In fact, under some conditions many of these misperceptions contribute to the maintenance of peace rather than the outbreak of war. Instead of examining all possible kinds of misperceptions, we will focus primarily on those that have the greatest and most direct impact on decisions for war. These include misperceptions of the intentions and capabilities of both adversaries and third states, as well as other forms of misperception that affect decisions for war or peace through their impact on these variables.[113]

The exaggeration of the hostility of the adversary's intentions is one of the most common and most important forms of misperception. Here it is useful to distinguish between short-term and long-term misperceptions. Each can affect the outbreak of war, but through different causal mechanisms. In short-term crisis situations, the exaggeration of adversary hostility can lead to the expectation of an adversary attack and a decision to act preemptively to gain the advantages of striking first and to minimize the costs of a war which is perceived to be inevitable. If in such a situation each adversary actually prefers other options to war, these misperceptions of adversary intentions would be a primary cause of the war. There is substantial evidence that most of the great powers exaggerated the hostility of their adversaries' intentions in the 1914 crisis, leading many scholars to conclude that these misperceptions were a leading cause of the war (North, 1967; Fay, 1928; Snyder, 1985; Van Evera, 1985).[114]

The overestimation of the hostility of adversary intentions can also be important over the long term. They lead to a greater effort than necessary to increase one's own military capabilities in order to deter aggression or to prepare for war in the event deterrence fails. This generally induces the adversary to respond in a similar manner, generating increased tensions and an increased likelihood of a conflict spiral, arms race, and perhaps even war. The diplomacy in the decade leading up to World War I is often characterized in terms of such an action-reaction cycle, as is the diplomacy leading up to the Seven Years' War in North America (1756–1763), which Smoke (1977:Chap. 8) describes as involving "no offensive steps by any player at any time."[115] In addition, a declining state's exaggeration of the permanent hostility of a rising challenger may erroneously convince the declining power that a future war is inevitable and thus increase its temptation for a preventive war under more favorable circumstances now (Levy, 1987).

It is also possible, although perhaps less common, for states to underestimate the hostility of the adversary. This can increase the likelihood of war, but through different causal paths. Underestimation of the adversary's resolve in a crisis often leads to the erroneous expectation that the adversary will back down, which may reduce one's own incentives to compromise or even lead one to undertake additional coercive measures. The result is often the hardening of the adversary's resolve and the generation of a conflict spiral and increased likelihood of war, as demonstrated by Lebow's (1981:Chap. 4) case studies of 13 brinkmanship crises. Over the long term, the underestimation of the hostility of the adversary leads to complacency and lack of preparedness, which against certain adversaries can increase the likelihood of war by undermining deterrence (Levy, 1983b:89–90). The assumption, of course, is that actions and policies undertaken to reinforce deterrence would have been successful. This is probably not the case with respect to the appeasement of Hitler prior to World War II. It is much more plausible that deterrent threats would have been successful in the cases of the U.S. underestimation of the hostility of North Korean intentions toward the South in 1950, Israeli complacency in 1973 (Stein, 1985b), and British underestimation of the hostility of Argentine intentions in 1982 (Hastings and Jenkins, 1983).

Other forms of misperceptions are important because of their effect on the misperception of adversary intentions. One is the misperception of the adversary's value structure and how she defines her vital interests (Jervis, 1983:5–6; Levy, 1983b:90). This is related to the misperception of the adversary's definition of the situation and the nature of the threats that situation poses to her values, which in turn is related to the adversary's perceptions of one's own intentions and capabilities and the threats that they pose. Such misperceptions bias one's expectations regarding the adversary's likely intentions, her response to one's own actions, and hence the consequences of one's own actions. The U.S. misperception of Chinese resolve during the 1950 Korean crisis, and hence of the intensity of the likely Chinese response to the U.S. expansion of the war, derived largely from the U.S. failure to understand the importance to China of preventing the establishment on its borders of a unified Korean regime under U.S. influence (George and Smoke, 1974:Chap. 7). Similarly, the United States exaggerated the effectiveness of a coercive bombing strategy against North Vietnam by underestimating the value that country placed on unifying the Vietnamese nation under its own control.

An important dimension of the adversary's definition of the situation, but one given insufficient attention in the literature, is its view of the future. Decision makers' "field of expectations" about future reality (Smoke 1977:270) may be as important as perceptions of present reality. Misperceptions of the adversary's future expectations can lead to serious misperceptions of her current intentions. The failure to recognize that the adversary perceives that the future is bleak, and hence that the present status quo is unsatisfactory, can result in the failure to appreciate her incentives to undertake what would otherwise seem to be unlikely actions now, including war. One reason for U.S. misperceptions of Japanese intentions in 1941 was the failure to understand how bleak the continuation of the status quo looked to the Japanese (Russett, 1967). A related point is that the failure to recognize that the adversary sees itself as a declining power results in an underestimation of the likelihood that it will initiate a preventive war (Levy, 1987).

The adversary's value structure and definition of the situation may also include an important domestic component, and a failure to recognize the importance of domestic considerations can lead to serious misperceptions of adversary intentions. The failure to recognize the seriousness of the current and future domestic threats to the political security of the adversary's regime may be particularly important in this regard and may lead to an underestimation of the likelihood of external military action that would not be expected on the basis of national security interests alone. The failure to recognize that domestic pressures can lead to the use of force in spite of the existence of an otherwise credible deterrent threat is emphasized by Lebow (1981) and others (Stein, 1985a, 1985b).[116] A related point concerns the nature of the adversary's decision-making process. There is a tendency to perceive that the adversary's political processes are more centralized than they actually are and to impute excessive intentionality to the actions of the adversary (Jervis, 1976). The failure to recognize that certain hostile actions may be the product of bureaucratic infighting or domestic politics and do not necessarily indicate a sustained policy of aggression may lead to overreaction and a conflict spiral.[117]

Another secondary category of misperception, which can affect one's expectations of the likely outcome of war and in this way expectations regarding adversary intentions, is misperception of the kind of war the adversary intends on fighting (Jervis, 1983:7-8). The adversary may recognize that it would almost certainly lose an all-out war but nevertheless perceive that it could secure its objectives through more limited forms of military action. Japan, for example, believed that the United States would fight in response to Pearl Harbor but that it would not fight an all-out war, preferring to negotiate and agree to Japanese hegemony in East Asia. Similarly, Hitler believed that Britain and France would fight over Poland but terminate the war after an initial German victory. Although it is difficult to argue that correct perceptions, particularly in the second case, would have made a difference, there are other situations in which these misperceptions can contribute causally to the outbreak of war. They can induce complacency and a failure to reinforce deterrence and readiness against a fait accompli or limited military action. Israel, for example, probably could have deterred an Egyptian attack in 1973 had it recognized that a limited move across the Suez Canal into the Sinai was perceived as a viable option by the Egyptians, whereas an all-out war against the Israelis was not (Stein, 1985*a*, 1985*b*). Erroneous perceptions of this kind can also lead states to undertake coercive measures under the false assumption that the adversary has no military options at its disposal, and those coercive measures may provoke the adversary into an attack. Some interpret U.S. economic sanctions against Japan in 1941 in this way. This point is consistent with the more general argument of George and Smoke (1974) that deterrence can fail in a variety of ways, that the adversary can often "design around" a deterrent threat, and that strategies of coercive diplomacy and crisis management require a range of usable military options (as well as diplomatic incentives).[118]

Misperceptions of adversary capabilities may be as important as misperceptions of intentions. The underestimation of the adversary's capabilities relative to one's own is critical and historically common, as Blainey (1973), Lebow (1981), and others have demonstrated. Statesmen tend not only to exaggerate the likelihood of victory, but also to underestimate the duration and the costs of the war. In August 1914 Kaiser Wilhelm stated that the war would be over "before the leaves have fallen from the trees," a belief that was shared in each of the major European capitals (Tuchman, 1962:142; Farrar, 1973:3–7); after his victory over Poland, Hitler told his generals that "a campaign against Russia would be like a child's game in a sandbox by comparison" (Speer, 1970:238); and numerous other cases of comparably extreme misperceptions have been identified. The existence of such misperceptions does not necessarily mean that they had a causal impact, of course, and the problems involved in inferring causality are admittedly difficult (Levy, 1983*b*; Stein, 1982). There are numerous cases, however, in which historians have concluded (although not without controversy) that misperceptions of relative capabilities did have an important impact on the processes leading to war. With respect to the Peloponnesian War, for example, Kagan (1969:355) argues that "all of the leading statesman expected a short war. . . . They all failed to foresee the evil consequences that such a war would have. . . . Had they done so they would scarcely have risked a war for the relatively minor disputes that brought it on." In spite of similar conclusions by historians in other cases (Farrar, 1973), the conceptual and methodological problems involved in reaching such conclusions have yet to be resolved.

The overestimation of one's relative strength includes misperceptions of military potential in a protracted war as well as immediately available military capabilities. The adversary's military potential might also be underestimated through the misperception of the impact of the war on the cohesiveness of the adversary's population and on the adversary's morale, and hence on the ability of the adversary's leadership to mobilize additional resources for the war effort (Levy, 1983*b*:83). It is particularly common for statesmen to assume erroneously that certain disenchanted ethnic minorities within the adversary state will rise up against the regime in power or even join the invading army in the event of war, leading to an excessively optimistic evaluation of the military balance. This is illustrated in the case of Iraq in her war against Iran, Hitler in his invasion of the Soviet Union, and numerous other cases.

It is also possible for decision makers to overestimate the adversary's capabilities relative to one's own. Although such misperceptions often lead to a more conciliatory policy and peace (unless this passivity is mistaken for weakness and encourages aggression by the adversary), they can also lead to war, but through different causal paths. Because adversary capabilities are often used (consciously or otherwise) by statesman as an indicator of adversary intentions, overestimation of adversary capabilities may lead to an exaggeration of the hostility of his intentions, which can trigger defensive measures, arms races, conflict spirals, and perhaps war.

Decision makers' expectations of the likely outcome of war and, hence, their decisions regarding the initiation of war, are affected not only by their perceptions of the dyadic balance of military power between themselves and their adversary, but also by their expectations regarding the likelihood of third state intervention and the impact of that intervention on the outcome of the war. Thus, misperception of the intentions and relative capabilities of third states constitute important forms of misperception. There is a common tendency to exaggerate the likelihood that the adversary's friends will stay neutral while one's own friends will come to one's aid (Blainey, 1973; Levy, 1983b:91–93). This helps generate the false expectation that a contemplated war can be "localized" and won with minimum costs, and this military overconfidence can be an important cause of the war. There is also a tendency to underestimate the relative military capabilities of potential enemies and consequently to minimize their impact on the outcome of the war should they intervene. Hitler's belief that the United States would probably not intervene and that if it did it would have only marginal impact is one example (Shirer, 1959:1170). Thus, an erroneous sense of military overconfidence generated by misperceptions of the intentions and capabilities of third states can under certain conditions, contribute to decisions for war.[119] As in the case of adversaries, misperceptions of the value structures of third states, their definition of the situation, and how they perceive threats contributes to misperception of their intentions.

Although numerous scholars have concluded that misperceptions have had an important role in the processes leading to numerous wars, it is not an easy task to define exactly what a misperception is, determine what historical phenomena should or should not be classified as misperceptions, or to evaluate the causal impact of misperceptions relative to that of other variables. Although considerable progress has been made since some of the earlier work on misperception and war (White, 1968; Stoessinger, 1978), some central analytical problems have yet to be solved. Lebow's (1981:90) statement still holds: "Nobody has been able to provide a clear, empirically useful and generally accepted definition of the concept."

One problem is whether misperception is best conceptualized as an outcome or as a process (Jervis, 1976, 1988a). Is a misperception simply a perception that is inconsistent with "objective" reality, or is misperception best conceptualized as reflecting a decision-making process that deviates from a standard rational model of information processing? It would make sense to focus on the accuracy of perceptions and define misperception as a discrepancy between the psychological environment of decision makers and the operational environment of the real world (Levy, 1983b; Sprout and Sprout, 1965). It is not easy, however, to determine an actor's perceptions with any degree of precision, much less the accuracy of those perceptions, given rather serious methodological problems involving data availability and access. Even if we have complete access to all the documents, however, the question of intentions may still be unresolved. The release of nearly all of the official documents of most of the great powers in the 1914 case, for example, has not precluded a continuing debate about German intentions in 1914 (Fischer, 1961, 1975; Koch, 1972; Moses, 1975). Decision makers' diplomatic, bureaucratic, and domestic political incentives to misrepresent their true perceptions in order to influence others' perceptions and behavior must be considered in evaluating the validity of the evidence, and their concern for their image in history must be considered in using later autobiographies as evidence. Problems of interpretation are compounded further by the fact that perceptions may vary for different actors and may change over time.

The identification of an actor's perceptions of another actor's intentions, as well as the actual intentions of the second actor, is particularly difficult and raises conceptual as well as methodological problems. The very concept of intentions implies that action is purposive and that the actor plans to act in definite ways under certain future contingencies. But individuals do not always have transitive preference orderings that facilitate predictable, rational, value-maximizing behavior, so that individuals are not always certain of their own intentions (Kahneman et al., 1982; Nisbett and Ross, 1980). Moreover, their intentions may change over time. The problem of purposive behavior is compounded for collective decision-making bodies, where different actors have different preferences, where there is often no transitive preference ordering for the collective decision-making body as a whole, and where resulting decisions are often determined by unpredictable political trade-offs and by the social-psychological dynamics of small-group behavior (Allison, 1971; Janis, 1982).

The determination of the accuracy of perceptions of relative capabilities is also difficult. Indicators of strength include not only relative objective indicators of numbers of troops, weapons systems, and the like, but also estimates of the impact of leadership, training, and morale and other more subjective factors. The ultimate measure of the accuracy of perceptions of relative military capabilities is the test of an actual war, which reflects the impact of both objective and subjective elements of military strength and also the uncertainties or "fog of war" (von Clausewitz, [1832] 1968).

The uncertainties inherent in any war raises an important conceptual problem relevant to the determination of the accuracy of perceptions of capabilities. Because of uncertainty, perceptions of relative capabilities are best conceptualized as subjective probability judgments involving some expected probability distribution of the expected outcomes of war. Perceptions of adversary intentions should be conceptualized in a similar way, as a probability distribution of expected behaviors of the adversary. Low probability outcomes (regarding adversary behavior and the outcome of the war) will occasionally happen, and when they do it should not necessarily be inferred that a misperception occurred. Thus, Levy (1983b:95) asks how we can distinguish between misperception and bad luck. Is it meaningful to say that the Spanish misperceived the military balance in launching the Spanish Armada in 1588 when, in fact, unfavorable winds had much to do with their defeat? Because issues of war and peace involve perceptions and situations that are, for all practical purposes, unique events, it is not really possible to compare the accuracy of some expected distribution of outcomes with the distribution of actual outcomes in a way that is comparable to the accuracy of economic forecasts. Thus, if we treat perceptions of adversary capabilities and intentions as subjective probability judgments, the concept of misperception becomes very problematic.[120]

One possible way around this dilemma is the use of a "third-party" criterion as a substitute for a truly objective measure of the accuracy of perceptions. In assessing the accuracy of X's perception of the intentions and relative capabilities of Y, it is useful to examine how other states (or other actors in different roles within the same state) perceive Y. If most other actors share X's perceptions of the intentions and capabilities of Y, then one probably could conclude that those perceptions are "correct"; if not, one could conclude that misperceptions were involved. The careful use of the third party criterion is a way of controlling for motivated biases and inferring whether perceptions (whether "correct" or ""incorrect") are a rational judgment under conditions of uncertainty or whether they reflect motivated biases resulting from historical antagonisms, ideological differences, wishful thinking, or other factors.[121] The fact that few other observers in 1982 shared Argentina's belief that Great Britain would not respond with military force to an Argentine seizure of the Falklands/Malvinas suggests that the Argentine view was a misperception driven by motivated biases based on the strategic or domestic political needs of the Argentine military elite.

There is no guarantee, of course, that the third party criteria can fully control for all motivated biases. The perceptions of various actors could be disproportionately influenced by the views of one "leader" rather than emerging from a number of independent assessments of the evidence, in which case the congruence of perceptions must be discounted as an indicator of their accuracy. There was a transnational "cult of the offensive" prior to World War I that led nearly all military and civilian elites to perceive (incorrectly) that military technology favored the offense (Van Evera, 1984a). It is possible that the lone view is the correct one, as illustrated by Churchill's pessimistic minority view of Hitler's intentions in the late 1930's. Finally, the state in question may base its beliefs on different information than do third parties (if a state is more directly engaged in an issue it presumably would have an incentive to devote more resources to the collection of intelligence), and it is not clear whether the variation in beliefs is due to motivated biases or asymmetrical information.[122]

Intractable problems such as these lead Jervis (1976:7; 1986) to suggest that the analyst focus not on the accuracy of perceptions but instead on the question of "How was it derived from the information available?" The implication is that decisions based on a sensitivity to risks and uncertainties and a reasonable use of information available or potentially available given resource and time constraints should not be judged to involve misperception, even if such decisions lead to an undesired outcome. The criterion for evaluation is how closely the actual decision-making process conforms to a "rational model" of judgment and decision under conditions of risk and uncertainty. The precise operational criteria by which deviations from a rational model would have to be specified, since the rational model is an ideal type that is never perfectly satisfied in practice and because there are several models of "bounded rationality" representing different degrees of departure from the ideal type (Simon, 1955; March, 1978). Note that in this approach the explanation of decisions and behavior is shifted from misperceptions, which can no longer be identified because there is no standard against which they can be measured (Levy, 1983*b*:78–80), to psychological, organizational, political, and systemic variables that explain departures from a rational decision-making calculus. In this formulation (although Jervis does not phrase it this way) misperceptions are an intervening variable between these prior conditions and processes and certain policy outcomes. Misperception itself is an unobservable hypothetical construct, but one that has observable behavioral antecedents and consequences.

The question of how to define and identify misperceptions is just one of several conceptual and methodological problems involved in the analysis of misperception and war. Another is that the existence of misperception does not necessarily affect an actor's decision, so that the causal impact as well as the existence of misperception must be established (Stein, 1982; Levy, 1983*b*).[123] Hitler clearly misperceived the intentions of Britain and France when he invaded Poland in 1939 (Taylor, 1961), but it is more questionable whether those misperceptions had any impact on his decision.

An analysis of the causal impact of misperception on the outbreak of war is complicated by the problem of finding adequate comparison groups for the purposes of a controlled scientific analysis. The ideal research design would require not just cases of misperceptions accompanied by war, but also cases of wars that occur in spite of the presence of relatively accurate perceptions, cases of misperceptions that fail to result in war, and cases of accurate perceptions associated with nonwar. As Jervis (1988a) notes, there has been less research on cases of nonwar than on cases of war,[124] and cases of mutually accurate perceptions are relatively rare. In the absence of these comparison groups it is difficult to show either that the presence of misperception contributed to war or that war would not have occurred in the absence of misperception. Even with such comparison groups the problem of dealing with the confounding effects of systemic, institutional, and societal variables and of determining the relative weight of misperceptions in the processes leading to war would remain.

Still another problem is that misperception can contribute to peace as well as to war. A state that erroneously perceives that the dyadic balance of military power favors the adversary may, for that reason, refrain from initiating a war that it otherwise might have desired. A declining state that erroneously perceives that its rising adversary will be conciliatory once it achieves superiority may refrain from initiating a preventive war that it might otherwise find desirable. This makes it all the more necessary to differentiate among different kinds of misperceptions and the distinct causal paths through which they affect decisions for war or peace, which I have tried to do here.

In part because of the severity of these conceptual and methodological problems, there has been relatively little systematic empirical research on the more general theoretical question of the causal impact of misperceptions and their importance relative to that of other variables. This is true in spite of the historical evidence suggesting that misperceptions of the intentions and capabilities of adversaries and third states frequently occur and that they may be important in a number of individual historical cases.

Implications for the Nuclear Era

As noted earlier, there is a significant gap between the theoretical literature on the causes of war and the writings of contemporary strategists. Those who theorize about the causes of war have made little attempt to adapt their theories of war to the nuclear age, and contemporary strategists have made little effort to base their strategic theories and policy prescriptions on traditional theory and historically confirmed propositions. Many of the first group engage in what Morgenthau (1967) and Jervis (1984) call the "conventionalization" of nuclear weapons. This refers generally to the attempt to understand the contemporary world through the intellectual tools of the prenuclear era, and more specifically to the assumption that nuclear weapons represent a quantitative but not qualitative change in the nature of military technology. If this were true, the only change in a theory of the causes of war would be a change in the parameters for military technology variables and for the interaction effects involving military technology.

It is not possible in our limited space to provide a complete and systematic analysis of the extent to which the nuclear revolution has affected the causes of interstate war. This is an extraordinarily difficult question for which there is unfortunately no definitive empirical evidence by which theoretical propositions can be tested. The literature provides little guidance here. Much of this literature focuses on the question of the general effects of the nuclear revolution on world politics rather than on the more specific question of how it has affected the causes of war. With regard to the second question, scholars are strongly divided. As noted earlier, some insist that nuclear weapons and associated long-range delivery vehicles have had a significant causal impact in reducing the likelihood of a war between the superpowers, while others insist that the effects have been minimal. Here I will develop an argument based on the current state of my own thinking on the question, as influenced by Schelling (1966), Jervis (1984, 1988b), and others. These views should be regarded as tentative until a more comprehensive and systematic study can be undertaken and until a rapidly growing literature can be assimilated.[125]

Although there can be little doubt about the increased destructiveness of nuclear weapons or the scale or speed of that destruction, at a slightly higher level of abstraction the most important change in military technology concerns the capacities of the states to defend their populations from external attack, as emphasized by Brodie (1946), Schelling (1966), Art (1982), Jervis (1984, 1989), and others. To put it simply, population defense was possible in the prenuclear era but not in the nuclear era. That is, throughout most of world history it has been technologically feasible and financially practical for the strongest states in the system to defend their populations from external military attack. The capacity to defend was a function of the dyadic balance of military capabilities between two adversaries, as modified by the offensive/defensive balance of military technology, loss of strength gradients, geographical considerations, and other variables. People were only vulnerable if their military forces were defeated on the battlefield, allowing their territorial frontiers to be penetrated by enemy forces. A sufficiently decisive military victory was necessary to inflict pain on the adversary population (Schelling, 1966:Chap. 1).

This is no longer true. As a consequence of the development of nuclear weapons and long-range delivery systems, population defense is no longer feasible even for the superpowers, at least for the present and for the near future.[126] Because it is now possible for strategic forces to strike directly at enemy populations without first defeating their military forces, military victory is no longer necessary to inflict pain on enemy populations and to protect one's own population from the miseries of war (Schelling, 1966). As a result, the direct link between disparities of strength and capacity for defense has been weakened (Art, 1982). Even the strongest states in the system can be utterly devastated by war.

The consequences of this change are enormous. Historically, the capacity for population defense meant that it was possible for a state, if it were sufficiently strong, to defeat its adversary's military forces, take what it wanted, and use threats of further force to compel the adversary to relinquish other assets and to change its behavior in desired ways. At the same time, one's own costs could be limited to the military costs of prosecuting the war and tolerable level of economic and social disruption at home. Thus, war *could* be rational, in that a state could be better off fighting than not fighting.[127] It could achieve a military outcome that could be translated into political gains.

Although such a positive expected outcome (relative to the status quo) is not totally inconceivable today, it is far less likely than in the past, at least with regard to an all-out nuclear war. It is hard to imagine a situation in which a superpower could emerge from such a war in a better overall position than it would if it had avoided fighting, even at the cost of making significant political concessions.[128] It would be little consolation if its adversary had suffered even greater damage. Even if one's power position relative to the adversary were to improve, it is hard to believe that the benefits of that would be sufficient to justify the death of tens or even hundreds of millions of its citizens, the destruction of most of its economic infrastructure, the long-term ecological as well as medical effects of the war (Chivian et al., 1982; Peterson, 1983), the wrenching disruption of its social structure, the destruction of its culture and heritage, and other effects.[129] As Charles de Gaulle noted, after a nuclear war the "two sides would have neither powers, nor laws, nor cities, nor cultures, nor cradles, nor tombs" (in Jervis, 1989). For these reasons, the concepts of victory and defeat become problematic for an all-out nuclear war. All major participants would almost certainly be losers. As Ronald Reagan and Mikhail Gorbachev have affirmed: "A nuclear war cannot be won and must never be fought" (*New York Times*, 22 November 1985).

By eliminating the capacity for population defense in the nuclear age and almost certainly making victory in war impossible, the nuclear revolution has had enormous consequences for the nature of the political interactions between states in the international system. On the most general level, the imperative of avoiding nuclear war and the significant risks of escalation to nuclear war have created historically unprecedented incentives for cooperation between the superpowers (George, 1988), at least at the strategic level, and have significantly reduced the likelihood of a major war between them. Situations that would have led to a major war in previous historical eras have had a peaceful outcome in the nuclear age.[130] But it has also created a number of paradoxes.

One paradox is that while mutual vulnerability has created incentives to avoid conflictual outcomes, at the same time it has created incentives to attempt to exploit an adversary's fear of mutual conflict to extract political concessions. The basic purposes of strategic doctrine have changed in fundamental ways. The traditional concern to maintain some reasonable balance between maintaining a capacity to fight a war and an ability to deter it has shifted significantly in the direction of the latter. In Schelling's (1966:35) words, "Military strategy can no longer be thought of . . . as the science of military victory. It is now . . . the art of coercion, of intimidation and deterrence."[131]

Another paradox created by the nuclear revolution is what Snyder (1965) and Jervis (1984:31) call the "stability-instability" paradox, which concerns the consequences of stability at the strategic level for stability at other levels of violence. If stability at the strategic level is ensured because of the balance of terror, threats of escalation to the nuclear level are too costly to implement. Consequently, they are not credible and therefore not useful for deterrence at the conventional level, undermining stability at the conventional level. On the other hand, there is a small chance that any conventional conflict might escalate, whether through the conscious strategy of using a "threat that leaves something to chance" (Schelling, 1960:Chap. 8) or the risk of loss of control or inadvertent escalation. This risk, in conjunction with the enormous costs involved, might be sufficient to reinforce deterrence and stability at lower levels. It is not inherently obvious which of these propositions is correct, and behavior under such conditions of uncertainty is not easily predictable. It depends in part on how the superpowers calculate both the magnitude of the risks involved and also the extent to which they can be controlled over the course of the crisis (George and Smoke, 1974). Past U.S.-Soviet behavior in issues directly affecting each other's interests has been sufficiently cautious, however, as to support the hypothesized deterrent effects of strategic stability at lower levels.

It is not possible here to explore these paradoxes in greater detail or to provide fuller justification for my arguments concerning the consequences of nuclear weapons. Nor is it possible to examine the questions of the possibility of a "limited" nuclear war, the proclivities of superpowers to intervene with military force in smaller wars, or the likelihood that such conflicts might escalate to a major superpower conflict. These were not the primary tasks of this chapter, and other papers in this series give greater attention to these questions.

There is one question, however, that requires some additional comment. In spite of recent efforts to think rigorously and systematically about the impact of the nuclear revolution, and in spite of the general belief that the probability of a war between the superpowers is very small, much less attention has been devoted to the question of the conditions or processes under which such an admittedly low probability event might still occur.[132]

I argued that a situation of mutual overkill means that it is almost certain that the costs of an all-out nuclear war will exceed any possible benefits from that war, that political leaders recognize this, and that consequently they would prefer peace, even peace with significant political concessions *if* they were ever faced with such a stark choice. This does not mean, however, that they would never rationally initiate a nuclear war. A preference for peace does not necessarily entail a preference for a strategy of noninitiation, however, for such a strategy could result not in peace but instead in a war initiated by the adversary rather than by oneself. If one superpower were nearly certain that such an attack would occur regardless of one's own actions, it might choose to preempt and initiate a nuclear war. Of all the causal sequences that might lead to an all-out nuclear war, the one involving preemption is the most likely. This directs our attention to the conditions under which preemption might be perceived as a viable option.[133]

The basic condition for preemption is a prisoner's dilemma situation in which each side has an incentive to strike first. The prevailing characteristics of military technology—the potential for enormous destruction, the invulnerability of a significant proportion of retaliatory forces, and the incapacity for population defense—guarantee a viable second strike capability,[134] which in turn eliminates any incentive to strike first. Such a condition could obtain in a crisis situation only if military technology were to change in such a way as to undermine the invulnerability of retaliatory forces or to create a population defense that is viable against a limited retaliatory strike. Such a scenario is unlikely in the foreseeable future, but it is not impossible.

Even in the absence of an objective incentive to strike first, it is conceivable that political leaders could come to the erroneous conclusion that war is inevitable, and that while the consequences would be devastating, war would be less devastating if the initial blow were struck by oneself rather than by the adversary. The specification of precisely how these beliefs could arise is an essential component of any theory of nuclear war. Two variables seem to be particularly important: perceptions of the inevitability of war (which would involve misperceptions of adversary intentions), and misperceptions of one's own military capabilities relative to those of the adversary. I have argued earlier that both of these processes are theoretically important and that they have occurred in numerous historical cases. Many of the sources of such beliefs and misperceptions continue to operate, including the anarchic structure of the international system, the ideological and cultural differences that distort states' perceptions of each other, and many of the psychological processes—especially under conditions of stress—that lead to distorted information processing. These factors are inherent in the structure of the international system and in the human mind, and there is little reason to believe that they will cease to operate in the nuclear age.

Although these factors are unlikely to disappear, new developments may be altering their likely impact. One is the widespread belief among political elites that the objective probability of an all-out war between the superpowers is much lower than in previous historical eras. For this reason, it is far more difficult for the self-fulfilling prophecies discussed above to get started. This effect is reinforced by the psychological tendency for political and military leaders to reduce their expected probability of an all-out war because the cost of that event would be so great. Psychological research has shown that estimates of the likelihood of events are not made independently of the value of those outcomes, so that statesmen have numerous mechanisms of wishful thinking, avoidance, and denial to lead them to lower the expected likelihood of an outcome with very negative consequences (Nisbett and Ross, 1980). The result is to reduce the likelihood of self-fulfilling prophecies regarding the inevitability of war. That likelihood is not zero, however, and one of the most urgent tasks for future research is the identification of the conditions and processes under which war comes to be perceived as inevitable.

Misperceptions of the relative military balance will undoubtedly continue to occur, as they have throughout history, but the consequences of those misperceptions are more difficult to predict. As emphasized earlier, misperception can occur without having a causal impact on decisions. It is probable that decision makers today as compared to those in the past will have much less confidence that a certain degree of military superiority can be translated into military victory with acceptable costs. The potential costs of a miscalculation are so great that even a relatively small risk of error almost certainly will be sufficient to induce caution. Admittedly, however, this again raises the question of the risk orientations of decision makers, for highly risk-acceptant actors might behave differently. The situational and dispositional factors contributing to extreme risk acceptance, particularly in the domain of extremely low probability events involving extraordinarily high costs, is another urgent area for further research.[135]

For these reasons it is reasonable to conclude that the likelihood that statesmen in a crisis situation will come to believe that war is inevitable, that they have military superiority that assures victory with acceptable costs, or that their second-strike capability is no longer viable, and that therefore they have an incentive to strike first, is considerably lower in the nuclear era than in previous historical periods.

There are, of course, other conceivable paths to nuclear war. One would be a model of crisis-induced stress, flawed decision making, loss of control, and inadvertent war (Lebow, 1987), based on the literature on the psychological and organizational determinants of crisis decision making. Space constraints have precluded a detailed discussion of that literature (see Holsti's chapter in this volume) and, therefore, of the loss of control/inadvertent war sequence, but the question of nonrational escalation to nuclear war is an important area of ongoing research. There have also been recent efforts to construct models of crisis escalation based on assumptions of rationality (O'Neill, 1986; Maoz, 1989:Chap. 4; Brams and Kilgour, 1989; Powell, 1987). Some of these models are particularly interesting because they show how rational behavior at each step of an escalating sequence can lead to outcomes that are highly undesirable for all parties involved.

The analysis of the impact of the nuclear revolution on other causal sequences leading to a major war between the superpowers is more difficult. It is probably true that the likelihood that other causal sequences will lead *directly* to decisions for war has been significantly reduced because of the irrationality of initiating a war for any purposes other than preemption. There is little reason to believe, however, that these traditional causes no longer operate in such a way as to create tensions and even crises between states and occasionally to bring them to the brink of war (Jervis, 1989:Chap. 1). Consequently, the importance of the causes of war surveyed here may now lie primarily in the way that they generate crisis situations in which preemption can be perceived as one possible policy option.

Conclusions

We have examined structural systemic theories, societal-level theories, and decision-making theories; general theories, middle-range theories, and bivariate hypotheses; and formal axiomatic theories and more traditional conceptualizations. We have also examined some of the evidence relevant to the validity of these theories, ranging from large-N correlational analyses to controlled comparative studies and individual case studies. It is hard to avoid the conclusion that there is little agreement on the identity of the most important causes of war, the methodology through which these causes might be discovered, the conceptual framework that might permit the integration of these factors into a general and logically consistent theory of war, or even the criteria by which one theory might be said to be better than another.

Instead, we find a number of dilemmas. Many of the hypotheses linking a certain variable to war can be paired with equally plausible hypotheses linking that same variable to peace. This is true not only for hypotheses deriving from fundamentally different research paradigms, such as liberal and Marxist-Leninist theories regarding the impact of capitalist economic systems on peace and war, but also for those generally associated with the same paradigm. The realist paradigm, for example, includes both the parity hypothesis and the preponderance hypothesis, and some balance of power theorists contend that multipolarity is stabilizing while other balance of power theorists argue that it is destabilizing. Because of these theoretical ambiguities it is perhaps not surprising that empirical research has demonstrated that in some historical periods certain variables are associated with peace but in other historical periods it is associated with war. It is obvious that under some theoretical conditions a particular factor has stabilizing effects while under other conditions it has destabilizing effects, but there has been too little theoretical and empirical research directed toward the specification of these conditions.[136]

This failure to specify the conditions under which many important relationships hold is compounded by the problem of equifinality—the fact that there are several distinct sets of conditions and causal sequences leading to the same outcome: war. Whereas some wars appear to result from the deliberate and careful calculation that the use of military force will bring strategic and economic gains with minimal costs, other wars appear to be the product of an inadvertent process of escalation involving the loss of control by political leaders and the absence of anything resembling a rational decision-making process. In the attempt to devise a general theory of war applicable in all cases, there has been too little work attempting to identify these distinct causal sequences or the conditions under which each is most likely to arise. The fact that many variables occur in more than one of these causal sequences makes it all the more difficult to test hypotheses regarding the causes of war, for simple correlational analyses that fail to incorporate interaction effects with key variables or capture the dynamic sequences leading to war are doomed from the start.

There is also the opposite problem, multifinality, in which a single set of conditions or a single causal sequence can have more than one possible outcome. Given a set of preferences or national interests and a set of international and domestic constraints, war may be but one of several possible means or strategies selected to optimize those preferences. Whether war or some other policy is selected is determined by a number of specific contextual and perhaps psychological variables. Such variables have not been incorporated into most of our theories of the causes of war, however, and these theories consequently are unable to specify with much precision when war as opposed to other policy options will be selected (Most and Starr, 1984). Recall that the theory that claims to have the highest degree of empirical confirmation,

Bueno de Mesquita's (1981a, 1985) expected utility theory of war, attempts to specify necessary rather than sufficient conditions. It attempts to predict only when war will *not* occur, not when it will occur. More general structural realist theories, such as Waltz's (1979) version of balance of power theory, specify even broader limits within which behavior is likely to fall, and consequently have less precise predictive power.

One reason for the absence of serious efforts to increase the level of precision of explanation is the concern by many political scientists for general, elegant, and parsimonious theories of behavior. There is a trade-off between explanatory completeness and parsimony, with the inclusion of additional variables increasing explanatory power but, in the process, also increasing the complexity of the theory and making it far more difficult to apply in a wide variety of historical circumstances. To the extent that factors idiosyncratic to a particular case need to be included, the possibility for a general theory of the causes of war is greatly restricted. There is no single answer as to how this trade-off between explanatory completeness and parsimony should be made, in part because of the different purposes for which theory can be used.

From the perspective of the policymaker, however, elegant and parsimonious theories lacking in more specific diagnostic power are of much less value than contingent generalizations that attempt to specify the likely outcomes of particular classes of situations, even if the emergence of those situations is not explained and even though these generalizations are not universally applicable (George and Smoke, 1974; George, 1976). The emphasis on general theory has distracted attention from the kinds of middle-range theories that might generate such conditional generalizations. This concern for general theory affects the policy relevance of the international conflict literature in another way, by contributing to the bias toward structural systemic theories that may be parsimonious but that tend to be based on variables that are not easily manipulable by policymakers.

We have seen that the utility of the traditional theoretical and empirical literature on the causes of war for policymakers is also diminished by the general failure of scholars to adapt traditional theories of war to the nuclear age and by the failure of contemporary strategists to ground their strategic theories and policy prescriptions more solidly on empirically confirmed knowledge about the behavior of states in previous eras. Both the propositions—that little has changed in the nuclear era or that everything has changed in the nuclear era—are undoubtedly incorrect. The truth, presumably, is somewhere in between. We still live in a decentralized, anarchic state system in which there are certain propensities toward war deriving from systemic, societal, institutional, and psychological pressures. At the same time, the development of nuclear weapons has profoundly altered the cost-benefit calculations of political leaders. This dilemma is captured by Howard (1983:21). He states that "the causes which have produced war in the past are operating in our own day as powerfully as at any time in history," yet on the following page insists that decisions for war are based on rational calculations and that "the odds against such a course [of going to war] benefiting their state or themselves or their cause will be greater, and more *evidently* greater, than in any situation that history has ever had to record." The task for theorists is to incorporate both sets of considerations into an integrated and comprehensive theory of war in the nuclear age.

Notes

This research has been supported by the Stanford Center for International Security and Arms Control, the Carnegie Corporation, the University of Minnesota and by a Social Science Research Council/MacArthur Foundation Fellowship in International Peace and Security. The views expressed here do not necessarily represent those of the supporting agencies. I have benefitted enormously from the criticisms and suggestions of a number of scholars regarding earlier versions of this chapter and I would like to thank them for their help: Alexander George, Robert Jervis, Kimberly Marten, Cliff Morgan, Kurt Weyland, seven anonymous reviewers, and the editors of this volume. I especially thank Brian Job for his particularly insightful and challenging comments. I alone, of course, am responsible for the final product.

1. One analyst estimates that there were approximately 860 wars between 1100 A.D. and 1925, involving about 35 million deaths (Sorokin, 1937). That does not even include World War II, which resulted in roughly 50 million military and civilian deaths (Beer, 1981:38), or the large number of international and civil wars over the last half century.

2. It is estimated that global military spending reached $900 billion in 1987 (Sivard, 1987).

3. This discussion is not meant to suggest that the social scientific research that influences policy necessarily represents the dominant view of the academic community or that it utilizes this research in the appropriate way.

4. The better of these reviews include Waltz (1954), Brodie (1973:Chap. 7), Blainey (1973), Gallie (1978), Nelson and Olin (1979), Bueno de Mesquita (1980*a*), Zinnes (1980), Brown (1987), and Vasquez (1987).

5. It has been increasingly common over the last decade for theoretical and empirical studies of war to begin at this point in history (Wright, 1965; Modelski, 1978; Levy, 1983*a*; Modelski and Thompson, 1988; Kennedy, 1987). Most wars in previous eras have far less relevance for contemporary theory or policy, the most notable exception being the Peloponnesian War.

6. Great powers are differentiated from other states on the basis of their military power and potential and their ability to project that military power for use in offensive as well as defensive operations; their more extensive interests, including their interests

in the structure and stability of the international system itself; their perceived status; and their regularized patterns of interaction with other great powers. Although there is some agreement regarding the identity of the great powers in the past, the concept and therefore the identity of the great powers has become somewhat more ambiguous in the nuclear age (Levy, 1983a:Chap. 2).

7. Here war is defined as substantial armed and violent conflict between the organized military forces of independent political entities (Levy, 1983a:Chap. 3), with "substantial" being defined to include a minimum of 1,000 battle casualties (Singer and Small, 1972) among the great powers.

8. The number of colonial or imperial wars is difficult to count precisely because their small size blurs the distinction between *wars* and lesser forms of violent conflict and because their protracted nature often makes it difficult to define when one war stops and another starts. One estimate is that there have been about 90 imperial or colonial wars since 1500 (Levy and Morgan, 1984).

9. For compilations of small wars from the 1815 to the present, see Small and Singer (1982). Other compilations for the post-1945 period include Butterworth (1976) and Kende (1971).

10. There do not appear to be any significant cyclical trends in the *frequency* of war of various types (Sorokin, 1937:352–360; Singer and Small, 1972:205–207; Singer and Cusack, 1981), but there is evidence that the *magnitude* or severity of war has been somewhat cyclical over the last five centuries (Singer and Small, 1972; Modelski, 1978; Thompson and Zuk, 1982). Goldstein (1985, 1988:Chap. 11) in particular emphasizes the cyclical nature of major warfare. Because of the historical, theoretical, and policy relevance of general wars (also referred to as hegemonic, global, or systemic war), the question of whether they have followed a cyclical pattern has attracted particular attention. Modelski (1978, 1987b) and Thompson (1983a) insist that there are 100-year cycles of global wars over the last five centuries, and the latter has presented some fairly strong supporting evidence (Thompson and Rasler, 1988; Thompson, 1988). However, their data base excludes some important major land-based wars that involved nearly all the European great powers and had enormous consequences for the structure of the system (for example, the Thirty Years' War), and the inclusion of these would undercut the notion of regular cycles (Levy, 1985a).

11. There are sociological as well as intellectual reasons for the great power bias among scholars. A disproportionate amount of scholarship on war and international relations is done by scholars in states that are currently or were historically great powers. These scholars compound the bias by failing to acknowledge some significant scholarship in smaller and non-Western states (Holsti, 1985).

12. The World War I analogy may be particularly misleading because the prevailing views of historians (but not political scientists) regarding the causes of the war have shifted in the last two decades. Whereas a significant number of political scientists still regard World War I as the classic case of an inadvertent war that was sought by none of the leading great powers (Holsti, 1972), many historians now accept some version of the Fischer (1961, 1975) thesis that Germany deliberately aimed for war in order to become a world power and to solve her domestic socioeconomic crisis (Kaiser, 1983; Berghahn, 1973).

13. One of the better efforts here is Smoke's (1977) historical study of hypotheses on escalation.

14. Although most studies of intervention have been focused on specific historical cases, there has been a growing body of literature that aims at more general hypotheses. Some of these have been limited to particular states (Tillema, 1973; Duner, 1985; Schmid, 1985) and some constitute one part of larger studies of the coercive use of force short of war (Blechman and Kaplan, 1978; Kaplan, 1981). There are a number of data bases for the study of intervention (Eckhardt and Azar, 1978; Pearson, 1988).

15. Depending on the classification of China in 1950, the Korean War might be one such case.

16. Of the 10 general wars of the last five centuries, the following clearly involved escalation from local conflicts or civil wars: War of Dutch Independence, Thirty Years' War, Seven Years' War in North America, the French Revolutionary wars, and World War I. In an earlier era, the Peloponnesian War also arose from the escalation of several local conflicts.

17. Some exceptions include Stoll (1982), Huth and Russett (1984, 1988), Huth (1988), and Morgan and Ray (1988).

18. This is not to say that individual belief systems, personalities, cognitive processes, and the like are not important causes of war. Their importance can be determined, however, only if they are considered separately rather than being aggregated into an all-inclusive and residual concept of human nature.

19. Fay's (1928) two-volume study of *The Origins of the World War* includes one volume on underlying causes going back to 1871 and one volume on immediate causes beginning with the assassination of the archduke.

20. The leading alternative paradigms include liberalism and Marxism-Leninism (Gilpin, 1975; Holsti, 1985).

21. The actors need not necessarily be nation-states but, instead, can be the dynastic states of sixteenth or seventeenth century Europe, the city-states of ancient Greece or the Italian Renaissance, or any territorially based political entities.

22. Few realists deal directly with the problems created by the assumption that *states* have well-defined interests that can be expressed as a transitive preference order (if A is preferred to B and B is preferred to C, then A is preferred to C), particularly the logical problems involved in establishing a social preference order for any collectivity (Arrow, 1951; Ordeshook, 1986:Chap. 2). Exceptions include Bueno de Mesquita (1981*a*) and Morrow (1988).

23. The *as if* assumption is an important one and I will return to it later.

24. Realists who focus on the international political economy rather than the international security system give far more emphasis to economic dimensions of power (Gilpin, 1975; Krasner, 1976; Keohane, 1984).

25. Wolfers (1962:Chap. 1) is most explicit about this and compares states in the international system to individuals in a house on fire; one does not need elaborate psychological theories to predict their behavior.

26. Most states that have the means to do so prefer to provide for their own security rather than rely on allies, because allies naturally give priority to their own interests, which are rarely fully congruent with one's own. Most alliances have historically been short-term solutions to immediate security threats rather than long-term solutions to

one's security needs (Liska, 1962). The nature of the trade-offs between the accumulation of military capabilities and the formation of alliances for the purposes of enhancing one's security is an important research question that only recently has begun to receive serious attention (Wagner, 1986). The trade-off between increased security and the loss of autonomy resulting from alliances is analyzed by Morrow (1987).

27. This reflects the more general problem that what is rational for the individual may not be rational for society (Barry and Hardin, 1982; Schelling, 1978), which gives rise to the problem of collective action (Olson, 1965; Hardin, 1982). There have been numerous attempts to describe these types of situations with prisoners' dilemma models (Rapoport and Chammah, 1965; Schelling, 1960; Snyder and Diesing, 1977; Axelrod, 1984; Brams and Kilgour, 1988), but these are discussed elsewhere in this series and will not be treated here.

28. Alternatively, if one state is much more committed to peace than another—and particularly if the former is more sensitive to the dangers inherent in the security dilemma than its rival, leading it to fear the consequences of firmness more than those of conciliation—anarchy and the security dilemma may facilitate the exploitation of "peace-loving" states by rival aggressors.

29. Thus, Mansbach and Vasquez (1981) suggest that attention be shifted "from the issue of power to the power of issues." For the importance of issues, see Keohane and Nye (1977), Zimmerman (1973), and Vasquez and Mansbach (1984). The importance of linkages between issues in strategic interaction has also been neglected (Morrow, 1986; Morgan, 1988).

30. It should also be emphasized that not all who recognize the importance of international anarchy are realists as defined here. The "idealist" tradition, often associated with classical liberalism, acknowledges that the anarchic structure of the system exacerbates the misunderstandings that frequently arise between states and suggests that the ultimate solution to the problem of conflict in the world is to replace the anarchic system with world government. A central issue that separates realists from idealists, however, is that the former see the world in zero-sum terms and recognize that genuine conflicts of interests do exist, whereas idealists assume an underlying harmony of interests in a nonzero-sum world (Gilpin, 1975:Chap. 1). For more on the realist-idealist debate see Jacobson (1960:Chap. 4) and Wolfers (1962:Chap. 6).

31. There are some recent exceptions that attempt to derive logically consistent balance of power models from a small set of axioms, but these assumptions are quite restrictive, and these models have not been tested against empirical reality (Zinnes, 1967; Wagner, 1986; Niou and Ordeshook, 1986, 1987).

32. Kaplan's (1957) essential rules of a balance of power system, for example, have been widely criticized for their inconsistency (Riker, 1962:159–187).

33. Although a major difference between balance of power theory and power transition theory is the latter's emphasis on the internal sources of military power and deemphasis on the importance of alliances, there is a general recognition by balance of power theorists that internal balancing may be important, particularly in bipolar systems (Waltz, 1979:Chap. 8). Bueno de Mesquita (1980a:370) is wrong to suggest that balance of power theory excludes internal increases in military power as a balancing mechanism or as a means by which the international distribution of power is altered.

34. Any discussion of threats of hegemony or dominance must specify the geo-

graphic scope of the system under consideration and the basis of power in the system (Levy, 1985a), but this is not always made explicit. Balance of power theories conceive of power primarily in terms of land-based military power and of hegemonic threats in terms of dominance over the European continent. The great powers have historically perceived the most serious threats to their security as emanating from land-based continental powers rather than sea powers, regardless of the global strength of the latter. Thus, it was the rising power of Germany in 1914, and not that of the United States, that was perceived by the other great powers as the primary threat to their interests and, consequently, it was against Germany rather than the United States that great power blocking coalitions were formed.

35. Other general wars involving nearly all the great powers may have occurred in spite of the absence of any clear threat of hegemony, including the War of Jenkins' Ear/Austrian Succession (1739–1748) and the Seven Years' War (1755–1763). See Levy (1985a).

36. Relatively isolated regional subsystems may share some of the characteristics of great power systems, and many balance of power propositions may be applicable to such systems.

37. Similarly, theories that specify the maintenance of the independence of states as the goal of balance of power systems do not see the partitioning or elimination of small or even medium states as undermining the stability of the system (Gulick, 1955; Kaplan, 1957:23–24). Propositions about the relationship between the dyadic balance of power and the outbreak of war between pairs of states, however, may be as applicable to secondary states as to great powers. On balancing and bandwagoning, see Walt (1987).

38. Hegemonic stability theory (Kindleberger, 1973; Gilpin, 1975; Krasner, 1976; Keohane, 1980, 1984) also deals with the relationship between power distributions and international stability. In contrast to scholars involved in the parity/preponderance debate, however, it defines the independent variable in terms of the distribution of economic power in the international system and the dependent variable in terms of the stability of the international political economy. Thus, it deals with a different set of theoretical questions and will not be discussed here. Only Gilpin (1981) attempts to extend hegemonic stability theory to the international security system, and his work will be discussed in the section on theories of hegemonic war.

39. This has been done in some of the quantitative empirical literature (Singer et al., 1972).

40. One exception is Bueno de Mesquita and Lalman (1988a).

41. Many of the hypotheses as to the systemic effects of polarity are similar to those of the effects of the size of the system. If size is defined as the number of great powers in the system, the size of the system is analytically distinct from the distribution of power. It appears, however, that regardless of precisely how the size of the system is defined, there is no evidence of a relationship between the size of the system and the frequency or seriousness of war in the system, either for the post-1815 period (Ostrom and Aldrich, 1978) or for the last five centuries (Levy, 1984b).

42. The debate over bipolarity and multipolarity generally ignores the phenomenon of unipolarity, probably because balance of power theorists assume that balancing

mechanisms work effectively to prevent any single state from achieving a position of dominance.

43. Note that the concept of risk orientation has a specific technical meaning: it is a measure of the shape of an actor's utility function. Utility functions are linear for risk-neutral actors, concave (downward) for risk-adverse actors, and convex for risk-acceptant actors (Ordeshook, 1986:46). Faced with the choice of (1) a gamble involving two possible outcomes with an expected value of x (for example, a 50-50 chance of nothing or $100, with an expected value of $50), and (2) a certain return of $50, risk-neutral actors are indifferent, risk-adverse actors prefer the certainty equivalent (x) of $50, and risk-acceptant actors prefer the gamble. For a good application to international relations, see Morrow (1987).

44. Contrary to Bueno de Mesquita (1981b), at extremely high levels of power concentration, where the threat of hegemony is for all practical purposes a sufficient condition for the emergence of a blocking military coalition to oppose the threatening state, it is unlikely that risk propensities have more than a marginal impact.

45. A word is in order regarding the data bases utilized in these studies. All quantitative empirical studies of the systemic distribution of power and war, and in fact nearly all studies of war over the past century and a half using aggregate data, are based on the Correlates of War data generated by Singer and Small. See Singer (1972) for a summary of the Correlates of War project, Singer and Small (1972) for the war data and a discussion of the procedures by which they were generated, and Levy (1983a, 1988b) for an extension of the war data back to the end of the fifteenth century. See Singer and Small (1966a) for the alliance data and Levy (1981) for an extension of the alliance data back three centuries. An overview of the capability data can be found in Stuckey and Singer (1973) or Singer (1988). The six Correlates of War capability indicators include two demographic measures (total population and urban population), two industrial indicators (energy consumption and iron or steel production), and two military measures (active armed forces personal and military expenditures), all equally weighted (Singer, 1988).

For good critiques of the project see articles by Job and Ostrom, Duvall, and Starr in Hoole and Zinnes (1976), and for a recent summary of the project's findings see Vasquez (1987). Note that the most recent stages of the Correlates of War project are the Militarized Interstate Dispute (MID) project and the Behavioral Correlates of War (BCOW) project. For summaries of the projects and of their data, see Maoz (1982a), Gochman and Maoz (1984), Gochman and Leng (1988), and Leng and Singer (1988). One important macrohistorical research program in international relations that uses aggregate data methods but not the COW data is long cycle theory, which relies on the sea power data of Modelski and Thompson (1988).

46. Levy's (1985b) quantitative study of the relationship between polarity and war over five centuries incorporates the bipolar period of the early sixteenth century. He finds that unipolar systems have historically been the least stable, bipolar systems have been the most stable, and multipolar systems have been of intermediate stability, suggesting a curvilinear relationship between the distribution of power in the system and the outbreak of major war. The value of the historical scope of the study is diminished, however, by the failure to use operational indicators in the measurement of polarity.

47. This argument requires the assumption that likely victims of aggression are more likely to have allies than likely aggressors, or that the allies of victims are more likely to intervene militarily than are allies of aggressors. Otherwise, an alliance that helps deter an attack by A against B could undermine the deterrence of B's attack against A. Most balance of power theorists argue that defensive alliances are more common than offensive alliances, that offensive alliances tend to be fragile and unstable, and generally that alliances are more easily formed against a common threat than to achieve positive gains (Liska, 1968). Note that many alliance treaties stipulate that the obligation to come to the aid of one's ally is dependent on the initiation of the war by an outside state. This formal obligation is reinforced by (and, in fact, is often made in anticipation of) domestic political considerations.

48. Note Sabrosky's (1980) finding that states tend to honor their alliance commitments more in the twentieth century than in the nineteenth century.

49. Other factors affecting the probability of victory include geographical advantages, the degradation of military strength over distance (Boulding, 1962; Bueno de Mesquita, 1981*a*), the offensive/defensive balance of military technology (Quester, 1977; Levy, 1984*a*), and political and administrative factors (Knorr, 1970; Organski and Kugler, 1980:Chap. 2).

50. For one attempt to resolve these conflicting findings, see Morgan (1989).

51. There is some danger, however, that these studies have inadvertently underestimated the importance of the balance of military power and potential through selection biases in their research designs (Levy, 1988*c*, 1989*b*). The estimation of the magnitude of these biases is an enormously difficult task, but an important one for future research.

52. Blainey (1973) recognizes that other variables may have a secondary influence on the outbreak of war. The most important of these are expectations of the behavior of outside states, perceptions of unity or discord within the adversaries, the social and psychological impact of one's recent wars, nationalism and ideology, the ability of the economy to sustain the envisioned war effort, and the personality and experiences of key decision makers.

53. Some discussion is necessary regarding my classification of this as a systemic-level theory. Bueno de Mesquita has constructed a theory of the foreign policy behavior of a single state, not of the strategic interaction of two or more states, so it does not really generate propositions about systemic outcomes and processes. As I noted earlier, however, I am using the levels of analysis as a framework for the classification of the independent variable. Because a theory is defined not only by its logical structure but also by its empirical content (Hempel, 1966:Chap. 6; Nagel, 1961), because all of the variables in Bueno de Mesquita's theory are operationalized and measured with reference to systemic-level indicators and data, and because the theory basically black-boxes all decision-making processes, I have classified the theory along with other systemic-level theories. Bueno de Mesquita explicitly compares his expected utility theory with balance of power theory, and others regard his expected utility as a formalized and operational version of a realist theory of international politics.

54. I have benefited from Jim Morrow's comments on this section of the paper.

55. The assumption of the existence of a dominant decision maker is a way to make the simplifying assumption that states behave as if they were unitary actors. The unitary actor assumption is common to all structural theories of international politics. It is explicitly motivated here by the need to avoid the logical problems involved in establishing a single preference ordering for a collective decision-making body (Arrow, 1951). Whether bureaucratic and domestic politics and different belief systems and world views of decision makers invalidate the assumption of a dominant decision maker with respect to war and peace issues is an important theoretical and empirical question.

56. The rationality assumption postulates that individuals have a consistent set of preferences, that they know the intensity (utility) of those preferences, and that they always choose the strategy that maximizes their expected utility (the sum of utilities of each possible outcome, each weighted by its probability of occurrence).

57. Recent modifications in the theory allow for intermediate outcomes between victory and defeat (Morrow, 1985).

58. There is an important debate regarding both the empirical accuracy of the rationality assumption (Kahneman et al., 1972; Nisbett and Ross, 1980; Tversky and Kahneman, 1981; Hogarth and Reder, 1987) and the question of whether rational choice theories should be evaluated by the accuracy of their assumptions or the accuracy of their predictions (Friedman, 1953; Hogarth and Reder, 1987). This debate is primarily among economists and social psychologists, but it is beginning to attract more attention in the political science literature (Moe, 1979).

59. One technical flaw in *The War Trap* is that Bueno de Mesquita not only sets the utility of the status quo at zero, but also sets the utility of winning at +1 and the utility of losing at −1. This is mathematically incorrect, for utility theory provides only two degrees of freedom here (Wagner, 1984). The substantive implication is that the status quo is always midway between winning and losing, which may not be true. This problem is corrected in Bueno de Mesquita (1985), where a value for the status quo for each state is calculated from its risk orientation.

60. As we have seen, many of the Correlates of War studies of the relationship among the outbreak of war and power concentrations, alliances, and related balance of power variables find that many of these relationships reverse direction in the nineteenth and twentieth centuries (Singer et al., 1972; Singer and Small, 1974).

61. Note one consideration precluding a direct comparison of the empirical fit of these different studies: whereas many other empirical studies examine the ordinal or product-moment correlations between indicators of the key theoretical concepts, which reflect two-way associations, Bueno de Mesquita's empirical tests are based on one-way measures of association (appropriate for the analysis of necessary conditions), which is much less demanding.

62. This is not technically correct, for it does not capture the *utility* of various outcomes to the weaker state. If the utility of victory is sufficiently great, and if the costs of defeat are not too great, the expected utility of war can be positive even if the most likely outcome is defeat. Bueno de Mesquita's proposition is consistent with the historical evidence only because of the tendency for utilities to be defined in zero-sum terms in his theory (about 70 percent of the conflicts included in *The War Trap* are

zero sum). This limitation in the theory has subsequently been corrected (Bueno de Mesquita, 1985).

63. This proposition is based on the troublesome assumption of the possibility of interpersonal comparison of utilities. This assumption is eliminated from later versions of the theory and appropriate modifications in the theory are made (Bueno de Mesquita, 1985).

64. There are two reasons why a war between allies should be common, according to Bueno de Mesquita (1981a:73–83). One is that intervention by third parties on the side of the victim is reduced considerably if the attacker and victim are "allies," reducing the risks for the attacker (consider U.S. inaction during the Soviet invasion of Hungary in 1956). Another argument, which I find much less compelling, is that any future changes in the relationship between the two parties is more likely to be negative rather than positive (since the congruence of interests reflected by the alliance is more likely to decline rather than improve), providing the stronger ally with an incentive to act preventively.

65. Bueno de Mesquita (1983) has constructed a separate model of the costs of war. Although these costs have not been fully integrated into the theory, Bueno de Mesquita and Lalman (1986) have made some progress here.

66. A more serious charge in a very good review by Wagner (1984) that the theory itself is ad hoc and cannot be formally derived from its assumptions.

67. The unitary actor assumption may be more accurate for decisions undertaken once war is underway, given the unifying effect of war itself, but even that may be doubtful (Iklé, 1971; Mayer, 1959).

68. My view of the reasonableness of the *as if* assumption is based on a Lakatosian view of scientific progress (Lakatos, 1970). The *as if* assumption is not too damaging to a theory if and only if there does not exist an alternative theory that provides equally accurate empirical predictions and that is also based on assumptions that are more congruent with empirical reality. If such a theory exists, it constitutes a theoretically and empirically progressive problem shift with respect to the theory based on as if assumptions. It is not easy, of course, to compare the accuracy of predictions of different theories trying to explain slightly different phenomena, as Kuhn (1962) recognizes in his concept of the incommensurability of paradigms. With respect to Bueno de Mesquita, my view is that the nature of the political decision-making process is an important component of a theory of the causes of war and that his refusal to deal with that question can be justified only by the absence of alternative theories that give reasonable precise and accurate predictions. I would expect, however, that new theories providing comparable predictions but based on more reasonable assumptions will emerge in the future, so that Bueno de Mesquita's as if assumption will become increasingly more difficult to justify.

69. One problem concerns the assumptions that the Singer and Small (1966a) categories of defense pacts, nonaggression and neutrality pacts, and entente pacts constitute an ordinal scale reflecting a decreasing order of commitment and therefore of similarity of interests, and that consequently ordinal statistical methods are appropriate. There are some reasons to doubt the validity of the ordinality assumption,

although the extent of the deviations from a strict ordinal scale, and the sensitivity of Bueno de Mesquita's analysis to these considerations, is an empirical question. The nonaggression pacts are particularly suspect, for such formal assurances that two states will not use force against each other are often made under conditions of considerable mistrust and suspicion and where some symbolic form of reassurance is desirable. Entente pacts, which involve "consultation" and "cooperation" in the event of a crisis, do not formally specify the conditions under which military force will or will not be used, and sometimes may not reflect any commitment or similarity of interests between states. The Franco-German entente pact of 1938 is an obvious case in point. Moreover, the congruence of interests and similarities of policies between states is not always reflected in formal military alliances. Important economic bonds between states, as well as some ideological ties (for example, the U.S.-Israeli relationship), are not reflected by Bueno de Mesquita's alliance indicator and may actually involve higher degrees of congruence of interests than many formal military alliances (Levy, 1981:587–588).

70. Although Bueno de Mesquita argues that the congruence of states' alliance patterns reflects the similarities of their policy goals and therefore one state's utility for another's policy, it might also be possible to conceive of alliances as revealed preferences regarding whom one is willing to fight for. These two conceptions are not necessarily consistent, however.

Another operational problem concerns the assumption that alliances with all states are equally important for the purposes of calculating the congruence of alignment patterns between states, regardless of the military strength or strategic location of the states involved. Finally, the measurement of utilities in terms of alliances creates a problem if alliances are also used as independent variables in the theory.

71. This argument is similar in many respects to Galtung's (1964) rank-disequilibrium theory, which is a general structural theory designed to explain aggression in any social system. Galtung views the international system as a multidimensional system of stratification and argues that aggression is most likely when an actor's rankings on different dimensions of status in the system are nonconsistent. Rank disequilibrium gives rise to a sense of self-righteousness and the motivation toward equilibration and also provides the resources necessary for the struggle. He concedes, however, that rank disequilibrium is not a sufficient condition for aggression, for the existence of alternative means of equilibration and the absence of a cultural experience with violent aggression may be inhibiting factors. For an attempt to apply a status inconsistency model to the specific problem of international war, see Wallace (1973).

72. Note the contrast with balance of power theory, which suggests that major war is least likely under conditions of rough parity.

73. The most useful definition of hegemonic war (also referred to as global, general, or systemic war) is provided by Gilpin (1981:199–200): it is a direct contest between the leading power or powers and a rising challenger over the nature and governance of the system, global in geographical scope and fought with unlimited means, and involves all of the major states and most of the minor states in the system. See also Levy (1985a).

74. Modelski and Thompson identify Portugal as the world power in the sixteenth century, the Dutch in the seventeenth century, the British in the eighteenth and nineteenth centuries, and the United States in the twentieth century.

75. Long cycle theory identifies the following periods of global warfare: the Italian Wars (1494–1517), the War of Dutch Independence (1585–1609), the Wars of Louis XIV (1689–1715), the French Revolutionary and Napoleonic wars (1792–1815), and the two World Wars of this century (1914–1939).

76. Thompson (1983a:143) concedes that the dynamics of power concentration and deconcentration may be affected by factors other than uneven development, but in a recent paper (1986a) emphasizes the importance of the emergence and decline of leading economic sectors.

77. The one exception, although one from an earlier international system, is the victory of the land-based military power Sparta over Athenian sea power in the Peloponnesian War.

78. Because the rising regional challengers in the long cycle paradigm are identical to the declining leaders from a Eurocentric perspective emphasizing land-based military power, Kennedy's (1987) argument regarding the behavior of declining states is also relevant. States in decline tend to divert excessive resources from the economic sector to the military one, which only hastens their decline. All the major wars have been won by the state able to marshall the greatest economic resources. (Again, the Peloponnesian War from an earlier era is an exception.)

79. Recall the Singer, Bremer, and Stuckey (1972) finding that parity is associated with peace in the nineteenth century and with war in the twentieth century.

80. These findings are particularly significant in light of the concern that the Modelski and Thompson definition of global war in terms of its systemic consequences may introduce an element of circularity into the definition of global war, result in the exclusion of some enormously destructive and theoretically important wars from the class of global war (for example, the Thirty Years' War, War of the Austrian Succession, and Seven Years' War), and thus inadvertently bias the analysis in favor of the hypothesized 100-year cycles (Levy, 1985a).

81. Keohane (1984:39–41), for example, states explicitly that "the hegemonic power need not be militarily dominant worldwide," but need only possess enough military power to prevent the incursions by others into its economic sphere.

82. For example, Gilpin includes the primarily land-based Thirty Years' War as a hegemonic war and France as the leading power in the eighteenth century. Gilpin's (1981:200) list of hegemonic wars is similar to but not perfectly congruent with that of Modelski and Thompson.

83. One difficulty in testing power transition theories is the absence of good data on power capabilities over the last five centuries other than the Modelski and Thompson (1988) sea power data. A more serious problem concerns the partial incommensurability of the theories themselves (Kuhn, 1962). This incommensurability is a product of differences among the theories with respect to assumptions about the geographical scope of the system and the basis of power in the system, the definition of hegemony and the identification of the leading state and the challenger, the definition and identification of hegemonic wars, and the specific conditions that trigger the war.

Another complicating factor is the tendency to define hegemonic wars in terms of their systemic consequences. This confounds cause and effect, results in lists of hegemonic wars that are tied to theories in nearly tautological ways, and greatly complicates an independent empirical test of hypotheses on hegemonic war (Levy, 1985a).

84. This represented a significant departure form mercantilist theory, which argued that war and commerce were mutually reinforcing during the sixteenth through eighteenth centuries (Howard, 1976:Chap. 3).

85. Similarly, the inference that the military conflict in the 1930s and 1940s was the consequence of the decline of free trade and the rise of economic nationalism seriously underestimates the importance of the role of Hitler, Nazi ideology, the German determination to overturn the harsh Versailles peace settlement, and other political factors. The attribution of "long peace" between the great powers after World War II to the system of free trade under U.S. leadership underestimates the deterrent effect of nuclear weapons and the importance of the absence of territorial conflicts or other conflicts of intrinsic interests between the superpowers (as opposed to conflicts over power and other general interests).

86. One example of this is the quantitative literature that examines the relationship between national attributes and the war behavior of states (Rummel, 1968).

87. Marxist-Leninist international theory was developed primarily by Lenin ([1917] 1939), who borrowed from Hobson ([1902] 1954), Hilferding ([1910] 1981), and Luxemburg ([1913] 1951). Lenin links imperialism not with capitalism in general but with a particular stage of capitalist development: "imperialism is the monopoly stage of capitalism" (as opposed to capitalist free competition) and is defined by five basic features. These include the concentration of production and capital into monopolies; the merging of bank capital with industrial capital, leading to the dominance of "finance capital" under a financial oligarchy; the distinctive importance of the export of capital as opposed to the export of commodities; the formation of international capitalist monopolies that share the world among themselves; and the territorial division of the world among the biggest capitalist powers (Lenin, [1917] 1939:88–89). Imperialism has also been defined more loosely to include more general forms of economic, political, and even cultural penetration across state boundaries; military conquest and occupation; and more general relationships of dominance and dependence (Cohen, 1973). Many theories of imperialism are weakened by the ambiguity of this central concept. My use of the concept here refers to the broader definition of imperialism.

For some good treatments of Marxist-Leninist theories of war, see Lider (1977, 1979) and Semmel (1981).

88. One analytical problem here is that it has never been demonstrated that formal political control is necessary for international trade. The greater economic efficiency of free trade may outweigh whatever other advantages are offered by political control. Whether states attempt to increase their wealth through commerce or conquest (Rosecrance, 1986) cannot be determined by strictly economic considerations but also involves questions of the structure of the international political and economic systems and political factors internal to the state.

89. Lenin ([1917] 1939:Chap. 6) is more careful and emphasizes that the great

power dimension of the conflict does not arise until the world has been territorially divided among the major capitalist states (or monopolies), at which point further expansion becomes zero sum.

90. Although there have been few systematic studies of the relative likelihood of capitalist and noncapitalist states initiating or otherwise becoming involved in war, we will see in the next section that recent research has demonstrated that liberal democratic states rarely fight each other and are no more likely to initiate war or otherwise be involved in war than are nondemocratic states (Rummel, 1983; Chan, 1984). To the extent that liberal democracy coincides with capitalist economic structures, this empirical generalization runs contrary to Marxist-Leninist theory.

91. The lack of congruence between the primary colonial rivalries before the war and the military alignments of the war is inconsistent with the Marxist-Leninist interpretation of World War I. (The rivalries between Great Britain and France in Africa and Great Britain and Russia in Asia were as serious as those between Germany and both Great Britain and France in Africa.) Further doubts are raised by the overwhelming importance of military and strategic considerations confronting the great powers in 1914, particularly the growth of German power and the inability of the state system to accommodate it, the imperatives of the alliance system, the instability created by the ideology of the offensive and perceived incentives of the advantages of striking first, and the hostile images and serious misperceptions held by many European statesmen (Fay, 1928; Albertini, 1957). For an emphasis on the economic causes of the war, see Zilliacus (1946) and Hardach (1977).

92. Another relevant point is whether capitalist states always generate surpluses that cannot be absorbed domestically. Regardless of the correctness of its economic assumptions, Marxist-Leninist theory underestimates the political tendency of capitalist states to undertake the reforms necessary to maintain an adequate and stable level of internal consumption.

93. It is true that most of the major capitalist states during this period did engage in imperialist activity to one extent or another, although Switzerland and the Scandinavian countries provide notable exceptions. Many of the leading imperialist states of this period, including Russia, Italy, Japan, and Portugal, exported very little capital to their colonies and in other respects as well could hardly be described as capitalist. Most of the capitalist states pursuing imperialist policies did not reach the monopoly stage until after the peak of their imperialist expansion, and late nineteenth century imperialism was not dominated by monopolies (Aron, 1968). Industrial production and financial capital were more concentrated in Germany than in Great Britain and France (Cohen, 1973:66), but Germany was the last major European state to join the scramble for colonies. Regarding the destination of capital exports, less than a quarter of British exports and less than 10 percent of French and German exports went to their colonies (Cohen, 1973:63), just as today the vast majority of capitalist exports of commerce and capital goes to other capitalist states. The single major outlet for British exports was the United States, and most French and German exports went to Russia, Austria-Hungary, and Turkey.

94. There are variations of Marxist-Leninist theory that do attempt to explain the phenomenon of imperialism in the era prior to modern industrial capitalism. These focus more generally on the dynamics of class conflict and explain imperialist expan-

sion in terms of the efforts of the ruling class to advance their own economic interests at the expense of the weak both at home and beyond their borders. Some scholars, for example, trace the origins of the Peloponnesian War to Athenian economic imperialism (Cornford, 1907; Green, 1970). Wallerstein (1974) adopts a more systemic perspective, identifying a capitalist world system dating form the sixteenth century and tracing imperialism to the core-periphery division of labor and the struggle to monopolize world trade.

95. Although some have likened Robbin's argument to an economic security dilemma created by the anarchic structure of states, the model does not fit perfectly. Because one can relatively quickly respond to a rival's efforts to set up protected colonial trade zones with one's own, the advantage of being the first to defect from cooperative free trade arrangements are marginal. This would be an iterated prisoner's dilemma game, which under certain conditions generates cooperative behavior (Axelrod, 1984). A more plausible explanation is that the preference structures of all states do not fit the prisoner's dilemma model. Economically less efficient states cannot compete with more efficient states and those with greater resources, cannot rely on the law of comparative advantage and their trading partners' good will in bad diplomatic times as well as good, and prefer politically more secure markets, investment opportunities, and sources of raw materials to a cooperative free trade outcome. Only wealthy and efficient insular states (for example, Great Britain and then the United States) or those with security guarantees from such states are militarily secure enough to reap the economic benefits of free trade.

96. Snyder (1988) is one who attempts to integrate strategic, economic, and domestic political variables into a theory of imperialism, and Doyle (1986) is another.

97. Many of these studies were part of a larger research program on the relationship between national attributes in general and foreign conflict behavior. Hypotheses that certain political cultures, ideologies, or religions are more warlike than others have found little support in the quantitative empirical literature (Richardson, 1960:Chaps. 7–9; Haas, 1965; Rummel, 1968; Tanter, 1966). Attempts to trace war to *differences* between societies in their religions, languages, ideologies, and other characteristics have been slightly more successful, generally finding positive but weak relationships between societal differences and war. Most of the hypotheses under consideration, however, are basically ad hoc in nature and have not been integrated into a more comprehensive theoretical framework and, as a result, it is not clear how the findings should be interpreted. One problem is the lack of much attention to the causal mechanisms involved in the processes leading to war. Do societal differences contribute to war by generating conflicts of interests, or by creating misleading images of the adversary that lead to misperceptions of adversary intentions and a conflict spiral?

98. Rummel's (1983) research suggests that democratic states have been less war prone than nondemocratic states, but this finding is biased by his exclusion of extra-systemic (imperial) wars, his tendency to focus primarily on democratic pairs or nondemocratic pairs rather than mixed pairs of states, and the restriction of most of his analyses to the 1976–1980 period (Chan, 1984).

99. The War of 1812 might be one, had Great Britain been classified as democratic at that time.

100. One question is whether the nonoccurrence of war between democracies can

be "explained" statistically, given the relatively small number of democracies in the system, particularly for the first 100 years of the post-Vienna period. In addition, with a fairly large percentage of all democracies over the past 170 years existing in the post-World War II period and being associated with the United States, could the democracy-peace inference be spurious and derive from the stabilizing effects of bipolarity and American dominance within the free world?

101. There is some evidence that rally-round-the-flag effects for U.S. political leaders have half-lives of perhaps less than 2 months (Russett, this volume). If the war drags on, if it has a significant impact on society, if important national interests are not perceived to be at stake, and if the war effort is not perceived to be unambiguously effective, the war will have detrimental effects on the political leaders involved in initiating the war. This is demonstrated by Cotton's (1986) quantitative empirical study of five U.S. wars since 1898. It is not clear, however, whether these patterns apply to other states. The beneficial effects of war for the regime in power may be more extended, as illustrated by Khomeni's Iran in its war against Iraq, although the fact than Iran did not initiate the war may limit the relevance of this case. Note that the important consideration for our purposes is not the reaction of the public, but political leaders' expectation of that reaction in the period prior to the war. The tendency of political leaders to minimize the likelihood that forceful external actions short of war will actually escalate to war and their tendency to exaggerate the probability of a short, victorious, and relatively costless war (Blainey, 1973:Chap. 3; Levy, 1983a) would help explain the tendency toward scapegoating in spite of detrimental effects over time.

102. Exceptions to this general neglect can be found in the recent work by Lebow (1981, 1985b), Stein (1985a, 1985b), and Lebow and Stein (1987) on the impact of domestic politics on deterrence.

103. The similarity in these studies is because they were all highly influenced by Rummel's (1963) research design and specific indicators, and many use his data. For more detailed critiques of these studies, see Scolnick (1974), Mack (1975), and Levy (1989a).

104. These include the Falklands/Malvinas War (Hastings and Jenkins, 1983), World War I (Kehr, 1970; Fischer, 1975; Mommsen, 1973; Kaiser, 1983), the Crimean War (Anderson, 1967), and the French Revolutionary wars (Blanning, 1986:Chap. 5). See Levy (1988a) for a brief summary of some of the arguments.

105. For a more thorough critique of the diversionary theory of war and an attempt to specify some of the conditions under which scapegoating is most likely, see Levy (1989a).

106. These bodies of literature generally build on the work of March and Simon (1958), Cyert and March (1963), Allison (1971), and other early organizational theorists. They give little or no attention to recent developments in organizational theory. For surveys of recent developments see Pfeffer (1982), Perrow (1986), and Harmon and Mayer (1986).

107. My own view is that only the first of these arguments is plausible, and that apart from budgetary considerations equally plausible arguments can be made regarding the advantages of defensive doctrines for advancing organizational goals of uncertainty avoidance, autonomy, and morale.

108. A doctrine may call for no first strike but a strategy of deep territorial penetration if one is attacked, as in Israeli doctrine in 1973 and German military doctrine in the 1870s and 1880s (Langer, 1964).

109. Note that instead of offensive doctrines increasing the likelihood of war, the relationship may be reversed. The anticipation of war may lead to the formation of alliances for protection, which may lead states to adopt offensive military doctrines: the defense of one's allies often requires a doctrine calling for deep territorial penetration (France and Russia in 1914), and a state facing a two-front war may adopt a doctrine calling for the preemptive move against and quick defeat of one enemy before the other can enter the war in full force (Germany's Schlieffen Plan in 1914) (Levy, 1986:203–207, 1988d; Sagan, 1986).

110. Some of these hypotheses and analogies are probably also applicable to cases of Israeli mobilization, although the rigidity of Israeli mobilization plans derives from societal and economic constraints as much as strictly military considerations. There has been little systematic work on this question by political scientists (Horowitz, 1987).

111. This section is based in part on two of my earlier articles on misperception and war (Levy, 1983b, 1989c).

112. Among the factors emphasized by political scientists are tendencies to exhibit overconfidence, to ignore value trade-offs, to assimilate new information into preexisting belief systems, to overrely on historical analogies in general and past successes in particular, and to engage in wishful thinking, bolstering, cognitive dissonance, and similar patterns of behavior.

113. This framework is based on the conceptualizations in Levy (1983b, 1989c) and Jervis (1983, 1988a). For a discussion of types of phenomena that should *not* be classified as misperception, including beliefs and images, see Levy (1983b).

114. See Note 12.

115. For an alternative interpretation see Higonnet (1968).

116. It is more difficult in these situations for the analyst to make a causal link between misperception and war, for it is not clear that correct perceptions would lead to actions that would avoid war.

117. These misperceptions can cut both ways. Tzar Nicholas correctly perceived that Prime Minister Aberdeen had peaceful intentions on the eve of the Crimean War but erroneously perceived that he would be able to impose his views on a more hawkish cabinet (and stay in power).

118. The research of Huth and Russett (1984) and Huth (1988) on extended deterrence is relevant here. They find that the likelihood of attack is more affected by the local and immediate balance of military forces (proximate to the target) between the potential aggressor and the defender than by the overall balance of military forces or the ultimate military potential of the two adversaries.

119. It is often argued that Germany's perception that an Austro-Serbian war could be localized in the Balkans without Russian intervention and that Britain would not intervene in a continental war were important factors leading Germany to encourage the Austrian actions that precipitated the war (Lebow, 1981; Levy, 1988d). Similarly, Corinth's war against Corcyra, which led to the Peloponnesian War, was predicated on the erroneous assumption that Athens would not intervene (Kagan, 1969:351).

120. Whether political decision makers do in fact treat their perceptions of adversary capabilities and intentions as subjective probability estimates is an interesting research question. There may be a tendency, perhaps deriving from the avoidance of value trade-offs, overconfidence, bolstering, and generally from the use of a limited number of heuristics, for actors to deny the probabilistic nature of their estimates of adversary intentions and capabilities (Kahneman et al., 1982; Nisbett and Ross, 1980).

121. In this sense the third party criteria involves both accuracy and process criteria.

122. Jervis (1976:7) favors the careful use of the third-party criterion whereas Lebow (1981:91) is more skeptical of its utility. For an application of this method to the important question of German perceptions of British intentions in 1914, see Sagan (1986).

123. Stein (1982) uses a game-theoretic framework to analyze the conditions under which misperception affects behavior and concludes that "misperception creates conflict only in a narrowly circumscribed range of situations." It is possible, however, that this narrow range of theoretical conditions actually occurs quite frequently in international politics, but this is an empirical question requiring further research (Levy, 1983b:99fn).

124. This is changing, as more scholars within both the quantitative and qualitative traditions are dealing with the question of the conditions under which crises do and do not escalate to war and include cases of nonwar as well as war.

125. The following discussion is concerned with the nature of a major war between nuclear states. The nuclear revolution has had far less impact on the nature of warfare and the causes of war among other states, but space constraints preclude a more thorough examination of that question here.

126. The decline of population defense in fact has not been quite so sudden. Militarily powerful states have never been able to provide absolute protection for their citizens, and terrorist attacks across state territorial borders have occurred for millenia (Bell, 1975; Laqueur, 1978). The feasibility of population defense began to erode much more rapidly in this century, even before the development of nuclear weapons, with the emergence of technology and doctrine of strategic bombing in the 1920s and 1930s. This was recognized by Douhet ([1921] 1942) and other "air power" theorists at the time and emphasized by numerous theorists early in the nuclear age (Herz, 1957; Brodie, 1959; Quester, 1966). German "buzz bombs" and U.S. fire bombing were intended more to intimidate the enemy population and destroy their morale than to weaken their military forces, and these actions were possible prior to military victory. With only conventional explosives, however, such weapons were not decisive, and the outcome of the European war was decided in the old-fashioned way, by military forces on the battlefield, not by political bargaining based on coercive threats. It was not until the lessons of Hiroshima and Nagasaki began to sink in that it became clear that something new had occurred and that the erosion of population defense would have profound political implications.

127. This is different from the assertion that war has always been rational for at least one belligerent.

128. If political decision makers ever perceived their alternatives as being (1) all-out nuclear war or (2) political concessions so extensive as to negate the state's very

existence as a sovereign territorial entity, their choice might be less predictable. The behavior of the superpowers over the last four decade gives every reason to believe, however, that they would do everything possible to avoid confronting their adversary with such a stark choice.

129. Moreover, it is quite possible that one's overall position in the international hierarchy would actually decline relative to that of nonsuperpowers who were less directly impacted by the war.

130. Examples might include the Berlin crises of 1958 and 1961 and the Cuban missile crisis of 1962.

131. The function of military force in international politics has been transformed in other ways as well. As Art (1980:15) argues, for nuclear states "nuclear weapons have downgraded the function of defense, ruled out physical nuclear compellence, enhanced deterrence and nuclear swaggering, and left unclear the utility of peaceful nuclear compellence." Here "defense" refers to the deployment and use of military force to block an enemy attack, minimize the damage to oneself, and fight the war to a successful conclusion. Compellence refers to the use of force or the threat of force to persuade an adversary to change his behavior. Art thus argues that the use of force by nuclear states for compellent purposes is no longer viable, but that the utility of *threats* of force for compellent purposes (which Art misleadingly calls "peaceful" compellence) is not yet clear. Swaggering refers to the possession or demonstration of military force for the purposes of enhancing prestige.

132. One such effort to go beyond the question of the likelihood of a major war to that of its more specific causes is Jervis (1988*b*).

133. For studies of the incentives for preemption see Schelling (1960), Jervis (1978), Wagner (1983), Snyder (1985), and Betts (1985).

134. A second-strike capability involves the high likelihood that one has the capacity to absorb an initial first strike by the adversary, retaliate, and inflict unacceptable damage.

135. Research in social psychology suggests that risk orientations are highly unpredictable with regard to events with probabilities approaching zero or one. Kahneman and Tversky (1979), who present considerable evidence that individuals tend to be risk averse with respect to gains and risk acceptant with respect to losses, concede that these tendencies may reverse at very low probabilities, as the example of insurance suggests.

136. Two exceptions, from rather different methodological perspectives, come immediately to mind. One is George's emphasis on the development of conditional generalizations (George and Smoke, 1974). The other is Bueno de Mesquita's (1981*a*, 1988) attempt to resolve many of these inconsistencies by subsuming apparently contradictory hypotheses under a single expected utility framework.

References

Albertini, L. 1957. *The Origins of the War of 1914*. 3 vols. Trans. by I.M. Massey. London: Oxford University Press.

Allison, G.T. 1971. *Essence of Decision*. Boston: Little, Brown.
———. 1977. Questions about the arms race: Who's racing whom? A bureaucratic perspective. In J. Endicott and R.W. Stafford, eds., *American Defense Policy*, 4th ed. Baltimore: Johns Hopkins University Press.
Allison, G.T., A. Carnesale, and J.S. Nye, Jr., eds. 1985. *Hawks, Doves, and Owls*. New York: Norton.
Altfeld, M. 1983. Arms races? and escalation? A comment on Wallace. *International Studies Quarterly* 27:225–235.
Anderson, O. 1967. *A Liberal State at War*. New York: St. Martin's Press.
Aron, R. 1955. *The Century of Total War*. Boston: Beacon.
———. 1968. War and industrial society. In L. Bramson and G.W. Goethals, eds., *War*, pp. 359–402. New York: Basic Books.
Arrow, K.J. 1951. *Social Choice and Individual Values*. New York: Wiley.
Art, R. J. 1980. To what ends military power? *International Security* 4:3–35.
———. 1982. The role of military power in international relations. In B.T. Trout and J.E. Harf, eds., *National Security Affairs*, pp. 13–53. New Brunswick, N.J.: Transaction Books.
Ashley, R.K. 1980. *The Political Economy of War and Peace*. London: Frances Pinter.
Axelrod, R. 1976. *Structure of Decision*. Princeton: Princeton University Press.
———. 1984. *The Evolution of Cooperation*. New York: Basic Books.
Babst, D. 1972. A force for peace. *Industrial Research* 14:55–58.
Barringer, R.E. 1972. *War: Patterns of Conflict*. Cambridge, Mass.: MIT Press.
Barry, B., and R. Hardin, eds. 1982. *Rational Man and Irrational Society?* Beverly Hills, Calif.: Sage.
Beer, F.A. 1981. *Peace Against War*. San Francisco, Calif.: Freeman.
Beer, F.A., and T.F. Mayer. 1986. Why wars end: Some hypotheses. *Review of International Studies* 12:95–106.
Bell, J.B. 1975. *Transnational Terror*. Washington, D.C.: American Enterprise Institute.
Berghahn, V.R. 1969. *Militarism*. Cambridge, England: Cambridge University Press.
———. 1973. *Germany and the Approach of War in 1914*. New York: St. Martin's Press.
Betts, R.K. 1985. Surprise attack and preemption. In G.T. Allsion, A. Carnesale, and J.S. Nye, Jr., eds., *Hawks, Doves, and Owls*. New York: Norton.
———. 1987. *Nuclear Blackmail and Nuclear Balance*. Washington, D.C.: The Brookings Institution.
Blainey, G. 1973. *The Causes of War*. New York: Free Press.
Blair, B.G. 1985. *Strategic Command and Control: Redefining the Nuclear Threat*. Washington, D.C.: The Brookings Institution.
Blanning, T.C.W. 1986. *The French Revolutionary Wars*. London: Longman.
Blechman, B.M. 1985. *Preventing Nuclear War*. Bloomington, Ind.: Indiana University Press.
Blechman, B., and S.S. Kaplan. 1978. *Force Without War*. Washington, D.C.: The Brookings Institution.

Bloomfield, L.P., and A.C. Leiss. 1969. *Controlling Small Wars*. New York: Knopf.
Bodin, J. [1593] 1955. *Six Books of the Commonwealth*. Abridged and trans. by M.J. Tooley. Oxford: Basil Blackwell.
Boulding, K.E. 1962. *Conflict and Defense*. New York: Harper & Row.
Bracken, P. 1983. *The Command and Control of Nuclear Forces*. New Haven, Conn.: Yale University Press.
Brams, S.J., and D.M. Kilgour. 1988. *Game Theory and National Security*. New York: Basil Blackwell.
―――. 1989. Are crises rational? A game-theoretic analysis. New York University and Wilfrid Laurier University. Mimeo.
Bramson, L., and Goethals, G.W. 1968. *War*. New York: Basic Books.
Brecher, M. 1980. *Decisions in Crises*. Berkeley, Calif.: University of California Press.
Brueilly, J. 1985. *Nationalism and the State*. Chicago: University of Chicago Press.
Brodie, B. 1946. *The Absolute Weapon*. New York: Harcourt.
―――. 1959. *Strategy in the Missile Age*. Princeton, N.J.: Princeton University Press.
―――. 1973. *War and Politics*. New York: Macmillan.
Brody, R. 1984. International crises: A rallying point for the president? *Public Opinion* 6:41–43, 60.
Brown, S. 1987. *The Causes of War and the Prevention of Peace*. New York: St. Martin's Press.
Bueno de Mesquita, B. 1975. Measuring systemic polarity. *Journal of Conflict Resolution* 19:77–96.
―――. 1980a. Theories of international conflict: An analysis and an appraisal. In T.R. Gurr, ed., *Handbook of Political Conflict*, pp. 361–398, New York: Free Press.
―――. 1980b. An expected utility theory of international conflict. *American Political Science Review* 74:917–931.
―――. 1981a. *The War Trap*. New Haven, Conn.: Yale University Press.
―――. 1981b. Risk, power distributions, and the likelihood of war. *International Studies Quarterly* 25:541–568.
―――. 1983. The costs of war: a rational expectations approach. *American Political Science Review* 77:347–357.
―――. 1985. The war trap revisited: A revised expected utility model. *American Political Science Review* 79:157–176.
―――. 1988 The contribution of expected utility theory to the study of international conflict. *Journal of Interdisciplinary History* 18:629–652.
Bueno de Mesquita, B., and D. Lalman. 1986. Reason and war. *American Political Science Review* 80:1113–1130.
―――. 1988a. Empirical support for systemic and dyadic explanations of international conflict. *World Politics* 41:1–20.
―――. 1988b. The road to war is strewn with peaceful intentions. Paper presented at the annual meeting of the American Political Science Association, Washington, D.C.

Burns, A.L. 1957. From balance to deterrence: A theoretical analysis. *World Politics* 9:494–529.
Butterworth, R.L. 1976. *Managing Interstate Conflict, 1945–1974: Data with Synopses*. Pittsburgh, Pa.: University of Pittsburgh Center for International Studies.
Buzan, B. 1984. Economic structure and international security: The limits of the liberal case. *International Organization* 38:597–624.
Center for Defense Information. 1987. *Nuclear War Quotations*. Washington, D.C.: Center for Defense Information.
Chan, S. 1984. Mirror, mirror on the wall: Are the freer countries more pacific? *Journal of Conflict Resolution* 28:617–648.
Chatterjee, P. 1975. *Arms, Alliances and Stability*. Bombay, India: Macmillan.
Chivian, E., S. Chivian, R.J. Lifton, and J.E. Mack, eds. 1982. *Last Aid: The Medical Dimensions of Nuclear War*. San Francisco: Freeman.
Choucri, N., and R.C. North 1972. In search of peace systems: Scandinavia and the Netherlands, 1870–1970. In B.M. Russett, ed., *Peace, War, and Numbers*. Beverly Hills: Sage.
———. 1975. *Nations in Conflict*. San Francisco: Freeman.
———. 1986. Lateral pressure and international conflict: The case of Japan. Paper presented at the annual meeting of the American Political Science Association, Washington, D.C.
Claude, I.L., Jr. 1962. *Power and International Relations*. New York: Random House.
Cohen, B.J. 1973. *The Question of Imperialism*. New York: Basic Books.
Cornford, F. 1907. *Thucydides Mythistoricus*. New York: Greenwood.
Coser, L. 1956. *The Function of Social Conflict*. New York: Free Press.
Cotton, T.Y.C. 1986. War and American Democracy. *Journal of Conflict Resolution* 30:616–635.
Cyert, R.M., and J.G. March 1963. *A Behavioral Theory of the Firm*. Englewood Cliffs, N.J.: Prentice-Hall.
Deutsch, K., and J.D. Singer. 1964. Multipolar power systems and international stability. *World Politics* 16:390–406.
Douhet, G. [1921] 1942. *The Command of the Air*. Trans. by D. Ferrari. New York: Coward-McCann.
Doyle, M.W. 1983*a*. Kant, liberal legacies, and foreign affairs: Part 1. *Philosophy and Public Affairs* 12:205–235.
———. 1983*b*. Kant, liberal legacies, and foreign affairs: Part 2. *Philosophy and Public Affairs* 12:323–353.
———. 1986. *Empires*. Ithaca, N.Y.: Cornell University Press.
Duner, B. 1985. *Military Intervention in Civil Wars: The 1970's*. Aldershot, England: Gower.
Dupuy, R.E., and T.N. Dupuy. 1977. *The Encyclopedia of Military History*, rev. ed. New York: Harper & Row.
East, M.A., S.A. Salmore, and C.F. Hermann, eds. 1978. *Why Nations Act*. Beverly Hills: Sage.

Eckhardt, W., and E. Azar. 1978. Major world conflicts and interventions, 1945–1975. *International Interactions* 5:75–110.

Etheridge, L.S. 1985. *Can Governments Learn?* New York: Pergamon.

Falkowski, L.S., ed. 1979. *Psychological Models in International Politics.* Boulder, Col.: Westview.

Farrar, L.L., Jr. 1973. *The Short-War Illusion.* Santa Barbara, Calif.: ABC-Clio.

———. 1983. Reluctant warriors: Public opinion on war during the July crisis 1914. *East European Quarterly* 16:417–446.

Fay, S.B. [1928] 1966. *The Origins of the World War.* 2 vols., 2d ed., rev. New York: Free Press.

Ferrill, A. 1985. *The Origins of War.* London: Thames and Hudson.

Ferris, W. 1973. *The Power Capabilities of Nation States.* Lexington, Mass.: Lexington Books.

Fischer, F. 1961. *Germany's Aims in the First World War.* New York: Norton.

———. 1975. *War of Illusions.* New York: Norton.

Fleiss, P.J. 1966. *Thucydides and the Politics of Bipolarity.* Baton Rouge, La.: Louisiana State University Press.

Fox, T.R., ed. 1970. *Annals of the American Academy of Political and Social Science*, vol. 392; a special issue on war termination.

Frei, D. 1983. *Risks of Unintentional Nuclear War.* Totowa, New Jersey: Rowman & Allanheld.

Friedman, M. 1953. The methodology of positive economics. In M. Friedman, ed., *Essays in Positive Economics*, pp. 3–43. Chicago: University of Chicago Press.

Fromm, E. 1941. *Escape From Freedom.* New York: Rinehart.

Gaddis, J.L. 1987. *The Long Peace.* New York: Oxford University Press.

Gallagher, J., and R. Robinson. 1953. The imperialism of free trade. *Economic History Review*, Second Series 6:1–15.

Gallie, W.B. 1978. *Philosophers of Peace and War.* Cambridge, England: Cambridge University Press.

Galtung, J. 1964. A structural theory of aggression. *Journal of Peace Research* 1:95–119.

Garnham, D. 1976*a*. Dyadic international war, 1816–1965. *Western Political Quarterly* 29:231–242.

———. 1976*b*. Power parity and lethal international violence, 1969–1973. *Journal of Conflict Resolution* 20:379–394.

George, A.L. 1969. The "operational code": A neglected approach to the study of political leaders and decision-making. *International Studies Quarterly* 13:190–222.

———. 1976. Bridging the gap between theory and practice. In J.N. Rosenau, ed., *In Search of Global Patterns*, pp. 113–119. New York: Free Press.

———. 1980. *Presidential Decision Making in Foreign Policy.* Boulder, Col.: Westview.

———. 1983. *Managing U.S.-Soviet Rivalry.* Boulder, Col.: Westview.

———. 1984. Crisis management: The interaction of political and military considerations. *Survival* 26:223–234.

———. 1988. Incentives for U.S.-Soviet security cooperation and mutual adjustment. In A.L. George et al., eds., *U.S.-Soviet Security Cooperation*. New York: Oxford University Press.

George, A.L., D.K. Hall, and W.R. Simons. 1971. *The Limits of Coercive Diplomacy*. Boston: Little, Brown.

George, A.L., and R. Smoke. 1974. *Deterrence in American Foreign Policy*. New York: Columbia University Press.

Gilbert, M. 1967. *Churchill*. Englewood Cliffs, N.J.: Prentice-Hall.

Gilpin, R. 1975. *U.S. Power and the Multinational Corporation*. New York: Basic Books.

———. 1981. *War and Change in World Politics*. Cambridge, England: Cambridge University Press.

Gochman, C.S., and R. Leng. 1988. Militarized disputes, incidents, and crises: Identification and classification. *International Interactions* 14:57–64.

Gochman, C.S., and Z. Maoz. 1984. Militarized interstate disputes, 1816–1976. *Journal of Conflict Resolution* 28:585–615.

Goldstein, J.S. 1985. Kondratieff waves as war cycles. *International Studies Quarterly* 29:411–444.

———. 1988. *Long Cycles*. New Haven, Conn.: Yale University Press.

Gompart, D.C. 1977. Constraints of military power: Lessons of the past decade. Adelphi paper No. 133. International Institute for Strategic Studies, London.

Green, P. 1970. *Armada from Athens*. London: Hodder and Stoughton.

Gulick, E.V. 1955. *Europe's Classical Balance of Power*. New York: Norton.

Haas, E.B. 1953. The balance of power: Prescription, concept, or propaganda. *World Politics* 5:442–477.

Haas, E.B., and A.S. Whiting. 1956. *Dynamics of International Relations*. New York: McGraw-Hill.

Haas, M. 1965. Societal approaches to the study of war. *Journal of Peace Research* 4:307–323.

———. 1974. *International Conflict*. Indianapolis: Bobbs-Merrill.

Halperin, M. 1963. *Limited War in the Nuclear Age*. New York: Wiley.

———. 1974. *Bureaucratic Politics and Foreign Policy*. Washington, D.C.: The Brookings Institution.

Hardach, G. 1977. *The First World War, 1914–1918*. Berkeley: University of California Press.

Hardin, R. 1982. *Collective Action*. Baltimore: Johns Hopkins University Press.

Harmon, M. M., and R.T. Mayer. 1986. *Organizational Theory for Public Administration*. Boston: Little, Brown.

Hastings, M., and S. Jenkins. 1983. *The Battle for the Falklands*. New York: Norton.

Hempel, C.G. 1966. *Philosophy of Natural Science*. Englewood Cliffs, N.J.: Prentice-Hall.

Hermann, C.F., C.W. Kegley, Jr., and J.N. Rosenau, eds. 1987. *New Directions in the Study of Foreign Policy*. Boston: Allen & Unwin.

Herz, J. 1957. Rise and demise of the territorial state. *World Politics* 9:473–493.

Higonnet, P.L.R. 1968. The origins of the Seven Years' War. *Journal of Modern History* 40:57–90.

Hilferding, R. [1910] 1981. *Finance Capital*. London: Routledge & Kegan Paul.

Hobbes, T. [1651] 1962. *Leviathan*. M. Oakeshott, ed. New York: Collier Books.

Hobson, J.A. [1902] 1954. *Imperialism*. London: Allen & Unwin.

Hoffmann, S. 1968. Balance of power. In *International Encyclopedia of the Social Sciences*, Vol. 1, pp. 506–510. New York: Macmillan.

Hogarth, R., and M. Reder 1987. *Rational Choice*. Chicago: University of Chicago Press.

Holsti, K.J. 1985. *The Dividing Discipline: Hegemony and Diversity in International Theory*. Boston: Allen & Unwin.

Holsti, O.R. 1972. *Crisis, Escalation, War*. Montreal: McGill-Queens University Press.

Holsti, O.R., P.T. Hopmann, and J.D. Sullivan. 1973. *Unity and Disintegration in International Alliances*. New York: Wiley.

Hoole, F.W., and D.A. Zinnes. 1976. *Quantitative International Politics: An Appraisal*. New York: Praeger.

Horowitz, D. 1987. Strategic limitations of "a nation in arms." *Armed Forces and Society* 13:277–294.

Houweling, H., and J.G. Siccama. 1988. *Studies of War*. Dordrecht, the Netherlands: Martinus Nijhoff.

Howard, M. 1976. *War in European History*. Oxford, England: Oxford University Press.

———. 1983. *The Causes of Wars*. Cambridge, Mass.: Harvard University Press.

Huth, P. 1988. *Extended Deterrence and the Prevention of Wars*. New Haven, Conn.: Yale University Press.

Huth, P., and B. Russett. 1984. What makes deterrence work? Cases from 1900 to 1980. *World Politics* 36:496–526.

———. 1988. Deterrence failure and crisis escalation. *International Studies Quarterly* 32:29–46.

Huntington, S.P. 1958. Arms races: Prerequisites and results. In C.J. Friedrich and S.E. Harris, eds., *Public Policy*, Vol. 8, pp. 41–86. Cambridge, Mass.: Graduate School of Public Administration, Harvard University.

Iggers, G.G. 1984. *New Directions in European Historiography*, rev. ed. Middletown, Conn.: Wesleyan University Press.

Iklé, F.C. 1971. *Every War Must End*. New York: Columbia University Press.

Jacobson, H.K. 1960. *America's Foreign Policy*. New York: Random House.

Janis, I.L. 1972. *Victims of Groupthink*. Boston: Houghton Mifflin.

———. 1982. *Groupthink*, 2d ed. Boston: Houghton Mifflin.

Janis, I.L., and L. Mann. 1977. *Decision Making*. New York: Free Press.

Jervis, R. 1976. *Perception and Misperception in International Politics*. Princeton, N.J.: Princeton University Press.

———. 1978. Cooperation under the security dilemma. *World Politics* 30:167–214.

———. 1979. Deterrence theory revisited. *World Politics* 31:289–324.

———. 1983. Deterrence and perception. *International Security* 7:3–30.
———. 1984. *The Illogic of American Nuclear Strategy*. Ithaca, N.Y.: Cornell University Press.
———. 1988a. War and misperception. *Journal of Interdisciplinary History* 18:675–700.
———. 1988b. The political effects of nuclear weapons. *International Security* 13:80–90.
———. 1989. *The Meaning of the Nuclear Revolution*. Ithaca, N.Y.: Cornell University Press.
Kagan, D. 1969. *The Outbreak of the Peloponnesian War*. Ithaca, N.Y.: Cornell University Press.
Kahn, H. 1965. *On Escalation*. New York: Praeger.
Kahneman, D., P. Slovic, and A. Tversky. 1982. *Judgment under Uncertainty: Heuristics and Biases*. Cambridge, England: Cambridge University Press.
Kahneman, D., and A. Tversky. 1979. Prospect theory: An analysis of decision under risk. *Econometrica* 47:263–291.
Kaiser, D. 1983. Germany and the origins of the First World War. *Journal of Modern History* 55:442–474.
Kant, I. [1795] 1949. Eternal peace. In *The Philosophy of Kant*, pp. 430–476. C.J. Friedrich, ed. New York: Modern Library.
Kaplan, M.A. 1957. *System and Process in International Politics*. New York: Wiley.
Kaplan, S.S. 1981. *Diplomacy of Power: Soviet Armed Forces as a Political Instrument*. Washington, D.C.: The Brookings Institution.
Karsten, P., P.D. Howell, and A.F. Allen. 1984. *Military Threats: A Systematic Historical Analysis of the Determinants of Success*. Westport, Conn.: Greenwood Press.
Kegley, C.W., Jr., ed. 1989. *The Long Postwar Peace*. Glencoe, Ill.: Scott, Foresman.
Kehr, E. 1970. *Der Primat der Innenpolitik*. Berlin: Walter de Gruyter.
Kende, I. 1971. Twenty-five years of local wars. *Journal of Peace Research* 1:5–22.
Kennedy, P.M., ed. 1987. *The Rise and Fall of the Great Powers: Economic Change and Military Conflict from 1500 to 2000*. New York: Random House.
Keohane, R.O. 1980. The theory of hegemonic stability and changes in international economic regimes, 1967–1977. In O.R. Holsti et al., eds., *Change in the International System*, pp. 131–162. Boulder, Col.: Westview.
———. 1983. Theory of world politics: Structural realism and beyond. In A. Finifter, ed., *Political Science: The State of the Discipline*, pp. 503–540. Washington, D.C.: American Political Science Association.
———. 1984. *After Hegemony*. Princeton, N.J.: Princeton University Press.
Keohane, R.O., and J.S. Nye. 1977. *Power and Interdependence*. Boston: Little, Brown.
Khong, Y.F. 1984. War and international theory: A commentary on the state of the art. *Review of International Studies* 10:41–63.
Kindleberger, C.P. 1973. *The World in Depression, 1929–1939*. Berkeley, Calif.: University of California Press.

Kissinger, H. 1957. *Nuclear Weapons and Foreign Policy*. New York: Harper.
———. 1982. *Years of Upheaval*. Boston: Little, Brown.
Knorr, K. 1966. *On the Uses of Military Power in the Nuclear Age*. Princeton, N.J.: Princeton University Press.
———. 1970. *Military Power and Potential*. Lexington, Mass.: Heath.
———. 1977. On the international uses of military power in the nuclear age. *Orbis* 21:5–27.
Koch, H.W., ed. 1972. *The Origins of the First World War: Great Power Rivalry and German War Aims*. New York: Macmillan.
Krasner, S.D. 1976. State power and the structure of international trade. *World Politics* 28:317–347.
Krasner, S.D. 1983. *International Regimes*. Ithaca, N.Y.: Cornell University Press.
Kugler, J. 1984. Terror without deterrence: Reassessing the role of nuclear deterrence. *Journal of Conflict Resolution* 28:470–506.
Kuhn, T.S. 1962. *The Structure of Scientific Revolutions*. Chicago: University of Chicago Press.
Lakatos, I. 1970. Falsification and the methodology of scientific research programs. In I. Lakatos and A. Musgrave, eds., *Criticism and the Growth of Knowledge*, pp. 91–196. London: Cambridge University Press.
Langer, W.L. 1964. *European Alliances and Alignments, 1871-1890*, 2d. ed. New York: Vintage.
Laqueur, W., ed. 1978. *The Terrorism Reader: A Historical Anthology*. New York: New American Library.
Lebow, R.N. 1981. *Between Peace and War*. Baltimore: Johns Hopkins University Press.
———. 1984. Windows of opportunity: Do states jump through them? *International Security* 9:147–186.
———. 1985a. The deterrence deadlock: Is there a way out? In R. Jervis, et al., *Psychology and Deterrence*, pp. 180–202. Baltimore: Johns Hopkins University Press.
———. 1985b. Conclusions. In R. Jervis et al., *Psychology and Deterrence*, pp. 203–232. Baltimore: Johns Hopkins University Press.
———. 1987. *Nuclear Crisis Management*. Ithaca, N.Y.: Cornell University Press.
Lebow, R.N., and J.G. Stein. 1987. Beyond deterrence. *Journal of Social Issues* 43:5–71.
Leng, R.J. 1983. When will they ever learn? Coercive bargaining in recurrent crises. *Journal of Conflict Resolution* 27:379–420.
Leng, R.J., and J.D. Singer. 1988. Militarized interactive crises: The BCOW typology and its applications. *International Studies Quarterly* 32:155–174.
Lenin, V.I. [1917] 1939. *Imperialism*. New York: International.
Lens, S. 1970. *The Military-Industrial Complex*. Philadelphia: Pilgrim Press.
Levy, J.S. 1981. Alliance formation and war behavior. *Journal of Conflict Resolution* 25:581–614.
———. 1982. Historical trends in great power war, 1495–1975. *International Studies Quarterly* 26:278–300.

———. 1983a. *War in the Modern Great Power System, 1495-1975*. Lexington, Ky.: University Press of Kentucky.

———. 1983b. Misperception and the causes of war. *World Politics* 35:76–99.

———. 1984a. The offensive/defensive balance of military technology. *International Studies Quarterly* 28:219–238.

———. 1984b. Size and stability in the modern great power system. *International Interactions* 10:76–99.

———. 1985a. Theories of general war. *World Politics* 37:344–374.

———. 1985b. The polarity of the system and international stability. In A.N. Sabrosky, ed., *Polarity and War*, pp. 41–66. Boulder, Col.: Westview.

———. 1986. Organizational routines and the causes of war. *International Studies Quarterly* 30:193–222.

———. 1987. Declining power and the preventive motivation for war. *World Politics* 40:82–107.

———. 1988a. Domestic politics and war. *Journal of Interdisciplinary History* 18:653–673.

———. 1988b. Analytic problems in the identification of wars. *International Interactions* 14:181–186.

———. 1988c. When do deterrent threats work? *British Journal of Political Science* 18:485–512.

———. 1988d. The role of crisis mismanagement in the outbreak of World War I. Paper presented at the annual meeting of the American Political Science Association, Washington, D.C.

———. 1989a. The diversionary theory of war. In M.I. Midlarsky, ed., *Handbook of War Studies*. Boston: Unwin Hyman.

———. 1989b. Quantitative studies of deterrence success and failure. In P. Stern, R. Axelrod, R. Jervis, and R. Radner, eds., *Perspectives on Deterrence*. New York: Oxford University Press.

———. 1989c. War and perception. In R.O. Matthews, A.G. Rubinoff, and J.G. Stein, eds., *International Conflict and Conflict Management*, 2d ed., pp. 45–52. Englewood Cliffs, N.J.: Prentice-Hall.

Levy, J., and T.C. Morgan. 1984. The frequency and seriousness of war: An inverse relationship? *Journal of Conflict Resolution* 28:731–749.

Lider, J.1977. *On the Nature of War*. Farnborough, England: Saxon House.

———. 1979. *The Political and Military Laws of War: An Analysis of Marxist-Leninist Concepts*. Farnborough, England: Saxon House.

Liska, G.1962. *Nations in Alliance*. Baltimore: Johns Hopkins University Press.

Luxemburg, R. [1913] 1951. *The Accumulation of Capital*. London: Routledge & Kegan Paul.

Mack, A. 1975. Numbers are not enough: A critique of internal/external conflict behavior research. *Comparative Politics* 7:597–618.

Magdoff, H. 1969. *The Age of Imperialism*. New York: Monthly Review.

Majeski, S.J., and D.J. Sylvan. 1984. Simple choices and complex calculations: A critique of *The War Trap*. *Journal of Conflict Resolution* 28:316–340.

Mandelbaum, M. 1981. *The Nuclear Revolution*. Cambridge, England: Cambridge University Press.

Mansbach, R.W., and J.A. Vasquez 1981. *In Search of Theory: A New Paradigm for Global Politics.* New York: Columbia University Press.

Maoz, Z. 1982*a*. The expected-utility of international conflict: Some theoretical problems and empirical surprises in "The War Trap." University of Haifa. Mimeo.

―――. 1982*b*. *Paths to Conflict: International Dispute Initiation, 1816-1976.* Boulder, Col.: Westview.

―――. 1983. Resolve, capabililties, and the outcomes of interstate disputes, 1816–1976. *Journal of Conflict Resolution* 27:195–229.

―――. 1989. Paradoxes of war. New York University. Mimeo.

March, J.G. 1978. Bounded rationality, ambiguity, and the engineering of choice. *Bell Journal of Economics* 9:587–608.

March, J.G., and H.A. Simon. 1958. *Organizations.* New York: Wiley.

May, E. 1973. *Imperial Democracy.* New York: Harper Torchbooks.

Mayer, A.J. 1959. *Political Origins of the New Diplomacy, 1917–1918.* New Haven, Conn.: Yale University Press.

Mefford, D. 1987. Analogical reasoning and the definition of the situation: Back to Snyder for concepts and forward to artificial intelligence for method. In C.F. Hermann, C.W. Kegley, Jr., and J.N. Rosenau, eds., *New Directions in the Study of Foreign Policy,* pp. 221–244. Boston: Allen & Unwin.

Melman, S. 1970. *Pentagon Capitalism: The Political Economy of War.* New York: Oxford University Press.

Millis, W. 1956. *Arms and Men.* New York: Mentor Books.

Mills, C.W. 1956. *The Power Elite.* New York: Oxford University Press.

Mitchell, C.R., and M. Nicholson. 1983. Rational models and the ending of wars. *Journal of Conflict Resolution* 27:495–520.

Modelski, G. 1978. The long cycle of global politics and the nation-state. *Comparative Studies in Society and History* 20:214–235.

―――. 1987*a*. *Exploring Long Cycles.* Boulder, Col.: Lynne Rienner.

―――. 1987*b*. *Long Cycles in World Politics.* Seattle: University of Washington Press.

Modelski, G., and W.R. Thompson. 1988. *Seapower in Global Politics, 1494–1993.* Seattle: University of Washington Press.

Moe, T.M. 1979. On the scientific status of rational models. *American Journal of Political Science* 23:215–243.

Mommsen, W.J. 1973. Domestic factors in German foreign policy before 1914. *Central European History* 6:3–43.

Montesquieu, C.L. [1750] 1949. *The Spirit of the Laws.* Trans. by T. Nugent. New York: Hafner.

Morgan, T.C. 1984. A spatial model of crisis bargaining. *International Studies Quarterly* 28:407–426.

―――. 1988. Issue linkages in international crisis bargaining. Rice University. Mimeo.

―――. 1989. Power, resolve and bargaining in international crises. *International Interactions* (special edition).

Morgan, T.C., and J.S. Levy. 1986. The structure of the international system and the frequency and seriousness of war. In M.P. Karns, ed., *Persistent Patterns and*

Emergent Structures in a Waning Century, pp. 75–98. New York: Praeger.
———. 1989. Base stealers vs. power hitters: A nation-state level analysis of the frequency and seriousness of war. In C.S. Gochman and A.N. Sabrosky, eds., *Prisoners of War*. Lexington, Mass.: Lexington Books.
Morgan, T.C., and J.L. Ray. 1988. The impact of nuclear weapons on crisis bargaining. Rice University and Florida State University. Mimeo.
Morgenthau, H.J. 1967. *Politics Among Nations*, 4th ed. New York: Knopf.
Morrow, J. 1985. A continuous outcome expected utility theory of war. *Journal of Conflict Resolution* 29:473–502.
———. 1986. A spatial theory of international conflict. *American Political Science Review* 80:1131–1150.
———. 1987. On the theoretical basis of a measure of national risk attitudes. *International Studies Quarterly* 31:423–438.
———. 1988. Social choice and system structure in world politics. *World Politics* 41:45–97.
Moses, J.A. 1975. *The Politics of Illusion: The Fischer controversy in German Historiography*. London: George Prior.
Most, B.A., and H. Starr. 1984. International relations theory, foreign policy substitutability, and "nice" laws. *World Politics* 36:383–406.
———. 1987. Polarity, preponderance, and power parity in the generation of international conflict. *International Interactions* 13:225–262.
Mueller, J.E. 1973. *War, Presidents, and Public Opinion*. New York: Wiley.
———. 1988. The essential irrelevance of nuclear weapons: stability in the post-war world. *International Security* 13:55–79.
Nagel, E. 1961. *The Structure of Science*. New York: Harcourt.
Nelson, S.D. 1974. Nature/nurture revisited I: A review of the biological bases of conflict. *Journal of Conflict Resolution* 18:285–335.
Nelson, K.L., and S.C. Olin. 1979. *Why War?* Berkeley, Calif.: University of California Press.
Niou, E.M.S., and P. Ordeshook. 1986. A theory of the balance of power in international systems. *Journal of Conflict Resolution* 30:685–715.
———. 1987. Preventive war and the balance of power. *Journal of Conflict Resolution* 31:387–419.
Nisbett, R., and L. Ross. 1980. *Human Inference*. Englewood Cliffs, N.J.: Prentice-Hall.
Nogee, J. 1975. Polarity: An ambiguous concept. *Orbis* 18:1193–1224.
North, R.C. 1967. Perception and action in the 1914 crisis. *Journal of International Affairs* 21:103–122.
North, R.C., O.R. Holsti, and N. Choucri. 1976. A reevaluation of the research program of the Stanford Studies in International Conflict and Integration. In F.W. Hoole and D.A. Zinnes, eds., *Quantitative International Politics*, pp. 435–459. New York: Praeger Press.
Olson, M. 1965. *The Logic of Collective Action*. Cambridge, Mass.: Harvard University Press.
———. 1982. *The Rise and Decline of Nations*. New Haven, Conn.: Yale University Press.

O'Neill, B. 1986. International escalation and the dollar auction. *Journal of Conflict Resolution* 30:33–50.

Ordeshook, P.C. 1986. *Game Theory and Political Theory*. New York: Cambridge University Press.

Organski, A.F.K. 1968. *World Politics*, 2d ed. New York: Knopf.

Organski, A.F.K., and J. Kugler. 1980. *The War Ledger*. Chicago: University of Chicago Press.

Osgood, R.E. 1957. *Limited War*. Chicago: University of Chicago Press.

———. 1967. The expansion of force. In R.E. Osgood and R.W. Tucker, eds., *Force, Order, and Justice*. Baltimore: Johns Hopkins University Press.

———. 1979. *Limited War Revisited*. Boulder, Col.: Westview.

Ostrom, C.W., Jr. 1977. Evaluating alternative foreign policy decision-making models: An empirical test between an arms race model and an organizational politics model. *Journal of Conflict Resolution* 21:235–266.

Ostrom, C.W., Jr., and J.H. Aldrich. 1978. The relationship between size and stability in the major power international system. *American Journal of Political Science* 22:743–771.

Ostrom, C.W., Jr., and D.M Simon. 1985. Promise and performance: A dynamic model of presidential popularity. *American Political Science Review* 80:541–566.

Pearson, F.S. 1988. International military interventions. *International Interactions* 14:173–180.

Perrow, C. 1986. *Complex Organizations: A Critical Essay*, 3d ed. New York: Random House.

Peterson, J. 1983. *The Aftermath: The Human and Ecological consequences of Nuclear War*. New York: Pantheon.

Pfeffer, J. 1982. *Organizations and Organization Theory*. Boston: Pitman.

Posen, B.R. 1984. *The Sources of Military Doctrine*. Ithaca, N.Y.: Cornell University Press.

Powell, R. 1987. Crisis bargaining, escalation, and MAD. *American Political Science Review* 81:717–735.

Quester, G.H. 1966. *Deterrence before Hiroshima*. New York: Wiley.

———. 1977. *Offense and Defense in the International System*. New York: Wiley.

Rapkin, D.P., W.R. Thompson, and J.A. Christopherson. 1979. Bipolarity and bipolarization in the Cold War era: Conceptualization, measurement, and validation. *Journal of Conflict Resolution* 23:261–295.

Rapoport, A., and A.M. Chammah. 1965. *Prisoners' Dilemma*. Ann Arbor, Mich.: University of Michigan Press.

Rasler, K.A., and W.R. Thompson. 1983. Global wars, public debts, and the long cycle. *World Politics* 35:489–516.

———. 1985*a*. War making and state making: Governmental expenditures, tax revenues, and global wars. *American Political Science Review* 79:491–507.

———. 1985*b*. War and the economic growth of major powers. *American Journal of Political Science* 29:513–538.

Richardson, L.F. 1960. *Statistics of Deadly Quarrels*. Chicago: Quadrangle.

Riker, W. 1962. *The Theory of Political Coalitions*. New Haven, Conn.: Yale University Press.
Ritter, G. 1958. *The Schlieffen Plan*. Trans. by A. Wilson and E. Wilson. New York: Praeger.
———. 1970. *The Sword and the Scepter: The Problem of Militarism in Germany*. 4 vols., Trans. by H. Norden. Coral Gables, Fla.: University of Miami Press.
Robbins, L. 1939. *The Economic Causes of War*. London: Jonathan Cape.
Roderick, H., with U. Magnusson. 1983. *Avoiding Inadvertent War: Crisis Management*. Austin, Tex.: University of Texas.
Rogers, J.P. 1986. The Crisis Bargaining Code Model: The Influence of Cognitive Beliefs and Processes on U.S. Policy-making During Crises. Ph.D. dissertation, University of Texas, Austin.
Rogowski, R. 1983. Structure, growth, and power: Three rationalist accounts. *International Organization* 37:713–738.
Rosecrance, R. 1963. *Action and Reaction in World Politics*. Boston: Little, Brown.
———. 1966. Bipolarity, multipolarity, and the future. *Journal of Conflict Resolution* 10:314–327.
———. 1986. *The Rise of the Trading State*. New York: Basic Books.
Rosen, S. 1973. *Testing the Theory of the Military-Industrial Complex*. Lexington, Mass.: Heath.
Rosenau, J.N. 1966. Pre-theories and theories of foreign policy. In R.B. Farrell, ed., *Approaches to Comparative and International Politics*, pp. 27–92. Evanston, Ill: Northwestern University Press.
Rummel, R. 1963. Dimensions of conflict behavior within and between nations. *General Systems* 8:1–50.
———. 1968. National attributes and foreign conflict behavior. In J.D. Singer, ed., *Quantitative International Politics*, pp. 187–214. New York: Free Press.
———. 1983. Libertarianism and international violence. *Journal of Conflict Resolution* 27:27–71.
Russett, B.M. 1963. The calculus of deterrence. *Journal of Conflict Resolution* 7:97–109.
———. 1967. Pearl Harbor: Deterrence theory and decision theory. *Journal of Peace Research* 4:89–105.
Russett, B.M., and J.J. Monsen. 1975. Bureaucracy and polyarchy as predictors of performance. *Comparative Political Studies* 8:8–31.
Sabrosky, A.N. 1980. Interstate alliances: Their reliability and the expansion of war. In J.D. Singer, ed., *The Correlates of War: II*, pp. 161–198. New York: Free Press.
Sabrosky, A.N., ed. 1985. *Polarity and War*. Boulder, Col.: Westview.
Sagan, S.D. 1985. Nuclear alerts and crisis management. *International Security* 9:99–139.
———. 1986. 1914 revisited: Allies, offense, and instability. *International Security* 11:151–175.
Sarkesian, S.C., ed. 1972. *The Military-Industrial Complex: A Reassessment*. Beverly Hills, Calif.: Sage.

Schelling, T.C. 1960. *The Strategy of Conflict*. Cambridge, Mass.: Harvard University Press.
———. 1966. *Arms and Influence*. New Haven, Conn.: Yale University Press.
———. 1978. *Micromotives and Macrobehavior*. New York: Norton.
Schmid, A.P. 1985. *Soviet Military Interventions Since 1945*. New Brunswick, N.J.: Transaction Books.
Schumpeter, J.A. [1919] 1951. *Imperialism and Social Classes*. Trans. by H. Norden. New York: Augustus M. Kelley.
Scolnick, J.M., Jr. 1974. An appraisal of studies of the linkages between domestic and international conflict. *Comparative Political Studies* 6:485–509.
Semmel, B., ed. 1981. *Marxism and the Science of War*. New York: Oxford University Press.
Shakespeare, W. [1598] 1845. *Henry IV, Part I*. London: Shakespeare Society.
Shirer, W.L. 1959. *The Rise and Fall of the Third Reich*. New York: Fawcet Crest.
Silberner, E. 1946. *The Problem of War in Nineteenth Century Economic Thought*. Trans. by A.H. Krappe. Princeton, N.J.: Princeton University Press.
Simon, H.A. 1955. A behavioral model of rational choice. *Quarterly Journal of Economics* 69:99–118.
Simmel, G. 1956. *Conflict*. Trans. by K.H. Wolff. Glencoe, Ill.: Free Press.
Singer, J.D. 1961. The levels of analysis problem in international relations. In K. Knorr and S. Verba, eds., *The International System*, pp. 77–92. Princeton, N.J.: Princeton University Press.
———. 1972. The "Correlates of War" project: Interim report and rationale. *World Politics* 24:243–270.
———. 1979a. *Explaining War*. Beverly Hills, Calif: Sage.
———. 1979b. *The Correlates of War, I: Research Origins and Rationale*. New York: Free Press.
———. 1980. *The Correlates of War, II: Testing Some Realpolitik Models*. New York: Free Press.
———. 1988. Reconstruction the Correlates of War dataset on material capabilities of states, 1816–1985. *International Interactions*, 14:115–32.
Singer, J.D., S.A. Bremer, and J. Stuckey. 1972. Capability distribution, uncertainty, and major power war, 1820–1965. In B.M. Russett, ed., *Peace, War, and Numbers*, pp. 19–48. Beverly Hills, Calif.: Sage.
Singer, J.D., and T. Cusack. 1981. Periodicity, inexorability, and steersmanship in international war. In R. Merritt and B.M. Russett, eds., *From National Development to Global Community*, pp. 404–422. London: Allen & Unwin.
Singer, J.D., and M. Small. 1966a. Formal alliances, 1815–1939: A quantitative description. *Journal of Peace Research* 3:1–32.
———. 1966b. National alliance commitments and war involvement, 1818–1945. *Papers, Peace Research Society* 5:109–140.
———. 1968. Alliance aggregation and the onset of war, 1815–1945. In J.D. Singer, ed., *Quantitative International Politics*, pp. 247–286. New York: Free Press.
———. 1972. *The Wages of War, 1816-1965*. New York: Wiley.

———. 1974. Foreign policy indicators: Predictors of war in history and in the state of the world message. *Policy Sciences* 5:271–296.
Sivard, R.L. 1987. *World Military and Social Expenditures 1987.* Washington, D.C.: World Priorities.
Siverson, R.M., and M.P. Sullivan. 1983. The distribution of power and the onset of war. *Journal of Conflict Resolution* 27:473–494.
Siverson, R.M., and M.R. Tennefoss. 1984. Power, alliance, and the escalation of international conflict, 1815–1965. *American Political Science Review* 78:1057–1069.
Small, M., and J.D. Singer. 1976. The war-proneness of democratic regimes, 1816–1965. *Jerusalem Journal of International Relations* 1:50–69.
———. 1982. *Resort to Arms: International and Civil Wars, 1816–1980.* Beverly Hills, Calif.: Sage.
Smith, T.C. 1980. Arms race instability and war. *Journal of Conflict Resolution* 24:253–284.
Smoke, R. 1977. *War: Controlling Escalation.* Cambridge, Mass.: Harvard University Press.
Snyder, G. 1965. The balance of power and the balance of terror. In P. Seabury, ed., *The Balance of Power*, pp. 185–201. San Francisco: Chandler.
Snyder, G., and P. Diesing. 1977. *Conflict Among Nations.* Princeton, N.J.: Princeton University Press.
Snyder, J. 1984a. Civil-military relations and the cult of the offensive, 1914 and 1984. *International Security* 9:108–146.
———. 1984b. *The Ideology of the Offensive: Military Decisionmaking and the Disasters of 1914.* Ithaca, N.Y.: Cornell University Press.
———. 1985. Perceptions of the security dilemma in 1914. In R. Jervis et al., *Psychology and Deterrence*, pp. 153–179. Baltimore: Johns Hopkins University Press.
———. 1988. *Myths of Empire: Domestic Politics and Strategic Ideology.* New York: Columbia University. Mimeo.
Snyder, R.C., H.W. Bruck, and B. Sapin. 1954. *Foreign Policy Decision-Making.* Glencoe, Ill.: Free Press.
Sorokin, P.A. 1937. *Fluctuation of Social Relationships, War, and Revolution.* Vol. 3, *Social and Cultural Dynamics.* New York, American Book Co.
Spanier, J. 1985. *American Foreign Policy Since World War II*, 10th ed. New York: Holt.
Speer, A. 1970. *Inside the Third Reich.* New York: Macmillan.
Sprout, H., and M. Sprout. 1965. *The Ecological Perspective on Human Affairs.* Princeton, N.J.: Princeton University Press.
Stein, A.A. 1976. Conflict and cohesion. *Journal of Conflict Resolution* 20:143–172.
———. 1982. When misperception matters. *World Politics* 34:505–526.
Stein, J.G. 1985a. Calculation, miscalculation, and conventional deterrence I: The view from Cairo. In R. Jervis et al., *Psychology and Deterrence*, pp. 34–59. Baltimore: Johns Hopkins University Press.
———. 1985b. Calculation, miscalculation, and conventional deterrence II: The view

from Jerusalem. In R. Jervis et al., *Psychology and Deterrence*, pp. 60–88. Baltimore: Johns Hopkins University Press.

Stern, P.C., R. Axelrod, R. Jervis, and R. Radner, eds. 1989. *Perspectives on Deterrence.* New York: Oxford University Press.

Stoessinger, J. 1978. *Why Nations Go to War*, 2d ed. New York: St. Martin's Press.

Stohl, M. 1980. The nexus of civil and international conflict. In T.R. Gurr, ed., *Handbook of Political Conflict*, Chap. 7. New York: Free Press.

Stoll, R. 1982. Major power interstate conflict in the post-World War II era. *Western Political Quarterly* 35:587–605.

Stuckey, J., and J.D. Singer. 1973. The powerful and the warprone: Ranking the national by relative capability and war experience, 1820–1964. Paper presented at a conference on "Poder Social: América Latina en el Mundo," Mexico City.

Tanter, R. 1966. Dimensions of conflict behavior within and between nations, 1958–1960. *Journal of Conflict Resolution* 10:41–64.

———. 1954. *The Struggle for Mastery in Europe, 1848–1918.* London: Oxford University Press.

Taylor, A.J.P. 1961. *The Origins of the Second World War.* London: Hamilton.

———. 1969. *War by Time-Table.* London: McDonald.

Taylor, M. D. 1960. *The Uncertain Trumpet.* New York: Harper & Row.

Tetlock, P.E., and C.B. McGuire, Jr. 1985. Cognitive perspectives on foreign policy. In S. Long, ed., *Political Behavior Annual.* Boulder, Col.: Westview.

Thompson, D. 1962. *Europe Since Napoleon.* New York: Knopf.

Thompson, W.R. 1983a. Cycles, capabilities, and war: An ecumenical view. In Thompson, ed., *Contending Approaches to World Systems Analysis*, pp. 141–164. Beverly Hills, Calif.: Sage.

———. 1983b. Succession crises in the global political system: A test of the transition model. In A.L. Bergeson, ed., *Crises in the World-System.* Beverly Hills, Calif.: Sage.

———. 1983c. Uneven economic growth, systemic challenges, and global war. *International Studies Quarterly* 27:341–355.

———. 1986a. Leading sectors, systemic leadership and global war. Paper presented at the annual meeting of the American Political Science Association, Washington, D.C.

———. 1986b. Polarity, the long cycle and global power warfare. *Journal of Conflict Resolution* 30:587–615.

———. 1988. *On Global War.* Columbia, S.C.: University of South Carolina Press.

Thompson, W.R., and K.A. Rasler. 1988. War and systemic capability reconcentration. *Journal of Conflict Resolution* 32:335–366.

Thompson, W.R., and G. Zuk. 1982. War, inflation, and Kondratieff's long waves. *Journal of Conflict Resolution* 26:621–644.

Thucydides. [431–411 B.C.] 1954. *The Peloponnesian War.* Trans. by R. Warner. New York: Penguin.

Tillema, H.K. 1973. *Appeal to Force: American Military Intervention in the Era of Containment.* New York: Crowell.

Tilly, C. 1975. Western state-making and theories of political transformation. In C.

Tilly, ed., *The Formation of National States in Western Europe*, pp. 601–638. Princeton, N.J.: Princeton University Press.

Toynbee, A.J. 1954. *A Study of History*, Vol.9. New York: Oxford University Press.

Tuchman, B. 1962. *The Guns of August*. New York: Dell.

Turner, L.F.C. 1979. The significance of the Schlieffen Plan. In P.M. Kennedy, ed., *The War Plans of the Great Powers*, pp. 199–221. London: Allen & Unwin.

Tversky, A., and D. Kahneman. 1981. The framing of decisions and the psychology of choice. *Science* 211:453–458.

Vagts, A. 1956. *Defense and Diplomacy*. New York: King's Crown.

———. 1959. *A History of Militarism*, rev. ed. New York: Free Press.

Van Evera, S. 1984a. The cult of the offensive and the origins of the First World War. *International Security* 9:58–107.

———. 1984b. Causes of War. Ph.D. dissertation, University of California, Berkeley.

———. 1985. Why cooperation failed in 1914. *World Politics* 38:80–117.

Vasquez, J.A. 1983. *The Power of Power Politics*. New Brunswick, N.J.: Rutgers University Press.

———. 1986. Capability, types of war, peace. *Western Political Quarterly* 38:313–327.

———. 1987. The steps to war: Toward a scientific explanation of correlates of war findings. *World Politics* 40:108–145.

Vasquez, J.A., and R.W. Mansbach. 1984. The role of issues in global cooperation and conflict. *British Journal of Political Science* 14:411–433.

Vayrynen, R. 1983. Economic cycles, power transitions, political management and wars between major powers. *International Studies Quarterly* 27:389–418.

Veblen, T. 1915. *Imperial Germany and the Industrial Revolution*. New York: Macmillan.

von Clausewitz, C. [1832] 1968. *On War*. New York: Penguin Books.

von Ranke, L. [1833] 1973. The great powers. G.G. Iggers and K. von Moltke, eds., *The Theory and Practice of History*, pp. 65–101. Indianapolis: Bobbs-Merrill.

Wagner, R.H. 1983. The theory of games and the problem of international cooperation. *American Political Science Review* 77:330–346.

———. 1984. War and expected-utility theory. *World Politics* 36:407–423.

———. 1986. The theory of games and the balance of power. *World Politics* 38:546–576.

Wallace, M.D. 1973. *War and Rank Among Nations*. Lexington, Mass.: Heath.

———. 1979. Arms races and escalation: Some new evidence. *Journal of Conflict Resolution* 23:3–16.

———. 1981. Armaments and escalation: Two competing hypotheses. *International Studies Quarterly* 26:37–56.

Wallerstein, I. 1974. *The Modern World System I: Capitalist Agriculture and the Origins of the World-Economy in the Sixteenth Century*. New York: Academic Press.

———. 1984. *The Politics of the World Economy*. Cambridge, England: Cambridge University Press.

Walt, S.M. 1987. *The Origins of Alliances*. Ithaca, N.Y.: Cornell University Press.
Waltz, K.N. 1954. *Man, the State, and War*. New York: Columbia University Press.
———. 1967. International structure, national force, and the balance of world power. *Journal of International Affairs* 21:220–228.
———. 1979. *Theory of International Politics*. Reading, Mass.: Addison-Wesley.
Wayman, F.J. 1984. Bipolarity and war: The role of capability concentration and alliance patterns among major powers, 1816–1965. *Journal of Peace Research* 21:61–78.
Wayman, F.J., J.D. Singer, and G.Goertz. 1983. Capabilities, military allocations and success in militarized disputes. *International Studies Quarterly* 27:497–515.
Weede, E. 1976. Overwhelming preponderance as a pacifying condition among Asian dyads, 1950–1969. *Journal of Conflict Resolution* 20:395–411.
———. 1983. Extended deterrence by superpower alliance. *Journal of Conflict Resolution* 27:231–254.
White, R. 1968. *Nobody Wanted War*. Garden City, N.Y.: Anchor.
Wilkenfeld, J., ed. 1973. *Conflict Behavior and Linkage Politics*. New York: McKay.
Wohlstetter, A. 1959. The delicate balance of terror. *Foreign Affairs* 37:211–234.
Wolfers, A. 1962. *Discord and Collaboration*. Baltimore: Johns Hopkins University Press.
Wright, Q. 1965. *A Study of War*, rev. ed. Chicago: University of Chicago Press.
Yarmolinsky, A. 1971. *The Military Establishment*. New York: Harper & Row.
Zagare, F. 1982. Review of *The War Trap*. *American Political Science Review* 76:738–739.
Zilliacus, K. 1946. *Mirror of the Past*. New York: A. A. Wyn.
Zimmerman, W. 1973. Issue-area and foreign policy process. *American Political Science Review* 67:1204–1212.
Zinnes, D.A. 1967. An analytical study of balance of power theories. *Journal of Peace Research* 4:270–288.
———. 1980. Why war? Evidence on the outbreak of international conflict. In T.R. Gurr, ed., *Handbook of Political Conflict*, pp. 331–360. New York: Free Press.
Zinnes, D.A., R.C. North, and H.E. Koch, Jr. 1961. Capability, threat, and the outbreak of war. In J.N. Rosenau, ed., *International Politics and Foreign Policy*, pp. 469–482. New York: Free Press.

5

Methodological Themes and Variations

PHILIP E. TETLOCK

Levels of Analysis, 338
COGNITIVE AND AFFECTIVE PROCESSES OF INDIVIDUAL DECISION MAKERS, 341
SMALL GROUP PROCESSES, 344   DECISION MAKERS AS REPRESENTATIVES OF COMPLEX BUREAUCRATIC CONSTITUENCIES, 345   MANAGING COMPLEX MILITARY-POLITICAL SYSTEMS, 347   THE NATURE OF THE NATION-STATE, 348   THE STRUCTURE OF THE INTERNATIONAL SYSTEM, 349

Research Methods, 351
LABORATORY EXPERIMENTS AND SIMULATIONS, 353   MASS SURVEYS OF PUBLIC OPINION, 355   QUANTITATIVE STUDIES OF HISTORICAL DATA, 357   CASE STUDY METHODS, 358   FORMAL MATHEMATICAL MODELS, 361

The Quest for Linkages, 364
THEORETICAL LINKAGES, 365   METHODOLOGICAL LINKAGES, 370

Concluding Remarks: The Quest for Policy Relevance, 372
Notes, 378
References, 380

The future of civilization, perhaps of the human race, hinges on our ability to avoid nuclear war. This point has been made so repeatedly and occasionally so eloquently that it needs no amplification here (Dyson, 1984; Katz, 1982; Institute of Medicine, 1986; Sagan, 1983; Schell, 1980). The consensus, however, begins and ends on this point. There is wide disagreement on how likely nuclear war is, how such a war might occur, the forms it might take, and how it might best be prevented. Will nuclear war arise as the result of a "conflict spiral" between the nuclear superpowers—a self-reinforcing process driven by the tendency of each side to exaggerate the hostile intent of the other and to acquire ever more sophisticated weapons systems that increase the other side's sense of vulnerability and motivation to strike first in a crisis? Will nuclear war arise as a result of the failure of deterrence—a failure to convince the other side that one has both the political will and military capability to resist encroachments on "vital national interests"? Will nuclear war arise as a result of accident or miscommunication triggered by flaws in the command, control, and intelligence systems of the superpowers? Or has the causal role of the superpowers been overestimated? Will nuclear war arise from Third World conflicts of relatively remote relevance to U.S.-Soviet relations? And must nuclear war be an all-or-nothing proposition? Might limited nuclear wars periodically break out between particular powers or combinations of powers?

The contributions to *Behavior, Society, and Nuclear War* do not, of course, yield definitive answers to these questions. Given the multiplicity of potential determinants of the events in question and the imperfection of our knowledge of underlying causal processes, it is impossible to assign precise or even approximate probability estimates to alternative hypotheses concerning how nuclear war might occur (Allison et al., 1985). Accordingly, our goals here are both more modest and attainable. We draw on the behavioral and social sciences not to make precise predictions, but to underscore the enormous ambiguity and complexity of the threat of nuclear war, illustrate the types of research methods available for testing competing claims concerning how nuclear war might break out, highlight the limitations of simple single cause models of nuclear war, and clarify the variety of possible event sequences that could lead to such a war.

Intellectual honesty requires acknowledging that no one knows whether a nuclear war will occur or, if one occurs, what causes will have produced it or what forms the war will take. If nothing else, this acknowledgment serves as a sharp reminder to be wary of the pervasive human tendency to be overconfident in the correctness of one's forecasts and predictions (see Fischhoff, forthcoming). The acknowledgement should be taken, however, not as cause for epistemological despair, but as a useful starting point for analysis. There has never been a nuclear war. The only instance in which nuclear weapons have actually been used in warfare were the atomic bombings of Hiroshima and Nagasaki in 1945. The United States—which possessed an overwhelming superiority in conventional weapons and a global monopoly on nuclear weapons—used the atomic bomb to force the surrender of an isolated and embattled Imperial Japan. We do not, fortunately, have a large data base of previous nuclear wars that we can probe and search for preconditions, correlates, or causes of the decision to use these extraordinarily destructive weapons. But if we lack in direct historical precedents, we risk being overwhelmed by the massive amount of indirect evidence at our disposal. There is no shortage of systematic high-quality research on international conflict (Levy, this volume). And there is no shortage of high quality research on the psychological, organizational, and political processes that make various forms of interpersonal and intergroup conflict more or less likely and more or less severe. If one is willing to grant that the same basic processes that shape these less apocalyptic forms of conflict also bear on the likelihood of nuclear war, then we have a sound logical basis for linking the behavioral and social sciences to the problems of both identifying plausible pathways to nuclear war and plausible preventive measures for avoiding such a war. To be sure, the linkages must be made cautiously, with sensitivity to the unique features of the nuclear predicament confronting us in the late twentieth century (for example, the tremendous accuracy and destructive power of the weapons, the rapidity with which decisions in nuclear crises might have to be made, and the danger of "losing control" over extremely complex technological systems). But the alternative to cautious inductive inference from "relevant" findings in the behavioral and social sciences also needs to be kept in mind. To place nuclear war in a category of its own—in which all we know about human behavior and society is peremptorily deemed irrelevant—is both difficult to justify and, in its most extreme form, a counsel of despair. How can one prepare to avoid an event that transcends existing theoretical and empirical knowledge? This chapter and, indeed, the entire series are premised on the assumption that although there will always be residual uncertainty about whether any given finding or generalization would hold up in a particular nuclear war scenario, we have learned a good deal about behavioral and societal processes that bear on the likelihood of nuclear war and, a central theme of this chapter, we have also learned a good deal about how to learn more about these processes.

This chapter has four specific purposes. The first objective is to provide an overview of the wide range of levels of analysis relevant to the problem of nuclear war. The overview will be sketchy, not exhaustive. The intent is to give a sense of the diverse disciplinary perspectives represented in this series. For analytic convenience, these perspectives have been divided into six (by no means mutually exclusive) categories: cognitive and affective processes of individual decision makers, small group dynamics that emerge when decision makers interact, bureaucratic politics, problems of managing complex military-political organizations, domestic political processes, and the structure of the international system.

The second objective is to provide an equally broad overview of the research methods that investigators can employ to explore processes that could produce a nuclear war. We will consider the five most heavily used methods of generating such knowledge: laboratory experiments and simulations, mass surveys of public opinion, quantitative analyses of historical data, in-depth case studies, and formal mathematical models. The topic of research methods, it should, however, be stressed, cannot be approached in isolation from theoretical issues. One's theoretical assumptions are tightly coupled to one's methodological preferences. For example, investigators who believe that cognitive limits on rationality often play a key role in shaping national security decisions draw heavily from laboratory research on the judgment and choice processes of individual human beings; investigators who see such decisions as severely constrained by organizational and systemic processes draw heavily from research methods suited for studying more "macro" processes of that type (for example, single and comparative case studies and multivariate statistical studies of historical data).

The third objective is to highlight ways in which different research methods and theoretical perspectives complement and mutually enrich each other. It is tempting (especially given the insularity of citation practices in the behavioral and social sciences) to emphasize the difficulty of interdisciplinary communication. Researchers from different traditions often appear to speak different data-languages—languages so different that they cannot be translated into each other's language without egregious loss of meaning. This "incommensurability thesis" is too pessimistic. There is growing evidence of multimethod convergence on key causal propositions relevant to particular paths to nuclear war. There is also a strong logical and empirical case to be made for increased integration of theories in the behavioral and social sciences. "Macro" theories can benefit by building on more realistic assumptions concerning the nature of the human decision maker (Simon, 1985); "micro" theories can benefit by taking into detailed account the normative and institutional constraints on decision making and the nature of the problems with which decision makers must cope (Pfeffer, 1985).

The fourth and final objective is to explore the problem of "policy relevance." Behavioral and social scientists are typically concerned with identifying empirical generalizations and theoretical propositions that hold up over large classes of observations (whether the units of observation be individuals, institutions, nation-states, or even international systems). Policymakers, on the other hand, want to know how to deal with a specific adversary on a specific issue at a specific time. The chapter concludes by examining the complex conceptual and methodological obstacles that arise in applying behavioral and social science knowledge to specific policy controversies.

Levels of Analysis

The study of international conflict can be likened to looking through a microscope at different levels of magnification. At the highest levels of magnification, the focus is on the cognitive, emotional, and even psychophysiological responses of the individual decision maker (Axelrod, 1976; Etheredge, 1978; Holsti, 1976; Lebow, 1981; Jervis, 1976; Walker, 1977; Wiegele, 1979). As one reduces the magnification, one loses the ability to draw fine-grained inferences about individual states of mind but gains the ability to place events in successively broader systems contexts. Thus, one no longer has access to data that allow one to test detailed hypotheses concerning the content of individual belief systems, the nature of the decision rules used to rule out options, or the motives that underlie policy preferences. One gains, however, the ability to draw inferences concerning the impact of the surrounding context on the decision process. The key advisors to the central decision maker, and the interpersonal and group dynamics among them, initially come into focus (Janis, 1982). These small group processes affect both the options considered and the procedures used for assessing those options. Next, the key agencies of government—with individual policymakers now appearing as role representatives of powerful bureaucratic constituencies—come into focus (Allison, 1971; Halperin, 1974; Art, forthcoming). Next, the domestic political and economic environment surrounding the central government looms into view (Russett, this volume). In the case of the United States, we must now take into account Congress, public opinion, defense contractors, the news media, mass political movements, and the interactions among them. Finally, we are confronted by the international system: the complex web of economic, political, and cultural entanglements that define one nation's relationship to another. We must also consider the balance of power and the many variables impinging on that balance: the conventional and nuclear forces of one's own and of other nations, patterns of interaction among nations (trade, formation and dissolution of alliances), and the economic underpinnings of military strength (growth rates, technological development, access to critical natural resources).

It is not surprising that communication across levels of analysis is both difficult and rare. What excites the attention of investigators working at one level of analysis may well be invisible to investigators working at other levels of analysis. One can study foreign-policy decision making at a purely cognitive level of analysis without ever referring to research on group dynamics, role theory, bureaucratic politics, special interests, public opinion, trading patterns, or the balance of power. The substantive content of the decisions would, in a fundamental sense, be irrelevant. The "cognitivist" would be concerned solely with the types of decision rules employed, the strategies used to cope with uncertainty and trade-offs, the degree of openness to new evidence, etc. Conversely, one can study patterns of interaction among nations—alliance formation and dissolution, the waxing and waning of arms races—without ever referring to cognitive research on belief systems or judgmental heuristics. Researchers at these higher levels of analysis often feel comfortable working with very simple assumptions concerning the human decision makers involved. It suffices to posit a capability for "rational" thought, a concern for power and, perhaps, an attitude toward risk.

The levels-of-analysis problem is a familiar one to international relations researchers, and there is not much to be gained from an extended examination of this much debated and essentially unresolved controversy (Greenstein, 1975; Hoffman, 1960; Holsti, 1976; Jervis, 1976; Kelman and Bloom, 1973; Rosenan, 1966; Singer, 1972; Verba, 1961; Waltz, 1959). There is still little agreement on the relative contributions that different levels of analysis can make to the explanation of international conflict. There are, however, at least signs of growing tolerance among advocates of competing schools of thought. Many scholars now agree that the importance of any given level of analysis is not a constant but is likely to vary as a function of the configurations of variables at other levels and the types of questions we want answered (Holsti, 1976; Jervis, 1976; Levy, this volume). For instance, systemic variables may shape the major challenges confronting a nation's foreign policy and the overall direction its policy may take, but not its exact responses in a specific situation. Thus, economic and geopolitical pressures might have made a major European war in the early twentieth century very likely (Choucri and North, 1975), but a psychological analysis of crisis decision making and of the personalities involved may be needed to explain why World War I broke out in August 1914 (Holsti, 1972). Or, to take another example, systemic variables may exert a powerful constraining influence over the foreign policies of individual nations, but that constraining influence may not be sufficient when variables at lower levels of analysis take on extreme values (for example, Hitler's Germany of 1939, or Khomeini's Iran of the 1980s).[1]

A great deal of the research reviewed in *Behavior, Society, and Nuclear War* points to the need for complex or contingent generalizations of this sort

(George, 1980). Different levels of analysis, in this view, do not represent mutually exclusive ways of looking at the world. The intensity of international conflict and the diverse forms it takes are typically the product of interactions among variables at many levels of analysis. In Allison's (1971) metaphor, levels of analysis are best thought of not as rival theories but as "beacons" that sensitize investigators to different bodies of data, research methods, and potential explanations. Psychological explanations lead one to expect patterns of individual and small group behavior among policy elites that one simply would not have expected if one restricted theorizing to a realpolitik, balance-of-power framework. If one assumes that foreign policy is the product of unitary, rational, power-maximizing actors, there is no reason for expecting decision makers to fall prey to serious misperceptions (Holsti, this volume; Jervis, 1976; Stein, forthcoming) or to engage in self-defeating patterns of behavior in small groups (Janis, 1982) or to advocate narrowly defined bureaucratic interests at the expense of broader national policy objectives (Halperin, 1974). These latter findings can be quite readily explained, however, if one grants the possibility that certain basic laws of psychosocial functioning hold up in very different spheres of life (for example, in laboratory experiments and cabinet rooms). Conversely, systemic theories lead one to expect regularities in international conduct that individual-level theorists would probably have never anticipated. For instance, Bueno de Mesquita (1985) has shown that it is possible to achieve impressively accurate predictions of the initiation of war based on purely systemic indicators (balance-of-power measures) with the assistance of only the most rudimentary psychological assumptions. Modelski (1987) and others have demonstrated intriguing regularities in the outbreak of major wars over the last five centuries, tracing these patterns to fundamental political-economic processes that make the decline of hegemonic powers inevitable.

This "beacon" interpretation suggests that the best test of a level of analysis is the power of theories formulated at that level to stimulate the discovery of important findings that otherwise would have remained undiscovered. The central research challenge is not to debunk competing levels of analysis but to improve the quality of theoretical and empirical work at one's chosen level. Efforts to achieve decisive tests between levels of analysis may be superficially appealing (create the appearance of cumulative hypothetico-deductive science) but actually may be extremely misleading. Confrontations between levels of analysis are often premature. They presume methodological refinement that just does not exist. Demonstrations that variables from one level of analysis "outpredict" variables from another level may tell us little about the explanatory superiority of that level and a lot about the relative sophistication of theory development within the two levels at a given time or the relative sophistication of techniques for operationalizing variables within the two levels at a given time. It is unwise to draw strong conclusions about the long-term explanatory potential of levels of analysis from such studies. The risks of underestimating the explanatory potential of the early losers and of overestimating the potential of the early winners are too great. A more prudent strategy is to encourage investigators to put their own "theoretical houses" in order before trying to annex new explanatory territory. As we will see in *Behavior, Society, and Nuclear War*, investigators working at the same level of analysis frequently find themselves in sharp disagreement over what variables are most important, how variables interact, and how these variables should be assessed.[2]

Next, I briefly sketch the types of processes studied at each of six different levels of analysis and the types of methods used to study these processes.

Cognitive and Affective Processes of Individual Decision Makers

Many behavioral scientists take it to be self-evident that microlevel explanations—those that invoke the beliefs, values, perceptions, and feelings of individual decision makers—can contribute to our understanding of how to prevent nuclear war. What, indeed, could be more obvious? Policymakers are human beings. The behavioral sciences have been at least partly successful in identifying lawful regularities in human behavior. It seems to follow that the behavioral sciences are well positioned to shed light on both the causes of war in general and, by implication, the potential causes of nuclear war.

This reductionist argument probably proves too much. For, by the same logic, behavioral science is reducible to biochemistry (of what, after all, do people consist?) which, in turn, is reducible to subatomic physics (of what ultimately do complex protein chains consist?). It is not enough to assert a reductionistic claim; one must systematically document exactly how concepts and research methods from the putatively fundamental discipline help to clarify problems that arise at the next higher level of analysis.

Analysts of political decision making have attempted to do exactly that (Axelrod, 1976; George, 1980; Jervis, 1976). They have built a strong case that important similarities exist between decision making in foreign policy and in other spheres of life. Thus, they have noted the extraordinary difficulty of identifying a best or utility-maximizing solution to most foreign policy problems (Steinbruner, 1974). Policymakers must deal with incomplete and unreliable information on the capabilities and intentions of other states (sometimes even of their own states). The range of response options confronting them are indeterminate. The probable consequences of each option are shrouded in uncertainty. Policymakers must compare options on many conflicting, seemingly incommensurable, value dimensions (for example, the impact of options on economic interests, international prestige, domestic popularity, human rights, and even lives). Finally, to compound the difficulty of the task, policymakers must sometimes work under intense stress and time pressure (Holsti, this volume; Janis and Mann, 1977; Lebow, 1981; Stein, forthcoming; Suedfeld and Tetlock, 1977).

Advocates of information processing explanations argue that policymakers frequently resort to simplifying strategies to deal with the complexity, ambiguity, and painful trade-offs inherent in foreign policy problems (Fischhoff, forthcoming). These simplification strategies can take many forms: reliance on simple historical analogues or precedents in interpreting new situations (Neustadt and May, 1986), reluctance to modify preconceptions in response to challenging evidence (George, 1980; Jervis, 1976), perceiving situations in ways designed to minimize evaluative inconsistency and value trade-offs (Axelrod, 1976), and dependence on simple, easy-to-execute heuristics in assessing the likely future behavior of other states (Jervis, 1976). It is also argued that cognitive economy and efficiency frequently have a steep price: susceptibility to error. Reliance on simple historical analogies raises the risk of overlooking important differences between one's preferred precedent and the current problem (for example, the Vietnam War differs in many respects from the diverse contemporary conflicts to which it has frequently been compared: El Salvador, Nicaragua, Afghanistan, Lebanon, Angola, Ethiopia, and Cambodia). Reluctance to modify preconceptions raises the risk of clinging to incorrect assessments of situations in the face of unexpected developments (for example, U.S. analysts who firmly believed in the monolithic nature of the Communist movement were slow to recognize the strategic significance of the Sino-Soviet dispute). Intolerance of evaluative inconsistency raises the risk of failing to recognize flaws in policies one supports and virtues in policies one rejects. Dependence on simple attributional heuristics raises the risk of drawing too sweeping and confident inferences concerning how others are likely to act in the future.

Balancing the possible benefits of cognitive efficiency against the possible increases in error is a perplexing normative problem with no widely acknowledged solution. By contrast, documenting cognitive constraints on judgment and choice processes is a relatively straightforward empirical problem with a quite widely acknowledged methodological solution. The solution takes the following form: (1) demonstrating—largely through experimental research—that people rely on certain cognitive strategies to cope with complexity and uncertainty; and (2) demonstrating—largely through historical case studies and content analyses of policy deliberations—that foreign policy decision makers appear to rely on similar sorts of strategies. In short, one looks for multimethod convergence.

This research strategy is especially appealing because it builds on the complementary strengths of experimental research (the ability to test detailed process models of individual behavior and to eliminate alternative causal hypotheses) and of naturalistic research methods (much more immediate relevance to events and issues bearing on the likelihood of nuclear war). One is justified in holding greater confidence in generalizations concerning judgment and choice that successfully pass two so very different methodological screening tests. And there is considerable evidence that the generalizations mentioned earlier hold up quite well indeed (George, 1980; Jervis, 1976; Tetlock and McGuire, 1986).

Although multimethod convergence of this sort is encouraging, caution is still appropriate for two important reasons. For one thing, it is possible to have spurious convergence. Naturalistic researchers might wrongly conclude that foreign policy behavior that only superficially resembles a laboratory analogue is the product of the same underlying cognitive or affective process. Thus, policymakers may appear to rely on simple rules of thumb in drawing lessons from history, but they may actually be working with a far more subtle and sophisticated grasp of the situation. Policymakers may be using simple historical arguments (such as "no more Munichs" or "no more Vietnams") to rally support from wavering political constituencies and to preempt potential criticism from either the left or right. In a similar vein, policymakers may not actually be unaware of value trade-offs or of contradictory evidence but may find it politically useful to refuse to acknowledge them. Distinguishing between genuine and spurious multimethod convergence (or, in this case, between perceptual-cognitive and political impression management explanations) is often a very tricky judgment call that requires detailed knowledge of specific historical episodes.

It is also a judgment call that many contributors to our series must implicitly or explicitly make. Holsti (this volume), for example, needs to make such judgments in assessing whether crisis-induced stress really impairs the judgment of foreign-policymakers or whether foreign-policymakers are craftily trying to influence the calculations of other national leaders by persuading them that such impairment has occurred (see Schelling, 1966, on the rationality of occasionally appearing irrational). Stein (forthcoming) needs to make similar sorts of judgments in assessing whether the leaders of states that challenge deterrence are allowing motives and wishes to distort their perception of the choices available to them or whether they are cleverly trying to intimidate the status quo power by persuading it that they have no choice (given domestic pressures) but to persevere with confrontational policies. We confront variants of the same analytic dilemma in the Fischhoff (forthcoming) chapter. How can we assess, for example, whether decision makers in nuclear command, control, and communications systems are overconfident in their ability to avoid Type I errors (falsely conclude that an attack is occurring) and Type II errors (falsely conclude that an attack is not occurring) or whether these decision makers are self-consciously promoting a necessary social-political fiction? In short, it is no simple matter to determine whether one has discovered true multimethod convergence.

There is also a second major reason for caution. Multimethod divergence sometimes occurs. For most laboratory-based generalizations, it is fairly easy to identify numerous exceptions and qualifications in the "real world." Decision makers sometimes draw flexible, multidimensional lessons from history (Neustadt and May, 1986), confront trade-offs even in highly stressful situations (Maoz, 1981), and display a willingness to change their minds in response to new evidence (Tetlock, 1985b). Multimethod divergence of this sort does not, of course, mean that one set of findings must be "right" and the other "wrong." When radically different research methods are being compared, an enormous number of possible explanations exist for divergence. How people think may depend on a variety of boundary conditions: individual differences in cultural background, intellectual capacity, and cognitive and interpersonal style, and situational variables such as the nature of the decision-making task, task importance, small group processes, and role and accountability relationships. Each class of variable—by itself or in combination with others—may help to explain inconsistencies in the pattern of evidence.

Small Group Processes

Decision makers do not operate in a social or institutional vacuum. Most important national security decisions appear to be collective products—the result of often intensive interactions among small groups of decision makers, each of whom in turn represents major bureaucratic or political constituencies. The norms and operating procedures of these small groups thus become potentially important determinants of policy outcome.

Evidence at hand suggests that these small group processes can interact in many ways with individual dispositions to influence the decisions that policymakers reach. Janis (1982), for example, reviews a considerable body of both historical and experimental research that suggests that, under certain conditions (directive leadership, cohesive group, high external threat, etc.), group norms will emerge that exacerbate already dangerous trends in individual judgment. Far from checking bias and error in each other, policymakers in these "groupthink" situations behave in ways that encourage overconfidence, self-righteousness, cognitive rigidity, and excessive optimism and that discourage dissent and the expression of unpopular doubts or opinions. The result, according to Janis, is the undertaking of ill-thought-out foreign policy projects that frequently lead to disastrous consequences (for example, the pursuit of the defeated North Korean army deep into the Korean peninsula in 1950 and the provoking of Communist Chinese intervention or the abortive Bay of Pigs invasion of Castro's Cuba in 1961).

Small group processes do not always, however, make matters worse. Under other conditions (external accountability checks, nondirective leadership, institutional mechanisms for ensuring the representation of different points of view), group norms can facilitate complex, open-minded analyses of policy options (Janis, 1982; George, 1980: Chap. 11) and confer at least some protection against well-documented judgmental biases such as overconfidence, intolerance of evaluative inconsistency, and the tendency for first impressions to persevere in the face of later contradictory evidence (Tetlock, 1985b; Tetlock and Kim, 1987). Janis (1982) cites the development of the Marshall Plan and the handling of the Cuban missile crisis as exemplary models of how group processes can improve the quality of decision making (see also Holsti, this volume).

Investigators who seek to apply knowledge of small group dynamics to the problem of preventing nuclear war generally adopt the same methodological strategy as those who seek to apply knowledge of individual-level processes. On the one hand, there is a body of experimental research on topics such as conformity, coalition formation, leadership styles and effectiveness, minority influence, and the group-induced attitude polarization effect. On the other hand, there is a body of historical and archival research that probes the relevance of this work on "basic processes" for understanding the making of critical national security decisions (Burnstein and Berbaum, 1983; George, 1980; Janis, 1982; Tetlock, 1979). To the degree these very different strategies of inquiry point to compatible conclusions, our confidence in those conclusions should be reinforced. Nonetheless, all of the cautionary caveats appended to the multimethod convergence argument in the previous section apply here.

Decision Makers as Representatives of Complex Bureaucratic Constituencies

National security decisions can be viewed as outputs of complex military and political organizations—organizations such as the Department of State, Department of Defense, Central Intelligence Agency, National Security Council, and so forth. It is typically assumed that attributes of individual decision makers cease—at this level of analysis—to be terribly important; what matters are the complex bureaucratic and political perspectives and interests that these decision makers are expected to represent. Decision makers become role incumbents; as the saying goes, "where they stand depends on where they sit."

Research on organizational behavior and bureaucratic politics abounds with examples of policymakers shifting supposedly firm convictions on assuming new posts or after shifts in the prevailing political atmosphere (Halperin, 1974; Kaplan, 1982). Such shifts should not be too surprising. There are often overwhelming normative pressures on decision makers to adopt attitudes consistent with both their own career and institutional interests (pressures, for example, to promote institutional control over policy and to justify appeals for increased budget and staff). Moreover, the readiness with which many high-level decision makers strategically shift their views is very consistent with what is known of the readiness of ordinary people to modify their opinions and conduct to the social demands of the moment. Large experimental literatures exist on ingratiation, self-presentation, and strategic attitude shifts—all of which underscore the plasticity of beliefs, attitudes, values, and feelings that one might otherwise suppose to be central to people's self-concepts (Schlenker, 1985).[3]

From the perspective of understanding determinants of policy preferences (which, in turn, may bear on the likelihood of nuclear war), the appropriate focus is on the institutional coalitions or systems that key decision makers represent. There is, for example, much work on the ways in which the institutional interests of the military affect the processes of weapons development, weapons procurement, and the setting of budgetary priorities (Melman, 1970; Sarkesian, 1972; Yarmolinsky, 1970). In recent years, there seems to have been a general tendency to favor offensive systems and, within that category, to favor systems that will expand the budgetary and manpower requirements and the political influence of one's own branch of the services. From the standpoint of students of organizational behavior, the tendency of national security bureaucracies to behave this way is no more surprising than would be the tendency of individual decision makers to rely on simple heuristics to cognitive psychologists. A basic principle of organizational functioning—the tendency to defend and, when feasible, expand claims on resources through socially acceptable justifications—has once again been validated (Pfeffer, 1985).

Documenting cause and effect relationships in complex bureaucracies is, of course, difficult. The available data are not impressive. One must rely largely on detailed interviews with former policymakers—whose memories and motives may be suspect—and on careful checks of archival records to cross-validate conclusions drawn from interviews. Nonetheless, the data can be suggestive. Correlations can be documented—through qualitative or quantitative, cross-sectional or time-series methods—between institutional self-interest and institutional policy advocacy. For instance, if the positions taken by the Air Force and Navy on the military value (even morality) of countervalue nuclear strikes depends on the technological sophistication of the weapons systems available to those services at different times—namely, the accuracy of land-based international ballistic missiles (ICBMs) and the availability and, later, the accuracy of submarine-launched ballistic missiles (SLBMs)—that finding counts as suggestive evidence that institutional interests played a part in shaping critical national security estimates and priorities.

Managing Complex Military-Political Systems

High-level decision makers sit atop organizational systems of enormous complexity—systems whose intricacies it is unrealistic to suppose they can fully master given the multifarious demands on their time and their often brief tenures in key positions. As a result, decision makers may be unaware of how quickly they can lose control over the chain of causal events leading up to war. Once decision makers commit themselves to a particular line of action (for example, partial mobilization), that commitment may trigger a series of preprogrammed action-reaction cycles that make conflict all but inevitable. Historical analysts have made this argument repeatedly in the case of World War I (emphasizing the rigidity of mobilization schedules and railroad timetables); contemporary strategic analysts have made analogous arguments concerning current procedures for the command and control of nuclear forces (Blair, 1987; Bracken, 1983; Steinbruner, 1985, 1987). High-level decision makers can be easily overwhelmed by the technical complexity of the weapons systems, the tendency to decentralize authority over nuclear weapons in crises, the problem of "alert instability," and uncertainty concerning the "rules of engagement" for military forces.

Understanding how nuclear war might occur requires, from this perspective, absorbing a staggering amount of detailed technical information on how the military forces of the key nation-states actually function and of the forms that military-political coordination takes within those states. Research methods from the social sciences can, however, help us to cope with this potential information overload. Rigorous game-theoretic modeling can highlight how the adoption of particular policy proposals, such as highly accurate counterforce weapon systems (e.g., the MX) or various types of ballistic missile defenses, affect the incentives for each to launch preemptive strikes at various points in the escalation sequence (Brams, 1985; Shubik, forthcoming). Analyses of this sort can sensitize the policymaking community to how ostensibly purely "defensive" measures by one's own side can dramatically affect the relative attractiveness of options open to the other side.

Historical case studies of crisis decision making can also play a valuable role. It is useful, for example, to be reminded of how standard military operating procedures have led, in the past, to incidents that could have triggered dramatic escalations of crises (for example, the need for careful oversight of the implementation of the naval blockade of Cuba to prevent an early clash between U.S. and Soviet forces during the missile crisis). Complex military operations send out a variety of both advertent and inadvertent signals to prospective adversaries—signals that can be easily misinterpreted (Thies, 1984). The leaders of other states may see a message being sent where none is intended (for example, a pause in bombing during the Vietnam War due to poor weather might be seen as a conciliatory gesture), or they may seriously misinterpret a message that is actually being sent (for example, a partial activation of military units might be seen as a prelude to a full-scale attack, even though it is intended only to indicate firmness of resolve).

The Nature of the Nation-State

The notion that some nations are intrinsically more prone to war than others is a long-standing one in the study of international politics (Waltz, 1959). Hypotheses on this issue take many contradictory forms. It has been suggested, for example, that capitalist states have special economic needs for expansion or for disposing of surplus capital (needs that predispose them to war). And it has been suggested that capitalism in conjunction with free international trade is actually the best guarantee of peace. It has been proposed that democratic political institutions encourage peace, and it has been proposed that democracies are especially vulnerable to volatile swings in public opinion that make war more likely. Finally, it has been argued—by various investigators at various times—that internal political conflict increases, has no effect on, and decreases the likelihood of war. There is, in brief, no shortage of speculation on the subject (see Levy, this volume).

Research generally takes one of three distinct forms at this level of analysis. One common form is the case study. Do national leaders in specific historical situations feel compelled by domestic political imperatives to pursue policies that are likely to result in war? In her chapter in the second volume of this series Stein reviews considerable evidence that this does indeed sometimes happen.[4] A second common form of research is the multivariate correlational study that probes for relationships between attributes of large numbers of nation-states (their form of government, level of economic development and type of economic organization, intensity of internal conflict, governmental stability, etc.) and the involvement of these nations in war. The third genre of research is the survey. Using relatively standardized sampling and interviewing techniques, the goal is to understand fluctuations in public opinion on foreign policy issues over time (for example, does out-group threat increase support for in-group symbols of authority such as the presidency?) and the relationship between public opinion and foreign policy (see Russett, this volume).

It is worth noting that an interesting example of both multimethod convergence and divergence emerges at this level of analysis. On the one hand, multivariate correlational studies of war lead us to conclude that the relationships between internal conflict within nations and involvement in external conflict are extremely weak, even nonexistent. On the other hand, experimental research, survey research, and historical case study research point to a different conclusion. Experimental work suggests that in-group cohesiveness increases as a function of external threat under a fairly broad range of circumstances (Brewer and Kramer, 1985; Coser, 1956). Survey research documents a compatible finding—the tendency for support for presidents to increase immediately after the use of force abroad (Mueller, 1973; Russett, this volume). And historical case study research suggests that high-level decision makers have a good intuitive grasp of this rather robust social science generalization and are willing on occasion to risk and even to seek external conflict in order to promote internal political cohesion and, by implication, their own political positions (Rosecrance, 1963; Lebow, 1981; Stein, forthcoming).

How should the apparent inconsistency be explained? There are several possibilities. One is that the inconsistency is illusory. The temptation to use external conflict to promote internal cohesion is real, but national leaders act on the temptation only when a variety of elaborate preconditions are met (for example, alternative, less risky methods of reducing internal conflict do not exist, a plausible pretext does exist for picking a quarrel with another power, the costs of quarreling are not prohibitive, and the internal conflict has not reached a point where it impairs the nation's capability and resolve to engage in external conflict.). As a result, internal conflict by itself is not a powerful predictor of external conflict. There are just too many—and too difficult to operationalize—moderator variables of the relationship between internal and external conflict.

Another possibility is that the multivariate correlational studies suffered from serious flaws that undermined their power to detect true relationships between internal and external conflict. Most studies, as Levy (this volume) points out, were based on a narrow and remarkably peaceful period in international politics (1955–1960). Since it is obviously unwise to draw sweeping conclusions from so brief and unrepresentative a slice of time, final verdict on this issue must await better cross-sectional and time-series evidence.

The Structure of the International System

Theories that are derived from this most "macro" level of analysis pay little or no attention to the psychological, institutional, and political processes that we have considered at the lower levels. Whether a nation goes to war is studied without reference to the psychological processes of individual decision makers, small group dynamics among those decision makers, intragovernmental factionalism, the difficulties of managing enormously complex military-political systems, and domestic political conflicts within the state. The nation-state is treated as an undifferentiated atom—a unitary rational actor that attempts to maximize its influence within the constraints posed by the international system. Key explanatory variables from this viewpoint are system-level variables: the bipolarity versus multipolarity of the distribution of power (Waltz, 1979), the intensity of competition for raw materials and markets (Choucri and North, 1975), threats to the current balance of power (when one power appears close to achieving hegemony, a military coalition of other powers will often emerge to resist it), the relative rates of change in the military-economic power of key nation-states (Kennedy, 1987; Organski and Kugler, 1980), and the existence of alliances and the cohesiveness and stability of these alliances. Investigators can test systemic hypotheses using qualitative or quantitative data analytic techniques. Thus, research can take the form of detailed case studies of shifting international coalitions prior to a specific war or multivariate statistical studies of the power of systemic variables to predict the outbreak of war among large numbers of nations or over long periods of time (Choucri and North, 1975; Bueno de Mesquita, 1981, 1985; Organski and Kugler, 1980). Such studies have shed light on the conditions under which systemic processes such as competition for scarce resources or shifting balances of power lead to war—although theorists working at this level of analysis still disagree sharply not only over the magnitudes of particular effects but sometimes even over the directions of those effects (see Levy, this volume).

Other research possibilities also exist. For instance, it is possible—because of the strong assumptions some systemic theorists make concerning the unitary rationality of foreign policies—to explore the logical implications of systemic formulations through game-theoretic techniques. Granting that interdependency in the international environment takes a certain form (obviously a difficult judgment call), it is important to know whether there is a Nash equilibrium point in the payoff matrix, a set of policy postures from which no player would have a strong incentive to depart because of the substantial risk of shifting strategy (for example, the defect/defect option in the prisoner's dilemma game; see Shubik, forthcoming). It is also important to know whether the equilibrium point is Pareto-inferior (there are sets of policy postures that would leave at least some players better off at no one's expense *if* everyone acted in the prescribed way) or Pareto-superior (there are no sets of policy postures that yield better outcomes for *both* players). Many regularities observed at the systemic level—arms races, the formation of alliances, preemptive wars against would-be hegemonic powers—can be viewed as the result of a tendency for rational national actors to plan for the worst (what game theorists term the minimax strategy of trying to maximize the "goodness" of one's worst possible outcomes). Pursuit of a minimax strategy may be rational in the sense of protecting oneself from exploitation, but often only at the price of locking each side into a Pareto-inferior set of outcomes (for example, never-ending arms races and geopolitical competition) and of precluding the identification of Pareto-superior sets of outcomes (for example, verifiable arms control or troop reduction agreements).

Research Methods

Research relevant to the problem of preventing nuclear war covers an enormous range of methodologies. As already noted, one's choice of research method hinges, in part, on one's level of analysis which, in turn, is often related to the nature of the outcome (dependent variable) one is trying to explain. It is possible to conduct highly controlled laboratory tests of certain causal hypotheses (for example, those pertaining to the impact of information load on choice strategies or the impact of pursuing a fair-but-firm reciprocity strategy on behavior in a mixed-motive game), but not of others (for example, one cannot experimentally manipulate the bipolarity-multipolarity of an international system or the degree of economic interdependence within an alliance).

In addition, one's choice of research method depends on one's epistemological preferences. Some investigators advocate extending the hypothetico-deductive or covering-law model of explanation to the study of international conflict. According to this model, an event has been explained only when one has shown that the existence of the event could have been inferred—either deductively or with a high probability—"by applying certain laws of universal or statistical form to specified antecedent circumstances" (Hempel, 1965:229). Advocates of this explanatory approach generally put their methodological faith in controlled laboratory experimentation (what better way is there to test causal hypotheses of universal or statistical form?) and in quantitative studies of the historical record (what better way is there to determine whether predicted lawful regularities actually hold up in the real world?). A pithy expression of this epistemological view is to be found in S.S. Stevens' famous critique of qualitative research: "when description gives way to measurement, calculation replaces debate" (in Kaplan, 1964:174). The key to cumulative scientific progress lies in identifying and quantifying lawful regularities in the phenomena under study.

Other investigators are markedly less enthusiastic. Little can be learned, in their view, from attempting to extend the covering-law model from domains where it has served us well (in many areas of the physical and biological sciences) to domains where it is inappropriate—inappropriate because of the complexity, uniqueness, and perhaps even indeterminacy of the underlying processes at work (Almond and Genco, 1977; Cronbach, 1975; Gallie, 1968; Gergen, 1978). Variable-centered, nomothetic research cannot begin to capture the multiplicity of motives activated in particular foreign policy problems, the confusion and uncertainty that frequently infuse the decision process, the norms and implicit understandings that exist among key actors, the institutional constraints on decision makers, and so forth. If we want to understand how nuclear war might break out, we need to understand in rich, idiosyncratic detail how policymakers live and work. The goal should be the "thick description" of specific events (Geertz, 1973) or the development of "coherent whole explanations" (Walsh, 1967) that trace the connections among events and then reveal superordinate themes that give meaning and context to those events.

It is, to be sure, misleading to divide the epistemological universe into two hostile, hopelessly incompatible camps. It is possible to see value in both quantitative, variable-centered research and in qualitative, idiographic research; it is even possible that the two lines of inquiry will occasionally lead to similar conclusions. Patterns or themes that emerge from in-depth case studies are sometimes highly consistent with lawlike generalizations that emerge from experiments or multivariate field research (for examples, see Druckman and Hopmann, this volume; Holsti, this volume; Stein, forthcoming). Although the epistemological packaging is certainly different, there is presumably a common underlying reality to which practitioners of these different approaches are responsive.

Most investigators—including the contributors to this series—do not appear to have made absolute or dogmatic commitments to a particular method of generating knowledge. Most seem to be pragmatists who are willing to shift methodological strategies depending on the nature of the problem under investigation and the available data. There is also a growing recognition that the distinctions among alternative research methods are not as clear-cut as often implied. It is possible to test hypotheses derived from covering-law explanations through comparative case studies. (For discussion of the method of focused comparison, see George [1979] and George and McKeown [1985]; for use of that method to identify problems that arise in applying abstract deterrence theory to specific historical cases, see George and Smoke [1979].) And there is no reason why quantitative, variable-centered researchers cannot be more sensitive to potential boundary conditions on the applicability of their hypotheses or to the problems that arise in operationalizing abstract constructs in concrete situations. (See Druckman and Hopmann [this volume] on the need to strike a balance in content analyzing negotiations between sensitivity to the uniqueness of the particular case and to the need for theoretical generality.)

Next I consider the range of research methods that can be deployed to increase our understanding of how nuclear war might occur. These methods differ from each other in many ways. They vary in the degree to which they permit confident causal inferences (well-controlled, laboratory experiments conferring the greatest inferential power, single historical case studies generally the least, with multivariate field studies somewhere in between), in their immediate or obvious relevance to the problem of avoiding nuclear war (historical case studies of U.S.-Soviet relations possessing the most relevance, laboratory experiments of college students perhaps the least), in their reliance on qualitative versus quantitative forms of argument (laboratory researchers and game theorists tending to be the most mathematical, historical researchers, the least), and in their focus on individuals versus institutions (laboratory studies tend by necessity to be individualistic, other forms of inquiry tend to be more flexible). Moreover, it should be emphasized that there is a great deal of intracategory variability. Laboratory studies of cognitive, affective, and small group processes differ greatly among themselves—in the types of tasks presented, the measures collected, the subjects used, and the hypotheses tested. Historical case studies vary dramatically in the thoroughness and comprehensiveness of the examination of evidence, the rigor of the hypothesis testing, and the systematic use of "focused comparisons" with other cases. Multivariate statistical studies of international conflict rely on an enormous range of data bases (attributes of nations, events data, capabilities data, political rhetoric), use a variety of analytic techniques to process these data, and test hypotheses derived from all the major levels of analysis considered earlier. In short, this chapter can but skim the surface of these vast research literatures.

Laboratory Experiments and Simulations

Researchers have used experiments and simulations to explore a variety of psychological and social processes that, with minimal imagination, can be seen as relevant to the problem of avoiding nuclear war. Voluminous experimental literatures exist on decision making in general (Abelson and Levi, 1985; Einhorn and Hogarth, 1981; Kahneman et al., 1982) and decision making under high-stress conditions in particular (Janis and Mann, 1977; Streufert and Streufert, 1978), attitude formation, persistence, and change (McGuire,

1985; Nisbett and Ross, 1980), and bargaining and negotiation processes (Pruitt and Rubin, 1986). The internal validity advantages of exploring basic processes under controlled laboratory conditions are well known. Investigators are in a position to make relatively strong inferences concerning determinants of the response class of interest. They can isolate the effects of particular independent (experimentally manipulated) variables, control for potential confounding variables, systematically assess interactions among independent variables, and test detailed models of the processes hypothesized to mediate relationships between independent and dependent variables.

Experimental research can obviously take many forms, from highly schematized payoff matrix studies (for example, mixed-motive games such as the prisoner's dilemma) to much more elaborate and involving scenarios (for example, the inter-nation simulations). Regardless of form, however, skeptics have been more impressed by the dissimilarities than the similarities between laboratory studies and high-level political decision making. The skeptics note the many differences between the almost always college student subjects and top policymakers: maturity, background, training, and concern for doing the best possible job (policymakers are presumably extremely motivated; college student subjects may approach their experimental assignments with a more casual attitude). The skeptics also note the existence of organizational and systemic constraints on actual policymakers that are not present in the laboratory. Policymakers, unlike experimental subjects, are embedded in complex networks of intra- and interorganizational accountability and competition. Finally, the skeptics contrast the brief duration of experiments (typically an hour or two) with the protracted course of most foreign policy deliberations (most crises last for days). In short, it is trivially easy to identify a plethora of threats to the generalizability of experimental studies, each threat a potential boundary condition on the applicability of elegantly demonstrated experimental phenomena to the complex, confusing, even chaotic world of foreign policy.

Although it is easy to point out ways in which laboratory experiments differ from the "real thing," it is much more difficult to specify when the differences make a difference. How does one begin to close the yawning generalizability gap between the artificial world of the laboratory and the "real" world of international conflict? Our contributions have not found a simple, all-purpose solution to this problem. In general, they proceed cautiously and rarely rely solely on experimental evidence to make an important argument. Consider the following three examples from *Behavior, Society, and Nuclear War:*

> 1. Holsti (this volume) refers to the large body of experimental work that has revealed a inverted-U relationship between stress and judgment and choice processes. He notes that very high levels of stress (threat to important values

and information overload) are generally disruptive of complex cognitive functioning. But Holsti also invokes other work—in organizational theory, history, and political science—to support claims concerning the effects of crisis-induced stress on the foreign policymaking process.

2. Stein (forthcoming) draws on laboratory research on bargaining processes to highlight the limitations of a pure-threat deterrence posture and to underscore the importance of drawing on alternative influence tactics (Chertkoff and Baird, 1971). Stein, however, draws even more heavily on historical case studies. Similarly, Stein notes laboratory research on motivated distortion in social judgment (Janis and Mann, 1977), but again puts even more weight on historical case studies that suggest leaders of challenger states sometimes engage in wishful thinking when assessing the chances of their successfully challenging the deterrence posture of a status quo power.

3. Druckman and Hopmann (this volume) refer to a variety of experimental studies for potential insights into international negotiation—including work on the effects of reciprocity strategies (Wilson, 1971), the effects of role reversal (Walcott et al., 1977), and negotiator responsiveness (Pruitt and Rubin, 1986). But, they are willing to draw inferences for the conduct of foreign policy from these literatures only in the presence of converging evidence from historical studies of international conflict management.

Mass Surveys of Public Opinion

Surveys do not permit the kind of confident causal inferences possible in experiments. The representative sample survey is, however, the method of choice for investigating a large class of questions relevant to nuclear war. Surveys allow us to assess the breadth and depth of popular support for particular foreign and defense policies, attitudes toward key political events and personalities, and the degree of lability-stability in public sentiment on these questions. Insofar as public opinion constrains, and perhaps occasionally even drives foreign and defense policy, surveys can shed light on important inputs into the policymaking process.

Like experimentation, survey research can take diverse forms. Researchers can focus on interrelationships among variables at one time or across time; they can focus on a narrow or broad range of political issues; they can focus on the general public or political elites or both; they can assess the impact of major events on public opinion; they can focus on the complex feedback relationships that appear to exist between public opinion and public policy; they can even embed question-wording experiments into surveys to assess the susceptibility of public opinion to linguistic manipulation. These methodological variations illustrate the flexibility of survey research and the range of issues that can be addressed.

A variety of by no means intuitively obvious findings have emerged from survey research on U.S. national security attitudes (see Russett, this volume). Public opinion on such issues does not appear to obey the same rules of ideological constraint as elite opinion (Converse, 1964). Many Americans in the 1980s, for example, do not feel it is inconsistent to support both a "freeze" on nuclear weapons and President Reagan's Strategic Defense Initiative (SDI). Citizen support for particular policies also often depends greatly on the linguistic packaging of the policies. The insertion and deletion of affect-laden terms (the presidency, communism, national defense, the Soviet Union, etc.,) can have large effects on response distributions (Schuman and Presser, 1981). Similarly, so can the relative emphasis on the "gain" and "loss" components of a policy proposal. Questions that make one's own losses salient (for example, the missiles we are required to dismantle) or the other side's gains salient (e.g., the weapons systems they get to keep) will obviously evoke less popular support than questions that make the other side of the trade-off equation salient (Kahneman and Tversky, 1979).

It is especially important from a policy standpoint not to underestimate the magnitude and pervasiveness of question-wording effects. Pundits commonly speak of public opinion on issues such as the SDI or the nuclear freeze as though it were a straightforward matter to obtain a single-point estimate that, within confidence intervals set by sampling variability, reflects how the American people think about key national security issues. Matters are not, however, so simple. One can sometimes obtain very different estimates of public sentiment by posing only subtly different versions of the same questions. Not surprisingly, political partisans often disagree sharply over what constitutes the fairest phrasing of questions, with judgments of fairness suspiciously highly correlated with degree of public support elicited for preferred positions.

Unfortunately, there is no theory, accepted procedure, or standard approach for adjudicating disputes over question bias and fairness. To be sure, numerous methodological tactics might be deployed here. One might try to develop politically neutral versions of questions; one might ask many (biased) versions of the "same" question; one might assess the stability of opinion in response to "neutral" questions by assessing how much people are willing to change their attitudes when confronted with particular challenges or counterarguments. In each case, however, there is always room for the political prejudices of the investigator to contaminate the results. One can never be sure that one did not phrase the argument on one side more persuasively than the argument on the other. Our knowledge of how to construct unbiased samples from the general population of potential respondents has advanced much more rapidly than our knowledge of how to construct unbiased samples from the conceptual population of potential questions.

Quantitative Studies of Historical Data

Many investigators have attempted to extend the empirical grasp of behavioral and social science by quantifying archival data and then using these data to test hypotheses concerning correlates or determinants of war. This methodological approach is not linked to any specific level of analysis. Efforts at quantitative hypothesis testing using historical data occur at a psychological level of analysis (for example, content analysis studies of policy deliberations and diplomatic communications: Axelrod, 1976; Holsti et al., 1969; Tetlock, 1985a), at the level of the nation-state (for example, Singer's [1980] correlates of war project) and at the level of the international system (for example, Bueno de Mesquita's [1985] efforts to test his theory concerning the necessary conditions for the rational initiation of war by developing quantitative systemic indicators of the balance of power).

The advantages of quantification are well known: investigators must use explicit, consistent, and public rules for attaching numerical scale values to observations. And the disadvantages of quantification are equally well known, in large part because of these very strengths. In their efforts to represent complex theoretical constructs with simple empirical indicators, quantitative researchers often make assumptions about their data that many skeptics regard as politically naive at best and ridiculous at worst.

It is no simple matter, for example, to gauge the importance of "perceptions of capability" in the policy deliberations of decision makers prior to World War I. One possible indicator is the frequency with which policymakers discuss such issues in the archival records (Holsti et al., 1969), but the absence of such discussion is far from compelling evidence that perceptions of capability played no role in the crisis decision-making process (Jervis, 1970). Decision makers may not have bothered to express such concerns because they felt the relevant information was too widely known or obvious, or the archival record may just be incomplete. It is also no simple matter to gauge the impact of internal conflict within a state on its propensity to go to war. There are many possible indicators of internal conflict (civil disturbances, guerrilla warfare, attempted coups, labor unrest, inflation, unemployment, intensity of ethnic, religious, or political factionalism), indicators that are frequently only weakly intercorrelated. It is even very difficult to achieve consensus on superficially straightforward judgment calls such as who initiated or won a war. Critics of Bueno de Mesquita's (1981) expected utility theory argue that his tests of the theory rest on a number of dubious historical classifications (Majeski and Sylvan, 1984). For instance, Bueno de Mesquita operationally defines the initiator of a war as the first state to engage in sustained combat on the opponent's territory—a definition that adequately covers many cases but seriously oversimplifies others (for example, it is at least debatable that Israel was the sole initiator of the 1967 Six Day War). And it strikes many observers as odd to classify Serbia as the sole victor in World War I or Poland as a victor in World War II (see Levy, this volume).

The difficulty of interpreting many quantitative historical indicators does not, of course, mean that it is fruitless to try. It does, however, help to explain why it has proven so hard to identify a set of predictively powerful and uncontroversial laws of international conflict. The explanatory variables are often extremely complex, context bound, and resistant to precise, standardized operational definitions. Partly because of these concerns, many researchers interested in international conflict eschew quantitative methods in favor of more flexible, case-specific, qualitative methods.

Case Study Methods

Although case study methods are perhaps the least scientifically prestigious of the approaches to generating knowledge considered here, such methods play a critical role in research on the origins of international conflict. As George (1979) and Eckstein (1975) have argued, case studies can both build on and enrich experimental and statistical approaches to the study of political processes. Case studies can be used, for example, to stimulate new lines of theorizing (for example, George and Smoke's [1974] comparative historical studies of deterrence suggested a variety of hypotheses concerning the conditions under which threats of force are likely to elicit desired reactions from other states), to provide detailed, qualitative evidence that phenomena documented by experimental or statistical research do indeed occur in specific historical situations (for example, Jervis' [1976] widely acclaimed use of diplomatic history to show that policymakers fall prey to cognitive biases and errors documented by experimental psychologists), and to cast doubt on the general validity of particular generalizations or lawlike claims (for example, Lebow's [1981] use of case studies to challenge the deterrence theory claim that the most important cause of international aggression is the perception of the leadership of "challenger" states that "status quo" states lack the resolve or capability to defend commitments). In short, case studies can advance knowledge in diverse ways.

The contributors to this series frequently draw on case study evidence to formulate, support, and qualify theoretical claims. This reliance on case study evidence reflects, in large part, a recognition that experimental and statistical studies—notwithstanding their many strengths—fail to capture much of the subtlety and complexity of the actual conduct of foreign policy.

Case studies complement quantitative, variable-centered research by providing qualitatively rich and contextually detailed descriptions of the lives and events that we seek to understand. The explanatory goal is no longer the creation of statistical models that account for as much of the variance across cases as possible; the goal is the creation of conceptual models that organize the disparate themes and strands of meaning that run through particular historical events. Thus, if one wants to understand the dynamic ebb and flow of U.S.-Soviet talks on intermediate-range nuclear forces in Europe, it may help to be aware of experimental and quantitative field research on bargaining and negotiation. There is no substitute, however, for "thick description" of the specific events of interest (Geertz, 1973; Talbott, 1985).

Thick description entails much more than a complete behavioristic account of an event (who said what to whom, when, where, and how?); it requires an interpretive account of the "multiplicity of complex conceptual structures, many of them superimposed upon or knotted into one another" (Geertz, 1973:10) that give meaning and structure to foreign policy. One needs, for example, to appreciate the intricate sociopolitical systems within which arms control negotiations are embedded. One needs to be aware of the crosscutting personal and political ambitions and rivalries within the negotiating teams, the degree of autonomy granted the negotiating teams on specific issues by their respective governments, how the limits of that autonomy were negotiated and are now understood, the domestic political constraints within which key governmental decision makers must operate, intra- and interalliance politics, the views of key decision makers on the types of concessions it is realistic to hold out for, and so forth (Talbott, 1985). Any given act within a negotiation session is open to interpretation at any one or combination of these various levels of analysis—a state of affairs that strains the open-mindedness even of investigators who are exceptionally tolerant of ambiguity.

To achieve highly nuanced case descriptions of this sort, investigators must often proceed more by feel and improvisation than by plan and research design. They must sift through often complex and contradictory archival records and through interview protocols with policymakers that yield difficult to disentangle mixtures of candid revelation, distorted recall, and self-serving rationalization. As a result, it is extraordinarily difficult to be explicit and systematic about standards of data collection and interpretation in case studies. It is also extraordinarily unlikely that even two investigators working from exactly the same data set will reach identical conclusions. Sometimes the disagreements will revolve around differences in emphasis. The investigators will attach different weights to different data sources. Sometimes the disagreements will be more fundamental. The investigators will reach opposite conclusions about the necessity or usefulness of drawing on a particular level of analysis to make sense of the events in the case history.

This apparent lack of methodological rigor is at the heart of many objections to case study approaches. Verba (1967) notes, for example, that case studies do not add up easily. Although each study may be beautifully written and elegantly organize a wide range of historical facts, it is rarely possible—because of idiosyncrasies in methods of gathering and interpreting data—to derive reliable and valid theoretical statements. Without well-defined and consistent standards of evidence and procedure across cases, there is no clear way of determining whether the variables are being measured on the same "scales" or, for that matter, whether the same variables are even being measured. There are also relatively few checks on the intrusion of error and bias into the research process. It is hard to say how much emphasis researchers have put or should have put on particular items of information in drawing particular conclusions.

These differences in emphasis can, moreover, be theoretically consequential. For instance, whether one views an ambiguous historical case as consistent or inconsistent with "deterrence theory" may ultimately hinge on the credibility one believes the leadership of the challenger state attached to warnings or threats from the status quo state. This judgment, in turn, hinges on a rather precise reconstruction of the expected utility decision calculus of the leadership of the challenger state from rather crude historical clues (see, for example, the exchange between Lebow [1987] and Orme [1987]). How seriously did the challenger view certain statements by certain government officials of the status quo power? Did the challenger under- or overestimate the military capabilities or alliance cohesiveness of the status quo power? How seriously did the challenger view the military preparations of the status quo power? Did the challenger under- or overestimate the significance of domestic political opposition to deterrence within the status quo power? Analysts of the historical case must try to piece together answers to such questions from often fragmentary and inconsistent archival records. Confronted with such a complex and unstructured task, it would be surprising if even methodologically self-conscious investigators did not occasionally fall prey to the cognitive tendency to give more weight to hypothesis-consistent than hypothesis-inconsistent evidence in drawing conclusions from historical records (Nisbett and Ross, 1980).

Defenders of case study approaches have a number of possible defenses to these objections. George (1979) and Janis (1982) forcefully argue that many of the methodological and inferential flaws commonly linked to case study approaches are by no means intrinsic to this genre of research. Janis' (1982) comparative case studies of groupthink in foreign policy deliberations, and George and Smoke's (1974) comparative studies of deterrence in international relations demonstrate that investigators can sometimes capitalize on the distinctive strengths of both quantitative, nomothetic studies (for example, explicit statements of theoretical hypotheses and explicit efforts to test those hypotheses against the evidence) and qualitative idiographic studies (for example, sensitivity to the unique historical circumstances of each case). From this perspective, case studies are a major methodological means of advancing the search for general laws or patterns underlying international conflict. Case studies serve the same ultimate epistemic goal as laboratory and statistical field studies (subsuming new observations under Hempel-like covering laws or identifying exceptions to these covering laws that require developing more complex or contingent theoretical generalizations).

Other defenders of case study approaches might mount even more radical challenges to quantitative, variable-centered research. Well-executed case studies serve as sobering reminders of just how difficult it is (perhaps impossible) to know whether a given covering law applies in a given setting. To be sure, it is possible for quantitative content and event analysts to develop systematic schemes for coding negotiation behavior (Pruitt and Lewis, 1975; Stephenson et al., 1977), political rhetoric (Holsti et al., 1969; Tetlock, 1985a), and foreign policy actions (Leng and Wheeler, 1979; Leng, 1983). But these efforts at quantification are—from a radically idiographic perspective—profoundly misguided. Efforts to develop coding categories that place superficially very different acts in the same theoretical categories encourage investigators to downplay, even ignore, highly context-specific components of meaning. Harsh words exchanged at the negotiation table may reflect a personal animosity, a secret joke at the expense of other participants or higher-ups, a carefully orchestrated exchange designed to manipulate the press of other countries, a calculated effort by one or both parties to sabotage the talks, and so on. The possibilities are virtually endless and only diligent attention to the particulars of each case can clarify which interpretations make sense of the facts—indeed, can clarify which facts need to be made sense of. Mechanically coding what is said on the basis of strictly syntactic or semantic criteria (hostile-friendly, responsive-unresponsive, simple-complex, etc.) makes it possible for quantitative comparative investigators to achieve intercoder reliability, but only at the expense of validity—of doing extreme violence to the elaborate networks of context-specific understandings that participants in political settings have worked out among themselves.[5]

Formal Mathematical Models

A final method of generating knowledge about the sources of international conflict deserves mention. Whereas practitioners of case study methods emphasize the importance of "thick description" of the historical contexts within which events are embedded, practitioners of formal modeling emphasize the importance of precise understanding of the underlying structural processes that drive historical events—underlying processes that can be most parsimoniously and effectively described by game theory (Shubik, forthcoming), differential equations models (Intriligator and Brito, 1984), or other advanced mathematical tools.

Although work in this analytic tradition can take many forms, game theory analyses clearly predominate. As Shubik (forthcoming) notes, game theory provides a "formal tool" for exploring what happens when rational, goal-oriented individuals interact with each other in particular environments. These environments can be defined by payoff matrices that specify the outcomes each party can expect given the response options that both have chosen. Game theorists argue that it is possible to reduce the enormous complexity of international conflicts to a finite set of mathematically well-defined games such as the "prisoner's dilemma" and "chicken" (see Shubik, [forthcoming] for more detail). War, in this view, arises not because of the cognitive shortcomings of leaders or the political shortcomings of nations but because of the incentives and disincentives that are built into payoff matrices that, in turn, capture the essence of the international predicaments confronting national leaders.

By way of illustration, one game theorist, Brams (1985:145), has argued that many of the most intractable issues that divide the United States and Soviet Union can be understood as products of the "unforgiving nature" of certain two-person nonzero-sum games. He attempts to model nuclear deterrence, for example, with the game of chicken (see also Schelling, 1966). The basic task of a player who desires to deter an adversary is to make the choice of aggression sufficiently unattractive—through threats of retaliation—that the adversary will refrain from undertaking the act. The key difficulty with this strategy, especially in a world of mutually assured destruction, is the shared knowledge that the deterrer will inflict grievous harm on himself or herself as well as his or her adversary if he or she actually executes the threat of retaliation. An important task for game theorists then becomes the mathematical solution of the difficult problem of identifying an "optimal compromise" (Brams, 1985:147) between the need for deterrent threats that are both effective and credible. Brams (1985) also tries to model the nuclear arms race by employing the prisoner's dilemma game. Both sides in this game would be better off cooperating, he notes, but fear of exploitation keeps them in competition. An important task for game theorists here becomes the identification of a strategy of conditional cooperation in which each side has the monitoring capability to ensure that the other side cooperated when it said it would.

Game-theoretic analyses sometimes yield startlingly simple but logically compelling conclusions. For instance, Axelrod (1984) conducted a computer simulation study that pitted a large number of expert-recommended strategies for coping with the prisoner's dilemma against each other. The simplest submission—tit-for-tat—won the most points—a submission that, Axelrod argues, embodied four critical strategic attributes (it was nice, clear, forgiving, and retaliatory).[6] Jervis (1978) subjected the widely used concept of security dilemma to detailed logical analysis to probe the conditions under which competition or cooperation is most likely to occur in prisoner's dilemma types of international situations. Policies that decrease the potential losses of unrequited cooperation or the potential gains of unilateral defection appear most likely to encourage stable mutual commitments to the otherwise unstable "cooperate-cooperate" cell of the payoff matrix. Jervis (1988) also makes an observation of special interest, at a time when serious consideration is being given to a new technological generation of antiballistic missile systems. He notes that cooperation in prisoner's dilemma types of international environments is more likely, to the degree that defensive military systems can be readily distinguished from offensive ones.

Investigators have applied other formal modeling approaches as well to the study of international conflict. Most important perhaps have been the efforts to develop differential equation models of arms races and to identify the conditions under which arms races do and do not lead to war. Early work that suggested arms races are inherently destabilizing appears to have been superceded (Richardson, 1960). Intriligator and Brito (1984), for instance, have argued on the basis of their interesting mathematical model of competitive military buildups that arms races can lead to war *or* peace, depending on the initial configuration and balance of forces and on the nature of the race (whether "qualitative" advances in weapons technology such as equipping missiles with multiple independently targetable re-entry vehicles (MIRVs) occur). The critical determinant—of whether arms buildups (or, for that matter, arms reductions) increase the likelihood of war—is whether the two sides have moved into a "force space" in which one side can successfully attack the other. It should be noted, however, that such analyses as these are compelling only insofar as one is willing to grant the empirical reality of the underlying mathematical assumption. There are usually solid grounds for skepticism. For example, from the point of view of Intriligator and Brito's (1984) model, it makes no difference whether one passes through a region of instability (breakdown of mutual deterrence) as a result of an arms buildup or as a result of compliance with an arms reduction agreement; from a psychological and political point of view, it may make a great deal of difference.

Formal modeling, especially game-theoretic, approaches have attracted criticism from a variety of quarters. The most frequent criticism is paradoxically directed at what many defenders view as the greatest strength of formal models: the deductive simplicity and elegance of the formulations. To critics, this elegance bespeaks lack of psychological and political realism. People often lack clear goals, misperceive each other's actions and intentions, and miscalculate what is in their own best interest. Nations often send off unintended signals and respond as much to internal political necessities as to external systems of incentives. In short, skeptics can challenge the generalizability and relevance of game-theoretic "solutions" to international conflict in much the same way that they can challenge the generalizability and relevance of experimental research findings—by pointing to potentially powerful variables at work in the international environment that were not taken into account in the original research.

The methodological challenge is to make the connection between the austere formalisms of game theory and the messy world of international conflict. Oye (1986) offers a fascinating example of how this might be done. A series of six historical case studies was commissioned to test the impact of three game-theoretic structural variables on international conflict: the mutuality of interest (cooperation increases as a function of the relative strength of the payoffs to cooperate versus compete), the shadow of time (cooperation increases as the temptation to obtain short-term gains from competition decreases), and the number of players (the fewer players, the more cooperation). The results reveal both the strengths and limitations of a purely game theoretic approach. In Axelrod and Keohane's (1985:227) words, the three causal variables deduced from game theoretic analyses "help us to understand the success and failure of attempts at cooperation in both military-security and political-economic relations." They add, however, that the structural variables, either separately or jointly, are not sufficient for cooperation. There is a multitude of impediments to cooperation that are, at least at present, extremely difficult to capture in formal game theoretic models—including ideological and cognitive variables, organizational and bureaucratic variables, and domestic political variables (variables embedded within levels of analysis reviewed earlier in this chapter).

The Quest for Linkages

Readers of this series should expect both theoretical and methodological diversity. There is no single, unified theory of international conflict; there is, instead, a continuum of theoretical perspectives, ranging from the micro (psychological) to the macro (systemic), within which investigators can formulate hypotheses and conduct research. And there is no single set of methodological guidelines for studying international conflict; there is, instead, a broad range of methods that, depending on the level of analysis and the type of problem under investigation, researchers are likely to find more or less useful.

How should we react to this confusing plurality of theoretical and methodological perspectives? One possibility is that the confusion is temporary—a reflection of the immature ("preparadigmatic") state of theoretical and methodological development in research on international conflict. It is only a matter of time before one level of analysis and set of research methods come to dominate inquiry. One version of this "waiting for a paradigm" thesis is microreductionist. Investigators will eventually be able to show that macrophenomena such as wars among nations can be best understood in terms of basic (probably experimentally demonstrated) laws of individual behavior. The epistemological mirror image of this approach is, of course, macroreductionist (what Greenstein [1975] has aptly called the "actor dispensability thesis"). Investigators will eventually be able to explain conflict among nations in terms of the operation of institutional, cultural, domestic political, economic, or systemic forces, with recourse to only minimal assumptions concerning the nature of individual decision makers.

Another possibility is that this plurality of theoretical and methodological perspectives will be with us for a very long time indeed—a reflection not so much of the immaturity of the disciplines as of the complexity of the subject matter. From this perspective (and it is this perspective that has guided chapter selection for this series), it is unwise to assume that the causal nature of the micro-macro relationship can be known in advance or that this relationship is always and everywhere the same. A more reasonable starting point is to assume that micro- and macroprocesses typically interact to shape decisions bearing on war and peace, with the degree of linkage and exact balance of causal forces shifting from time to time and under different conditions.

This open-ended interactionist position suggests that searches for a fundamental or unifying level of analysis are misguided. Rather than seeking to fit all research efforts into a common reductionist mold, we should be content with: (1) looking for linkages across levels of analysis (ways in which different levels complement and mutually enrich each other); and (2) looking for linkages across research methods (assessing the degree to which practitioners of very different methods of research reach compatible or contradictory conclusions).

Theoretical Linkages

Advocates of different levels of analysis often seem to speak in different data languages—languages that are so different that they cannot be translated into each other without egregious loss of meaning. Balance-of-power theorists, for instance, are not interested in using or testing detailed process models of individual decision making; they feel that it is possible to achieve self-contained, internally consistent, and predictively powerful accounts of international conflict by relying on purely systemic indicators. Investigators in this tradition design studies to test which configurations of systemic variables best explain when, where, and why war breaks out (variables from other levels of analysis simply drop out of the empirical picture).

Although it is true that each level of analysis reviewed earlier has generated its own distinctive, self-contained research literature, it is also true that the distinctions between (and among) levels of analysis are not nearly as neat and tidy as academic writers sometimes imply. Levels of analysis "interpenetrate." One can make a strong case that variables operating at a micro- (psychological) level of analysis rarely directly determine policy outcomes; microlevel processes are constrained, shaped, and perhaps sometimes even transformed by the social systems within which individual decision makers must work and by the structure of the problems that they must confront. Conversely, one can make a strong case that our understanding of when and how macroprocesses shape policy outcomes would be much enhanced by drawing on more realistic assumptions concerning the nature of the individual decision maker.

Let us consider a few examples of how micro- and macroapproaches to the study of war and peace might be brought together. As noted earlier, it is frequently argued that how individual decision makers respond to policy problems reflects the operation of internal psychological processes—for instance, the tendency to rely on simple judgment and choice heuristics to reduce cognitive strain and the tendency in evaluating options to encode possible outcomes as gains or losses from a neutral reference point (Kahneman et al., 1982). Exactly how these response predispositions are expressed in a specific foreign policy setting may depend enormously on the surrounding social-political context. Many of these macro constraints are so obvious that they hardly need to be specified. The "content" of thought—the policy options considered (for example, arms control proposals), the consequences contemplated to arise from each option (for example, the impact on different parties' perceptions of the balance of power), and the bureaucratic and political constituencies to be placated—is largely dominated by the policymaker's perception of macrolevel variables.

It would be misleading, however, to conclude that the disciplinary division of labor is quite so simple, with cognitive psychologists specifying the abstract information processing rules used for interpreting events and making choices, and political scientists and historians specifying the "belief-content" on which those abstract rules operate. It is quite conceivable—available research indicates even likely—that the processing rules themselves can change as a function of the social-political environment. Much depends—as work on group dynamics and bureaucratic politics suggests—on the role and accountability relationships that exist among key decision makers.

These role and accountability relationships link individual decision makers to social systems and can increase or decrease, for example, the complexity of the cognitive strategies that decision makers use to make sense of the world (March, 1978; Halperin, 1974; Janis, 1982; Tetlock, 1985a; Weick, 1979). Much also depends on the nature of the problem confronting the decision makers and exactly how the problem is presented to them (Einhorn and Hogarth, 1981). For instance, although decision makers generally find trade-off reasoning aversive and tend to define situations in ways that deny or minimize trade-offs, there seem to be certain institutional and strategic environments in which trade-offs are so starkly obvious that they have become, in effect, undeniable. Steinbruner (1987:535) has advanced such an argument with respect to the command and control of nuclear weapons. The extreme destructiveness and rapid timing of these weapons has forced the superpowers to confront "unavoidable conflicts among fundamental objectives"—objectives such as maintaining control over one's nuclear forces in a crisis and retaining the ability to respond to a massive first strike. The "solutions" to profoundly difficult trade-offs of this sort are reflected in the institutional procedures that the superpowers have evolved to plan and direct their strategic operations. It would be extremely difficult to argue for a change in these institutional procedures without simultaneously acknowledging the importance of the major conflicting values in the trade-off equation.

Knowledge of response dispositions that exist at the microlevel is then helpful, but rarely sufficient. One can, moreover, make almost an identical argument with respect to knowledge of macrolevel processes. Macroprocesses surely constrain, sometimes sharply, the range of conceivable outcomes of policy deliberations. National leaders sometimes feel that "their hands are tied," that they have no choice (save resignation or waiting to be ousted from office) but to act in certain ways. President Kennedy reportedly felt that he had to succeed in removing Soviet missiles from Cuba or face impeachment (Allison, 1971). Macrotheorists have yet, however, to provide persuasive empirical demonstrations that they can reliably predict specific policy outcomes from the values of macrolevel variables. Too many exceptions exist. Policymakers sometimes resist pressures to represent narrowly defined bureaucratic interests when they feel a larger national objective is at stake; political leaders sometimes court disaster by advocating policies that antagonize important constituencies; national leaders do not always decide to go to war when the "expected utility of war" (as gauged by the sorts of systemic indicators used by Bueno de Mesquita, [1985]) is positive, even highly positive.

Macrocauses of war do not seem to operate the same way on different national leaders and in different situations. As soon as we come into contact with the historical record, simple bivariate hypotheses derived from macrotheories need to be qualified (Greenstein, 1975; Levy, this volume). The complexity arises, in part, because we live in a multivariate macroworld—a world in which many causes at the macrolevel are interactively shaping policy. A policymaker may refuse to yield to pressures from one constituency because he or she is under even greater pressure from another. Or the leader of a hegemonic state may refrain from preemptive war against a rapidly rising challenger state because of the looseness of his or her own state's alliance structure or the tightness of the alliance structure of the challenger.

The complexity also arises because we understand quite poorly exactly how: (1) macrovariables constrain processes at work at a microlevel; (2) microprocesses aggregate to produce macro-outcomes. For instance, systemic theories (the most macro of the macrotheories) assume that, in order to survive in an anarchic international system, states must attach "primacy to their security interests" (Levy, this volume). This assumption tells us very little about how risk-seeking or risk-averse states will be in their pursuit of power in different situations. Macrotheories could benefit in this regard by drawing on some empirically well-validated propositions concerning individual decision processes. For example, prospect theory (Kahneman and Tversky, 1979) leads one to expect leaders to be much more willing to take large risks in order to avoid major losses in national power than in order to expand national power. This tendency to loss aversion may help to explain why threats to the balance of power have been so strongly associated with the outbreak of general wars in the last five centuries. Wars frequently arise in such situations as a result of dominant states fearing loss of control and launching preemptive wars or as a result of weaker states coalescing to prevent a would-be hegemonic power from imposing its will on them.[7]

The tendency to loss aversion may also help to explain some intriguing patterns in public opinion data on support for national security policies. It has been argued, for instance, that the public is most willing to back hardline policies when "national pride" has been wounded (McClosky, 1967)—an explanation that has been invoked, albeit in post hoc fashion, to account for the receptiveness of the German public to nationalistic appeals in the wake of the Versailles Treaty and for the surge in American public support for defense spending in the aftermath of the Vietnam War, OPEC oil embargoes, and the Iranian hostage crisis. It has also been noted (Russett, this volume) that

American public support for defense policies tends to increase when those policies (SDI) are presented as means of avoiding potentially catastrophic losses (the destruction of U.S. cities). Avoiding an easily imaginable disaster seems to be a much more psychologically compelling objective than reaching a difficult-to-understand and perhaps even more difficult-to-justify arms control agreement.[8]

Explicating the microprocesses that link macrophenomena to foreign-policy decision making is a profitable but surprisingly underutilized way of exploring linkages among levels of analysis. From a psychological point of view, systemic theories are often woefully underspecified (Simon, 1985). It is not enough simply to posit the existence of rational national actors who maximize their interests within the constraints of the international system. One can derive very different predictions about the effects of important systemic variables depending on the auxiliary assumptions that one makes about the subjective probabilities or beliefs and utilities or preferences of the policymakers involved. Three examples—all highly relevant to the current geopolitical scene—must suffice to make this critical theoretical point.

1. *Is nuclear proliferation destabilizing?* Enormous concern has been expressed over the slowly but inexorably expanding number of nuclear powers. One can construct plausible systemic arguments that this concern is either justified or unjustified. One can argue that nuclear proliferation reduces the likelihood of war by inducing caution, increases the likelihood of war by increasing the incentives for preemption, or has no effect one way or another (because the former two effects cancel each other out). Which outcome one predicts hinges on the assumptions one chooses to make about the belief systems and utility functions of key national decision makers. (In extreme cases, it may even be necessary to redefine what is customarily meant by "rational." What happens, for example, if nuclear weapons fall into the control of messianic religious or political leaders who attach much higher value to destroying their enemies than they do to insuring their own survival?)

2. *Is parity destabilizing?* Organski and Kugler (1980) have challenged the widely held view that approximately equal distributions of power among major states are conducive to peace. They have argued that parity in power is actually destabilizing because it tempts each side to believe that it has a reasonable chance of winning. They have argued, moreover, that parity is particularly dangerous when the balance of power is in flux. Which position one takes depends in large part on one's assumptions about the accuracy with which policy elites can appraise shifting military–technological–economic balances of power. The Organski and Kugler position seems to leave more room for cognitively or motivationally driven forms of misperception than the traditional realpolitik position (Stein, forthcoming). Which position one takes may also depend on one's assumptions about key decision makers' attitudes toward risk

and uncertainty. The Organski and Kugler position seems to imply a greater willingness to take risks than the traditional realpolitik analysis.

3. *Are alliances destabilizing?* Levy (this volume) notes that there has been much controversy concerning when alliances increase versus decrease the likelihood of war. There is no single answer to this question. The impact of alliances depends almost certainly on the degree to which alliances simplify the calculations of would-be aggressors (uncertainty reduction), make war more or less attractive (by affecting the subjective probability of success), and make war seem more or less likely (by affecting perceptions of the hostility of the other side). Systemic theories can make predictions on this key geopolitical issue only by assigning implicit or explicit causal weights to each of these components of the individual and collective decision-making process.

Methodological Linkages

Just as communication across levels of analyses can be difficult, so too can communication across research methods. The difficulties are not, however, insurmountable. I have already mentioned several examples of multimethod convergence. Sometimes very different methods of inquiry yield compatible conclusions. Thus, laboratory studies of judgment and choice, quantitative content analyses of archival records, and qualitative case studies all point to a widespread tendency for decision makers to rely on simple, low-effort heuristics in interpreting new events and choosing among courses of action (Axelrod, 1976; George, 1980; Jervis, 1976; Nisbett and Ross, 1980). The same three categories of method—plus some game theoretic and computer-simulation work (Axelrod, 1984)—also point to a common conclusion concerning the relative effectiveness of different influence tactics in mixed-motive games. In general, some form of tit-for-tat (reciprocity) strategy is more effective than either bullying or appeasement as a method for achieving mutually beneficial compromise agreements (George et al., 1971; Leng and Wheeler, 1979; Pruitt and Rubin, 1986; Snyder and Diesing, 1977). Many additional examples of convergence could, moreover, be cited (Holsti, this volume; Stein, forthcoming).

The notion of seeking out multimethod convergence is deeply entrenched in the behavioral and social sciences (see Campbell and Fiske, [1959] on multiple operationism), so it should not be surprising to see the idea surface in a research domain where there is so much uncertainty concerning both what needs to be measured and how the measurement process should proceed. It seems only prudent not to put all of one's theoretical "eggs" in one methodological "basket"—to recognize that different methods often have complementary strengths and weaknesses and to look for patterns of convergence in the findings that emerge from applications of these methods. And it is reassuring that the search for multimethod convergence has occasionally been successful. Investigators working with quite different theoretical concepts and very different methodological tools have sometimes arrived at surprisingly similar conclusions.

There is, then, some cause for optimism that many of the emergent generalizations discussed in *Behavior, Society, and Nuclear War* are not method specific. Implementing a multimethod research strategy is not, however, a simple task, for a number of reasons. Part of the problem is the difficulty of determining whether multimethod convergence has indeed occurred; the other part of the problem is the difficulty of deciding what to do when one concludes that multimethod convergence has not occurred—when different methods yield inconsistent, even contradictory, results.

There is no fixed, objective rule for solving these problems. Consider, for instance, the difficulties that arise in assessing whether experimental research on mixed-motive games really converges on the same conclusions as qualitative and quantitative studies of the historical record. A "fair-but-firm" reciprocity strategy may have a precise operational definition in the laboratory, a fuzzier, more open-ended operational definition in quantitative event analysis studies, and a highly context-specific operational definition in historical case studies (a definition anchored in politically controversial assumptions about the perceptions and goals of specific actors at specific times in the flow of events). Similarly, judgmental biases such as belief perseverance typically have precise meanings in experimental studies but are notoriously resistant to precise or consensual definition in actual foreign-policy settings. (To what extent, for example, should observers of the Soviet Union have changed their minds after learning of the invasion of Afghanistan or after learning of the Soviet withdrawal?) The qualitative diversity of research methods makes it extremely difficult to determine whether practitioners of different methods are truly studying the same underlying phenomenon or whether we (the reviewers of interdisciplinary literatures) are imposing a false unity on these diverse research efforts. It is possible, as noted earlier, to have spurious multimethod convergence—to fail to recognize that superficially similar phenomena actually arise as a result of the operation of fundamentally different causes (for example, overconfidence in the validity of a simple historical analogy may arise not as a result of reliance on simple cognitive heuristics documented in laboratory work but rather from political pressures to appear "firm" to particular constituencies).

If identifying multimethod convergence poses problems, so too does interpreting multimethod divergence. When two different methods yield different conclusions, one confronts a plethora of interpretive options. One might question the usefulness of one method for testing a particular hypothesis or class of hypotheses. Thus, it could be argued that multivariate correlational studies are, for various reasons, just not as useful for exploring linkages between domestic conditions and foreign policy as comparative case studies (see Levy, this volume). Or, it could be argued that qualitative forms of content analysis are more useful than quantitative techniques for identifying subtle shifts in the thinking of key national leaders or for predicting shifts in government policies (George, 1959).

Another interpretive option is to concede that both methods are useful for testing a given hypothesis and to argue that the different results have arisen as a result of the operation of moderator variables to which one method is more sensitive than the other. Thus, comparative case studies of decision making may be better equipped than laboratory studies to identify institutional and political boundary conditions on the expression of cognitively rooted judgmental biases (thus helping to explain why decision makers do not exhibit such biases in certain cases). Neither method, from this standpoint, is yielding trivial or artifactual results. The two methods, in conjunction, help to reveal the range of circumstances under which the hypothesized information processing biases hold up.

The key point is that how one decides to weight data from different methodological sources is ultimately a judgment call. There is no integrative set of guidelines that tells us when to pay special attention to, and when to ignore, results from particular research methods. And it is misleading to think of such decisions as purely methodological. Such decisions ultimately rest on implicit or explicit theories concerning the causal mechanisms that produce both regularities and irregularities in the data. Methodological and theoretical choices are, as we have seen before, tightly linked.

Concluding Remarks: The Quest for Policy Relevance

There are obviously many gaps and inconsistencies in the research literatures from which we have drawn in these volumes. But assume, for the sake of argument, that behavioral and social science research on international conflict had advanced much further than it now has. Assume that we possessed an integrative theory of international conflict that specified—with reasonable precision—how processes from different levels of analysis interact to shape policy outcomes. Assume that we also possessed broad interdisciplinary consensus on the usefulness of different research methods for testing different aspects of this integrative formulation. Would we then be in a position to offer authoritative advice on how to avoid nuclear war?

The answer is still not an unqualified "yes." Although such an integrative theory would be enormously useful for organizing our thinking about problems of managing international conflict in general, it would not satisfy the needs of policymakers for guidance in coping with the myriad of specific real-world problems created by the introduction of nuclear weapons into international politics in 1945 and by the complex evolution and proliferation of such weapons and their delivery systems in the intervening 43 years. At their best, behavioral and social science theories yield conditional generalizations of the form: "Under circumstances x, y, and z, this type of intervention is likely to have these effects and under this other set of circumstances, the same intervention is likely to have this other set of effects." Such advice falls considerably short of telling policymakers whether it is a good idea to proceed with the development of a new weapon system or to accept a particular arms control proposal. Such advice falls short largely because it begs the question of how one determines whether the preconditions for adopting a given strategy have actually been met in a given situation. For example, it is one thing to claim that a firm-but-fair reciprocity strategy usually works better than alternative strategies (pure threat or appeasement) in promoting mutually advantageous solutions to conflicts of interest; it is quite another thing to claim that a reciprocity strategy is most appropriate in a particular political context. In Verba's (1967:116) words, "Generalizations fade when we look at particular cases." It is necessary to take into account the many circumstances unique to the case at hand, each circumstance not fully explored in the research underlying the original generalization, each circumstance thus a potential boundary condition for the "law" one seeks to apply. Caution is in order, for the history of the behavioral and social sciences abounds with examples of the simple causal generalizations of today becoming the first- and second-order interaction effects of tomorrow (Cronbach, 1975; Gergen, 1978; McGuire, 1985).

A set of predictively powerful, reliably documented generalizations is, in short, not enough; one needs some systematic way of assessing whether general principles apply to specific cases. In addition to an integrative theory, we require a diagnostic checklist for assessing whether the antecedent conditions for the activation of a given generalization are present. Such a checklist will not, moreover, be easy to devise (see Griffiths, forthcoming). The most divisive policy debates often focus on what we call from a theoretical point of view "antecedent conditions." In the post-World War II era, for instance, there has been enormous disagreement over what mixture of deterrence and reassurance is most appropriate in U.S. dealings with the Soviet Union. This debate has not hinged on the generic wisdom of a fair-but-firm strategy; it has hinged on the assessment of Soviet geopolitical intentions. Is the Soviet Union a dangerously expansionist power prepared to take large risks to achieve highly ambitious goals (R. Osgood, 1981; Wildavsky, 1983)? Or is the Soviet Union best thought of as a conservative status quo power preoccupied with minimizing internal and external threats to its own security (White, 1984)? Or is Soviet foreign policy guided by some complex mixture of defensive and opportunistic offensive motives, with the relative importance of motives depending on the issue domain and leadership period under consideration? How one answers these questions has important implications for the emphasis one places on deterrence versus reassurance in U.S. national security policy.

Linking up theory to practice requires methods for systematically sizing up specific situations. Here the behavioral and social sciences blur into the arts of diplomacy and conflict management. This is not to say that the behavioral and social sciences have nothing to offer to the practice of international relations. These disciplines offer a variety of qualitative and quantitative techniques for predicting future trends in the behavior of nation-states (Choucri and Robinson, 1978). These disciplines also highlight the dangers of cognitive conceit (of thinking we know more than we do), point to possible correctives of judgmental biases such as overconfidence and, most crucial of all, remind us of the importance of stating our hypotheses concerning the nature of the adversary in falsifiable form (be prepared to state what would make us change our minds). But the behavioral and social sciences can apparently take us only so far. Expert observers of the Soviet Union still disagree sharply at this time over what Soviet geopolitical goals were at the time of the invasion of Afghanistan or, for that matter, over what the long-term goals of Gorbachev's foreign policy currently are.

The inferential difficulties also do not end here. Even if one had a surefire method of determining that a general principle did apply to a specific case, one would still confront the profound problem of operationalizing the theoretical advice. For example, what exactly does it mean to say that the United States should pursue a reciprocity strategy in its dealings with the Soviet Union? Reciprocity can be operationalized in a seemingly infinite variety of ways. Does it mean adopting some variant of Osgood's (1962) graduated and reciprocal initiatives in tension reduction (GRIT) proposal in which one superpower attempts to defuse tensions through a series of carefully planned and announced concessions? And what exactly should those concessions be? Should the United States announce a no-first-use policy? Should the Soviet Union have persisted with its recent unilateral nuclear test moratorium? How does one know that in operationalizing a reciprocity strategy in a particular way that one has struck the right balance between conciliatoriness and resistance to exploitation? Presumably some kind of corrective feedback mechanism needs to be built into the policy formula. The key problem then becomes calibrating one's responses to those of the other side: how does one decide whether a given response by the other side is sufficiently conciliatory or refractory to warrant a response in kind?

Once again, the behavioral and social sciences can only take us so far. It is not possible to deduce specific policy prescriptions from these abstract bodies of knowledge (no more than it is possible to deduce a medical diagnosis of a particular patient from the biological sciences). The behavioral and social sciences do, however, highlight issues that prudent policymakers should take into account if they wish to avoid war in international confrontations. George's (George et al., 1971; George, 1980) work on the use of coercive diplomacy in the context of crisis management is an excellent illustration of work in this vein. In discussing the practice of coercive diplomacy in international politics, George did not presume to tell policymakers whether they should use force or threats of force in specific situations. On the basis of his own inductive-historical research, he did, however, identify several generic problems that policymakers need to solve if they are to be successful in a diplomatic crisis at both protecting "vital national interests" and avoiding war. For example, when considering the use of the strategy of coercive diplomacy, policymakers should ask themselves:

1. What are the risks (often considerable) of presenting an ultimatum that specifies a deadline for compliance? Can the risks be controlled?

2. How should one deal with the conflict between the need to pressure the opponent into compliance (cease attack, withdraw missiles) and the need to slow the pace of events to give the opponent time to evaluate the situation?

3. How should one calibrate the intensity and timing of threats?

4. How should threats be presented? (The linguistic, cultural, and political context can be critical determinants of whether threats backfire.) Should threats be coupled with rewards in a carrot-and-stick package that makes compliance the most attractive option? How threatening should the consequences of noncompliance be? How appealing should the consequences of compliance be? How can rewards and threats be designed to augment rather than negate each other?

These guidelines highlight the complexity of the issues and the variety of "things that can go wrong" in crisis decision making. To be sure, following these procedural guidelines is neither a necessary nor a sufficient condition for ensuring a good outcome. Policymakers may sometimes impulsively choose policies that, in hindsight, appear wise. And policymakers may sometimes carefully choose policies that, in hindsight, appear disastrous. These is no simple, all-encompassing formula for coping with the complexities of crisis management. Given what we know, however, of crisis decision making and intergroup negotiation under stress, it is reasonable to conclude that foreign-policymakers who heed these guidelines are less likely to make calamitous miscalculations than policymakers who ignore the guidelines. George's (1980) prescriptions for crisis management do not tell us what to do, but they do tell us how to structure our thinking. The guidelines are similar in this regard to the "fault trees" that engineers use to diagnose the diverse ways in which complex physical systems can fail (Fischhoff et al., 1978).

If it is indeed impossible and perhaps undesirable to "reduce" international relations to an exercise in applied behavioral and social science, where does this leave us?

A simplistic answer is that we are left with the necessity of individual judgment. It will not be possible any time in the foreseeable future to deduce "optimal policies" (optimal in the sense of maximizing policymakers' values) from theory or research in the behavioral and social sciences. Policymakers of the future will have to rely as they do now on subjective judgment and their own often implicit crude causal theories—theories that are sometimes as inchoate as "no more Munichs" or "no more Vietnams" (Neustadt and May, 1986). A more sophisticated answer is that although we may never escape the necessity of individual judgment, we can work to ensure that the judgments of policymakers are well informed by the richer, more explicit, more differentiated—albeit sometimes fallible—knowledge base provided by the behavioral and social sciences.

It is all too easy to puncture the prescriptive pretensions of the behavioral and social sciences. The power of these disciplines to yield solutions to societal problems often seems meager compared to the power of the biological and physical sciences. And a good case can be made that excessive claims have been made in the past on behalf of the behavioral and social sciences. But if hubris is a vice to be avoided so, too, is excessive modesty. A great deal of evidence has accumulated—on social judgment and choice processes, bargaining and negotiation processes, influence processes, the functioning of individuals and organizations under stress, and the dynamics of public opinion—that should be kept in mind in public debates on key issues of international security. The appropriate benchmark of comparison is not "Has research on war and peace attained the paradigmatic consensus that prevails in certain other sciences?" but rather, "If knowledge from the behavioral and social sciences is not used to inform these debates, what types of knowledge will be used?" There is no value-neutral option here. To withhold information is as consequential an act as to release it.

The behavioral and social sciences cannot replace individual judgment, but they can sharpen, refine, and inform it. Historians and political scientists have noted that the commonsense reasoning of foreign policy elites is far from infallible. Policymakers, it has been observed, are prone to essentially the same cognitive biases and errors as ordinary mortals. They are often too quick to draw strong conclusions from weak evidence and too slow to modify those conclusions in response to new evidence (George, 1980; Jervis, 1976; Neustadt and May, 1986). The result is often the drawing of sweeping, undifferentiated generalizations from currently salient historical precedents ("appeasement does not work" or "conventional armies cannot defeat guerrillas with strong indigenous support") and an insensitivity to differences between current problems and these popular historical precedents ("if we don't build this weapon system, we will be repeating the errors of appeasement," "if we do send troops into this country, we will be repeating the errors of Vietnam or Afghanistan"). The behavioral and social sciences have created a number of institutional checks on these types of sweeping, undifferentiated causal claims. It is incumbent on an investigator who advances such a claim to document its universal applicability and to state the claim with sufficient precision that other investigators will have a reasonably clear idea of what evidence will count either as support for or as refutation to the claim. Few claims survive this methodological screening process. Most generalizations, as is apparent from the contributions to *Behavior, Society, and Nuclear War*, have had to be qualified or circumscribed, often sharply so. Causation in international politics tends to be complex (to involve variables from a number of different levels of analysis), interactive (the effects of variables at one level of analysis often depend on the state of variables at other levels of analysis), and difficult to identify with confidence and precision (the limited number of observations, the large number of confounding variables, and the fallibility of our research methods make it difficult to disentangle competing causal hypotheses).

Behavior, Society, and Nuclear War illustrates that we have made tangible progress toward clarifying the underlying processes that affect both the likelihood of war in general and of nuclear war in particular. It also illustrates how difficult it is to make progress in this area. Readers who are looking for elegantly axiomatized theories and empirical consensus will be disappointed. Nonetheless, what has been achieved should not be minimized. We have learned a good deal on both the theoretical and the methodological fronts and, perhaps, most important, we have learned a good deal about the limits of our knowledge. Knowledge of our ignorance—especially in a policy domain where confident, even glib, causal assertions are so common—can be a major contribution in itself. The most important service the behavioral and social sciences can currently provide to the policymaking community may well be to make thoughtful skepticism respectable: to sensitize those who make key decisions to the uncertainty surrounding our understanding of international conflict and to the numerous qualifications that now need to be attached to simple causal theories concerning the origins of war.

In the same spirit, *Behavior, Society, and Nuclear War* should not be viewed as a final or definitive statement of our knowledge, but as a product of an ongoing process of inquiry. The process of adapting behavioral and social science methods to the study of international security issues is a massive undertaking that requires careful analysis of the strengths and weaknesses of different methods and, for many problems, the invention of hybrid approaches that combine the distinctive strengths of these methods (e.g., comparative case studies combined with game theoretic modeling or laboratory simulations). The process of formulating tentative theoretical generalizations and subjecting them to criticism and revision is an equally massive undertaking that requires careful and patient empirical evaluations of a confusing variety of claims, counterclaims, and revised claims. The volumes of *Behavior, Society, and Nuclear War* represent the initial stages of these efforts. Our goal has been to bring together those methodological and theoretical advances that, in our collective judgment, promise the most fruitful payoffs in the next stages of this ongoing process.

Notes

I would like to acknowledge the support of the MacArthur Foundations for my research and writing on international security issues. I also appreciate the support of the Institute of Personality Assessment and Research, the secretarial help of Alice Brilmayer, and the helpful comments of Alexander George, Irving Janis, Robert Jervis, Philip Converse, William K. Estes, and Paul Stern on an earlier version of this chapter.

1. It is worth noting that although scholars typically study processes at only one level of analysis (the departmental structure of research universities encourages such specialization), policymakers do not have this analytical luxury. They must deal with complex, real-world events that defy neat theoretical taxonomies. Policymakers need to have at least a crude intuitive understanding of when processes at one or another level of analysis have become particularly critical determinants of policy outcomes. They need to make judgments such as: Has the leadership of nation x misjudged our likely reaction to this policy? Is the leadership pursuing goals different from those that we initially supposed? How much latitude for maneuver does the leadership of nation x have given the domestic political and economic constraints within which it must work? Does this response of nation x reflect the intentions of the central leadership, or is it an act initiated by a particular influence group or bureaucracy within the government? One need only think of the vigorous policy debates within the United States that have been triggered by events such as the Cuban missile crisis, the Third World debt crises, and the Korean Airlines flight 007 disaster to recognize the enormous impact that level-of-analysis attributions can have on policy preferences.

2. Levels of analysis represent broad conceptual frameworks within which it is

possible to articulate and refine numerous testable "theories of the middle range" (Merton, 1957). Thus, there is no single psychological theory of individual decision making, no single organizational theory of bureaucratic politics, and no single systemic theory of how the balance of power affects the likelihood of war. This internal complexity of levels of analysis makes it extremely difficult, perhaps at present impossible, to falsify the claim that a particular level of analysis is necessary or sufficient for explaining a particular phenomenon. As soon as one has rejected hypotheses derived from one middle-range theory, another middle-range theory emerges to replace it. Presumably, a limit must be placed on this process; repeated failures to reconcile evidence with middle-range theories from a given level of analysis are reminiscent of what Lakatos (1970) described as "degenerative" research programs. When more intellectual energy goes into thinking of post hoc interpretations to defend existing theory than goes into thinking of ways of extending existing theory to new evidence, the time has probably come to reevaluate the viability of the entire research program.

3. We need to be careful not to assume that all role-induced attitude shifts are purely opportunistic. Changes in roles may expose policymakers to new evidence and analysis that, in turn, produce genuine shifts in intellectual perspective. It is difficult in any given case to disentangle opportunistic from information-driven attitude change.

4. Domestic political pressures do not, however, operate in only this direction. Historians have documented many cases in which, were it not for influential antiwar domestic constituencies, national leaders almost certainly would have pursued more bellicose policies (for example, Roosevelt prior to 1941 or the Johnson administration during the Vietnam War).

5. Advocates of quantitative, variable-centered research are not, of course, without counterarguments. If nomothetic researchers were simply measuring radically different properties of behavior in different situations and arbitrarily categorizing those properties under the same variable label, one would not expect statistically powerful or replicable relationships to emerge from studies conducted by these researchers. Since nomothetic research sometimes reveals powerful and replicable relationships, the critique is overstated. Advocates of qualitative idiographic approaches can still, however, claim that quantitative researchers typically treat context-specific meanings as statistical noise or error variance and that, as a result, seriously oversimplify reality. Phenomena that represent artifacts or nuisance variables from a nomothetic point of view may be of central interest from an idiographic perspective.

6. Although the tit-for-tat strategy accumulated large numbers of points against other response programs in Axelrod's computer simulation tournament, that does not mean tit-for-tat is the key to survival in the international environment (Jervis, 1988). One can raise a variety of objections to the strategy. From a "dovish" perspective, tit-for-tat may be too tough. Once one has entered into a competitive response cycle, it is unclear how tit-for-tat can get one out. Someone has to take the conciliatory initiative (see Osgood's [1962] discussion of GRIT; Larsen, 1987). From a "hawkish" perspective, tit-for-tat may be too soft. As Axelrod (1984) notes, tit-for-tat never actually won any individual game in the computer tournament. If the primary goal in international politics is defined as maximizing one's *relative* gain, a response strategy that can at

best tie loses much of its attractiveness. Finally, from a psychological point of view, tit-for-tat may simply not work very well in a world in which perceptual errors occur—in which decision makers frequently misclassify cooperative behavior as competitive and competitive behavior as cooperative (Are Gorbachevian arms control concessions motivated by the desire to reach a stable, mutually beneficial modus vivendi with the West? Or are the concessions attempts to gain breathing time for a political-economic system that, once recovered, will pose an even more severe threat to Western security?). From this analytic perspective key questions become "How high an error rate can tit-for-tat withstand?" and "How high is the actual error rate in international politics?" In brief, the game-theoretic analysis ultimately has to be grounded in psychological and political reality.

7. Even this pretty robust generalization requires qualification. For instance, Nazi Germany in 1939 and Imperial Japan in 1941 appear to have been willing to take very large risks to expand national power. These observations can, however, be readily reconciled with some form of subjective expected utility theory. Germany, it could be argued, sought to recover from the enormous losses of World War I (hence its willingness to take risks), and Japan, it could be argued, feared that the military-economic balance of power would shift progressively against it unless decisive action were taken (Russett, 1967).

8. Work on framing effects on decision making (Tversky and Kahneman, 1981) suggests that public support for arms control proposals that require complex trade-offs is likely to be volatile and to depend very much on how salient the question makes the "loss" and "gain" sides of the trade-off equation. This perspective also suggests that in a multidimensional, asymmetric strategic environment (in which the two sides possess distinctive and difficult-to-compare strengths and weaknesses [Steinbruner, 1985]), opponents of arms control will *ceteris paribus* have a built-in psychological edge in the battle for public opinion as a result of the tendency for losses to loom larger than gains.

References

Abelson, R.P., and A. Levi. 1985. Decision-making and decision theory. In E. Aronson and G. Lindzey, eds., *Handbook of Social Psychology*, Vol. 2. Hillsdale, N.J.: Erlbaum.

Allison, G.T. 1971. *Essence of Decision*. Boston: Little, Brown.

Allison, G.T., A. Carnesale, and J.S. Nye. 1985. *Hawks, Doves, and Owls: An Agenda for Avoiding Nuclear War*. New York: Norton.

Almond, G., and T. Genco. 1977. Clouds, clocks, and the study of politics. *World Politics* 29:489–522.

Art, R.J. Forthcoming. U.S. nuclear policy and the political process. In P.E. Tetlock, J.L. Husbands, R. Jervis, P.C. Strn, and C. Tilly, eds., *Behavior, Society, and Nuclear War*. Vol. 3. New York: Oxford University Press.

Axelrod, R. 1976. *Structure of Decision*. Princeton, N.J.: Princeton University Press.

———. 1984. *The Evolution of Cooperation*. New York: Basic Books.

Axelrod, R., and R.O. Keohane. 1985. Achieving cooperation under anarchy: Strategies and institutions. *World Politics* 38:226–254.

Blair, B.G. 1987. Alerting in crisis and conventional war. In A.B. Carter, J.D. Steinbruner, and C.A. Zracket, eds., *Managing Nuclear Operations*. Washington, D.C.: The Brookings Institution.

Bracken, P. 1983. *Command and Control of Nuclear Forces*. New Haven, Conn.: Yale University Press.

Brams, S. 1985. *Superpower Games*. New Haven, Conn.: Yale University Press.

Brewer, M., and R.M. Kramer. 1985. The psychology of intergroup relations and behavior. *Annual Review of Psychology*, 36:219–244.

Bueno de Mesquita, B. 1981. *The War Trap*. New Haven, Conn.: Yale University Press.

———. 1985. The war trap revisited: A revised expected utility model. *American Political Science Review* 79:157–176.

Burnstein, E., and M.L. Berbaum. 1983. Stages in group decision-making: The decomposition of historical narratives. *Political Psychology* 4:531–561.

Campbell, D.T., and D.W. Fiske. 1959. Convergent and discriminant validation by the multitrait-multimethod matrix. *Psychological Bulletin* 56:81–105.

Chertkoff, J.M., and S.L. Baird. 1971. Applicability of the big lie technique and the last clear chance doctrine to bargaining. *Journal of Personality and Social Psychology* 20:298–303.

Chertkoff, J.M., and J.K. Esser. 1976. A review of experiments in explicit bargaining. *Journal of Experimental Social Psychology* 12:222–236.

Choucri, N., and R.C. North. 1975. *Nations in Conflict*. San Francisco, Calif.: Freeman.

Choucri, N., and T.W. Robinson. 1978. *Forecasting in International Relations*. San Francisco, Calif.: Freeman.

Converse, P.E. 1964. The nature of belief systems in mass publics. In D.E. Apter, ed., *Ideology and Discontent*. New York: Free Press.

Coser, L. 1956. *The Function of Social Conflict*. New York: Free Press.

Cronbach, L.J. 1975. Beyond the two disciplines in scientific psychology. *American Psychologist* 30:116–127.

Dyson, F. 1984. *Weapons and Hope*. New York: Harper & Row.

Eckstein, H. 1975. Case studies in political science. In N. Polsby and F.I. Greenstein, eds., *Handbook of Political Science*, Vol. 6. Reading, Mass.: Addison-Wesley.

Einhorn, H., and R.M. Hogarth. 1981. Behavioral decision theory. *Annual Review of Psychology* 32:53–88.

Etheredge, L.S. 1978. *A World of Men*. Cambridge, Mass.: MIT Press.

Fischhoff, B. Forthcoming. Nuclear decisions: Cognitive limits to the thinkable. In P.E. Tetlock, J.L. Husbands, R. Jervis, P.C. Stern, and C. Tilly, eds., *Behavior, Society, and Nuclear War*, Vol. 2. New York: Oxford University Press.

Fischhoff, B., P. Slovic, and S. Lichtenstein. 1978. Fault trees: Sensitivity of estimated failure estimates to problem representation. *Journal of Experimental Psychology: Human Perception and Performance* 2:330–344.

Gallie, W.B. 1968. *Philosophy and the Historical Understanding*, 2d. ed. New York: Schocken.
Geertz, C. 1973. *The Interpretation of Culture*. Princeton, N.J.: Princeton University Press.
George, A.L. 1959. *Propaganda Analysis*. White Plains, N.Y.: Row, Peterson.
———. 1979. Case studies and theory development. In P.G. Laure ed., *Diplomatic History: New Approaches*. New York: Free Press.
———. 1980. *Presidential Decision-Making in Foreign Policy: The Effective Use of Information and Advice*. Boulder, Col.: Westview.
George, A.L., P.J. Farley, and A. Dallin. 1988. *U.S.-Soviet Security Cooperation: Achievements, Failures, Lessons*. Oxford, England: Oxford University Press.
George, A.L., D. Hall, and W. Simons. 1971. *The Limits of Coercive Diplomacy*. Boston: Little, Brown.
George, A.L., and T.J. McKeown. 1985. Case studies and theories of organizational decision making. In *Advances in Information Processing*, Vol. 2. Greenwich, Conn.: JAI Press.
George, A.L., and R. Smoke. 1974. *Deterrence in American Foreign Policy: Theory and Practice*. New York: Columbia University Press.
Gergen, K.J. 1978. Experimentation in social psychology: A reappraisal. *European Journal of Social Psychology* 8:507–527.
Greenstein, F.I. 1975. Personality and politics. In N. Polsby and F.I. Greenstein, eds., *Handbook of Political Science*, Vol. 2. Reading, Mass.: Addison-Wesley.
Griffiths, F. Forthcoming. Mutual perceptions of intentions among Soviet and U.S. policy elites. In R.E. Tetlock, J.L. Husbands, R. Jervis, P.C. Stern, and C. Tilly, eds., *Behavior, Society, and Nuclear War*, Vol. 3. New York: Oxford University Press.
Halperin, M. 1974. *Bureaucratic Politics and Foreign Policy*. Washington, D.C.: The Brookings Institution.
Hempel, C.G. 1965. *Aspects of Scientific Explanation*. New York: Free Press.
Hoffman, S. 1960. *Contemporary Theory in International Relations*. Englewood Cliffs, N.J.: Prentice-Hall.
Holsti, O.R. 1972. *Crisis Escalation War*. Montreal, Canada: McGill Queens University Press.
———. 1976. Foreign policy formation viewed cognitively. In R. Axelrod, ed., *Structure of Decision*. Princeton, N.J.: Princeton University Press.
Holsti, O.R., R.A. Brody, and R.C. North. 1969. The management of international crisis: Affect and action in American-Soviet relations. In D.G. Pruitt and R.C. Snyder, eds., *Theory and Research on the Causes of War*. Englewood Cliffs, N.J.: Prentice-Hall.
Institute of Medicine. 1986. *The Medical Implications of Nuclear War*. Washington, D.C.: National Academy Press.
Intriligator, M.D., and D.L. Brito. 1984. Can arms races lead to the outbreak of war? *Journal of Conflict Resolution* 28:63–84.
Janis, I.L. 1982. *Victims of Groupthink*, 2nd ed. Boston: Houghton-Mifflin.
Janis, I.L., and L. Mann. 1977. *Decision Making*. New York: Free Press.

Jervis, R. 1969. The costs of the quantitative study of international relations. In K. Knorr and J. Rosenau, eds., *Contending Approaches in International Politics*. Princeton, N.J.: Princeton University Press.

———. 1970. *The Logic of Images in International Relations*. Princeton, N.J.: Princeton University Press.

———. 1976. *Perception and Misperception in International Politics*. Princeton, N.J.: Princeton University Press.

———. 1978. Cooperation under the security dilemma. *World Politics* 30:167–214.

———. 1988. Realism, game theory and cooperation. *World Politics* 41:317–349.

Kahneman, D., P. Slovic, and A. Tversky, eds. 1982. *Judgment Under Uncertainty*. Cambridge, England: Cambridge University Press.

Kahneman, D., and A. Tversky. 1979. Prospect theory: An analysis of decision under risk. *Econometrica* 47:263–291.

Kaplan, A. 1964. *The Conduct of Inquiry*. Scranton, Penn.: Chandler.

Kaplan, F. 1982. *Wizards of Armageddon*. New York: Simon and Schuster.

Katz, A.M. 1982. *Life after Nuclear War: The Economic and Social Impacts of Nuclear Attacks on the United States*. Cambridge, Mass.: Ballinger.

Kelman, H., and A. Bloom. 1973. Assumptive frameworks in international politics. In J. Knutso, ed., *Handbook of Political Psychology*. San Francisco, Calif.: Jossey-Bass.

Kennedy, P. 1987. *The Rise and Fall of the Great Powers: Economic Change and Military Conflict from 1500 to 2000*. New York: Random House.

Lakatos, I. 1970. Falsification and the methodology of scientific research programs. In I. Lakatos and A. Musgrave, eds., *Criticism and Growth of Knowledge*. London: Cambridge University Press.

Larsen, D. 1987. Game theory and the psychology of reciprocity. Unpublished manuscript, Columbia University.

Lebow, R.N. 1981. *Between Peace and War*. Baltimore, Md.: Johns Hopkins University Press.

———. 1987. Deterrence failure revisited. *International Security* 12(1):197–213.

Leng, R.J. 1983. When will they ever learn: Coercive bargaining in recurrent crises. *Journal of Conflict Resolution* 27:379–420.

Leng, R.J., and H.G. Wheeler. 1979. Influence strategies, success, and war. *Journal of Conflict Resolution* 23:655–684.

Majeski, S.J., and D.J. Sylvan. 1984. Simple choices and complex calculations. *Journal of Conflict Resolution* 38:316–340.

Maoz, Z. 1981. The decision to raid Entebbe. *Journal of Conflict Resolution* 25:677–707.

March, J.G. 1978. Bounded rationality, ambiguity, and the engineering of choice. *Bell Journal of Economics* 9:587–603.

McClosky, H. 1967. Personality and attitude correlates of foreign policy orientation. In J.N. Rosenau, ed., *Domestic Sources of Foreign Policy*. New York: Free Press.

McGuire, W.J. 1985. The nature of attitudes and attitude change. In G. Lindzey and E. Aronson, eds., *Handbook of Social Psychology*, 3rd ed. Reading, Mass.: Addison-Wesley.

Melman, S. 1970. *Pentagon Capitalism: The Political Economy of War*. New York: Oxford University Press.
Merton, R.K. 1957. *Social Theory and Social Structure*. Glencoe, Ill.: Free Press.
Modelski, G. 1987. *Long Cycles in World Politics*. Seattle, Wash.: University of Washington Press.
Mueller, J.E. 1973. *War, Presidents, and Public Opinion*. New York: Wiley.
Neustadt, R.E., and E.R. May. 1986. *Thinking in Time: The Uses of History for Decision Makers*. New York: Free Press.
Nisbett, R.E., and L. Ross. 1980. *Human Inference*. Englewood Cliffs, N.J.: Prentice Hall.
Organski, A.F.D., and J. Kugler. 1980. *The War Ledger*. Chicago: University of Chicago Press.
Orme, J. 1987. Deterrence failures: A second look. *International Security* 11(3):3–40.
Osgood, C.E. 1962. *An Alternative to War or Surrender*. Urbana, Ill.: University of Illinois Press.
Osgood, R.E. 1981. *Containment, Soviet Behavior and Grand Strategy*. Berkeley, Calif.: Institute of International Studies.
Oye, K.A. 1986. *Cooperation Under Anarchy*. Princeton, N.J.: Princeton University Press.
Pfeffer, J. 1985. Organizations and organization theory. In E. Aronson and G. Lindzey, eds., *Handbook of Social Psychology*, Vol. 1. Hillsdale, N.J.: Erlbaum.
Pruitt, D.G., and S.A. Lewis. 1975. Development of integrative solutions in bilateral negotiation. *Journal of Personality and Social Psychology* 31:621–633.
Pruitt, D.G., and J. Rubin. 1986. *Social Conflict: Escalation, Stalemate and Settlement*. New York: Random House.
Richardson, L.F. 1960. *Arms and Insecurity*. London: Stevens and Sons Ltd.
Rosecrance, R. 1963. *Action and Reaction in World Politics*. Boston: Little, Brown.
Rosenau, J. 1970. Theories and pre-theories of foreign policy. In R.B. Farrell, ed., *Approaches to Comparative and International Politics*. Evanston, Ill.: Northwestern University Press.
Russett, B.M. 1967. Pearl Harbor: Deterrence theory and decision theory. *Journal of Peace Research* 4:89–106.
Sagan, C. 1983. Nuclear war and climatic catastrophe. *Foreign Affairs* 62:257–292.
Sarkesian, S.C., ed. 1972. *The Military-Industrial Complex: A Reassessment*. Beverly Hills, Calif.: Sage.
Schell, J. 1980. *The Fate of the Earth*. New York: Knopf.
Schelling, T.C. 1966. *Arms and Influence*. New Haven, Conn.: Yale University Press.
Schlenker, B. 1985. *The Self in Social Life*. New York: Academic Press.
Schumann, H., and S. Presser. 1981. *Questions and Answers in Attitude Surveys: Experiments on Question Form, Wording, and Context*. New York: Academic Press.
Shubik, M. Forthcoming. Models of strategic behavior and nuclear deterrence. In P.E. Tetlock, J.L. Husbands, R. Jervis, P.C. Stern, and C. Tilly, eds., *Behavior, Society, and Nuclear War*. Vol. 2. New York: Oxford University Press.

Simon, H.A. 1985. Human nature in politics: The dialogue of psychology with political science. *American Political Science Review* 79:293–304.

Singer, D. 1972. *The Scientific Study of Politics: An Approach to Foreign Policy Analysis*. New York: General Learning Press.

Singer, J.D. 1980. Accounting for international war: The state of the discipline. *Annual Review of Sociology* 6:349–367.

Snyder, G.H., and P. Diesing. 1977. *Conflict Among Nations: Bargaining Decision Making, and System Structure in International Crises*. Princeton, N.J.: Princeton University Press.

Stein, J.G.. Forthcoming. Deterrence and reassurance. In P.E. Tetlock, J.L. Husbands, R. Jervis, P.C. Stern, and C. Tilly, eds., *Behavior, Society, and Nuclear War*, Vol. 2. New York: Oxford University Press.

Steinbruner, J.D. 1974. *A Cybernetic Theory of Decision*. Princeton, N.J.: Princeton University Press.

———. 1985. U.S. and Soviet security perspectives. *Bulletin of the Atomic Scientists* 22:89–93.

———. 1987. Choices and trade-offs. In A.B. Carter, J.D. Steinbruner, and C.A. Zracket, eds., *Managing Nuclear Operations*. Washington, D.C.: The Brookings Institution.

Stephenson, G.M., B.H. Kniveton, and I.E. Morely. 1977. Interaction analysis of an industrial wage negotiation. *Journal of Occupational Psychology* 50:231–241.

Streufert, S., and S. Streufert. 1978. *Behavior in the Complex Environment*. Washington, D.C.: Winston & Sons.

Suedfeld, P., and P.E. Tetlock. 1977. Integrative complexity of communications in international crises. *Journal of Conflict Resolution* 21:169–184.

Talbott, S. 1985. *Deadly Gambits*. New York: Knopf.

Tetlock, P.E. 1979. Identifying victims of groupthink from public statements of decision-makers. *Journal of Personality and Social Psychology* 37:1314–1324.

———. 1985a. Integrative complexity of American and Soviet foreign policy statements: A time-series analysis. *Journal of Personality and Social Psychology* 49:1565–1585.

———. 1985b. Accountability: The neglected social context of judgment and choice. In B.M. Staw and L. Cummings, eds., *Research in Organizational Behavior*, Vol. 1. Greenwich, Conn.: JAI Press.

Tetlock, P.E., and J.I. Kim. 1987. Accountability and judgment processes in a personality prediction task. *Journal of Personality and Social Psychology* 52:700–709.

Tetlock, P.E., and C. McGuire. 1986. Cognitive perspectives on foreign policy. In S. Long ed., *Political Behavior Annual*, Vol. 1. Boulder, Col.: Westview. Reprinted in R. White, ed., 1986. *Psychology and the Prevention of Nuclear War*. New York: New York University Press.

Theis, W. 1984. *When Governments Collide*. Berkeley, Calif.: University of California Press.

Tversky, A., and D. Kahneman. 1981. The framing of decisions and the rationality of choice. *Science* 221:453–458.

Verba, S. 1961. Assumptions of rationality and non-rationality in the international system. In K. Knorr and S. Verba, eds., *The International System: Theoretical Essays*. Princeton, N.J.: Princeton University Press.

———. 1967. Some dilemmas in comparative research. *World Politics* 20:111–127.

Walcott, C., P.T. Hopmann, and T.D. King. 1977. The role of debate in negotiation. In D. Druckman, ed., *Negotiations: Social Psychological Perspectives*. Beverly Hills, Calif.: Sage.

Walker, S. 1977. The interface between beliefs and behavior: Henry Kissinger's operational code and the Vietnam War. *Journal of Conflict Resolution* 21:129–168.

Walsh, W.H. 1967. *Philosophy of History: An Introduction*. New York: Harper & Row.

Waltz, K.N. 1959. *Man, the State, and War*. New York: Columbia University Press.

———. 1979. *Theory of International Politics*. Reading, Mass.: Addison Wesley.

Weick, K.E. 1979. Cognitive processes in organizations. In B.M. Straw, ed., *Research in Organizational Behavior*. Greenwich, Conn.: JAI Press.

White, R. 1984. *Fearful Warriors: A Psychological Study of U.S.-Soviet Relations*. New York: Free Press.

Wiegele, T.C. 1979. Signal leakage and the remote psychological assessment of foreign policy elites. In L. Falkowski, ed., *Psychological Models in International Politics*. Boulder, Col.: Westview.

Wildavsky, A. 1983. *Beyond Containment: Alternative American Policies toward the Soviet Union*. San Francisco: Institute of Contemporary Studies.

Wilson, W. 1971. Reciprocation and other techniques for inducing cooperation in the prisoner's dilemma game. *Journal of Conflict Resolution* 15:167–195.

Yarmolinsky, A. 1970. *The Military Establishment*. New York: Harper & Row.

Contributors and Editors

DANIEL DRUCKMAN is a study director at the National Research Council and adjunct professor of conflict management at George Mason University. He has been a senior scientist at Booz Allen & Hamilton and the Mathtech Scientist at Mathematica, Inc. His primary interests are in the ares of interparty conflict resolution, international negotiations, nonverbal communication, political analysis, and modeling methodologies, including simulation. His publications include *Negotiations: Social-Psychological Perspectives* (Sage, 1977), *Nonverbal Communication: Survey, Theory, and Research* (Sage, 1982), and *Political Stability in the Philippines: Framework and Analysis* (University of Denver, 1986). Druckman received a Ph.D. in social psychology from Northwestern University.

OLE HOLSTI is a professor of political science at Duke University. His research interests include foreign policy, crisis decision making, public opinion and foreign policy, international relations, and international relations theory. He is author of *Crisis, Escalation, War* (McGill Queens University Press, 1972) and coauthor of *American Leadership in World Affairs: UN and the Breakdown of Consensus* (with James N. Rosenau; Allen & Unwin, 1984). Holsti received a B.A. from Stanford, an M.A.T. from Wesleyan University, and a Ph.D. in political science from Stanford University.

P. TERRENCE HOPMANN is a professor of political science and director of the Institute of International Studies at Brown University. His primary interests are in the areas of international negotiation, arms control, and the history of U.S.–Soviet arms negotiations. His publications include *Rethinking the Nuclear Weapons Dilemma in Europe* (Macmillan, 1988) and *Unity and Disintegration in International Alliances* (Wiley, 1973). He holds an A.B. from Princeton University and a Ph.D. in political science from Stanford University.

Jo L. Husbands is a senior research associate with the National Research Council. From 1982 to 1986, she was deputy director of the Committee for National Security in Washington, D.C. Her research interests include U.S. defense policy, international negotiations, and Third World security issues such as arms transfers and nuclear proliferation. Her recent publications include *Defense Choices: Greater Security with Fewer Dollars* (with William W. Kaufman; Committee for National Security, 1986) and "The Conventional Arms Transfers Talks" (with Anne H. Cahn) in *Arms Transfers Limitation and Third World Security* (Thomas Ohlson, ed.: Oxford University Press, 1988). She received a Ph.D. in political science from the University of Minnesota.

Robert Jervis is a professor of political science and a member of the Institute of War and Peace Studies at Columbia University. He is currently working on problems of psychology, decision making, and cooperation. Among his publications are *Perception and Misperception in International Politics* (Princeton University Press, 1976), and *Psychology and Deterrence* (with Richard Ned Lebow and Janice Stein; Johns Hopkins University Press, 1985). He received a Ph.D. in political science from the University of California at Berkeley.

Jack S. Levy is a professor of political science at Rutgers University. His research focuses on the question of the causes of war from several different theoretical and methodological perspectives. He is the author of *War in the Modern Great Power System, 1495–1975* (University Press of Kentucky, 1983) and has contributed articles to numerous scholarly journals. Levy received a B.S. in physics from Harvey Mudd College, and M.A. and Ph.D. degrees in political science from the University of Wisconsin, Madison.

Bruce Russett is Dean Acheson professor of international relations and political science at Yale University. He is also the editor of *The Journal of Conflict Resolution*. His research interests include constraints and opportunities concerning security policy in democratic political systems and systematic comparative studies of the conditions of success and failure of deterrence policy. Russett's publications include *What Price Vigilance? The Burdens of National Defense* (Yale University Press, 1970) and *The Prisoners of Insecurity: Nuclear Deterrence, the Arms Race, and Arms Control* (Freeman, 1983). He holds a Ph.D. in political science from Yale University, a diploma in economics from King's College, Cambridge University, and a B.A. in political economics from Williams College.

PAUL C. STERN is study director of the Committee on Contributions of Behavioral and Social Science to the Prevention of Nuclear War and staff officer at the National Research Council. His current research is on the formation of social attitudes about environmental policy. His publications include *Evaluating Social Science Research* (Oxford University Press, 1979) and *Energy Use: The Human Dimension* (with Elliot Aronson; Freeman, 1984). Stern received a B.A. from Amherst College, and M.A. and Ph.D. degrees in psychology from Clark University.

PHILIP TETLOCK is professor of psychology and director of the Institute of Personality Assessment and Research at the University of California at Berkeley. His major research interests include the study of international conflict, judgment and choice processes, and impression management. His recent publications include "Psychological advice on foreign policy: What do we have to contribute?" (*American Psychologist*, 1986) and "Monitoring the integrative complexity of American and Soviet foreign policy rhetoric: What can be learned?" (*Journal of Social Issues*, 1988). Tetlock received B.A. and M.A. degrees from the University of British Columbia and a Ph.D. in psychology from Yale University.

CHARLES TILLY is distinguished professor of sociology and history at the New School for Social Research, where he also directs the Center for Studies for Social Change. Most of his recent research and writing concerns political aspects and consequences of large-scale social change. His most recent books are *Big Structures, Large Process, Huge Comparisons* (Sage, 1985), *The Contentious French* (Harvard University Press, 1986), and *States, Coercion, and Capital* (forthcoming). Tilly received his Ph.D. in sociology from Harvard University.

Index

Accommodation, in crisis, 54, 55
Adversary's intentions and capabilities, misperceptions of, 280–285
Affective processes of individual decision makers, 341–344
Afghanistan, Soviet intervention in, 62, 63, 86, 120, 121, 180, 191, 342, 371, 374
Alliances
　ad hoc vs. permanent, 236
　role in balance of power theory of, 235–236
　as structural factors in international negotiations, 128–131
　tensions between crisis management and alliance management, 60, 61
Allison, G. T., 274
American Institute of Public Opinion (AIPO), 181, 185
Angola, 342
Antiballistic missile (ABM) treaty (1972), 185
　popular support for, 196
　SDI and, 52, 53
Antisatellite (ASAT) weapons, 51, 64, 95
Appeasement, 54
Arab nations, 60, 61
Argentina, 279, 281, 287
Arms control negotiations
　effect of economic downturn on, 191
　as type of international security negotiations, 93–96
Arms race, differential equation models of (research method), 363
Art and Science of Negotiation, The (Raiffa), 162
Atomic bombing of Japan, 193, 336

Attention span, reduced, 30
Austria-Hungary, 39
Axelrod, R., 110

B-1 bomber program, 62
Backtranslating messages, 49
Balance of power theory of war, 228–243, 338
　assumptions of, 230
　central proposition of, 230–231
　criticism of, 251
　dyadic balance of power, 240–243
　military capabilities of, 231–235
　other variables in, 236–240
　role of alliances in, 235–236
Ball, George, 36
Ballistic missile defense (BMD), 52
Bargaining, 49
　as crisis management prescription, 56
　in international negotiations, 107–119
　　debate and role reversal, 115–119
　　models of, 91–93
　mutual security negotiations and, 91–93
Bargaining process analysis (BPA), 116–117, 149, 156, 158–163
Bay of Pigs, 345
Begin, Menachem, 98, 144
Belgium, 38
Bentham, Jeremy, 263, 268
Berlin blockade (1948–1949), 44
Berlin "deadline" crisis (1958–1959), 61
Best alternative to a negotiated agreement (BATNA) model for bargaining, 92
Bipolar systems, balance of power theory and, 233–234
Bismarck, Otto von, 45

"Boundary role conflict" in international negotiations, 99
Bounded rationalist, decision maker as, 22
Brezhnev, Leonid, 191
Brzezinski, Zbigniew, 120
Bueno de Mesquita's expected utility theory of war, 243–251, 357–358
Bureaucratic constituencies, 338, 345–347
  impact on crisis decision making of, 14–15, 16–19

Cambodia, 20, 178, 342
Camp David negotiations (1978), 98
  as example of "single negotiating test" strategy, 144
Carter, Jimmy, 62, 144
  popular support for hawkish behavior of, 177
  SALT II agreement and, 191
Case studies (research method), 348, 349, 358–361
Causes of war, 210–335
  balance of power theory, 228–243
  crisis management theories and, 54–57
  decision making theories, 222, 274–289
    misperception and war, 279–289
    organizational politics and processes, 275–277
    rigidity of military doctrines and war plans, 277–279
  democracy and war, 267–270
  domestic politics in, 271–274
  expected utility theory, Bueno de Mesquita's, 243–251
  historical and theoretical context, 213–223
    historical record, 213–215
    organizing framework, 219–223
    theories of international conflicts, 215–219
  implications for the nuclear era, 289–295, 335
  incapacity for population defense, 290–292
  lateral pressure theory, 258–260
  liberal economic theories, 260–262
  Marxist-Leninist theories, 263–267
  misperceptions of military balance, 294
  nonrational escalation, 295
  paradox of mutual vulnerability, 291–292, 293
  power transition and hegemonic war theories, 251–258
  preemption as condition for war, 293–295
  realist paradigm, 224–228
  "stability-instability" paradox, 292
  scapegoat hypothesis, 271–274
  societal-level theories, 222, 262–274
  systemic-level theories, 222, 223–262
China. See People's Republic of China (PRC)
Churchill, Sir Winston, 269, 287
Civil wars, 214, 219
Coalitions, 128–131
Coercion, theory of, 211
Coercive diplomacy, 62, 375
Cognitive processes of individual decision makers, 341–344
Cognitive rigidity, 6, 44
  stress and, 30–31
Colonial expansion, lateral pressure theory and, 260
Command, communication control, and information (C^3I) systems
  crisis decision making and, 64–65
  need for improvements in, 198–200, 343–344
Committee on the Present Danger, 62–63
Conference on Security and Cooperation in Europe (CSCE), 129
Content analysis in negotiation research, 149, 155–163
Conventional Arms Transfer (CAT) talks, 105
"Conventionalization" of nuclear weapons, 289–290
Coolidge, Calvin, 33
Cooperation between superpowers, incentive for, 291–292
Crisis, 12–13
  definition of, 12
  as surrogate for war, 46–47
Crisis decision making, 5, 9–84
  bureaucratic organization, 14–15, 16–19
  coercive management in, 375
  crisis management, 48–59
    assessment, 57–59
    prescriptive theories, 53–57
  decision-making groups, 14–15, 19–22
  in foreign policy crises, 37–48
    Cuban missile crisis, 41–43
    1914 crisis, 37–40
    other international crises, 43–48
  government officials in, 63–64
  individual decision makers, 14–15, 22–27
  impact of stress on, 25–37, 375–376
    cognitive rigidity, 30–31
    constricted search, 32–33
    reduced span of attention, 30
    time perspective, 31–37
  nation-state, as unit of analysis, 13–16

Index

tensions between crisis management and alliance management, 60, 61
since World War II
  crises as surrogates for war, 46–47
  decreased dangers of "routinized" crises, 47
  impact of nuclear weapons, 46
Crisis-induced stress, 6, 11–13, 25–37, 44, 45, 375–376
  cognitive rigidity and, 30–31
  reduced span of attention and, 30
  time perspective and, 31–37
Crisis management, 48–59, 211
  appeasement of expansionist powers, unwarranted, 54
  assessment of, 57–59
  control of events and, 55
  crisis avoidance and, 58–59
  effective communications and, 49–50, 56
  escalation, mutually undesirable, 54–55
  force structures and, 56–57
  knowledge, transference of, 63–64
  partisan and ideological tenor of U.S. politics and, 63–65
  prescriptive theories of, 53–57
  "prisoners' dilemma" scenario and, 48–49, 50
  tensions between alliance management and, 60, 61
  time pressures for policy makers, 50–53
  U.S. electoral cycle as impediment to, 62–63
Crisis stability, 211
Cruise missiles, 52
Cuba, sanctions against, 187
Cuban missile crisis, 60, 110, 211, 274, 348, 367
  bureaucratic decision making in, 18
  communications problems during, 49
  as effective crisis management, 20, 41–43, 59
  effect on test ban negotiations of, 125
  stress induced by, 26, 35, 36
  successful "groupthink" decisions and, 21
  tensions between alliance management and crisis management during, 61
Cultural factors in international negotiations, 131–137
Culture, effects of fear of war on, 197
Czechoslovakia, 62

"Decapitation" strategy, 51
Decision makers
  impact on crisis decision making of, 14–15, 19–22
  as intuitive scientists, 22–23
  managing military-political systems, 347–348
  as representative of bureaucratic constituencies, 345–347
  three conceptions of, 22–23
Decision making. *See* crisis decision making
Decision-making theories of war, 222, 274–289
  misperception and war, 279–289
  organizational politics and processes, 275–277
  rigidity of military doctrines and war plans, 277–279
Defect/defect option in the "prisoners' dilemma" game, 350
Defense spending, mass opinion and, 179–180, 181
Defensive doctrines, distinction between offensive doctrines and, 276–277
"Defensive economic imperialism" theory, 266
Democracy
  causes of war in, 187–191, 267–270
  electoral politics and international conflicts, 187–188
  foreign policy as symbolic politics, 186–187
  mass opinion in, 179–185
  rational leaders in, 185–191
  reactions to nuclear weapons and nuclear war, 192–198
    disarmament and trust, 194–195
    effects of fear of war, 197–198
    no first use of weapons, 192–194, 374
    yearning for protection, 195–196
    strengthening command and control, 198–200
Destructiveness of warfare, 213–214
Détente, decline of, 180
Deterrence, 4, 5–6, 49–50, 62, 211, 276–277
  dyadic balance of power and, 241, 242–243
  nation-states and, 16
Diplomacy, 97, 100
  coercive, 62, 375
  importance of prenegotiation phase in, 104, 105
  theory of international negotiations and, 137–145
Disarmament, in mass opinion, democracy, 194–195
Domestic political imperatives of nation-states, 348

Domestic political imperatives (*continued*)
  international conflicts and, 189–190
  theories of war and, 271–274
Domestic structural factors of international negotiations, 126–128
Doves, 175–176, 177
  vulnerability of C³I systems and, 198
Dulles, John Foster, 11
Dyadic balance of power, 240–243
  perceptions of, 285, 287
  population defense and, 290

Economic downturn
  arms control treaties and, 191
  rationality of voters and leaders regarding, 186–187, 188, 191
  U.S. involvement in international conflicts and, 189, 191
Economic "misery index," 188
Eden, Anthony, 11, 34
Egypt, 97, 283
Eighteen Nation Disarmament Conference (1962–1963), 117, 153
Eisenhower, Dwight, crisis decision making and, 10, 47–48
Electoral politics, international conflicts and, 187–188
El Salvador, 342
Escalation
  effect on crisis decision making of, 45
  of local conflicts, 214–215, 216–217
  mutually undesirable, 54–55
  nonrational, 295
Essence of Decision (Allison), 274
Ethiopia, 342
Eurocentric state system, 213
Evolution of Cooperation, The (Axelrod), 110
Expansionist powers, unwarranted appeasement of, 54
Expected utility theory of war, Bueno de Mesquita's, 243–251, 357–358
External influences on international negotiations, 119–126, 230

Falklands/Malvinas war, 279, 281, 287
Fallout shelters, 199–200
Fatigue, 44
Fear of war, 196
  effects of, 197–198
First-strike advantage, 48, 95
  opposition to, 192–194, 374
Force structures as crisis management prescription, 56–57
Ford, Gerald, 62

Foreign policy
  crisis decision making in, 37–48
    Cuban missile crisis, 41–43
    1914 crisis, 37–40
    other international crises, 43–48
  domestic political imperatives and, 189–190, 271–274, 348
  effect of economy on, 186–187, 188
  electoral politics and, 187–188
  nation-state decision making and, 16
  as symbolic politics, 186–187
Formal mathematical models (research method), 361–364
France, 129, 260
  balance of power theory and, 231
  crisis management and, 54
  Hitler's misperceptions of, 288
  1914 crisis and, 38, 39
  opposition to first-use in, 192–193, 194
Franco, Francisco, 120
Franco-Prussian War, 252, 253

Game theory analyses (research method), 362–364, 370
  for mutual security negotiations, 97–98
Genscher, Hans Dieter, 131
Germany, 260. *See also* Hitler, Adolf; West Germany
  imperial overextension of, 267
  nationalism as cause of war, 272
  1914 crisis and, 38, 39, 278
Gilpin's theory of hegemonic transitions, 256–258
  balance of power theory and, 229–230
Global wars, 255–256
Goldwater, Barry, 12
Gorbachev, Mikhail, 374
  cultural effects on U.S.-Soviet negotiations and, 132, 133
  INF treaty and, 51, 86–88, 104, 150–151
  nuclear disarmament and, 195
Graduated reduction in international tensions (GRIT), 49, 124, 374
  in bargaining process, 113
Great Britain, 260
  bureaucratic crisis decision making and, 18–19
  crisis management and, 54
  Hitler's misperceptions of, 283, 288
  imperial overextension of, 267
  misperceptions as cause of war, 279, 281, 287
  nationalism as cause of war, 272
  1914 crisis and, 38

opposition to first-use in, 192–193, 194
U.S. missiles deployed in, 86
Great power wars, 213–215, 219
  Marxist-Leninist theory and, 264–266
Grenada, 179, 187
Gromyko, Andrei, 45
Gross national product (GNP)
  defense spending as percentage of, 179
  U.S. involvement in international conflicts and, 189
"Groupthink" situations, 21, 344–345
Gulf of Tonkin incident, 178
Guns of August (Tuchman), 41

Hapsburg-Valois rivalry, 235
Hawks, 175–176, 177
  vulnerability of C^3I systems and, 198
Hegemonic transitions, Gilpin's theory of, 256–258
  balance of power theory and, 229–230
Hiroshima, 336
Historical record of warfare, 213–215
  quantitative studies of, 357–358
  reliance on, 342
Hitler, Adolf, 34, 276
  as individual decision maker, 22
  underestimation of hostility of intentions of, 281
  World War II misperceptions of, 283, 284, 285, 287, 288
Hoffman Report on SDI, 52
Hostility of adversary's intentions, exaggerating, 280–283
Hot line, establishment of, 49
Hull, Cordell, 33
Humiliation, avoiding actions that provoke, 54–55
Hungary, 11

Imperialism
  Marxist-Leninist theory of, 264–266
  theory of "defensive economic imperialism," 266
Imperial overextension, 267
Imperial wars, 214, 219
Individual decision makers
  cognitive and affective processes of, 341–344, 367
  and on crisis decision making, 14–15, 22–27
  responses of, 338
  systematic bias constraints on, 23–25
Indo-China, 20. *See also* Vietnam War
Inflation, 186–187, 188, 191
In-group/out-group hypothesis, 272

Integrative complexity, 45
Interaction process analysis (IPA), 158–159
Intercontinental ballistic missiles (ICBMs), 52, 143
  Soviet, 95
Intermediate-range Nuclear Force (INF) Treaty (1987), 51, 86–88, 94, 104, 136, 150–151, 178
Internal balancing of power, 230
International conference on oil tanker standards, 141–142
International conflict theories, 215–219. *See also* causes of war
International Crisis Behavior Project, 43–44
International negotiations. *See* negotiation
International systems, 338
  structure of, 349–351
Interstate wars, 219
Intervention, 215, 216
Iran, 185, 284
Iranian hostage crisis, 180, 368
Iran-Nicaraguan Contra scandal, 175, 178
Iraq, 284
Isolationists, 175, 179
Israel, 60, 61, 97, 281, 282, 358
  opposition to use of nuclear weapons in, 193
Italy
  opposition to first-use in, 192–193, 194
  U.S. missiles deployed in, 86

Japan
  lateral pressure theory and, 259, 260
  U.S. and
    atomic bombing, 193, 336
    misperceptions of Japan, 282, 283
    pre-Pearl Harbor policy, 54–55
Johnson, Lyndon B., 178, 179
Joint Soviet-U.S. control center, 49

Kant, Immanuel, 263, 268
Keegan, John, 53
Keesing's Contemporary Archives, 121
Kennedy, John F., 112, 125, 151
  crisis decision making and, 41, 42, 46, 59, 211, 367
  Partial Nuclear Test Ban Treaty and, 109, 145
Kennedy, Robert, 35
Khrushchev, Nikita, 133
  crisis decision making and, 26, 41, 42, 46
Kissinger, Henry, 120
  on difficulties of effective crisis management, 59–60

Kissinger (*continued*)
  SALT II and, 124
  "shuttle diplomacy" of, 97
Korean Airlines flight 007, 24, 62
Korean War, 10, 32, 196, 345
  crisis decision making and, 20
  U.S. misperceptions of, 279, 281, 282

Laboratory experiments (research method), 353–355
Lateral pressure theory of war, 258–260
Lebanon, 243
"Lens-model" paradigm in negotiations, 143
"Lessons learned" exercises, 149
Levels of analysis, 338–351
  bureaucratic constituencies, 345–347
    impact on crisis decision making, 14–15, 16–19
  complex military-political systems, 338, 347–348
  individual decision maker
    cognitive and affective processes of, 341–344, 367
    impact on crisis decision making, 14–15, 22–25, 27
    internal system, 349–351
  macro and micro, 152–153, 366–368
  nation-state, 348–349
    impact on crisis decision making, 13–16
    in negotiation research, 152–153
  small group processes, 338, 344–345
    impact on crisis decision making, 14–15, 19–22
  theoretical linkages across, 365–370
Liberal economic theories of war, 260–262
Liberal internationalists, 175, 179
Libya, 187
Limited nuclear war, 50–51, 199–200, 292, 335
Limited war, 211, 216
Long cycle theory, 254–256
Long-term causes of war, 221–222
Louis XIV, King, 231

McKinley, William, 271
McNamara, Robert, 41
Marshall Plan, 21, 345
Marx, Karl, 263
Marxist-Leninist theories of war, 263–267, 270
Mass opinion, 179–185
  attitude change, 181–184
  on defense spending, 179–180, 181
  the elite versus the masses, 179–180

hawks versus doves, 175–176, 177
  interest and information, 184–185
  opinion change and policy change, 181
  surveys of, 355–356
Mathematical models (research method), 361–364
Means-ends rationality model, 18
Metternich, Prince Klemens, 45
Middle East crisis, 44, 97
  importance of prenegotiations diplomacy in, 104, 105
Military doctrines, rigidity of, 277–279
Military-political systems, 338, 347–348
  balance of power theory and, 238
Misperception in theories of war, 279–289
  adversary's capabilities, 283–285
  contributing to peace, 289
  defining, determining, and evaluating accuracy of misperceptions, 285–289
  of hostility of adversary's intentions, 280–283
  intentions and capabilities of third states, 285, 287–288
  long-term misperceptions, 280–281
Multiattribute value theory, 142–143
Multiple independently targetable reentry vehicle (MIRV) technology, 50
Multipolar systems, balance of power theory and, 233–234
Multivariate correlational study of nation-states, 348, 349
Munich agreements of 1938, 54
Mutual and Balanced Force Reduction (MBFR) negotiations, 94, 99, 119, 152, 154
  BPA applied to, 159
  communications during, 139–141
  influence of external events during, 121–123
  structural factors in, 128–129, 130–131
Mutual assured destruction (MAD), 52
Mutually undesirable escalation, 54–55
Mutual security negotiations. *See* negotiations on mutual security
Mutual vulnerability of superpowers, 291–292, 293

Nagasaki, 336
Nasser, Gamal Abdel, 34
National Command authority (NCA), C^3I systems and, 198, 199, 200
Nationalism
  as cause of war, 271–272
  public support for hardline policies and, 368–369

National Opinion Research Center (NORC), 181
National Security Council, 41, 47
National Security Decision Memorandum, 242, 251
Nation-state, 348–349
  impact on crisis decision making of, 13–16
Negative expected-utility hypothesis, 245–246
Negative feedback, crisis decision making and, 35
Negotiations on mutual security, 86–163
  arms control, 93–96
  bargaining models for, 91–93, 98–99
  bargaining processes, 107–119
  contextual influences, 119–137
  cultural factors, 131–137
  diplomacy, in theory of, 137–145
  dynamic approach, in research, 153–155
  external influences, 119–126, 230
  game theoretic models, 97–98
  international context, 91–96
  international systems models, 100–102
  levels of analysis and, 152–153
  prenegotiation phase, 104–107
  problem-solving aspects of, 143–144
  processes and influences, 103–137
  research methodology, 102–103, 151–163
  security dilemma, security regimes, and, 89–91
  social psychological models, 98
  static approach, in research, 153–155
  structural factors in, 126–131, 349–351
  theoretical framework for policy analysis, 146–151
  theories of, 96–102
  as three-stage process, 93
Netherlands, the, 259
New Times (Soviet Union), 121
New York Times, The, 121
Nicaragua, 175, 178, 179, 192, 342
Nicolson, Harold, 131
1914 crisis
  decision making deficiencies during, 37–40, 41, 42
  losing control of events during, 55
Nixon, Richard
  crisis decision making and, 9, 10
  popular support for conflictual behavior of, 178
No-first-use policy, 192–194, 374
Nonpolarized alliance systems, 236
Nonrational escalation to nuclear war, 295
North Atlantic Council (NAC), 128

North Atlantic Treaty Organization (NATO), 86, 185
  first-use and, 192
  INF Treaty and, 150
  MBFR negotiations and, 99, 128, 130–131
North Vietnam, bombing of, 177
Nuclear "balance of terror," 48
Nuclear freeze, 356
  SDI and, 194–195
Nuclear Nonproliferation Treaty, 94
Nunn, Sam, 62

Offensive doctrines, linkage of war and, 276–277
OPEC oil embargoes, 368
Organizational bargaining models for international negotiations, 98–99
Organski's power transition theory, 251–256
  incorporation into the long cycle theory, 254–256
Overestimation of hostility of adversary's intentions, 280–281

Panama Canal Treaty, 97, 142
Parity, 232
Partial Nuclear Test Ban Treaty (1963), 94, 98, 145, 153
  computerized content analysis system used in, 157–158
  influence of external events on, 121–123
  responsiveness of negotiators in, 109–110
  stress and, 124–125
Pearl Harbor, 32, 54–55
Peloponnesian War, 3, 224, 284
  Organski's power transition theory and, 252, 253
People's Republic of China (PRC)
  border war with Soviet Union, 10
  Korean War and, 10, 279, 281, 282
  "prisoners' dilemma" scenario in Soviet dealing with, 49
  U.S. and
    change of mass opinion toward (1953–1986), 181–184
    cultural effects on negotiations, 132
    diplomatic recognition, 120
    rejection of nuclear weapons use, 47–48
Pershing II missiles, 51
Philip II (king of Spain), 230–231
Philippines, base-rights negotiations with U.S., 97–98, 142
Plato, 262
Poland, 97, 250, 358
  Hitler's invasion of, 276, 283, 284, 288

Polarity/stability debate, 233–235
Polarized alliance systems, 236
Population defense, incapacity in nuclear war for, 290–292
Positive expected-utility hypothesis, 245–246
Posturing in bargaining process, 113–114
Power preponderance theory, 232–233
Power transition theory of war, Organski's, 251–256
  incorporation into long cycle theory, 254–256
Preemption and initiation of nuclear war, 293–295
Prenegotiation phase, 104–107
Prescriptive theories of crisis management, 53–57
  assessment convergence in, 57–58
  constraints on rationality, 55–57
  losing control of events, 55
  provoking mutually undesirable escalation, 54–55
  transference of relevant crisis knowledge, 63–64
  unwarranted appeasement of expansionist powers, 54
Presidential Directive, 59, 51
Presidential popularity, 177–179
Preventive war theory, 253–254
Prisoners' dilemma situations, 48–49, 50
  as basis of preemptive conditions for war, 293–295
  as cause of war, 222, 223
  defect/defect option in, 350
  strategies for coping with, 363, 370
Problem-solving aspects of negotiations, 143–144
Process debriefing, 63
Proxy wars, 216
  between superpowers, 214–215
Psychopathological foreign policy leaders, 11–12
Public opinion. *See* mass opinion

Quantitative studies of historical data (research method), 357–358
Quemoy-Matsu crises (1954–1955 and 1958), 61

Raiffa, H., 162
Rand Corporation, 57–58
Rationality, assumption in realist paradigm, 224–225
  bounded, in decision making, 22
  constraints on, and theories of crisis management, 55–57
  means-ends model, 18
Rational leaders in a democracy, 185–191
Reagan, Ronald, 132, 291
  defense budget of, 180
  INF Treaty and, 51, 86–88, 104, 150–151
  limited nuclear war and, 199
  popular support for, 177–179
  Reykjavik summit meeting and, 64
  SDI program and, 51, 52, 194–195, 356
Realist paradigm theory of war, 224–228
  balance of power theory and, 228, 229
Reduced span of attention, 30
Research methods, 351–364
  case studies, 348, 349, 358–361
  content analysis in negotiations research, 155–163
  formal mathematical models, 361–364
  laboratory experiments and simulations, 353–355
  mass surveys of public opinion, 355–356
  negotiation research, methodological issues, 102–103, 152–155
  quantitative studies of historical data, 357–358
  theoretical linkages across methods, 370–372
Responsiveness of negotiators in bargaining processes, 107–115
Reykjavik summit meeting (1986), 64, 86–87, 136, 178
Rigid military mobilization and war plans, 277–279
Role reversal in bargaining process, 115–119
Roper Organization, 177
"Routinized" crises, 47
Rumania, 129
Russia, 260. *See also* Soviet Union
  1914 crisis and, 38, 39
Russo-Japanese War, 39, 252, 253

Sadat, Anwar el-, 98, 112, 144
Safety-valve hypothesis, 264
SALT I, 120, 185
  BPA applied to, 159
  cultural effects on, 132
SALT II, 62, 63, 94, 185, 191, 195
  BPA applied to, 159
  cultural effects on, 132
  external influences on negotiations during, 120–121
  stress and, 124
Scandinavia, 259

Scapegoat hypothesis, 272–273
Schelling, Thomas, 92
Schlieffen Plan, 38, 39, 278
Schmidt, Helmut, 131
Scowcroft Commission, 50
Seabeds Denuclearization Treaty, 128, 129, 149
Secondary states, wars between, 219
Second-strike posture, 200
Security dilemma in negotiations, 89–91
   realist paradigm theory and, 226–227
Self-presentation debate, 115–116
Serbia, 38, 250, 358
Seven Years' War (1756–1763), 281
Short-term causes of war, 221, 222
Short-term misperceptions, 280–281
Shultz, George, 104
Shuttle diplomacy, 97
Signaling and bargaining with the adversary, 56
Simulations (research method), 353–355
Sinai War (1973), 283
"Single negotiation text" strategy, 144
Six Day War (1967), 28, 358
Skybolt missile crisis, 18–19
Small group processes, 338, 344–345
   impact on crisis decision making of, 14–15, 19–22
Small state wars, 214
   as route to superpower confrontations, 214–215
Social imperialism, 267
Social psychological models for international negotiations, 98
Societal-level theories of war, 222, 262–274
   democracy and war, 267–270
   domestic politics and the scapegoat hypothesis, 271–274
   Marxist-Leninist theories, 263–267
   nation-state level of analysis, 348–349
Solidarity Union, 97
South Africa, 187
Soviet Union. *See also* Cuban missile crisis; *names of specific arms reduction negotiations and treaties*
   border war with China, 10
   "the China card" and, 120
   crisis stability and, 62–63
   effect of economic adversity on arms control treaties, 191
   effects of fear of war on children and adolescents, 197
   geopolitical objectives of, 4, 374
   intervention in Afghanistan, 62, 63, 86, 120, 121, 180, 191, 342, 371, 374
   limited nuclear war policy and, 50–51
   nuclear strike capabilities of, 39
   "prisoners' dilemma" scenario in dealings with U.S. and China, 49
   U.S. and
      arms control negotiations, 86, 94–96, 104, 109–110
      changing U.S. popular attitudes, 177–179, 181–184, 193–194
      cultural effects on negotiations, 132–137
      sanctions against, 187
      SDI program, 52–53, 132–137
      security dilemma in arms race, 89–91
Spain, base-rights negotiations with U.S., 108, 120, 121, 149
Spanish-American War, 271
Spanish Armada, defeat of, 287
SS-20 missiles (Soviet), 50, 86
"Stability-instability" paradox, 292
Stalin, Joseph, 21, 133
Stanford General Inquirer program for political analysis, 157–158
Star Wars. *See* Strategic Defense Initiative (SDI)
State, the, realist paradigm theory and, 224–228. *See also* nation-state
Static approach to negotiations research analysis, 153–155
Stevenson, Adlai, 42
Strategic Arms Reduction Talks (START), 94, 95
   multiattribute value theory as model for, 142–143
Strategic Defense Initiative (SDI), 51–53, 64, 136, 178, 356
   as antidote to nuclear freeze movement, 194–195
   crisis stability and, 62
   divided opinion on feasibility of, 51, 52–53
   effects on U.S.-Soviet negotiating processes, 132–137
   fear of war and, 198
   popular support for, 196, 369
Strategy of Conflict, The (Schelling), 92
Stress, crisis-induced, 6, 11–13, 25–37, 44, 45, 375–376
   cognitive rigidity and, 30–31
   as external influence on negotiating behavior, 123–126
   impairment of evaluation, 33
   moderate levels of, 28
   reduced span of attention and, 30

Stress *(continued)*
  time perspective and, 31–37
Structural factors in international negotiations, 126–131, 349–351
  domestic structure, 126–128
  international structures, 128–131
Suez Canal crisis (1956), 11
  bureaucratic crisis decision making and, 18–19
Supreme Headquarters of the Allied Powers in Europe (SHAPE), 128
Surrogates for war, crises as, 46–47
Surveillance satellites, 48
Surveys of public opinion (research method), 355–356
Symbolic politics, 186–187, 198
Syria, 97, 178
Systematic biases as constraints on individual decision makers, 23–25
Systemic-level theories of war, 222, 223–262
  balance of power theory, 228–243
  Bueno de Mesquita's expected utility theory, 243–251
  lateral pressure theory, 258–260
  liberal economic theories, 260–262
  realist paradigm, 224–228
  theories of power transition and hegemonic war, 251–258

Television commentators, mass opinion and, 183
"Tensions-first approach" to mutual security negotiations, 87
Terrorism, 219
Thatcher, Margaret, 59
Theories of international conflict, 215–219. *See also* causes of war
  policy relevance of, 220–221, 337–338, 372–378
Third World, 4
"Threshold adjustment," 108
Thucydides, 3, 221, 224, 252, 253
Time perspective, 41, 45
  two-way relationship between stress and, 31–37
Tit-for-tat strategy in bargaining process, 49, 110–111
  combination of unilateral initiative and, 112–113
  "prisoners' dilemma" and, 336, 370
Trade-offs, 6, 43, 44
Truman, Harry S., 33, 34
  popular support for conflictual behavior of, 179

Tuchman, Barbara, 41, 211
Type I errors, 344
Type II errors, 344

Underestimation. *See* misperception
Unemployment, 186–187, 188, 191
Unilateral initiatives in bargaining process, 111–115
Unitary actor assumption in realist paradigm theory, 224–225
United States (U.S.). *See also* Cuban missile crisis; *names of specific arms reduction negotiations and treaties*
  attitudes toward nuclear disarmament in, 194–196
  Berlin blockade and, 44
  bureaucratic crisis decision making and, 18–19
  China and
    change of mass opinion toward (1953–1986), 181–184
    cultural effects on negotiations, 132
    diplomatic recognition, 120
    rejection of nuclear weapons use, 47–48
  C^3I systems vulnerability and, 64–65
  effects of fear of war on children and adolescents, 197
  electoral cycle as impediment to crisis management, 62–64
  geopolitical objectives of, 4, 373–374
  involvement in international conflicts as reflection of GNP, 189
  Japan and
    atomic bombing, 193, 336
    pre-Pearl Harbor policy, 54–55
  limited nuclear war policy and, 50–51
  missiles deployed in Europe, 86
  misperceptions of
    toward Japan, 282, 283
    in Korean War, 10, 279, 281, 282
    in Vietnam War, 282
  nuclear strike capabilities of, 39
  opposition to first-use in, 192–194
  -Philippines base-rights negotiations, 97–98, 142
  security dilemma in arms race, 89–91
  Soviet Union and
    arms control negotiations, 86, 94–96, 104, 109–110
    changing U.S. popular attitudes, 177–179, 181–184, 193–194
    cultural effects on negotiations, 132–137
    "prisoners' dilemma" scenario in dealings, 49

sanctions against, 187
SDI program, 52–53, 132–137
-Spain base-rights negotiations, 108, 120, 121, 149
tensions between crisis management and alliance management in, 60, 61
U.N. Special Session on Disarmament (UNSSOD), 129–130, 136
U.S. Foreign Service Institute, "lessons learned" exercises of, 149
U.S.S.R. *See* Soviet Union

Vietnam War, 368
bombing of North Vietnam, 177
changes in mass opinion toward, 179–180, 185
crisis decision making and, 20
dangers of comparing contemporary conflicts with, 342
escalation of, 177, 178
U.S. misperceptions of, 282
Von Ranke, Leopold, 215
Von Tirpitz, Admiral, 40

War gaming, 63
Warner, John, 62
War of Jenkins' Ear (1739–1748), 272
War plans, rigidity of, 277–279

Warsaw pact, 106
MBFR negotiations and, 99, 130–131
Wars of intervention, 215, 216–217
Watergate, 10
West Germany
MBFR negotiations and, 131
opposition to first-use in, 192–193, 194
U.S. missiles deployed in, 86
Wilhelm, Kaiser, 33, 38
Wilson, Woodrow, 268
"Window of vulnerability," 50
World War I, 215
balance of power theory and, 237
Marxist-Leninist theory of, 264–265
misperceptions as cause of, 280, 281, 287
1914 crisis leading to
decision making deficiencies during, 37–40, 41, 42
losing control of events, 55
Organski's power transition theory and, 252
rigidity of military doctrines and war plans and, 276, 277–279
World War II, 252
role of world-wide depression in, 257
World War III, 196

Yearning for protection, 195–196
Yom Kippur War (1973), 61
Yugoslavia, 129